To Have and to Hold

This volume analyzes how, why, and when pre-modern Europeans documented their marriages – through property deeds, marital settlements, dotal charters, church court depositions, and other indicia of marital consent. The authors consider both the function of documentation in the process of marrying and what the surviving documents say about pre-modern marriage and how people in the day understood it. Drawing on archival evidence from classical Rome; medieval France, England, Iceland, and Ireland; and Renaissance Florence, Douai, and Geneva, the volume provides a rich interdisciplinary analysis of the range of material customs, laws, and practices in Western Christendom. The chapters include freshly translated specimen documents that bring the reader closer to the actual practice of marrying than the normative literature of pre-modern theology and canon law.

Philip L. Reynolds is Aquinas Professor of Historical Theology in the Candler School of Theology at Emory University and a Senior Fellow in the Center for the Study of Law and Religion at Emory University. His publications include *Marriage in the Western Church: The Christianization of Marriage during the Patristic and Early Medieval Periods* (1994) and *Food and the Body: Some Peculiar Questions in High Medieval Theology* (1999).

John Witte, Jr. is the Jonas Robitscher Professor of Law and Director of the Center for the Study of Law and Religion at Emory University. A world-class scholar of legal history, marriage, and religious liberty, he has published 120 articles, 8 journal symposia, and 19 books, including *From Sacrament to Contract: Marriage, Religion, and Law in the Western Tradition* and *God's Joust, God's Justice: Law and Religion in the Western Tradition*. His writings have appeared in German, French, Italian, Hebrew, Spanish, Russian, Ukrainian, and Romanian translations.

To Have and to Hold

MARRYING AND ITS DOCUMENTATION IN
WESTERN CHRISTENDOM, 400–1600

Edited by

PHILIP L. REYNOLDS
Emory University

JOHN WITTE, JR.
Emory University

CAMBRIDGE
UNIVERSITY PRESS

CAMBRIDGE UNIVERSITY PRESS
Cambridge, New York, Melbourne, Madrid, Cape Town, Singapore, São Paulo

Cambridge University Press
32 Avenue of the Americas, New York, NY 10013-2473, USA

www.cambridge.org
Information on this title: www.cambridge.org/9780521867368

First published 2007

Printed in the United States of America

A catalog record for this publication is available from the British Library.

Library of Congress Cataloging in Publication Data

To have and to hold : marrying and its documentation in Western Christendom, 400–1600 /
edited by Philip L. Reynolds.
p. cm.
Includes bibliographical references and index.
ISBN-13: 978-0-521-86736-8 (hardback)
ISBN-10: 0-521-86736-3 (hardback)
1. Marriage – History.   2. Marriage – History – Sources.   3. Marital property – History.
4. Marriage – Religious aspects – Christianity – History.   5. Marriage law – History.
I. Reynolds, Philip Lyndon, 1950–   II. Witte, John, 1959–   III. Title.
HQ503.T6   2007
306.8109182′10902 – dc22   2006018203

ISBN   978-0-521-86736-8 hardback

CONTENTS

LIST OF CONTRIBUTORS

AGNES S. ARNÓSDÓTTIR is Associate Professor in the Institute of History and Area Studies at the University of Aarhus, Denmark.

ART COSGROVE is Professor Emeritus of History and former President of University College Dublin.

JUDITH EVANS-GRUBBS is Professor of Classics at Washington University in St. Louis.

R. H. HELMHOLZ is Ruth Wyatt Rosenson Distinguished Service Professor of Law at the University of Chicago.

MARTHA C. HOWELL is Miriam Champion Professor of History at Columbia University.

DAVID G. HUNTER is Monsignor James A. Supple Professor of Catholic Studies at Iowa State University.

CYNTHIA JOHNSON is currently at the University of Toulouse-Mirail, France, completing her second doctorate in history, and she is an associated member of the research group FRAMESPA in the Centre National de la Recherche Scientifique.

THOMAS KUEHN is Professor and Department Chair of History at Clemson University.

LAURENT MORELLE is Director of Studies at the École Pratique des Hautes Études (division of historical and philological sciences), Paris.

FREDERIK PEDERSEN is Lecturer in History at the University of Aberdeen, Scotland.

PHILIP L. REYNOLDS is Aquinas Professor of Historical Theology at Candler School of Theology, Emory University and a Senior Fellow of Emory's Center for the Study of Law and Religion.

JOHN WITTE, JR. is Jonas Robitscher Professor of Law and Director of the Center for the Study of Law and Religion at Emory University in Atlanta.

Preface and Acknowledgments

Throughout much of the West today, marriage formation requires the execution of a written marriage contract – usually a marriage certificate that is signed by the couple and their witnesses and registered with a government official. These publicly registered marriage contracts can be anticipated by private engagement and prenuptial contracts respecting the parties' property, custodial, and other rights before, during, and after the marriage. Marriage contracts may also be accompanied by public notices and invitations; elaborate liturgies or ceremonies; ritual exchanges of promises, rings, and other property; and lavish parties and lush honeymoons. But none of this is essential to the validity of the marriage today: the properly signed marriage certificate is enough to make a marriage.

In the pre-modern West, both the documentation and the formation of marriage were considerably more complex and variegated. Most so-called marriage contracts in the Middle Ages were, in fact, primarily marriage *settlements*: they recorded agreements about transfers of marital property, and although they often referred to the mutual consent of the parties to form a marital union, they did so only to situate the settlement in its proper context. Moreover, the relationship between written marriage contracts and the contract of marriage per se varied considerably over time and across cultures. Some of the documents recorded the marriage itself; some did not. Some of them were intended for use at weddings; some were not. Some of the documents included commentary on the legal, ethical, or religious function of marriage; some did not. Finally, prior to the sixteenth century, marital liturgies, weddings, and feasts were not essential to the validity of a marriage contract, and when they did occur, they were subject to endless local variations.

This volume analyses how, why, and when pre-modern Europeans documented their marriages – through deeds, settlements, and charters, through the depositions used in episcopal and consistory courts, and through other surviving indicia of the couple's agreement to marry. We consider both the function of documentation in the process of marrying and what the surviving documents say about pre-modern marriage and about how people in the day understood it. The marital documents that have survived are a rich source of information about the marital

[ix]

norms and customs of pre-modern Europeans. They are closer to the actual practice of marrying than the normative literature of pre-modern theology and canon law, about which we have long known a good deal. Indeed, the value of marital documents surpasses that of any historical theory or generalization that we can glean from them, for they record moments in the lives of real persons. Sometimes these individuals would be well known to us in any case, but usually they would otherwise be quite forgotten or, at best, known only to biographers.

We make no pretense that this volume provides a comprehensive survey of the forms and norms of marriage formation and documentation in pre-modern Christian Europe: the surviving evidence is too scattered and spotty, and it is subject to too many different methods of interpretation, to make such a claim. Instead, the chapters that follow offer a fair representation of the range of customs, laws, and practices surrounding the formation and documentation of marriages in pre-modern Europe, and the range of legal, social, and religious modes of scholarly analysis that can be responsibly applied to the documentary evidence that has survived.

We have chosen the chronological bookends of 400 through 1600 under advisement. The theological syntheses of St. Augustine and other post-Nicene Church Fathers, and the legal syntheses of the Roman jurists working from the reigns of Constantine through Justinian, were foundational to Western marriage for more than a millennium. The chapters illustrate how this antique marriage paradigm was adopted in various eras and areas of Western Christian Europe and then adapted in response to widely variant customs, languages, liturgies, and property schemes. Though church and state battled intermittently over marital jurisdiction from the fifth to the sixteenth centuries, the basic norms and forms of marriage inherited from the fifth and sixth centuries were not seriously challenged until the eighteenth- and nineteenth-century Western Enlightenment.

The sequence of chapters takes the reader on a pleasant and instructive journey through the surviving data. In Chapter 1, "Marrying and Its Documentation in Pre-Modern Europe: Consent, Celebration, and Property," Philip L. Reynolds provides an overview of some of the main themes, terms, and trends that readers will encounter in making this journey. He shows how the doctrine of marital consent gradually became the sine qua non of valid betrothal and marriage. He sifts through the complex marital liturgies and ceremonies that were developed in the Christian West, certain forms of which eventually were mandated by the Council of Trent in 1563 and by various Protestant civil laws. And he sketches an interdisciplinary map of the exceedingly intricate legal systems of marital property.

In Chapter 2, "Marrying and Its Documentation in Later Roman Law," Judith Evans-Grubbs recalls the salient features of Roman marriage law in late antiquity, but she focuses in a novel way on actual written contracts, using papyrological evidence as much as possible and spreading her net over a wide geographical and cultural area within the Roman Empire (including Africa, Egypt, and the near East) to compensate for lack of surviving *tabulae nuptiales* from Europe.

In Chapter 3, "Marrying and the *Tabulae Nuptiales* in Roman North Africa from Tertullian to Augustine," David G. Hunter analyzes the Roman dotal instrument, which was the precursor of the dotal charters on which several later chapters focus. He also shows that in Augustine's Christian world, domestic wedding ceremonies (which often included the reading and signing of *tabulae*) were customary steps in the process of getting married, but that church liturgies were not. The varying relation between dotal instruments and nuptial liturgies is a thread running through the collection.

In Chapter 4, "Dotal Charters in the Frankish Tradition," Philip L. Reynolds focuses on the formulae for dotal charters in the standard collection of Merovingian and Carolingian formulae by Karl Zeumer. They range from the sixth to the eleventh centuries. Reynolds first considers the Frankish dowry and its place in the nuptial process; next, he analyzes the diplomatic form of the charters; then, in the main part of the article, Reynolds focuses on eleven "sacred" formulae, which include (chiefly in preambles) an account of the sanctity of marriage and its place in God's plan. Such formulae are witnesses to a robust theology of marriage that is closely allied to liturgical ministry (the blessing of "rites of passage"). By including within the scope of the study some actual Northern-French dotal charters (rather than formulae) from the late eleventh through twelfth centuries, Reynolds tentatively outlines the evolution of the sacred dotal charter in Northern France.

In Chapter 5, "Marriage and Diplomatics: Five Dower Charters from the Regions of Laon and Soissons, 1163–1181," Laurent Morelle meticulously analyzes the diplomatic form and the religious message of the charters, which churchmen used to express their own concerns about marriage. He then applies his expertise in biographical research to identify the spouses and the signatories and to suggest the significance of the marriages in relation to lineage and to the spheres of influence of different castellanies.

In Chapter 6, "Marriage Agreements from Twelfth-Century Southern France," Cynthia Johnson focuses on seven marriage charters, dating from 1127 to 1197, which she puts in the context of some sixty comparable texts. She shows the standard and variable elements in these documents, particularly in their discussion of property transfers by both gift and devise. She also points to evidence that developments in civil law influenced the texts and that the spouses did not consider themselves to be actually married until they began to live together (or at least until the gifts had become truly the property of the recipient).

In Chapter 7, "Marriage Contracts in Medieval England," R. H. Helmholz outlines criteria for what should be counted as marriage contracts. Helmholz distinguishes between two sorts of marriage contract: secular marriage contracts (of which ten examples, from the eleventh through fifteenth centuries, appear in an appendix) and the religious marriage contracts that came before and were enforced in ecclesiastical courts. The former were written, the latter oral. Helmholz finds that, at least in medieval England, the two sorts were usually analogous but independent instruments that often did not mention each other.

In Chapter 8, "Marriage Contracts and the Church Courts of Fourteenth-Century England," Frederik Pedersen analyzes the documentary evidence of marriage from English consistory courts, especially York. He observes how lay people were able to exploit canonical procedures for their own personal ends, and he notes the respective roles of clergy and notaries in the formation of marriage and the interaction between religious and civil authorities.

In Chapter 9, "Marrying and Marriage Litigation in Medieval Ireland," Art Cosgrove focuses on depositions presented in Irish church courts dealing with marriage litigation in the late Middle Ages. He conveys a vivid sense of the (mainly quite ordinary) people named in the documents and their lives, values, and expectations. Cosgrove's study reveals the kinds of complaints that the laity brought to court, the grounds cited in depositions as evidence of marriage contracts, and the social attitudes presupposed thereby.

In Chapter 10, "Marriage Contracts in Medieval Iceland," Agnes S. Arnórsdóttir observes the form and evolution of marriage settlements beginning from the twelfth century (when written contracts first appeared). She considers the written contracts in relation both to the Icelandic and Norwegian legal codes and to the influence of European canon law. In their older form, these contracts were between the kinsfolk on both sides as well as between the partners themselves; the partners retained separate ownership of their respective properties and the bond was soluble. After the twelfth century, there was more emphasis on the agreement of the partners themselves; they held the property in common and the bond was indissoluble. She also notes that church weddings and the involvement of clerics in nuptials were neither legally necessary nor universally observed.

In Chapter 11, "Contracting Marriage in Renaissance Florence," Thomas Kuehn begins with the famous clandestine union of Giovanni della Casa and Lusanna di Benedetto, using that as a foil to examine typical marriage contracts in Florence. Marriages there usually ran through a three-step process: betrothal (*sponsalitium*), exchange of vows (*matrimonium*), and delivery of dowry, and each step might be recorded in a distinct notarial document. This process, along with the public transport of the bride to her husband's house (*traductio*), ensured that the marriage was distinguishable from clandestine unions and concubinage. In that regard, Florentines, even those of fairly modest circumstances, contracted marriages in a remarkable written form, whereas clandestine unions like that of Giovanni and Lusanna remained entirely oral. Kuehn finds that most Florentine marriages prior to Trent were little influenced by ecclesiastical forms and rules (other than the clear written assertion that marriage was contracted *per verba de praesenti*), and that churches and clergy had only an ancillary role in the formation of marriages.

In Chapter 12, "Marriage Property Law as Socio-Cultural Text: The Case of Late-Medieval Douai," Martha C. Howell considers marriage as a property arrangement. Viewing property law as a witness to the social and cultural meanings of marriage, Howell exploits the unusual wealth of matrimonial documents from Douai, an important French-speaking city in the medieval county of Flanders. The laws and customs of Douai, Howell argues, shed light on other regions of the North (where the evidence is usually more patchy) and on the differences between the North and South. Howell focuses on a form of marriage settlement known as the *ravestisse-ment*, whereby the spouses became a single social unit and had equal rights to matrimonial property. She contrasts the *ravestissement* with the more detailed (and male-centered) marriage contract that eventually superseded it.

In Chapter 13, "Marriage Contracts, Liturgies, and Properties in Reformation Geneva," John Witte, Jr., considers some matrimonial documents from John Calvin's Geneva, including the new marriage liturgy, several new statutes, and two marriage contracts, and he sets these in the context of contemporaneous developments in Reformed marriage law and theology. Both of the marital contracts analyzed in his chapter are essentially property transfers, with only incidental reference to the theology and law of marriage. Witte emphasizes the interplay of secular and religious concerns in the new marriage liturgy of Geneva and outlines the archaic gifts and other tokens of betrothal and marriage that, while ancient, were still customary in this period.

Most of the chapters conclude with an appendix of specimen documents. Here, one hears echoes of what pre-modern individuals said, heard, and negotiated in the process of getting married. The appendices are not an afterthought but were an essential component of the project from the beginning. Even narrative summaries would have lost the immediacy and verisimilitude of the original texts. To save the immediacy of such material, as well as to make it more accessible, we have translated the appended documents into English (although we have reproduced the original text when it is not available in a printed edition). To be sure, translation puts the reader at one remove from the original texts (most of which are in Latin), but today one cannot assume that every interested reader will be able to read the original texts fluently. Moreover, although most of these texts are rudimentary on a merely grammatical and syntactical level, their correct construal requires specialist expertise and familiarity with the material. Translation has the advantage, too, of bringing problems of interpretation to the surface and requiring the historian or commentator to be explicit about what the text means in his or her judgment.

Three of the chapters included herein are versions of previously published articles and appear by kind permission of the publishers. Chapter 3 is a revised version of David G. Hunter, "Augustine and the Making of Marriage in Roman North Africa," *Journal of Early Christian Studies* 11:1 (2003): 63–85, © The Johns Hopkins University Press. Chapter 5 is a translation of Laurent Morelle, "Mariage et diplomatique: Autour de cinq chartes de douaire dans le Laonnois-Soissonnais 1163–1181," *Bibliothèque de l'École des chartes* 146 (1988): 225–84. Chapter 9 is a revised and augmented version of an article first published as "Marriage in Medieval Ireland" in Art Cosgrove (ed.), *Marriage in Ireland* (Dublin: College Press, 1985), 25–50.

We wish to thank M. Wallace McDonald for preparing a working translation of Laurent Morelle's article (Chapter 5), Joseph Goering for translating from Latin the charters appended to Chapter 5 and Kendra Willson for translating from Icelandic the documents appended to Chapter 10. We are grateful to Professor Stephen D. White at Emory University for helping us find English equivalents for some French feudal terminology. We are grateful, too, for the frequent and generous counsel of Professor David Bright at Emory University and Professor Joseph Goering at the University of Toronto regarding the correct translation and interpretation of passages in several of the Latin texts and manuscripts analyzed throughout this volume. And we give thanks to the sharp-eyed Emory doctoral students who checked the sources and citations in the chapters: Tracey Billado, Claire Bischoff, Colleen Flood, Mark DelCogliano, Andrew Gallwitz, and Jennifer Thompson.

This anthology is one of a series of new volumes to emerge from the project called "Sex, Marriage, and Family & the Religions of the Book," undertaken by the Center for the Study of Law and Religion at Emory University. The project seeks to take stock of the dramatic transformation of marriage and family life in the world today and to craft enduring solutions to the many new problems it has occasioned. The project is interdisciplinary in methodology: it seeks to bring the ancient wisdom of religious traditions and the modern sciences of law, health, public policy, the social sciences, and the humanities into greater conversation and common purpose. The project is interreligious in inspiration: it seeks to understand the lore, law, and life of marriage and family that are characteristic of Judaism, Christianity, and Islam in their genesis and in their exodus, in their origins and in their diasporas. The project is international in orientation: it seeks to place current American debates over sex, marriage, and family within an emerging global conversation.

We wish to express our deep gratitude to our friends at The Pew Charitable Trusts in Philadelphia for their generous support of our Center for the Study of Law and Religion. We are particularly grateful to Pew's President Rebecca Rimel and program officers Luis Lugo, Susan Billington Harper, Diane Winston, and Julie Sulc for masterminding the creation of our Center, along with sister "centers of excellence" at ten other American research universities – a bold and visionary act of philanthropy that is helping transform the study of religion in the American academy. We also wish to express our deep gratitude to our Emory Center colleagues April Bogle, Eliza Ellison, Anita Mann, Amy Wheeler, and Janice Wiggins for their extraordinary work on this project, which is scheduled to yield thirty other volumes besides this one.

We wish to express our gratitude to Dr. Craig Dykstra and his colleagues in the Lilly Endowment, Inc., for a generous grant that provided John Witte, Jr., with release time and research support to work on his contribution to this volume.

We wish to thank John Berger and his colleagues at Cambridge University Press for taking on this volume and working assiduously to see to its timely publication. And we thank one of our contributors, Professor Dr. Helmholz, as well as the two anonymous readers of the manuscript engaged by Cambridge University Press, for their expert critique and counsel on how to shape the volume.

JOHN WITTE, JR.   PHILIP L. REYNOLDS

List of Abbreviations

CCL   *Corpus Christianorum, series latina* (Turnhout, 1953–)

CCM   *Corpus Christianorum, continuatio medievalis* (Turnhout, 1966–)

CP   York Cause Papers, Borthwick Institute, York

CSEL   *Corpus Scriptorum Ecclesiasticorum Latinorum* (Vienna, 1866–)

MGH   *Monumenta Germaniae Historica*

PL   J. P. Migne (general editor), *Patrologia Latina* (Paris, 1844–64)

X   *Liber extra* (Decretals of Gregory IX), in Emil Friedberg (ed.), *Corpus Iuris Civilis*, 2 vols. (Leipzig, 1879–81), vol. 2

CHAPTER ONE

MARRYING AND ITS DOCUMENTATION IN PRE-MODERN
EUROPE: CONSENT, CELEBRATION, AND PROPERTY

Philip L. Reynolds

This anthology focuses on the agreements that marrying entailed in Western Christendom from 400 to 1600, and on the documentation of such agreements. It is
appropriate at the outset, therefore, to reflect synoptically on the process of marrying. What agreements were made and who made them? What was the function of
such agreements in the process of marrying? Which agreements were documented
and which were oral? What other actions did the process of marrying entail, as well
as agreements, and what were *their* functions? The following sketch is intended
to provide an overarching historical and conceptual framework for the specialized
chapters that follow, to explain some of the terms, concepts, and institutions that
the authors presuppose, and to direct the reader to some of the pertinent secondary
literature.

Marriage brought about three kinds of social change, pertaining respectively
to a core relationship, to a redistribution of property, and to a reconfiguration of
family connections. First, and most fundamentally, a man (or boy) and a woman
(or girl) entered into the core relationship that was marriage itself. They became,
in certain respects, a social unit, forming a partnership (*societas*) characterized by
a cluster of sexual, collaborative, parental, and familial obligations. Because the
couple became a new family unit, marriage severed a son from his parents even in
virilocal societies. Thus according to Genesis 2:24, a text that surely presupposed
a virilocal norm, the man who marries leaves his father and mother to be united
with his wife: he does not need to leave his parents' *home*, but he does leave their
embrace.[1] Those who construed marriage as belonging to the natural law considered
its chief *raison d'être* to be the procreation, rearing, and education of children,
and they sometimes compared human marriage with sexual bonding in other
animals.[2] As Augustine was fond of pointing out (see Chapter 3, by David Hunter),

---

[1] Compare Genesis 24 (on the marriage of Isaac and Rebekah), which clearly depicts virilocal marriage.
[2] See Ulpian in *Digest* 1.1.1.3 (cited by Thomas Aquinas in his discussion of the precepts of the natural
law in *Summa theologiae* I^aII^ae, q. 94, art. 2, resp.); Cicero, *De officiis* I.4.11; and Thomas Aquinas,
In IV Sent., d. 26, q. 1, art. 1, resp.

Roman dotal instruments customarily referred to marriage as a relationship entered into *liberorum procreandorum causa*, that is, for the sake of begetting *legitimate* children or one's *own* children (i.e., one's heirs). With his own concubine and illegitimate son in mind, Augustine observed that whereas one married in order to have children, children were begotten only accidentally outside marriage, although they sometimes forced their fathers to love them.[3]

Second, marriage was an occasion for the transfer (and thus the redistribution) of property. The husband might endow his wife with a marriage gift, and the wife might bring a dowry from her family into the marriage. Once the partners were married, their respective contributions might either be merged as a single resource or remain under the separate control of the husband and his wife (or their respective families). The wife might also acquire a dower interest in a portion of her husband's property, which would support her in the event of her widowhood. Eventually, property from both sides would normally pass to the children after their parents' deaths, so that dotation was a means by which wealth devolved from grandparents to grandchildren.

Third, marriage rearranged interfamilial relationships and created new ones. For example, a husband might gain influence through becoming associated with his wife's family, or he might manage real estate that she had brought into the marriage, or two families might become more closely allied as a result of their children's marriage.

Changes of the third sort require no further comment here (although they will feature in the chapters by Laurent Morelle, Cynthia Johnson, Martha Howell, and John Witte). But it is appropriate to comment at the outset on changes of the first and second sorts (pertaining respectively to status and to property), for these were intrinsically contractual and were therefore the subject of distinct oral or written agreements. Contracts of two sorts, therefore, attended marrying in premodern Europe. On the one hand, there were agreements to marry (i.e., to form the core relationship), whether in the future or with present effect. On the other hand, there were agreements by which one party conferred betrothal gifts or marital "assigns" on the other.

Nothing more is meant by the term "contract" here than a binding agreement that came under the purview of a system of law (whether codified or customary, written or oral) and was thereby (at least ostensibly) enforceable. This mild use of the term "contract" does not necessarily imply that there was a codified system of contract law, or that there was a formal juridical procedure for enforcing contracts, or even that the existence of a written contract would have been the decisive factor in the resolution of conflicting claims. Although little evidence of the use of matrimonial documents in litigation has survived, their form presupposes that they were legally enforceable. Nor does this use of the term "contract" imply that people considered marriage to be a contract, for it is one thing to posit marriage as the object of a contract and quite another to construe marriage itself as a contract with some

---

[3] Augustine, *Confessions* IV.2(2), CCL 27, 41.

other object (a distinction of cardinal significance in the history of marriage as a sacrament).[4]

In regard to the first aspect of marrying – the formation of the core relationship – something needs to be said, first, about the role of "consent" (*consensus*) in the process of marrying, and second, about the intervention of the clergy in this process. The intervention in question here is not the regulation of marriage in canon law (although that is part of the story) but rather the active participation of clergy in marrying (for example, by administering the liturgical celebration of marriage).

In regard to the second aspect of marrying, something needs to be said here about the various marital assigns and their economic function, and about the place of dotation in the nuptial process. With all that in mind, one is in a position to appreciate how marriages were documented and the respective functions of written and oral agreements.

CONSENT AND THE NUPTIAL PROCESS

When scholars of marriage in Roman law or in the Middle Ages refer to marital "consent," the term is a literal rendering of the Latin *consensus*, and it is not used in its usual modern sense. In modern English, the word "consent" usually connotes permission or compliance with the will of another. To be sure, what counted as *consensus* in medieval marriage was often, in fact, only compliance with the will of families or parents (especially where daughters were concerned), but the Latin term implied that the two parties were of one mind, and its prefix implied mutuality. What is in question here, therefore, is at least putatively an active rather than a merely passive consent. More precisely, it is the kind of agreement that creates a bond of commitment or obligation between the two parties. Furthermore, the marital consent of medieval canon law and theology was always an *act* of agreement – an event – whereas in classical Roman law, the marital consent that established a valid marriage did not necessarily require any such act. As long as the partners were qualified to marry and there was no serious misalliance of class, evidence that they regarded each other as man and wife or with "marital affection" sufficed, under Roman law, to establish that they were, in fact, man and wife.[5]

---

[4] During the high-medieval period, canon lawyers (with the "conjugal debt" of 1 Cor. 7:3 in mind) were inclined to construe marriage itself as a contract, but theologians were more cautious and preferred to say that marriage was *like* a contract: see Georges Le Bras, "Mariage: La doctrine du mariage chez les théologiens et les canonistes depuis l'an mille," *Dictionnaire de théologie catholique* 9/2 (Paris, 1927), 2123–2317, at 2182–84; ibid., "Le mariage dans la théologie et le droit de l'Église du XIᵉ au XIIIᵉ siècle," *Cahiers de civilisation médiévale* 11 (1968): 191–202, at 194.

[5] See Philip L. Reynolds, *Marriage in the Western Church: The Christianization of Marriage during the Patristic and Early Medieval Periods* (Leiden, 1994), 35–38. It seems that the betrothal (*sponsalia*) envisaged in classical Roman law was a consensual act, but that the legal concept of marital *consensus* was inductive, i.e., any reliable indication that the partners regarded each other as man and wife, whether it be found in an event or in an attitude, sufficed to establish that the partners were of

During the early Middle Ages, the act of mutual agreement formally required for marriage was prospective: it created a contract that would be fulfilled at length when the spouses came together as man and wife. In other words, it was a betrothal.[6] The usual Latin term for this agreement in the early Middle Ages was *desponsatio*, although the classical term *sponsalia* (denoting a promise to marry) was sometimes used in the same sense. Notwithstanding some equivocation about the precise function and the effect of betrothal, the notion of an act of agreement in the present tense that immediately creates a marriage did not become explicit until the twelfth century. To appreciate the function of betrothal, therefore, one needs to appreciate its relation to the process that it initiated.

A remarkable letter that Pope Nicholas I wrote to Boris, the Khan of Bulgaria, in 866 provides us with a good point of departure for understanding the early medieval nuptial process.[7] Boris was trying to decide whether his people should join the Orthodox or the Roman branches of the church, and Nicholas explained, among other matters, how people married in the West. It is a unique record, for references to marriage during this period usually presupposed a common understanding.

The process outlined in the letter begins with betrothal (*sponsalia*), which Nicholas defines as an agreement to marry in the future. Next, the *sponsus* gives the *sponsa* a ring as a pledge (*arrha*) of his intent and as a symbol of their undivided fidelity, and he confers upon her, by means of a written agreement, a dowry that is acceptable to both sides. All of these steps may occur before the partners are of marriageable age. At length, when they are old enough, they are blessed and veiled in a church ceremony. Nicholas adds that, in contrast with Eastern practice, there is no sin if any of these formalities are omitted, for formal marriages are expensive and many cannot afford them; only the acts of agreement (*consensus*) are strictly necessary.[8] But he says nothing about anyone's agreement in the wedding phase of the process. Agreement is expressed chiefly in the betrothal, which he

---

one mind in the relevant sense. Because marriage in pre-Christian Roman law was dissoluble and the law defined no conjugal rights or obligations (although there were social norms and customary expectations), the main consequence of a valid marriage was that its offspring were legitimate.

[6] On the early medieval betrothal, see Reynolds, *Marriage in the Western Church*, 315–27; and on the meaning of *desponsatio* in early Christian usage, see ibid., 316–23.

[7] Nicholas I, *Epist.* 99 (*Responsa ad consulta Bulgarorum*), c. 3, in MGH *Epist.* 6, *Epistolae Karolini Aevi* 4 (1925), p. 570. The passage of the letter referred to here is translated subsequently in ch. 4 (at n. 37), and there is a translation of the sections of the letter on marriage and sexual morality in Jacqueline Murray (ed.), *Love, Marriage, and Family in the Middle Ages: A Reader* (Peterborough, Canada, 2001), 234–41. For commentary, see Michael M. Sheehan, "The bishop of Rome to a barbarian King on the rituals of marriage," in Steven B. Bowman and Blanche E. Cody (eds.), *In iure veritas: Studies in Canon Law in Memory of Schafer Williams* (Cincinnati, 1991), 187–99; reprinted in Michael M. Sheehan, *Marriage, Family, and Law in Medieval Europe: Collected Studies*, James K. Farge (ed.) (Toronto, 1996), 278–91; and Angeliki E. Laiou, "*Consensus facit nuptias – et non*: Pope Nicholas I's *Responsa* to the Bulgarians as a source for Byzantine marriage customs," *Rechtshistorisches Journal*, 4 (1985): 189–201, reprinted in eadem, *Gender, Society and Economic Life in Byzantium* (Aldershot, 1992).

[8] *Epist.* 99, p. 570, lines 16–21.

says is "celebrated with the consent both of those who are contracting the marriage and of those in whose power they are." Here Nicholas is echoing an opinion of the third-century Roman jurist Paulus regarding consent to marry: marriage (*nuptiae*), Paulus says, is not valid "unless all give their consent, that is, those who come together and those in whose power they are."[9] Nicholas emphasizes mutual agreement, too, when he mentions the dowry. But he treats bride and groom at the wedding as passive recipients: they are brought (*perducuntur*) to the wedding ceremony and placed (*statuuntur*) at the hand of a priest, and they receive (*suscipiunt*) the priest's blessing and the veil.

The difference between Nicholas's notion of marrying and our modern notion is fundamental. We are accustomed to regard marrying as an event consisting essentially of an exchange of vows with immediate effect. Before the exchange, the partners are unmarried (albeit probably "engaged"). After the event, they are married. Anyone approaching medieval or even early modern marriage with that assumption in mind would find much that is confusing or puzzling. Normative accounts of marrying by theologians and canon lawyers from the high (i.e., central) and late Middle Ages might seem largely consistent with it, but sources that are closer to practice during the period indicate that people still regarded marrying as a process or a series of steps, even when canon law defined a particular point or event that was, in itself, a sufficient condition for marriage. What has sometimes been called the "processual" view of marriage was deeply rooted in Western tradition, and the innovations of high-medieval theologians could not uproot it.[10]

Betrothal, then, was an agreement between the partners and between their respective parents or kinsfolk that created an obligation that would be fulfilled when the partners eventually came together. Courtship, negotiations, or pourparlers might occur before the betrothal, but once the partners were betrothed, they were contractually bound together, albeit not indissolubly (for they could dissolve their betrothal on numerous grounds as well as by mutual consent). Although the partners could become betrothed before they were of marriageable age (in theory, from the age of seven), it was chiefly through this prospective agreement that the parties expressed the consensual, contractual aspect of marriage. Clearly, this was not a norm that emphasized the genuine consent of the partners themselves, although (as Nicholas notes) their consent, too, was supposedly required. If all went according to plan, there was no need to repeat at a wedding the agreement that had already been expressed in the betrothal, although subsequent steps (such as dotation) would confirm the agreement and keep it on track. Marriage was

---

[9] *Dig.* 23.2.2. Cf. *Dig.* 23.1.7.1 and 23.1.11, which state that the consents required for betrothal (*sponsalia*) are the same as those for marriage. The person in power is normally the *paterfamilias*.

[10] See Reynolds, *Marriage in the Western Church*, 315–61; Mia Korpiola, "An act or a process? Competing views on marriage formation and legitimacy in medieval Europe," in Lars Ivar Hansen (ed.), *Family, Marriage and Property Devolution in the Middle Ages* (Tromsø, 2000), 31–54; and Alan Macfarlane, *Marriage and Love in England: Modes of Reproduction* 1300–1840 (Oxford, 1986), 291–317.

completed at length in the coming together of the partners in a shared life, an occasion marked by the "handing over" (*traditio*) of the wife to her husband, when the husband was said to lead (*ducere*) his wife in marriage. Whereas she had formerly been his betrothed (*sponsa*) and a wife-to-be, she was now fully married (*nupta*). Their coming together was the presumptive occasion for the sexual consummation of their marriage, but prior to Gratian, it seems, there was no definitive doctrine that consummation was a formal requirement for marriage. Ideally, as Nicholas indicates, a church ceremony or at least a priestly blessing would precede or mark the occasion of their coming together, but the term *nuptiae* does not necessarily denote a liturgical event, despite its etymological connection with veiling.

The Christian understanding of the nuptial process during the early Middle Ages was therefore closely akin to the Jewish one, although the betrothed woman in Judaism was arguably even more "married" than her Christian counterpart, and the process was typically quicker. Marrying among Jews began with *kiddushin* (betrothal), which created an inchoate marriage.[11] The betrothed woman continued to live in her parents' home, but her status in other respects was that of a married woman. (If she was unfaithful, she was in the fullest sense an adulteress.) After sufficient time had elapsed for the necessary preparations,[12] the marriage was concluded in *nisuin*, when the partners came together as husband and wife. Thus, according to the Vulgate version of Matthew's Gospel (Matt. 1:18), Mary was betrothed (*desponsata*) to Joseph when she conceived Jesus, but they had not yet "come together" (*convenirent*). Yet the implications of that crucial precedent were ambiguous, and attempts to resolve the ambiguity by theologians and canonists of the high Middle Ages were not entirely successful. Augustine observes that an angel called Mary Joseph's wife (*coniux*) as soon as they were betrothed (*ex prima desponsationis fide*), even though Joseph would never "know" her.[13] Is a betrothal (*desponsatio*) a promise to do something in the future or an act that has immediate effect?

In the twelfth century, the canonist Gratian defined the nuptial process formally by characterizing betrothal as *matrimonium initiatum*: a marriage that had begun. Marriage was perfected and rendered legally valid (*ratum*), according to Gratian, through subsequent coitus (the "knowing" to which Augustine referred).[14] Gratian

---

[11] See Boaz Cohen, *Jewish and Roman Law: A Comparative Study*, vol. 1 (New York, 1966), 279–348; and Mordechai A. Friedman, *Jewish Marriage in Palestine: A Cairo Genizah Study* (2 vols., Tel-Aviv and New York, 1980–81), vol. 1, 192–93.

[12] According to Friedman (ibid., 193), the standard period for a first marriage was twelve months, and for subsequent marriage thirty days, although a longer period might be permitted for a very young bride.

[13] *De nuptiis et concupiscentia* I.11 (12), CSEL 42, 224.

[14] *Decretum*, C. 27, q. 2, cc. 34–39, in Emil Friedberg (ed.), *Corpus Iuris Canonici*, vol. 1 (Leipzig, 1879), 1073–74, especially dictum post c. 34 (1073) and dictum post c. 39 (1074). On Gratian's theory, see John A. Alesandro, *Gratian's Notion of Marital Consummation* (Rome, 1971); Le Bras, "Doctrine du

presented his theory as a way of reconciling two sets of dicta from the church Fathers and later Christian authorities. On one side were the "consensual" proof texts, which, taken together, implied not only that consensus alone was sufficient for marriage but also that the partners became man and wife as soon as they were betrothed. On the other side were the "coital" proof texts, according to which a woman was not married and did not participate in the nuptial mystery of Christ and the church (Eph. 5:32) until her marriage had been sexually consummated.[15] In fact, although it probably did not seem so to Gratian, the two sets of *auctoritates* were not evenly matched, for while the dossier on the consensual side was genuine and mostly apropos, the chief texts on the other side were spurious, corrupted, or misappropriated.[16] Be that as it may, Gratian found his solution in the notion of *matrimonium initiatum*: yes, spouses were married as soon as they were betrothed, but only by *matrimonium initiatum*, and not by *matrimonium ratum*.

Gratian's theory was congruent not only with the traditional customs and expectations of his day[17] but also with the key biblical premise that marriage is a union of "two in one flesh" (Gen. 2:24). Yet although the position that he advocated was not without precedent in patristic and medieval thought, it defined the role of coitus in the formation of marriage with a clarity that was quite new in continental Europe, and it therefore provoked debate. Scholars have often assumed that Gratian's coital theory originated in Germanic law, but the evidence regarding continental Europe is wanting.[18] Some twelfth-century scholars of Roman civil law maintained that

---

mariage" (n. 4 earlier) 2149–51; and James A. Brundage, *Law, Sex, and Christian Society in Medieval Europe* (Chicago, 1987), 235–39. Gratian probably completed the *Decretum* in the early 1140s, but the process of its composition was complicated, and Gratian remains a shadowy figure: see Anders Winroth, *The Making of Gratian's Decretum* (Cambridge, 2000).

[15] Needless to say, if the wife did not participate in the mystery, neither did her husband, but in fact the crucial texts happened to frame the issue as one pertaining only to the wife, for the germ of the dossier was a letter by Pope Leo I regarding a man's marriage to a girl who had been his slave or servant. See Reynolds, *Marriage in the Western Church*, 162–67, 355–56, 390–91.

[16] The germ of the dossier was a text from Pope Leo I. Hincmar of Reims misappropriated the text, and through a misreading of Hincmar, variants of the text became ascribed to Augustine and appear in this guise in Gratian and elsewhere (including the MGH edition of Hincmar). On Leo and Hincmar, see Reynolds, *Marriage in the Western Church*, 328–61, but my treatment of Hincmar (353–61) should be corrected or supplemented in the light of Gérard Fransen, "Le lettre de Hincmar de Reims au sujet du mariage d'Étienne," in R. Lievens, E. Van Mingroot, and W. Verbeke (eds.), *Pascua Mediaevalia*, Mediaevalia Lovaniensia series I, studia X (Leuven, 1983), 133–46. On the history of the false dossier in the early twelfth century, see Nicholas M. Haring, "The *Sententiae Magistri A* (Vat. ms lat. 4361) and the School of Laon," *Mediaeval Studies* 17 (1955): 1–45; and Heinrich J. F. Reinhardt, *Die Ehelehre des Schule des Anselm von Laon,* = *Beiträge zur Geschichte der Philosophie und Theologie des Mittelalters* N.F. 14 (Münster, 1974), 86–93.

[17] See Jean Gaudemet, *Le mariage en occident: Le mœurs et le droit* (Paris, 1987), 185–88.

[18] The role of coitus – or rather, bedding – in marrying is expressed with unusual clarity in early Icelandic law: see Andrew Dennis, Peter Foote, and Richard Jenkins (eds. and trans.), *Grágás II: Laws of Early Iceland*, vol. 2 (Mannitoba, 2000), add. 147, p. 243: "A wedding is celebrated in accordance with law if a legal administrator betroths the woman and there are six men at least at the wedding and the bridegroom goes openly into the same bed as the woman." (*Grágás* is the collective term for written

the "handing over" (*traditio*) of the bride or her being led into her husband's home (*deductio*) was the moment at which marriage was complete, whether or not consummation ensued immediately, and although this was a minority opinion (at a time when scholarly opinions became polarized between the consensual and coital theories of marriage formation), it was probably a better reflection of the traditional view.[19]

There was still some tension, if not outright inconsistency, between Gratian's theory and the teaching of Augustine, who, for complex theological and ideological reasons, had taught not only that agreement alone created a marriage but that Mary and Joseph had been married in the fullest sense.[20] Gratian's attempt to interpret Augustine in the light of his conciliatory position was astute but not entirely convincing, although it must be said that Augustine's own intentions had been pastoral and ideological: he had never intended to resolve canonical or juridical issues regarding the formation of a valid marriage.

An alternative position arose in the schools of twelfth-century Paris, where its first proponents were theologians. (The relationship between the theory and contemporaneous jurisdiction in Paris at that time remains obscure.) Where Gratian tried to conciliate between coital and consensual theories of marriage formation, Hugh of St. Victor and Peter Lombard took the consensual theory of marriage formation to its logical extreme. With good support from Augustine, Hugh developed his theory in two works composed in the 1130s. The first was a polemical treatise on the virginity of Mary, in which he rebutted an unnamed adversary who held views similar to Gratian's.[21] He later incorporated the theory of marriage developed there into his comprehensive treatment of marriage in the *De sacramentis Christianae fidei*, the first of the great theological *summae*.[22] Hugh maintained, on the one hand, that Mary and Joseph were truly married, and on the other hand, that Mary was a virgin not only in body but also in mind, which is to say that

---

Icelandic laws originating before the Iceland's submission to Norway in 1262/64.) In twelfth-century Iceland, a legal marriage required three things: betrothal (*festar*), the wedding feast (*bryllup*), and witnessed bedding or consummation. There would usually be some delay (normally not more than twelve months) between the betrothal and the conclusion of the marriage (in the wedding feast and bedding). On the role of consummation in Icelandic marriage, see Roberta Frank, "Marriage in twelfth- and thirteenth-century Iceland," *Viator* 4 (1973): 473–84, at 475; and Jenny Jochens, "The church and sexuality in medieval Iceland," *Journal of Medieval History* 6 (1980): 377–92, at 380.

[19] See Charles Donahue, Jr., "The case of the man who fell into the Tiber: The Roman law of marriage at the time of the glossators," *American Journal of Legal History* 22 (1978): 1–53; and Brundage, *Law, Sex, and Christian Society*, 266–67.

[20] See Reynolds, *Marriage in the Western Church*, 254–57, and 339–45 passim.

[21] *De beatae Mariae virginitate*, in P. Sicard (ed.), *L'Oeuvre de Hugues de Saint-Victor*, vol. 2: *Super Canticum Mariae* [etc.], with commentary and translations by Bernadette Jollès (Turnhout, 2000), 183–259. For the Migne version, see PL 176:857–76.

[22] *De sacramentis Christianae fidei*, I, 8, c. 13 (PL 176:314C–318A); ibid., II, 11, c. 2 (482A–D). Hugh devotes the whole of part 11 of Book II (479–520) to marriage. Both treatises date from the period 1130/31–37, but the treatise on Mary was written before the *De sacramentis*: see remarks by B. Jollès in *Super canticum Mariae* [etc.], 8–9.

she made her marriage vows while intending not to consummate her marriage (a problematic position under medieval canon law). Hugh carefully expounded Genesis 2:24: "Wherefore a man shall leave father and mother, and shall cleave to his wife, and they shall be two in one flesh." According to Hugh's analysis, the dictum clearly implies that husband's union with his wife excludes a prior bond with his parents. Therefore the husband must take something from one side to give it to the other. Clearly this cannot be coitus or the conjugal debt; nor can it be cohabitation, given that marriages are often virilocal. Instead, it is a bond of mutual intimacy. The union of "two in one flesh" is indeed sexual union, but that union is another, superadded component in marriage. Hugh shared with Gratian the assumption that only sexual union can establish the union of two in one flesh.

Hugh's rationale for his theory was based on the novel premise (still only some three decades old) that marriage was a sacrament,[23] although he made no attempt to apply to marriage the general theory of the sacraments that he worked out elsewhere in the *De sacramentis*. (According to the latter theory, each sacrament contains or confers what it signifies.)[24] Instead, he predicated his argument on the symbolism of marriage. Conceding that only consummated marriage could be the "great sacrament" of Christ and the church (Eph. 5:32), Hugh argued that there was a deeper, spiritual relationship in marriage that was a still "greater sacrament," namely, that of the union between God and the soul. The greater sacrament was more valuable and could thrive in a celibate, unconsummated marriage, such as that of Mary and Joseph.

Peter Lombard codified (and brought down to earth) Hugh's theory in his *Sentences*, composed in the 1150s, construing marriage not as two sacraments but

---

[23] The term *sacramentum* enjoyed a long history in the theology of marriage prior to the twelfth century and was especially important in Augustine, where the *sacramentum* in (not of!) marriage was the trait of indissolubility that distinguished Christian from non-Christian marriage: see Reynolds, *Marriage in the Western Church*, 280–311. But the notion that marriage should be counted as one of the sacraments along with baptism, eucharist, and the rest first appears in early twelfth-century sentential literature associated in modern scholarship (arguably for no good reason) with Anselm of Laon and his school. Most notable in this development was a treatise on marriage known by its incipit, *Cum omnia sacramenta*, the much-quoted opening passage of which (which Hugh himself appropriated in *De sacramentis* I, 11, c. 1, PL 176:479–80) explicitly compares and contrasts marriage with the other sacraments: see F. Bliemetzrieder (ed.), *Anselms von Laon systematische Sentenzen*, = *Beiträge zur Geschichte der Philosophie des Mittelalters* 18.2–3 (1919), 129–51, at 129: "Cum omnia sacramenta post peccatum et propter peccatum sumpserunt exordium, solum coniugii sacramentum ante peccatum etiam legitur institutum, non ad remedium, sicut cetera, sed ad officium." On marriage in early twelfth-century sentential theology, see Reinhardt, *Die Ehelehre des Schule des Anselm von Laon* (n. 16 earlier); Hans Zeimentz, *Ehe nach der Lehre der Frühscholastik* (Düsseldorf, 1973); and Bernd Matecki, *Der Traktat "In primis hominibus,"* Adnotationes in Ius Canonicum 20 (Frankfurt a.M., 2001). It took more than a century for the problems and inconsistencies entailed in construing marriage as one of the sacraments of the New Covenant (the church's "sacred medicaments") to be fully resolved. The best historical summary of marriage as a sacrament is still Le Bras, "Doctrine du mariage" (n. 4 earlier).

[24] On the theory, see Hugh, *De sacramentis* I, 9, c. 2 (PL 176:317D).

as a single sacrament that signified two aspects of Christ's union with the church, respectively spiritual and incarnate.[25] By this time, Gratian's position was well known, and Lombard wrote in opposition to it. Peter Lombard was less interested than Hugh in the spirituality of chaste marriage, but he was more diligent about tying up canonical loose ends. Lombard deduced that agreement (*consensus*) alone was sufficient to create a sacramental and indissoluble marriage.

Crucial for both Hugh and Peter Lombard was a distinction between the agreement to marry in the future and the agreement to marry with present effect, which first appears early in the twelfth century.[26] Gratian was apparently unaware of this distinction. Canon law had always recognized that at a certain point in the process of marrying, a compact that had been dissoluble became indissoluble. For the followers of Gratian, that point was consummation. For Peter Lombard, the point was an agreement about the present (*consensus de praesenti*), and the compact could be dissolved only as long as it was merely prospective. According to Lombard, a simple agreement was sufficient to create a binding, sacramental marriage, regardless of consummation, but only if the agreement was expressed (i.e., stated orally) in words of the present tense, and only if it was a genuine (rather than coerced) expression of intent. An agreement expressed in words of the future tense, therefore, did not make a marriage at all:

The efficient cause of matrimony is agreement [*consensus*], not of any sort, but expressed in words; and not as to the future [*de futuro*], but as to the present [*de praesenti*]. For if they agree about the future, saying, "I shall take you as a husband," and "I shall take you as a wife," this is not the agreement that is effective of matrimony.[27]

The position that Hugh and Peter Lombard advocated was innovative not only in emphasizing the distinction between the two kinds of consent but also in positing an agreement that was not prospective at all but rather had immediate effect. It became possible to marry suddenly and casually, without any preparations, negotiations, or permission.

Canonists as well as theologians during this period were preoccupied with the necessity of the partners' consent to their own marriage,[28] but the Parisian position was consensualist not only in the obvious sense that agreement was sufficient for marriage but also in the subtler sense that it emphasized the consent of the partners

---

[25] Peter Lombard, *Sententiae in IV libris distinctae*, bk. IV, d. 27, cc. 2–5, and d. 28, c. 3 (Grottaferrata edition, vol. 2 [1981], 422–24 and 434–35). For discussion of Lombard's theory, see Penny S. Gold, "The marriage of Mary and Joseph in the twelfth-century ideology of marriage," in Vern L. Bullough and James A. Brundage (eds.), *Sexual Practices and the Medieval Church* (Buffalo, 1982), 102–17.

[26] See Korbinian Ritzer, *Le mariage dans les Églises chrétiennes du Ier au XIe siècle* (Paris, 1970), 373–77; and Zeimentz, *Ehe nach der Lehre*, 119–24. Ritzer (following Portmann) suggests that Ivo of Chartres (d.1116) was the "father" of the distinction.

[27] *Sent.* IV, d. 27, c. 3.1 (422).

[28] See John T. Noonan, Jr., "Power to choose," *Viator* 4 (1973): 419–34; Brundage, *Law, Sex, and Christian Society*, 238–40.

themselves. Betrothals were typically agreements negotiated between parents, families, and kinsfolk, and children could become betrothed well before marriageable age. Once the distinction between *consensus de futuro* and *consensus de praesenti* was in place, families negotiating a marriage had little to gain by jumping precipitously to the final stage, while couples wishing to marry despite the wishes of their families had nothing to gain by agreeing to marry *de futuro*. By requiring an exchange of vows in the present tense (or something presumptively equivalent), the clergy required persons who were marrying to speak up for themselves. Children who were the subject of a prospective marriage contract drawn up by their parents or families while they were still underage would confirm their own consent when they came of age, sometimes with the help of clergy.[29]

The divergence of opinion regarding the role of coitus in the formation of marriage had great jurisdictional implications. These concerned not only the point of no return at which the marriage bond became indissoluble, but also such questions as whether someone's consummated marriage to one person would automatically abrogate a prior unconsummated but solemnized marriage to another person. During the second half of the twelfth century, canonists presented Gratian's position as the law of Bologna or of Italy, and Peter Lombard's as the law of Paris or of the "church of the French" (*ecclesia Francorum*).[30]

The logic of Peter Lombard's theory, with its clear distinction between betrothal and matrimony, seems to subvert any notion of processual marriage. There is an underlying distinction between promising to do something and actually doing it. As soon as the partners exchanged words of present consent, and not before, they were married, and no actions prior to that consent were necessary. Contrariwise, not only was betrothal merely a promise to marry in the future, but marrying was, itself, an act of agreeing. In other words, betrothal was an agreement *de futuro* to agree *de praesenti*. Whether Lombard really regarded betrothal in that light (as we do today) is not clear. Notoriously, people found the distinction between *de futuro* and *de praesenti* agreements hard to understand. The resulting confusion is evident in terminology. During the high Middle Ages, the traditional terms for betrothal, such as *desponsatio* and *sponsalia* (or in English, "spousals"), could also denote an agreement *de praesenti* or even the exchange of vows at a wedding. At the same time, the partners' coming together and the consummation of their marriage remained important in the secular view of marriage. The fifteenth-century canonist Panormitanus (Nicholas de Tudeschis) noted that a woman was not said to be *nupta* until her husband had "led" her into his house, and that the partners were customarily not called husband and wife (*vir* and *uxor*) until they had consummated their marriage; until then, they were still called *sponsi*. Panormitanus

---

[29] Such confirmation appears in two of the fourteenth-century English cases discussed in ch. 8: *Percy c. Colvyle* (CP E 12), and *Marrays c. Roucliff* (CP E 89).

[30] The relevant sources are conveniently collected in Joseph Freisen, *Geschichte des kanonischen Eherechts bis zum Verfall der Glossenliteratur* (Paderborn, 1893; repr. Aalen, 1963), 182–90.

regarded these matters of usage as at least somewhat relevant to the interpretation of local statutes about dowries, although his opinion seems not to have affected his adherence to the canonical position that agreement alone was sufficient to create a sacramental marriage.[31] Canon law did not prevent the secular authorities from applying narrower, local definitions of a complete marriage to the regulation of dotal transactions (for example, by requiring *deductio* or consummation).[32]

Subsequent modifications of the consensual theory in canon law restored the processual aspect of marrying that Gratian had definitively articulated without altering the principle that *consensus de praesenti* was sufficient in itself to create a valid marriage. Thus Pope Alexander III supplemented the Parisian theory in two ways.[33] First, Alexander ruled that an agreement *de futuro* became a binding marriage if it was sexually consummated. Some canonists construed consummation in that case as a presumptive expression of *consensus de praesenti*, but that was a legal fiction. In effect, Alexander had saved Gratian's notion of *matrimonium initiatum*.[34] Second, a marriage created by *consensus de praesenti*, according to Alexander, could be dissolved in some circumstances before, but not after, it was consummated. In particular, either partner could dissolve a valid marriage unilaterally at this stage by entering the religious life, leaving the other free to remarry.[35] This opportunity was not as improbable as it may seem: David d'Avray has shown that, in fact, there was often a delay between marrying (by *consensus de praesenti* or a liturgical exchange of vows) and the partners' coming together (a further indication that *consensus de praesenti* could still retain the function of betrothal).[36] Later popes extended the principle by investing themselves with the power to dissolve valid but unconsummated marriages.[37]

Although Hugh of St. Victor and Peter Lombard did not envisage any role for coitus in the formation of the marriage bond, canonists and theologians found it easy to adapt Hugh's theory of the twofold sacrament to explain why unconsummated marriage was still dissoluble (under special circumstances) but consummated marriage was indissoluble. For example, one could argue that

---

[31] See Charles Donahue, Jr., "Was there a change in marriage law in the late Middle Ages?" *Rivista Internazionale de Diritto Comune* 6 (1995): 49–80, especially 54.

[32] Ibid., 55–56.

[33] See Charles Donahue, Jr., "The policy of Alexander the Third's consent theory of marriage," in Stephan Kuttner (ed.), *Proceedings of the Fourth International Congress of Medieval Canon Law*, = *Monumenta Iuris Canonici*, series C, subsidia 5 (Vatican City, 1976), 251–81.

[34] See Gaudemet, *Le mariage en occident* (n. 17 earlier), 180–81; and Joannes Mullenders, *Le mariage presumé*, Analecta Gregoriana 181 (Rome, 1971). See also Anne Lefebvre-Teillard, "Règle et réalité dans le droit matrimonial à la fin du moyen-âge," *Revue de droit canonique* 30 (1980): 41–54, especially 43–45 (on the survival of *matrimonium initiatum*) and 47–49 (on marriages resulting from the consummation of *de futuro* spousals).

[35] On dissolution by profession of religious vows, see George H. Joyce, *Christian Marriage: An Historical and Doctrinal Study*, 2nd edition (London, 1948), 452–65.

[36] David d'Avray, *Medieval Marriage: Symbolism and Society* (Oxford, 2005), 180–88.

[37] Joyce, *Christian Marriage*, 430–52; d'Avray, *Medieval Marriage*, 195–99.

unconsummated marriage symbolized the dissoluble union between God and the soul, while consummated marriage symbolized the permanent union between the incarnate Christ and the church.[38] Whereas Gratian had equated *matrimonium ratum* with consummated marriage, churchmen now distinguished between *matrimonium ratum* (effected by an exchange of vows in the present tense) and *matrimonium consummatum* or *perfectum* (effected by subsequent coitus).

While saving the role of coitus in the formation of marriage, Alexander underscored the principle of "consent alone" in another sense: in his judgment, no formality, solemnity, or ceremony was necessary for the formation of a valid marriage, nor was the permission of parents or lords; nor was there any impediment to a marriage between free and unfree persons (as there was in Roman law) as long they both knew about the difference in status when they married. The rationale for his position was partly theological, but Charles Donahue suggests that Alexander's chief motive was to limit the influence of family and feudal lords, even at the cost, which the pope must surely have foreseen and regretted, of encouraging clandestine marriage.[39] Churchmen may also have been influenced by a desire to bring all marriages within the ambit of ecclesiastical regulation, including marriages among the unfree and the nameless poor and misalliances that would traditionally have amounted, at most, to concubinage.[40] Medieval consensualism equalized marriage among different levels of society: on the one hand, marriage of the poorest persons became fully valid and subject to the rules of canon law, while on the other hand, members of the nobility were empowered to marry informally, regardless of family and property.

Notwithstanding the apparent downgrading of betrothal in the high Middle Ages, it was sometimes a solemn event carried out in the presence of a priest. Yet betrothal rites remain a rather shadowy presence in the history of medieval marriage.[41] Efforts by clergy to supervise and regulate *de futuro* agreements seem to have been strongest in northern France. According to the statutes of Eudes de Sully, Bishop of Paris at the beginning of the thirteenth century, *betrothal* (rather than marriage) should be preceded by the reading of banns.[42] Charles Donahue

[38] See Le Bras, "Doctrine du mariage" (n. 4 earlier), 2199–2201; Seamus Heaney, *The Development of the Sacramentality of Marriage from Anselm of Laon to Thomas Aquinas* (Washington, D.C., 1963), 16–20; Thomas Aquinas, *In IV Sent.*, d. 27, q. 1, art. 3, qu^a 2, resp.

[39] Donahue, "Policy." See Charles Duggan, "Equity and compassion in papal marriage decretals to England," in Willy van Hoecke and Andries Welkenhuysen (eds.), *Love and Marriage in the Twelfth Century* (Leuven, 1981), 59–87, at 82–83, where Duggan argues that Donahue's explanation must be wrong because Alexander III categorically condemned clandestine marriage (but the argument seems to involve a non sequitur).

[40] See M. M. Sheehan, "Theory and practice: Marriage of the unfree and the poor in medieval society," in idem., *Marriage, Family, and Law* (n. 7 earlier), 211–46.

[41] See Geneviève Ribordy, *"Faire les nopces": Le mariage de la noblesse française (1375–1475)*, Studies and Texts 146 (Toronto, 2004), 48–56.

[42] M. M. Sheehan, "Marriage theory and practice in the conciliar legislation and diocesan statutes of medieval England," in *Marriage, Family, and Law*, 118–76, at 139. Sheehan points out (139–41) that

has pointed out that whereas most of the English episcopal marriage cases in the high and late Middle Ages were civil actions (i.e., instance cases) regarding *de praesenti* agreements, most of the French cases were criminal actions (i.e., office cases) regarding *de futuro* agreements.[43] In the latter case, a court prosecutor (*promotor*) brought an action to enforce the betrothal. Donahue mentions a French case in which partners who had informally promised to marry *de futuro* "were fined a pound of wax each 'for the clandestinity' and ordered to solemnize their marriage within a week."[44] Donahue proposes an explanation involving cultural differences: in the more individualistic ethos of England, the church courts focused on resolving disputes between individuals, whereas in the more communitarian ethos of northern France, they focused on law enforcement and were, in some sense, co-opted as a means by which families controlled their children.[45]

Notwithstanding the clerical view of marital consent, families continued to negotiate marriages for their children, especially among the aristocracy and minor gentry (but probably among much lower orders as well). Daughters in particular were subject to their parents' will, and it is likely that few seriously considered resistance.[46] Yet canon law left open the possibility for partners to escape the control of their families and to marry informally, whether casually or out of love.[47] Such marriages were not necessarily clandestine, given that the ecclesiastical rules for public marriage had nothing to do with dowry negotiations or parental permission, but a Romeo and Juliet would hardly have had the banns read in their parish church on three consecutive Sundays. An unresolved tension between social control and filial obedience, on the one hand, and the apparently "individualistic" basis of canon law, on the other, is evident in late-medieval England.[48] But even a bride who unwillingly fulfilled her parents' wishes did not necessarily vitiate the consent that canon law required. Agreement to marry did not need to be happy or deeply felt, nor did it need to be the expression of considered personal conviction

---

although a Worcester statute of 1229 seems to make the same ruling, other English references to the reading of banns prior to *sponsalia* may reflect only confusion regarding the terms *matrimonium* and *sponsalia*, which became interchangeable in this period.

[43] Charles Donahue, Jr., "English and French marriage cases in the later Middle Ages: Might the differences be explained by differences in the property systems?" in Lloyd Bonfield (ed.), *Marriage, Property, and Succession* (Berlin, 1992), 339–66. Donahue notes that there was also a long-term trend away from cases involving informal *de praesenti* marriages to separation cases in late-medieval England (344).

[44] Ibid., 342.

[45] Ibid., 362–66.

[46] See Ribordy, *Faire les nopces*, 97–111; and Shannon McSheffrey, "'I will never have none ayenst my faders will': Consent and the making of marriage in the late medieval diocese of London," in Constance M. Rousseau and Joel T. Rosenthal (eds.), *Women, Marriage, and Family in Medieval Christendom: Essays in Memory of Michael M. Sheehan, C.S.B.* (Kalamazoo, 1998), 153–74.

[47] See Geneviève Ribordy, "The two paths to marriage: The preliminaries of noble marriage in late medieval France," *Journal of Family History* 26 (2001): 323–36.

[48] See Jacqueline Murray, "Individualism and consensual marriage: Some evidence from medieval England," in Rousseau and Rosenthal, *Women, Marriage, and Family*, 121–51.

or commitment. It needed only to be genuine in a merely contractual sense. The impediment of "force and fear" (*vis et metus*) invalidated the agreement, but only if it was sufficient to move a "constant man" (*vir constans*). Such legislation was borrowed from contract law.[49] Depositions in *Katherine Dowdall c. Christopher Verdon* (Chapter 9, Doc. 5) vividly illustrate the tensions and emotional turmoil that might eventually result in a daughter's attempt to get her marriage annulled on the grounds of force and fear. The sentence of the court has not survived, but her parents' threats seem to have been sufficient to move a constant man, and her lack of consent both at her betrothal and at her wedding is painfully obvious. Readers are bound to grieve over Katherine's wretched plight, but the disarmingly frank admissions of her parents stir sympathy for them as well. They were doing their best, faced with modest means, to find an advantageous match for one of their several daughters.

The Intervention of Clergy in Marrying

Marriage during the Middle Ages came under the jurisdiction of the "church" (i.e., the clergy, canon law, and bishops with their consistory and episcopal courts), which defined the general conditions for valid marriage and judged whether marriages were valid in particular cases.[50] In theory, the church had this power throughout the Middle Ages, but the clergy's control over marrying became broader and deeper during the eleventh and twelfth centuries, and it was virtually complete by the beginning of the thirteenth.

Georges Duby has drawn attention to two "models" of marriage, respectively aristocratic and ecclesiastical, in high-medieval France.[51] The aristocracy favored endogamy, divorce, and family control, whereas the clergy favored exogamy and indissolubility and maintained that the consent of the partners themselves was not only necessary but sufficient for marriage. Although any theory involving a battle played out between two opposing forces is inevitably too simple to capture the complexity of what went on in fact (and one should keep in mind that the laity as well as the clergy constituted the "church"), subsequent studies have generally

---

[49] See Brundage, *Law, Sex, and Christian Society* (n. 14 earlier), references under "Impediments, marital: force and fear" and "Constant man standard" in the index. In most of the English cases, the litigant is a wife complaining that her parents forced her into the marriage, although in a few cases, the husband is accused of forcing his wife into marriage: see Sara M. Butler, " 'I will never consent to be wedded with you!': Coerced marriage in the courts of medieval England," *Canadian Journal of History* 39 (2004): 247–70.

[50] On the early development of the idea that marriage is subject rather to divine law than to civil or national laws, see Reynolds, *Marriage in the Western Church*, 121–55. On ecclesiastical jurisdiction over marriage cases in the Middle Ages, see Joyce, *Christian Marriage* (n. 35 earlier), 215–44, and Gaudemet, *Le mariage en occident* (n. 17 earlier), 139–45.

[51] Georges Duby, translated by Elborg Forster, *Medieval Marriage: Two Models from Twelfth-Century France* (Baltimore, 1978).

corroborated Duby's insight. Nor was what Duby called the "aristocratic" model limited to the highest social level. (Thus historians referring to his theory often substitute the term "secular" for "aristocratic.") The doctrine of indissolubility, although necessarily inconvenient and at odds with practical and even pastoral considerations, was a crucial component of the ecclesiastical understanding of marriage in the West. Marriage in high-medieval canon law could not be dissolved by mutual consent (although that had been permissible in the early Middle Ages). Ecclesiastical courts could annul a marriage (i.e., declare it invalid) or grant a legal separation (such as the *divortium a mensa et thoro*: "divorce from table and bed"), but they could not dissolve a fully constituted marriage. In other words, neither partner in a valid marriage could remarry as long as the other was alive.

Yet, although the clergy's role in the regulation of marriage was clear, their role in the formation of marriage was much less clear. As members of a learned, professional class, clerics sometimes assisted as matchmakers, and they sometimes mediated in interfamilial conflicts over marital property, but these roles were not exclusively clerical. Priests alone were entitled to administer the liturgical celebration of marriage, yet the nuptial liturgy or priestly blessing was never a condition for valid marriage in the West, as it had become in the East by the ninth century.[52] From time to time, someone proposed on moral or theological grounds that a priestly blessing or some other ecclesiastical formality was necessary for the formation of a valid, legitimate, or sacramental marriage. In the Carolingian period, the authors of forged decretals and capitularies (such as those collected under the name of Benedictus Levita) insisted that all the customary secular and sacred formalities, including dowries and the nuptial liturgy, were necessary for a legitimate marriage. The doctrine was congruent with the chief aim of this spurious literature, which was to insist on the authority of the clergy and especially bishops.[53] In the sixteenth century, Melchior Cano and others argued that priestly blessing was the form of the sacrament of marriage, whereas the spouses' agreement was only its matter. According to this theory (for which there was a good theological case), an unblessed marriage would be a valid contract or quasi-contract but not a sacrament.[54] But such theories never supplanted the deeply entrenched belief that people made their

---

[52] See Reynolds, *Marriage in the Western Church*, 401–12; Cyrille Vogel, "Les rites de la célébration du mariage: Leur signification dans la formation du lien durant le haut Moyen Âge," in *Il matrimonio nella società altomedievale*, Centro italiano di studi sull'alto Medioevo (Spoleto, 1977), vol. 1, 397–465; and Eve Levin, *Sex and Society in the World of the Orthodox Slavs, 900–1700* (Ithaca, 1989), 83–88. The Byzantine Emperor Leo VI (866–912) ruled that the ritual of nuptial benediction by a priest (including the ceremony of crowning for first marriages) was necessary for a valid marriage: see Kallistos Ware, "The sacrament of love: The orthodox understanding of marriage and its breakdown," *Downside Review* 109 (1991): 79–93, at 83–86. A useful resource for the Byzantine canon law of marriage is Patrick D. Viscuso, "A Byzantine Theology of Marriage: The *Syntagma kata stoicheion* of Matthew Blastares" (dissertation, Catholic University of America, 1989).

[53] See Ritzer, *Le mariage*, 340–53; Reynolds, *Marriage in the Western Church*, 404–9.

[54] Melchior Cano, *De locis theologicis* VIII.5 (Padua, 1762, p. 218). See Le Bras, "Doctrine du mariage," 2235, 2255–56.

own marriages. (In the developed Eastern view, on the contrary, a priest joined the spouses, and no expression of their consent was required at the ceremony.)[55] The clergy in the early medieval period declined to bless second marriages or the marriages of *corrupti* (persons who had already experienced coitus), but there was nothing to suggest that such marriages were invalid. Augustine, whose extensive writing on marriage was the basis of the medieval theology of marriage as a sacrament, never mentioned a nuptial liturgy or blessing. (As David Hunter points out in Chapter 3, this was probably because there was no such liturgy in North Africa in Augustine's day.) During the high Middle Ages, churchmen insisted more and more that "clandestine" marriage was sinful and that people should marry *in facie ecclesiae* (i.e., "before the church," or perhaps "in front of a church"), but clandestine marriage was only illicit (forbidden, sinful, and punishable) and not invalid (i.e., nonexistent under canon law). Part of the reason for this situation, as we shall see subsequently, was that even when people did solemnize their marriages in church, they often did so *after* they had privately but validly exchanged marriage vows in the present tense. Eventually, the Council of Trent put an end (wherever it was promulgated) to the medieval regime by ruling in the explicitly innovative decree *Tametsi* (1563) that henceforth a clandestine marriage would be invalid. Trent's rules for marriage *in facie ecclesiae* included the reading of the banns on three previous Sundays or other feast days, and the presence of a parish priest (or his representative) and of two or three other witnesses at the exchange of vows. The priest was to marry the couple with a formula such as "I join you in marriage [*ego vos conjungo*] in the name of the Father, the Son, and the Holy Spirit," or whatever else was customary in the region; and he was to record in a book the date and place of the wedding and the names of the spouses and witnesses. Yet even so, the essential function of the priest, according to Trent, was not to join the couple or to administer the sacrament but rather to witness the partners' own actions.[56] The bishops at Trent permitted pressing pastoral concerns to override theological ones by ruling that what the church had not formally witnessed, regardless of other evidence, did not exist. One can hardly understand medieval marriage without taking account of the liturgy, yet it remains in an odd way at the periphery of practice, and it rarely intrudes upon the theology of marriage as a sacrament.

Most of the traditional rites, symbols, and tokens of the medieval nuptial liturgy – such as the ring, the kiss, the joining of right hands (*dexterarum iunctio*), and the bridal veil – are still familiar today.[57] The ring, the handclasp, and the

---

[55] Ware, "The sacrament of love," 83–84.

[56] For the decree, see Norman P. Tanner (ed.), *Decrees of the Ecumenical Councils* (London, 1990), vol. 2, 755–56. On Trent's deliberations over marriage, see Le Bras, "Doctrine du mariage," 2233–47; and on the decisions of the council, see ibid., 2248. On the intentions behind the decisions, see Jean Bernard, "Le décret *Tametsi* du Concile de Trente: Triomphe du consensualisme matrimonial ou institution de la forme solennelle du mariage?" *Revue de droit canonique* 30 (1980): 209–234.

[57] See Jean-Baptiste Molin, "Symboles, rites et textes du mariage au moyen âge latin," in Giustino Farnedi (ed.), *La celebrazione cristiana del matrimonio*, = *Studia Anselmiana* 93, Analecta liturgica

kiss passed from the betrothal into the wedding itself. The ring and the handclasp were originally features of agreements of all sorts, but their specialized incorporation into the nuptial process gave them new meaning. (The ring, for example, became a symbol of undivided fidelity.) Two conspicuous features of the medieval marriage ceremonies that are no longer customary today are the *pallium* and the blessing of the bedchamber. The veiling of the couple under a cloth called a *pallium* to symbolize their union was more significant than the veiling of the bride alone, although the practice of the bridal veil (now a white veil to symbolize purity instead of the red *flammeum* of pre-Christian Rome) must have continued as well, for it was conspicuous in the quasi-nuptial ceremony by which consecrated virgins and nuns took their solemn vows as brides of Christ.[58]

The complicated history of nuptial rites and liturgies involves not only the rite of veiling but also several ancillary rites that were originally domestic but became Christianized and attached to the liturgy.[59] The veiling was always linked to blessing, and the terms *velatio* and *benedictio* are virtually synonymous in the early liturgical texts. The surviving evidence suggests that the rite of nuptial veiling and blessing began in Rome. The ancillary rites had regional origins elsewhere, and some of them (most notably the bedding rituals) may be characterized, for want of a more precise term, as Germanic. Priestly or ecclesiastical involvement in marrying generally occurred toward the end of the process

11 (Rome, 1986), 107–27, a succinct survey that covers the joining of hands, the veil, the ring, the dotal charter, betrothal coins, the kiss, the symbolic feast and common cup, the bedchamber rite, the expression of consent, and certain minor rites. For a more specialized and detailed account (with emphasis on archaeological evidence), see Henri Leclercq, "Mariage," *Dictionnaire d'archéologie chrétienne et de liturgie* (Paris, 1907–53), vol. 10/2, 1843–1982, especially 1889–90 (on the crown), 1891–93 and 1931–43 (on the ring), and 1893–95 (on the kiss). See also Reynolds, *Marriage in the Western Church*, references under "betrothal tokens" in the index. Medieval discussions of the ritual and symbolic elements of the nuptial liturgy are generally limited to repetitions of Isidore of Seville, but Guilelmus Durandus, *Rationale divinorum officiorum* (ca. 1286), the most popular of the high-medieval liturgical treatises, includes a brief account of marriage as one of the sacraments: see I.9, nos. 7–17, CCM 140 (1995), 114–19. Durandus explains the meaning of the veil (I.9.9, p. 116) and of the ring (I.9.10–11, pp. 116–17).

58 René Metz is the authority on such rituals: see idem, *La consécration des vièrges dans l'Église romaine* (Paris, 1954); idem, "La consécration des vièrges en Gaul des origines à l'apparition des livres liturgiques," *Revue de droit canonique* 6 (1956): 321–39; idem, "L'Église franque d'après la plus ancienne vie de sainte Pusinne (VIII–IXe siècle)," *Revue des sciences religieuses* 35 (1961): 32–48.

59 On the western nuptial liturgy from its origins through the early medieval period, see Korbinian Ritzer, *Formen, Riten und religiöses Brauchtum der Eheschliessung in den christlichen Kirchen des ersten Jahrtausends* (Münster, Westfalen, 1962); second edition, revised by Ulrich Hermann and Willibrord Heckenbach (Münster, 1981). Among English-speaking scholarly communities, the French translation is better known and more widely cited: *Le mariage dans les églises chrétiennes du Ier au XIe siècle* (Paris, 1970). For the later period (but in France and Anglo-Norman England alone), see Jean-Baptiste Molin and Protais Mutembe, *Le rituel du mariage en France du XIIe au XVIe siècle*, Théologie historique 26 (Paris, 1974). Kenneth Stevenson, *Nuptial Blessing: A Study of Christian Marriage Rites* (London, 1982, and New York, 1983), although not always reliable, contains many helpful insights. Much the same may be said of the handy compendium of translations, Mark Searle and Kenneth W. Stevenson (eds.), *Documents of the Marriage Liturgy* (Collegeville, 1992).

of marrying, and it was associated symbolically, albeit ambiguously, with sexual union.

The earliest clear evidence of a nuptial liturgy of veiling and benediction comes from Italy during the late fourth and early fifth centuries. This ritual was reserved for first marriages and indeed for *incorrupti* (virgins of both sexes).[60] What are probably the earliest explicit references to the Roman nuptial blessing appear *passim* in the writings of the fourth-century theologian known today as Ambrosiaster, who assumed that the bride alone was blessed and associated the Christian practice of blessing with Jewish precedents.[61]

The earliest extant liturgical text for the blessing of marriage occurs in the *Veronense* (sometimes known as the *Leonine Sacramentary*), a collection of mass propers for the Roman rite. This collection survives in a single early seventh-century manuscript but drew on Roman material from the fifth through sixth centuries. The marriage rite consists of a sequence of six prayers headed *Incipit velatio nuptialis* ("Here begins the nuptial veiling"). This rubric may refer to the veiling of the couple, although the only petition for specifically *marital* blessings in the sequence pertains to the bride alone (in accordance with the early Roman norm).[62]

Such sources provide prayers for a marriage service (typically a nuptial mass) but provide little information about any other symbols, tokens, gestures, or rituals that would have been customary. Isidore of Seville (ca. 560–636), in his *De ecclesiasticis officiis*, provides us with glimpses of these other aspects as practiced in Visigothic Spain, although his intention was not to describe what happened but to explain the meaning of customs with which his readers were familiar.[63] Isidore explains that the betrothal ring, which the *sponsus* gives to the *sponsa* and places on her fourth finger (whence a vein runs to the heart), symbolizes their mutual fidelity and the union of both their hearts. He mentions that the phrase "for the sake of procreating children" (*causa procreandorum liberorum*) is inscribed on the dotal instrument (*tabulae dotales*), although here he may be merely echoing Augustine. The bride comes to the wedding accompanied by a brideswoman (*pronuba*), who has been married only once, and she wears a veil, called a *mafors* in the vulgar tongue, to symbolize her subjection to her husband.

After the nuptial blessing, according to Isidore, a deacon (*levita*)[64] links them together with a bond (*vinculum*) that symbolizes their indissoluble union. Isidore next explains that "the same *vitta*" is made from a mixture of white and reddish

---

[60] Ritzer, *Le mariage*, 222–26.

[61] Ambrosiaster, *Comm. in I Cor.* 7:40 (CSEL 81/2, 90); *Comm. in I Tim.* 3:12–13 (CSEL 81/3, 268) and 5:3 (278–79); *Quaestiones novi et veteris Testamenti CXXVII* 127.3 (CSEL 50, 400).

[62] See Leo C. Mohlberg, L. Eizenhöfer, and P. Siffrin (eds.), *Sacramentarium Veronense*, Rerum ecclesiasticarum documenta, series major, fontes 1 (Rome, 1956), 139–41; or Ritzer, 421–44.

[63] Isidore of Seville, *De ecclesiasticis officiis* II.20 (CCL 113:89–97). See especially sections 6–9, pp. 91–93.

[64] The rank of deacons or lay-ministers was unusually important in Spain, especially in cathedrals: see *Lexikon für Theologie und Kirche* (Freiburg, 1957–65), vol. 6, 996, and *Dictionnaire d'archéologie chrétienne et de liturgie* (Paris, 1907–53), vol. 8/2, 2996.

(*purpureus*) material: white and red symbolize purity and procreation respectively, and thus the alternation of abstinence and sexual relations in marriage (following Paul's advice in 1 Cor. 7:5).[65] Classical precedents would lead one to expect that the *vitta* was a headband or chaplet worn by the bride to her wedding. According to the most natural reading of this text, therefore, Isidore is referring to two different symbols: the *vinculum* (a band or cord linking the bride and groom) and the *vitta* (a chaplet). In that case, the point of the word "same" (*eadem*) would be that one and the same *vitta* is made from two kinds of material. But scholars usually assume that the *vinculum* and the *vitta* in this passage are the same thing, and that the word "same" equates the latter with the former. According to this interpretation, the deacon links the bride and groom with a bond (*vinculum*) consisting in a ribbon or cord (*vitta*) of cloth made from a mixture of white and reddish material. The reason for preferring this unlikely reading is that rubrics in eleventh-century Spanish *ordines* for the nuptial mass refer to the "veiling" of bride and groom together by what is variously called a *iugale*, a *palleum*, and a *sippa*. According to these rubrics, the *iugale* (perhaps a band of cloth) was made from white and scarlet material and was draped across the head of the bride and the shoulders of the groom.[66]

In his *responsa* to Boris, Pope Nicholas I describes how the *sponsus* and *sponsa* are finally brought to a church with "oblations," where a priest joins their right hands, veils them, and blesses them. Nicholas finds precedent for veiling and benediction both in Genesis 1:28, in which God blessed the first couple and commanded them to "be fruitful and multiply," and in the prayers of Tobias and Sarah (Tob. 8:4, 6–9). Finally, they leave wearing crowns (*coronae*) that are kept in the church.[67] By alluding to the story of Tobias, Nicholas construes the nuptial blessing as a pious deferment of consummation, for that is the point of the story: Tobias and his bride waited for three days, praying instead of consummating their marriage. The

---

[65] *De eccl. officiis* II.20.7 (92): "Quod autem nubentes post benedictionem a leuita uno inuicem uinculo copulantur, uidelicet ne conpagem coniugalis unitatis disrumpant. At uero quod eadem uitta candido purporeoque colore permiscitur; candor quippe ad munditiam uitae, purpora ad sanguinis posteritatem adhibetur, ut hoc signo continentiae lex tendenda. . . . " Interpretation turns on the whether the word *eadam* in the second sentence looks forward to *permiscitur* or backward to *uinculum*. It is possible that *vitta* is a mistaken reading of some Visigothic term (cf. *mafors*).

[66] See Brian F. Bethune, "The Text of the Christian Rite of Marriage in Medieval Spain" (dissertation, University of Toronto, 1987), 296 (for texts) and 181 (for commentary); and Ritzer, *Le mariage*, 303. The same rubric, borrowed from the *Sacramentary of Vich*, occurs in the *Pontifical of Arles* (fourteenth century): see Molin and Mutembe, *Le rituel*, 229–230 (for discussion) and *Ordo* XII, 301 (for the rubric).

[67] Nicholas says earlier in the passage that bride and groom in the West do not wear a *ligatura* ("band") made of gold, silver, or some other metal when they enter into "nuptial agreements" (*nuptialia foedera*). There are at least three solutions to this apparent contradiction: first, that the *ligatura* in question was not a crown; second, that Nicholas's point was that bride and groom in the West did not wear crowns at the beginning of a wedding or during it, as in the East, but only afterwards (see Sheehan, "Bishop of Rome," in *Marriage, Family, and Law* [n. 7 earlier], at 285–86); or third, that the *coronae* mentioned here were not crowns but wreaths or garlands (a plausible translation).

blessings of Tobias's marriage appear in both dotal charters and nuptial liturgies,[68] in which they served both as precedents for liturgical blessing and as proof that marriage was a blessed and not a sinful state. In some regions, the clergy encouraged newlyweds to observe the "Tobias nights," by postponing consummation during the first night or first three nights of their marriage. The origins of the custom are obscure, but the earliest unequivocal references to it date from the Carolingian period.[69] Nicholas's choice of biblical precedents, therefore, like the mixing of colors in the Spanish *vitta* or *iugale* (according to Isidore's interpretation), holds sex and chastity together in a tension that is balanced and yet not without ambiguity. Are the spouses supposed to regard coitus as a sacred duty or a regrettable desecration? Certainly it was the normal and expected outcome of marriage, yet perhaps the clergy expected decent persons to blush at the prospect.

In fifth-century Gaul, as among other regions where recently converted Germanic people were dominant, the blessing of the bedchamber (*benedictio in thalamo* or *ordo in thalamo*) seems to have been the earliest way in which clergy were involved in marrying.[70] The ritual would have occurred at the conclusion of a domestic wedding ceremony. The nuptial prayers in the *Bobbio Missal*, which probably reflect Gallican practice during the Merovingian period (although the possibility of Visigothic influence cannot be ruled out), were intended exclusively for the bedchamber rite.[71]

By the late eighth century, if not before, the Franks were using the Roman rite, which centered on blessing and veiling in a nuptial mass. The *Hadrianum* (the Gregorian sacramentary that Pope Adrian I sent to Charlemagne) includes the petitions for a nuptial mass under the rubric, *Oratio ad sponsas velandas* ("Prayer for the veiling of brides").[72] Because the *Hadrianum* was the basis of Charlemagne's liturgical reforms, one may assume that its nuptial rite became standard among the Franks. There is a similar rite, adapted from Roman forms, in the so-called

---

[68] See references under "Tobie (bénédiction de)" in the index to Molin and Mutembe, *Le rituel*, 345. On the three nuptial blessings in the Book of Tobit and their influence, see Reynolds, *Marriage in the Western Church*, 371–75. There are allusions to Tobit in some dotal contracts appended to this chapter: see ch. 4, Doc. 14, and ch. 5, Charters 1 and 3.

[69] See Molin, "Symboles, rites et textes" (n. 57 earlier), 123–24; Ritzer, *Le marriage* (n. 59 earlier), 281–82; Henry G. J. Beck, *Pastoral Care of Souls in South-East France during the Sixth Century*, Analecta Gregoriana 51 (Rome, 1950), 232–33; Reynolds, *Marriage in the Western Church*, 334, 336–37, 374, 391. The custom is sometimes depicted today as morbidly puritanical, but in circumstances that were common in the early Middle Ages (e.g., child brides, virilocal marriage), it would have been charitable.

[70] See Ritzer, *Le mariage*, 273–76.

[71] For the nuptial prayers, see E. A. Lowe (ed.), *The Bobbio Missal: A Gallican Massbook*, vol. 2, Henry Bradshaw Society [hereafter HBS] 58 (London, 1920), 167–68; or Ritzer, *Le mariage*, 431. On the missal as a whole, see Yitzhak Hen and Rob Meens (eds.), *The Bobbio Missal: Liturgy and Religious Culture in Merovingian Gaul* (Cambridge, 2004).

[72] See Jean Deshusses (ed.), *Le sacramentaire grégorien: Ses principales formes d'après les plus anciens manuscrits, edition comparative*, vol. 1, Spicilegium Friburgense 16, 3rd edition (Fribourg, 1992), 308–11; or Ritzer, *Le mariage*, 427–29.

Old Gelasian Sacramentary, which was written in the scriptorium of the convent of Chelles, near Paris, in the mid-ninth century. Here the ritual appears under the rubric *Incipit actio nuptialis* ("Here begins the nuptial rite") and includes a blessing for the couple (rather than for the bride alone as in Roman practice).[73]

These *ordines* from Francia provide only the nuptial prayers to be used in a mass. The earliest written *ordo* that mentions other ritual and symbolic aspects of marrying is the combined wedding and coronation for Judith, daughter of Charles the Bald, on the occasion of her marriage to Ethelwulf, King of Wessex, in 856.[74] (Its author may have been Hincmar of Rheims.) In the nuptial part of the ceremony, which comes first, there is a prayer for blessings upon the marriage gifts (*dotes*), which is followed by a rite for conferral of the betrothal ring: "Accept the ring, a sign of fidelity and love and a bond of conjugal union, so that man should not separate those whom God has joined together [Matt. 19:6, Mark 10:9]." Then the priest joins the bride and bridegroom in betrothal, thus:

I espouse you to one man, a chaste and modest virgin, a wife-to-be, as the holy women were to their husbands – Sarah, Rebekah, Rachel, Hester, Judith, Anna, Naomi – with the favor of the author and sanctifier of marriage, Jesus Christ our Lord, who lives and reigns for ever and ever.[75]

The nuptial rite concludes with a petition for nuptial blessing (*Deus qui in mundi crescentis*) that appears also in the *Old Gelasian* form. It evokes Genesis 1:28, in which God blessed the first couple and commanded them to procreate. The remarkable combination of betrothal practices (dowry, ring, and *desponsatio*) with nuptials seems to anticipate the Anglo-Norman rites of the high Middle Ages, but the setting and the ceremony (a combination of betrothal, marriage, and coronation) were unusual.

In England and northern France, the ceremonies of the ring and the bedchamber became attached to the nuptial blessing as ancillary rites. But although a priest sometimes blessed the bedchamber and the couple (placed on or in the bed) after a church wedding,[76] it seems that the *benedictio in thalamo* could still function as the only priestly intervention in the process, as in Merovingian times. The latter pattern is probably presupposed in the nuptial sections of the so-called *Egbert Pontifical* (from tenth-century England), which provides prayers for general blessings and

---

[73] See Leo C. Mohlberg, L. Eizenhöfer, P. Siffrin (eds.), *Liber Sacramentorum Romanae Aeclesiae ordinis anni circuli (Sacramentarium Gelasianum)*, Rerum ecclesiasticarum documenta, series major, fontes 4 (Rome, 1960), 208–10; or Ritzer, *Le mariage*, 424–26.

[74] A. Boretius and V. Krause (eds.), MGH, *Capitularia Regum Francorum*, vol. 2 (1890–97), no. 296, pp. 425–27.

[75] Ibid., (426): "Despondeo te uni viro virginem castam atque pudicam, futuram coniugem, ut sanctae mulieres fuere viris suis, Sarra, Rebecca, Rachel, Hester, Iudith, Anna, Noëmi, favente auctore et sanctificatore nuptiarum Iesu Christo domino nostro, qui vivit et regnat in saecula saeculorum."

[76] Ritzer, *Le mariage*, 314–17.

specific prayers for blessings upon the bedchamber, the couple, the ring, and the bed but contains nothing to suggest a nuptial mass.[77] The former pattern is probably presupposed in the nuptial rite of the *Benedictional of Archbishop Robert*, which reflects Anglo-Norman practice of the eleventh century. This rite combines the Roman nuptial mass in its Gregorian form with prayers for the blessing of the ring and its conferral. The concluding prayers seem to have been intended for the bedchamber rite, and the last two prayers in this sequence occur also in the bedchamber rite of the *Egbert Pontifical*.[78]

The blessing of the bedchamber was conspicuous in nuptial liturgies from the Visigothic and Mozarabic tradition of Spain, but here it occurred before the marriage. This is the most distinctive trait of a distinctive tradition, and it survived the influx of Gallican norms during the high Middle Ages. Another distinctive trait of the Spanish rite was the ritual blessing of *arrha*s, which preceded the bedchamber rite. The Spanish *arrha* was originally a betrothal gift and not a ring, as in the Roman tradition; sometimes it was a gift of coins. (Compare the thirteen pennies of the Salian Franks.) When the Spanish *ordo arrharum* became fused with the nuptial rite in the eleventh century, rings replaced coins, but here too the Spanish tradition was distinctive, for whereas the groom alone gave a ring in other cultures, here bride and groom exchanged rings.[79]

A new style of nuptial liturgy developed in England and northern France during the high Middle Ages, and the innovative Anglo-Norman model influenced the rest of Europe. The innovations stemmed from the clergy's keenness to oversee marriages and to make sure that they were consistent with ecclesiastical norms. The same desire is manifest in the clergy's efforts to eliminate "clandestine" marriage. These concerns sometimes expressed themselves in excessive, unrealistic demands that could not endure. A synod at Rouen in 1012 condemned the practice of marrying secretly (*in occulto*) and decreed that before any marriage, there should be careful inquiry into the relationship of the partners (lest they marry within the prohibited degrees). The partners should prepare themselves for the wedding by

---

[77] Ibid., 312–13. For the texts, see H. M. J. Banting (ed.), *Two Anglo-Saxon Pontificals (the Egbert and Sidney Sussex Pontificals)*, HBS 104 (London, 1989), 133–34, 140.

[78] See Mark Searle and Kenneth W. Stevenson, *Documents* (n. 59 earlier), 107–08; and Ritzer, *Le mariage*, 312. For the rite, see Ritzer, 443–45, or Henry A. Wilson (ed.), *The Benedictional of Archbishop Robert*, HBS 24 (London, 1903), 149–51.

[79] The best known and most elaborate of the Spanish rites is that of the *Sacramentary of Vich*, which was compiled at the cathedral of Vich (or Vic) in the eleventh century. (The spelling "Vic," a result of the standardization of Catalan orthography, has replaced the traditional form "Vich" only since the 1970s.) The text is in Ritzer, *Le mariage*, 435–41, but the best source of information about the Spanish nuptial liturgy is the unpublished dissertation by Brian Bethune, cited earlier in n. 66. Bethune collates the rubrics and prayers from several sources (210 ff.), ranging from Vich and the eleventh-century *Liber ordinum* (extant in codices probably written in the monasteries of Santo Domingo de Silos and of San Prudencio de Monte Laturce in the Rioja) to late-medieval sources. On the distinguishing features of the Spanish nuptial liturgy, see ibid., 140–209.

fasting in a monastery or church, and the wedding was to be a solemn occasion that included a nuptial blessing.[80]

The most distinctive feature of the Anglo-Norman model was the preliminary rite at the door of a church or in the porch, which developed during the eleventh and twelfth centuries.[81] This rite typically included the blessing and conferral of a ring, the exchange of other tokens, and the handing over of the bride by her sponsor or patron (*traditio puellae*). The preliminary rite incorporated or reiterated (but did not necessarily supersede) elements of the betrothal process, including dotation, but it was above all an opportunity for a clerical inquiry, usually conducted in the vernacular. As well as inquiring into the conditions and circumstances of the marriage, the priest had to establish that the partners freely consented to it. The preliminary ritual itself was sufficient to establish that the marriage had been made *in facie ecclesiae* and was not clandestine, but it would ideally be followed by a nuptial mass in the church itself. There the couple would begin by prostrating themselves before the altar, and at length the priest would bless them and join them under the *pallium*. After the church ceremony, there might be a domestic celebration that included the bedchamber rituals.[82]

The nuptial *ordo* in a late-twelfth-century pontifical from Canterbury known as the *Magdalen Pontifical* (after the library that holds the manuscript) provides a convenient snapshot of the preliminary rite during that period, for the relevant rubric is precise and detailed:

At spousals [*desponsationes*], the bridegroom [*sponsus*], the bride [*sponsa*],[83] and the bridesmen [*paranymphi*] are stood in front of the door of the church. The priest asks them whether the bridegroom and bride can legitimately come together, lest, that is, they are joined by consanguinity or by some spiritual relationship.[84] When these matters have been established, the priest inquires of the bridegroom, using his proper name, thus: "N., do you will[85] this woman?" If he responds, "I do," the priest says to him, "Do you will to look after her in God's faith and in your own, in health and in sickness, as a Christian man ought to look after his wife?" He inquires of the bride likewise, and if she responds, "I do," the priest and the bride's patron give her to the bridegroom by

---

[80] Ritzer, *Le mariage*, 390–91.

[81] See Molin and Mutembe, *Le rituel*, 32, 34, 35–37, 80; Michael M. Sheehan, "Choice of marriage partner in the Middle Ages: Development and mode of application of a theory of marriage," in idem, *Marriage, Family, and Law* (n. 7 earlier), 87–117, at 111–12; and Christopher N. L. Brooke, *The Medieval Idea of Marriage* (Oxford, 1989), 248–57.

[82] Compare the rite from a Bury St. Edmunds missal (dated 1125/35) in Molin and Mutembe, *Le rituel*, 289–91, Ordo V.

[83] The term *sponsus/sponsa* is used to mean both bridegroom/bride and husband/wife in this passage.

[84] Spiritual affinity was a quasi-parental relationship contracted by sponsoring someone at baptism or confirmation. For example, a man could not marry his goddaughter or her mother.

[85] The verb is *velle*. The English verb "to will" formerly had the same transitive sense, which survives today only in archaic idioms such as "do what you will."

the right hand. Then the bridegroom gives a dowry to his bride with a knife.[86] Then the ring is placed with the spousal pennies on a shield, and they are blessed. "Let us pray: Creator [and sustainer of the human race, giver of spiritual grace. . . .]"[87] After the blessing of the ring, the bridegroom takes the ring and repeats after the priest: "*N.*, with this ring I honor you, and this silver I give to you, and with my body I espouse you, in the name of the Father (on the thumb), and of the Son (on the index finger), and of the Holy Spirit (on the middle finger)." [There follow further prayers.] After this they all go into the church singing, "Blessed are all they who fear the Lord" up to the end with "Glory be to the Father" and "Our Father". . . .[88]

The most effective manifestation of the Anglo-Norman trend toward clerical supervision during this period was the practice of the banns.[89] The parish priest would announce the forthcoming marriage on several (typically three) previous Sundays or feast days, so that anyone who knew of an impediment could come forward. At the same time, the priest was expected to make his own inquiries. In 1215, the Fourth Lateran Council, in a decree on clandestine marriages, made the practice obligatory for the whole church (as well declaring that any cleric who participated in a clandestine union would be punished at minimum by suspension from office for three years).[90] Henceforth, the proper execution of the banns was the chief feature distinguishing a licit from a clandestine marriage.[91] The conclusion of the banns was incorporated into the preliminary rite at the church door.[92] But although scholars have often assumed that the Fourth Lateran Council required couples to say their vows in church or *in facie ecclesiae* or at least in the presence of

---

[86] *per cultellum.* Compare Stephen D. White, *Custom, Kinship, and Gifts to Saints: The Laudatio Parentum in Western France, 1050–1150* (Chapel Hill, 1988), 32 and 249 n. 101 (with the citations given there). White observes that during the ceremonial giving of property to a monastery, "a staff, a knife, a glove, a hammer, a book, or some other object suddenly charged with symbolic meaning was passed by hand from the abbot or prior to the lay donor." The cartulary of the monastery of St. Vincent of Le Mans records gifts made *per cultellum* (with a knife), *per baculum* (with a staff), *per denarium* (with a penny), *per furcam* (with a fork), *per candalabrum* (with a candlestick), *per librum* (with a book), *per cartam* (with a charter), etc.

[87] The text of this standard nuptial prayer is spelled out in full after the rubric.

[88] H. A. Wilson (ed.), *The Pontifical of Magdalen College*, HBS 39 (London, 1910), 202. Although the text is entirely in Latin, the priest would presumably have conducted the dialogue in the vernacular (i.e., in English or French).

[89] See James B. Roberts, *The Banns of Marriage: An Historical Synopsis and Commentary*, Catholic University of America Canon Law Studies 64 (Washington, D.C., 1931); and Michael M. Sheehan, "Marriage theory and practice in the conciliar legislation and diocesan statutes of medieval England," in *Marriage, Family, and Law*, 118–76, at 145–54.

[90] Canon 51. For the text (edited by Giuseppe Alberigo et al.) and a translation, see Tanner, *Decrees of the Ecumenical Councils* (London, 1990), vol. 1, 258.

[91] See Donahue's explanation of the senses of "clandestine" in "The policy" (n. 33 earlier), 258, n. 33.

[92] See the elaborate fourteenth-century preliminary rites of the *Missal of Rouen* and the Cistercian abbey of Barbeau (diocese of Sens) in Molin and Mutembe, *Le rituel, Ordo* XIV, 303–5, and *Ordo* XV, 305–8.

a priest, there is nothing in the decree about how weddings should be conducted, and there is evidence that a record made by a notary, even in the absence of liturgy or clergy, sufficed to make a marriage fully licit in Italy.[93]

In the nuptial rites of the late Middle Ages and the Reformation period, an active, dialogical expression of consent ("I, *N.*, take you, *N.*") sometimes superseded the passive, interrogatory form noted above ("Do you, *N.* take this woman/man, *N.*?"). In that case, bride and groom would repeat the words after a priest instead of merely replying "I do" to his questions. The trend toward greater agency on the part of the spouses is manifest also in the changing meaning of the bride's being "given in marriage," for whereas the bride was traditionally given by her father or guardian, the bride and groom were now sometimes said to give themselves in marriage.[94] The mid–sixteenth-century Sarum liturgy includes both interrogatory and dialogical forms within the preliminary rite (which is performed at the church door). The interrogatory form (wherein bride and groom respond, "I will") occurs first, but later they repeat after the priest the words of the dialogical form ("I, *N.*, take thee, *N.*, to my wedded wife, to have and to hold," and so on).[95] Yet the role of the priest was conspicuous in the formula, "ego vos coniungo" ("I join you in marriage"), which first appears in the late fifteenth century. The formula seems to imply that the priest is the minister of the sacrament (as in Orthodox practice), although the Council of Trent resisted that logic.[96]

Peter Lombard taught that when partners marry, they should clearly express their intent in words of the present tense such as "I take you as my husband," and "I take you as my wife." (It was the sense that mattered, according to Lombard, and not the precise formulation: agreement should be expressed "in these words or in others signifying the same.")[97] Other churchmen made similar prescriptions.[98] But in what setting did the clergy envisage the speaking of such formulae? Because churchmen in northern France were advocating marriage *in facie ecclesiae* when

[93] See David d'Avray, "Marriage ceremonies and the church in Italy after 1215," in Trevor Dean and K. J. P. Lowe (eds.), *Marriage in Italy, 1300–1650* (Cambridge, 1998), 107–15. Compare the notarized *matrimonia* documents from Renaissance Florence appended to ch. 11 (Docs. 2, 5, and 8).

[94] See Molin and Mutembe, *Le rituel,* 77–116.

[95] A. Jefferies Collins (ed.), *Manuale ad usum percelebris Ecclesie Sarisburiensis,* HBS 91 ([Chichester], 1960), 44–59. See also Searle and Stephenson, *Documents* (n. 59 earlier), 163–77 (for the rite in contemporaneous English), and Jacqueline Murray, *Love, Marriage, and Family in the Middle Ages: A Reader* (Peterborough, Ontario, 2001), 261–70 (for a rendering in modern English).

[96] See Joanne Pierce, "A note on the 'Ego vos conjungo' in medieval French marriage liturgy," *Ephemerides liturgicae* 99 (1985): 290–99; and A. Duval, "La formule *Ego vos conjungo* au Concile de Trente," *La Maison-Dieu* 99 (1969): 144–53. The formula first appears in Rouen in 1455.

[97] *Sent.* IV, d. 27, c. 3.1 (423): "Accipio te in virum et ego te in uxorem, matrimonium facit." Ibid., d. 28, c. 4.2 (435): "Cum igitur sic convenient, ut dicat vir: *Accipio te in meam coniugem,* et dicat mulier: *Accipio te in meum virum,* his verbis vel aliis idem significantibus, exprimitur consensus." Compare Hugh's formulation of a typical *desponsatio de praesenti* in *De sacramentis* II.11.5 (PL 176:488A–B): "... ille dicit: Ego te accipio in meam, ut deinceps et tu uxor mea sis, et ego maritus tuus, et illa similiter dicit: Ego te accipio in meum, ut deinceps et ego uxor tua sim, et tu maritus meus."

[98] Molin and Mutembe, *Le rituel,* 104.

Peter Lombard wrote the *Sentences*, one might assume that he had in mind the exchange of marriage vows at a church service, or more precisely during the preliminary Anglo-Norman rite at the church door. But that is unlikely, for in Peter Lombard's Paris, the partners would probably have expressed their consent at the wedding only passively and in response to the priest's inquiries, replying "I do" at the appropriate moments. Molin and Mutembe's evidence suggests that the full-fledged dialogical form, wherein each partner (following the priest) states that he or she accepts the other, does not appear in nuptial liturgies until the fourteenth century.[99] By the sixteenth century, the active, dialogical form was prevalent in northeastern and southern France, but the passive form still prevailed in a large central area of France that included Paris.[100]

I suggest, therefore, that Peter Lombard and others who directed the laity to use such formulae as "I take you as my husband" were not thinking of the nuptial liturgy but of agreements made privately or in domestic settings. If a cleric was present at a domestic marriage, he could lead the couple in a dialogue, but it was also incumbent upon the clergy to teach the laity how to contract marriage properly even when no cleric was present, as was often (probably usually) the case. The laity would also have learned by example, imitating privately what they heard occasionally in church. There is ample evidence from the depositions of England and Ireland that even if people did not always fully understand the distinction between *de futuro* and *de praesenti* spousals, many of them knew how to exchange vows *de praesenti* in a manner that would satisfy the church courts. A church wedding might follow at a later date. One of the rules stated by Trent in *Tametsi* was that spouses must not begin to live together until a priest had solemnized their marriage in church.[101] The rule presupposes that many had been living together before their marriages were solemnized. Studies of post-Reformation England, indeed, have shown that despite the best efforts of the clergy, many couples began to cohabit once they had been espoused *de futuro* and did not see anything wrong with that.[102]

The church's position on the solemnization of marriage was in this respect analogous to its position on baptism. Bishops and synods in northern France during the high Middle Ages urged parish priests to teach the laity how to baptize a newborn child if the child's life was at risk and no priest was available. This simple act required nothing more than the threefold sprinkling with water in the name of Father, Son, and Holy Spirit. If the child survived, the parish priest would in due course ascertain that the correct form had been used and would then complete the ceremony (with the rituals of salt, chrism, and so forth).[103] But whereas baptism

[99] Ibid., 106–09.

[100] Ibid., 110.

[101] *Tametsi*, in Tanner, *Decrees of the Ecumenical Councils*, vol. 2, p. 756, lines 24–25.

[102] See Macfarlane, *Marriage and Love in England* (n. 10 earlier), 304–06.

[103] See Kathryn A. Taglia, "The cultural construction of childhood: Baptism, communion, and confirmation," in Rousseau and Rosenthal, *Women, Marriage, and Family* (n. 46 earlier), 255–87, at 261–69.

by a priest was the norm and bishops permitted lay baptism only as an emergency measure, lay marrying seems to have been the norm, and not only in a statistical sense, for even when there was a church wedding, it would often follow a private but valid exchange of vows in the present tense.

A deposition in the York Cause Papers that Frederik Pedersen analyzes (CP E 79) includes a good example of the use of the dialogical method in a private setting, although the relaxed attitude to nuptial formalities evinced here might have been more typical of England than of France during the period (see Chapter 8, Appendix B.1–2). In 1351, Robert Midleton and Elizabeth Frothyngham were married privately in her father's chapel. The chaplain, Richard Wynsted, explained to the partners how to plight their troth in words of the present tense. Repeating after the chaplain, Robert said: "I take thee Elizabeth as my wife, to hold and to have until the end of my life, and on this I give thee my pledge." Likewise Elizabeth said: "Here I take thee Robert as my husband to hold and to have until death has separated us, and on this I give thee my pledge." Had the process stopped at that point, the marriage would have been valid yet clandestine and illicit. In fact, the banns were subsequently published for three successive Sundays in the parish churches of Frysmersk and Burton, and the marriage was finally solemnized in the presence of many distinguished guests in Frysmersk, the nearest church that was large enough for the wedding. The family chaplain, Richart Wynsted, must have helped them to make the arrangements. Because they regarded marriage as a process rather than an event, they fulfilled the requirements sequentially and not all at once.

The late-medieval depositions from Armagh appended to Chapter 9 show that the laity had learned how to exchange their vows properly when there was no cleric present to say, "repeat after me.…" Even if these witness statements (which depended on memory) were not accurate, it is notable that lay witnesses recalled exchanges of vows that were perfectly congruent with canon law and church doctrine. When John McCann married Anisia FitzJohn privately in a garden (Doc. 1), Niall O'Moregan, a laborer, was their only witness, yet they exchanged vows that they might have heard in church weddings: "John married the said Anisia and she similarly him with words in the present tense, saying, 'I take you as my wife,' and she similarly, 'I take you as my husband until death do us part'." William Kelly, a layman, played the role of minister rather well when he "married" Margaret Keran and John O'Kele (Doc. 2). Having first ascertained that there was no impediment of relationship, William joined their right hands, and they exchanged vows in the present tense, saying "I John take you Margaret as my lawful wife and thereto I give you my faith," and "I Margaret take you John as my lawful husband and thereto I give you my faith." Having plighted their troth, John and Margaret kissed each other. Marriage vows spoken in a private, secular setting could be as refined as those spoken in church, as when Harry Palmer married Kateryn Boys in a barn or storehouse (Doc. 4): "I Harry Palmer take thee Kateryn Boys to my ryghtfull wyf to have and to hold unto my lyfe's end and thereto y plyght thee my trouthe," and

"I Kateryn Boys take thee Harry Palmer to my lawfull spouse to have and to hold unto my lyfe's end and thereto y plyght thee my trouthe." What more need they have said?

DOTATION

The term "dotation" is used very broadly here, so as to cover any transfer of wealth or property to a spouse or couple that is peculiarly marital. There were several sorts of matrimonial assign in medieval Europe, given in various combinations, and the regimes varied considerably among different cultures and over time. Somewhat artificially, one may divide the typical assigns into four sorts: (1) brideprice or bridewealth, which a suitor or husband gave to the woman's father (such as the Lombard *meta* or *metfio* and the Burgundian *wittimon*); (2) gifts from a husband (or his father or parents) to a betrothed woman (or her representatives) to confirm their betrothal; (3) gifts from a husband to his newlywed spouse, such as the *morgengabe* (morning gift), supposedly once given after consummation as the price of virginity; and (4) endowments transferred with the bride from her father, parents, or kinsfolk.[104]

The distinction between the second and third types is not always clear (the Frankish dowry, for example, fulfilled both roles), and from a merely economic point of view, their function was usually the same. Hence, one may reduce the list to three types. In the convenient terminology of anthropologists, these are (1) bridewealth, (2) indirect dowry, and (3) direct dowry. Bridewealth passed from the husband's side to his wife's parents or family. Indirect dowry passed from the husband or from others on his side (such as his father) to his wife. Direct dowry passed from the wife's side (i.e., from her father, parents, family, kinsfolk, or guardian) to the wife herself or to the couple.[105]

Yet dotal contracts of the period record arrangements that were more complicated than any threefold or fourfold division might suggest. For example, the contract might state that the bride's father transferred wealth to the bride herself, or to her husband, or to her father-in-law; or the dowry might be divided among

[104] See Régine Le Jan, "Aux origines de douaire médiévale (VIᵉ–Xᵉ siècle)," in eadem, *Femmes, pouvoir et société dans le haut Moyen Âge* (Paris, 2001), 53–67, especially the chart on p. 60. On the Germanic assigns, see Reynolds, *Marriage in the Western Church*, 80–87. There is a wealth of information on early medieval dotal regimes in François Bougard, Laurent Feller, and Régine Le Jan (eds.), *Dots et douaires dans de haut moyen âge*, Collection de l'École française de Rome 295 (Rome, 2002), a collection that may be said to represent the "state of the art" in this field of legal history. For the post-medieval period in France, see Jacqueline Musset, *Le régime des biens entre époux en droit normand du XVIᵉ siècle à la Révolution française* (Caen, 1997).

[105] See Jack Goody, *The Development of the Family and Marriage in Europe* (Cambridge, 1983), references under "brideprice," "bridewealth," and "dowry" in the index; and idem, "Bridewealth and dowry in Africa and Eurasia," in Jack Goody and S. J. Tambiah, *Bridewealth and Dowry*, Cambridge Papers in Social Anthropology 7 (Cambridge, 1973), 1–58.

them (for example, the bride's father might give so much to her father-in-law and so much to her husband). It is not always possible to ascertain the purpose or eventual destiny of such transfers.

The term "dowry" is problematic, for the corresponding Latin term, *dos*, was applied both to direct and to indirect dowries during the medieval period. Many historians today reserve the term "dowry" (or in French, *dot*) for property that a wife brought into a marriage from her family.[106] Most distinguish categorically between dowry and dower, treating them as an opposing pair. Some historians refer to any marriage gift from husband to wife as a "dower" (or in French, *douaire*), but many reserve that term exclusively for the "widow's portion," that is, a wife's interest in a portion of her husband's property, to which she will receive a life estate or usufruct if he predeceases her. Such conventions, which are apparent in several of the following chapters, are perfectly acceptable, but one should keep in mind that they are a result of modern stipulations (usually unstated) and do not replicate medieval usage. In medieval Latin, the term *dos* could denote any of these assigns, even including the widow's portion, and a glance at the entries under "dowry" and "dower" in the *Oxford English Dictionary* suggests that the two terms (both of which derived from the Latin *dotarium* via the French *douaire*) were interchangeable in late-medieval English. Moreover, although the medieval terminology can be revealing, one should not depend on it or assume that it was consistent, for the more predictable the rules and expectations in practice, the less the terminology mattered.

The Economics of Dotation

Scholars approach medieval dotation from various points of view. Some legal historians focus on law codes and charters, attending especially to the precise terms used for the various assigns in order to determine a society's rules or dotal "regime." Social historians consider dotation within the broader context of its social setting (for example, regarding the family or gender). Anthropologists consider dotation and its function comparatively, by considering norms and customs in diverse societies. Although they are chiefly preoccupied with ethnographic evidence, some of them (most notably Jack Goody) have taken the history of dotation in premodern Europe into account and have even contributed to this field of study.[107] In general, anthropologists have tended rather to refine the categories and to generate questions than to produce overarching explanations. Some economists have tried to explain patterns of dotation by reducing them to predictive, quantified models,

---

[106] Because the English word "dot" (= "dowry") is no longer current, the word "dowry" has to serve as the equivalent of the French *dot*, although (like "dower") it came from the French *douaire*.

[107] As well as Goody's *Development of the Family and Marriage*, see idem, *The European Family* (Oxford, 2000), especially ch. 5, "European Patterns and Medieval Regimes" (57–67), and ch. 7, "Dowry and the Rights of Women" (86–99), where Goody summarizes and reviews his previous work on such topics.

and again, some of these economists have included medieval dotation within their purview.

Bridewealth is property that a suitor or husband gives to his bride's family or kin as a condition for receiving her in marriage. Some historians still use the term "brideprice" in this sense, and such assigns were sometimes referred to as *pretium* ("price," "cost") in early medieval sources. Yet because the term seems to suggest that men bought and sold women like chattels, most scholars today follow Jack Goody's lead in preferring the more neutral term, "bridewealth." Anthropologists and economists generally assume that the function of bridewealth is to compensate the bride's family or kinsfolk for the loss of her productive and reproductive value, although ethnographic evidence shows that bridewealth is sometimes involved in a circulating fund, wherein what a group acquires in exchange for daughters it pays out again to acquire daughters-in-law. Bridewealth may compensate the bride's family, therefore, but in cultures wherein it is systematic and well developed, it also regulates the giving and receiving of brides.[108]

Some of the Germanic races of Europe seem to have practiced bridewealth during late antiquity and the early Middle Ages, although it is hard to show that such assigns remained with the bride's family rather than passing eventually to the bride herself, and the importance of bridewealth in our collective historical imagination is inflated. Germanic husbands or their families or representatives sometimes gave wealth (construed today as bridewealth or brideprice) in return for a power over the bride known as *munt* (or in Latin as *mundium*), which passed from father to son-in-law. Such was the case among some East German races during the early Middle Ages (especially the Burgundians and Lombards). The *mundr* of medieval Iceland (discussed by Agnes Arnórsdóttir in Chapter 10) seems likewise to have been brideprice or bridewealth. But evidence of bridewealth among West German races, such as the Alammani, Thuringians, and Franks, is at best tenuous. Diane Owen Hughes, in an extraordinarily influential article, assumes that brideprice had "fallen from prominence" among the tribes that lived on the fringes of Empire by the end of the first century AD, and that it had "generally disappeared" from West German practice by the time written codes of Germanic law were drawn up (in Latin). But she assumes that it must once have existed in the unwritten prehistory of these races, and that some customary betrothal gifts, such as the *solidus* and *denarius* of the Salian Franks, were vestiges of it.[109]

The purpose of medieval dowries (whether direct or indirect) is largely a matter for speculation, but likely reasons are not hard to find. The dowry insured a wife

---

[108] See Goody, "Bridewealth and dowry," 5.

[109] Diane Owen Hughes, "From brideprice to dowry in Mediterranean Europe," *Journal of Family History* 3 (1978): 262–96, at 266 ff. The article is reprinted in Marion A. Kaplan (ed.), *The Marriage Bargain: Women and Dowries in European History* (New York, 1985), 13–58. See also Goody's critical references to this article in *Development of the Family*, Appendix 2: "From Brideprice to Dowry?" 240–61 passim.

against separation resulting from misuse, divorce, or widowhood, and it was a contribution to the economy of married life. The direct dowry compensated the husband for the cost of marriage. The conferral of dowries might confirm or establish a relationship between two families or kin groups. Less obviously, dowry could be a means of social or economic advancement. For example, a family that had recently become wealthy might use a direct dowry to enable a daughter to move upward into a family of higher social standing and influence, whereas a family of high status but inferior wealth might hope to reestablish themselves economically and socially by attracting a daughter-in-law who would bring a large dowry. Finally, dowry was a means of passing wealth from generation to generation. Thus, dowry was in some sense a "premortem inheritance," or rather should be considered one means of devolution among others. As Jack Goody puts it, "both dowry and inheritance [are] ... part of an intergenerational process of devolution in which daughters have access to parental property."[110]

When one considers the history of dotation across the medieval period, the most conspicuous feature is a trend from direct to indirect dowry during the early Middle Ages and then a revival of the direct dowry in the high Middle Ages.[111] The dowry (*dos*) of classical Roman law was wealth that a wife brought into a marriage from her parents. This assign was not strictly a gift (*donatio*), for under Roman law, the wife remained a member of the family that had raised her even after her marriage, and her family could recover the dowry (for example, if she died without offspring). But the husband might contribute a marriage gift to his wife before their marriage (the *donatio ante nuptias* or *sponsalitia largitas*). After Justinian had lifted the ban on gifts between spouses, a husband could endow his wife after they were married (in which case, the gift was called *donatio propter nuptias*).[112] During late antiquity, the importance of the husband's gift in Roman society increased. Legislation that was intended to cap its maximum value at that of the direct dowry is evidence that there was a trend toward inflated gifts on the husband's side.[113]

In early medieval Europe, the husband's gift to his wife was the principal assign. People called it a *dos*, and the direct dowry largely disappeared from written records. This change can be explained in part as a result of Germanic influence: Tacitus had observed that among the Germans, it was not the wife who offered the dowry to

---

[110] Goody, *European Family*, 86–87.

[111] See David Herlihy, "The medieval marriage market," in Dale B. J. Randall (ed.), *Medieval and Renaissance Studies*, no. 6: *Proceedings of the Southeastern Institute of Medieval and Renaissance Studies, Summer, 1974* (Durham, N.C., 1976), 3–21; reprinted in Herlihy, *The Social History of Italy and Western Europe, 700–1500: Collected Studies*, Variorum Reprints (London, 1978), XVI. Hughes discusses the revival of (direct) dowry in "Brideprice to dowry," 276 ff. But see Jack Goody, *Development of the Family and Marriage*, Appendix 2 (240–61). On the regime of the *dos ex marito*, see André Lemaire, "La *dotatio* de l'épouse de l'époque mérovingienne au XIIIᵉ siècle," *Revue historique de droit français et étranger*, 4th series, 8 (1929): 569–80.

[112] See Judith Evans-Grubbs's discussion of these gifts in ch. 2.

[113] Herlihy, "Marriage market," 5–6.

her husband, but the husband who offered it to his wife.[114] But the trend affected even cultures and regions in which Roman influence remained strong. Thus Pope Nicholas I, explaining Western marriage practices to Boris of Bulgaria in A.D. 866, described the *dos* as a gift that the *sponsus* (the husband-to-be) gave to his *sponsa* (his betrothed). Nicholas also said that both sides – i.e., the respective families, friends, or representatives of bride and groom – agreed to its terms, and that the agreement was recorded in writing.[115]

Direct dowry regained its importance during the first half of the twelfth century.[116] This trend coincided with the renewed influence of Roman law, following the rediscovery of Justinian's *Corpus Iuris Civilis* in the late eleventh century, but it is very unlikely that such influence alone could have so profoundly affected prevailing norms and customs. What might explain these opposite trends?

The social historian David Herlihy has proposed a theory of the "marriage market" to account for these trends. According to this theory, endowment compensates for the relatively low value of men or women on the market, so that contributions from the husband's side (as bridewealth or indirect dowry) are dominant when more marriageable men are available than women, whereas direct dowries are dominant when more marriageable women are available than men. In fact, there is good evidence from other indications (mainly circumstantial, although there are some demographic data) that such was the case: that marriageable men outnumbered marriageable women in the early Middle Ages, whereas marriageable women outnumbered marriageable men in the high and late Middle Ages.[117] The relative level of availability of men or women in medieval Europe was not only a function of absolute numbers in the population. Factors such as celibacy (clerical and monastic) and the tendency for men to marry later than women would have reduced the number of men available on the marriage market.

Herlihy's theory is generally consistent with theoretical models developed by the economist Gary Becker. Expressed in terms of Becker's "rational choice" approach, the function of marital assigns is to equalize the respective values of marriageable men and women and thereby to clear the marriage market.[118] But two other rational choice economists, Maristella Botticini and Aloysius Siow, have proposed an alternative theory predicated on Goody's notion of dowry as premortem inheritance.[119] The authors object that according to the marriage market theory, a fall in

---

[114] *Germania* 18.1: "Dotem non uxor marito, sed uxori maritus offert."

[115] Nicholas I, *Epist.* 99, MGH *Epist.* 6, p. 570.

[116] Herlihy, "Marriage market," 7–8.

[117] Ibid., 5–19. Herlihy touches on the population imbalance *passim* in two other essays reprinted in *Social History* (n. 111 earlier): "Women in medieval society" (IX), and "Life expectancies for women in medieval society" (XIII).

[118] See Gary S. Becker, *A Treatise on the Family* (Cambridge, Mass., 1981; revised edition 1991).

[119] Maristella Botticini and Aloysius Siow, "Why dowries?" *American Economic Review* 93 (2003): 1385–98. Throughout the article, the authors contrast dowry (i.e., direct dowry) with "brideprice," but they seem to include indirect dowry under the latter term.

the importance of endowment from the husband's side should always be accompanied by an increase in the importance of endowment from the other side, which (beyond the medieval European context) is not always the case.[120] The crucial factor favoring direct dowry, in their view, is not the ratio between marriageable men and marriageable women but rather whether or not marriage is virilocal. Their theory centers on the stake that sons have in nurturing the family's assets. Suppose, for example, that there are two children, a son and a daughter, and that their parents would like, other things being equal, to divide the family's wealth equally between them. If the daughter marries but her portion remains for the time being with the family's assets (while she retains her right to eventual ownership), there would be a disincentive to the son, who must work to nurture the family's capital. The authors claim that their model has good predictive or explanatory value across a wide range of societies, including those of premodern Europe. But the theory is most convincing when a daughter's receipt of a direct dowry excludes her from further inheritance, which (as Goody himself notes) was not always the case in premodern Europe.[121]

Another economist, Duran Bell, is critical of some of the assumptions underlying such theories.[122] For example, Bell objects to Goody's notion that the dowry is a premortem inheritance.[123] In part, his objection is to an improper use of the term "inheritance," which properly denotes a "system . . . in which the claims upon a person's estate are *socially prescribed* by unambiguous rules of devolution." According to Bell, the bequest, rather than inheritance, was the dominant mode of devolution in medieval Europe, because of the influence of the clergy (who wished to divert wealth to themselves). Someone who makes a bequest owns full rights to alienate the property in question. But Bell also objects that in many cultures, the direct dowry is not received by the bride in her own right but instead becomes joint or family property. And Bell objects to marriage market theories in general because they presuppose that the direct dowry and the value of women are inversely related. Bell counters that in many societies, the opposite is the case: dowry is a "prestige practice," and the greater the social value of a bride, the greater her dowry.[124] It

---

[120] The authors also object (1385b) that the marriage market theory "cannot account for why in many dotal societies the timing of intergenerational transfers is gender specific, with parents assigning dowries to their daughters and leaving bequests to their sons." Yet if one assumes that parents want to leave wealth to both sons and daughters (in a roughly equal distribution), the marriage market theory would explain precisely why, during a period in which women were at a premium, it would make sense to pass wealth to daughters prematurely in the form of dowries.
[121] See Goody, *European Family*, 86–87.
[122] Duran Bell, "Wealth transfers occasioned by marriage: A comparative reconsideration," in Thomas Schweizer and Douglas R. White (eds.), *Kinships, Networks, and Exchange* (Cambridge, 1998), 187–209.
[123] Ibid., 204–05.
[124] Ibid., 206–07.

remains to be seen whether Bell's insights have much relevance for medieval historians because his avowed aim is to study bridewealth and dowry as exchanges pertaining to "corporate groups" rather than to individuals, and the more individualistic presuppositions that he shuns may apply tolerably well to medieval Europe.[125]

Indirect dowries during the high and late Middle Ages often included or consisted in a widow's right to receive a portion (such as half or a third) of her late husband's estate.[126] Such rights might be defined in a written contract, or they might be undocumented and automatic. The custom was widespread in high- and late-medieval Europe, and it was especially well developed in England and Northern France. The origins of the widow's portion should probably be sought in the *tercia* of the Franks and Burgundians (a widow's right to a third of her husband's estate). There may have been some historical connection between the *tercia* and customary caps on indirect dowries and morning gifts, such as the Lombardic *quarta* and the Visigothic *decima*.[127] The widow's portion usually consisted only in usufruct, so that it was in effect her life estate and would pass eventually to her husband's heirs rather than to her own (if there was a distinction).

Direct and indirect dowries predominate in the chapters that follow. Apart from the *mundr* of medieval Iceland (a brideprice that was distinct from a husband's gift to his wife), bridewealth appears only in passing. The dotal instruments of late antiquity discussed in the first two chapters define direct dowries (although Evans-Grubbs in Chapter 2 describes as well the husband's *arrha* and *donatio ante nuptias*). The Merovingian and Carolingian dotal charters discussed in Chapter 4 define the husband's gift, here called a *dos*. The dotal charters of twelfth-century northern France discussed in Chapter 5 define the same gift, although in this era it was called *dotalicium, sponsalicium, donatio propter nuptias*, or *donatio nuptialis*. The twelfth-century Occitanian charters of Chapter 6 state both a direct dowry (sometimes called a *dos*) and a husband's gift (variously called *donatio propter nuptias* or *dotalicium*; the term *sponsalicium* was applied here to gifts of both sorts). The Occitanian husband's gift was typically half of his property or real estate, although as Cynthia Johnson explains, it was always subject to specification or exemption in the written agreement. The English dotal charters appended to

---

[125] Ibid., 188. A corporate group is "a set of individuals who have socially recognized claims ... to consume or use a specific [and scarce] resource or set of resources," so that "the rightful claim of an individual must be limited to a share of that resource."

[126] See Hughes, "Brideprice to dowry," 270; Laurent Feller, "*Morgengabe, dot, tertia*: Rapport introductif," in Bougard, Feller, Le Jan, *Dots et douaires*, 1–25; and Janet S. Loengard, "'Of the gift of her husband': English dower and its consequences in the year 1200," in Julius Kirshner and Suzanne F. Wemple (eds.), *Women of the Medieval World: Essays in Honor of John H. Mundy* (Oxford, 1985), 215–55.

[127] Compare Hughes, "Brideprice to dowry," 269–70.

R. H. Helmholz's Chapter 7 define gifts from either side.[128] The documents from late-medieval Iceland appended to Chapter 10 define bilateral exchanges, and the dotal regimes that appear in the remaining chapters are likewise bilateral.

To characterize a dowry fully, one would have to state not only its source and whether it was direct or indirect but also the nature of the woman's right to it. Even when the direct dowry belonged to the wife, the husband would typically manage it during the marriage and could profit from it. When a husband contributed an indirect dowry, whether in the form of a defined gift or as a widow's portion, his wife sometimes (but not always) had only usufruct rights to it, so that her portion was a life interest in property that remained part of her husband's patrimony.[129] In some high- and late-medieval dotal regimes, marital assigns were fused into a common fund that belonged jointly to the couple but was managed by the husband. Property regimes in northern France during the late Middle Ages tended to be communitarian: generally, all children inherited equal portions of their parents' estate, and the couple held property in common.[130] In England, on the contrary, property devolved by preference to the oldest male offspring, and spouses held marital property separately, so that the husband could not alienate or bequeath his wife's property. But this pattern is clearest in the case of real estate. In England, the husband was sometimes entitled to alienate his wife chattels, and dotal agreements in France were qualified by the division of wealth into inherited land, acquired land, and movables.[131] Although direct dowries typically belonged to the wife or her family, local statutes in Italy during the high and late Middle Ages gave more control over the dowry to the husband, so that he could keep a portion of it if his wife predeceased him. But some doctors of the *ius commune* (the body of canon and Roman laws and jurisprudence supposedly common to all of Christendom) resisted this trend because a woman and her family retained ownership of her dowry under Roman law.[132] In a late-medieval variant of the dotal regime, which emerged in civil law in many parts of Europe, a portion of the direct dowry, sometimes called the "marriage portion," was reserved for the wife and her family after the wedding, whereas the remainder was merged with the common property.

Both common and separate property regimes appear in the chapters that follow. The implications of such trends for the politics of gender are very hard to

---

[128] Docs. 1–2 (twelfth century) and 9 (fifteenth century) define gifts from the husband's side; Docs. 3 (twelfth century), 5 (thirteenth century), 7 (fourteenth century), and 10 (fifteenth century) state the parental or direct dowry (although in Doc. 10, the donor is the bride's brother); and Doc. 8 (fourteenth century) includes gifts from both sides.

[129] On the question of a wife's usufruct vs. full ownership of her assigns, see Hughes, "Brideprice to dowry," 270–72.

[130] This is merely a generalization. Some northern cities maintained systems of primogeniture, and many gave priority to all male offspring over females. Moreover, testamentary freedom permitted parents to favor some children and to disinherit others.

[131] See Donahue, "English and French marriage cases" (n. 43 earlier), 348–50.

[132] See idem, "Was there a change in marriage law" (n. 31 earlier), 58–59.

disentangle. Martha Howell in Chapter 12 explains how, in late-medieval Douai, a common property regime gave way to a norm of separate property. In the older regime, spouses who had begotten at least one child were automatically considered to have created a *ravestissement par sang,* whereby their property became merged into a common fund. (The tradition seems to imply that the begetting of a child, rather than consummation, completed the marriage.) A married couple could also draw up a written *ravestissement,* in which case the common fund applied "whether or not there is an heir" (Doc. 1). But during the fourteenth and fifteenth centuries, there was a trend toward a system of separate property that was, in some respects, akin to the old Roman dotal regime. Each spouse would bring his or her contribution (*portement*) to the marriage, and although the fund would be merged and placed under the husband's control during the life of their marriage, each contribution remained marked as separate property. Written contracts, drawn up at least forty days before the wedding, defined the wife's *portement* in meticulous detail (see Docs. 2–3). Agnes Arnórsdóttir in Chapter 10 describes an opposite trend in medieval Iceland, where a twelfth-century norm of separate ownership gave way to a thirteenth-century norm of joint ownership called *félag,* an institution that existed as well in Denmark and Norway.[133] In the Icelandic case, the trend seems to have been allied to a greater focus on the agreement of the spouses rather than of their fathers or families in the contracting of marriage.

Dotation and Documentation in the Process of Marrying

In any study of marrying and its documentation, the ritual significance of dotation is as important as its economic function. Gifts or agreements marked steps in the process of marrying, ensured that the marriage was honorable, and sometimes helped to distinguish between a true marriage and a casual relationship. Thus even a vestigial or token gift (such as the gift of a flower in Renaissance Florence mentioned by Thomas Kuehn in Chapter 11) could be significant in the absence of wealth.

Bishops, canonists, and other churchmen, from late antiquity and throughout the early Middle Ages, insisted that formal dotation, as well as public nuptials, was a necessary step in contracting a legitimate marriage. Churchmen often quoted the maxim, "There can be no marriage without a dowry [*dos*]." The maxim seems settled and orthodox, although it is ambiguous: does it imply that marriages without dotation are invalid (and therefore void), or only that they are illicit (and perhaps for that reason voidable)? Nor is it clear whether it was the dowry per se that was

---

[133] See Stig Iuul, *Fællig og hovedlod: studier over formueforholdet mellem ægtefæller i tiden før Christian V's danske lov* (Copenhagen, 1940); Frederik Pedersen, "The *fællig* and the family: The understanding of the family in Danish medieval law," *Continuity and Change* 7 (1992): 1–12; Kathrine Græsdal, "Joint ownership in medieval Norway," in Lars Ivar Hansen (ed.), *Family, Marriage and Property Devolution* (n. 10 earlier), 81–97; and Ragnhild Ormøy, "Inheritance and division of wealth on the death of a husband," ibid., 99–106.

important or rather its written record, for the dotal charter seems to have been the only written record of marriage during the early Middle Ages. The force of the maxim began to wane in the eleventh century, although canonists continued to pay lip service to it. Gratian, in the mid-twelfth century, treated dotation as optional.[134] In any case, it is likely that such prescriptions applied mainly to persons of substance, who alone have left written traces for historians to study. The maxim seems never to have expressed a necessary condition for the validity of marriage. Nevertheless, in cultures that recognized concubinage alongside marriage, the lack of dotation and documentation underscored the informality of the partnership, although disparity of class was a more important indicator. Such was the concubinage of classical Rome (a relationship *not* entered into *liberorum procreandorum causa*). Judith Evans-Grubbs (Chapter 2) argues that under Justinian's reign, matrimonial documents became the "indicators of morality" needed to show that a relationship between a man of high status and a lowborn woman was indeed a marriage. Contrariwise, Giovanni di ser Lodovico della Casa, in Renaissance Florence, married Lusanna without dowry or documentation (albeit in the presence of several guests, including two clerics) and later denied that the marriage existed (see Chapter 11).

Some written dotal agreements were linked to the betrothal and others to marriage. There is no obvious difference in function between the two sorts. Similarly, although the Jewish *ketubah* is usually signed at the wedding or at the time of coming together, it was written at the time of betrothal during the early Tannaitic period (i.e., at the beginning of the classical period of Jewish law, corresponding roughly to the beginning of the Christian era).[135] The Roman dotal instrument was associated rather with marriage than with betrothals, although in most cases, such instruments would probably have been drawn up before the marriage. Representatives of the two sides may well have discussed the dowry and had the instrument drawn up during the pre-marital negotiations or at the betrothal (*sponsalia*); or they might have concluded the agreement at any time between betrothal and marriage. Yet there is no reason to associate Roman dotal instruments specifically with betrothals, and the terms used for them (such as *tabulae nuptiales* and *tabulae matrimoniales*) imply an association with marriage. The jurist Scaevola says that the tablets were often not actually *signed* until after the marriage itself had begun (*Dig.* 24.1.66 pr.), and David Hunter, in Chapter 3, suggests that the signing of a dotal instrument was a conventional feature of domestic wedding ceremonies among North African Christians around the fifth century AD.

In the early Middle Ages, dotal agreements were associated with betrothal but treated as a subsequent pre-marital formality (i.e., as another stage in the process). This association was probably in part a result of Germanic influence, but even under

---

[134] See André Lemaire, "Origine de la règle *Nullum sine dote fiat coniugium*," in *Mélanges Paul Fournier* (Paris, 1929), 415–24; idem, "La *dotatio* de l'épouse" (n. 111 earlier); and Patrick Corbet, "Le douaire dans le droit canonique jusqu'à Gratien," in Bougard, Feller, and Le Jan, *Dots et Douaires*, 43–55.

[135] See Boaz, *Jewish and Roman Law* (n. 11 earlier), vol. 1, 304.

Roman law, betrothal became more significant and more binding in late antiquity, so that breaking a betrothal became legally actionable. Under such conditions, it would have been advisable for the parties involved to state the financial terms of the proposed marriage during the negotiation phase of marriage. Pope Nicholas I, in his rescript to Boris of Bulgaria, describes agreement about dowry as occurring after the betrothal, but continuation of the promise to marry must have depended on reaching such agreement. Hence the Frankish indirect dowry or betrothal gift coalesced with the antenuptial gift (*donatio ante nuptias*) of Roman law and came under rules about the latter in the *Theodosian Code* and the Visigothic *Breviary*, which were the chief written sources of Roman law during the early medieval period. (The *arrha* of Roman law probably also influenced the Germanic dowry, but the early medieval *arrha* usually took the form of a ring, the value of which was more symbolic than economic.)

The Frankish dotal charters discussed in Chapter 4 (which survive as formulae) recorded an agreement made after the betrothal, but the dotal charter was apparently the only documentation of that betrothal. The *sponsus* recalled in the dotal contract that the betrothal had already taken place, and he looked forward to the wedding, when the bride's rights to her indirect dowry would come into effect. One finds the same pattern in two tenth-century dotal charters from northern Aquitaine (which, like the Frankish formulae, defined a gift from husband to wife).[136]

In other examples, the dotal charter itself embodied an agreement to marry *de futuro*. This is the pattern that seems most logical and predicable when one considers the manner in which a marriage was negotiated during the high and late Middle Ages, for, in general, negotiations between families and kin naturally concluded in a *de futuro* agreement, whereas the clergy were chiefly interested in *de praesenti* agreements. Several of the English deeds appended to R. H. Helmholz's Chapter 7 (Docs. 6–10, ranging from the thirteenth through fifteenth centuries) explicitly state *de futuro* agreements to marry. Hence the remarkable separation between "secular" and "spiritual" contracts that R. H. Helmholz discusses in Chapter 7 is, to some extent (although not entirely), explicable as a product of the distinction between *de futuro* and *de praesenti* agreements. In a study of marrying among the French aristocracy during the fourteenth and fifteenth centuries, Geneviève Ribordy describes how negotiations would be concluded in a betrothal contract stating the agreement to marry in the future, the marriage gift, and other conditions.[137] According to René Girard, marriage contracts in Avignon in the later fifteenth century began with the rubric, "A betrothal has been made by words in the future tense [*sponsalia facta sunt per verba de futuro*]" and included a promise to marry *in facie ecclesiae*, as well as defining the direct dowry and other marriage gifts. The *sponsalitium* of Renaissance Florence (see Chapter 11, Docs. 1, 4, and 7)

---

[136] See Philippe Depreux, "La dotation de l'épouse en Aquitaine septentrionale du IXe au XIIe siècle," in Bougard, Feller, and Le Jan, *Dots et douaires*, 219–44, at 241–42, nos. 1 (ca. 975) and 2 (ca. 990).

[137] Ribordy, *Faire le nopces* (n. 41 earlier), 10–13.

was likewise a document that recorded both a *de futuro* agreement to marry and
the financial settlement (pertaining especially to the earnest money pledged by the
sponsus to his wife-to-be).

Other dotal charters embodied an agreement to marry with present effect.[138]
Such are the deeds from twelfth-century northern France appended to Chapter 5
and those from twelfth-century Occitania appended to Chapter 6. The northern-
French deeds seem to have been intended for use in the preliminary rite at the
church door. The situation of the Occitanian charters in relation to the nuptial
process is less clear, although Cynthia Johnson notes that there was sometimes a
delay between the agreement *de praesenti* embodied in the charter and the partners'
coming together in a common home, which was probably the point at which the
laity, if not the clergy, would have regarded the marriage as complete.

THE DOCUMENTATION OF MARRIAGE

Most of the documents appended to the chapters that follow are records that were
intended (at least ostensibly) to provide evidence of a marriage or of its circumstances for some legal process, such as the resolution of a dispute or the enforcement
of an agreement. Documents that fit this broad description include records used
by episcopal and consistory courts in marriage litigation. These describe, among
other things, the contracting of marriages through an oral exchange of vows. Most
of these documents are depositions, that is, witness statements that proctors of the
court took down for use as evidence in marriage cases. (The witnesses themselves
rarely appeared in person, although in the later medieval period, documents from
marriage cases sometimes include the recorded testimony of parties at the trial.)
Such documents seem to have survived in significant quantities only from certain
dioceses in England,[139] Ireland,[140] and (to a lesser extent) northern France[141] during

---

[138] Another of Depreux's examples, dated 1083, is of this type: see no. 4, 243–44.
[139] The classic study of the English evidence is R. H. Helmholz, *Marriage Litigation in Medieval England*
(London and New York, 1974). See also Michael M. Sheehan, "The formation and stability of
marriage in fourteenth-century England: Evidence of an Ely register," in idem, *Marriage, Family,
and Law* (n. 7 earlier), 38–76 (article first published in *Mediaeval Studies* 33 [1971], 228–63); Frederik
Pedersen, *Marriage Disputes in Medieval England* (London, 2000), a work now supplemented by
Prof. Pedersen's chapter in this volume; Shannon McSheffrey (ed. and trans.), *Love and Marriage
in Late Medieval London* (Kalamazoo, 1995); eadem, "I will never have none ayenst my faders will"
(n. 46 earlier); and Donahue, "Policy" (n. 33 earlier).
[140] See the article by Art Cosgrove reproduced in this volume (ch. 9).
[141] See Anne Lefebvre-Teillard, *Les officialités à la veille du Concile de Trente* (Paris, 1973); Beatrice
Gottlieb, "Getting Married in Pre-Reformation Europe: The Doctrine of Clandestine Marriage and
Court Cases in Fifteenth-Century Champagne" (doctoral dissertation, Columbia University, 1974);
Charles Donahue, Jr., "The canon law on the formation of marriage and social practice in the later
Middle Ages," *Journal of Family History* 8 (1983): 144–58; and idem, "English and French marriage
cases" (n. 43 earlier). See also Geneviève Ribordy, *Faire les nopces* (n. 41 earlier) – but while taking the
above studies into account, Ribordy relies mainly on secular proceedings (i.e., Parlement de Paris,
Registre de Trésor des Chartes) because extant documents on marriage from French ecclesiastical
courts are rare (see xviii, n. 21).

the high and late Middle Ages. Depositions constitute much of the evidence used in Chapters 8 and 9 (respectively by Frederik Pedersen and Art Cosgrove), and examples of depositions are appended to these chapters. Such documents include records of marriage contracts, yet the contracts per se were not written but oral. The courts rarely used written marriage deeds to substantiate a marriage.

The other main class of marriage documents consists in deeds, or *acta*. These record marital agreements between the two "sides" involved in the marriage: on the one side, the groom or his parents, kinsfolk, or representatives, and on the other side, the bride or her parents, kinsfolk, or representatives. Most of these deeds not only recorded but also embodied the agreement, inasmuch as the parties committed themselves to the agreement by signing the deed in the presence of witnesses (although in some cases, as Agnes Arnórsdóttir explains in Chapter 10, the deed and its witnesses testified to an earlier, oral agreement). Marriage deeds, too, provided evidence that might, in principle, be used in some legal process, although one can rarely show that they served that purpose in fact. Whatever the intention and expectations surrounding them, deeds were ostensibly actionable in law.

Documents of this sort, with which most of the essays in this anthology are chiefly concerned, are commonly (and not incorrectly) called "marriage contracts." Yet this term can be misleading because the chief object of such agreements is usually dotation rather than marriage per se, although as R. H. Helmholz points out, many of these "settlements" also express or refer to the agreement to marry. (This may have been why phrases such as "to have and to hold" passed from property agreements into the nuptial liturgy and marriage vows.)

It is remarkable that the dotal contract of pre-modern Christendom was never a medium for the full expression of marriage vows. Whereas the Jewish *ketubah* recorded not only the marriage settlement but also the husband's or spouses' marital obligations (such as his duty to honor and provide for his wife according to the law),[142] the medieval dotal contract seems never to have recorded the spouses' commitment to the fundamental obligations of marriage. If the spouses articulated these obligations at all, they did so *viva voce*, whether formally in a nuptial liturgy or haphazardly in private vows.

In the early Middle Ages, a dotal charter might record that a betrothal had occurred at an earlier date (see Chapter 4), but there seems to have been no written record of the betrothal itself. Likewise, the expression of agreement *per verba de praesenti* on which the high-medieval doctrine of marriage focused was for the most part a strictly oral contract, or at least it was so in northern Europe. Thomas Kuehn notes (Chapter 11) that in Renaissance Florence, where secular notarial culture was unusually advanced and prominent, marriage itself was sometimes recorded in a document called a *matrimonium*. Such documents recorded the (oral) marriage

---

[142] See Friedman, *Jewish Marriage in Palestine* (n. 11 earlier). Although the Babylonian *ketubah* expressed the husband's obligations alone, the Palestinian *ketubah* expressed the wife's obligations as well: see ibid., vol. 1, pp. 19, 43, 181–91.

vows alone and said nothing about transfers of wealth or property.[143] And Trent required parish priests to record in a book the marriages solemnized in the parish church. Yet it is remarkable that north-European clergy considered the agreement to marry to be a strictly oral contract notwithstanding the close association between clerical office and literacy in that society (an association that has left its mark in the shared etymology "clergy" and "clerk"). The supposition was congruent with the high-medieval theology of marriage as a sacrament, given that every sacrament was supposed to be caused and actively constituted by its "word" or "form" (such as the invocation of the Trinity in baptism and the words of consecration in eucharist), although neither canon lawyers nor theologians ever prescribed any determinate formula for marriage: it was the meaning and the intent that counted, not the precise words. Mutes were permitted to use nonvocal signs, and canon law recognized the local significance of such ritual gestures as the handclasp. In R. H. Helmholz's discussion of marriage contracts in medieval England (Chapter 7), the "secular" marriage contracts, which focused on dotal arrangements, were written deeds, whereas the "spiritual" contracts (i.e., the contracts considered by the episcopal courts) were strictly oral. Frederik Pedersen (Chapter 8) describes how the English episcopal courts' dependence on oral evidence in marriage cases was so thorough that even when they did take the existence of a written deed into account, only oral testimony about the deed, and not the deed itself, was entered into evidence. Nevertheless, most oral testimony reached the court only via written depositions, since the witnesses rarely appeared in person.

For the most part, the medieval "marriage contract" in the narrowest sense of that term – the agreement to marry as such – remains hidden from us because it was only rarely a written agreement. Like the judges in ecclesiastical courts, we know about it only indirectly, for example, through the documentation of oral testimony.

---

[143] See Docs. 2, 5, and 8 appended to ch. 11.

CHAPTER TWO

Marrying and Its Documentation in Later Roman Law

Judith Evans-Grubbs

"Marriage is the joining of male and female and a partnership [*consortium*] for all of life, a sharing of divine and human law," wrote the jurist Modestinus early in the third century.[1] The lawyer thus expresses the Roman idea of marriage as a joint enterprise, in which each partner has both emotional and financial interests (*consortium* can also connote a business relationship), a view found also in literary sources.[2] A similar but more sentimental depiction of marriage appears in funerary inscriptions for a deceased spouse, with whom the dedicator is said to have lived for years "without any complaint" (*sine ulla querela*), and on sarcophagi depicting the couple clasping hands in a gesture of marital solidarity.[3] Whatever the realities of married life for individuals, Roman public and private ideology clearly espoused the idea of marriage as a mutual and balanced partnership.

It is fitting to begin with a quotation from one of the great legal minds of the imperial period, for any study of Roman marriage will of necessity draw heavily on legal evidence. The sources available to scholars of marriage in the medieval and

---

[1] *Digest* 23.2.1 (see n. 5 for text used): "Nuptiae sunt coniunctio maris et feminae et consortium omnis vitae, divini et humani iuris communicatio." All translations are my own unless otherwise noted. Most of the legal sources cited here are translated in Judith Evans-Grubbs, *Women and the Law in the Roman Empire: A Sourcebook on Marriage, Divorce, and Widowhood* (London, 2002), hereafter WLRE. Other abbreviations in the notes that follow: TAPA = *Transactions of the American Philological Association*; FIRA = *Fontes Iuris Romani Antejustiniani*, ed. S. Riccobono, J. Baviera, et al., 3 vols., 2nd edition (Florence, 1968–72). I am grateful to Antti Arjava and Agnes Arnórsdóttir for comments on this chapter.

[2] Tacitus, *Annales* 3.34 (ed. C. D. Fisher, Oxford Classical Texts, 1906) describes a debate in the Senate on whether wives should accompany provincial governors to their posts; proponents cite the benefits of a marital "partnership [*consortium*] of favorable and adverse things." On Roman marriage in the classical period (first century BCE to third century CE), see Susan Treggiari, *Roman Marriage: Iusti Coniuges from the Time of Cicero to the Time of Ulpian* (Oxford, 1991). For late antiquity, see Judith Evans-Grubbs, *Law and Family in Late Antiquity: The Emperor Constantine's Marriage Legislation* (Oxford, 1995); Antti Arjava, *Women and Law in Late Antiquity* (Oxford, 1996); and Philip L. Reynolds, *Marriage in the Western Church* (Leiden, 1994). On marriage as a partnership, see Treggiari, *Roman Marriage*, 249–51.

[3] Treggiari, *Roman Marriage*, 243–49; Evans-Grubbs, *Law and Family*, 58 and 78–88.

early modern periods – cartularies, parish records, local and episcopal archives, private diaries, letter exchanges, and so on – do not exist here (apart from the epistles of famous political or religious figures, which are literary or theological works rather than intimate correspondence).[4] Certainly, in antiquity, people of property made wills, registered their children's births with the authorities, wrote personal letters, and often recorded marriage or divorce agreements in writing, but time and weather have destroyed most of the documents. Those that do survive (see the subsequent discussion on marriage documents on papyri and wood) are from Greco-Roman Egypt and, to a much lesser extent, from elsewhere in the Middle East; none survives from Europe.

In this chapter, I examine what defined marriage in the Roman imperial period (which began with the reign of Augustus, 31 BCE to 14 CE), with emphasis on developments in the fourth through early sixth centuries CE. The chapter focuses on those aspects of most relevance to medieval marriage: questions of consent, marital assigns (dowry and prenuptial gifts), and the use of written records and deeds (*acta*). All of these issues relate to one basic question: how could one tell whether a relationship was marriage? In other words, what distinguished a legally sanctioned union from a non-legal alternative?

LEGISLATION AND SOCIAL HISTORY

The lack of primary source material noted previously makes the legal evidence all the more valuable, because there we can at least find references to wills and marriage agreements, even when the actual documents have perished. This is especially true for the *Digest*, the most important source for the classical period of Roman law.[5] Compiled under the emperor Justinian (reigned 527–65) as part of his *Corpus Iuris Civilis*, the *Digest* is a collection of excerpts from the most important jurists of the late Republic and earlier Empire, with the majority of citations from the second and early third centuries.[6] Jurists were legal experts, not judges or

---

[4] The private letters of Cicero are an exception (and Treggiari uses them to good effect in her *Roman Marriage*), but he was writing before the period on which this chapter focuses.

[5] Scholars refer to the period ca. 100 BCE to ca. 235 CE, when the jurists in the *Digest* wrote, as "classical." Law of the fourth and fifth centuries is called "post-classical" or "late antique." The most accessible text of the *Digest* (hereafter *Dig.*), and the one cited here, is Alan Watson (ed.), *The Digest of Justinian*, 4 vols. (Philadelphia, 1985): this is a reprint of the Latin edition of Theodor Mommsen and Paul Krueger (Berlin, 1868) with facing English translation.

[6] Justinian intended his corpus to have legal validity in his own day, 300 years after the jurists wrote; passages dealing with obsolete laws or issues regarding which the law had changed were thus deleted. An earlier generation of scholars believed that the compilers interpolated many words and ideas from the sixth century into the classical texts that they assembled. In recent work, the hunt for interpolations has largely ceased. We can mainly trust the *Digest* to be the words of the jurists themselves, though in an incomplete and abbreviated form. See David Johnston, *Roman Law in Context* (Cambridge, U.K, 1999), 17–22; and Tony Honoré, *Tribonian* (London, 1978), 248–51.

lawmakers; in this period the emperor was the only real source of law. But some jurists did receive special authority from the emperor, so that their opinions carried great weight. The jurists quoted in the *Digest* often discuss specific cases on which they had been consulted, such as disputes over dowry or over the validity of marriages.

There are valuable details about individual cases in another part of Justinian's corpus as well, the *Codex Justinianus*, which preserves legislation of emperors from the second century up to Justinian's reign. Almost all the constitutions in the *Codex* from before the reign of Constantine (307–37 CE) are *rescripta*, that is, rulings on particular points of law given in response to petitions from imperial subjects (including women and non-elite provincials).[7] They inform us about the sorts of legal issues that concerned ordinary people, including matters of marriage and dowry, inheritance rights, and questions regarding status. Unfortunately, the petitions themselves do not survive, but it is still possible to see the individuals behind the emperors' responses, and to understand how the ambiguities inherent in Roman legal principles played themselves out in real life.

For legislation from Constantine up to 438, there is the *Codex Theodosianus*, compiled and promulgated under Theodosius II and later used by Justinian for his code; for the later fifth century, some post-Theodosian imperial laws (*novellae*) also survive.[8] Unlike the brief responses to petitions found in second- and third-century rescripts, late antique legislation was in the form of "general laws" (*leges generales*), intended to have application for the population at large. The laws were addressed to imperial and provincial officials or to government bodies such as the Senate, and the recipients were then supposed to relay the emperor's rulings down the chain of command to the local level.[9] The laws in the *Theodosian Code* represent imperial attempts to craft a uniform policy for issues that in the past had received more nuanced and individualized responses. They also served ideological and propaganda purposes and were therefore highly rhetorical, setting out what the emperor believed was just and moral along with harsh penalties for the disobedient.[10]

---

[7] Tony Honoré, *Emperors and Lawyers*, 2nd ed. (Oxford, 1994). The standard edition of the *Codex Justinianus* (hereafter CJ) is that of Paul Krueger, in the second volume of the *Corpus Iuris Civilis* (Zurich, originally published 1877, reprinted many times).

[8] Theodor Mommsen and Paul Meyer edited the *Theodosian Code* (hereafter CTh) with the *novellae* and the Sirmondian Constitutions (Berlin, 1905). For a useful English translation, see Clyde Pharr, *The Theodosian Code* (Princeton, 1952).

[9] See Jill Harries, *Law and Empire in Late Antiquity* (Cambridge, U.K., 1999); and John Matthews, *Laying Down the Law: A Study of the Theodosian Code* (New Haven, 2000).

[10] The wording of the laws was the responsibility of the head of the imperial chancellery (the *quaestor sacri palatii*), who (especially in the fourth century) was more likely to have rhetorical and literary skills than legal training: see Tony Honoré, *Law in the Crisis of Empire 379–455 AD: The Theodosian Dynasty and its Quaestors* (Oxford, 1998); and Harries, *Law and Empire*, 36–53. How much input an emperor actually had in the laws made under his name depended on his age and competence. For convenience, even child emperors are credited here with authority for laws made in their name.

Law is, by its nature, prescriptive, and clearly we cannot assume that people always followed these laws. But late Roman legislation did more than simply regulate the processes of making marriage; it also expressed certain assumptions and beliefs about the betrothal bond and the respective roles of father, mother or other relatives, guardians, and the *sponsa* herself. Late Roman emperors not only introduced new elements into the Roman law of marriage, they also enunciated the traditional ideology more explicitly than the jurists of the earlier Empire had done. Unfortunately, the compilers abridged the laws in the *Theodosian Code*, and therefore we cannot see the full ideological impulse that motivated late antique emperors or their specific reasons for enacting particular laws.[11]

However, unlike the Justinianic Corpus, which retained only legislation still applicable in Justinian's day, the *Theodosian Code* preserves laws that had been annulled or modified by later rulings. This allows us to see the evolution of imperial responses to issues such as prenuptial gifts, divorce, or quasi-marital unions between slave and free, and to see how the eastern and western halves of the late Empire differed in their policies. Until the death of Theodosius I in 395, laws made under one emperor would be accepted by his imperial colleagues, but the division between eastern and western Empire became permanent in the fifth century (apart from the brief period of Justinian's reconquest in the mid-sixth century), and the two halves diverged in their policies.[12] In the socially more cohesive East, emperors were more likely to follow classical Roman law than were rulers in the rapidly disintegrating West, and eastern law schools (such as the famous one in Beirut) fostered that tendency.[13] Thus laws of eastern emperors are often more liberal on matters such as divorce, the rights of illegitimate children, and the need for proof of marital status, whereas in the West, where rulers were trying to stem intense social and economic change, imperial attitudes appear harsher.

For a study focusing on marrying and matrimonial documents in the Middle Ages, an understanding of the Roman law of marriage is essential, because of the enormous impact Roman law had on medieval canon and civil law. Issues such as consent to marriage, dowry and prenuptial gifts, and the use of pledges

[11] Unlike the abridged versions of laws in both the Theodosian and Justinianic codes, the *novellae* have been preserved in full. Some of the laws abbreviated in the *Theodosian Code* have also been fully preserved in a compilation of sixteen laws relating to the Christian church now known as the *Sirmondian Constitutions*, and comparison of the two versions can provide an idea of what the compilers left out. The *Sirmondian Constitutions* are found in vol. 1.2 of Mommsen-Meyer and are translated in Pharr, *Theodosian Code*.

[12] Although the headings of laws of both the Theodosian and Justinianic Codes give the names of all emperors reigning when the law was made, for most of the period from Constantine's death in 337 to the deposing of the last emperor in the West in 476, each emperor had his own consistory and enacted legislation for his own part of the Empire. It is usually possible to determine which emperor was responsible for a law by noting either its place of promulgation (e.g., Milan or Ravenna for western laws, Constantinople for eastern laws) or the position of the official to whom the law was addressed.

[13] Honoré, *Law in the Crisis of Empire*.

(*arrhae*) as betrothal guarantees, are all rooted in Roman law.[14] Canon law itself drew heavily on Roman law, and the revival of Roman classical law beginning in the late eleventh century gave the ancient jurists an even greater authority than they had enjoyed in their own time. In the early Middle Ages, the *Theodosian Code* strongly influenced the early "barbarian" law codes; indeed, the *Breviarium* of Roman law prepared under the Visigothic king Alaric is based on the *Theodosian Code* and contains so many Theodosian laws that we use it to supply texts now missing from manuscripts of the *Code* itself.[15] The *Theodosian Code* and the *Breviarium* remained the standard sources of Roman law until the "rediscovery" of Justinian's Corpus in the late eleventh century (when the *Digest* began to exert enormous influence on legal scholars and to shape civil and canon law).

THE MEANING OF MARRIAGE: LAW AND IDEOLOGY

According to a legal handbook written around the year 300:

Legitimate marriage occurs if the right to marry [*conubium*] exists between those who are contracting marriage, and the male is as mature as the female is capable [of sexual intercourse], and if they both consent, if they are legally independent, or their parents also consent if they are under [paternal] power. *Conubium* is the ability to take a wife by law.[16]

The key concepts here are *conubium* and consent: if these elements were present and there were no legal impediments to a marriage between two particular people, then the marriage existed. Girls could legally marry at age twelve; there was no corresponding age limit for boys, although it was understood that they had to have reached puberty. Betrothal could take place when the parties were as young as seven, although such early and long betrothals probably occurred mainly among the elite.[17] No ceremony was required, apart from the "escorting into the home" (*deductio in domum*) whereby the bride was taken to the residence of the groom (a practice suggesting that at least the Romans of classical Italy considered marriage to be virilocal). Even then, it was not strictly necessary for the new husband himself to be present at his bride's entry into the marital home, as long as *she* was physically there.[18]

---

[14] See the chapters by Hunter, Reynolds, and Kuehn in this volume.

[15] On the Germanic codes in relation to Roman law, see Reynolds, *Marriage*, 66–70; and Antti Arjava, "The survival of Roman family law after the Barbarian settlements," in Ralph W. Mathisen (ed.), *Law, Society, and Authority in Late Antiquity* (Oxford, 2001), 33–51.

[16] *Regulae Ulpiani* 5.2–3, in FIRA, vol. 2, 268. The *Regulae Ulpiani* (also called the *Tituli Ulpiani*), though ascribed to the early third century jurist Ulpian, actually date from the late third or early fourth century.

[17] *Dig.* 23.2.4 (Pomponius); *Dig.* 23.1.14 (Modestinus).

[18] *Dig.* 23.2.5 (Pomponius). But *Dig.* 23.2.6 (Ulpian) appears to contradict this. See Evans-Grubbs, WLRE 82–83 and 287 n. 3. Compare Scaevola at *Dig.* 24.1.66.

No written record of the marriage was needed for proof of its validity.[19] Nor was it necessary for the bride to bring a dowry. Nevertheless, at least among the propertied classes, both dowry and documentation were common, as was a ceremony of some sort to mark the event. Indeed, marriage alliances among the elite (the only class for whom we have substantial evidence) involved a complex process of discreet inter-family negotiation and assessment of the social, moral, and financial suitability of prospective spouses, conducted not only by the *paterfamilias* (the oldest surviving male ascendant) but by other relatives and friends as well.[20]

Nevertheless, marriage was not simply a private matter, a contract conducted between two kin groups. Marriage was also important to the Roman government, given that well-ordered households created a well-ordered state, and the continued strength and survival of the Empire depended on a steady supply of children, who were likely to be reared and properly socialized only within marriage. When Augustus achieved sole power after more than a generation of civil wars and evolved into the first Roman emperor, he turned his attention to the institution of marriage, which he believed was in crisis.

Like many another leader of a socially fractured state, Augustus attacked per-ceived immorality and turned to promotion of "family values" as a way of instilling social cohesiveness and discouraging nonconformity with his objective of rebuild-ing Roman might and manpower. In 18 BCE, he enacted two laws that brought the state into the citizen's bedroom (to the dismay of the Roman elite, who resented the claims of one man, however powerful, to regulate what had always been a family matter). The first law, the *lex Julia de adulteriis coercendis* (Julian law on repressing adulteries), made extramarital sex by or with a married woman a criminal offense, open to prosecution by any male citizen and punishable by exile for both parties. Although sexual misbehavior by a woman of respectable status had always been subject to opprobrium, the judge of such behavior prior to Augustus had been the woman's family headed by her *paterfamilias*, along with her husband. The second law, the *lex Julia de maritandis ordinibus* (Julian law on the marrying of the social orders), required that all Roman citizen males between the ages of twenty-five and sixty, and all citizen females between twenty and fifty, were to be married; wid-ows and divorcées were to remarry within a short period of time. Anyone not in compliance would forfeit any legacies he or she received from those outside the sixth degree of kinship (by Roman calculation, the level of second cousin or great-uncle/aunt), and spouses could receive no more than a tenth of each other's estate unless they had a child in common.[21]

Such a penalty would affect only those likely to give or receive legacies outside of their immediate family – in other words, the propertied elite, at whom the laws were primarily aimed. In the absence of demographic data, we cannot know how

[19] *Dig.* 20.1.4 (Gaius). Compare *Dig.* 22.4.4 (idem).
[20] Treggiari, *Roman Marriage*, 124–60.
[21] See ibid., 37–80 and 277–98; Evans-Grubbs, *Law and Family*, 103–12 and 202–16. A later law, the *lex Papia-Poppaea* (9 CE), modified the original law.

effective Augustus's laws were, but they also had propaganda value, demonstrating imperial concern for morality and for maintenance of the seedbed of the state, the family. They remained in force for more than three centuries, until repealed by the emperor Constantine.

At the same time the Roman government was actively encouraging marriage and procreation in general, it was also setting limits on who could have *conubium*, the legal ability to marry. Restrictions on the right of two people to marry were based mainly on considerations of kinship or status. Spouses could not be related within three degrees (as calculated in Roman custom), which ruled out marriage between siblings or between parent and child; marriage between a man and his sister's daughter was also forbidden.[22] Originally, these restrictions had not applied to provincials who were not Roman citizens, and whose own marriage customs might differ; for instance, in many parts of the Greek east, marriages between close kin (including uncle–niece unions, and even brother–sister marriage in Egypt), were acceptable and common.[23] But in 212, the emperor Caracalla granted Roman citizenship to virtually all free inhabitants of the entire Empire, and the Roman law of marriage now applied throughout, superseding local rules that ran counter to it. This attempt to instill Roman *mores* among non-Romans was only partially successful: documentary evidence from Egypt does show a dropping-off in brother–sister marriages, but later legislation against close-kin unions indicates that as late as Justinian there were pockets of the Empire where the practice persisted.[24]

Other marriage prohibitions were based on legal status. Slaves did not have *conubium* with each other or with free people. Monogamous unions formed by slaves were called *contubernium* and had no legal consequences; the children of a slave woman would automatically belong to her owner, who could break up the family at any time. But if both partners were freed, the union automatically became *iustum matrimonium*, so that children born after that time would be freeborn and legitimate and would come under their father's legal power. The transition from *contubernium* to *matrimonium* did not require any documentation, although the births of all legitimate children (and after the mid-second century, of illegitimate children as well) were supposed to be recorded in the public *acta*.[25]

Unions between those of vastly disparate statuses were subject to disapproval, particularly if a freeborn woman had a relationship with a slave.[26] Yet the law did

---

[22] Previously, marriage of a man with his brother's daughter had been illegal, too, but in 49 CE the law was changed so that the emperor Claudius could marry his niece Agrippina.

[23] Evans-Grubbs, *Law and Family*, 97–101 with references cited there; Roger Bagnall and Bruce Frier, *The Demography of Roman Egypt* (Cambridge, U.K., 1994), 127–34.

[24] For example, an edict of the pagan emperor Diocletian: see WLRE 140–43. There seems to have been an amnesty for those who had been married before 212.

[25] Jane Gardner, "Proofs of status in the Roman world," *Bulletin of the Institute of Classical Studies* 33 (1986), 1–14. It does not follow that all were, in fact, registered.

[26] A decree of the Senate under Claudius (41–54 CE) said that a free woman in *contubernium* with someone else's slave would become the slave of her lover's owner if the latter had not known about the union, or his freedwoman if he had consented to it; and her children would become his slaves. Justinian finally annulled the law. See Judith Evans-Grubbs, "'Marriage more shameful

not penalize men's relationships with slaves. Adultery, a crime under Augustus's legislation (mentioned earlier), was defined as sex between a married woman and anyone other than her husband, so that a man who confined his extramarital activities to slaves of either sex or to prostitutes (who were usually of servile status) had nothing to fear from the law. Nevertheless, unions between a free man and a slave had no legal validity, and any children whom a slave woman bore were also slaves. If a man wanted to have a relationship with his own slave legally recognized, he could free her and marry her, and any children subsequently born would be free and come under his paternal power. Many men did free their slaves in order to marry them, as evidenced both by numerous funerary inscriptions commemorating such marriages and by the attention jurists gave to the topic.[27] Such marriages were quite acceptable both legally and socially, except in the case of men and women of senatorial status (that is, a senator or his children or grandchildren), who were prohibited under Augustus's legislation from legal marriage with a freed person (*libertinus/libertina*), an actor or actress, or someone who had been an actor or actress.[28] In such unions, the woman would be a concubine, not a wife, and their children would be illegitimate.[29]

Even when a man was not prohibited by law from marriage with a woman, *concubinatus* (concubinage) might still be more socially appropriate if there was a great disparity in their status.[30] *Concubinatus* with a former slave or other woman of low status also provided a way to have a long-term sexual partnership without worrying about the main consequence of *iustum matrimonium*: legitimate children who were their father's natural heirs.[31] It could be an attractive option for widowers who already had children and wanted to avoid splitting their estate further, or for young men who were not yet ready to take on the responsibilities of marriage and child rearing. Roman *concubinatus* was a monogamous, long-term relationship, an alternative rather than a supplement to marriage. It had no legal standing, but neither the man nor his *concubina* would be liable to adultery charges if she was clearly of low status and was not married to someone else.

Yet in a society that did not require a legal ceremony or written documentation of marriage, the availability of such nonmarital yet monogamous relationships

---

than adultery': Slave-mistress relations, 'Mixed Marriages,' and late Roman law," *Phoenix* 47 (1993): 125–54.

[27] See WLRE 192–94. Unlike other wives, a freedwoman whose former master had freed her in order to marry her could not remarry someone else if she left him against his will.

[28] *Dig.* 23.4.44 pr (Paulus). Influential senators might get imperial permission to marry a freedwoman: see *Dig.* 23.2.31 (Ulpian). Freeborn Romans could not have *iustum matrimonium* with prostitutes, pimps, or convicted adulteresses. See Thomas A. J. McGinn, *Prostitution, Sexuality, and the Law in Ancient Rome* (Oxford, 1998), 70–104.

[29] Beryl Rawson, "Roman concubinage and other de facto marriages," TAPA 104 (1974): 279–305; Susan Treggiari, "Concubinae," in *Papers of the British School at Rome* 49 (1981): 59–81.

[30] Ulpian (*Dig.* 25.7.1 pr) says it is more "honorable" (*honestius*) for a man's freedwoman to be a concubine than a respectable married woman (*materfamilias*).

[31] All children by a legal wife, male and female, inherited equally if a man died intestate; if he left a will, he had to leave something to all his children unless he disinherited them.

could raise problems. According to the jurist Ulpian, the only difference between a wife and a concubine was their rank (*dignitas*).[32] This opinion raises an important issue. Was the difference always evident? When a man of senatorial status lived in a monogamous union with a former slave, it would naturally be assumed that the relationship was *concubinatus*, not marriage. Not only the legal prohibition on such marriages but also the extreme disparity in status would make that assumption reasonable. But there were other cases in which the relationship might be more doubtful, for example, if a man of respectable but not exalted status were living with his own freedwoman. Was she his wife or his concubine? The jurist Paulus said that the question was to be judged on the basis of "the mind's intention" alone.[33] How did the couple appear to regard each other? Did they display *affectio maritalis*, a "marital frame of mind"?[34] If the woman had provided a dowry, the couple had reared children, and the man treated his wife as a social equal, one could reasonably conclude that their union was a marriage, unless there were known legal prohibitions preventing *conubium*.

There might be good reason to want to assess the nature of the relationship. If the woman's status was high enough that she could be a wife, some might attempt to classify the relationship as *stuprum* (illicit sex), punishable under the adultery law.[35] Those who hoped to receive legacies from friends or distant relatives would need to be married according to the Augustan law. And in the case of a widower or divorcé with children by a prior marriage, questions of inheritance might arise.

A concubine and her children did not have any automatic inheritance rights, but a man could leave legacies to his children by a concubine, and he could even give her gifts during the relationship, whereas paradoxically, gifts between husband and wife were invalid.[36] As the jurist Papinian noted:

It is agreed that gifts to a concubine are not able to be revoked nor, if marriage has later been contracted between the same parties, does what was previously valid become invalid. Moreover, I replied that weight must be given to whether marital honor and *affectio* earlier preceded [the gift], and after the persons had been compared and their joining of life had been considered: for tablets do not make a marriage.[37]

Papinian had been asked about a woman who had received a gift from a man with whom she had a relationship. If she was his concubine, the gift was legal; if she was his wife, it was not. How to tell? One must compare the relative social status of

---

[32] *Dig.* 32.49.4.

[33] *Dig.* 25.7.4.

[34] On *affectio maritalis*, see Treggiari, *Roman Marriage*, 51–57; eadem, "Concubinae," at 61–64; John T. Noonan, "Marital affection in the canonists," *Studia Gratiana* 12 (1967): 481–509.

[35] See Thomas A. J. McGinn, "Concubinage and the *lex Iulia* on adultery," TAPA 121 (1991): 335–75. *Dig.* 34.9.16.1 (Papinian) discusses such a case.

[36] The ban on gifts between spouses is explained in *Dig.* 24.1.1–3 pr (Ulpian and Paulus). See WLRE 98–100; Treggiari, *Roman Marriage*, 366–74.

[37] *Dig.* 39.5.31 pr. Not all jurists liked the idea that concubines were able to receive gifts when wives could not: see Ulpian at *Dig.* 24.1.3.1 and *Dig.* 24.1.32.28.

the couple, and determine whether *affectio maritalis* had existed when the gift was given; if the intent to be married had come later, then the gift was still valid. The presence (or absence) of *tabulae nuptiales* was basically irrelevant.

In the face-to-face society of classical Rome, neighbors and acquaintances would usually have enough information about the partners and their behavior towards each other to "just know" what the status of the relationship was, without the need for written documentation of intent.[38] Only in the more heterogeneous, socially fluid world of late antiquity did reliance on community standards begin to break down, after the extension of citizenship to all provincials and the upheavals of the third century. Then lawmakers sought explicit proof that a relationship was indeed *iustum matrimonium*, and written records became more significant.

In most respects, the large-scale social and religious changes of the later Empire, most notably the rise of Christianity, had little immediate impact on the making of the marriage bond. This is not to deny that changes did occur. In regard to marriage, the most significant was the emergence of perpetual celibacy as a socially acceptable alternative to the married state. Ever since Paul had expressed his preference for celibacy over marriage (1 Cor. 7:1, 7), an influential strain of Christian thought had favored virginity and considered sex an essentially sinful activity that should at the very most be limited to married couples who desired to have children.[39] With the legitimation and victory of Christianity, both men and women had the option of leading a celibate life dedicated to God and removed from the cares and temptations of "the world." Needless to say, men had always been able to eschew legitimate marriage for nonmarital relationships, either with a low-status concubine or more promiscuously with slaves or prostitutes. But freeborn women had traditionally been expected to marry at least once (the handful of Vestal Virgins in Italy hardly constitute an exception), and they were under legal and often familial pressure to remarry if widowed or divorced while still of childbearing age. Thus the alternative of Christian virginity or dedicated widowhood represented a real change for women of all classes.

Late Roman law reflects this rise of a celibate lifestyle, while not always approving its manifestations. In 320, Constantine abolished the penalties on unmarried men and women that Augustus had mandated over three centuries earlier. Constantine was probably more concerned with pleasing the senatorial aristocracy of Rome (who had always objected to the law) than with promoting the Christian ideal of celibacy, but Christians certainly took advantage of the new law.[40]

---

[38] It appears that if the nature of the relationship was particularly unclear, the partners might make an attestation (*testatio*) as to its purpose: see *Dig.* 25.7.3.1 (Marcian; usually considered an interpolation). See E. Karabélias, "La forme de la *testatio* (*ekmartyrion*) matrimoniale en droit romain classique et post-classique," *Revue historique de droit français et étranger* 62 (1984): 599–603; cf. McGinn, "Concubinage," 361.

[39] Peter Brown, *The Body and Society: Men, Women, and Sexual Renunciation in Early Christianity* (New York, 1988).

[40] CTh 8.16.1; see Evans-Grubbs, *Law and Family*, 103–39.

Post-Constantinian laws recognized the existence of Christian celibates, punishing those who tried to abduct consecrated virgins and widows for the purpose of marriage.[41]

Other laws, too, appear to have had a Christian genesis. A law of 388 banning marriage between Jews and Christians can plausibly be attributed to pressures on the emperor Theodosius I from Christian advisors, perhaps the powerful bishop of Milan, Ambrose, who had great influence over the emperor.[42] A case can also be made for Christian influence on restrictions to unilateral divorce, which first appear with Constantine. But not all scholars would see the workings of church teaching even there.[43]

Christianization of marriage was gradual, as traditional practices were adapted to the new ideology. Church leaders criticized members of their flock who continued to celebrate marriages in the time-honored fashion. Thus John Chrysostom, Bishop of Constantinople, thundered:

Nowadays on the day of a wedding people dance and sing hymns to Aphrodite, songs full of adultery, corruption of marriages, illicit loves, unlawful unions, and many other impious and shameful themes. They accompany the bride in public with unseemly drunkenness and shameful speeches. How can you expect chastity of her, tell me, if you accustom her to such shamelessness from the first day, if you present in her sight such actions and words as even the more serious slaves should not hear?[44]

In Italy, Bishop Paulinus of Nola adapted the Greco-Roman wedding hymn to a Christian mould when he celebrated the marriage of Julian, Bishop of Eclanum (an opponent of Augustine's doctrine of original sin). Paulinus cites the marital model of Rebecca and Isaac and also invokes Genesis 2:23–24 (on the creation of Eve from Adam's rib) to illustrate the bonding of man and wife. The biblical exempla, perhaps adapted from contemporary sermons on marriage, bring to mind the preambles to some medieval dotal charters.[45]

---

[41] The full version of a law of Honorius in 420 punishing abduction of celibate women, preserved in the *Sirmondian Constitutions*, reveals that it was actually prompted by the *suggestio* of a Christian priest. See J. Evans-Grubbs, "Virgins and widows, show-girls and whores: Late Roman legislation on women and Christianity," in Mathisen, *Law, Society and Authority* (n. 15 earlier), 220–41.

[42] CTh 3.7.2; CTh 9.7.5. See Hagith S. Sivan, "Why not marry a Jew? Jewish-Christian marital frontiers in late antiquity," in Mathisen, *Law, Society and Authority*, 208–19.

[43] For doubts about Christian influence, see Antti Arjava, "Divorce in later Roman law," *Arctos* 22 (1988): 5–21; Roger Bagnall, "Church, state, and divorce in late Roman Egypt," in Karl-Ludwig Selig and Robert Somerville (eds.), *Florilegium Columbianum: Essays in Honor of Paul Oskar Kristeller* (New York, 1987), 41–61. I would argue that Christian thinking influenced Constantine, although his law cannot be termed a "Christian" law: see Evans-Grubbs, *Law and Family*, 253–60.

[44] John Chrysostom, *Sermon on Marriage*, translated by Catharine Roth, in eadem and David Anderson, *St. John Chrysostom on Marriage and Family Life* (Crestwood, N.Y., 1986), 82–83. See Hunter in this volume on the evidence for Christian marriage rituals during this period.

[45] Paulinus of Nola, *Carmen 25* (written ca. 405), translated by David Hunter, *Marriage in the Early Church* (Minneapolis, 1992), 128–140. On the medieval charters and their sacred preambles, see Philip Reynolds's chapter in this volume.

Even with the social and religious changes of late antiquity, however, the over-arching prerequisites of *iustum matrimonium* continued to be the consent of all parties and the lack of legal impediments attributable to kinship or status. Indeed, a feature of late Roman law is the intensification of these elements: the demand for paternal consent in cases where it had not previously been necessary, the (re)emergence of betrothal as a binding contract, and increased concern about distinguishing legitimate marriage from nonlegal concubinage.

CONSENT TO MARRIAGE

The essential feature of both betrothals and marriages under Roman law was con-sent (*consensus*). Thus, according to the jurist Paul, "Marriage is not able to occur unless all consent, that is, both those who join together and those in whose power they are."[46] To be *matrimonium iustum*, a marriage had to be made with the con-sent of each partner's *paterfamilias* (the father or, if he was still alive, the paternal grandfather), who wielded paternal power (*patriapotestas*) over his children. The *paterfamilias* was responsible for arranging suitable marriages for his children; indeed, Augustus's marriage law said that fathers who prevented their children from marrying or refused to provide a dowry could be forced to do so.[47] Fathers were expected to take their children's wishes and best interests into account when arranging their marriages; after all, the main goal of marriage was the production of legitimate children, who would be heirs to their father (or to *his* father, if he was still alive), and a union in which at least one of the partners was unhappy was not as likely to produce children.

Sons would generally have much more say in their own marriage arrangements than would daughters. For one thing, they would be significantly older. Among the elite, women married in their early teens and men in their early to mid-twenties; below the elite, the age at first marriage would be a few years later for men and women.[48] By the time a Roman was twenty-five, his or her *paterfamilias* was proba-bly dead, and, he – or she – would be legally independent (*sui iuris*) and would need

---

[46] *Dig.* 23.2.2 (Paulus): "Nuptiae consistere non possunt nisi consentiant omnes, id est qui coeunt quorumque in potestate sunt." On consent, see Treggiari, *Roman Marriage*, 170–80; eadem, "Consent to Roman marriage: Some aspects of law and reality," *Echoes du Monde Classique/Classical Views* 26, n.s. 1 (1982): 34–44; Guillaume Matringe, "La puissance paternelle et le mariage des fils et filles de famille en droit romain," in *Studi in onore di Edoardo Volterra*, vol. 5 (Milan, 1971), 191–237; Judith Evans-Grubbs, "Parent-child conflict in the Roman family: The evidence of the Code of Justinian," in Michele George (ed.), *The Roman Family in the Empire: Rome, Italy, and Beyond* (Oxford, 2005), 92–128.

[47] *Dig.* 23.2.19 (Marcian).

[48] Richard Saller, "Men's age at marriage and its consequences in the Roman family," *Classical Philology* 82 (1987): 21–34; Keith Hopkins, "The age of Roman girls at marriage," *Population Studies* 18 (1964): 309–27; cf. Brent Shaw, "The age of Roman girls at marriage: Some reconsiderations," *Journal of Roman Studies* 77 (1987): 30–46.

no one's permission to marry.[49] Because they married later, men were more likely to have become legally independent before marrying, and because they were not kept to the same strict sexual conventions as unmarried girls (who were strongly expected to be virgins at their first marriage), they might well have had premarital sexual experiences with slaves or prostitutes. Women in their teens, on the contrary, would probably still be under *patriapotestas* and would have led a much more sheltered existence, and they would therefore be dependent on their fathers for their marriage arrangements. Such dependence on a male might continue after marriage, given that there was an average age difference between husband and wife of about ten years. Nevertheless, a wife did not strictly come under her husband's legal control: although she would live with her husband, she remained under her father's *potestas* until he died or emancipated her (unless the paternal grandfather survived, in which case he was the *paterfamilias*).[50]

Children whose *paterfamilias* was still alive were supposed to consent to their marriage. Lack of refusal constituted consent, particularly for daughters, who were not even supposed to object to their father's choice of a husband unless he was "shameful or of unworthy character."[51] Tacit consent could work in the opposite way: if a daughter got married without her father's knowledge, the union was nonetheless valid if he did not object when he found out about it.[52] But if a *paterfamilias* actively objected to his child's union or died without knowing about it, it would not be *iustum matrimonium*, and the couple's offspring would not be legitimate.[53]

Rescripts in the *Code of Justinian* show worried men and women petitioning the emperor about the validity of unions made in the absence of a father's consent. For instance, Alexander Severus (reigned 222–35) replied to a woman named Maxima: "If, as you claim, the father of your former husband, in whose paternal power he was, did not object to your marriage after he had learned of it, you should not fear that he will not acknowledge his own grandson."[54] Probably Maxima's husband

---

[49] Richard Saller, *Patriarchy, Property, and Death in the Roman Family* (Cambridge, 1994).

[50] *Manus* marriage, under which a wife entered her husband's legal control, had died out by the imperial period, and when a wife became legally independent upon her father's death, she could divorce. Until Constantine imposed restrictions on unilateral repudiation of a spouse in 331 (CTh 3.16.1), divorce was available to both men and women.

[51] *Dig.* 23.1.12 (Ulpian). As regards sons, see *Dig.* 23.2.22 (Celsus) and cf. 23.2.21 (Terentius Clemens).

[52] *Dig.* 23.1.7 (Paulus, citing Julian). Compare *Sententiae Pauli* 2.19.2 (FIRA 2, 345), attributed to Paulus but actually written ca. 300 CE: "Eorum qui in potestate patris sunt sine voluntate eius matrimonia iure non contrahuntur, sed contracta non solvuntur: contemplatio enim publicae utilitatis privatorum commodis praefertur." Although this probably referred to a second-century imperial ruling that a father could not force his child to divorce, by the early Middle Ages it seems to have been understood as recognizing marriages made without paternal consent. See Paulo Merêa, "Le mariage *sine consensu parentum* dans le droit romain vulgaire occidental," *Revue Internationale des droits de l'antiquité* 5 (1950): 203–17; Matringe, "La puissance" (n. 46 earlier), 203 n. 52 and 215.

[53] See Matringe, "La puissance," and Evans-Grubbs, "Parent-child conflict" (n. 46 earlier).

[54] CJ 5.4.5.

was dead; they might have been divorced, but her concern with recognition of her child by his paternal grandfather suggests that there was no longer a living link between them. Maxima feared that her father-in-law's initial ignorance of his son's marriage jeopardized the union's validity. If her husband was still under paternal power when he died, anything that he possessed belonged legally to his father, and the husband's own legitimate children would be under the *potestas* of their grandfather. Therefore what was at stake in Maxima's inquiry was not only her son's legitimacy, but also his right to inherit.

Marriage arranged by the *paterfamilias* with at least the nominal consent of all parties continued to be the socially and legally approved norm in late antiquity. And as in the earlier period, young people usually acquiesced in their parents' plans, at least for their first marriage. Macrina, sister of Basil of Caesarea and Gregory of Nyssa, was betrothed by her father before she turned twelve to a young man whose character and oratorical talents served as bride-gifts (*hedna*) to recommend him. Macrina herself "was not ignorant" of her father's plans, but raised no objection until after her fiancé died, at which point she refused any other match, pointing out that she was happy with the spouse her father had chosen, whom she would eventually see in the resurrection.[55] Like Macrina, Melania the Younger preferred a life of consecrated virginity, but she was married "with much force" to her relative Pinianus, when she was fourteen and he was about seventeen. She tried to get her husband to live in a celibate marriage, but he persuaded her to wait until they had heirs, and because they belonged to the highest and wealthiest level of the Roman senatorial aristocracy, there was a lot at stake. After the death of two children (the second born prematurely), Melania succeeded in convincing Pinianus to accept celibacy, to the annoyance of the couple's parents, who wanted grandchildren and were concerned for the family's reputation.[56]

Sons, too, were subject to parental pressure to marry: Paulinus of Pella was forced into marriage at age twenty by his parents, who were concerned about his sexual activities in the slave quarters, where he had fathered more than one child.[57] Bishop Ambrose of Milan wrote to a son, Cynegius, whose father Paternus had arranged a marriage between Cynegius and his own niece (daughter of Cynegius' sister). The son had objected to the match but reluctantly agreed out of filial duty (*pietas*). Ambrose interceded for Cynegius with his father, pointing out that the marriage went against not only imperial law (Paternus expected to receive special dispensation from the emperor) but also biblical teachings. It is not clear whether

[55] Pierre Maraval (ed.), *Grégoire de Nysse: Vie de Sainte Macrine* (Paris, 1971), 152–57.

[56] Denys Gorce (ed.), *Vie de Sainte Melanie* (Paris, 1962), 131–41; translated from Greek by Elizabeth A. Clark, *The Life of Melania the Younger* (New York, 1984).

[57] Paulinus of Pella, *Eucharisticus*, lines 170–85, in H. G. Evelyn-White (ed.), *Ausonius II*, Loeb series (Cambridge, Mass., 1921).

or not the marriage took place.[58] Ambrose also wrote to a man named Sisinnius, whose son had married without paternal consent. Sisinnius had originally been very angry, but Ambrose had persuaded him to forgive his son and accept his new daughter-in-law. Ambrose points out the advantages of the marriage for Sisinnius: not only was he relieved of responsibility for arranging his marriage (with the attendant risk of making the wrong decision), but now both son and daughter-in-law will be particularly anxious to please Sisinnius.[59]

Ambrose's letter to Sisinnius illustrates the possibility that children, especially sons, could marry without paternal permission but later obtain it after the *fait accompli*. Such a possibility was abhorrent to the emperor Constantine, who attacked a marriage strategy that was an alternative to betrothal arranged by the *paterfamilias*: abduction marriage (*raptus*).[60] The law was directed against any man who had not made a marriage agreement with a girl's parents, but instead had "seized her when she was unwilling or led her away when she was willing." The consent of an abducted girl was worthless, and indeed, she was to be punished also. A willing *rapta* (presumably one who had connived in her "abduction" in order to evade paternal objection) would suffer the same penalty as her *raptor*.[61] Unwilling victims would still be deprived of inheritance rights from their parents, and parents who agreed after the fact to their daughter's marriage were to be deported because (said the law) they of all people should have sought revenge on the abductor. Constantine's law was so harsh – indeed, unworkable – that his successors reduced the penalty for an abductor to a "capital penalty" and put a five-year statute of limitations on prosecution.[62] Justinian abolished the penalty for the girl and her parents, though he forbade marriage after an abduction and encouraged the hunting-down of abductors.[63]

It is doubtful whether Constantine or later emperors were effective in abolishing bride-theft, but the laws do provide interesting evidence for an alternative to the legally approved norm of marriage by betrothal pact. Although marriage by abduction is attested in classical literature and late-antique church rulings, it goes largely unnoticed in earlier Roman law, probably because it was uncommon

---

[58] Ambrose, *Epistles* 58 and 59 (Latin texts in CSEL 82.2)

[59] Ambrose, *Epistle* 35 (in CSEL 82/1).

[60] CTh 9.24.1 (dated 320 or 326). See Judith Evans-Grubbs, "Abduction marriage in antiquity: A law of Constantine (CTh IX.24.1) and its social context," *Journal of Roman Studies* 79 (1989): 59–83.

[61] The law as preserved in the *Theodosian Code* does not specify the penalty, but it was presumably an aggravated form of death, such as burning or condemnation to the arena.

[62] CTh 9.24.2 (Constantius, 349); CTh 9.24.3 (Valentinian, 374). The "capital penalty" would probably still be death, but by simple execution rather than in one of the forms mentioned earlier n. 61. (Condemnation to the arena and crucifixion had been abolished in any case.) In an earlier period, capital penalty might include exile.

[63] CJ 9.13.1 (dated 533). Justinian's Code retains only one sentence of Constantine's original law (at CJ 7.13.3) regarding the reward for slaves who report an abduction.

among the urban elite who were the focus of classical law. Constantine's law is an
example of the "vulgarization" of the imperial purview, an attempt to regulate the
customs of those below the upper classes.[64]

The law on abduction presupposed that a girl's father would make her betrothal,
and for a first marriage this would generally be the case. But a woman married
in her teens might find herself a widow before she was twenty-five, particularly if
her husband had been significantly older. A widow would have more sexual and
social autonomy than an unmarried virgin still living in her parents' home, and
she might want to take a more active role in arranging a new marriage. But what
if a widowed daughter's wishes collided with those of her father? And if her father
was dead, whose choice of spouse should prevail: her own or that of older relatives
who would be expected to know best?

Western laws of Valentinian and Honorius during the later fourth and early
fifth centuries addressed these questions. A law of Valentinian I (reigned 364–75)
addressed to the Senate of Rome begins in a rather vehement manner:

Widows under twenty-five, even if they enjoy the freedom of emancipation, are not
to enter upon a second marriage without their father's agreement or in opposition to
him. Therefore the go-betweens and marriage-brokers shall cease, the secret messengers
and corrupt reporters of information! No one is to purchase noble marriages, no one
is to cause a disturbance, but a marriage alliance is to be deliberated publicly, and a
multitude of suitors is to be summoned.[65]

The law says that where the widow's choice differed from that of relatives other
than her father, there was to be a judicial hearing "as has been ordained in the
marriage of women minors whose fathers are dead," so that in cases where suitors
were "equal in birth and morals," the woman's own decision would prevail. Close
relatives, who would be in line to inherit from the widow, were not to prevent her
making an "honorable" remarriage.

A woman who (as the law put it) "enjoyed the freedom of emancipation" had
been formally released from paternal power by her *paterfamilias*; she was therefore
sui iuris, as she would have been if she lost her *paterfamilias* through death (for
instance, if there were no surviving paternal grandfather and her father died).
It was not uncommon in late antiquity for fathers to emancipate their children,

---

[64] Evans-Grubbs, *Law and Family*, 330–42. Abduction marriage also occurred, under different legislative
norms, in the Germanic kingdoms that arose after the demise of the western Empire and drew on
late Roman legislation for their own law codes: see Reynolds, *Marriage*, 101–08 and 394–401.

[65] CTh 3.7.1 (cf. CJ 5.4.18), dated 371. Matringe, "La puissance" (n. 46 earlier), 209 claims that
Valentinan's law did not introduce anything new, because even in the classical period an emancipated daughter would need the permission of her father, who would still be her *tutor legitimus*
(legal guardian). But women did not need a *tutor*'s consent to marriage, only for undertaking
financial transactions (such as providing a dowry).

particularly those who were grown or had married.[66] A woman might have been married while under paternal power, subsequently emancipated, and then widowed while her father was still alive. Once she was *sui iuris* she would not have needed his consent to a second marriage.[67] Her father might refuse to provide a dowry, but as a legally independent woman, his daughter could own her own property, which she might have inherited from her mother or her first husband. It is easy to see the potential for father–daughter conflict over a second marriage in such a situation, particularly when the daughter was still legally a minor. Valentinian supported the father, declaring that an underage daughter still required her father's consent to marriage.

Valentinian's law was addressed to the Senate, and may have been in response to complaints he had heard of third parties (*sequestres* and *interpretes*)[68] interfering in the marriage plans of wealthy young widows. Although professional matchmakers were known in Greek society, in the Roman elite, *patresfamilias* and their friends and kinsmen made marriage alliances by a delicate process of negotiation and networking.[69] Perhaps infringement of such senatorial etiquette by outsiders or subordinates trying to "purchase noble marriages" had prompted a complaint. In fact, unmarried women whose wealth made them vulnerable to fortune hunters were the focus of another ruling of Valentinian, on Christian virgins and widows who were courted by clerics and monks hoping to benefit from the celibate women's generosity.[70] In that law too, the emperor upheld the right of kinsmen (*propinqui*) to safeguard an unmarried woman's property in the interests of her family. The fourth century saw the social resurgence of the Roman senatorial elite, many of them extremely wealthy; and at the same time the Christian ascetic movement was gaining adherents among both men and (especially) women of the elite.[71] Although Valentinian's relationship with the Senate was far from

---

[66] See Arjava, *Women and Law*, 41–42; idem, "Paternal power in late antiquity," *Journal of Roman Studies* 88 (1998): 147–65.

[67] Modestinus, *Dig.* 23.2.25.

[68] The vocabulary is Ciceronian: the *Oxford Latin Dictionary* (Oxford, 1982), 947, cites the first speech against Verres, 36: *sequestres aut interpretes corrumpendi iudici*. This suggests that the quaestor who composed this law was familiar with classical oratory.

[69] David Noy, "Matchmakers and marriage-markets in antiquity," *Echoes du Monde Classique/Classical Views*, 38 n.s. 9 (1990): 375–400; Treggiari, *Roman Marriage*, 125–45 on earlier period. In late antiquity, even bishops might play a role in match-making: see Arjava, *Women and Law*, 30; and for Augustine on this topic, see Hunter in this volume.

[70] CTh 16.2.20, dated 370. The law said male celibates were not to visit unmarried women or receive anything from them unless they were relatives. They could be "expelled by public trials" if any of the women's kinsmen wanted to bring an accusation against them. See Evans-Grubbs, "Virgins and widows" (n. 41 earlier) on this law.

[71] On the late-Roman senatorial elite, see John Matthews, *Western Aristocracies and Imperial Court, A.D. 364–425* (Oxford, 1975). On the ascetic movement, see Brown, *Body and Society* (n. 39 earlier); and Elizabeth A. Clark, *Ascetic Piety and Women's Faith* (Lewiston, N.Y., 1986).

smooth, it was in the interests of both parties to maintain senatorial fortunes and lineages.

The western emperor Honorius (reigned 393–423) reiterated the classical legal position that a daughter still under paternal power required her father's consent to marriage, adding that if a woman under twenty-five was legally independent, *her* consent was necessary. If her father was dead, her mother and relatives could have a say. But Honorius adds that:

if, orphaned of both parents, she is placed under the protection of a *curator* and perhaps a contest between honorable competitors for marriage should arise . . . if the girl because of concern for her sense of shame [*verecundia*] has not wished to bring forth her own will, it shall be permitted for a judge in the presence of her kinsmen [*propinqui*] to determine to whom the young woman is better joined.[72]

Fatherless women (and men) below twenty-five would be under the guardianship of either a *tutor* or a *curator*.[73] Both Valentinian and Honorius cite the need for a judicial decision in regard to the marriages of such women, as does a rescript of the emperors Septimius Severus and Caracalla on a specific case in which the *tutor*, mother, and *propinqui* of a fatherless girl disagreed over choice of husband.[74] So much importance was placed on properly arranged marriages, at least among the elite, that there was a policy of referring disputes to a judge.

Honorius was also irritated by the audacity of men who tried to get an imperial dispensation to marry a woman who would otherwise be off-limits to them:

Certain people, neglecting the rule of ancient law, think that a marriage which they understand they do not deserve should be requested from us by creeping up with their entreaties, pretending that they have the girl's consent. For this reason we prohibit such a kind of betrothal by the decision of the present law. . . .[75]

Anyone who has managed to obtain imperial permission for a forbidden marriage is to be deprived of his property and deported, and children of the union are illegitimate. But Honorius made an exception for those who had been allowed to marry first cousins (forbidden under Theodosius I but permitted by his sons

---

[72] CJ 5.4.20 (dated 408–09), not found in CTh.

[73] All males less than age 14 and females less than 12 who were no longer under *patria potestas* were required to have a guardian (*tutor impuberum*) to manage their property and make sure no one was taking advantage of them. In later antiquity, fatherless minors who were past puberty but below 25 were to have a *curator*, whose responsibilities were less than a *tutor's* but who was still supposed to protect them from the unscrupulous.

[74] CJ 5.4.1 (dated 199). Two other rescripts on disputed marriages of fatherless minors under a *curator* (and therefore over the age of puberty) say that the decision is up to the minor himself or herself, rather than the *curator* or relatives: *Dig.* 23.2.20 (Paulus), quoting another rescript of Severus and Caracalla; and CJ 5.4.8, a rescript of the emperor Gordian dated 241. It may be that a court judgment was previously resorted to only when the person concerned was a very young girl, and that Valentinian's law extended the policy to cover widows under 25 who were not under paternal power.

[75] CTh 3.10.1 (cf. CJ 5.8.1). This may have been part of the same law as CJ 5.4.20.

Honorius and Arcadius) and for "those who desire to fulfill the betrothal made by parents for the marriage of their daughters, or who ask that betrothal gifts, that is, those given in the name of pledges [*arrae*], be returned to them with the quadruple penalty." In cases in which a betrothal pact had been made but later broken, a rejected *sponsus* may petition the emperor for a judgment, particularly if the parents of his *sponsa* had been the original party to the pact. Presumably, the emperor would order the defaulting party to go through with the marriage or repay the pledges with the penalty.[76]

In another law, Honorius declared that if a father arranged his daughter's betrothal but died before the marriage took place, the agreement had to be honored and the woman's guardian must not make a new pact for her: "For it is very unjust that the decision of a *tutor* or *curator*, who was perhaps bribed, should be admitted against a father's will, since often the intention of even the woman herself is found to be working against her own best interests."[77] The law does not state the consequence of disregarding a betrothal made by a deceased father and marrying another: would the marriage lack legal validity, as it would if she had married without the consent of a living *paterfamilias*? In fact, the penalty may have been purely financial: loss of the dowry that she would have received, and forfeiture of any gifts that her father had given or received as a guarantee that the marriage would take place.[78]

As the laws suggest, the marriage plans of women under twenty-five whose father was dead posed a particular problem, given that there was no *paterfamilias* to arrange or to enforce a betrothal pact for them, and they were still young and presumably innocent of the ways of the world. Needless to say, mothers had always had great authority, and in the absence of fathers, frequently did oversee the arrangements for the marriages of both female and male children.[79] We need only think of the thirty-year-old Augustine's willingness for his mother Monnica to arrange his marriage (with a girl who was still two years short of the legal marriageable age), even though it meant the dissolution of his long-term monogamous relationship with a concubine. But without the clout and social network of a *paterfamilias*, widowed mothers and their daughters might be vulnerable to adventurers, as we see in Sidonius Apollinaris's story of a widow who did not properly vet her daughter's suitor.[80]

The laws of Valentinian and Honorius were designed to prevent such problems from happening, but they innovated by ruling against a young woman's freedom

---

[76] On *arrhae sponsaliciae* and the quadruple penalty, see subsequent discussion.

[77] CTh 3.5.12 (= CJ 5.1.4), enacted at Ravenna, 422. This was part of a longer law of which two other excerpts are preserved elsewhere in the code: CTh 3.13.3 (cf. CJ 5.18.11 and 5.19.1), on return of dowry after a husband's death; and CJ 5.9.4, on the fate of betrothal gifts from a deceased husband after his widow remarries.

[78] Matringe, "La puissance" (n. 46 earlier), 211–12. See subsequent discussion on such guarantees.

[79] See Suzanne Dixon, *The Roman Mother* (Norman, Okla., 1988).

[80] On Monnica and Augustine, see *Confessions* VI.13.23. On Sidonius, see n. 149 in this chapter.

of decision. In classical law, a fatherless woman, of whatever age, would be legally independent (*sui iuris*) and could not be forced to go ahead with a marriage previously arranged by her now deceased father. In the early third century, the jurist Paulus had discussed a case in which a man and his wife had agreed to the marriage of their children from previous marriages (his daughter, her son) and had drawn up a document stipulating a penalty for anyone who opposed the union. After the man died, his daughter did not want to go through with the marriage. Paulus, asked to decide whether the man's heirs (who would include his daughter) were liable to the penalty if she did not marry her stepbrother, ruled they were not because the stipulation had not been made "according to good morals" and "because it seemed dishonorable for marriages, whether in the future or already contracted, to be tied by the bond of punishment."[81] But late-antique emperors did tie marriages "by the bond of punishment," not only by penalizing unilateral divorce, but also by enforcing betrothal pacts made by a *paterfamilias*, even after his death.

It is likely that these laws were prompted by particular cases, but the circumstances are unknown. We do hear of conflict between parents and daughters over marriage plans, but always when a daughter refused a proposed marriage not so that she could marry another, but in order to live in Christian asceticism. Men such as Jerome (whose *Epistle* 22 to the virgin Eustochium is a classic statement of the advantages of maidenhood over marriage) and Ambrose (who wrote several tracts for and about holy virgins) encouraged young women to remain virgins. It is a *topos* of these works that daughters had to face intense opposition from their parents, who preferred them to marry and have children.[82] Ambrose complains that he knows many virgins who wanted to remain unmarried but were forbidden to by their mothers, and worse yet, by *widowed* mothers, whom he addresses directly: "For indeed if your daughters wanted to love a *man*, they could legally choose whom they wanted. And so they are permitted to choose a man, but not to choose God?" He relates a salutary story about a noble girl whose father was dead, and who had fled to the church altar after being pressured to marry by her relatives. One kinsman asked her, "What if your father were alive: would he allow you to remain unmarried?" She responded, "And indeed perhaps he died so that no one would be able to present an impediment." The uncooperative kinsman himself died soon afterwards, and the other relatives, learning from his example, let her have her way.[83] Although Ambrose would not go so far as to tell a living

---

[81] *Dig.* 45.1.134. The daughter could bring an *exceptio doli mali* to any attempt to enforce the pact. It was not the proposed marriage itself that went against *boni mores* (for marriage between step-siblings was legal) but the existence of a penalty for those who objected to it. Compare CJ 5.1.1, a rescript of Diocletian and Maximian dated 293.

[82] See earlier on Macrina and Melania, and the works of E. Clark and P. Brown cited nn. 39 and 71 earlier. Although there were already monastic establishments in which celibate women lived communally, such women often lived at home with parents or other relatives during this period.

[83] Ambrose, *De virginibus* I.10–11 (*Patrologia Latina* 16).

paterfamilias that he could not marry off his own daughter, he has no compunction about supporting a girl over any other relatives.

By the mid-fifth century, some parents were following the recommendations of Christian leaders. The western emperor Majorian (457–61) condemned parents who prevented the marriages of their daughters and consigned them instead to a life of Christian celibacy.[84] They did this ostensibly for religious reasons, but really (according to the emperor) to avoid having to give their daughters the same share of their patrimony as their brothers.[85] Not only did such action deprive the state of legitimate children, but it could lead to unfortunate results: "For what good does it do if virginal desire, repressed by paternal power, conceives deep within a deceitful desire for marriage and, restrained from legitimate union, is drawn to illicit allurements?"[86] Majorian's solution was to forbid a woman to take the veil until she was forty, by which time, one presumes, her sexual urges would have receded. Parents (both fathers and mothers) who did not obey were to be fined a third of their property, as was a legally independent woman who wished to be consecrated before the requisite age. Daughters who had married against their parents' wishes and had been disinherited or had been left only the minimum amount required by law were to inherit equally along with their siblings.[87]

There is a "disconnect" here between imperial and ecclesiastical goals. Despite Theodosius I's establishment of Nicene Christianity as the official religion of the Empire and the espousal of Christian asceticism by many members of the elite, emperors still strongly promoted traditional Roman ideals.[88] There was ancient precedent for Majorian's solution in the Augustan marriage law, which had said that a father could be forced to allow his children to marry. He also harked back to another part of Augustus's legislation by demanding that childless widows who did not remarry after five years (because they wished to pursue a life of Christian celibacy) had to make over their property to their relatives.[89] But these reforms were as short-lived as Majorian himself: he was deposed in 461, and his laws were rescinded.

---

[84] *Novel* 6, enacted at Ravenna Oct. 26, 458. Text in Mommsen-Meyer, CTh, vol. 2 (n. 8 earlier).

[85] A daughter's children born in legitimate marriage would come under the *patria potestas* of her husband (or his father, if still alive), and therefore any property that she passed on to her children would leave her natal family. But a son's children came under his *potestas* (or his father's), and property passed on to them would stay in his family. This was presumably what motivated parents to deprive their daughters of the right to have children by pledging them to lifelong virginity.

[86] Majorian, *Novel* 6 pr.

[87] The minimum would be her share of the "Falcidian fourth." Roman law required that in a man's will, at least one-fourth of his estate go to those who would have inherited in full if he had died intestate, i.e., all his legitimate children (male and female). Each child had a right to an equal share of this quarter of the estate. A child who did not receive his or her share could bring suit for "undutiful will."

[88] See Evans-Grubbs, "Virgins and widows" (n. 41 earlier). For Theodosius I's law, see CTh 16.1.2 (380).

[89] Augustus's law had required remarriage within two or three years of widowhood, but in 320, Constantine had rescinded the Augustan penalties on celibacy (CTh 8.16.1).

THE *ARRHAE SPONSALICIAE*, PRENUPTIAL GIFTS, AND DOWRIES

Marrying entailed several assigns, especially the dowry (which the wife brought with her into the marriage) but also gifts from a man to his future bride. The latter provided some recompense when either partner failed to fulfill the betrothal promise, although none of the assigns was strictly necessary for a valid marriage.

Betrothal had been a legally actionable contract in pre-classical Roman law, but by the first century BCE this was no longer the case. The jurist Paulus remarked that it did not matter whether or not the betrothal pact (*sponsalia*) was witnessed by others or put in writing.[90] (The same was true of marriage itself in the classical period.) Nor were there any legal penalties in pre-Constantinian law for breaking an engagement in order to marry another, as long as the rejected party was notified.[91] But there could certainly be social repercussions, particularly for the *sponsa*. Her reputation might be adversely affected if she was repudiated because others might suspect that it had been because of unchastity or sexually questionable behavior. The North-African literary figure Apuleius made much of the damaged reputation of the daughter of one his legal opponents. According to Apuleius, the young woman had been "circulated" among rich young men, and even given over to certain suitors "to make trial of her." Repudiated by her fiancé, she would have sat at home "a widow before she was wed" had she not found a naïve young man (Apuleius's stepson Pontianus) willing to marry her. These allegations need not be taken as fact, though Apuleius does remind his audience that they themselves witnessed the young woman's shameless behavior.[92] But a betrothed woman who had been repudiated was at risk for being considered "damaged goods," and this could pose a serious obstacle to her making another match and could harm her family's social position.

A key aspect of the betrothal agreement was arrangement of the bride's dowry. Dowry was by far the most important marital assign in the classical period, although it was not a legal necessity. In the Roman world, including the eastern provinces, dowry always came from the bride or her family.[93] It could be in the form of jewelry, money, or other movable possessions such as slaves; among the elite, at least in the West, it could also include land. Dowry belonged to the husband for the duration of the marriage when, as the wife's contribution, it helped to

---

[90] *Dig.* 23.1.7 pr.

[91] Being betrothed to two people simultaneously was punished as bigamy, as was entering a new betrothal pact with someone else without properly notifying the person to whom one was already betrothed. The penalty was *infamia*, entailing loss of certain legal privileges such as the right to represent others in court: See *Dig.* 3.2.1 and 3.2.13.1–2.

[92] *Apologia* 76, in Vincent Hunink, *Apuleius of Madauros: pro Se de Magia (Apologia) edited with a Commentary* (Amsterdam, 1997). He also claimed that his opponent had pimped for his own wife and blackmailed her customers by threatening to prosecute them for adultery.

[93] On dowry, see Treggiari, *Roman Marriage*, 322–64; Evans-Grubbs, WLRE 91–98.

defray the "burdens of marriage." Upon divorce or the death of either spouse, the wife or her heirs could reclaim it, with deductions sometimes made if there were children (whose support was the father's responsibility). The possibility of reclamation would discourage squandering by the husband, whereas he would get the profits from careful investment or cultivation of the dowry during the marriage. Wives might also bring other property into the marriage or acquire it afterwards, primarily through family inheritance. (In Roman law, all legitimate children were their father's heirs, and at least among the elite, daughters would receive something in their parents' wills beyond their dowry.)[94] Unlike dowry, this property remained in the wife's possession.

Betrothal also offered an opportunity to bestow other gifts, which would then legally belong to the recipient once the marriage took place. It was not unusual for a prospective bridegroom to offer his betrothed a token of his esteem or intention to marry, for example, a ring. Sometimes these gifts would then go into the bride's dowry.[95] In Roman law, gifts between husband and wife *during* marriage were illegal, and therefore it was important that a gift clearly be given before the wedding, not afterwards. The jurist Paulus discussed a tricky case in which a man had given a silver basket to his virgin bride on the day when he married her: was it a valid gift? It all depended on whether the *donatio* had preceded or followed the *deductio* (her being escorted to her new husband's home). Paulus thought the case required a legal judgment.[96]

Classical law put prenuptial gifts (both those from *sponsus* to *sponsa* and those from *sponsa* to *sponsus*) into two legal categories: (1) smaller gifts of affection or esteem, which were not returnable if the marriage did not take place; and (2) gifts given "for the sake of contracting marriage" (*adfinitatis contrahendae causa*), which were to be returned if the match fell through.[97] But if the giver was responsible for breaking the engagement, he or she would forfeit even gifts of the latter sort.[98] The difference between the two kinds of gifts was not clear-cut, and by the third century it evidently eluded many people in the Empire, most of whom would have been quite unfamiliar with Roman family law. Confused subjects, both men and women, petitioned the emperor for help in retrieving gifts they had given for a marriage that had not materialized, or conversely, for legal support in refusing to return gifts

---

[94] Although a daughter's dowry was not her entire inheritance portion, she might be asked to put her dowry back into "the pot" if her father died intestate, so that there would be an equal distribution of all paternal assets to all children. Such aggregation was known as *collatio dotis*.

[95] See *Dig.* 6.2.12 pr (Paulus, citing a rescript of Antoninus Pius), CJ 5.3.1, and CJ 5.3.14.

[96] *Fragmenta Vaticana* 96 (FIRA 2, 488). The passage does not use the word *deductio*, but it is implied. In regard to the ban on gifts (discussed subsequently), cf. *Dig.* 39.5.1 pr (quoted earlier at n. 37) and CJ 5.3.6 (Aurelian).

[97] *Dig.* 39.5.1 (Julian). See Lucien Anné, *Les rites des fiançailles et la donation pour cause de mariage sous le Bas-Empire* (Louvain, 1941); Percy E. Corbett, *The Roman Law of Marriage* (Oxford, 1930), 18–23; Treggiari, *Roman Marriage*, 152–53.

[98] See Papinian in *Fragmenta Vaticana* 262 (FIRA 2, 519).

they had received.[99] In view of the diversity of practice throughout the Empire, it is not surprising that an emperor like Constantine, who wanted to promote unity and orderly legal procedure, would revamp the Roman law of donations. His legislation established the foundation for two centuries of lawmaking, and it introduced one of the most innovative features of late Roman marriage law: regulation of nondotal marital assigns.[100]

In 319, Constantine ruled that whoever was responsible for breaking a betrothal forfeited *any* gifts given or received, thus applying the policy for gifts *adfinitatis contrahendae causa* to all betrothal gifts. On the one hand, if the *sponsus* broke off the match, he could not take back what he had given, and if the gift was still in his possession, he had to hand it over to his ex-fiancée. On the other hand, if the decision not to marry lay with the *sponsa* or the person who had *potestas* over her (i.e., her *paterfamilias*), she had to return the gifts. The same applied for gifts given by the *sponsa* to her betrothed. There were to be no reasons given as to why the betrothal was broken off, nor imputations as to birth or character, given that such issues should have been investigated before the betrothal had been made.[101] Refusal to hear excuses for breaking a betrothal had several purposes: it cut down on petitions to the emperor regarding the legal status of gifts, it discouraged feuding between families over the fate of gifts, and it enabled the *sponsus* to save face and the *sponsa* to preserve her reputation.[102]

This law addressed only the fate of betrothal gifts and did not legislate for gift exchange in general. But four years later, Constantine went further and overhauled the classical law of donations.[103] To be valid, a gift had to be attested by a written document giving the name of the donor and the property being given; there had to be a physical, publicly witnessed handing-over (*traditio*) of the gift (in the case of immovable property, the donor had to vacate the land); and lastly, the transaction had to be recorded in the public *acta*. According to the law's preamble, the emperor had learned that many lawsuits had arisen regarding donations because of uncertainty about exactly when and how gifts had been made. In 333, the emperor reiterated the necessity for registering gifts in the public records, even gifts between

---

[99] For example, CJ 5.3.2 (222–35); CJ 5.3.10 (294–304); and a rescript of Valerian and Gallienus (ca. 257) in FIRA 2, 656–57. See Evans-Grubbs, *Law and Family*, 157.

[100] For what follows, see esp. Anné, *Les rites*; Corbett, *Roman Law of Marriage*; Evans-Grubbs, *Law and Family*, 156–83; Arjava, *Women and Law*, 52–62.

[101] CTh 3.5.2 (cf. CJ 5.3.15), posted at Rome, Oct. 27, 319.

[102] Another law of Constantine (CTh 3.5.4, dated 332) said that if a *sponsus* allowed two years to pass without marrying his *sponsa*, she could enter another union without penalty because "in hastening her marriage she did not suffer her vows to be mocked any longer."

[103] *Fragmenta Vaticana* 249 (FIRA 2, 513–16), MS dated 316 but redated to 323 by Mommsen. Part of the law is at CTh 8.12.1, although the preamble is found only in the *Vatican Fragments*. See Elizabeth Meyer, *Legitimacy and Law in the Roman World: Tabulae in Roman Belief and Practice* (Cambridge, 2004), 280–84; and Evans-Grubbs, *Law and Family*, 117–18; cf. ibid. 114–20 for other laws on gifts and inheritance.

parents and children (who did not, however, need to observe formal *traditio*). Later emperors followed suit.[104]

Constantine was willing to make an exception to his new rule requiring registration of gifts. In 330, he ruled that when a man had handed over a gift to a fiancée who was still a minor (i.e., below the legal age of twenty-five), the fact that he had not registered the gift in the *acta* should not mean that he could then reclaim it after "marital affection [*caritas*] has been dissolved," that is, after divorce.[105] The possibility that a man might cheat his future wife of the promised betrothal gift arises again in a law of Justinian, who states that he had received "many appeals for help" against deceptive husbands who intentionally omitted to enter prenuptial gifts in the *acta*, thereby nullifying them, and then proceeded to profit from their wives' dowries.[106]

In a law of 335 addressed to the vicar of Spain, Constantine returned to the subject of betrothal gifts. If a betrothed couple had exchanged a kiss (*osculo interveniente*), and one of them subsequently died before marriage took place, half of the gifts given by the *sponsus* were to go to the surviving partner and half to the family of the deceased. If there had not been a kiss, all gifts returned to the giver or his heirs. Any gifts given by the *sponsa* were to return to her (or her heirs) whether or not a kiss had been exchanged. The law notes that the giving of betrothal gifts by *sponsa* to *sponsus* "rarely occurs": evidence that prenuptial gifts usually came from the bridegroom's side only.[107]

This law apparently refers to an aspect of the *sponsalia* in which the future spouses kissed in a public ceremony, thus cementing the agreement. The only extant references to such a kiss before this law appear in writings of the North-African Christian apologist Tertullian, who mentions it along with the joining of hands by the betrothed couple. But there is evidence for the exchange of a kiss (between men and women who were related or between husbands and wives) to mark the solemnity of agreements in the pre-Christian classical period. Thus, although the use of an *osculum* to mark a betrothal may have had special significance for Christians, it was not an exclusively Christian custom. No other extant law of the fourth or fifth century mentions a betrothal kiss, but both the *Breviarium* of Alaric and the *Code of Justinian* retain Constantine's law, and the *osculum* appears

---

[104] For the law of 333, see CTh 8.12.5. Compare CTh 8.12.6 (Constans, 341) and CTh 8.12.8 (Theodosius II, 415). In CTh 8.12.9 (417) Theodosius II also abolished the need for physical delivery of gifts, and CTh 3.5.13 of 428 repeats this specifically in regard to betrothal gifts.

[105] CTh 3.5.3, to Valerianus, acting vicar of the prefect of Rome, 330. The ruling appears in part at CJ 1.18.1. A year later, Constantine made a law against unilateral divorce (CTh 3.16.1). At the same time, he upheld the ban on gifts between spouses during marriage (*Frag. Vat.* 273 [315]).

[106] CJ 5.3.20 (533). Compare CTh 3.5.7 (345), 3.5.8 (363), and 3.5.13 (428).

[107] CTh 3.5.6 (= CJ 5.3.16). Vicars were imperial officials who oversaw a grouping of provinces called a diocese. The law was probably sent to other imperial officials also, but the copy received in Hispalis was the one used by the code's compilers.

again in early medieval dotal charters.[108] It may have been a fairly localized custom, confined to provincials of Spain and North Africa.

Whatever its origins, Constantine clearly considered a betrothal *osculum* to have a contractual meaning. The fact that gifts from the *sponsa* to *sponsus* were to be returned in full suggests that, as in Constantine's law of 319, betrothed women who did not end up marrying their *sponsi* were in a particularly sensitive position. Whether or not the *osculum* was accompanied by other intimacies, a young woman's reputation might be compromised if marriage did not follow such a betrothal. Indeed, another law of Constantine describes the groom's *donatio maritalis* as a "reward for chastity" (*praemium pudicitiae*). Here the gift serves the same purpose as the Germanic *morgengabe* is supposed to have had.[109] Concern for the preservation of a young woman's premarital virginity is found in other Constantinian laws[110] and reflects a very traditional Greco-Roman view. As Apuleius had said, virginity was the only thing brought by a bride to her marriage that she could not retrieve when the marriage ended; unlike the dowry, it would always remain with the husband.[111]

Constantine's laws spoke of "gifts" (*donationes*) or "things given" (*res donatae*): he did not use any special term to describe a betrothal gift, apart from his reference to the *donatio maritalis* as the "reward for chastity." His laws presupposed two functions of such gifts: they guaranteed that the marriage would take place and would therefore be forfeited if it did not; and they were the bridegroom's contribution to the marriage, whereas the bride, who "rarely" gave such gifts, was expected to provide a dowry. Later emperors distinguished between these functions in legislation: gifts that served as surety that the marriage would take place were called *arrhae* (or *arrae*) *sponsaliciae*, from the Greek *arrha* (meaning "earnest" or "surety"), whereas the *sponsus*'s gift to the *sponsa* came to be called a "gift before marriage" (*donatio ante nuptias*). Both sides could give *arrhae sponsaliciae*, although the laws focus exclusively on those the *sponsa* received.[112] The *donatio ante nuptias* always came from the *sponsus*. The bridegroom's gift may originally have

---

[108] See chapters by Hunter and Reynolds in this volume; also Reynolds, *Marriage*, 387–88; Treggiari, *Roman Marriage*, 149–51; Evans-Grubbs, *Law and Family*, 148 and 171, noting also a jet plaque, probably for a pendant, found in Roman Britain and dating to the third or fourth century, which shows a couple kissing and may have been a betrothal gift.

[109] CTh 9.42.1 (321). On the *morgengabe* see Diane Owen Hughes, "From brideprice to dowry in Mediterranean Europe," in Marion A. Kaplan (ed.), *The Marriage Bargain: Women and Dowries in European History* (New York, 1985), 13–58, at 27–28. Similarly, Valentinian III's law on return of betrothal gifts (*Novel* 35.8–9, quoted subsequently at n. 119) said that if a husband died without children and his parents were dead, his widow could keep "everything she received in return for her modesty [*pudor*]."

[110] For example, CTh 9.8.1 (326), which says that the guardian of a fatherless girl about to be married has to prove that her virginity is intact or shall be held responsible for its loss (see Evans-Grubbs, *Law and Family*, 193–202).

[111] Apuleius, *Apologia* 92. Compare Pliny, *Epistle* 1, 14; Juvenal, *Satire* 6, 203–05.

[112] It may be that only *sponsi* gave *arrhae*, these being, in effect, a portion of the prenuptial gift that was given as a surety. See Arjava, *Women and Law*, 56.

been a Greek or eastern practice, but *donatio ante nuptias* appears in both eastern and western imperial legislation of the fifth century. A clear distinction between *arrhae* and *donatio ante nuptias* is not found in law until the fifth century; before then, both the terminology and the concepts were still fluid, and both were called *sponsalia*.

The earliest extant legal mention of *arrhae* comes in a law of Theodosius I dated 380, which uses the terms *sponsalia* and *arrhae* synonymously.[113] Theodosius refers to an "old law" that had established a fourfold penalty for the *sponsa* if, after *sponsalia* had been given, the marriage did not take place. Presumably this repayment of four times the amount received applied only when the *sponsa* or her family broke the betrothal. The law of 380 remitted this fourfold penalty when the girl had not yet reached the age of ten (i.e., she was more than two years away from the legal age for marriage). If she was between ten and twelve, her father or whoever was responsible for her was liable to the fourfold penalty if he believed that the "pledges" (*pignera*) should not be returned. If the girl was over twelve and her *paterfamilias* was dead, she herself was penalized. But she could bring a legal action against her mother, relative, or guardian if she could show that she had been compelled to receive *arrhae* (and thus forced into the betrothal).[114] Both the term *arrhae* and the fourfold penalty must pre-date the beginning of Theodosius's reign in 379 and may go back to a law of Constantine that is no longer extant. The penalty remained in effect until the eastern emperor Leo replaced it with a double penalty if the *sponsa* was legally independent and had turned twenty-five.[115]

Meanwhile, the *donatio nuptialis* had become better defined in both East and West. Divorce laws indicate the betrothal gift's growing importance: in Constantine's law punishing those who illegally repudiate their spouse, the offending party forfeits only the dowry; by the fifth century, loss of the *donatio* is mentioned alongside the dowry.[116] Emperors came to require that the *donatio ante nuptias* and the dowry should be equivalent, and that both eventually would go to the couple's children. Two years after his law on *arrhae*, Theodosius I ruled that a remarried widow had to pass on to her children by her first marriage everything she received from her first husband, including *sponsalia*. Remarried widowers were "admonished," but not commanded, to do the same with what they received from their first wife, which would include her dowry.[117] Fifty-seven years later, the eastern emperor

---

[113] *Dig.* 23.2.38 pr, which mentions *arrhae*, is interpolated. See Corbett, *Roman Law* (n. 97 earlier), 18–23.

[114] CTh 3.5.11 (380). Another part of the law (preserved in CJ 5.1.3) said that if either the *sponsus* or the *sponsa* died after *arrhae sponsaliae* had been given, what had been given was to be returned, "unless the deceased person has already given cause not to celebrate the nuptials." This seems to run counter to Constantine's law of 335 (CTh 3.5.6).

[115] CJ 5.1.5 (472). If she was under twenty-five and someone other than a parent or grandparent had received *arrhae* in her name, she was only liable to the "single penalty."

[116] CTh 3.16.1 (Constantine, 331); cf. CTh 3.16.2 (Honorius and Constantius II, 421) and CJ 5.17.8 (Theodosius II, 449).

[117] CTh 3.8.2 (dated 382), repeated in CJ 5.9.3 with some changes. This is one of several Theodosian laws that encouraged widows not to remarry and safeguarded the rights of their children by their first

Theodosius II repeated his grandfather's ruling, this time *requiring* a remarried man to pass on the dowry that he had received from his first wife to her children, even if the first wife had incorporated the prenuptial gift she had received from him into her dowry, "as usually happens."[118]

Western emperors, too, considered the husband's prenuptial gift to be a counterweight to the wife's dowry. Valentinian III (reigned 425–55) ruled that if a man died without children, his wife was to return half of his betrothal gift to his parents and keep the other half; if his parents were dead, she could keep everything. Likewise, if his wife predeceased him, a man was to return half of her dowry to her parents and keep half for himself. Nevertheless, the law continues, "the wife's side ought to give back as much as the husband had brought in betrothal gifts, so that there be an equal condition of giving and receiving, lest an acceptable future marriage be a source of gain to one, but a detriment to the other."[119] The dowry should be worth as much as the prenuptial gift, so that neither family uses the marriage to advance its own financial and social position.

Another western emperor, Majorian (457–61), had the same concern. Claiming that he wanted to increase the number of children born "for the increase of the Roman name" and therefore was seeking what was advantageous to them, Majorian demanded that a wife's dowry be equal in value to the husband's prenuptial gift.[120] According to him, parents of nubile girls were demanding large gifts from men who were "aroused by the desire of future marriage," and then refunding the gift to their daughter in the form of dowry or even keeping it for themselves. This use of prenuptial gifts from the man's side to enhance the parental dowry is also mentioned in an earlier eastern law, which says this is sometimes done either "in ignorance" or "with cunning," but it does not condemn the practice.[121] Majorian saw it as a despicable ploy on the part of a girl's family to take advantage of infatuated youths. But Majorian's law went even further, decreeing that if there was no dowry, the couple would be "branded with the stains of infamy" and their children would be illegitimate.

For the first time in Roman law, therefore, Majorian had made a dowry a requirement for a marriage's validity. In the past, dowry had always been advisable (and usual, at least among the propertied classes), but not necessary. Lack of dowry in cases in which the woman was of significantly lower social status than the man could suggest that the relationship was concubinage, not marriage, but the real indicator would be whether or not the couple had marital intent (*affectio maritalis*). But

---

husband. Compare CJ 5.10.1 (392), which allows a remarried mother the usufruct of the prenuptial gift from her first husband, but nothing else.

[118] *Novel* 14, 439, = CJ 5.9.5. Compare CJ 5.9.4 (Honorius, 422): the *sponsalicia largitas* a remarried woman received from each husband goes to her children by that husband.

[119] *Novel* 35.8–9 of Valentinian III, dated 452 (a western law).

[120] *Novel* 6.9–10 of Majorian, 458.

[121] CTh 3.5.13 (Theodosius II, 428). Compare *Novel* 14 of Theodosius II (439), which allows the practice.

Majorian's purpose was not, apparently, to ensure that the parties were of appropriate social status. Rather, he was concerned about a decrease in the population of well-born Romans at a time when imperial power in the West was shrinking. (We have already seen how he was concerned about parents who forced their daughters to remain virgins.) Because he was deposed and killed three years later and his legislation was annulled, his ruling on the necessity of dowry may have had have little effect, although it has been suggested that his contemporary, Pope Leo, was recalling Majorian's law in his response to an inquiry about a man's relationship with a servile concubine.[122]

Ten years later, in the East, the emperor Leo ruled that although dowry and prenuptial gift did not have to be equal in amount, the amount of the gift that a wife kept if her husband predeceased her was to equal the amount of dowry that her husband would retain if she died first.[123] Finally, in 533, Justinian completed the legal equation of dowry (*dos*) and *donatio*. He noted that he had received "many requests for help against husbands" from wives whose husbands had cheated them by neglecting to register the gift in the *acta* so that it did not take effect. The husbands would benefit from their wives' dowry, whereas wives were "left without a nuptial aid." To remedy this situation, Justinian decreed that the husband's gift would no longer be called *donatio ante nuptias* ("gift *before* marriage") but rather *donatio propter nuptias* ("gift *on account of* marriage"), so that it could be given at any time during the marriage, just as dowry could. For why, he wondered, should there be a difference in the legal treatment of *dos* and *donatio*, given that "it would be better to come to the aid of women, because of the weakness of their sex, rather than to the aid of males."[124]

Justinian realized that allowing a *donatio* to be made after a marriage had already taken place ran counter to the classical legal prohibition on gifts between husbands and wives. But he reasoned that the ancients had forbidden such gifts because they had been made from motives of lust or because of the poverty of one party, and not because of what he called *nuptiarum affectio* (by which he presumably meant *affectio maritalis*, the intent to be married and to regard one's partner as a spouse). Under the new law, either party could add to his or her contribution during the marriage, so that *dos* and *donatio* could maintain equilibrium, and if one was greater than the other, an amount would be deducted from it and given to the other so that the two contributions would be equal.[125] Thus, rather than demanding that husband and wife bring an equal amount to the marriage in the form of *dos* and *donatio*, Justinian ensured they would *become* equal after the marriage.

---

[122] The suggestion is that of Diane Owen Hughes, "Brideprice to dowry" (n. 109 earlier), 17; but cf. Reynolds, *Marriage*, 166. A. Lemaire, "Origine de la règle *Nullum sine dote fiat conjugium*," in *Mélanges Paul Fournier* (Paris, 1929), 415–24, thought that Leo was interpreting CTh 3.7.3 (Theodosius II, 428).

[123] CJ 5.14.9 (468). Compare 5.14.10 (529) of Justinian, which expands on Leo's law.

[124] CJ 5.3.20.1 (533). Compare CTh 3.5.3 of Constantine, discussed at n. 105 earlier.

[125] This reaffirmed CJ 5.14.9 of Leo (468) and 5.14.10 (529) of Justinian himself.

Two hundred years after its first appearance in Roman law, the bridegroom's nuptial gift had become a requisite part of the marriage settlement in both East and West. In the eastern Roman Empire, *dos* and *donatio* existed side by side as equal contributions. In the Germanic kingdoms of western Europe that were no longer under Roman control but whose own legislation had been influenced by Roman law, the bridegroom's gift was the customary marital assign, not the bride's dowry. Thus the word *dos*, which in Roman law had always referred to the wife's contribution, came to be used of the husband's contribution, which in classical Rome had played a very minimal role.[126]

THE BOND OF BETROTHAL

Late Roman laws on betrothal suggest that emperors considered the marriage pact to be a binding contract, one that should be kept even if the *paterfamilias* who had arranged it had died. Whatever the size or nature of the *arrhae*, these gifts signified intent to marry on the part of both giver and recipient, and would be forfeited by the defaulting party. The *sponsus*'s prenuptial gift could also be seen as a *praemium pudicitiae*: a reward to his future wife for having remained chaste before marriage.

In placing increased importance on the betrothal bond, late Roman law reflects contemporary *mores*. The rulings (canons) of local church councils held in the fourth century reveal that ecclesiastical leaders were concerned not only to prevent the dissolution of marriages by adultery or divorce, but also to maintain the betrothal bond. (They also offer a rare glimpse into the less regulated sexuality of young people outside the elite classes, where a girl's virginity might not be so closely guarded.) In the early fourth century, the Council of Elvira in Spain ordered parents who had broken off their children's *sponsalia* to abstain from communion for three years, unless they had done it because either *sponsa* or *sponsus* had committed a "serious crime."[127] But if the partners had "polluted themselves" by premarital sex, it was definitely wrong of the parents to break the betrothal.[128] In the East in 314, the Council of Ancyra (Ankara) ruled that betrothed girls abducted by others were to

[126] Hughes, "Brideprice to dowry"; Arjava, *Women and Law*, 56–62; idem, "Survival of Roman family law" (n. 15 earlier), 40. See Reynolds in this volume on the Frankish *dos*. But parental dowry does occur even among northern peoples later, in part because of a renewal of Roman law, and in part because of the influence of canon law (see chapter by Arnórsdóttir in this volume).

[127] Canon 54, in José Vives, Tomás M. Martínez, and Gonzalo M. Díez (eds.), *Concilios visigóticos e hispano-romanos* (Barcelona, 1963), 1–15. The Council apparently took place in the first decade of the fourth century. Maurice Meigne, "Concile ou collection d'Elvire?" *Revue de l'histoire ecclésiastique* 70 (1975): 361–87, argues that some of the canons attributed to Elvira (including canon 54) were actually from later councils. But even so, the canon would still be relevant in a study of betrothal in the fourth and fifth centuries.

[128] Compare canon 14: a girl who slept with a man and then married him is readmitted to communion without penance after a year, but if she had sex with more than one man, she must do five years' penance.

be returned to their fiancés unless they had suffered violence, and the council also dealt with a case in which a man had gotten his fiancée's sister pregnant; after the betrothed couple went ahead and married, the sister killed herself.[129] Later in the fourth century, Basil of Caesarea repeated Ancyra's policy on returning abducted girls to their fiancés, but he added that if a girl who was *not* betrothed was abducted, she was to be returned to her family, who could decide whether or not they wanted her to marry her abductor.[130] Clearly, Constantine's law against abduction marriage was aimed at an actual practice, but the Christian canonist's policy differed radically from the emperor's.

A letter of 385 by Pope Siricius further stresses the importance that the church placed on betrothal, at least when it involved the participation of clergy. Siricius was replying to an inquiry from Himerius, the bishop of Tarragona, who had asked "if a man could take in marriage a girl who was betrothed [*desponsata*] to another." Siricius said definitely not, "since if that benediction that a priest places on a woman about to marry [*nuptura*] is violated by any transgression, it is among the faithful like a sort of sacrilege."[131] The pope was referring to a ritual in which a priest blessed the couple, and he equated such a ritual with the beginning of marriage itself.[132] Such a conception of betrothal is actually rather different from the legal focus on an agreement made between families and cemented by the exchange of *arrhae*, but both the ecclesiastical and legal conceptions consider betrothal (*sponsalia*) to be a much more binding agreement than it had been in earlier Roman law.[133]

Nor were emperors and Christians the only ones to disapprove of a broken betrothal. The great pagan senator Symmachus, a contemporary of Siricius, wrote to an acquaintance, Julianus, who had previously contracted *pactae nuptiarum* for his daughter with another senator, Herculius. Julianus was now having second thoughts about the match, and Symmachus, who had favored the marriage and worked behind the scenes to promote it, reminds Julianus that breaking a betrothal would be a serious breach of senatorial faith (*fides*).[134] The letter ends

---

[129] Canon 11 (abduction); canon 25 (seduction and suicide), in Karl J. Hefele and Henri Leclerq, *Histoire des conciles d'après les documents originaux* (Paris, 1907), 298–326.

[130] Basil of Caesarea, *Epistle* 199, canon 22 (375 CE). Compare canon 30 on penalty for abductors. Text in Roy J. Deferrari (ed.), *Saint Basil: The Letters*, vol. 3 (Cambridge, Mass., 1962), 113–15 and 123. The problem continued: in 451, the Council of Chalcedon anathematized laymen and demoted clerics who abducted women.

[131] Text in PL 56:556–57. Himerius had actually sent his letter, asking about a number of thorny pastoral issues, to Siricius's predecessor Damasus, who had died in 384.

[132] Compare Reynolds, *Marriage*, 321–22; and see Hunter's chapter in this volume, on nuptial blessing in Rome and Italy. It is noteworthy that Himerius was bishop of Tarragona, in Spain. Compare Constantine's law on the *osculum* sent to an imperial official in Spain (discussed earlier at n. 107), and canon 54 of the Council of Elvira. Betrothal may have had a particular importance there.

[133] See Reynolds, *Marriage*, 315–27, on the strong Christian conception of betrothal in late antiquity.

[134] Symmachus, *Epistle* 9, 43, in Jean-Pierre Callu (ed.), *Symmaque Lettres Tome IV (livres IX–X)* (Paris, 2002). For Symmachus's promotion of the match, cf. *Epistle* 6, 44, in Callu (ed.), *Symmaque Lettres Tome III (livres VI–VIII)* (Paris, 1995).

by reminding Julianus that he has already approved a "pledge" (*pignus*) of the contract (*foedus*): this probably refers to *arrhae sponsaliciae* given by Herculius to Julianus or his daughter, which Julianus would be obliged to return with a fourfold penalty.[135] Symmachus does not mention the legal penalty; clearly, an appeal to senatorial fidelity and proper behavior was more likely to persuade the reluctant Julianus.

These legal, patristic, and literary references all suggest that in the late Empire, the betrothal bond received greater significance than in earlier times. This did not happen overnight or from any one cause. Well before Constantine, there had been a trend toward assimilating the legal status of betrothal to that of marriage in certain respects. Nevertheless, *sponsalia* were never considered equivalent to *nuptiae* in Roman law, even in late antiquity.[136] Not even pope Siricius goes that far in his response to Himerius.

THE DOCUMENTATION OF MARRIAGE

Late Roman laws on *arrhae sponsaliciae* and prenuptial gifts presuppose the use of written documentation; several laws refer to the registration of gifts in the public records (*acta*), and the possibility of litigation over return of *arrhae* or gifts would encourage both parties to make sure that written documents existed. These documents are variously called dotal tablets (*tabulae dotis* or *dotales*) or nuptial tablets (*tabulae nuptiales* or *matrimoniales*). *Tabulae* were wooden diptychs coated with wax, which would be written on with a metal stylus. Among Romans in the Latin-speaking western Empire, it appears that *tabulae* were the usual medium for a marriage document. A recent study of *tabulae* in Roman law and culture has shown that wax tablets had a value as evidence above that of other types of documents and were used in specific kinds of transactions, including marriage and dotal pacts.[137] The use of *tabulae* as the medium for marriage documents indicates the significance that these agreements had for Romans, whether or not we want to call them "marriage contracts." They resembled the modern "prenuptial agreements," setting out the financial stake that each party had in the marriage and making provision for divorce or the death of one of the partners. Such documents would be drawn up before marriage took place, although the jurist Scaevola noted that the *tabulae dotis* often were not signed until after marriage had been contracted.[138]

---

[135] Theodosius I's law on *arrhae sponsaliciae* (CTh 3.5.11, dated 380) uses the word *pignera* as a synonym for *arrhae*. For another nonlegal reference to *arrhae*, written around the same time as Symmachus's letters, see Evans-Grubbs, *Law and Family*, 175.

[136] Evans-Grubbs, *Law and Family*, 172–73; Jean Gaudemet, "L'orginalité des fiançailles romaines," in idem, *Sociétés et mariage* (Strasburg, 1980), 15–45 (article originally published in 1955).

[137] This is the central thesis of Meyer, *Legitimacy and Law* (n. 103 earlier).

[138] *Dig.* 24.1.66 pr.

Paulus said that marriage pacts would reflect the wishes of the particular couple, and that they might make financial arrangements that differed from the norm, such as "that a woman is to support herself with the promised dowry, and the dowry is not to be requested from her as long as she is married, or that she is to offer a certain sum of money to her husband and is to be supported by him."[139] In many cases, however, the parties would not draw up any written agreement at all, especially if there was no property changing hands.

The earliest extant reference to *tabulae* involves the notorious case of Messalina, wife of the emperor Claudius (reigned 41–54).[140] Messalina had been having an affair with the senator Gaius Silius, and she decided to divorce Claudius in order to marry her lover, but without notifying Claudius of her intention. While the emperor was out of town, she and Silius went through a full-fledged marriage ceremony, including *tabulae* signed by witnesses who had been summoned for the occasion; they declared that they "came together for the sake of rearing children" (*suscipiendorum liberorum causa*), they performed a sacrifice to the gods, and they spent the customary wedding night together. Under ordinary circumstances such behavior would have been thought inconsiderate to the woman's ex-husband (the polite thing would be to notify him of his own divorce before it became public knowledge), but it was not illegal as long as Messalina had made clear her intention to divorce before remarrying. But in this case, Silius was seen as attempting to usurp not only Claudius's wife but his throne. The bewildered Claudius was informed of his divorce by the imperial freedman Narcissus, who declared that the emperor should not even request back the slaves and other items that Messalina had removed from the imperial household into her new home: "rather, let him enjoy these things, but return the wife and break the marriage tablets." Breaking the *tabulae nuptiales* would signify intention to dissolve the marriage, just as drawing up tablets signified the intent to marry. (In the end, both Silius and Messalina were executed, and Claudius married his niece Agrippina, after changing the incest law.)

Other references to *tabulae dotales* or *tabulae nuptiales* turn up in Latin literature of the second century. Juvenal, in his satire on married life, refers to a wife as "contracted and joined to you with legitimate *tabellae* [= *tabulae*]," and elsewhere he describes a marriage ceremony between males in which tablets were signed.[141] In the *The Golden Ass* (a novel by the North African writer Apuleius), a young woman claims that her fiancé could be called "husband" even before the wedding by virtue of the *tabulae* and her parents' consent.[142] Particularly valuable is Apuleius's

---

[139] *Dig.* 23.4.12.1. Normally, the dowry remained in the husband's possession during marriage.

[140] Tacitus, *Annales* 11.26–30; also Suetonius, *Divus Claudius* 26.2, who refers to a dowry agreement being signed (*dote...signata*); cf. Juvenal, *Satire* 10, 336. Treggiari, *Roman Marriage*, 140 n. 72 says this is "the first attested example" of *tabulae nuptiales.*

[141] Juvenal, *Satire* 6, 200; same-sex ceremony: *Satire* 2, 119–20.

[142] Apuleius, *Metamorphoses (The Golden Ass)* 4.26.

narrative of the marital vicissitudes of his wife, Aemilia Pudentilla, a wealthy widow and landowner in the province of Tripolitania in North Africa.[143]

Pudentilla had earlier been married to a fellow citizen of the town of Oea, Sicinius Amicus, by whom she had two sons. After Amicus's death, her father-in-law Sicinius Aemilianus pressured her to marry another of his sons, Sicinius Clarus (presumably to keep her wealth accessible to his family). As their paternal grandfather, Aemilianus was the *paterfamilias* of her sons, and he threatened to disinherit them if she married an "outsider." Pudentilla therefore agreed, and even drew up *tabulae nuptiales* with Clarus, but she managed to evade actual marriage. Eventually Aemilianus died and the inheritance rights of his grandsons were safe. Thus Pudentilla, who had been a widow for fourteen years and whose health was allegedly suffering from long-term celibacy, felt free to break the betrothal to Clarus and to look around for another husband. Just then Apuleius was visiting town while on a speaking tour of the province. When he fell ill, he was taken in by Pudentilla's older son, Pontianus, who knew Apuleius from their university days in Athens. According to Apuleius, Pontianus suggested that he could marry his mother, thereby solving her gynecological problems and at the same time, he hoped, avoiding the problem of an unsympathetic stepfather with designs on his mother's fortune. The proposed marriage caused much resentment on the part of Pudentilla's former in-laws, now led by another ex-brother-in-law, the younger Sicinius Aemilianus. In order to avoid family unpleasantness, and to avoid having to provide the common people of Oea with "goody baskets" (*sportulae*), Apuleius and Pudentilla married quietly in the country, where they signed *tabulae nuptiales*.[144] Apuleius claims that the tablets not only specified an unusually small dowry for such a wealthy woman (300,000 sesterces),[145] but also maintained the rights of Pudentilla's sons by her first marriage. Despite such precautions, Apuleius was perceived as a young fortune hunter who had inveigled an older woman into marriage by illegally using erotic magic.

As a legally independent widow with money, land, and several hundred slaves to her name, Pudentilla would have wanted a written instrument setting out the terms of the marriage, including whatever she chose to bring as dowry.[146] The *tabulae* with Sicinius Clarus were drawn up in advance of the marriage, probably at the time of betrothal; they obviously did not serve as proof of an actual marriage, since in the end no marriage took place. Perhaps they did not

---

[143] This is Apuleius's defense speech when on trial for using magic to bewitch Pudentilla into marrying him. He actually presented the tablets from his marriage with Pudentilla in court as evidence for his assertions. For his use of *tabulae* as evidence, see Meyer, *Legitimacy and Law* (n. 103 earlier), 238–41.

[144] *Apologia* 67–69 and 87–88. Latin text in Vincent Hunink (ed.), *Apuleius of Madauros: Pro se de magia (Apologia)* (Amsterdam, 1997).

[145] In order to stay in the equestrian class (the highest social class after senators), a man had to have a net worth of 400,000 sesterces. Apuleius should not be taken at face value.

[146] Her *paterfamilias* was dead; she had a legal guardian (*tutor mulierum*), who gave his consent to the dowry (she did not need his consent for the marriage itself).

even *sign* the tablets.[147] The *tabulae nuptiales* of Pudentilla and Apuleius were signed (*consignatae*) in a country villa, and the distinctly private nature of this transaction occasioned criticism. Apparently marriage tablets were supposed to be signed in public with a number of witnesses (a Latin contract from Egypt had seven witnesses; discussed later), but equally apparently the lack of publicity did not invalidate the document or the marriage.

Pudentilla and both her husbands were natives of Roman North Africa, and it may be that marriage tablets had greater importance there than elsewhere in the West. In Carthage, a few decades after Apuleius wrote his *Apologia*, the Christian rhetor Tertullian mentions *tabulae nuptiales* as a standard part of contemporary marriage customs. Two centuries later, the North-African bishop Augustine (who attended school in Apuleius's hometown of Madaura) refers frequently to *tabulae* in his writings (including sermons to his congregation); clearly he saw them as a very significant part of contracting marriage.[148]

Writing in the 470s, the Gallo-Roman aristocrat Sidonius Apollinaris tells a salutary tale of the abuse of marriage tablets. A young man, Amantius, from Sidonius's region of the Auvergne, had left home without the knowledge or consent of his stingy father. In Marseilles, Amantius ingratiated himself with a wealthy widow and her pre-adolescent daughter; when the girl had reached marriageable age, he asked for her hand. *Tabulae nuptiales* were drawn up, in which were mentioned many estates back in the bridegroom's native region, included as his part of the marriage settlement although they were not, in fact, in his possession. Amantius then returned to his home with his rich wife and the property that he had received in return (presumably as dowry) from his mother-in-law. When the widow realized that the *sponsalicia donatio* was largely imaginary, she began a legal action against Amantius. But by then there were grandchildren, and apparently she was ultimately reconciled to her swindler son-in-law. And she was not the only one who failed to check Amantius's credentials; Sidonius recounts the story in some chagrin, as he was also taken in and had earlier recommended Amantius to his correspondent as a likely young man.[149] Marriage tablets were only as reliable as the people who drew them up.

Marriage Documents on Papyri and Wood

No *tabulae nuptiales* have survived from anywhere in the Latin-speaking West (encompassing southern Europe, Britain, and North Africa west of Egypt) before the time of the barbarian kingdoms. There is a fifth-century *tabula dotis* from Vandal North Africa (discussed subsequently) on which the text has been directly

---

[147] Compare Scaevola (*Dig.* 24.1.66): *tabulae dotis* are often signed after marriage.

[148] See Hunter's chapter in this volume. Note also the *tabula dotis* from Vandal Africa (discussed subsequently at n. 179).

[149] *Epistle* 7, 2, written in the 470s. Compare *Epistle* 6, 8, the letter of recommendation. Texts in W. B. Anderson (ed.), *Sidonius, Letters III–IX*, Loeb edition (Cambridge, Mass., 1965).

written in ink. In the East, Egypt, the Judaean desert, and the military outpost of Dura Europos (on the Euphrates frontier with Persia) alone have yielded matrimonial documents. Unlike the wax tablets of Italy and North Africa, which have not survived, these were written on papyrus (a paper-like material made from the papyrus reed), and most were written in Greek.[150] This distribution of evidence is a result of the materials used for the documents and the environmental conditions under which they can survive. It does not imply that people elsewhere in the Empire did not draw up similar documents. Although this volume focuses on western and northern traditions, therefore, we must turn to papyri from the Roman East for actual examples akin to the matrimonial documents discussed previously.

In Egypt, the custom of drawing up a marriage contract long preceded the country's incorporation as a Roman province in 31 BCE. Both native Egyptians and the Greek settlers who arrived in Egypt in the late fourth century BCE, after Alexander the Great's conquest, made use of written instruments to record dowries, to set out expectations for the couple, and to make arrangements in the event of death or divorce. Amost all the marriage documents from Roman Egypt are written in Greek and reflect Greek marriage practices and law. Native Egyptians also drew up contracts in demotic (the Egyptian language), and those few Roman citizens living in the province before 212 (mostly provincial administrators or military men) used Latin. We have dozens of Greek marriage contracts from Roman Egypt for the first and second centuries, but only about a dozen altogether from the third, fourth, and fifth centuries.[151]

The Egyptian marriage documents show regional variation in wording and format, but virtually all of them mention a dowry (*pherne*) provided by the bride or her family, which might include clothing, jewelry, or other items. (A rare exception is a third-century contract attesting the marriage of two embalmers of mummies; the lack of dowry is probably attributable to the couple's low socio-economic level.)[152] Like the Roman *dos*, the Egyptian *pherne* was in the husband's ownership during the marriage and returned to the wife only upon divorce. Documents of the imperial

---

[150] Wax tablets are known from Roman Egypt for other types of documents. In what follows I use the standard abbreviations for editions of papyri as found in the online *Checklist of Editions of Greek, Latin, and Coptic Papyri, Ostraca, and Tablets,* http://scriptorium.lib.duke.edu/papyrus/texts/clist.html. (version last updated April 2005). For a list of marriage papyri with links to texts, see D. Instone-Brewer, *Marriage & Divorce Papyri of the Ancient Greek, Roman and Jewish World,* at http://www.tyndale.cam.ac.uk/Brewer/MarriagePapyri/Index.html.

[151] See Uri Yiftach-Firanko, *Marriage and Marital Arrangements: A History of the Greek Marriage Document in Egypt, 4th century BCE–4th century CE* (Munich, 2003); Hans J. Wolff, *Written and Unwritten Marriages in Hellenistic and Post-Classical Roman Law* (Haverford, Pa., 1939). For translations of the papyri see WLRE 122–30 and 210–16; and Jane Rowlandson (ed.), *Women and Society in Greek and Roman Egypt: A Sourcebook* (Cambridge, 1998).

[152] P. Oxy. XLIX.3500. Greek text in A. Bulow-Jacobsen and J.E.G. Whitehorne (eds.), *The Oxyrhynchus Papyri XLIX* (London, 1982). Translation: WLRE 129.

period mention two other types of property from the bride, which remained hers during the marriage: *parapherna*, comprising smaller personal items that the wife used for her own adornment or comfort;[153] and *prosphora*, which could include land and slaves. As was the case with Roman dowry, however, none of these forms of marital assets was required for a marriage to be valid. The documents' main purpose was to record and make provision for these properties, which would, in almost all cases, return to the wife or her family upon the marriage's dissolution. In addition, some papyri mention the marital duties expected of husband and wife (financial support on the part of the husband, proper behavior on the part of the wife) and make arrangements for the care of children born to the couple in case of divorce or the death of the husband. Not all contracts include these additional provisions, which vary according to time period and locality.[154]

Another aspect of marriage that appears in the papyri is the act of *ekdosis*, the "giving-over" of the bride to the groom. The documents attest *ekdosis* by the bride's father, mother, and even "self-*ekdosis*" by the bride herself. Not all marriage documents mention *ekdosis*, and it may not have been part of every marriage.[155] *Ekdosis* is roughly analogous to Roman *deductio in domum*, although it did not always involve the movement of the bride to the groom's home (for instance, in the case of brother–sister marriages, in which the couple might continue to live with their parents).

Some documents refer to a phenomenon known as "unwritten marriage." Early in the twentieth century, scholars thought that "unwritten marriages" were less than complete marriages, perhaps undertaken for a trial period. But Hans Julius Wolff disproved that thesis, and a recent study of marriage in Greco-Roman Egypt shows that the only apparent difference between an "unwritten" and a "written" marriage was that the father of a child born in an unwritten marriage had powers over the child that he would not have in a written marriage.[156] Many people would see no need for documentation, for instance, very poor people who had no dowry or other marital assigns to record, or those in brother–sister marriages, which were quite common (about twenty percent of all marriages in the first two centuries CE) but usually less prone to family concerns over "his" and "hers."[157] Sometimes a couple would live in an unwritten marriage for many years and only draw up a contract when circumstances arose that made documentation useful.

---

[153] Also known to Roman law as a Greek phenomenon: see *Dig.* 23.3.9.3 (Ulpian) and CJ 5.14.8 (Theodosius II).

[154] Yiftach-Franko, *Marriage and Marital Arrangements*, 105–95.

[155] Yiftach-Franko, *Marriage*, 41–54, believes *ekdosis* occurred even when not mentioned in the documents, contra Wolff, *Written and Unwritten Marriages*, 25–30, who sees a decline in the practice in the Roman period.

[156] Yiftach-Franko, *Marriage*, 81–102; Wolff, *Written and Unwritten Marriages*.

[157] Not that all sibling marriages were harmonious or without property disputes: cf. P.Kron. 52, the divorce agreement of Kronion's son and daughter.

Only two Latin marriage contracts survive from Egypt, both on papyrus, both fragmentary.[158] They record the marriages of Roman citizens, who comprised only a small minority of residents in Egypt before 212. Both contracts state that the father of the bride is giving her in marriage "for the sake of producing children" (*liberorum procreandorum causa*) according to the Augustan law *de maritandis ordinibus*, and both list a dowry consisting of jewelry (valued by weight) and clothing. The more fragmentary of these also mentions cooking utensils.[159] The more complete Latin contract dates to some time in the second century.[160] Here the dowry includes not only clothes and jewelry, but also a bronze statuette of Venus (mentioned in several Greek marriage contracts and evidently intended as an aid to wifely sexiness and fertility), land, and a "paternal slavewoman" (perhaps an old family retainer who had once been the bride's nurse). The bride also has a small *parapherna*, but no *prosphora*. (The items that would be found in a Greek-Egyptian *prosphora*, i.e., land and slaves, are part of the dowry in this Latin contract.) This contract also mentions a contribution from the groom consisting of some land from his father's family: a very early attestation of the husband's prenuptial gift, which becomes standard from the fourth century onward. On the back of the papyrus were the signatures of seven witnesses.

Nine marriage documents recording marriages between Jews and dating to the late first or early second centuries have been found in the Roman provinces of Judaea and Arabia (largely coterminous with modern Israel and Jordan). Five of these are in Greek, the rest in Aramaic. The Greek contracts reveal an interesting fusion of Greek and Jewish elements, whereas the Aramaic documents are traditional Jewish *ketubat*. In one of the Greek documents, hidden along with other papyri in the "Cave of Letters" on the Dead Sea during the second Jewish revolt from Rome, the bride's father gives his daughter Shelamzion in marriage to another Jew of the same

---

[158] Two other documents are often identified as marriage-related: one, a wax tablet (P.Mich. VII.444, late second century), was said by its editor to be a "Fragment of a marriage contract or attestation," but it is so fragmentary that there is no way of knowing what it is. The other, a papyrus (P.Mich.442, second century) has been variously identified as a marriage contract, a betrothal contract, or an acknowledgment of receipt of dowry. It concerns a soldier (who was forbidden to marry while in service) and a woman who had been married to him before he joined up and by whom he had two children. Its purpose was evidently to attest to the marriage and the legitimacy of the children, and to safeguard the dowry previously given by the woman. See R. O. Fink, "P.Mich. VII.422 [*sic*] (inv.4703): Betrothal, marriage, or divorce?" in A. E. Samuel (ed.), *Essays in Honor of C. Bradford Welles* (New Haven, 1966), 9–17.

[159] PSI VI.730, in *Papiri greci e latini*, vol. 6 (Florence, 1920), dated by the editor to the first century after Christ. Text is also in Robert Cavenaile (ed.), *Corpus papyrorum latinarum* (Wiesbaden, 1956–58), 207. On the phrase *liberorum procreandorum causa*, see Hunter's chapter in this volume.

[160] P.Mich. VII.434 + P.Ryl. IV.612 (= *Corpus papyrorum latinarum*, 208–09). There are three fragments, two in the University of Michigan collection of papyri and one in the Rylands Library in Manchester. One should not use the original publication of the Michigan pieces in TAPA 1938, because the editor, H. A. Sanders, did not know of the Manchester fragment. The most recent publication of the Latin text is in A. Bruckner and R. Marichal (eds.), *Chartae Latinae Antiquiores* IV (Olten, 1967), no. 249, 49–53. Translation: WLRE 126–27.

village in Roman Arabia. She provides a *phosphora* valued at 300 denarii, and the groom contributes another 300 denarii, which is to go into the dowry (here called a *proix*, the word used for "dowry" in classical Athens).[161]

Another marriage document from outside Egypt was found at Dura Europos, a Roman military outpost on the Euphrates at the border with the Persian Empire. Written in Greek and dated 232 (about twenty years prior to the destruction of Dura by invading Persians), it is the marriage contract of a Roman soldier and a woman named Marcellina, who "has given herself from widowhood for the partnership of marriage." Her dowry includes the usual clothing, jewelry, and household implements (all assigned a monetary value) as well as money in silver. As in the Jewish contract from Arabia, the groom also contributes money to the dowry (here also called a *proix*).[162]

Roman marriage law did not much affect local marriage practices in these regions after 212 (when all free provincials became Roman citizens and came under Roman law), except that practices that were clearly illegal, such as sibling marriage, seem to have died out in Egypt. Documents continued to be written in Greek; a well-preserved papyrus from Oxyrhynchus dated in 260 retains the same features as earlier contracts from the same city.[163] The bride's mother (who is presumably a widow; she is "assisted" by a male who may be a relative) gives her daughter in marriage, and the papyrus describes a substantial dowry. Provisions are made in case of divorce for return of the dowry or of its appraised value at the time of the wedding.

In a Greek document dated 304, a mother states that she has given her daughter, who is described as "present and consenting" in marriage "according to the Papion-Pappaeon [*sic*] law."[164] This is a reference to the centuries-old *lex Papia Poppaea* of the emperor Augustus, which was to be repealed by Constantine sixteen years later. The bride's mother also provides the dowry, including clothing, linen, "female implements," and two slaves. The groom is represented by a guardian (*curator*), which indicates that his *paterfamilias* is dead and that he is below the age of majority (twenty-five). Because the last part of the papyrus is lost, it is not clear whether the groom contributed any goods. Nevertheless, a later marriage contract (discussed later) and several fourth-century documents relating to the break-up of marriages mention the groom's prenuptial gift, called *hedna*.[165]

---

[161] P. Yadin 18, part of the "Babatha archive." Greek text is in Naphtali Lewis (ed.), *The Documents from the Bar Kokhba Period in the Cave of Letters: Greek Papyri* (Jerusalem, 1989). For a translation of the outer (lower) part of this text, see WLRE 132–33.

[162] P. Dura 30, translated in WLRE 134.

[163] P. Oxy X.1273. Greek text in B. P. Grenfell and A. S. Hunt (eds.), *The Oxyrhynchus Papyri X* (London, 1914), 207–10. Translation: WLRE 127–29.

[164] P. Vind. Bosw. 51, dated 304. Repeal of Augustan penalties: CTh 8.16.1 (320).

[165] *Hedna* are mentioned in P. Grenf. II.76, dated 305/06 (a divorce agreement), and in four complaints from aggrieved spouses suffering marital problems: P. Oxy. LIV.3770 (334), P. Cairo Preis.2 (362), P. Lond. V. 1651 (363), and P. Lips. 41 (later fourth century).

An unusual contract from mid–fourth-century Egypt provides evidence for a marital arrangement otherwise unattested in antiquity, though found in much later Byzantine documents.[166] The groom, who is said to be "destitute," not only moves into the home of the bride's father but also admits that he does not have the "power" to leave her or her father; essentially he is entering into service with his father-in-law. The bride's contribution is called a "wedding gift," not a dowry. Another unique feature of this marriage agreement is the presence of a Christian priest (*papas*), who signs the contract for the groom and the bride's father. No other matrimonial documents of this period mention Christian clergy, but two long complaints by wives detailing the abuse that they received from their husbands mention clergy as mediators who attempt to reconcile the spouses.[167]

A more traditional Greek contract of 363 describes the bride's dowry and mentions *hedna*.[168] The document sets out the same duties as found in earlier marriage documents from the same region in Egypt: the husband is to provide his wife with clothing and the necessities of life, and the wife should keep herself blameless and free from accusation of immoral conduct. The now fragmentary end of the document would have made provisions for return of the dowry to the wife or her father in the event of separation.

Only one Greek contract from fifth-century Egypt is preserved, in a very fragmentary state. It is in the form of a *homologia*, a reciprocal declaration by the spouses of their intention to marry and of the usual duties of each: for the husband to care for and clothe his wife, and for the wife to love her husband. As we have it, the papyrus does not mention marital assigns and gives no indication of the circumstances in which the marriage took place.[169] A much more complete Jewish *ketubah* survives from the city of Antinoopolis, written in Aramaic and Greek (using Hebrew characters) and dated 417. Samuel declares that he is taking Metra, daughter of Leazar, as wife. Metra's duties follow, and then an inventory of goods that have been given to her by her mother as dowry. Samuel and Leazar each get a copy of the contract. Great importance is placed on the dowry, which is mentioned before the groom's contribution, the *mohar* (here actually called by the Greek name *hedna*). This stress on the dowry shows Greco-Roman

[166] P. Ross. Georg. III.28. Greek text in G. F. Zereteli and P. Jernstedt (eds.), *Papyri russischer und georgischer Sammlungen III: Spätrömische und byzantinische Texte* (Tiflis, 1930). Translation: WLRE 130. On the marital arrangement, see Joëlle Beaucamp, *Le statut de la femme à Byzance (4ᵉ–7ᵉ siècle): II. Les pratiques sociales* (Paris, 1992), 108–09.

[167] P. Oxy. L. 3581 (fourth/fifth century); P. Oxy. VI.903 (fourth century) in Rowlandson, *Women and Society*, 207–09 (n. 151 earlier); Bagnall, "Church, state, and divorce" (n. 43 earlier). See Hunter's chapter in this volume on bishops signing *tabulae matrimoniales* in Augustine's North Africa.

[168] P. Stras. 131, from the Arsinoite nome. Because of the lacunose state of the papyrus, it is unclear who is giving the *hedna* (I assume the groom), and it may be that the *hedna* remain in the keeping of the bride's father.

[169] P. Iand. Inv. 507 = SB 13886, dated 489/90. See Beaucamp, *Le statut*, 112.

influence on the contract, though in some other respects it adheres to rabbinical norms.[170]

Nine Greek marriage documents (several very fragmentary) survive from sixth-century Egypt.[171] In an agreement from Antinoopolis dating between 566 and 573, the husband, a soldier and "porter" (*ostiarius*) named Flavius Horouonchis, begins by declaring that he has found his bride's virginity intact and therefore owes her a certain amount of money as "*hedna* or gifts on behalf of marriage."[172] Here the groom's gift is made after the beginning of marriage, as Justinian had said it could be, and is therefore *donatio propter nuptias* rather than *donatio ante nuptias*.[173] It is analogous to the Germanic *morgengabe* or the Roman *praemium pudicitiae*.

Whereas marriage documents of the earlier Empire focus on property matters, most of this contract is devoted to recording the expectations for the conduct of both spouses. The husband's behavior receives more attention; the wife's obligations are much vaguer and more generic. Presumably it went without saying that she should be sexually faithful to her husband and that any hint of impropriety would be construed as disrespectful and liable to penalty.[174] The circumstances in which either spouse must pay a fine to the other for breach of obligations are essentially the same as the causes allowed for unilateral divorce in contemporary law, and presumably in such circumstances Horouonchis and Scholastikia would divorce, although this is not explicitly stated.[175] After these undertakings for proper marital behavior, the groom adds, almost as an "afterthought,"[176] that he will not bring into the home any "strange" women in addition to Scholastikia, and that he will pay the aforementioned penalty if he does. Another sixth-century contract contains a similar clause, in which the husband agrees not to take another woman or concubine.[177]

[170] Text in C. Sirat et al., *Le Ketouba de Cologne: Un contrat de mariage juif à Antinoopolis*, Papyrologia Coloniensia 12 (Opladen, 1984). See S. R. Llewelyn (ed.), *New Documents Illustrating Early Christianity*, vol. 9 (Grand Rapids, 2002), 82–98 for an English translation with discussion of this contract as well as of earlier Jewish contracts.

[171] See Beaucamp, *Le statut*, 106 for a list of sixth- and seventh-century contracts, to which add P. Berol. Inv. 21334, published by Kuehn (n. 178 later), and P. Cair.inv.s.r. 3733, published by A. Hanafi in Isabella Andorlini (ed.), *Atti del XXII Congresso Internatzionale di Papirologia* (Florence, 2001), 571–75. There are also at least three extant marriage contracts from sixth- and seventh-century Palestine (Nessana).

[172] P. Lond. V.1711, completed by the draft, P.Cair.Masp. III.67310. Greek texts in J. Maspero (ed.), *Papyrus grecs d'époque byzantine: Catalogue général des antiquités égyptiennes du Musée du Caire*, vol. 3 (Cairo, 1916); and H. I. Bell (ed.), *Greek Papyri in the British Museum*, vol. 5 (London, 1917). Translation: Rowlandson, *Women and Society*, 210–11.

[173] Compare CJ 5.3.20 (533). The contract uses the Greek equivalent.

[174] Beaucamp, *Le statut*, 87–88.

[175] Ibid., 87. For contemporary divorce law, cf. Justinian, *Novel* 117.8–9 (542).

[176] As noted by H. I. Bell, editor of P.Lond. V.1711. The sentence does not appear in the draft but was added in the final version.

[177] P. Cair. Masp. I.67006v, cited by Beaucamp, *Le statut*, 84.

Interestingly, although the *hedna* is described at the beginning of the document, there is no mention of a dowry. That does not mean that Scholastikia did not bring a dowry; this document is in effect an acknowledgement by the husband that he owes his wife the nuptial gift, as are several other marriage documents of this period.[178] Another document may have recorded receipt of the dowry, perhaps drawn up before marriage. Dowry is mentioned in other marriage and divorce papyri of the sixth century, and clearly was still an important marital assign in Byzantine Egypt. But the *donatio ante/propter nuptias* (or *hedna*) played an important role in early medieval eastern marriage arrangements, just as equivalent gifts did in the Germanic kingdoms in the West.

In contrast, a Latin marriage document from Vandal North Africa features the bride's dowry. The *tabula dotis* of Geminia Januarilla was one of forty-five wooden tablets, written in ink with a reed pen and deposited in terracotta jars, which were buried in a cave in the border area between Tunisia and Algeria. The tablets date from the reign of the Vandal king Gunthamund (484–96) and apparently were hidden during one of the native Berber upheavals of the late fifth century.[179] Apart from the *tabula dotis*, these documents concern sales of parcels of land that were part of the *dominium* of a certain Flavius Geminius Catullinus and his heirs. The Latin syntax and spelling are poor, and many of the participants are said to be illiterate, but the transactions continue to use the classical Roman *stipulatio* formula; evidently the writers had access to formularies without necessarily understanding the legal technicalities.[180] We do not know who deposited the tablets, nor do we know what was the relationship of Geminia Januarilla and her *sponsus* Julianus to the people mentioned in the other tablets (although her *nomen* indicates that she was related in some way to Flavius Geminius Catullinus).[181]

The document begins, "In the ninth year of our lord, the unconquered king, on the fifteenth day before the Kalends of October [Sept. 17], the dowry tablet of Geminia Januarilla, *sponsa*, together with Julianus, for the sake of procreating children (*infantium procreandorum cause*)...." The ancient Roman formula indicating the purpose of marriage still survives, although rather than the classical *liberorum*, the tablet uses *infantium* (which had replaced *liberi* as the generic

---

[178] C. A. Kuehn, "A new papyrus of a Dioscorian poem and marriage contract: P. Berol. Inv. No. 21334," *Zeitschrift für Papyrologie und Epigraphik* 97 (1993): 102–15, at 105.

[179] *Les Tablettes Albertini: Actes privés de l'époque Vandale* edited with commentary by C. Courtois, L. Leschi, C. Perrat, and C. Saumagne (Paris, 1952). The *tabula dotis* is Tab. Albertini I (p. 215). Most of the tablets are palimpsests and are either triptychs or diptychs; the *tabula dotis* is one of the few single-leaved examples.

[180] Courtois et al., *Tablettes*, 206–07. On the survival of the *stipulatio* in late antiquity see Meyer, *Legitimacy and Law* (n. 103 earlier), 264.

[181] The sellers of the land parcels may have been tenants who had owned the rights to work land on the estate of Catullinus but had failed to cultivate it and had to sell back the property (the prices paid are very low). See Bruce Hitchner, "Historical text and archaeological context in Roman North Africa: The Albertini Tablets and the Kasserine Survey," in David B. Small (ed.), *Methods in the Mediterranean* (Leiden, 1995), 124–42.

word for "children").[182] The dowry's contents are then listed, consisting entirely of clothing, jewelry, and implements for weaving wool (the traditional Roman female activity). The dowry amounts in total to 12,000 folles. By far the most expensive item is a "pure African dalmatic": a long-sleeved tunic mentioned in other late imperial marriage documents. Its value of 2000 folles is particularly surprising when compared to the highest price paid for land in the other tablets: 1500 folles, eight times *less* than the total value of Januarilla's dowry! The summation of the values of all the items is given as 11,500 folles, to which another 500 is added "for the purpose of embellishing the dowry." The document does not say whether this topping-off of the dowry comes from the bride's side or the groom's. It may be Julianus's *donatio ante nuptias* (although it is by no means equivalent to the dowry, as expected by contemporary law). The last line is almost unreadable but appears to record Julianus's acceptance of the dowry.

Geminia Januarilla and Julianus were apparently "Romano-Berbers," descendants of Roman settlers who had intermarried with native North Africans centuries earlier. They were not Vandals, and their legal and social practices seem untouched by the Vandal occupation, probably because they live in a remote area and have relatively modest financial means. The editors of the published text rather condescendingly compared the items found in Januarilla's dowry with the adornments worn by brides among contemporary Kabyle (in 1952).[183] We might instead compare it to the dowries of women in late Roman Egypt or third-century Dura Europus. Clearly the *dos* of the heiress of a wealthy senatorial family would have been far greater and would have included land (absent from Januarilla's dowry), but this sole surviving *tabula dotis* is surely more typical of what the average Roman bride brought to her marriage.

Documents and Unequal Unions: The Late Roman Legal Attitude

As the papyri show, whatever the classical Roman tradition said about a marriage's validity resting on consent and *conubium* alone, there were parts of the Empire where written marriage documents had long been the rule. In the third century, after the emperor Caracalla granted Roman citizenship to all provincials, new citizens might well be confused about what did and did not make their marriage legal. Several third-century rescripts to petitioners worried about the status of their marriage illustrate this confusion. Probus (reigned 276–82) told a man named Fortunatus that if it was common knowledge among his neighbors and others that he had "a wife at home for the sake of producing children" (*liberorum procreandorum causa*), and if indeed he and his wife had a child, the lack of both *nuptiales tabulae* and documentation of his daughter's birth did not diminish the marriage's validity

---

[182] Apparently the dative *caus[a]e* is used rather than the ablative *causa*. See Courtois et al., *Tablettes*, 80.

[183] Ibid., 207.

86 Judith Evans-Grubbs

or the girl's legitimacy.[184] The expression "for the sake of producing children" is found also in Latin marriage documents and may have been used in the Augustan marriage law to describe the purpose of *iustum matrimonium*. Fortunatus and his wife obviously have demonstrated *affectio maritalis* by their raising of children, and that fact, combined with the "knowledge of neighbors," is evidence enough that their union is marriage. Similarly, Septimius Severus and Caracalla reassured a woman named Trophima, "If your father consented to the marriage, the fact that he did not sign an instrument pertaining to the marriage will not make a difference."[185] Indeed, as a rescript from Diocletian and Maximian put it, just as the absence of written documentation did not invalidate an otherwise legitimate marriage, so also the fact that there *were* documents did not prove that marriage existed "if the truth of the matter is otherwise."[186]

Whereas classical law did not privilege documents over the oral testimony of reliable witnesses, later legal sources increasingly refer to the use of *instrumenta* as an alternative or supplement to witnesses.[187] Late Roman laws frequently refer to *acta publica*, that is, archives where documentation of property transfers could be checked in cases of dispute. As we have seen, Constantine required all gifts to be recorded in the *acta publica* in order to be valid, including prenuptial gifts (with an exception for underage women whose husbands had neglected to register the gifts). The *acta* were repositories for other sorts of records as well, including declarations by widowed mothers that they would not remarry (a condition they had to meet if they wished to serve as their children's guardian) and the proceedings of trials and criminal investigations.[188] This emphasis on the use of public archives is part of a trend in late antiquity to give more authority to the written word, whether in laws posted in public places, or in holy Scripture, or in private transactions.[189]

There is no indication in fourth- or fifth-century laws that marriage documents (apart from prenuptial gifts) or dowry agreements had to be recorded in the *acta publica*. But in late antiquity, some emperors did question the classical legal position that consent and the presence of *affectio maritalis* were the only true constitutive elements of marriage, and in the fifth-century West, there were attempts to require some visible manifestation of intent to marry. As we have seen, the emperor Majorian demanded that the bride provide a dowry that was to be no smaller than

---

[184] CJ 5.4.9. Compare Quintilian, *Institutes* 5.11.32 (cited in Treggiari, *Roman Marriage*, 54).
[185] CJ 5.4.2, dated between 197 and 211.
[186] CJ 5.4.13, dated between 292 and 305.
[187] Jane F. Gardner, *Being a Roman Citizen* (London, 1993), 182–83.
[188] On *acta publica*, see Harries, *Law and Empire* (n. 9 above), 70–76. On increased use of written documents in court, including (but not only) *tabulae*, see Meyer, *Legitimacy and Law* (n. 103 earlier), 241–49, who notes that in late antiquity other kinds of written documents (*instrumenta* in general) came to receive the same authority as *tabulae* had had earlier.
[189] Harries, *Law and Empire*, 57; Matthews, *Laying Down the Law* (n. 9 earlier), 190–91. This heightened regard for the written word appears at a time when general literacy was in decline: see William V. Harris, *Ancient Literacy* (Cambridge, Mass., 1989), 285–322.

the prenuptial gift she required from the groom. He was not the first western emperor to look for external evidence of marital intent. About thirty years earlier (ca. 426), a law of Valentinian III decreed that "those [children] who were brought forth into the light by a legitimate joining without honorable celebration of matrimony [*quos sine honesta celebratione matrimonii procreatos legitima coniunctio fuderit in lucem*]" be classified as *naturales* (i.e., illegitimate).[190] But the law made an exception for soldiers, who were permitted "the free capacity of contracting marriage with freeborn women without any solemnities of marriage."[191]

The paradoxical wording of Valentinian's law betrays its novelty in Roman legal thought: how could children of a "legitimate joining" not be legitimate themselves? The emperor was aware that he was stretching the term *naturales* beyond its customary meaning, for he goes on to say, "It is obvious by law itself, moreover, that slaves are born from the womb of a slavewoman, although by force of nature the name of *naturales* cannot be taken away even from them. . . ." Classical law used the term *naturalis* to describe a man's biological child, whether or not conceived in legal marriage. This category included (but was not confined to) the child of a free man by a slave woman, either his own slave or someone else's. (The child of a slave mother was born a slave, regardless of the father's status.)[192] Valentinian III wanted to use the term *naturalis* to describe any child born to any relationship not clearly shown to be marriage by external criteria. His law does not explicitly require *tabulae* or other documents, but only some visible manifestation of intent to marry. Nevertheless, the drawing up of such documents would surely have served as an act of *honesta celebratio*. In this respect, Valentinian III's law can be seen as consistent with a general trend toward favoring *instrumenta* to "prove" what previously had been ratified by verbal contracts.

Yet, in the eastern Empire, this attempt to require proof of marriage did not sit well with the more classicizing legal attitude of the administration of Valentinian's uncle in Constantinople, Theodosius II, who rejected the western policy a year or so later:[193]

---

[190] CTh 4.6.7 (not in CJ). The date has not been preserved, but Valentinian III did not take the throne until 425, and the addressee (the praetorian prefect Bassus) held office in 426/27. Although in the names of both reigning emperors, it is a law of Valentinian alone, but because he was then only about seven years old, he was presumably not responsible for its contents. (The eastern emperor, Arcadius's son Theodosius II, was likewise still a child.)

[191] CJ 5.4.21, undated. Like CTh 4.6.7, this is addressed to the western praetorian prefect Bassus, and it is reasonable to conclude that they were part of the same law.

[192] On use of the term *naturalis* to describe slave-born children of a free man, cf. *Dig.* 36.1.80.2 (Scaevola), *Dig.* 42.8.17.1 (Julian); *Dig.* 19.5.5 pr (Paulus). See Marian Niziolek, "Meaning of the phrase *liberi naturales* in Roman law sources up to Constantine's reign," *Revue internationale des droits de l'antiquité* 22 (1975): 317–44, modifying H. J. Wolff, "The background of the post-classical legislation on illegitimacy," *Seminar* 3 (1945): 21–45.

[193] On the classicism of fifth-century eastern law in contrast with western law, see Honoré, *Law in Crisis* (n. 10 earlier).

If documents [*instrumenta*] of prenuptial gifts or dowry have been lacking, and even the procession or other celebration of marriage is omitted, let no one think that on account of this, stability is lacking to a marriage that has been entered into correctly in other respects. Nor should anyone think that the rights of legitimate [children] can be taken away from children born of this [marriage], since between persons equal in honor no law impedes a union, which is confirmed by the consent of [the partners] themselves and the good faith of their friends."[194]

Theodosius II upheld the classical doctrine that consent makes a marriage, not *instrumenta* or ceremonies. But while denying the necessity of such external evidence, the eastern law does include an important proviso: the couple should be "equal in honor" (*pares honestate*), that is, of equal status. And, in fact, that is what the western law of Valentinian III was also seeking. For although Valentinian's law was influenced by the general trend toward favoring written documents over oral agreements, its real purpose was to prevent the children of unions of high-ranking men with low-born women from being considered legitimate heirs.

   Valentinian's law was part of a much larger body of legislation, going back to Constantine, which forbids and penalizes such marriages, and restricts the inheritance rights of children born from them. Although Constantine had abrogated the part of Augustus's marriage law (the *lex Julia de maritandis ordinibus*) that mandated marriage and child bearing, he had actually expanded those provisions of the same law that banned marriage between members of the senatorial class and former slaves.[195] Furthermore, he had forbidden any attempt by men of rank to give gifts or legacies to such women or any children they had by them, whereas in earlier law, men had been able to leave legacies to their concubines and illegitimate children (though such children could not inherit upon intestacy), and had even been able to give gifts to a concubine. Later emperors, probably prompted by complaints from men who wanted to leave property to their children by concubines, modified Constantine's policy so that illegitimate children could inherit some of their father's estate, particularly when there was no heir by a legal marriage.

   The laws of Valentinian III and Theodosius II discussed previously are two of many laws "on natural children and their mothers," which are mainly concerned with the right of illegitimate children to inherit from their fathers.[196] Late Roman emperors, especially in the West, were anxious to distinguish legitimate marriage, which resulted in children who were their parents' heirs, from concubinage, which

---

[194] CTh 3.7.3 = CJ 5.4.22 (to the eastern praetorian prefect Hierius and given at Constantinople, February 21, 428), to be joined with CTh 4.6.8, CTh 3.5.13 (on which see nn. 104 and 106 earlier), and CTh 3.13.4 (= CJ 5.11.6), which says no formal stipulation is necessary for validity of a dowry, and several other extracts from the Codes.

[195] CTh 4.6.3 = CJ 5.27.1 (336). Other laws of Constantine punished unions between free and slave (especially free women and slave men); see Evans-Grubbs, "Marriage more shameful than adultery" (n. 26 earlier); eadem, *Law and Family*, 261–316.

[196] Evans-Grubbs, *Law and Family*, 300–04; Arjava, *Women and Law*, 213–17. The amount *naturales* could receive and under what circumstances fluctuated over 200 years.

resulted in illegitimate children, and therefore they tried to discourage unequal unions. Requiring dowry or prenuptial gifts or a document that recorded such exchanges was one way to ensure that both partners had roughly equal economic and social standing, and that the union was intended to be a permanent *matrimonium* and not a temporary *concubinatus*, which one partner could later abandon in order to make a "real" marriage. Thus Theodosius II's law, while stating that a marriage "between equals" did not need *instrumenta* attesting dowry or prenuptial gift, nor any ceremony, implied that any union between those who were *not* socially equal *did* require such external proof of intent.

Emperors devised another way to encourage marriage between social equals and discourage concubinage: by allowing retroactive legitimation of wives and children in relationships that should have been marriage, not concubinage, in the first place. In the fourth century, Constantine had encouraged men to marry their *freeborn* concubines, and allowed them to legitimate children previously born from such women. His policy was revived more than a century later by the eastern emperor Zeno.[197] Zeno's law (presumably following Constantine's, which is no longer extant), says that "as soon as marriage has been celebrated with their mothers," illegitimate children become legitimated and come under their father's *potestas*. The law does not specify what such "celebration" would entail; a modern scholar assumed it was referring to the drawing up of *tabulae nuptiales*.[198]

When Theodosius II published his *Code* in 438, his law was the last entry under the title "On natural children and their mothers" and therefore superseded Valentinian III's law in the West as well as the East. Thus, as with Majorian's law, Valentinian's requirement of external evidence for marriage was short-lived. But Alaric retained Theodosius's law in his *Breviarium*, and the same law seems to have influenced a decision of Pope Leo that made its way into medieval canon law collections and Gratian's *Decretum*.[199]

Leo's decision is found in a letter to Bishop Rusticus of Narbonne, who had asked the bishop of Rome for his opinion on several different ecclesiastical issues that were creating controversy in the church at Narbonne. Among Rusticus's concerns was whether a cleric could give his daughter in marriage to a man who had already been in a sexual relationship with another woman, by whom he had even had children. Leo's response makes it clear that the other woman was something less than a legally married wife:

Not every woman joined to a man is the man's wife, since not every child is his father's heir. Moreover, the marriage pacts [*foedera*] between freeborn persons are legitimate and between equals; the Lord decided this very thing long before the beginning of

---

[197] Zeno's law is CJ 5.27.5, dated 477. Constantine's original law may have been CTh 4.6.1 (which is missing). See Evans-Grubbs, *Law and Family*, 296–98.

[198] Wolff, "Background" (n. 192 earlier), 39.

[199] See Lemaire, "Origine de la règle" (n. 122 earlier).

Roman law existed. Therefore a wife is one thing, a concubine another; just as a slave-woman is one thing, a free woman another.... [Leo then cites the Old Testament precedent of Abraham and his bastard son by his slavewoman Hagar, who was not his father's heir, and invokes the apostle Paul to the effect that marriage was more than a union of the sexes, it was also a "sacrament of Christ and the Church."] Therefore it must be accepted that a cleric of whatever place, if he has given his daughter in marriage to a man who has a concubine, has not given her as to a married man – unless by chance that woman, having both been made freeborn and legitimately endowed, seems to have been made honorable by means of public nuptials."[200]

The concubine in question is either a slave or slaveborn; in any case, certainly not the social equal of her cleric partner. The fact that there are children of the union is irrelevant, as they are not their father's heirs. Leo's next two responses, on the same issue, state that a daughter so married by "paternal will" is blameless, and that the man who has "ejected his slavewoman from his bed and received a wife of certain free birth" is not to be considered twice-married, but rather as having now embarked on the honorable course of marriage. The concubine's slave birth evidently precludes her eligibility as a cleric's wife, but in certain cases, the concubine could gain the legitimacy that would enable her to be a wife, if she was "made freeborn" by the legal process known as *restitutio natalibus* (restoration to free birth) and then given a dowry and married in a publicly witnessed ceremony.[201] Leo's criteria for legal marriage are thus the same as Valentinian III's, except that he also imbues the legal union with a spiritual meaning that concubinage does not have. Leo does not say that dowry and ceremony are necessary for all marriages, but he believes the presence of these elements clearly signifies that a relationship between a man and his social inferior is intended as marriage, and that they are therefore necessary in cases where the relationship would more naturally be construed as concubinage. In that respect, his ruling echoes the law of Theodosius II, which implied that when a union was not "between equals," some sort of visible manifestation of marital intent was needed.

Pope Leo believed that there was an intrinsic difference between the relationship of a man with a lowborn woman, even one that was monogamous and had produced children, and true marriage with a social equal. There is nothing intrinsically Christian about this distinction (despite Leo's use of Pauline citations to support it); rather, it reflects ancient Roman ideas about status and social honor. Christian leaders concurred with imperial attempts to distinguish marriage from concubinage, in part for moral reasons, but in part because they shared the emperors'

[200] Leo, *Epistle* 167 (written 458 or 459), resp. 4, PL 54:1204–1205. See also resp. 5–6 on the same topic.
[201] Only the emperor could effect such restoration. By the third century, even those obviously of slave birth could receive *restitutio*: see *Dig.* 40.11.2 (Marcian); Fergus Millar, *The Emperor in the Roman World* (Ithaca, 1977), 488–90. Jerome, *Epist.* 69, 5 (CSEL 54) refers to this procedure in the case of men who receive an imperial rescript enabling them to give their slave concubine a *stola* (the garment of married women), unlike poor men, who cannot.

assumptions about class and status. Ambrose, who had served as governor of Aemilia and Liguria before his ordination as bishop of Milan and whose father had been one of the highest ranking officials in the Empire, warned catechumens preparing for baptism that although the patriarch Abraham was to be imitated in other respects, they should not follow his marital arrangements or "join to themselves those who are not their equals" because the children of such unions could not be heirs.[202]

Other fourth- and fifth-century Christian writers indicate that it was not unusual, especially among the elite or would-be elite, for young men not yet ready for marriage to sow their wild oats in sexual relationships with lowborn women. Paulinus of Pella, before being married off by the age of twenty by his anxious parents, had frequented the slave quarters and fathered at least one illegitimate child (though he was glad to say that he had never actually seen any of his bastards). Sidonius Apollinaris, a contemporary of Leo and Paulinus, told a correspondent (a bishop) of a young man who, after living in *contubernium* with a slave girl, had finally considered his reputation and his responsibility to pass on his name and property and married a wealthy girl of good birth.[203] There were dissident voices: Jerome objected to the fact that a widower who remarried after baptism could not become a bishop, unlike a man whose concubine had died before he was baptized and who then took a wife after baptism. To distinguish in such a way between wife and concubine, said Jerome, was to interpret the apostle (Paul) as saying that it was *coniugales tabulae* and dotal rights, not *coitus*, that stood in the way of ordination to the episcopacy.[204]

The most famous example of such premarital cohabitation is the young Augustine, who lived for about fifteen years with a woman whose status and background apparently made her legally or socially ineligible to be a wife to a man of curial (municipal elite) status, even rearing the child whom he had by her. When the upwardly mobile Augustine did decide to marry, at around the age of thirty, he dismissed his concubine well before the projected marriage. (The girl was still only ten years old and could not marry for two years.) Such behavior, which readers today consider cavalier and which Augustine himself was to condemn in later years, was quite typical and unexceptional by traditional Roman standards. No doubt Ambrose understood.[205]

---

[202] *De Abraham* 1.3.19 (in CSEL 32/1). For the attitude of Callistus (Bishop of Rome, early third century), see Evans-Grubbs, *Law and Family*, 309–16; and Reynolds, *Marriage*, 159–62.

[203] Paulinus, *Eucharisticus*, lines 159–72; Sidonius, *Epistle* 9, 6 (to Bishop Ambrosius).

[204] *Epistle* 69, 5. Jerome also claims that "we see many men decline the burden of wives because of excessive poverty and have their own slavegirls in place of wives, and bring up the children conceived from them as their own." Compare Council of Toledo, canon 17 (ca. 400): a man can have "either wife or concubine" as long as he has only one woman.

[205] See Augustine, *Confessions* IV.2 and VI.15 on his concubine; and cf. *De bono coniugali* 5 (CSEL 41) for his later view. On Augustine's background, see Brent Shaw, "The family in late antiquity: The experience of Augustine," *Past and Present* 115 (1987): 3–51, at 8–10. On his relationship, see Danuta

Sixth-century legislation in the East continued to wrestle with the distinction between marriage and concubinage. In 517, the emperor Anastasius allowed men who had no legitimate children and had children by a woman "in the place of a wife" (*uxoris loco*) to consider them *legitimi* and give or bequeath whatever they liked to the children without fear of his relatives objecting "under the cunning and subtle pretext of laws and imperial constitutions." But there was an important proviso to Anastasius's decree: in the future, those who wished to have such a woman "in place of a wife" had to draw up "dotal instruments."[206] Anastasius's successor Justin condemned the law, which he saw as condoning unions originally made from lustful motives: "But in future all should know that legitimate progeny are to be sought from legitimate marriage, as if the aforementioned law had not been issued. For no pardon in the future shall defend lustful desires. . . . "[207] Nevertheless, not long afterward, Justin himself, clearly prompted by his nephew and effective co-ruler, Justinian, abrogated the ancient law of Augustus that had prohibited marriage between senators and showgirls (generally considered to be no better than prostitutes). As long as there were dotal instruments, the participants in such a marriage had no reason to fear its validity. Yet in other cases of marriage between those of different social rank, *dotalia instrumenta* were no longer necessary, "as long as the women are free or freeborn, and there has been no suspicion of wicked (i.e., adulterous) or incestuous unions."[208] The main beneficiary of the new law was Justinian himself, now able to marry the ex-showgirl Theodora.[209]

Justinian's own legislation after his accession in 527 further blurred the distinction between *iustum matrimonium* and *concubinatus*, by extending to *naturales liberi* policies that had previously applied only to legitimate children. If a man lived happily with a free woman in a union without *dotalia instrumenta* and then, with the same *affectio*, turned the relationship into marriage by drawing up *nuptialia instrumenta*, children born after this point should not have any more inheritance rights than those born before.[210] But some interpreted Justinian's law with "an empty subtlety" by claiming that it applied *only* if there were also children born

Shanzer, "*Avulsa a latere meo:* Augustine's spare rib – *Confessions* 6.15.25," *Journal of Roman Studies* 92 (2002): 157–76.

[206] CJ 5.27.6 (517). For this interpretation of the problematic text (which changes the punctuation found in Krueger's edition), see C. van de Wiel, "La légitimation par mariage subséquent, de Constantin à Justinien: Sa réception sporadique dans le droit byzantin," *Revue internationale de droits de l'antiquité* 25 (1978): 307–50, at 324–29. For the idea of a concubine as a woman who took the place of a wife (*uxoris loco*), cf. *Dig.* 50.16.144 (Paulus).

[207] CJ 5.27.7 (519); quotation is from paragraph 3.

[208] CJ 5.4.23 (520–23); quotation is from paragraph 7. Justinian reiterated this ruling in Greek in CJ 1.4.33.2 (534).

[209] See David Daube, "The Marriage of Justinian and Theodora: Legal and theological considerations," *Catholic University Law Review* 16 (1967): 380–99.

[210] CJ 5.27.10, dated 529. This policy did not extend to the illegitimate (*spurii*) children of freeborn women of high rank, "for whom the observation of chastity is especially required": see CJ 6.57.5 (originally part of the same law as CJ 5.27.10).

after the conversion to marriage. As Justinian remarked when he eliminated the loophole, this was an absurd legal quibble, but it reveals that not everyone agreed that children born before documentation of a marriage were to be treated in exactly the same way as their postmarital siblings.[211] Another law made inroads into the Augustan prohibition on marriage between a senator and a freedwoman by refusing to annul such a marriage if it had begun before the man attained senatorial status: "For it is better to repress the severity of the Papian law . . . rather than in following it to destroy men's marriages not because of the sin of a woman and her husband, but because of the good fortune of one party."[212] If a man did not have a legal wife but kept his slavegirl (*ancilla*) "under the name of concubine" until his death, she and her children by him did not become the property of his heirs, but became free upon his death.[213] Moreover, a man could declare in the *acta* that a slave was his son (presumably by such a slave concubine), and this would be taken as a tacit manumission of the son, though not as actual adoption.[214] (The unions of free women with slaves were not granted the same status.)[215] Another law of 533 made it clear that if a man received a woman "with marital affection" (*maritali affectu*) with her parents' consent or her own (if they were dead), even if there was no dowry or *dotalia instrumenta*, the marriage was just as valid as if there had been dotal documents, "for marriages are contracted not by dowries, but by affection."[216]

Justinian's laws enacted after the publication of the Code in 534 continued to repeal earlier prohibitions on marriage between high-ranking men and low-born women and at the same time set forth the circumstances in which documents and dowry were necessary for a marriage to be legitimate. In 538, while admitting that ancient law had accepted as valid those marriages formed on the basis of *affectus* alone, he decided that from now on everyone except those of "abject life" had to have a document attesting their marriage registered with church authorities.[217] A year later, he ruled that if a man of any rank wanted to make his slavewoman a legal wife, he had only to manumit her and draw up "nuptial documents." Marriage between a man and his former slave had always been possible (except when the man was of senatorial status), but Justinian innovated in declaring that as soon

---

[211] CJ 5.27.11, dated 530; to be joined with CJ 5.29.4 (allowing fathers to appoint in their will guardians for illegitimate as well as legitimate children) and CJ 5.35.3 (allowing mothers to serve as guardians to their *naturales liberi* as well as their legitimate ones).

[212] CJ 5.4.28 (531 or 532).

[213] CJ 7.15.3 (531). This did not apply to men who had wives *and* concubines.

[214] CJ 7.6.1.10, from the same law as 7.15.3. Compare *Institutes* 3.11.12, citing an alleged precedent in early Roman law mentioned by the elder Cato.

[215] Although Justinian abolished the decree of the Senate under Claudius (see n. 26 earlier), he wanted masters to break up unions of their slaves with free women and to punish the slaves: CJ 7.24.1 (cf. *Institutes* 3.12.1).

[216] CJ 5.17.11 pr, dated 533.

[217] *Novel* 74.4. Noonan, "Marital affection," 482–83 (n. 34 earlier); Arjava, *Women and Law*, 206.

as such "dotal documents" had been written, children born while their mother was still a slave (who were therefore slaves themselves) automatically became free and were to enjoy exactly the same inheritance rights as their siblings born after the marriage.[218] The reference to "dotal documents" indicates that dowry was as necessary a component of such a marriage as documentation; indeed, the two went together. And given that it was unlikely that a former slave or woman of low degree could provide her own dowry, the man himself would do it. This is the situation that Pope Leo had described almost a century earlier, in which a former slave was "made freeborn" and endowed by her husband.

Finally, a law of 542 abolished the need for documentation of marriage except in the case of men of the highest rank (*illustres*); others, including those who held lesser honors, could marry with dotal instruments if they desired, but they did not have to do so. (An exception was made for high-ranking barbarians as well, who could marry *nudo affectu*.) Moreover, a man had only to write in a document (witnessed and signed by three men of good faith) that a child born to him by a free woman was his, and *not* add that the child was *naturalis* (Greek *physikos*), and no other proof was required that the child was legitimate and could inherit. A woman who had lived with a man without documents but with marital *affectus* had rights to his property even if he dissolved the marriage and married another woman *with* dotal instruments. And finally, Justinian abolished the law of Constantine that had forbidden marriage between men of rank and women of "lowly" birth or occupation; several years earlier he had remarked that parts of the Constantinian law were obsolete anyway.[219]

Justinian did away with all the earlier rules that had prohibited men from having *iustum matrimonium* with women of lower status. Now a man had no excuse for taking a woman as a concubine rather than a wife; to do so could only be immoral. But the age-old problem of how to tell whether a woman whose status was significantly lower than her man's was a wife or a concubine remained. Therefore, in cases in which a man was of high status (and would, under earlier law, have been prevented from marrying a lowborn woman at all), he had to produce written evidence that marriage was his intention.[220] Matrimonial documents now were more than records of financial transactions: they had become indicators of morality.

---

[218] *Novel* 78.3–4 (539).

[219] *Novel* 117.2–6. For the earlier law, see *Novel* 89.15, dated 539.

[220] On this development, see Wolff, *Written and Unwritten Marriages* (n. 151 earlier) 92–103; van de Wiel, "La légitimation par mariage subséquent" (n. 206 above), 341–43.

CHAPTER THREE

MARRYING AND THE *TABULAE NUPTIALES* IN ROMAN NORTH AFRICA FROM TERTULLIAN TO AUGUSTINE

David G. Hunter

In his *Life of St. Augustine*, Possidius, Bishop of Calama, observed that Augustine as bishop was reluctant to involve himself in certain worldly activities, such as arranging marriages, writing letters of recommendation for men entering military careers, and accepting dinner invitations. The reasons for this reticence, which Possidius attributed to the influence of Bishop Ambrose, were as follows: "lest spouses quarrel and curse the one who had brought them together ... lest the man recommended for the military turn out badly and blame his backer; and lest the habit of temperance be lost through frequent attendance at banquets with fellow townsmen." In the case of episcopal involvement in marriages, Possidius records one important qualification: "but he also said that when spouses were in agreement, the bishop should, if asked, be present so that their compacts or agreements might be ratified or blessed."[1]

Possidius's description of Augustine's (somewhat qualified) interest in Christian weddings provides a helpful entry into the topic of this essay. What precisely do we know about the ceremony of marriage among Christians in North Africa in the time of Augustine? The question is important not only for the history of liturgy but also for an understanding of Augustine. No Christian writer has exerted greater influence on the development of the Western theology of marriage than Augustine. Whereas much scholarly discussion has been devoted to Augustine's theological understanding of the "sacramentality" of marriage and, more recently, to his views of sexuality and sin, comparatively little attention has been paid to the specific ritual or liturgical practices that may have accompanied the formation of a Christian

---

[1] *Vita Augustini* 27.4–5. Text in *Vita di Cipriano, Vita di Ambrogio, Vita de Agostino*, edited by A.A.R. Bastiaensen (Milan, 1975), 199–201. Translation (but significantly altered) is by Matthew O'Connell, in John E. Rotelle (ed.), *The Life of Saint Augustine* (Villanova, 1988), 105.

This chapter is a revised version of the following: Hunter, David G. "Augustine and the making of marriage in Roman North Africa," *Journal of Early Christian Studies* 11:1 (2003), 63–85. © The Johns Hopkins University Press. Reprinted with permission of The Johns Hopkins University Press.

marriage as Augustine knew it. If the principle of *lex orandi, lex credendi* holds, attention to Augustine's practice may shed light on his theology of marriage as well.[2]

Yet investigation of this question founders on one significant fact: Augustine says virtually nothing about a Christian marriage liturgy. This silence is especially puzzling because it contrasts with the extensive evidence from late–fourth-century Italy, especially Rome, which indicates that Christians regularly celebrated rituals in which the bishop placed a veil over the head of the bride and offered a nuptial blessing. Augustine's contemporaries, Ambrose of Milan and Pope Siricius, both referred explicitly to these practices, as did Ambrosiaster.[3] Paulinus of Nola even mentioned that Christian weddings sometimes took place within a church building.[4] Nothing comparable can be found in Augustine's writings. Not once in his many extensive discussions of marriage did Augustine speak explicitly of the practices of veiling or blessing by a bishop.[5]

How should we interpret this silence? Should we assume that Augustine and the North African church followed procedures that were similar to those used in fourth-century Rome and Italy, despite the lack of evidence? Such an assumption seems unwarranted, in view of the possibility of regional variation in liturgical practice, especially in an area as vaguely defined as marriage. I shall argue that even by Augustine's day, there is still little evidence of any specifically Christian rituals of marriage in North Africa. But this inquiry will highlight incidentally the significance of dotal instruments (*tabulae matrimoniales* or *tabulae nuptiales*) in marriage as Augustine understood it, a topic that is germane to one of the principal themes of this volume: the documentation of marital contracts.

Much depends on how one interprets the evidence from the earlier North African tradition. On the one hand, if it can be demonstrated that Christians in North Africa

---

[2] Good introductions to Augustine's theology of marriage can be found in Philip L. Reynolds, *Marriage in the Western Church: The Christianization of Marriage during the Patristic and Early Medieval Periods* (Leiden, 1994), 241–311; Émile Schmitt, *Le mariage chrétien dans l'oeuvre de saint Augustin: Une théologie baptismale de la vie conjugale* (Paris, 1983); and Theodore Mackin, *The Marital Sacrament* (New York, 1989), 196–231.

[3] Ambrose, *Epist.* 62.7 (CSEL 82/2:124): "Nam cum ipsum coniugium velamine sacerdotali et benedictione sanctificari oporteat, quomodo potest coniugium dici, ubi non est fidei concordia?" See also Siricius, *Epist.* 1.4.5 (PL 13:1136–37), who speaks of both the "conjugal veil" and the blessing "which the priest bestows on the woman who is to be married." Further references to the practices of a nuptial blessing and nuptial veiling can be found in Siricius, *Epist.* 1.9.13 (PL 13:1142) and *Epist.* 7.3 (PL 13:1171). The nuptial blessing is also mentioned a number of times by Ambrosiaster, who restricts it to first marriages: *In epist. ad Cor. primam* 7:40 and 11:3 (CSEL 81/2:90 and 120); *In epist. ad Timotheum primam* 3:12 and 5:3 (CSEL 81/3:268 and 278); and *Quaestiones veteris et novi testamenti* 127.3 (CSEL 50:400). For a discussion of these passages, see Korbinian Ritzer, *Le mariage dans les Églises chrétiennes du Ier au XIe siècle* (Paris, 1970), 222–37; and Mackin, *Marital Sacrament*, 153–56.

[4] Paulinus of Nola, *Carmen* 25 (CSEL 30:238–45), esp. verse 201, which speaks of the service taking place "before the altar" (*ante altaria*). See the discussion in H. Crouzel, "Liturgie du mariage chrétien au Ve siècle selon l'Epithalame de saint Paulin de Nole," in *Mens concordet voci* (Paris, 1983), 619–26. See Ritzer, *Le mariage*, 224: "D'après cette description, c'est à l'église qu'a lieu la cérémonie."

[5] As we shall see, there is one ambiguous passage that may contain a reference to a marriage blessing by a bishop: see at n. 40, which follows.

had begun to adopt Christianized marriage rituals prior to the fourth century, it will be reasonable to assume that Augustine continued to follow these customs, despite his silence. On the other hand, if no evidence of such practices exists, then it is more likely that Augustine's silence indicates the continued lack of such practices. Therefore, before proceeding to my discussion of Augustine, it is necessary to examine the evidence for Christian marriage practices prior to the late fourth century.

NORTH AFRICAN MARRIAGE PRACTICE PRIOR TO AUGUSTINE

Prior to Tertullian, there are only vague and scattered allusions to marriage practice anywhere in early Christian literature. The most explicit statement regarding church regulation of marriage was the following advice given to Bishop Polycarp of Smyrna by Ignatius of Antioch (ca. 107): "It is right for men and women who marry to be united with the consent of the bishop, that the marriage be according to the Lord and not according to lust."[6] But Ignatius says nothing about a Christian ritual of marriage; he only insists that marriages be contracted with the permission or approval of the bishop. Needless to say, second-century Christians showed considerable concern for the moral dimensions of married life. For example, the question of remarriage after the death of a spouse and the possibility of penance after adultery occupied a number of authors such as Hermas and Athenagoras.[7] But before Tertullian there are no unambiguous references to Christian marriage procedures or rituals.[8] Even an author such as Clement of Alexandria, who devoted considerable attention to the question of Christian conduct in marriage, says nothing about any specifically Christian marriage rituals.[9]

The earliest relevant sources, then, are the writings of Tertullian. There are a number of places in his works where Tertullian seems to refer to Christian rituals of marriage. In two passages, Tertullian indicated that Christian marriages might have required some sort of public permission or affirmation from the clergy or the wider Christian community. In his treatise *De monogamia*, written at some time after 213, when he was fully under the influence of the "New Prophecy," Tertullian

---

[6] Ignatius, *Polyc.* 5.5.2, translated by Kirsopp Lake, *The Apostolic Fathers*, Loeb Classical Library (Cambridge, Mass., 1912), 1:273.

[7] Hermas, *Mand.* 4.29–32; Athenagoras, *Leg.* 33.

[8] I can find no support for Kenneth Stevenson's assertion that "Athenagoras knows of a definite procedure regarding marriage, and that he is referring to a recognized form, involving some sort of liturgy." See his *Nuptial Blessing: A Study of Christian Marriage Rites* (New York, 1983), 14. Athenagoras simply states that "according to the laws that we have laid down," Christians marry only for procreation.

[9] Clement, *Paed.* 3.63.1, refers to a presbyter laying hands on the head of a woman, but this is not necessarily a reference to a nuptial blessing, *contra* Stevenson, *Nuptial Blessing*, 15. For a discussion of the passage, see J. P. Broudéhoux, *Mariage et famille chez Clément d'Alexandrie* (Paris, 1970), 95–96, who correctly observes, "on ne peut s'autoriser pour affirmer l'existence de pareille cérémonie du seul passage où Clément parle d'une imposition des mains faite par le presbytre sur la tête de la femme: les circonstances de cette bénédiction ne sont précisées d'aucune manière" (96).

addressed the following words to Catholic critics of his view that second marriages
were forbidden to Christians:

So, then, you propose to *marry in the Lord*, as the law and the Apostle require –
supposing that you bother about this at all. But how will you dare request the kind of
marriage which is not permitted to the ministers from whom you ask it, the bishop
who is a monogamist, the presbyters and deacons who are bound by the same solemn
obligation, the widows whose way of life you repudiate in your own person? Our
adversaries, it is plain, will give husbands and wives in marriage indiscriminately, as
they dole out pieces of bread, for thus they understand the text: *Give to everyone that
asketh of you.* They will join you together in a virgin church, the one spouse of the one
Christil.[10]

Here Tertullian appears to assume that it was common practice for Christians to
"request marriage" (*matrimonium postulans*) from an ecclesiastical official.

Similarly, in *De pudicitia*, also a work written during his Montanist period,
Tertullian noted that in order to avoid the suspicion of fornication, all Christians
should profess their marriages publicly "before the church" (*apud ecclesiam*):

And so, among us, secret marriages, also, that is to say, those which are not first contracted before the church, run the risk of being judged the next thing to adultery and
fornication. Nor may they, under the appearance of marriage, escape the charge of
crime when they have been contracted because of it.[11]

Both passages suggest that Christians at Carthage (both Catholics and Montanists)
may have sought some kind of ecclesiastical permission to marry. The passage from
De pudicitia may allude to a practice peculiar to Montanists, that is, some sort
of profession of marriage *apud ecclesiam*, since Tertullian speaks of what happens
"among us" (*penes nos*). The text of *De monogamia*, by contrast, refers to a Catholic
practice of "requesting" a marriage of the church.[12]

But what precisely was this practice? In *De monogamia* Tertullian said only that
a Christian might "request marriage" from a bishop, presbyter, deacon, or widow.

---

[10] Tertullian, *De monogamia* 11.1–2 (CCL 2:1244), translated (slightly altered) by William P. Le Saint,
Tertullian: Treatises on Marriage and Remarriage, Ancient Christian Writers 13 (New York, 1951), 93. I
have followed the dating of Tertullian's works given in René Braun, *Deus Christianorum: Recherches
sur le vocabulaire doctrinal de Tertullien* (Paris, 1962), 567–77.

[11] Tertullian, *De pudicitia* 4.4 (CCL 2:1287), translated by William P. Le Saint, *Tertullian: Treatises on
Penance*, Ancient Christian Writers 28 (New York, 1959), 62.

[12] Henri Crouzel, "Deux textes de Tertullien concernant la procédure et les rites du mariage chrétien,"
Bulletin de littérature ecclésiastique 74 (1973): 3–13. Crouzel's article was a response to Ritzer (*Le
mariage*, 85–90), who had argued that Tertullian was describing practices that were Montanist, but
not Catholic. It makes sense that Montanist Christians might have required a more public profession
of marriage, since they prohibited second marriages. Nevertheless, it is best not to draw too sharp a
distinction between "Montanists" and "Catholics" in this period. See David Rankin, *Tertullian and
the Church* (Cambridge, 1995), 31–32, who observes that expressions such as *penes nos* may signify
nothing more than a distinct Montanist group within the broader Christian community at Carthage,
rather than a formal rupture or schism.

The addition of the last group, widows, is intriguing. Tertullian seems to have introduced widows only to reinforce his polemic against second marriages. That is why he listed the various groups to whom second marriages were forbidden: the higher ranks of the clergy (bishop, presbyter, and deacon) and, by definition, the widows. Tertullian's primary aim in *De monogamia* was to stress a moral or ascetical point, not to describe a ritual. The most that can reasonably be said is that couples intending to marry would seek some sort of permission (probably from the bishop) and that this may have involved a public announcement to the community. The latter is what Tertullian would have meant by *apud ecclesiam professae*. If my reading of these texts is correct, then Christians in Tertullian's North Africa had not moved very far beyond Ignatius of Antioch's prescription that Christians should marry only with the permission of the bishop. Seeking permission to marry and a public announcement of intent to marry do not necessarily imply a specifically Christian liturgy of marriage.[13]

This brings us to another highly controversial passage, *Ad uxorem* 2.8. In this early work, written ca. 204, before he had been thoroughly influenced by the New Prophecy, Tertullian addressed his wife, urging her to avoid a second marriage. Yet by Book 2 he had turned to the question of a (second) marriage with a non-Christian. In the context of warning about the dangers of a mixed marriage, Tertullian spoke in glowing and highly rhetorical terms about the beauties of a marriage between Christians:

How shall we ever be able adequately to describe the happiness of that marriage which the church arranges, the offering strengthens, upon which the blessing sets a seal, at which angels are present as witnesses, and to which the Father gives his consent? For not even on earth do children marry properly and legally without their fathers' permission.[14]

At first glance, it would appear that Tertullian might be referring to Christian rituals, such as a eucharistic "offering" (*oblatio*) at a wedding or the pronouncement of a liturgical "blessing" (*benedictio*), and, indeed, some scholars have interpreted his words in this way.[15]

Yet the situation is more complex. Part of the difficulty lies in the fact that Tertullian deliberately employed technical terms drawn from Roman marriage customs. For example, when he spoke of "that marriage which the church arranges" (*quod ecclesia conciliat*), Tertullian was referring to the role of the *conciliator* in arranging the match. Such a function, as Susan Treggiari has noted, particularly involved "the bringing about of an initial meeting, not only by family members

---

[13] This reading of Tertullian and the earlier writers is confirmed by Marcel Metzger, "Apports de l'histoire de la liturgie à la théologie du mariage," *Revue de droit canonique* 42 (1992): 215–36, at 218: "dans les écrits d'Ignace d'Antioche, de Tertullien ou de Clément d'Alexandrie, on ne trouve que de vagues allusions, qui intéressent plutôt le droit canonique que la liturgie."

[14] *Ad uxorem* 2.8.6 (CCL 1:393), translated (slightly altered) by Le Saint, *Treatises on Marriage and Remarriage*, 35.

[15] For example, Crouzel, "Deux textes de Tertullien," 3–13; Stevenson, *Nuptial Blessing*, 16–19.

such as a father or father-in-law, but by unrelated parties."[16] When he referred to that marriage which "the offering strengthens" (*confirmat oblatio*), Tertullian was probably drawing a parallel to the Roman practice of the bride and groom's offering a sacrifice or *confarreatio* on the morning of their wedding: "In a marriage by *confarreatio*, the offering was one of fruits and a wheaten loaf. At a later period, it was more usual to offer a bloody sacrifice."[17] And when Tertullian spoke of that marriage upon which "the blessing sets a seal" (*obsignat benedictio*), he may have been referring to a seal placed on the written marriage documents, the *tabulae nuptiales* that he mentioned elsewhere.[18]

It is clear that Tertullian wished to draw a parallel between aspects of traditional Roman marriage ceremonial and the practice of a Christian marriage, but a number of questions remain. Was he actually describing Christian ritual practices, such as a eucharistic offering (*oblatio*) on the day of a wedding between Christians? Was an official blessing (*benedictio*) pronounced on that occasion by a member of the clergy or merely by the father or male guardian? By speaking of an "offering," Tertullian could have meant simply the couple's shared liturgical life, rather than a specific eucharist for marriage. Similarly, the "blessing" may refer only to the generic blessing of marriage in Genesis, something to which Tertullian often alluded. Moreover, the term *benedictio* in Tertullian sometimes denoted the praise of God in a general sense, rather than a specific liturgical blessing. In this case, the words *obsignat benedictio* would refer to the Christian couple's common worship of God. In other words, Tertullian's use of the technical terminology could be simply metaphorical.[19]

Such use of metaphor would not be uncharacteristic of Tertullian. It was a common rhetorical pattern in Tertullian's thought to contrast pagans and Christians by re-describing the Christian in pagan terms. For example, in the famous passage from *De idololatria* Tertullian proclaimed, "there is no agreement between the divine and the human sacrament, between the standard of Christ and the standard of the devil, between the camp of light and the camp of darkness."[20] When we read such texts, we do not assume that Christians actually lived in their own military encampments, carried their own standards, or swore oaths in the manner of Roman legionaries. Similarly, we should not assume that the parallels Tertullian

---

[16] Susan Treggiari, *Roman Marriage: Iusti Coniuges from the Time of Cicero to the Time of Ulpian* (Oxford, 1991), 136–37; cf. Le Saint, *Treatises on Marriage*, 132, n. 143.

[17] Le Saint, *Treatises on Marriage*, 132, n. 144. See also Treggiari, *Roman Marriage*, 21–24.

[18] *Ad uxorem* 2.3.1 (CCL 1:387); *De virginibus velandis* 12.1 (CCL 2:1221). These dotal contracts were an important legal component of marriage and were often ratified or sealed at the wedding. Their sealing by the witnesses was normally a prominent feature of the marriage ceremony. For a more extensive discussion, see the chapter by Judith Evans-Grubbs in the present volume.

[19] For this interpretation, see Ritzer, *Le mariage*, 114–19, whom I have followed closely in this paragraph. A similar reading of the *Ad uxorem* passage can be found in Mackin, *The Marital Sacrament*, 126–29.

[20] *De idololatria* 19.2 (CCL 2:1120): "Non convenit sacramento divino et humano, signo Christi et signo diaboli, castris lucis et castris tenebrarum."

drew between Roman and Christian marriage practices should be taken literally. In *Ad uxorem* 2.8, Tertullian certainly wished to contrast a marriage between Christians with a marriage between a Christian and a pagan, but it is far from clear that he was describing a specifically Christian ritual of marriage.[21]

Another argument that can be adduced for this minimalist reading of Tertullian on the Christian marriage liturgy is the fact that he referred on several occasions to traditional Roman marriage ceremonies, that is, the rituals that would have been shared by pagan and Christian alike. In most instances, he plainly assumed that Christians usually took part in the common rituals. For example, in *De idolatria* 16, Tertullian argued that Christians were allowed to participate in traditional ceremonies of betrothal (*sponsalia*), nuptials (*nuptialia*), and name-giving (*nominalia*), because these ceremonies were not directly involved in idolatrous activity. In connection with the betrothal, he mentioned specifically the giving of a ring and observed: "God no more prohibits nuptials to be celebrated than names to be given."[22]

By contrast, in *De corona* Tertullian rejected the practice of placing crowns on the heads of the married couple because he believed the crown carried idolatrous connotations.[23] In several other places, he pointed out that it was common custom for women to take a veil upon their betrothal, and perhaps also to exchange a kiss with their intended bridegrooms.[24] Moreover, as mentioned earlier, Tertullian also occasionally referred to the *tabulae nuptiales*, that is, to the written marriage documents by which spouses formally ratified their marriages.[25] The sum of this evidence suggests that Christians in North Africa usually celebrated their betrothals and nuptials with the same rituals as did non-Christians; Tertullian plainly approved of such practices, as long as idolatrous activity was not directly involved. Here again, I would argue, we have further confirmation that specifically Christian rituals of marriage had not yet evolved in Roman North Africa by the time of Tertullian.

The remainder of the evidence from third-century North Africa drives us to a similar conclusion. Cyprian's collection of biblical *Testimonia ad Quirinum* contains two chapters on marital law, but no reference to marriage liturgy.[26] In *De habitu virginum* Cyprian urged Christian virgins not to attend wedding ceremonies

[21] It should also be noted that in *Ad uxorem* 2.8.6 (CCL 1:393), Tertullian refers to the presence of angels as witnesses to the Christian marriage (*angeli renuntiant*) and to the ratification of the marriage by the Father (*pater rato habet*). In these two instances, Tertullian cannot be referring literally to a marriage ceremony, *contra* Stevenson, *Nuptial Blessing*, 19.

[22] *De idolatria* 16.3 (CCL 2:1117).

[23] *De corona* 13.4 (CCL 2:1061): "Coronant et nuptiae sponsos. Et ideo non nubemus ethnicis, ne nos ad idololatrian usque deducant, a qua apud illos nuptiae incipiunt."

[24] *De virginibus velandis* 12.1 (CCL 2:1221); *De oratione* 22.4 (CCL 1:269–70). See Treggiari, *Roman Marriage*, 147–53, who questions whether Tertullian's statements represented common practice.

[25] See n. 18 earlier.

[26] *Testimonia ad Quirinum* 3.62 (CSEL 3/1:166–67); 3.90 (CSEL 3:175).

because of the frankly erotic banter that usually took place there. "What place is there at a wedding for one whose mind is not set on a wedding?" Cyprian argued.[27] There is no indication that Cyprian had in mind only pagan wedding ceremonies; his objections have entirely to do with moral dangers of such attendance to female virgins, not the religious danger of idolatry. On the contrary, the most reasonable assumption would appear to be that Cyprian was referring to the wedding ceremonies of Christians that differed in no way from the celebrations of their pagan counterparts. He discouraged virgins from attending, but assumed that other Christians would be present.[28]

As we move into the fourth century, the dearth of evidence for a Christian marriage ritual becomes ever more pronounced. In the North African conciliar literature from the fourth century there are only a few canons that refer to marriage, and not one of these alludes to a Christian marriage ceremony. For example, the Council of Carthage in 397 determined that "the children of bishops or of any other clerics should not be joined in marriage with pagans, heretics, or schismatics."[29] Other canons required that lectors, upon reaching puberty, should either marry or take vows of celibacy. But such legislation implies only that bishops tried to exercise some control over the marriages of their fellow clerics (and of their children). Nothing is said about a Christian wedding ceremony even for clerics.[30] In the entire corpus of canons from North Africa published in *Corpus Christianorum* by Munier, there is only one reference to a nuptial blessing by a bishop; but this is found in the *Statuta ecclesiae antiqua*, a collection that originated in fifth-century Gaul, not in North Africa.[31]

---

[27] *De habitu virginum* 18 (CSEL 3/1:200): "Quis illi in nuptiis locus est cui animus ad nuptias non est."

[28] My argument on the Cyprianic material follows the interpretation of Victor Saxer, *Vie liturgique et quotidienne à Carthage vers le milieu du IIIᵉ siècle: Le témoignage de saint Cyprien et de ses contemporains d'Afrique* (Rome, 1969), 325–26.

[29] Canon 12 (CCL 149:37). This prohibition is frequently repeated in the North African conciliar literature.

[30] Canon 2 of the Council of Hippo in 393 (CCL 149:20–21). See also canon 18 of the Council of Carthage in 397 (CCL 149:38). By contrast, in Italy at this time married clerics were required to have been married with a blessing bestowed by a bishop. See Siricius, *Epist.* 1.9.13 (PL 13:1142): "Qui accessu adolescentiae usque ad tricesimum aetatis annum, si probabiliter vixerit, una tantum, et ea, quam virginem communi per sacerdotem benedictione perceperit, uxore contentus, acolythus et subdiaconus esse debebit." None of the North African canons speaks of a nuptial blessing for clerics.

[31] Canon 13 in C. Munier (ed.), *Concilia Africae A. 345 – A. 525* (CCL 149:345): "Sponsus et sponsa cum benedicendi sunt a sacerdote, a parentibus suis vel a paranymphis offerantur, qui cum benedictionem acceperint, eadem nocte pro reverentia ipsius benedictionis in virginitate permaneant." As Munier has observed: "Sub inscriptione Concilii Carthaginensis quarti, ab episcopis quattuordecim, era 436 (=398), habiti, editores conciliorum . . . quoddam documentum adferunt, cuius originem gallicam, non autem africanam, fuisse nemo est qui dubitet" (CCL 149:342). Munier has attributed the canons of the so-called "Fourth Council of Carthage of 398," also known as the *Statuta ecclesiae antiqua*, to Gennadius of Marseilles, c.475. As Jane E. Merdinger has observed, no African council met in 398, on account of the revolt of Gildo. See her article, "Councils of North African Bishops," in Allan D. Fitzgerald (ed.), *Augustine through the Ages* (Grand Rapids, 1999), 249. I should like to acknowledge Professor Merdinger's assistance on this question.

I should add that this lack of evidence of Christianized marriage rituals from the North African church does not seem to reflect a general disinterest in liturgical ritual itself within North African Christianity. For example, from the later fourth century, we do have evidence of ecclesiastical rituals for the blessing and consecration of virgins in North Africa.[32] It is clear from several North African canons that this ritual included both a blessing and a veiling by the bishop, as it did elsewhere in the West. The rite of virginal consecration is a vivid example of the Christianization of the Roman marriage ceremony, though in the paradoxical form of a profession of celibacy and marriage to Christ. But there seems to have been no Christian equivalent for a regular human marriage in North Africa. Arguments from silence are always weak, but none of the available evidence suggests anything more than we saw in the writings of Tertullian, namely, that it was common practice for Christians to seek approval of their marriages from a bishop or presbyter. We do not yet find evidence of any distinctively Christian rituals of veiling, blessing, or other liturgical ceremony for Christian marriages in North Africa.

AUGUSTINE AND THE *TABULAE MATRIMONIALES*

This silence regarding any Christianized rituals of marriage persisted in the writings of Augustine. In one place, he mentioned the role of the "best man" (*paranymphus*), whom he described as an exceptionally close friend of the bridegroom (*amicus interior, conscius secreti cubicularis*).[33] For Augustine, the *paranymphus* was an apt image for John the Baptizer in his role as forerunner of Christ the Bridegroom. Elsewhere Augustine showed that he was aware of the following features of the traditional Roman wedding ceremony: the giving away of the bride by her father, the pronouncing of vows, the celebration of a wedding feast, the appraisal of the dowry, and the signing of marriage contracts.[34] But Augustine never referred explicitly to any of the Christian rituals of marriage that were becoming common elsewhere in the West at this time. That is, he mentioned neither the offering of a nuptial blessing by the bishop nor the imposition of a nuptial veil at the hands of the bishop, the practices that are explicitly discussed by Ambrose, Siricius, Ambrosiaster, and (at a slightly later date) Paulinus of Nola. Because of the absence of these practices from the prior North African tradition as well, it is best to conclude that they had not become established in the churches of North Africa before or during Augustine's lifetime.

---

[32] See, e.g., canon 3 of the Council of Carthage in 390 (CCL 149:13–14); canon 34 of the Council of Carthage in 397 (CCL 149:42).

[33] *Sermo* 293.7 (PL 38:1332). Augustine also referred to the *paranymphus* in *De civitate dei* 14.18 (CCL 48:441).

[34] *De genesi ad litteram* 11.41.57 (CSEL 28/1:376).

Yet the writings of Augustine do not leave us completely in the dark regarding Christian marriage practice. There is one aspect of Roman marriage ceremonial that Augustine mentioned with some regularity. I refer to the *tabulae matrimoniales*, which Augustine cited on more than a dozen occasions.[35] The frequency with which Augustine spoke of the *tabulae matrimoniales*, as well as the way in which they figure into his discussions of marriage, suggests that this was one feature of the wedding ceremony that had begun to be "Christianized" in some way. Certainly, this was the one part of the marriage ceremony that had made an impact on Augustine's perception of Christian marriage. Attention to Augustine's discussion of the *tabulae matrimoniales*, therefore, sheds light both on the making of marriage among North African Christians and on Augustine's understanding of Christian marriage.

The *tabulae matrimoniales* (also known as *tabulae nuptiales* or *tabulae dotales*) were written contracts that were an important (though not essential) legal component of Roman marriages. As Susan Treggiari has observed: "Obviously the contract was drawn up carefully in advance of the wedding. It contained a statement of the contents of the dowry and agreements about what would happen to the dowry at the end of the marriage."[36] Although the contract was primarily concerned with dotal and property arrangements, it also was a public declaration of the intent to marry. In one extant marriage contract, a fragmentary papyrus dating to ca. 100 CE, there are found the signatures and seals of seven witnesses. In addition to the intent to marry and the contents of the dowry, this document also stated the purpose of the marriage: "for the sake of producing children" (*liberorum procreandorum causa*), a phrase that was to be of considerable significance to Augustine.[37]

Of all the features of Roman marriage practice, the signing of the *tabulae matrimoniales* is the one that Augustine mentioned most often. On two occasions, Augustine referred to the recitation of the *tabulae matrimoniales* before witnesses (e.g., "recitantur tabulae, et recitantur in conspectu omnium attestantium").[38]

---

[35] A valuable survey of most of Augustine's references to the *tabulae matrimoniales* can be found in Marcello Marin, "Le *tabulae matrimoniales* in s. Agostino," *Siculorum gymnasium* 29 (1976): 307–21. See also Wunibald Roetzer, *Des heiligen Augustinus Schriften als liturgie-geschichtliche Quelle* (Munich, 1930), 205–08.

[36] Treggiari, *Roman Marriage* (n. 16 earlier), 165. For most of this paragraph, I am indebted to Treggiari's fine study.

[37] H. A. Sanders, "A Latin marriage contract," *Transactions and Proceedings of the American Philological Association* 69 (1938): 104–16. For an English translation of this document, see Judith Evans-Grubbs, *Women and Law in the Roman Empire: A Sourcebook of Marriage, Divorce, and Widowhood* (New York, 2002), 126–27. As Evans-Grubbs notes (126–27 and 294–95, n. 99), "[liberorum procrea]ndorum causa" is an "almost certain" reconstruction. The letters in square brackets are absent from both extant copies of the documents; *causa* is apparently present in both, and the ending "*ndorum*" only in one. In her contribution to the present volume, Judith Evans-Grubbs observes that both of the Latin marriage contracts now extant in papyrus fragments employ the phrase *liberorum procreandorum causa* and that a similar expression is found in the *tabula dotis* of Geminia Ianuarilla preserved in the Albertini Tablets.

[38] *Sermo* 51.22 (PL 38:345). See *Confessiones* 9.9.19 (Bibliothèque Augustinienne 14.110): "illas tabulas, quae matrimoniales vocantur, recitari audissent."

In *Sermon* 332, Augustine explicitly stated that it was common for the bishop to be present and to sign the marriage contracts.[39] In another place, Augustine spoke of the indissoluble marriage bond as a pair of "shackles" that is reinforced by "the hands of the bishop." Although the mention of the bishop's "hands" could refer to a nuptial blessing, it is more likely a reference to the signature of the bishop on the marriage contract.[40] The practice of reading, signing, and sealing the *tabulae matrimoniales* was perceived by Augustine to be so central to the making of a marriage that he could speak of "those contracts by which a man takes a woman as a wife [*ipsas tabulas... quibus eam ducit uxorem*]."[41]

Augustine's frequent references to the *tabulae matrimoniales*, together with his complete silence regarding any other aspect of Christian marriage ceremony, suggests that the most common way in which the church in North Africa recognized and participated in the unions of Christians was through the presence of the bishop at the signing of the marriage contracts. On that occasion, as Possidius suggests, the bishop may have pronounced a blessing, although Augustine himself did not say so explicitly and the testimony of Possidius is ambiguous.[42] In short, in Augustine's day, we find the practice of marriage among Christians to be essentially the same in form and content as that of their non-Christian contemporaries. Only the presence of a bishop in the family home would have distinguished a pagan wedding from a Christian one. And the bishop's signature on the *tabulae matrimoniales* would have been the only visible sign that the Christian church recognized this marriage to be a Christian one.[43]

If my argument thus far has been correct, Christians in North Africa seem to have differed from those in Italy in their manner of formalizing marriage arrangements. References to veiling and blessing by the bishop (the practices mentioned most often by Ambrose, Siricius, and others) were absent in North Africa, whereas Augustine prominently features the signing of the *tabulae matrimoniales*. Further confirmation of the centrality of the marriage contracts in Augustine's view of marriage can be found in the many references to these documents in his writings. Augustine spoke of the *tabulae matrimoniales* in a variety of different contexts, and

---

[39] *Sermo* 332.4 (PL 38:1463): "Verum est: istis tabulis subscripsit episcopus: ancillae vestrae sunt uxores vestrae, domini estis uxorum vestrarum."

[40] *Enarrationes in psalmos* 149.15 (CCL 40:2190): "Tales compedes consolidant vobis et episcopi manus."

[41] *Sermo* 51.22 (PL 38:345).

[42] In the *Vita Augustini*, Possidius stated that the bishop was present "so that their compacts or agreements might be ratified or blessed [*ut vel eorum iam pacta vel placita firmarentur vel benedicerentur*]" (see n. 1 earlier). His use of the passive *benedicerentur* does not necessarily indicate the bestowal of a liturgical blessing by the bishop.

[43] See the observations of A.-G. Hamman, *La vie quotidienne en Afrique du Nord au temps de saint Augustin* (Paris, 1979), 91: "La célébration du mariage entre chrétiens devait ressembler à s'y tromper à celle de deux païens.... On lit publiquement devant les témoins les actes du contrat matrimonial (*tabulae matrimoniales*). C'est la pièce maîtresse, souscrite par l'évêque et rédigée avec son concours." Stevenson, *Nuptial Blessing*, 29–30, dramatically overstates the case when he attempts to describe the "wedding service conducted by the great North African bishop."

it is clear that this custom influenced his thinking on marriage in significant ways. In the remainder of this essay I examine these references and explore the impact of this marriage practice on Augustine's thought.

The feature of the *tabulae matrimoniales* mentioned most frequently by Augustine is their reference to procreation as the primary purpose of the marriage. As already noted, the statement that the marriage was being formed *liberorum procreandorum causa* is a common feature of the extant marriage contracts.[44] Although the centrality of procreation to marriage was a commonplace in antiquity, it is significant that Augustine often appealed to the *tabulae matrimoniales* when he wished to assert the validity of procreation within marriage. For example, in his book *De moribus ecclesiae catholicae et de moribus Manichaeorum*, Augustine attacked the Manichean practice of allowing marriage to the "auditors" while forbidding procreation. The Manichaean avoidance of procreation, Augustine argued, violated the declared purpose of marriage as stated in the *tabulae matrimoniales*:

Marriage, as the marriage contracts themselves declare, joins the male and female together for the sake of procreation. Therefore, whoever says that it is a greater sin to procreate children than to have intercourse, forbids marriage itself. Such a one makes a woman not a wife, but a mistress who, by the exchange of a few gifts, is joined to a man simply to gratify his lust.[45]

Similarly, in his treatise *Contra Faustum Manichaeum*, Augustine argued that the Manichees made legitimate wives into adulterers by prohibiting procreation:

They take wives, according to the law of marriage, that is, "for the sake of producing children," as the contracts proclaim.... But they are unwilling to receive children, although this is the sole purpose of conjugal intercourse. As the apostle predicted long ago (1 Tim. 4:3), you have indeed forbidden marriage, when you try to remove from marriage the very purpose of marriage.[46]

In these writings against the Manichees, Augustine appealed explicitly to the wording of the *tabulae matrimoniales* in order to argue that the legal definition of marriage itself required the willing acceptance of children. To attempt to avoid procreation as the Manichees did, according to Augustine, was to deny the very reason for marital intercourse (*propter quod solum coniugia copulanda sunt*). By denying the true purpose of marriage, Augustine argued, the Manichees violated the marriage contracts.

A similar polemical use of the *tabulae matrimoniales* can be found later in several of Augustine's anti-Pelagian writings. But in these works, the wording of the marriage contracts was adduced in order to underscore the essential goodness of sexual intercourse for procreation, in contrast to the corruption of the sexual urge

[44] See n. 37 earlier.
[45] *De moribus ecclesiae et de moribus Manichaeorum* 2.18.65 (PL 32:1372).
[46] *Contra Faustum manichaeum* 15.7 (CSEL 25/1:429).

that has been introduced by original sin. For example, in *De gratia Christi et de peccato originali*, Augustine noted:

Marital intercourse, which according to the marriage contracts takes place "for the sake of producing children," is in itself a good without qualification, not merely in comparison with fornication. Even though, on account of the "body of death" which has not yet been renewed by the resurrection, this [marital intercourse] cannot take place without a kind of bestial motion, which causes human nature to blush, nevertheless intercourse itself is not a sin, when reason uses lust for a good purpose and is not diverted to a bad purpose.[47]

Similarly, in his *Contra Iulianum*, Augustine argued that marital chastity involved a constant struggle against the impulses of concupiscence. "If this marital chastity has such strength and is so great a gift of God that it carries out what the marriage contracts prescribe, it wages war in a fiercer conflict upon the marriage bed itself so that concupiscence does not entice the body of the husband beyond what is sufficient for begetting children."[48] Simply to follow the marriage contracts and restrict acts of intercourse to procreation, Augustine observed, required a great gift of God.

The tendency for married people to go beyond the limits of their *tabulae matrimoniales* and to engage in intercourse without the intention to procreate was a persistent theme in Augustine's sermons as well. For example, in *Sermon 51* Augustine argued that sex beyond the need of procreation is a violation of the *tabulae matrimoniales*. The passage is worth quoting in full because it shows that Augustine could count on his audience to be familiar with the wording of the marriage contracts:

But anyone who desires his wife's body for more than is prescribed by this limit (the purpose of procreating children) is going against the very contract with which he married her. The contract is recited, it is read out in the presence of all the witnesses, and what is read out is: "for the sake of procreating children"; and it is called the matrimonial contract. Unless this were what wives are given away and taken for, who with any sense of shame would give away his daughter to another's lust? But to save parents from being ashamed when they give away their daughters, the contract is read out, to make them fathers-in-law, not whoremongers. So what is read out in the

---

[47] *De gratia Christi et de peccato originali* 2.38.43 (Bibliothèque Augustinienne 22:252–54). Augustine drew a similar contrast between the good of procreation, as proclaimed in the *tabulae matrimoniales*, and the evil of lust in *De civitate dei* 14.18 (CCL 48:441).

[48] *Contra Iulianum* 3.43 (PL 44:724), translated (slightly altered) by Roland Teske, *Answer to the Pelagians, II*, The Works of Saint Augustine (Hyde Park, 1998), 363. See *De nuptiis et concupiscentia* 1.4.5 (CSEL 42:215–16), where Augustine argues that non-Christians cannot attain true marital chastity, even if they follow the marriage contracts and restrict all acts of intercourse to procreation. Their chastity is deficient because they do not intend to raise their children as Christians.

contract? "For the sake of procreating children." The father's brow clears, his face is saved when he hears the words of the contract.[49]

Here, as elsewhere in his sermons, Augustine cited the authority of the *tabulae matrimoniales* to show that sexual intercourse in marriage, when it exceeds the limit needed for procreation, violates the marriage contract and thus should be regarded as a sin.[50]

Yet, despite this rigorism, Augustine had no illusions about the ability of married people to follow this demanding (and limited) view of sex. In one sermon he even acknowledged that it was unlikely that anyone actually followed the mandates of the marriage contracts and restricted sex to procreation: "Is there any married man who uses his wife only for the purpose of having children? For this is why she was given: the contracts which were drawn up in marriage convict you."[51] To deal with the gap between theory and practice, Augustine developed the notion of a "venial fault" (*venialis culpa*) in conjugal intercourse. He derived the idea from reading 1 Corinthians 7:5–6, in which Paul counseled married couples to abstain from sex temporarily for prayer but then "to come together again so that Satan may not tempt you because of your lack of self-control." Paul made this statement, Augustine noted, "by way of concession [*secundum veniam*], not of command." What was "conceded" to married people was not sex for the purpose of procreation (which, being wholly good, did not require a concession), but rather sex instigated by the concupiscence of the flesh and apart from procreation. The "fault" or "sin" in such actions is allowed, Augustine argued, because of the good of marriage itself.[52]

Because Augustine could assume that his congregation was familiar with the *tabulae matrimoniales*, he often cited them to remind his flock of the ways in which they fell short of perfection on a daily basis. In one sermon, he referred to the violation of the marriage contracts as an example of one of the "daily sins" (*quotidiana peccata*) that can be absolved by the practice of daily almsgiving: "When you wish to use your wife more than the need of procreation demands, it is a sin. And it is sins such as these that daily almsgiving cleanses."[53] In another sermon he

---

[49] *Sermo* 51.22 (PL 38:345), translated (slightly altered) by Edmund Hill, *Sermons III (51–94) on the New Testament*, The Works of Saint Augustine (Brooklyn, 1992), 33–34.

[50] See also *Sermo* 9.18 (CCL 41:143): "Cum ipsa uxore si exceditur concumbendi modus procreandis liberis debitus, iam peccatum est. Ad hoc enim ducitur uxor: nam id etiam tabulae indicant ubi scribitur: Liberorum procreandorum causa."

[51] *Sermo* 278.9 (PL 38:1272).

[52] Augustine discussed the *venialis culpa* in many places. See, e.g., *De bono coniugali* 4.4–6.6 (CSEL 41:191–95) and *Sermo* 354A.7–9 (text in François Dolbeau, *Vingt-six sermons au peuple d'Afrique* [Paris, 1996], 80–81). I have recently discussed the significance of this Dolbeau sermon in the development of Augustine's teaching on marriage, including the *venialis culpa*: see David G. Hunter, "Augustine, Sermon 354A: Its place in his thought on marriage and sexuality," *Augustinian Studies* 33 (2002): 39–60.

[53] *Sermo* 9.18 (CCL 41:143–44): "Quando tu uti uxore amplius quam necessitas procreandorum liberorum cogit volueris, iam peccatum est. Et ipsa talia peccata quotidianae elemosinae mundant."

recommended the daily recitation of the Lord's Prayer as the proper remedy for the exercise of conjugal rights beyond the limits of the marriage contracts.[54] In yet another sermon Augustine urged his listeners to take the *tabulae matrimoniales* as a subject for the examination of their consciences:

In order to learn why you take a wife, do not read my arguments, but your own marriage contracts. Read them, study them, and if you do anything beyond them, blush! Read, and I too will listen. I have to do this because of you. Certainly this is what you read: "for the sake of producing children".... Therefore, if you are married and do not want the apostle to concede anything to you by way of pardon, do not exceed the limits of your [marriage] contracts.[55]

The consistent thread in all of these references to the *tabulae matrimoniales* is that they were a well-known and public statement of the purpose of marriage, *liberorum procreandorum causa*. Therefore, in his preaching, Augustine could make frequent and comprehensible appeals to the marriage contracts whenever he wished to remind his congregation of the purpose of their marriages.

Another theme that emerges in Augustine's discussions of the *tabulae matrimoniales* is that the marriage contracts reinforce the subordination of wives to their husbands. This topic is found much less frequently than the references to procreation, but it does occur on at least four occasions. In several sermons, Augustine observed that a good wife should regard her husband as a master (*dominus*) and herself as his obedient servant (*ancilla*), and he cited the *tabulae matrimoniales* to back this up. For example, in *Sermon 37*, in the middle of an allegorical treatment of the church as the "valiant woman" of Proverbs 31:10–31, Augustine noted that:

Every good wife calls her husband "master." Indeed not only does she call him this, but she really thinks so and means it, she bears it in her heart and professes it with her lips. She regards the marriage contracts as the documents of her purchase [*instrumenta emptionis suae*].[56]

Likewise, in *Sermon 332* Augustine observed that when the bishop signed the *tabulae matrimoniales*, wives became the *ancillae* of their husbands, and husbands became their *domini*.[57]

Perhaps the most vivid account of this theme is the famous passage of the *Confessions* where Augustine described the advice his mother Monica gave to the women of Thagaste who suffered beatings from their angry husbands.

Monica, speaking as if in jest but offering serious advice, used to blame their tongues. She would say that since the day when they heard the so-called matrimonial contracts

---

[54] *Sermo* 278.10 (PL 38:1272); cf. *Sermo* 354A.12 (Dolbeau, 83).

[55] *Sermo* 354A.9 (Dolbeau, 81–82).

[56] *Sermo* 37.7 (CCL 41:454). See *Sermo* 392.5 (PL 39:1712).

[57] *Sermo* 332.4 (PL 38:1463): "Verum est: istis tabulis subscripsit episcopus: ancillae vestrae sunt uxores vestrae, domini estis uxorum vestrarum."

read out to them, they should reckon them to be legally binding documents [*tamquam instrumenta*] by which they had become servants. She thought they should remember their condition and not proudly withstand their masters.[58]

The presence of these several references to the marriage contracts as legal documents (*instrumenta*) that declared wives to be the "servants" of their husbands and the husbands to be "masters" raises an important question: did the *tabulae matrimoniales* in Augustine's day, at least in North Africa, contain some provision for the subordination of women to their husbands? Some scholars have asserted that this is so, but in my opinion it is unlikely.[59] We do not have independent corroboration for such an expression in an extant marriage contract, as we do for the phrase *liberorum procreandorum causa*. Nor did Augustine explicitly say that the marriage contracts contained a verbatim affirmation of the husband's "lordship" over the wife in the same way that he asserted the presence of the language regarding procreation. It is possible that Augustine was simply drawing a parallel between the matrimonial contracts and other deeds of purchase, such as documents of slave ownership, which were also called *tabulae*. For example, in one place, Augustine stated "in order to manumit a slave, you break his contracts."[60] When speaking of women and their duties to their husbands, Augustine seems to have slipped easily between speaking of the *tabulae matrimoniales* and speaking of other types of *tabulae* or "deeds of purchase" (*instrumenta emptionis*).[61] It is far from certain that the marriage contracts themselves actually designated the husband and wife as *dominus* and *ancilla* respectively.[62]

Another way in which Augustine utilized the *tabulae matrimoniales* was in his allegorical treatment of the marriage between Christ and the church. In three sermons, Augustine referred to this spiritual marriage and explicitly cited the *tabulae matrimoniales*, and in each of these, his argument is the same. Because Christ is the Bridegroom and the church is the Bride, their wedding contracts will reveal their true identity and the true nature of their union. The *tabulae matrimoniales* of Christ and the church are the gospels:

---

[58] *Confessiones* 9.9.19 (Bibliothèque Augustienne 14:110), translated (slightly altered) by Henry Chadwick, *The Confessions, Saint Augustine* (New York, 1992), 168–69.

[59] Ritzer, *Le mariage*, 78, believes so: "D'après lui, elles doivent avoir contenu, au moins à son époque et dans sa patrie, une clause qui attribuait au mari un *dominium* sur sa femme et obligeait celle-ci à le servir." Marin, "Le *tabulae matrimoniales*," 314 (n. 35 earlier) cites Ritzer but does not commit himself to this view.

[60] *Sermo* 21.6 (CCL 41:282), cited in Marin, "Le *tabulae matrimoniales*," 317.

[61] See *Sermo* 392.5 (PL 39:1712): "Pretium suum attendat, tabulas suas legat."

[62] In a response to this chapter, Judith Evans-Grubbs also noted that it is highly unlikely that the Latin marriage contracts explicitly referred to husband and wife as *dominus* and *ancilla*. As she observed, such a concept would have been contrary to classical Roman ideology, which extolled the "companionate" marriage.

Thus the holy reading of the gospel each year reveals to us the true Christ and the true church, so that we do not make a mistake in respect to either of them, by presenting the wrong bride to the holy bridegroom or by presenting the holy bride with someone other than her true husband. Therefore, so that we do not err regarding either of them, let us listen to their marriage contracts in the gospel.[63]

For Augustine, Luke 24:46–47 contained the essentials of the marriage contract between Christ and the church. The essential message about Jesus is that "it was necessary for Christ to suffer and to rise again from the dead on the third day" (Luke 24:46). The essential message about the church is that "repentance and forgiveness of sins is to be proclaimed in his name to all nations beginning from Jerusalem."[64] The former message protects the church from the heresy of Docetism, Augustine argued, and the latter from the error of the Donatists.[65]

The appearance of the *tabulae matrimoniales* in Augustine's discussion of the marriage between Christ and the church is further evidence of the centrality of these documents in the North African marriage ceremony. In this case, it was not so much the content of the marriage contracts (e.g., the endorsement of procreation) that influenced Augustine as the contractual nature of the documents themselves. That is, Augustine could liken the gospels to the marriage contracts because, like the *tabulae matrimoniales*, the gospels were written documents that publicly attested to the type of relationship that existed between the Bride and her Bridegroom. Here again Augustine could slip easily between speaking of marriage contracts and speaking of other forms of contractual obligation. For example, in *Sermon* 340A, Augustine referred to the same passage from Luke 24:46–47 as *tabulae*, but in this instance he meant a "document of purchase": "We were all bought together, one price was paid to acquire us. The records [*tabulae*] of our price are being read out, the instrument of our purchase is the holy gospel."[66] Elsewhere in this sermon Augustine could even describe "the Lord's contracts" (*tabulas dominicas*) as both an "instrument" and a "testament of our inheritance." When the contracts are properly understood, Augustine argued, there will be no room for heretical error or sectarian division: "Let us read them, let us understand them, why should we litigate?"[67]

---

[63] *Sermo* 238.1 (PL 38:1125).

[64] *Sermo* 183.11 (PL 38:991–92); *Sermo* 238.3 (PL 38:1125–26); *Sermo* 268.4 (PL 38:1233).

[65] See *Sermo* 183.11 (PL 38:992): "Ad nuptias venimus, tabulas legamus, et non litigemus. Ergo si tu dicis, Christus est sponsus partis Donati; ego tabulas lego, et invenio esse Christum sponsum ecclesiae diffusae toto orbe terrarum."

[66] *Sermo* 340A.11, G. Morin (ed.), Miscellanea Agostiniana 1 (Rome, 1930–31), 573: "Simul emti sumus, uno pretio comparati sumus; pretii nostri tabulae recitantur, nostrae emtionis instrumentum sanctum est evangelium." See *Sermo* 21.6 (CCL 41:282): "tabulae tuae evangelium sunt, ubi est sanguis quo comparatus es."

[67] *Sermo* 340A.11 (574): "Tabulas dominicas lego, instrumentum vel potius testamentum hereditatis nostrae lego; legamus, intellegamus: quare litigamus?"

Conclusion

In this essay, I have argued that there is little evidence of any specifically Christian rituals of marriage in North African Christianity from the time of Tertullian to that of Augustine. Even in Augustine's day, there was nothing to distinguish a Christian marriage from a pagan one, except for the presence of a bishop at the family nuptials. Bishops were sometimes (perhaps often) invited to be present and to sign the marriage contracts (*tabulae matrimoniales*), although there is no evidence that this was a requirement for the validity of a marriage. On that occasion, the bishop may have pronounced a blessing on the couple, though the evidence for this practice is very slight, being limited to the ambiguous comments in Possidius's *Vita Augustini*. By contrast, Christians elsewhere in the West, especially in Italy, had already developed the custom of celebrating marriage with rituals of veiling the bride and blessing at the hands of a bishop. In this respect, marriage customs in North Africa seem to have been less "Christianized" than they were elsewhere in the West.[68]

Yet, although he never alluded to rituals of marriage, Augustine referred on numerous occasions to the reading and signing of the marriage contracts. Because they were signed by a bishop, the *tabulae matrimoniales* indicated that the covenant between the spouses was being accorded ecclesiastical recognition in some form. Although these documents were largely secular in their orientation, dealing with matters of dowry and inheritance, they were of great significance to Augustine. Because they contained the phrase "for the sake of producing children," the *tabulae matrimoniales* served to define the essential purpose of sex and marriage for Augustine and (he hoped) for his congregation. The similarity between the marriage contracts and other forms of property agreements (*instrumenta emptionis*), especially deeds of slave ownership, suggested to Augustine that the relationship between husband and wife could be understood in similarly proprietary terms: the husband was to be considered the *dominus* and the wife the *ancilla*. Moreover, this proprietary character of the *tabulae matrimoniales* suggested to Augustine a theological point as well: the church was to be seen as the Bride of Christ, purchased at a great price. Like a human marriage, the spiritual marriage between Christ and the church had its own form of public affirmation, its own *tabulae matrimoniales*: the sacred scriptures.

---

[68] The only possible exception that I have found is a passage from *Epist.* 23 (CSEL 34:169), in which Augustine says that a Christian couple usually pledged mutual fidelity "through Christ." Commenting on the tragic divisions within families created by the Donatist schism, Augustine wrote: "Nonne ingemiscimus, quod vir et uxor, ut fideliter iungant corpora sua, iurant sibi plerumque per Christum et ipsius Christi corpus diversa communione dilaniant?" Ritzer, *Le mariage*, 96, cites this text and suggests that Augustine is the earliest witness for an exchange of vows that contained an explicit invocation of God or Christ. If this is the case, it is puzzling that Augustine does not speak more about these vows.

Finally, I should note, there is an important connection between the points that I have argued here and part of Judith Evans-Grubbs's discussion in this volume. As Evans-Grubbs has demonstrated, Roman emperors of the fourth and fifth centuries increasingly resorted to written contracts (*instrumenta*) in order to verify agreements, including marriages, that previously had relied on mainly verbal testimony. She argues that Roman emperors during this period, in both East and West, were motivated by their anxiety to distinguish legitimate marriage, which produced heirs, from concubinage, which resulted in "natural" (i.e., illegitimate) children (*naturales*). Requiring dowry or prenuptial gifts, in part because such financial exchanges would have been documented, was a way to ensure not only that both partners had roughly equal economic and social standing, but also that the union was a permanent marriage (*matrimonium*) and not only a temporary concubinage (*concubinatus*), given that a man might subsequently abandon his concubine in order to enter into a "real" marriage.[69]

Yet, by the time of Justinian, as Evans-Grubbs has shown, such documentation had become something different, namely, a means to facilitate the entry of men of high status into legitimate marriages with women of low status and thereby to eliminate any moral grounds for concubinage. The *tabulae matrimoniales*, in Justinian's legislation, had become "indicators of morality" as well as "records of financial transactions."[70] Augustine's intense interest in the documentation of marriage can thus be set within the broader context of the development of the *tabulae* as moral and not merely legal documents. As evidence of marital intent, these documents were also indicators of moral behavior, insofar as they served to distinguish a legitimate marriage from other sexual liaisons. Perhaps Augustine, who knew intimately the difference between marriage and concubinage, was especially sensitive to this distinction.[71] Looking much further forward, we shall see the same theme in Thomas Kuehn's chapter on Renaissance Florence, where written dowries and other notarized records (rather than religious rituals) distinguished marriage from concubinage.

---

[69] See earlier, 91–94.

[70] See earlier, 94.

[71] I am grateful for comments on this paper from Philip L. Reynolds, as editor of the volume, and especially from Judith Evans-Grubbs, who provided a formal response and suggested the ideas found in my final paragraph.

CHAPTER FOUR

DOTAL CHARTERS IN THE FRANKISH TRADITION

Philip L. Reynolds

The dotal charter of this essay was a written deed (*actum*) whereby a man agreed to give a marriage gift, usually called a dowry (*dos*), to his betrothed.[1] It was a northern successor to the Roman *tabulae nuptiales* discussed in the previous chapters, although the donor was the betrothed man and not the bride's father or parents. I shall consider the form and content of such charters in a Frankish tradition that ranged from the Merovingian period through the Carolingian period and continued into eleventh-century northern France.

One must assume that many such charters did not survive, and that what remains for us to examine is a small fraction. A dotal charter ceased to be relevant, at least in respect to the purpose for which it had been drawn up, when the dowered wife died. When a dotal charter or its content did survive, it was usually because someone put it to another use. In the early Middle Ages (roughly from the Merovingian period into the eleventh century), the content of some survived because a scribe made a revised copy to be used as a formula (i.e., a model or exemplar). Most of the dotal charters that have survived from the tenth and later centuries did so because a church or monastery retained them (usually as copies) in a cartulary, probably in view of some connection with the institution's own interests in the property.[2]

---

[1] I am grateful to the editors of *Recherches de théologie ancienne et médiévale* and of its successor, *Recherches de théologie et philosophie médiévales*, for permission to use some passages that appeared in Philip L. Reynolds, "The dotal charter as theological treatise," *Recherches de théologie ancienne et médiévale* 61 (1994): 54–68. I am grateful to Édouard Jeauneau for help with the original article, to Laurent Morelle and David Hunter for comments on the present chapter, and to David Bright for corrections and suggestions regarding the appended translations.

[2] On the circumstances of such retention, see Georges Duby, *Le chevalier, la femme et le prêtre: Le mariage dans la France féodale* (Paris, 1981), 103–07; or idem, *The Knight, the Lady and the Priest*, translated by Barbara Bray (New York, 1983), 95–99. Duby states that although people continued to draw up dotal contracts (*sponsalitia*), church archivists no longer copied them into cartularies after about 1030–40, and he reasons that this was because "legal procedures were changing; it was no longer necessary to produce written evidence before tribunals, since those who had to pass judgment now relied on oral testimony or on proofs of the judgment of God" (translated by Bray, 99). By the latter phrase, Duby refers to trials by ordeal (fire or water) or combat (see n. 22). But the logic

Comparable exemplars for dotal charters during this later period are to be found also in high-medieval *ars dictandi* manuals.[3]

Karl Zeumer's *Formulae Merowingici et Karolini Aevi* includes some thirty formulae for dotal charters in the Frankish tradition, ranging from the sixth through the eleventh centuries.[4] These documents provide vivid glimpses of marriage among wealthy, landed families, and some are witnesses to a distinctive theology of marriage. (It is the last feature that chiefly interests me in this chapter.) I have based the following discussion mainly on Zeumer's hoard, and I have described in an appendix all the dotal formulae from the Frankish tradition contained in this collection, with complete or partial translations of many.[5]

It may seem arbitrary to focus on a single nineteenth-century volume of the *Monumenta Germaniae Historica*. There may be comparable early medieval examples awaiting our attention in manuscripts. But Zeumer's collection of formulae and formularies was remarkably thorough, and the dotal formulae contained therein must at least amount to an excellent sample. Moreover, because citations to Zeumer's dotal formulae appear frequently in scholarly footnotes (usually without any synoptic analysis of their form and content), I intend this chapter to serve partly as a practical introduction or guide to them: a "handbook," as it were. Nevertheless, to complete the picture and to extend the study into a later period, I take into account as well some copies of actual dotal charters (rather than formulae) from the same tradition, dating from the tenth through twelfth centuries.[6]

---

of the argument is unclear, and in any case, the empirical observation is based exclusively on two collections: the *Recueil des chartes de l'abbaye de Cluny* (ed. Bernard and Bruel), and the *Cartulaire de Saint-Vincent de Mâcon* (ed. Ragut).

[3] The *Aurea gemma "gallica,"* a French *ars dictandi* manual from the mid-twelfth century, includes two dotal formulae. The manual has been edited and translated by Steven M. Wight for *Scrineum*, an online documentary resource from the University of Pavia, using two MSS: Admont, Stiftsbibliothek, cod. 759, fols. 59^r–91^v (letter collection fols. 91^v–117^r), twelfth century; and Brugge, Stadsbibliotheek (Bibliothèque de la Ville, = Stedelijke openbare Bibl.), cod. 528, fols. 7^v–15^v, twelfth century. For the dotal charters, see http://dobc.unipv.it/scrineum/wight/index.htm, texts 2.28–32 and 3b.82–84. In a footnote to the first text, Wight notes that there are three other examples in a collection of model charters associated with Bernard de Meung's *Flores dictaminum*. On *ars dictandi* manuals in general, see Martin Camargo, *Ars Dictaminis, Ars Dictandi*, Typologie des sources du moyen âge occidental 60 (Turnhout, Belgium, 1991).

[4] Karolus Zeumer (ed.), *Formulae Merowingici et Karolini Aevi*, MGH *Legum* V, *Formulae* (Hanover, 1886). In my references to Zeumer's fomulae, the "Document" numbers are those of the appendix that follows, whereas the abbreviations for the formularies and collections (*And., Aug.* B, etc.) are those of Zeumer's edition (see ibid. p. IX and the tables that follow).

[5] I include those formulae intended for the Carolingian Alamanni (such as *Aug.* B 24, pp. 357–58). Zeumer's collection includes Visigothic formulae compiled in the seventh century under Sisebut, King of the Visigoths in Spain. Among these, *Vis.* 14–20 (pp. 581–85) are dotal charters, but because they belong to a different tradition and are quite different in form from the Frankish examples, I do not discuss them here.

[6] For these additional sources, I am dependent mainly on the following: Laurent Morelle, "Mariage et diplomatique: Autour de cinq chartes de douaire dans le Laonnois-Soissonnais 1163–1181," *Bibliothèque de l'École de chartes* 146 (1988): 225–84 (now translated as the chapter that follows);

Dotal charters in this tradition were of two sorts, which I characterize as secular and sacred respectively. Only eleven of Zeumer's Frankish formulae fall clearly into the sacred category. The essential function of the two sorts was the same, for the secular matter, pertaining to a donation of property, was the raison d'être of any dotal charter. The difference is a simple matter of content. The secular formulae may use conventional expressions of piety (such as "in the name of God," "in the name of the Lord," "God willing," or "with Christ's favor"), but they say nothing about the religious aspects of marriage. The sacred formulae presuppose a basic secular form, but they supplement it (mainly in preambles) with religious and moral commentary, explaining the sanctity of marriage and its place in God's plan. (Some of the sacred preambles affirm as well that legitimate marriage is in accordance with civil law.)[7] Written by monks or clerics, and sometimes incorporated into the celebration of a wedding, dotal charters were a medium through which churchmen could express their own, properly religious concerns about marriage.

My plan in this essay is twofold: first, to consider the charters generally, analyzing their diplomatic form and showing how they were situated in relation to the process of getting married; and second, to focus on the religious or theological import of sacred dotal charters.

Formulae and Dotal Charters

Formulae were examples of administrative or official documents, especially of letters and legal charters. During the early Middle Ages, the use of such models was not only for the sake of style; rather, it was essential to the practice of law, which depended then not on theory or jurisprudence but on imitation and tradition. And the traditions were remarkably constant: the form and much of the phraseology of these dotal charters remained the same over some three centuries, throughout the Merovingian and Carolingian periods. We know little about the men who studied, collected, and composed charters for deeds for the laity in northern Europe during the early Middle Ages, but we may presume that most were either monks or diocesan clergy.

The redactors usually based the dotal formulae on actual charters. Sometimes they even retained proper names, but they usually replaced the proper names of persons and places with indefinite signs such as *ille, illa, nomine ille,* and so on (which I have translated with expressions such as "*So-and-So*" in the appendix); or they might signify a personal name by the sign *N.* (for *nomen*), or simply leave

and Philippe Depreux, "La dotation de l'épouse en Aquitaine septentrionale du IXe au XIIe siècle," in François Bougard, Laurent Feller, and Régine Le Jan (eds.), *Dots et douaires dans le haut Moyen Âge* (Rome, 2002), 219–44.

[7] See *Bit.* 15 (Doc. 6), *Extr.* I 11 (Doc. 13), and *Extr.* I 14 (Doc. 16).

a blank space. Likewise, they usually replaced quantities with indefinite signs such as *tanta* ("so many").

The nuptial gift in these formulae is usually called a *dos*. The corresponding written deed is therefore called *libellum dotis, carta dotis,* or (less commonly) *epistola dotis*: phrases signifying a dotal certificate, charter, or document.[8] The word *osculum* is sometimes used in the same sense, because of the influence of the phrase *interveniente osculo* in the *Theodosian Code*.[9] (Properly, the term denoted the ceremonial kiss that confirmed the betrothal, the nuptials, or gifts associated with these compacts.)[10] The term *tandono* (with its variants) appears occasionally as a synonym for *libellum dotis* (see *Merk.* 15, Doc. 9).[11] It may be a corruption of the Latin phrase *tantum donum* ("a gift of such-and-such an amount"), which appears as a variant in a few manuscripts. Some dotal formulae are simply entitled *cessio* or *donatio*, and two are entitled *traditio*:[12] these are generic terms for any gift.

Beginning around the late tenth century, terms such as *sponsalicium, donatio propter/ante nuptias, donatio nuptialis,* and *dotalicium* gradually superseded (without entirely replacing) the term *dos* as the name for the husband's gift or for the written agreement defining it, but they do not appear in Zeumer's fomulae. *Sponsalicium* is the neuter substantive form of an adjective meaning "pertaining to betrothal," from the classical word *sponsalia* ("betrothal"). The word *sponsaliciae* (apparently a feminine noun) occurs in the Merovingian formula *And.* 1c (see Doc. 1), but only in a garbled echo of the phrase *sponsalicia largitas* ("betrothal gift") in the *Theodosian Code*. Otherwise, the term *sponsalicium* is absent from these early medieval formulae, although it would have been quite appropriate.[13] The use of terms such as *sponsalicium* and *donatio propter nuptias*, rather than *dos*, to denote

---

[8] See the entries under *dos* in Zeumer's index. The neuter form *libellum* is standard, rather than the classical *libellus* (masculine).

[9] See *Tur.* app. 2 (p. 164, line 12), and *Extr.* I 9 and 10 (p. 539, lines 9 and 37). See the article on *osculum* in Jan F. Niermeyer, C. van de Kieft, and J. W. J. Burgers, *Mediae Latinitatis Lexicon Minus*, 2nd rev. ed. (Leiden, 2000).

[10] See *Cod. Theod.* III.5.6 (= *Breviary* III.5.5), a law determining what happens to the antenuptial gift (*donatio ante nuptias*) once the kiss has been exchanged (*interveniente osculo*) if one of the betrothed partners dies before the marriage. (It is to be divided equally between the survivor and the heirs of the deceased.) On the nuptial kiss in Roman tradition, cf. Tertullian, *De virginibus velandis* 11.3, CCL 2, 1220–21; idem, *De oratione* 22.10, CCL 1, 271. On the history of the betrothal kiss, see Henri Leclercq, "Mariage," *Dictionnaire d'archéologie chrétienne et de liturgie* 10/2 (1932), 1843–1982, at 1893–95 (and on the *osculum* as a written instrument, see ibid., 1894).

[11] See also *Marc.* II 15 (p. 85, line 6); *Big.* 6 (p. 230, line 1); *Merk.* 15 (p. 246, line 35; p. 247, lines 4 and 7); and *Merk.* 17 (p. 248, line 2, copied from *Marc.* II 15).

[12] *Tur.* 15 (p. 143) and *Tur.* app. 3 (p. 164). The term seems to be used here in its generic sense (i.e., to denote a formal act of cession, a legally constituted gift), and not to denote the "handing over" of the bride in marriage.

[13] See the article on the adjective *sponsalicius* in Niermeyer et al., *Mediae Latinitatis Lexicon Minus*. For examples of this term used to denote the agreement or gift in the tenth and later centuries, see Duby, *Le chevalier, la femme et le prêtre*, 106–15, passim.

the husband's gift in post-Carolingian northern-French sources may have been a result of a revived influence of Roman law (perhaps partly via canon law) or, indeed, a result of the revival of the parental dowry, for in terms of Roman law, the Frankish dowry would be a *donatio ante nuptias* or perhaps an *arrha*, but not a *dos*. Similarly, the use of newly coined terms such a *dotalicium* after the eleventh century may have served to distinguish the husband's gift from a revived bridal dowry (now called a *dos*, as in Roman law).

THE FRANKISH DOWRY

The *dos* of the Frankish charters was not the bridal dowry of Roman law, which the wife brought into the marriage from her parents, but rather a dowry that the husband gave to his wife (a *dos ex marito*), albeit one promised before their marriage in confirmation of the betrothal. The Roman historian Tacitus had considered this practice, whereby the bride received a dowry from her husband rather than from her *paterfamilias*, to be a distinguishing trait of the *Germani*. Forms of the Germanic *dos ex marito* supplanted the parental dowry throughout Europe during the early Middle Ages as the chief assign in marriage, even in regions where Roman influence was strong, and even when parents continued to confer dowries upon their daughters.[14] The Frankish dowry appears in the charters as a required matrimonial settlement that was solemnly pledged and legally binding. It was evidently a normal precondition for marriage, at least among the landed classes.

Many historians today arbitrarily reserve the term "dowry" (or in French, *dot*) exclusively for the Roman-style, parental *dos*. At the same time, although some historians call any marital gift from the husband's side a "dower" (or in French, *douaire*), most reserve that term exclusively for a widow's right to a certain portion of her late husband's estate (the "widow's portion"). Although there is virtue in having a consistent terminology, these modern conventions would leave no convenient English term for the *dos* of the Frankish charters. I persist in calling it a dowry for two reasons. First, Jack Goody, an anthropologist who has written extensively on marriage and dotation in the Middle Ages, defines dowry in general as *any* "property transferred to a woman when she marries," and he distinguishes between direct dowry (from parents to daughter) and indirect dowry (from husband to wife).[15] In Goody's terms, the Frankish *dos* was an indirect dowry. Second,

---

[14] On the regime of the *dos ex marito*, see André Lemaire, "La *dotatio* de l'épouse de l'époque mérovingienne au XIIIᵉ siècle," *Revue historique de droit français et étranger*, 4th series, 8 (1929): 569–80; and Philip L. Reynolds, *Marriage in the Western Church* (Leiden, 1994), 80–87. But please note that on p. 81, with reference to Tacitus (*Germania*, 18.1), I said exactly the opposite of what I meant to say, which was that among the Germans, according to Tacitus, "the husband gives the dowry to his wife, whereas among the Romans the wife gives it to her husband."

[15] For the definition of dowry, see Jack Goody, *The European Family: An Historico-Anthropological Essay* (Oxford, 2000), 187. The direct/indirect dowry distinction occurs passim in Goody's article

and more important, there is virtue in consistently replicating in English the terminological pattern of the Latin sources, so that there is a one-to-one correlation between more or less technical terms in each vocabulary. It is significant that when Germanic culture came into contact and blended with Roman culture, those who recorded Germanic practices in Latin considered the husband's gift to be a dowry and used the term *dos* to denote it (instead of *donatio ante nuptias*, for example). Clearly, they considered the two assigns – the Roman dowry and the Germanic marriage gift – to be functionally equivalent in certain respects.

The Frankish dotal charters concern this (indirect) dowry alone. There are no formulae in Zeumer's collection for marital assigns of other sorts. It does not follow that such assigns did not exist. Frankish parents may have endowed their daughters at marriage even in the early Middle Ages, but if they did so, the parental dowry must not have been a written gift, nor a gift deemed to be an especially significant step in the process of marrying. The same would be true of any trousseau that the bride took with her when she married. Likewise, widows may have automatically received, in addition to the written dowry, some customary portion of their late husbands' estates (or at least usufruct rights to it), such as the Frankish one-third (*tercia*).[16] Philippe Depreux has noted evidence for a *douaire* of this sort (a customary widow's portion) in northern Aquitaine during the early eleventh century.[17] There would have been no need to document a customary, virtually automatic right (nor any reason *not* to document it). Be that as it may, the topic of this chapter is rather dotal charters than dotal regimes, and the charters are exclusively concerned with a defined indirect dowry (*dos ex marito*).

The dowry of the Frankish charters is usually given by the *sponsus* to the *sponsa* in confirmation of their betrothal (although in an unusual dotal charter in Marculf's formulary, it is the father of the *sponsus* who gives the dowry to his daughter-in-law).[18] The Frankish dowry seems to have absorbed the morning gift, which the bride would have received from her husband on the morning after their wedding

"Bridewealth and dowry in Africa and Eurasia," in J. Goody and S. J. Tambiah, *Bridewealth and Dowry*, Cambridge Papers in Social Anthropology 7 (Cambridge, UK, 1973), 1–58, and in Goody's *The Development of the Family and Marriage in Europe* (Cambridge, UK, 1983).

[16] See Diane Owen Hughes, "From brideprice to dowry in Mediterranean Europe," *Journal of Family History* 3 (1978): 262–96, at 270.

[17] Depreux, "La dotation de l'épouse" (n. 6 earlier), 225.

[18] *Marc.* II 15 (p. 85, lines 5–6): "Donat igitur illi honeste puelle, norae [= nurui] suae lei [*sic*], sponsa filio suo illo, ante die nuptiarum donantisque animo transferet atquae transcribit, hoc est in tanodono...." See Laurent Feller, "'Morgengabe', dot, *tertia*: rapport introductif," in Bougard, Feller, and Le Jan, *Dots et douaires*, 1–25, at 11–12. Feller suggests that this was a counter-gift of some sort, perhaps to compensate for a gift from the *sponsus* or from the father of the *sponsa*. The *libellum dotis* of *Marc.* 15 is called a *tanodono*, and according to Feller (if I understand him correctly), that term was specific to dotation of this sort (i.e., from a father-in-law to his son's bride). But in the other charters wherein the term occurs (*Merk.* 15 and *Big.* 6), it is the *sponsus* himself who gives the dowry. (I discount here *Merk.* 17, which seems to be based on *Marc.* II 15. Moreover, this text is garbled, and it is not clear who gives the dowry!)

night, for although Merovingian sources still mention both dowry and morning gift, these are lumped together and no longer distinguishable.[19] Yet the dowry was also a betrothal gift, for the betrothed man (*sponsus*) conferred it as final confirmation of the betrothal, although the *sponsa* would not usually receive or become entitled to the estate until she became his wife (*uxor*). The charters show that the Franks assimilated their dowry to the ante-nuptial gift (*donatio ante nuptias*) of the *Theodosian Code* and *Breviary*, for that too was a gift from the *sponsus* that confirmed a betrothal and was supposed to be recorded in writing.[20] Thus, two distinct Roman transactions merged in the Frankish dotal charter: written ante-nuptial gifts; and dotal instruments (sometimes called *tabulae nuptiales*), which, among Romans, had been a record of the bridal dowry and the signing of which was sometimes a feature of the domestic wedding ceremony.[21]

Scholars have argued that the Germanic *dos ex marito* evolved from or supplanted brideprice or bridewealth. On this view, a gift that had been a suitor's fee to a woman's parents as the price (*pretium*) of their daughter (or more precisely of their power over her: the *munt* or *mundium*) now went instead to the wife herself. Thus Diane Owen Hughes construes the *dos ex marito* as a version of the morning gift, which (according to her theory) grew in size and significance as it superseded brideprice. Hughes argues, with the presumed sexual significance of the morning gift in mind, that the development tended to emphasize the "formal consummation" of a marriage in coitus.[22] Again, the Frankish dowry may have evolved from bridewealth under the influence of the Roman ante-nuptial gift, a development that perhaps accompanied greater recognition of a bride's right of consent to her marriage.[23] These are plausible theories worthy of serious consideration, but they are at best highly speculative, and the slight evidence hardly supports the weight of interpretation. Evidence of brideprice at any period in the history of the West German races (such as the Alamannians, the Thuringians, and the Franks) is at

---

[19] See Régine Le Jan, "Aux origines du douaire médiéval (VIᵉ–Xᵉ siècle)," in eadem, *Femmes, pouvoir et société dans le haut Moyen Âge*, Les médiévistes français 1 (Paris, 2001), 53–67, at 57–59 passim.
[20] Compare the echoes of *Cod. Theod.* III.5 (on betrothals and antenuptial gifts) in the preambles to *Tur.* 14 and *Tur.* app. 2 (pp. 142 and 163). The regime of the *donatio ante nuptias* was a means to penalize either partner for breach of promise, given that someone failing to fulfill the betrothal (except by mutual consent) would forfeit the gift and might pay multiples of it in compensation: for a very brief summary of these rules, see Reynolds, *Marriage in the Western Church*, 6–7 and 26–27.
[21] On written confirmation of the antenuptial gift, see *Cod. Theod.* III.5.2, interpr. The documentation of such gifts may have usually been included in the dotal instrument. On the dotal instrument in Roman law, see the chapters by Evans-Grubbs and Hunter in this volume. Important older studies include Hans J. Wolff, *Written and Unwritten Marriages in Hellenistic and Post-Classical Roman Law*, Philological Monographs, American Philological Society, no. 9 (Haverford, Philadelphia, 1939); and Carlo Castello, "Lo strumento dotale come prova del matrimonio," *Studia et documenta historiae et iuris* 4 (1935): 208–24.
[22] Hughes, "Brideprice to dowry" (n. 16 earlier), 274a and 275–76. For critiques of Hughes's theory, see Reynolds, *Marriage in the Western Church*, 85–86, and Jack Goody, *Development of the Family and Marriage* (n. 15 earlier), App. 2, 240–61.
[23] See Le Jan, "Aux origines," 57–58.

best tenuous. Written records provide no evidence of such a gift, only of things that one might construe as vestiges of it (such as the Salic gift of a solidus and a denarius, by which a *sponsus* confirmed his betrothal).[24] Even the earliest Merovingian dotal formulae define a husband's gift to his wife and say nothing of brideprice or bridewealth.

DOTATION AND THE NUPTIAL PROCESS

The notional speaker in dotal charters (the "I" of the intitulation) is usually the *sponsus*, who pledges to confer the dowry upon the girl or woman to whom he is already betrothed, his *sponsa*. There are no exact equivalents in modern English to the terms *sponsus* and *sponsa* as used here. The old-fashioned English term "betrothed," used as a substantive, is close enough, although it is does not have distinct male and female forms.[25] The terms "fiancé" and "fiancée," as used in modern English, are too weak, for the early medieval betrothal was more binding and more marriage-like in its degree of commitment than is a mere engagement to be married.

The noun *sponsus* is the past participle of *spondere* ("to promise," "to pledge oneself," "to betroth"). The *sponsus* and *sponsa* are persons who have been promised in marriage but are not yet married: they are husband-to-be and wife-to-be. During the early Middle Ages, the terms *sponsa* and *sponsus* applied only to betrothed persons *before* their union in marriage. The usage became confused from the twelfth century, when terms such as *desponsatio*, *sponsalia*, and *matrimonium* were applied both to marriage vows said *per verba de praesenti* and to betrothals said *per verba de futuro*, and then *sponsus* could mean "betrothed," "bridegroom," or "spouse." (Hence the English word "spouse" is derived, via French, from *sponsus*.) Because the bride and groom at early medieval weddings were still *sponsa* and *sponsus*, "bridegroom" is an apt translation of *sponsus* in some contexts even here, but in the Merovingian and Carolingian dotal formulae, the dotal act expressed in the charter presupposes that the marriage is still some way off in the future.

The *desponsatio* envisaged in Frankish dotal charters contained and expressed the consensual element of the normal nuptial process. It was the public agreement of all legally interested parties (not only of the persons getting married but also of their parents and even their kinsfolk) that the marriage would take place. Although the consent of the partners was supposedly required, they might be still very young when their families betrothed them. (Perhaps they had to be at least seven years old, as under Roman law, but there seems to have been no clearly defined minimum age in practice.) Marrying was a process that began with the betrothal (*desponsatio*) and was completed in marriage (*nuptiae*): in other words, the process began with

---

[24] See Hughes, "From brideprice to dowry," 266b–67a.
[25] Modern French has better equivalents in the adjectival nouns *promis* and *promise*.

an agreement to marry and ended with a coming together in marriage. At the betrothal, by promising that the partners would come together eventually as man and wife, the parties expressed the mutual agreement that was essential to the compact of marriage. Each subsequent stage in the process tied the partners more securely to each other and increased the difficulty of separation.[26] The parents and kinsfolk and even the betrothed partners themselves would confirm their continued consent (or compliance) through fulfillment of the subsequent stages, especially dotation.

To confirm the betrothal itself, either on the same occasion or soon afterwards, the *sponsus* might give the *sponsa* a ring (construed as the *arrha sponsalicia* of Roman law), or the *osculum* might take place; but it is difficult to know whether to interpret that as a kiss, an oath, or even a documentary *actum*. Among the Salian Franks, as we shall see in some of the charters that follow, he would give a solidus and a denarius or thirteen pennies to her (or perhaps to her parents) to clinch the betrothal.[27] Some Merovingian sources mention a gift of shoes or slippers as another step of confirmation in the nuptial process.[28]

Dotation occurred functionally in the middle of the process. The *sponsus* recalls in the dotal charter that the betrothal has already taken place, and he looks forward in the same charter to the forthcoming marriage (*nuptiae*).[29] The *sponsus* concludes the act by stating that the *sponsa* shall have, hold, and possess the estate described previously in due course, usually when their marriage takes place. But it does not follow that dotation occurred *chronologically* in the middle of the process. The signing of the dotal charter may have occurred as a final formality on the occasion of the betrothal, yet the wording of the charters suggests that dotation was originally supposed to occur at some considerable time after the betrothal. The charters consistently refer to the betrothal in the past tense, and the *sponsus* often declares in the charter that the foregoing betrothal is well known to many: why remind those present of something that they had just witnessed? Because the partners could become betrothed long before marriageable age, there might be some considerable delay before the conclusion of their marriage, and it would be reasonable to leave the financial arrangements unsettled until the donor and his kinsfolk could be confident about what they would have to offer when the

[26] On betrothal in Germanic law, see Reynolds, *Marriage in the Western Church*, 75–80. On betrothal, consummation, and nuptial benediction as stages in the nuptial process in the early medieval church, see ibid., 315–85; and on the nuptial process in the Frankish church in particular, see ibid., 386–412. On the concept of the nuptial process or "processual" marriage, see also Mia Korpiola, "An act or a process? Competing views on marriage formation and legitimacy in medieval Europe," in Lars Ivar Hansen (ed.), *Family, Marriage and Property Devolution in the Middle Ages* (Tromsø, 2000), 31–54.

[27] See *Big.* 6 (p. 230), *Merk.* 15 (Doc. 9), *Lind.* 7 (p. 271), *Pith.* 55 (p. 597), *Pith.* 60 (p. 598), and *Extr.* I 12 (Doc. 14).

[28] See Reynolds, *Marriage in the Western Church*, 386–89.

[29] The same manner of situating dotation in relation to betrothal and marriage appears in two tenth-century dotal charters appended to Depreux, "La dotation de l'épouse" (n. 6 earlier): see documents 1 and 2 on pp. 241–42 (dated ca. 975 and ca. 990). On dotation in Germanic law, see Reynolds, *Marriage in the Western Church*, 80–87.

marriage was concluded. But Frankish dotal charters may be construed as betrothal documents in a broad sense, for they were apparently the only written record of the betrothal, and dotation confirmed the betrothal.

Marriage was completed in the "handing over" (*traditio*) of the woman to her husband, when he was said to lead her into matrimony (*ducere eam in matrimonium*). The marriage became a fact in the fullest sense when the partners began to live together (and consummation was presumed to occur). Thus, the nuptial process envisaged here proceeded from voluntary to corporeal union: it began with a union of wills, and it was completed in a union of lives and bodies. The cession of property was an interim step leading from one terminus to the other.

The dotal charters look forward to a *dies nuptiarum*, a phrase that one might translate either as "day of the marriage" or "wedding day." And in general, one might translate the word *nuptiae* in the dotal formulae either as "marriage" or as "wedding." The ambiguity would have been insignificant if, in the normal course of events, the final formality before their coming together was a public celebration of their marriage and cohabitation or consummation usually followed at once. But one cannot always be sure that a wedding was a *church* event. In the earliest, Merovingian formulae (such as *And.* 1 c, Doc. 1), the wedding envisaged was probably still a civil, domestic celebration, after which a priest might have accompanied the couple to their bedchamber and blessed them and their bed. In the Carolingian examples, because of the introduction of Roman norms, there would ideally have been a church wedding followed by a domestic celebration (at which, again, a priest would have blessed the bedchamber).[30] In that case, what was called the *velatio nuptialis* (a rite of priestly blessing that was linked, in a way that is not always obvious, to the veiling of the bride or the couple) was the ecclesiastical prelude to what it both symbolized and ritually postponed: the union of two in one flesh that followed the "handing over" (*traditio*) of the bride to her husband and her being "led" to her new home. But one should assume that these were ideal norms, applicable mainly to the highest social stratum. In many marriages, priestly involvement, if any, would have been limited to participation in domestic wedding celebrations, especially the rite of the bedchamber.

Some legal historians assume that when a dotal charter refers to the wife's coming into possession "on the day of the marriage," it means that the gift would become hers only after consummation, as may once have been the case with the morning gift.[31] But in my view, this stretches the evidence too far. My sense is that a *sponsa*

---

[30] See Michael M. Sheehan, "Choice of marriage partner in the Middle Ages: Development and mode of application of a theory of marriage," in idem, James K. Farge (ed.), *Marriage, Family, and Law in Medieval Europe: Collected Studies*, (Toronto, 1996), 87–117, at 110–11. On getting married in the Frankish tradition, see Korbinian Ritzer, *Le mariage dans les Églises chrétiennes du Iᵉʳ au XIᵉ siècle* (Paris, 1970), 267–88.

[31] See Le Jan, "Aux origines," p. 59, citing *Tur.* 14. Similarly, Depreux, in "Le dotation de l'épouse," 222, interprets the phrase *in die nuptialem et cupulationis nostre* in a dotal charter as a reference to sexual consummation; but *copulatio* is a generic term for union and need not specifically imply sexual intercourse.

became an *uxor* when the couple began to live together or even at the wedding. People *presumed* that sexual consummation would occur immediately thereafter, but that issue would surface only in cases of nonconsummation, when the presumption failed; and then the canonical and legal status of the marriage was ambiguous and troubling, as we see in some deliberations by Archbishop Hincmar of Reims in the ninth century: the partners seemed neither married nor unmarried.[32]

What I have outlined was the process presupposed by the Frankish dotal charters, but it was not peculiarly Frankish. Pope Nicholas I, to whom Hincmar appealed for counsel and final decisions in several marriage cases, outlined much the same process in a famous rescript that he sent to Boris, the king or khan of Bulgaria, in AD 866.[33] A recent convert to Christianity, Boris was trying to decide whether his own people should be Catholic or Orthodox. Thus the Pope explained, among other things, how people got married in the West. As befits the Bishop of Rome, Nicholas speaks here with a strong "Roman accent," keeping closely to the terminology and tenets of Roman law, but the gift that he describes, as among the Franks, is a *dos ex marito*. One passage is worth quoting in full here, for the process depicted therein, at least in respect of its general outline, is probably very similar to that presupposed by the Carolingian dotal formulae:

after the betrothal [*sponsalia*] is celebrated (which is the promised compact of a future marriage,[34] and which is celebrated with the consent of both of those who are contracting the marriage and of those in whose power they are),[35] and after the *sponsus* betroths the *sponsa* to himself by putting on her finger a ring, the sign of fidelity, as an *arrha*, and [after] he has conferred upon her, in the presence of those invited by both sides, a dowry that is acceptable to both [sides] with a document stating the agreement – then, either soon afterwards or at an appropriate time (that is, lest they should presume to do such a thing before the time defined by law), both are brought to the nuptial compact. First, they are placed at the hand of the priest in a church of the Lord, with offerings that they should present to God. Then at last they receive the blessing and the celestial veil. This is in imitation of the Lord, who, having placed the first human beings in paradise, blessed them and said, "Increase and multiply," and so on [Gen.1:28]. And indeed we read that Tobias, before he knew his wife, prayed to God along with her [Tob. 8:4, 6–9]. . . . After this, they leave the church wearing crowns [*coronae*] on their

---

[32] On the consummation of marriage, especially as churchmen understood it, see Reynolds, *Marriage in the Western Church*, 328–61.

[33] On the interpretation of this letter, see Michael M. Sheehan, "The bishop of Rome to a barbarian King on the rituals of marriage," in Steven B. Bowman and Blanche E. Cody (eds.), *In iure veritas: Studies in Canon Law in Memory of Schafer Williams* (Cincinnati, 1991), 186–99; reprinted in Sheehan, *Marriage, Family, and Law in Medieval Europe*, 278–91.

[34] Compare *Dig.* 23.1.1.

[35] An echo of an opinion by the Roman jurist Paul regarding marriage (*nuptiae*), according to which a marriage is not valid "unless all give their consent, that is, those who come together and those in whose power they are" (*Dig.* 23.2.2). Compare *Dig.* 23.1.7.1 and 23.1.11, which state that the consents required for betrothal (*sponsalia*) are the same as those for marriage.

heads. It is customary always to keep these in the church. And thus, after the nuptials have been celebrated, they are directed [by the priest] to lead henceforth an undivided life[36] with God's help.[37]

Nicholas's reference to Tobias is notable here because allusions to the story appear later in some dotal charters in the Frankish tradition.[38] Prayers for nuptial blessing from the Book of Tobit influenced the early nuptial liturgies.[39] It is significant that the story both confirms the goodness of marriage and teaches restraint, for Tobias and Sarah prayed for three nights instead of consummating their marriage. Thus clergy sometimes encouraged newlyweds to observe the "Tobias nights," by abstaining from coitus during the first night or first three nights of marriage.[40] The origins of the custom are obscure, but the earliest unequivocal references to it date from the Carolingian period. The custom is usually seen today as morbidly puritanical, but in circumstances that were common in the early Middle Ages (e.g., child brides, virilocal marriage), it would have been charitable.

Dotation is the only stage in Nicholas's account that he says is recorded in writing. Likewise, there are no formulae in Zeumer's collection for the recording either of betrothals or of nuptials (or for that matter of direct dowries or of widow's portions), although there are formulae for the dissolution of a marriage by mutual consent.[41] It seems that dotal charters would have provided the only documentary evidence of marriage. Perhaps this was why churchmen often cited the maxim, "There can be no marriage without a dowry [*dos*]."[42]

---

[36] An echo of Modestinus's famous definition of marriage, stated in Justinian's *Institutes*, 1.9.1: "Marriage or matrimony is the union of a man and a woman comprising an undivided way of life."

[37] Nicholas I, *Epist.* 99 (*Responsa ad consulta Bulgarorum*), c. 3, in MGH *Epist.* 6, *Epistolae Karolini Aevi* 4 (1925), p. 570.

[38] There are allusions to Tobit in Doc. 14 appended to this chapter, and in Charters 1 and 3 appended to Chapter 5.

[39] See under "Tobie (bénédiction de)" in the index to Jean-Baptiste Molin and Protais Mutembe, *Le rituel du mariage en France du XIIe au XVIe siècle*, Théologie historique 26 (Paris, 1974), 345. On the three nuptial blessings in Tobit and their influence, see Reynolds, *Marriage in the Western Church*, 371–75.

[40] See Jean-Baptiste Molin, "Symboles, rites et textes du mariage du moyen âge latin," in Giustino Farnedi (ed.), *La celebrazione cristiana del matrimonio*, = *Studia Anselmiana* 93, = Analecta liturgica 11 (Rome, 1986), 107–27, at 123–24; Ritzer, *Le mariage* (n. 30 earlier), 281–82; Henry G. J. Beck, *Pastoral Care of Souls in South-East France during the Sixth Century*, Analecta Gregoriana 51 (Rome, 1950), 232–33; Reynolds, *Marriage in the Western Church*, 334, 336–37, 374, 391.

[41] *And.* 57 (p. 24), *Marc.* II 30 (94), *Tur.* 19 (145–46), and *Merk.* 18 (248). These provide for dissolution in the full sense (with the possibility of remarriage), rather than for legal separation (*divortium a mensa et thoro*) or annulment (declaration that an apparent marriage is invalid and nonexistent). For an English translation of *And.* 57, see Francis A. Laine, *The Angevin Formulae: A Translation with Linguistic Commentary, A Summary of a Thesis* (Nashville, 1951), 19–20. There is a partial translation of *Marc.* II 30 in Philip L. Reynolds, "Marriage, sacramental and indissoluble: Sources of the Catholic doctrine," *Downside Review* 109 (1991): 105–50, at 146.

[42] See André Lemaire, "Origine de la règle *Nullum sine dote fiat coniugium*," in *Mélanges Paul Fournier* (Paris, 1929), 415–24; idem, "La *dotatio* de l'épouse" (n. 14 earlier); and Patrick Corbet, "Le douaire dans le droit canonique jusqu'à Gratien," in Bougard, Feller, and Le Jan, *Dots et Douaires* (n. 6 earlier), 43–55.

Yet one should not presume that every Christian wife in the early Middle Ages had a written dowry, or any dowry at all. Pope Nicholas goes on to say that in contrast with Eastern practice, there is no sin if any of the formalities are omitted, for formal marriages are expensive, and many cannot afford them: only the acts of agreement (*consensus*) are strictly necessary.[43] Even nuptial blessing by a priest was never a necessary condition for a canonically valid marriage in the medieval West, as it was in the East.[44] The Pope's perspective was no doubt an ecclesiastical or canonical one, but he seems to have gone out of his way to include in his account of western practice the customs of ordinary people of modest means.

How, then, should one interpret the maxim that there is no marriage without a dowry? Perhaps a small or merely symbolic gift would have sufficed, without any written record. Or perhaps dotation was a necessary condition for validity only within the context of certain presumptions: that among persons of a certain elite class, written dotation and the other formalities were obligatory and perhaps were what distinguished legitimate marriage from concubinage, mere cohabitation, or a love affair. But that is a weak thesis because of the presumptions surrounding it. Brides from the elite class marrying honorably would always have had dowries. Contrariwise, we do not know how early medieval people would have regarded a marriage between persons of wealth and comparable status if there was no dowry. Ancient Germanic traditions had permitted a man subsequently to legitimize a relationship following an elopement (a legitimization that was strictly prohibited under Roman law), or even following forcible abduction, by providing an indirect dowry or compensation or both. But that custom was designed as much to resolve conflict, obviate vendettas, and restore honor as it was to bring about matrimonial legitimacy per se.[45]

Most of the dotal formulae in Zeumer's collection define very large gifts, often including homesteads or extensive tracts of land with everything situated upon them. One should expect standard, stereotypical lists to be inclusive, so that items could be left in or omitted according to circumstances (much as today we strike items from pro forma contracts). And perhaps it seemed fitting to use a grand dotal formula as an exemplar even for more modest charters. But even so, it looks as though it was mainly persons of substance who used dotal charters. It is likely that

---

[43] *Epist.* 99, p. 570, lines 16–21.

[44] See Reynolds, *Marriage in the Western Church*, 401–12; Cyrille Vogel, "Les rites de la célébration du mariage: Leur signification dans la formation du lien durant le haut Moyen Âge," in *Il matrimonio nella società altomedievale*, Centro italiano di studi sull'alto Medioevo (Spoleto, 1977), vol. 1, 397–465; and Eve Levin, *Sex and Society in the World of the Orthodox Slavs, 900–1700* (Ithaca, 1989), 83–88.

[45] See Reynolds, *Marriage in the Western Church*, 101–08. The *raptus* of Roman law was really elopement (i.e., a man's running off with a girl without her parents' consent), for the girl's own consent only made her complicit in the crime and did not mitigate *his* guilt. Germanic law, on the contrary, generally distinguished between elopement (when the girl consented) and abduction (when she did not), and it treated abduction as far worse, although one could remedy any injury by sufficient compensation under Germanic legal traditions.

written dowries, therefore, were a normal part of the nuptial process not universally, but only among wealthy, landed families. (The same was probably true of church weddings and nuptial blessings.) It is very likely that among such families, written dotation was an expected stage in the nuptial process leading from betrothal to marriage, but it is not clear that the absence of a dowry, written or otherwise, would ever have formally invalidated a marriage in the judgment of clergy or episcopal courts.

THE PRINCIPAL PARTS

It is convenient to distinguish four principal parts of the typical dotal charter or formula in this tradition: the preamble, the exposition, the disposition, and the penalty clause.[46] (I have indicated these divisions in the translations appended later.) The essential parts are the exposition and disposition, and neither the preamble nor the penalty clause is always present. The diplomatic form of dotal formulae is closely akin to that of other gifts between spouses, such as the *interdonatio* whereby a childless husband and wife left their entire estates to each other.[47] Indeed, the form of a father's cession or bequest to a son is very similar.[48]

The typical form of a dotal charter, then, is as follows. In the *exposition* (which includes the functions of intitulation, address, and narrative), the *sponsus* identifies himself and his *sponsa* by name (and sometimes by the names of their parents as well), addressing his *sponsa* and recalling that he has already betrothed her before witnesses with the consent of their parents and kinsfolk. Some expression of his great affection for the *sponsa* is customary either here or at the beginning of the disposition.

The *disposition* (the heart of any charter) begins when the *sponsus* says that he wills to give the following items to his *sponsa* as her dowry (although the beginning of the disposition is not always distinguishable from the exposition). Next, he itemizes the gift. Finally, concluding the disposition, he confirms the gift and states when she will get the dowry, what are the terms or conditions under which she will possess it, and what will happen to it when she dies. Notwithstanding a prevalent assumption among scholars that wives had only the usufruct of a husband's marriage gift, some formulae grant the wife unrestricted power over the dowry,

---

[46] My terminology is tolerably consistent with that proposed by the Commission Internationale de Diplomatique – see Milagros Cárcel Ortí (ed.), *Vocabulaire international de la diplomatique* (València, 1997), 53–68 – but the Commission's nomenclature does not cover the peculiarities of dotal charters. What English-speaking scholars call the intitulation of a charter and French scholars call the *suscription* ("superscription") is the self-identifying statement of the subject, usually in the form "I, So-and-So".

[47] Compare *Marc.* I 12 (pp. 50–51), *Marc.* II 7 (79–80), *Tur.* 17 (144–45), *Merk.* 16 (247), and *Lind.* 13 (275–76). See also *Aug.* B 1 (347–48) and *Aug.* B 2 (348–49), which are similar, although the couple gives their property to a monastery or church.

[48] Compare *And.* 58 (pp. 24–25), *Arv.* 6 (31), *Tur.* 4 (137–38), *Sen.* 23 (195), *Big.* 10 (231–32), and *Big.* 12 (232).

allowing her to do with it whatever she wills.[49] This would have left a widow free to give it to a church or a monastery, or to take it with her as a monastic dowry if she herself became a nun after her husband's death. But it is not clear whether a wife ever had control over her estate in fact while her husband lived, or whether on the contrary he managed it but was supposed to maintain the principal as her trust fund. (Nothing in the dotal charters would settle this point.) Some formulae say that she is to have and to hold the estate as long as she lives but that it will then revert to her husband or (if he has not survived) pass to their children: this probably implies that she enjoys only the usufruct.[50] A few formulae state explicitly that she is to have the usufruct of the property.[51] In such cases, the dowry estate would remain part of her husband's patrimony.

Next, as further confirmation of the dotation, there may be a penalty clause. Such clauses seem to be directed rather against legal contesting of some sort than against simple delinquency, trespass, or misappropriation. They remind us that it was entirely possible for two or more parties to have some legal claim (even a legitimate claim) to the same property. The clause prohibits anyone (including the *sponsus*) from making an action against the dotation or contesting or undoing it. (Here the *sponsus* often adds parenthetically that he can hardly imagine that such a thing would happen.) And the clause imposes a sanction: the "opposed" person will be subject to a specified fine (ranging from a few ounces of gold to the current value of the entire estate or even multiples thereof). Penalty clauses in grand charters (such as for the foundation of a monastery) sometimes include curses, and there is the hint of one in *Extr.* I 12 (Doc. 14): anyone who contests the wife's possession will suffer the wrath of him who instituted marriage. The penalty clause often concludes by saying that the dowry will nevertheless stand firm, a statement that functions both as the conclusion of the penalty clause and as final confirmation of the act as a whole.

Some other standard items appear occasionally. For our purposes, the most interesting is the preamble, which may say something about legitimacy and the need for dotation to be written down (in secular charters), or about the goodness of marriage and its place in God's plan (in sacred charters).[52] Before that, there might

---

[49] *And.* 1c (Doc. 1), *And.* 34 (Doc. 2), *Sen.* 25 (Doc. 7), *Merk.* 15 (Doc. 9), *Lind.* 7 (p. 272), *Extr.* I 12 (Doc. 14).

[50] *And.* 54 (p. 23), *Tur.* 14 (Doc. 4), *Sang.* 18 (p. 388), *C. Sang.* 18 (p. 407). On full possession vs. usufruct of dowries, see Le Jan, "Aux origines" (n. 19 earlier), 61–66.

[51] *And.* 40 (p. 18, line 1); *Aug.* B 24 and 25 (p. 358, lines 4 and 21–22). *And.* B 24 explicitly states that the dotation is done under Alamannian law, and the same probably applies to *And.* B 25 as well.

[52] On the composition and evolution of preambles, see Michel Parisse, "Préambles de chartes," in Jacqueline Hammesse (ed.), *Les prologues médiévaux: Actes du colloque international organisé par l'Academia Belgica et l'École Française de Rome avec le concours de la F.I.D.E.M. (Rome, 26–28 mars 1988)*, Textes et études du moyen âge 15 (Turnhout, 2000), 141–69. See also Michel Parisse, "Arenga et pouvoir royal en France du Xᵉ au XIIᵉ siècle," in Jürgen Petersohn (ed.), *Mediaevalia Augiensia: Forschungen zur Geschichte des Mittelalters*, Vorträge und Forschungen, Bd. 54 (Stüttgart, 2001), 12–27.

be an invocation. Only one of the dotal formulae in Zeumer's collection begins with an invocation strictly so called, namely, *Extr.* I 11 (Doc. 13), which begins by invoking the Trinity. Yet most of the sacred charters name God at the beginning of the preamble (albeit in the nominative, not the vocative case), producing a similar effect. Before the disposition (either in the preamble or in the exposition), to emphasize the happiness of the occasion, there may be what I have called an exultation: a stereotypical statement about how good marriage is, or how good a thing it is that these two persons are getting married. At the end, there may be a subscription, with signatures or spaces for them.

And. 1 c (Doc. 1), based on a sixth-century Angevin charter, is a good and very old example of the basic type, without a preamble, but including a penalty clause (with a final confirmation). The gift includes a homestead with its land and everything upon it, domestic animals, and personal movables such as jewelry and a bedspread. (Compare *Sen.* 25 [Doc. 7], where the marriage gift includes several bedspreads. Some scholars regard the bedspread as a symbol of marital union, but it may have been customarily included in marriage gifts rather because it was especially valuable.) The penalty in *And.* 1 c is huge (according to interpretation, either three or four times the value of the entire estate). *And.* 34 (Doc. 2), from the same era, has the same form but is briefer and confers a more modest gift on the *sponsa*. The only item mentioned here as her dowry is a house (*casa*), and the penalty for contesting the deed is merely *so many* solidi.

Tur. 14 (Doc. 4), a secular formula probably from the mid-eighth century, is exemplary. Its wording is unusually clear and precise; it has all the principal parts, including a secular preamble and a penalty clause; its preamble notes the importance of *written* dotation; and it situates the act of dotation clearly in relation both to the previous betrothal and to the forthcoming marriage, when the wife will at last receive as her dowry the usufruct of the estate. This is probably the most frequently cited formula in scholarly literature on early medieval dotation. Would that they all presented so clear a picture!

THE TIMING OF DOTATION

As I noted earlier, dotation occurred functionally *in medias res*, between the betrothal and the marriage. But the timing of the act of dotation in relation to the marriage is not always clear. Nor is it always clear when the woman would receive the estate. Crucial in this regard is the interpretation of certain stereotypical time references, in which the *sponsus* says either when he gives the dowry to his partner or when she comes into possession. These occur mainly in the confirmation (i.e., the conclusion of the disposition), but also in the exposition. Phrases such as "from the present day" and "before the wedding day" occur frequently. (The phrase *ante dies nuptiarum* is reminiscent of the terminology of antenuptial gifts in Roman law.) We do not know enough about the customary use of such charters to interpret these time references securely. Such phrases may have mattered little in practice, being little more than archaic verbal ornaments. Circumstances and customary expectations would have been more decisive.

Among the formulae that include specific time references, some simply state that the woman will get the dowry on the occasion of their future marriage.[53] When the *sponsus* says that he gives or confers the dowry "on the present day" or "from the present day," this may mean only that the act of *dotation* occurs now, although the recipient will not actually come into possession until the future, when the two marry. Such is probably the sense of *Extr.* 1 10,[54] in which the *sponsus* begins the disposition by saying, "Accordingly it has pleased me before the day of the marriage from the present day [*ante diem nuptiarum a die praesente*] that I should bestow upon her something from my own estate." It is clearly the case in *Tur.* 14 (Doc. 4), in which the *sponsus* recalls in the exposition that his intention has been to confer a dowry "before the wedding day" (*ante dies nuptiarum*) but states in the confirmation that the *sponsa* will come into possession in the future, when they marry.[55] Some formulae state that he has promised (or now promises) to give a dowry *before* the wedding day, and that he therefore gives it to her now, from *this* day.[56] Perhaps here, too, only the act of dotation occurs at once. But some state that the woman will actually receive the estate or have power over it "before the wedding day"[57] or "from the present day."[58] In some others, the time references are muddled and ambiguous.[59]

In the absence of clear documentary evidence, one may be permitted to speculate. In principle, the Frankish dowry was the last condition to be fulfilled before the partners were ready for marriage. (Contrary to some scholars, I assume that it was more akin to the Roman *donatio ante nuptias* than to a morning gift.) Insofar as a dowry consisted in moveable goods such as cash, jewelry, or clothing, therefore, its actual conferral might have occurred shortly before a wedding or as part of the ceremonies. But insofar as it consisted in entitlements of ownership or usufruct, the marriage itself would have been the point at which a woman came into possession of what had been promised at the betrothal or in the dotal instrument, so that, in fact, the relation was reversed: marriage was the precondition for actual possession of the dowry, and not vice versa. Indeed, possession in fact might not have come until the husband died.

---

[53] *Big.* 6 (p. 230), *Merk.* 15 (Doc. 9), *Lind.* 7 (p. 272), *Sang.* 16 (p. 387).
[54] Zeumer, *Formulae*, p. 539.
[55] This is probably the sense of *And.* 40 (pp. 17–18)
[56] *Tur.* 15 (p. 143), *Tur.* app. 2 (164), *Tur.* app. 3 (164).
[57] *Marc.* II.15 (p. 85, lines 5–6, 12).
[58] *Aug.* B 25 (p. 358, lines 20–21).
[59] *Bit.* 15 (p. 175), *Sen.* 25 (196).

DOWRY CHARTERS AT WEDDINGS

Later dotal charters and formulae seem to have been intended for use at weddings.[60] This impression is consistent with what is known about the evolution of the nuptial liturgy during the period, for by the late eleventh century, weddings in northern France and England began with a rite at the entry to the church that included the blessing of a ring and the conferring of the agreed *dos* and other gifts.[61] Rubrics sometimes mention the transfer or blessing of dowries or other assigns at this stage, but if the gift was substantial, the transaction must have involved the reading or signing of a charter rather than a transfer of actual property. Some rubrics use terms that imply or explicitly denote use of a dotal charter.[62] The appearance of dotation in the preliminary nuptial ritual may be construed as a liturgical incorporation of elements of the betrothal into the wedding, but it was above all the result of the practice of clerical interrogations, whereby a priest had to ascertain whether all the proper requirements, conditions, and preliminaries for marriage had been met before proceeding. The coalescence of dotation and weddings may indeed have occurred during a much earlier period. An actual dotal charter from northern Aquitaine ca. 975 retains the general form noted previously, whereby the dotal agreement is situated between betrothal and marriage. The *sponsus*, Alcher, recalls that the betrothal has already taken place and that he willed then to give her a dowry on their wedding day (*in dies nuptiarum*). But having itemized the gift, he confirms that he gives it to her today (*ad diem praesentem*).[63] In that case, there may be an ambiguity regarding the *giving* of a dowry: perhaps it was given on the present day as regards the act of dotation, and would be given on the wedding day (still in the future) as regards actual possession (a pattern that we have seen in earlier formulae). Be that as it may, a late–eleventh-century dotal charter from this region (dated 1083) is virtually a contract of marriage with present intent, and the *sponsus* invokes the name of God. The disposition begins thus: "Accordingly, I

---

[60] See Laurent Morelle, "Mariage et diplomatique," 233 (or see Chapter 5 here, 173). Morelle suggests that the four sacred charters that he discusses were intended to be read at the entrance of the church prior to the nuptials, and that the secular charter (no. 5) was for an already-married couple.

[61] See Molin and Mutembe, *Le rituel du mariage* (n. 39 earlier), 32, 34, 35–37, and 80; Sheehan, "Choice of marriage partner in the Middle Ages" (n. 30 earlier), 111–12; and Christopher N. L. Brooke, *The Medieval Idea of Marriage* (Oxford, 1989), 248–57.

[62] See section C in the following twelfth-century rituals quoted by Molin and Mutembe, *Le rituel du mariage*: Ordo II, from Rennes, p. 285 (*dotalitium*); Ordo III, from Évreux(?), p. 286 (*recapitulatio de dote mulieris*); Ordo IV, from Avranches, p. 288 ("Primo legitur dotalium"); Ordo V, from Bury St. Edmunds, p. 289 ("tunc proferantur dos et alia dona, sicut inter illos ante pactum fuerit, et dentur mulieri"). Compare Ordo VII, from Albi, p. 293 ("sacerdos, lecta carta sponsalicii, benedicat arras").

[63] See Depreux, "La dotation de l'épouse," 241 (for the charter), and 221–22 (for Depreux's commentary).

Alberic, my dearest Audeburgis, in the name of almighty God, join you to myself as my wife [*uxor*], and I give to you a dowry" (the details of which follow).[64] The statement certainly sounds like part of a liturgy.

I suggest that *Extr.* I 11–15 (Docs. 13–17) in Zeumer's collection were intended for use at weddings too, for here the *sponsus* bestows the dowry at once, and any references to the marriage as still forthcoming seem perfunctory and merely conventional. This interpretation would explain in part why the sacred preambles in most of the *Extravagantes* are especially developed, and why they have a liturgical cadence. *Extr.* I 13–15 appear in effect to be wedding contracts. *Extr.* I 13 (Doc. 15) concludes with a prayer that the woman should serve her partner dutifully: he is still called her *sponsus*, but she could hardly serve him dutifully until they were married. In *Extr.* I 14 (Doc. 16), the *sponsus* expresses his will to take the *sponsa* in marriage (*in matrimonium ... ducere*). In *Extr.* I 15 (Doc. 17), he says that he wills to have her as his wife (*in uxorem habere*) and therefore confers the dowry. The reading and signing of such charters, therefore, may have been a prelude to a church wedding, perhaps done at the entrance to the church or in the porch. Perhaps a cleric read the charter, but it seems likely that the *sponsus* himself (the notional speaker of the act in any case) either read out the charter or at least repeated parts of it, for who else would have said, "I, *So-and-So*"?

Laurent Morelle tentatively suggests that northern-French dotal charters, having formerly been read at the entrance to a church as part of the nuptials, lost their "nuptial" character in the later twelfth century, becoming purely "juridical" again (i.e., concerned only with property).[65] Theological commentary had no place in such charters, although it is likely that in northern France, these charters, too, were composed by clerics from cathedral chancelleries, and not by secular lawyers or notaries.

Secular Preambles

Five of the formulae have purely secular preambles: *And.* 54, *Marc.* II 15, *Tur.* 14 (Doc. 3), *Tur.* app. 2, and *Sang.* 12. In the brief preamble to *Sang.* 12, the *sponsa*'s father (who states the agreement on behalf of the *sponsus*) remarks that the purpose of marriage is to maintain the race of mortal human beings.[66] The other secular preambles say something about the status of marriage and dotation in law, or about the need for dowries to be written down.

Thus the preamble to *And.* 54 states that in accordance with both the law of happiness (*lex felicitatis*) and Roman law, and because the custom of the district

---

[64] Ibid., p. 243.

[65] Morelle, "Mariage et diplomatique," 234 (later in this volume, 174).

[66] Compare Justinian, *Novel* 22, pr.; and Plato, *Symposium* 206e–207d.

(*pagus*) agrees with this, and given that royal jurisdiction (*principalis potestas*) does not prohibit it, the *sponsus* is going to transfer the items listed below to his betrothed on their wedding day. The high-sounding but untranslatable preamble to *Marc.* II 15 begins with echoes of phrases from the Roman law of marriage,[67] adding that a dowry must be stated in writing if it is to stand firm. The preamble to *Tur.* 14 (Doc. 4) is similar: "Law and custom demand that whatever has been promised or bestowed between *sponsus* and *sponsa* for their forthcoming marriage, whether by the consent of their parents or their own if they are independent, should be solemnly confirmed in writing." This statement is a variant of a passage from the *Theodosian Code*, but taken out of context. (The original passage regards the *sponsa*'s right to keep her antenuptial gift if the *sponsus* voluntarily breaches his promise to marry her, but only if the gift has been properly recorded in writing.)[68] The preamble to *Tur.* app. 2 covers the same ground as that of *Tur.* 14, explicitly appealing to the authority of the *Theodosian Code.*[69]

SACRED PREAMBLES

The sacred preambles among Zeumer's dotal formulae fall naturally into two sorts, respectively, rudimentary and elaborate. The rudimentary group includes *Bit.* 15, *Sen.* 25, *Big.* 6, *Merk.* 15, and *Sang.* 16. The preamble to *Extr.* I 14 (Doc. 16) is rudimentary too, although, in some respects, it is akin to the more developed formulae. The elaborate preambles all belong to *Extravagantes*, namely, *Extr.* I 9, 11, 12, 13, and 15.

The dating of these formulae is problematic, especially the *Extravagantes*. There are no internal references to datable events. The dating of the manuscript, if reliable, would tell us when the *copy* was made, but that would be only the *latest* possible date for the original charter. But in regard to the *Extravagantes*, some of these supposedly latest dates seem much too early. *Extr.* I 13 (*Summus et ineffabilis pater*, Doc. 15), the dotal formula with the most elaborate preamble, is a case in point. It is

---

[67] P. 85, lines 1–2: "De disponsandis maritandisque ordinibus hac procreatione liberorum causis. . . ." These words, while virtually meaningless in context, are derived from *Lex Iulia de maritandis ordinibus* (the Augustan legislation of 18 BC regulating marriages between different social orders) and the *Lex Papia Poppaea* (the amendment of AD 9 that introduced incentives for begetting children; the two laws merged in subsequent legislation). The epithet *liberorum procreandorum causa* ("for the sake of begetting legitimate children"), or one of its variants, was included in Roman *tabulae nuptiales* (dotal instruments), in which it distinguished marriage from concubinage (wherein a man's offspring did not count as his own children): see Reynolds, *Marriage in the Western Church*, 17 and 303–04, as well as David Hunter's chapter in this volume.

[68] *Cod. Theod.* III.5.2, interpr.

[69] Zeumer, *Formulae*, p. 163, lines 26–27: "sicut in Theodosiano codice 'de sponsalibus et ante nuptias donationibus' narrat auctoritas. . . ." The phrase is from the title to *Cod. Theod.* III.5.

extant in a codex held in Leiden.[70] Zeumer's date for the hand in which it is written is late tenth century.[71] Karel Adriaan de Meyier, in his authoritative catalogue of the Leiden collection (published in the 1970s), says that the hand is from the ninth century.[72] But so early a date is hardly credible. The eleventh century seems more probable.

I am not qualified to say anything about the material dating of the manuscripts themselves, but the results of a study by Michel Parisse corroborate the later date. Parisse surveys the preambles to several hundred royal *acta* spanning the period from the reign of Charles III the Simple (898–922) to the reign of Louis VI the Fat (1108–1137). At first, a brief preamble of some three lines is typical. Then around 1020 or 1030, the preambles become longer and more elaborate, with more references to the church and the Christian faith and more citations from Scripture. But they diminish sharply again in the early twelfth century, around 1110.[73] On that basis, one might hazard that while the rudimentary sacred preambles in Zeumer's collection date from the ninth century (or perhaps from as late as the tenth), the elaborate ones date from the eleventh century.

The Rudimentary Sacred Preambles

These preambles are composed mainly of scriptural references in the form both of quotations (often rather free) and of allusions to well-known biblical episodes. Most of the quotations and allusions pertain in one way or another to the origin of marriage in the beginning, when God created the first human beings. Only *Sen.* 25 (Doc. 7) uses a scriptural passage that is not linked to the origin of marriage, namely, the Wedding at Cana (John 2:1–11), at which Jesus confirmed the sanctity of marriage by his presence and by turning water into wine. (The wedding at Cana with its moral will become a topos in later dotal charters and marriage sermons.)

Three of these preambles – *Bit.* 15 (Doc. 6), *Big.* 6 (Doc. 8), and *Merk.* 15 (Doc. 9) – cite the dictum, "For this reason a man shall leave his father and mother and cleave unto this wife, and they shall be two in one flesh." The dictum links the story of Eve's formation (Gen. 2:7–24) to Jesus's counsel against divorce (Matt. 19:4–9, Mark 10:5–12), for it occurs not only when God gives Eve to Adam as his wife and helpmeet (Gen. 2:24), but also in the New Testament, when Jesus cites the text as evidence of the permanence of marriage in the beginning (Matt. 19:5 and Mark 10:7–9).[74] Both *Big.* 6 (Doc. 8) and *Sen.* 25 (Doc. 7) cite the moral that Jesus himself

---

[70] Universitatsbibliothek, Vossianus latinus, fol. 70, 81 v.

[71] Zeumer, *Formulae*, p. 541.

[72] K. A. de Meyier, *Codices Vossiani Latini*, Part 1: *Codices in Folio* (Leiden, 1973), 144.

[73] Michel Parisse, "Arenga et pouvoir royal en France" (n. 52 earlier), especially 14 and 24–25.

[74] There are minor variations among these texts in the Vulgate: Gen. 2:24: "Quam ob rem relinquet homo patrem suum et matrem et adherebit uxori suae et erunt duo in carne una." Matt. 19:5: "Propter hoc dimittet homo patrem et matrem et adherebit uxori suae et erunt duo in carne una." Mark 10:7–8: "Propter hoc relinquet homo patrem suum et matrem et et adherebit ad uxorem suam

draws from the story of Eve's formation: "What God has joined, man should not separate" (Matt. 19:6, Mark. 10:9). Yet Genesis 2:24 seems to stand in the early dotal formulae rather for union per se than for indissolubility. Hence it is the core of the preamble to *Marc.* I 12 (Doc. 3), an *interdonatio* that a childless couple enacted in the presence of the king, whereby they bequeathed their respective estates to each other. The point of the text here is to show that it quite proper for husband and wife, having in some sense left their respective parental families to be united with each other, to be entirely devoted to each other. (That there was a need for some justifying rationale implies that dowries were supposed to be the means by which wealth passed from grandparents to grandchildren.)

Bit. 15 (Doc. 6), as well as citing Genesis 2:24, refers to Adam's need of a woman as his helpmeet (Gen. 2:18, 20). *Sang.* 16 (Doc. 11), which is unusual in its choice of texts, quotes Scripture as saying, "A wife will be prepared for the man by the Lord." This dictum is from the Old Latin version of Proverbs 19:4, although it conveys a message implicit in the narrative of Eve's formation. *Bit.* 15 refers also to the benediction in Genesis 1:28, when God blessed the first man and woman and said, "Increase and multiply." *Sang.* 16 conveys the same message with a dictum that seems to be Leviticus 26:9 conflated with Genesis 1:28 (or Gen. 9:1): "Increase and multiply, and I shall establish my covenant with you."

These preambles do not draw out the moral of the biblical references, and there is no pastoral discourse. The preamble to *Bit.* 15 (Doc. 6) affirms that persons should not marry incestuously or illicitly, but instead of deriving this moral from Scripture, it attributes it to the Holy Spirit speaking through the "sacred emperors," an allusion to *Codex Theodosianus* III.12. The impression that springs naturally from these biblical citations, which are presented without any pastoral or legal explication, is that marriage is a union whereby two persons, from different families, become a single social unit; that God instituted marriage at the dawn of creation; that Jesus reconfirmed it; and that legitimate monogamy is the proper means of procreation. The forthcoming marriage of two present-day individuals is universalized by being linked immediately to the primordial marriage of Adam and Eve, which God ordained when the world began. As long as one marries legitimately and with honorable intentions, one fulfills God's original plan.

At least as important as the choice of biblical texts is the rhetorical trajectory of most of these preambles. *Sang.* 16 (Doc. 11) is exceptional, but the others – *Bit.* 15 (Doc. 4), *Sen.* 25 (Doc. 7), *Big.* 6 (Doc. 8), and *Merk.* 15 (Doc. 9) – begin at the beginning, recounting how God instituted marriage and putting the name of God close to the start of the preamble, simulating an invocation. Moreover, two of these preambles refer to God as the creator: he is the "almighty God, creator of heaven

---

et erunt duo in carne una." The dotal formulae quote Scripture rather freely in any case, but they seem to prefer the Genesis version of this passage, even when they attribute it to Jesus: see, for example, *Bit.* 15 (p. 174): "et Salvator intonuit: 'Quam ob rem relinquid homo patrem et matrem et adherebit uxore suae, et erunt dui in carne una'."

and earth," according to *Bit.* 15 (Doc. 6); and he is the "Lord almighty, creator of heaven and earth," according to *Merk.* 15 (Doc. 9). Hence the rhetorical shape of these early sacred charters is threefold: they begin with a quasi-invocation of God as the Lord, as the almighty, or as creator; then they commemorate the institution of marriage in the beginning (mainly by recounting the story of Adam and Eve), noting too that Jesus himself reconfirmed the institution of marriage; and at last they turn to the forthcoming marriage of the two present-day individuals whose names follow (in the intitulation that comes next).

This rhetorical shape is congruent with diplomatic norms, for charters often begin with an invocation and then state a narrative before getting to the disposition. The shape is also reminiscent of the creeds. But I tentatively suggest that the redactors borrowed the form from nuptial blessings performed by priests (probably in the course of a liturgy).

Was the tripartite structure a feature of liturgical nuptial blessings that were contemporaneous with our formulae, or at least with the origin of the traditions or norms for sacred preambles? Here the argument becomes somewhat tenuous. On the one hand, the dating of the formulae themselves is doubtful: at best, as noted previously, we know only the dates of the copies, not of the originals (although it is likely that these are Carolingian formulae, composed in the ninth century, or at least between the eighth and the tenth). On the other hand, the evidence of nuptial liturgies in France during the relevant periods is patchy. Yet it is clear that the tripartite structure discernable in the sacred preambles is a traditional feature of early nuptial liturgies.

The Talmudic nuptial benediction has the same general shape,[75] and one finds essentially the same tripartite form (invocation of almighty God as creator of all things; narrative of the primordial marriage; petition for blessings on the present marriage) in Tobias's prayer for God's blessing upon his marriage with Sarah, a petition that Sarah herself completes:

And Tobias said: Lord God of our fathers, may the heavens and the earth, and the sea, and the fountains, and the rivers, and all thy creatures that are in them, bless thee. Thou madest Adam of the slime of the earth, and gavest him Eve for a helper. And now, Lord, thou knowest that not for fleshly lust do I take my sister to wife, but only for the love of posterity, in which thy name may be blessed for ever and ever. Sara also said: Have mercy on us, O Lord, have mercy on us, and let us grow old both together in health. (Tob. 8:7–10)[76]

---

[75] For a translation of this benediction, see Gary Anderson, "Celibacy or consummation in the Garden? Reflections on early Jewish and Christian interpretations of the Garden of Eden," *Harvard Theological Review* 82 (1989): 121–48, at 132. Translations may also be found in the following: *The Authorized Daily Prayer-Book* (New York, 1946), 1013; Maimonides, *The Code of Maimonides, Book Four: The Book of Women*, translated by Isaac Klein (New Haven, 1972), 62; and Mark Searle and Kenneth W. Stevenson, *Documents of the Marriage Liturgy* (Collegeville, Minn., 1992), 27–28.

[76] Quoted from the Douay-Rheims version (Challoner revision). On the blessings in Tobit and their influence, see references in nn. 38–40 earlier.

An elaborated version of the same tripartite form is manifest in the nuptial prayer *Pater mundi conditor* ("Father, creator of the world"), which is included in the *Veronense* and the *Gelasian Sacramentary.*[77] Whereas the former is a collection of Roman mass booklets (*libelli*) from the fifth and sixth centuries, the *Gelasianum* is a Frankish sacramentary based on a Roman model and prepared in the mid-eighth century by the nuns of Chelles, near Paris. The *Pater mundi conditor* is a magnificent prayer, replete with theological reflection. The priest celebrating the marriage begins by invoking God as the Father, the creator of the world, and the source of all life. Next, he recounts how God made the first man, and how God made the first woman from the man, so that they were marvelously different: for while the man was made like God, the woman was made like the man. From that couple, all humankind would proceed, so that generation would succeed generation, all human beings would be kinsfolk, and the human race would continue indefinitely despite the brief span of mortal life. Finally, the priest asks God to sanctify the woman, as the weaker partner, so that she may be more concerned with remaining faithful to her marriage vows than with the license that marriage permits. There follows a sequence of petitions for the bride alone.[78]

A nuptial blessing with the same outline appears in the *Hadrianum*, the Gregorian-style sacramentary that Pope Adrian I gave to Charlemagne ca. 790, and which was the basis of Charlemagne's liturgical reforms.[79] Here the priest begins by addressing God "who by the power of your strength have made all things from nothing." He then recounts the creation of man in God's image, the formation of woman from the man's flesh as his helper, and their indissoluble union. Finally, after some theological reflections (very rare in the western liturgical tradition) on marriage as a blessed state that prefigured the mysterious union (*sacramentum*) between Christ and the Church, the priest offers a series of petitions for blessings upon the bride alone.

Few of the blessings and prayers in Molin and Mutembe's study of nuptial liturgies in France from the twelfth through sixteenth centuries have the same tripartite structure. Yet the structure is discernable in a marriage blessing (perhaps based on Raguel's blessing in Tob. 7:15) that occurs in the *Benedictional of Archbishop Robert* and in several other sources from the tenth through eleventh centuries:

---

[77] For the Latin text, see Ritzer, *Le mariage* (n. 30 earlier), 422–23 (section 6a). For the Gelasian rite, see ibid., 426 (section 8a), in which Ritzer simply refers back to the Verona text. See ibid., 239–41 for commentary on the prayer. For the prayer in the Gelasian rite, another source is *Liber sacramentorum Augustodunensis*, CCL 159B, 204. For an English translation of the prayer, see Searle and Stevenson, *Documents of the Marriage Liturgy*, 42–43 (section 6a). On the Leonine and Gelasian blessings and their structure, see Reynolds, *Marriage in the Western Church*, 375–79.

[78] In the Gelasian rite, a blessing over the couple (rather than over the bride alone, as in the Roman tradition) follows at this point: see Ritzer, *Le mariage*, 426, section 9: this may be a Gallican insertion.

[79] Ritzer, *Le mariage*, 427–28, sect. 6. For translation and commentary, see Reynolds, *Marriage in the Western Church*, 379–80.

Almighty and eternal God, who by his own power created our first parents, Adam and Eve, and sanctified them by his blessing, and joined them in holy association, may he sanctify your hearts, and join you in the association and affection of true love. Amen.[80]

There is no explicit mention of God as creator in this particular variant, but the creation of the universe is connoted by the word "almighty" (for Christians confess belief in "one God, the Father almighty, creator of heaven and earth").

How might one explain the similarly between the tripartite form of the sacred preambles and that of the aforementioned precedents, especially the *Pater mundi conditor*? Among several possible explanations, two seem to me to be the most probable. First, nuptial blessings, perhaps even from contemporaneous liturgies that are no longer extant, may have influenced the preambles. It is possible that the influence occurred in the Carolingian period and that the theme continued to occur in the preamble tradition more or less independently of the liturgy. Second, Tobias's prayer itself (Tob. 8:7–10) may have influenced both the liturgies and the preambles. Numerous echoes of the Book of Tobit find their way both into the nuptial liturgies and into the preambles of dotal charters, in part because the book provided proof texts both for the blessedness of marriage and for the practice of nuptial blessing. In any case, there seems to have been some association between the sacred preambles and the nuptial liturgy.

Be that as it may, there can be no doubt about the rhetorical force of the three-fold pattern, whereby a marriage of two present-day individuals is linked to the archetypal first marriage and thereby to the origin of the world. The *Extravagentes*, to which we now turn, take the same tripartite form and elaborate it, raising the preamble to extraordinary heights of theological and philosophical reflection.

The Elaborate Sacred Preambles

The Latin of the sacred preambles among the *Extravagantes* is high and ornate. Here, too, we find passages from Scripture regarding the original institution of marriage. But whereas the rudimentary sacred formulae leave the biblical texts to speak for themselves, these more developed examples explicate the message of the texts. Moreover, they are not limited to citation: they fill out the sacred-historical data, producing a continuous theological argument, and they add commentary and pastoral discourse, including counsel on sexual morality. The quasi-liturgical resonance, noted earlier, becomes even more apparent in the *Extravagantes*, and especially in *Extr.* I 13 (Doc. 15), which concludes with a prayer of petition for the bride and an Amen. Likewise, the *Fiat* with which *Extr.* I 14 (Doc. 16) concludes is another way of saying, "Amen."

---

[80] See Molin and Mutembe, *Le rituel du mariage* (n. 39 earlier), 323–24 (n. 23), 202 (d), 267 (c); Ritzer, *Le mariage*, 442 (VI.1) and 444 (9). Versification of the Book of Tobit is that of the Vulgate and Douai versions (which differs from that of modern versions such as the New Revised Standard Version).

The *Extravagantes* use the same dossier of citations as we found in the earlier preambles, but they amplify it. *Extr.* I 9 and 15 (Docs. 12 and 17) tell how God fashioned Adam from the dust of the ground (Gen. 2:7). *Extr.* I 9 also recalls Adam's need for a helpmeet (Gen. 2:18, 20). *Extr.* I 9, 12, 14, and 15 (Docs. 12, 14, 16, and 17) recount the formation of Eve from Adam's rib (Gen. 2:21–22). *Extr.* I 9 and 12 (Docs. 12 and 14) recall the benediction of Genesis 1:28, when God said, "Increase and multiply." Five of these six preambles (*Extr.* I 11–15, Docs. 13–17) cite some version of the text, "For this reason a man shall leave his father and mother and cleave unto his wife, and they shall be two in one flesh" (Gen. 2:24, Matt. 19:5, Mark. 10:7–9). *Extr.* I 11 (Doc. 13) recalls as well the lesson that Jesus draws from this dictum: "What God has joined, man should not separate" (Matt. 19:6, Mark 10:9). According to *Extr.* I 13 (Doc. 15), not only the account of Adam and Eve's marriage in Genesis but also numerous other passages in the Old and New Testaments, which are too obvious to need citing, show that marriage is indissoluble.

These preambles emphasize the goodness of marriage. *Extr.* I 12 (Doc. 14) recalls how an angel blessed Tobias's marriage (cf. Tob. 9:8–12). *Extr.* I 12, 13, and 15 (Docs. 14, 15, and 17) tell of the Wedding at Cana (John 2:1–11), when Jesus confirmed the blessedness of marriage both by his physical presence and by performing there the first of his "signs," or miracles (John 2:11). They draw out the moral of that narrative, rebutting any heretical contempt for marriage, as among encratite sects. According to *Extr.* I 13, the episode shows that "legitimate marriage is a sacred compact and not a crime."[81]

The *Extravagantes* also warn that marriage is good and blessed only insofar as one enters into it legitimately and intending to generate children rather than to satisfy sexual desire. According to *Extr.* I 11 (Doc. 13), Scripture teaches us how good a thing is legitimate marriage. According to *Extr.* I 15 (Doc. 17), one should marry "in the hope of offspring, not motivated by lust." The expositions in *Extr.* I 13 and 15 (Docs. 14 and 16) characterize the proper motive for marriage as love for the procreation of children: the use of the term "love" (*amor*) sharpens the contrast between a promiscuous, merely carnal motive for marriage, and a responsible, decent, properly Christian motive. Such admonitions echo Tobias's prayer, "Lord, thou knowest that not for fleshly lust do I take my sister to wife, but only for the love of posterity, in which thy name may be blessed for ever and ever" (Tob. 8:9). They echo too Isidore of Seville's counsel that as regards the choice of a good partner and the formation of a good marriage, people should marry to have children and not out of lust (*libido*), because marriage was instituted not to satisfy carnal desire

---

[81] This way of construing the marriage at Cana (as an affirmation that marriage is no sin) is a topos in thirteenth-century marriage sermons. For examples, see David d'Avray, *Medieval Marriage Sermons* (Oxford, 2001), 132–33 (nos. 10–11), 211, 249, and 301. Gérard de Mailly, O.P. (ibid., 249) and Hughes de Saint-Cher, O.P. (132, no. 10) explicitly direct the interpretation against heretics (perhaps with the Cathars in mind).

but for procreation, and the dotal tablets themselves proclaim that a man takes a wife "for the sake of procreating children."[82]

St. Paul's pastoral discourse on marriage appears here, too. *Extr.* I 15 affirms that marriage is good because it is a way to avoid fornication, citing 1 Corinthians 7:2: "Let each one have own wife because of fornication." (*Sen.* 25, *Doc.* 7, alluded to this text, too, but only to affirm monogamy.) *Extr.* I 9 (*Doc.* 12) cites Ephesians 2:25: "Husbands, love your wives, as Christ also loved the Church." Then, citing 1 Corinthians 7:4, this preamble speaks of the conjugal debt.

Extr. I 15 (*Doc.* 17) takes up the vexed issue of clandestine marriage: when a man takes a wife, they should perform all the proper formalities, including the written dowry. They should not marry secretly, as do the Gentiles, who know nothing of God. This passage implies that the written dowry is integral to the publicity of a formally established marriage, and it construes publicity as a distinguishing feature of the *Christian* way of marriage.

The authors of these formulae connect their thoughts into a continuous theological narrative that begins with almighty God and proceeds through creation and the institution of the first marriage to arrive at *this* marriage. (We have already noted this quasi-liturgical trajectory in the earlier, less elaborate preambles.) *Extr.* I 13 (*Doc.* 15) and 15 (*Doc.* 17) weave the creation and fall of the angels in this narrative, reasoning (as *Extr.* I 15 explains) that God created human beings to take the place of the fallen angels.[83] That doctrine not only explains why God created human beings; it also shows the proper function of procreation in God's plan, and by showing how procreation is part of God's plan, the preambles prepare the way for saying *how* procreation should occur – not promiscuously, lecherously, or accidentally, but legitimately and monogamously, and with chaste intentions.

The extraordinary preamble to *Extr.* I 13 (*Doc.* 15) expands the argument into a little treatise. The author begins (in a quasi-invocation) by calling God as creator the "supreme and ineffable Father." In language derived from Pseudo-Dionysius via John Scottus (also known as Eriugena), he characterizes God's nature as the "superessence" (i.e., that which is beyond being, the *hyperousia*).[84] The author contrasts the true doctrine of a single transcendent first principle with the materialism of certain philosophers, according to whose absurd teachings the world

---

[82] Isidore of Seville, *De ecclesiasticis officiis* II.20.9–10 (CCL 113, 92–93): "Illae sunt autem certae nuptiae quae in coniugio non libidinem sed prolem requirunt. Neque enim sic institutae sunt ut carnis uoluptatibus seruiant, sed tantum ut fructum propaginis quaerant. Nam et ut ipsae dotales tabulae indicant, 'causa procreandorum liberorum' ducitur uxor." See n. 67 earlier.

[83] Compare Augustine, *Enchiridon* 9 (29), CCL 46, 65; idem, *De civitate Dei* XXII, l, CCL 48, 807; and Anselm of Canterbury, *Cur Deus homo* I, cc. 16–18, in F. S. Schmitt (ed.), *Opera Omnia*, vol. 2 (Edinburgh, 1946), 74–84.

[84] John Scottus uses the terms *superesse* and *superessentialis* (although not *superessentia*) to denote the reality that transcends being: see Édouard's Jeauneau's note in his edition of Jean Scot, *Homélie sur le Prologue de Jean*, Sources Chrétiennes 151 (Paris, 1969), 323–24. Fulbert of Chartres (d. 1028) speaks of the "superessence of the deity" in a letter dated 1003 (*Epist.* 2, PL 141:190C).

originated from two first principles: the atoms and the void. (These philosophers were the Epicureans, whom John of Salisbury criticizes in very similar terms.)[85] The preamble goes on to explain how through the second Person of the Trinity (the Father's "consubstantial wisdom"), God the Father created the Empyrean (the "resplendent abode of highest heaven") for ten choirs of angels. The angels named after Lucifer, the "light bearer," were the most excellent and the subtlest in nature, but they fell because of pride. Then the other angels, seeing with consternation the fall of Lucifer's choir, were confirmed in their goodness, freely choosing to give up free will. God created human beings so that they might ascend to the spiritual heights from which Lucifer's choir had fallen.

Although the theory that God created human beings to take the places of the fallen angels is common in patristic and medieval theology, the implied numerology here, although perfectly logical, is unusual: our author assumes that there were originally ten choirs of angels, and that God created human beings to replace the fallen tenth choir, so that they would eventually join the nine choirs of good angels in bliss and restore the decad. The root of the idea may have been Pope Gregory the Great's mystical reading of the parable of the lost drachma in Luke 15:8–10. Gregory explains that the woman had ten drachmas because God first created nine choirs of angels and then created human beings to complete the "number of the elect." But in Gregory's reading, it is human beings, not a choir of angels, who are the lost drachma: they are the ones who fell, and whom Christ has restored.[86]

The theology of *Extr.* I 13 is remarkably detailed and precise. The author even includes some theodicy, explaining that God gave the angels the capacity to err not because he wanted some to fall, but so that they were free and able to earn their own reward. And he mentions that the dictum of Genesis 2:24 ("For this reason, a man shall leave his father and mother and cleave unto his wife, and they shall be two in one flesh") was spoken by God *through* Adam. This is in accordance with patristic interpretations of the text, according to which Adam uttered the dictum, but speaking as a prophet, for he uttered it after awaking from a prophetic trance (the "deep sleep" of Gen. 2:21).[87]

In *Extr.* I 13–15 (Docs. 15–17), the preambles are the point of the formulae, and other material is neglected. *Extr.* I 15 substitutes the phrase *ista et ista* ("such and such") for the entire itemized dowry. In *Extr.* I 14 (Doc. 16), there are three blank

---

[85] See John of Salisbury, *Metalogicon* II.2, CCM 98, p. 58, lines 9–12: the Epicureans (according to John) taught that the world was not made by God but rather evolved from atoms and the void, a typical example of the lack of skill in reasoning among philosophical sects. The same idea appears in a twelfth-century commentary on Book VIII of Martianus Capella's *De nuptiis Mercurii et Philologiae*: see Édouard Jeauneau, *Lectio philosophorum: Recherches sur l'École de Chartres* (Amsterdam, 1973), p. 20: "Epicurus et sui ponebant duo principia rerum: athomos et inane."

[86] Gregory the Great, *Homiliae in Evangelia* II, hom. 34, 6, CCL 141, 303–05, lines 137–47 (or PL 76:1249, C6–D4).

[87] See Reynolds, *Marriage in the Western Church*, 282–93.

lines where the disposition should be. In *Extr.* I 13, the *sponsus* merely says that he wills to give her a dowry, without saying anything about its content or terms: "And I will to bestow upon you something from what I possess, so that, the union of marriage having been performed according to custom, you shall by my oath have these things as your rightful dowry." A concluding prayer for blessings upon the wife follows immediately (in the form of an elegiac couplet): "May you always render to your *sponsus*, who has done this, / Dutiful service and loving fidelity. Amen. Blessed be God!" The effect is manifestly liturgical.

THE EVOLUTION OF THE SACRED PREAMBLE

By adding to Zeumer's formulae some examples of actual dotal charters, one can get some idea of how the sacred preamble evolved and mutated over the Carolingian period, through the period of the *Extravagantes*, and into the twelfth century.

The rudimentary preambles, as we have seen, simply cite the biblical texts, which they leave to speak for themselves. One finds the same technique taken a step further in three actual dotal charters from northern Aquitaine, on which Philippe Depreux has commented. Two of these date from the late tenth century, and the other from the mid-eleventh.[88]

All three of these preambles begin by naming God as the almighty creator. In the dotal charter from Alcher to Raingardis (or Raingaldis), ca. 975, the preamble next recounts how God joined man and woman in the beginning (Gen. 2:22), how a man leaves his father and mother and cleaves unto this wife (Gen. 2:24), and how Jesus said, "What God has joined, man should not separate" (Matt. 19:6, Mark. 10:9).

The preamble to the charter from Fulk to Arla, ca. 990, which is more continuously woven, recalls how God created man to his own image and likeness in the beginning, placing him in Paradise; how God judged that the man should not be alone and made a helpmeet for him (Gen. 2:18); how he blessed them, telling them to be fruitful and multiply (Gen. 1:28); how he commanded man to leave his father and mother and cleave unto his wife (Gen. 2:24); and how, by the grace of the Holy Spirit, this command remained with "the prophets and patriarchs and perfect faithful men of the holy Church," so that their progeny continues even unto the present day.

The preamble to the third charter, from Alberic to Audeburgis (dated February 4, 1083), notes how pleasing marriage is to God; how God formed woman from man's side (Gen. 2:21–22), so that each man has his own wife (1 Cor. 7:2); and how Jesus confirmed the goodness of marriage at Cana, and not only by his presence but

---

[88] Depreux, "La dotation de l'épouse," 241, 242, 243 (nos. 1, 2, and 4). The third example in Depreux's appendix is a secular charter.

by performing there the first of his miracles (John 2:11) in response to his mother's beseeching (John 2:3).

Laurent Morelle has compared the sacred preambles in two sets of dotal charters: on the one hand, some tenth- and eleventh-century charters preserved at Cluny and two others for dukes of Normandy; and on the other hand, four mid–twelfth-century sacred charters from the dioceses of Laon and Soissons, in the Archdiocese of Reims.[89] His study reveals further development and then a shift in the twelfth century, with a different method and some new themes.

The preambles in the earlier group are composed chiefly of Scriptural passages, assembled to demonstrate the sanctity of marriage and the importance of legitimate marriage. The references are the same as those we have seen in Zeumer's formulae. Genesis 2:24 (or Matt. 19:5, Mark 10:7–8) and Matthew 19:6 (= Mark 10:9) are the most popular texts (according to which a man leaves his parents and cleaves to his wife, and no man should separate what God has joined). Other texts include Genesis 1:28 or 9:1 ("increase and multiply"), Genesis 2:18 (Adam's need for a helpmeet), Genesis 2:21 and 2:23 (the story of Eve's formation), John 2:1–11 (the miracle at Cana), 1 Cor. 7:2 (each should have his own spouse because of fornication), and Ephesians 5:25 (the husband should love his wife as Christ loves the Church). The sacred preamble to a Mâcon *sponsalitium* of 994, whereby a count named Oury (or Ulric) endowed his *sponsa* Ermengarde, weaves such quotations into a continuous argument by supplementing and glossing them, yet it is modest and restrained by the standards of Zeumer's *Extravagantes*.[90] The style and composition of this entire charter, as well as of its preamble, is notably similar to that of the earlier, "rudimentary" sacred dotal charters in Zeumer's collection.

The two dotal charters for dukes of Normandy are still more developed, with longer quotations and a still more filled-out, continuous argument.[91] One of them (dated 1026 or 1027) begins by explaining how the "ineffable clemency of almighty God" would not suffer the number of angels to remain diminished and imperfect, and how God created man in his own image and likeness to take the places left vacant by those angels who had fallen because of their pride.[92] The same argument, as we have seen, is a feature of *Extr.* I 13 and 15 (Docs. 15 and 17).

---

[89] Morelle, "Mariage et diplomatique," at 235–42 (later in this volume, 174–81).

[90] Auguste Bernard and Alexandre Bruel (eds.), *Receuil des chartes de l'abbaye de Cluny* (Paris, 1876–1903), vol. 3, no. 2265. Duby, who summarizes and comments on the deed in *Le chevalier, la femme et le prêtre*, 106–107 (translated by Bray, 97–99), describes the preamble (p. 106) as "[un] long et pompeux préambule [qui] expose la théorie ecclésiastique du bon marriage." There is an English translation of this deed by Paul Hyams in Paul Halsall (ed.), *Internet Medieval Source Book*, at http://www.fordham.edu/halsall/source/endow1.html.

[91] For editions of these charters, see Marie Fauroux, *Recueil des actes des ducs de Normandie de 911 à 1066*, Mémoires de la Société des antiquaires de Normandie, t. 36 (Caen, 1961), 82–85 (for charter 11, dated 996–1008), and 180–82 (for charter 58, dated January, 1026/1027).

[92] Ed. Faroux, ibid., 181.

The four sacred preambles from the later twelfth century, on the contrary, make little use of citation, developing instead a continuous pastoral argument, and focusing on what Morelle calls "the progressive institution of the sacrament of marriage."[93] They all begin by invoking the name of the Trinity, as does *Extr.* I 11 (Doc. 13). Then, in the preamble, they call marriage a sacrament, and one of them (n. 2, from Soissons, dated 1170) calls marriage a sacrament of Christ and the Church. All of them not only mention the Wedding at Cana but explicitly cite it to attack the heresy of those who despise marriage. Three of the preambles allude to Augustine's idea that exogamy and procreation extend the bonds of friendship.[94] These are witnesses to a new tradition, with little relation to the one that we have been examining, although one should not assume that the older form fell into disuse.[95]

The *Extravagantes* preambles are advanced examples of the earlier of these two types. They are very similar in method, style, and content to the two charters for the dukes of Normandy from the early eleventh century (although the theological argument is even more developed). They still rely on the dossier of standard biblical citations. There is little sign yet of any interest in Augustine on marriage, and they mention nothing about marriage as a sacrament. These are traits of the systematic theology of marriage that developed in the twelfth century, which was based on a recovery of Augustine but was centered on a new idea: that marriage is not only a sign of Christ's union with the Church (Eph. 5:32) but is one of the sacraments of the New Covenant, along with Baptism, Eucharist, and the rest.

THE THEOLOGY OF THE SACRED CHARTERS

The sacred preambles are didactic as well as ritual statements, designed to express what the clergy regarded as the salient features and the most important notes of marriage from the perspective of faith and morals. What theology or religious doctrine, then, do they convey? The gist or "moral" of all the sacred preambles in Zeumer's collection is the same: that God created monogamy in the beginning, that it is the proper means of procreation, and that it is a blessed state. These might seem

[93] Morelle, "Mariage et diplomatique," 238 (later in this volume, 177). For the texts of the twelfth-century charters, see 266–83 (195–212).
[94] See Morelle, ibid., appendix, 258–66. Compare Augustine, *De bono coniugali* 1 (1), CSEL 41, 187.
[95] Compare the two twelfth-century *ars dictandi* formulae edited by Steven M. Wight (n. 3 earlier), both of which have short sacred preambles succinctly expressing a theology of marriage. The more traditional example (2.30) states that marriage is a remedy for human frailty, cites Gen. 2:24 (the union of two in one flesh), and adds that Jesus "consecrated" marriage by his presence at Cana (cf. John 2:11). But the other example (3b.84), which occurs only in the Admont MS, is less literal in its allusions to the Bible: noting that the "nuptial sacrament" has been commended through the counsel of "upright men" (*probi homines*), it goes on to explain how, by forming the first woman from man's side, God marvelously revealed the oneness (*identitas*) of marriage and the union of two persons in one flesh.

commonplace observations but for two things: the contrast with a quite different approach to marriage, Augustinian in inspiration, which was to become central to the theology of marriage as a sacrament in the medieval schools; and the rhetorical, quasi-liturgical form of the preambles. To appreciate the distinctive theology of marriage in these sacred preambles, therefore, one must risk anachronism by distancing them from a later theology with which medievalists and church historians today are more familiar.

The doctrine of the Fall and concupiscence; the theory that the "time to embrace" (Eccles. 3:5) ended with Christ, when celibacy became the norm of holy living; the construal of Christian marriage rather as a remedy against lust than as the means of procreation (cf. 1 Cor. 7): these are the salient features of Augustine's theology of marriage. It is in such terms that he expounds the goodness of marriage in the *De bono coniugali* and the *De nuptiis et concupiscentia*.[96] On this view, although marriage is by nature and even by definition a compact that one enters into "for the sake of procreating legitimate children" (*liberorum procreandorum causa*), marriage after Christ is justifiable chiefly as a remedy for lust among those not strong enough to lead a life of Christ-like celibacy, which is a much more effective way to populate the Kingdom of God and to reach the mystical number of the elect (and thus the world's end). Marriage might have been and indeed once was a duty (*officium*) for the healthy, Augustine argues in a much-quoted passage, but it is now a remedy (*remedium*) for the sick.[97] This doctrine rarely appears in the marriage liturgies surviving from the Middle Ages, but perhaps only because the written liturgies did not usually include didactic statements. (A sermon would have been a more appropriate setting.)

A recovery of Augustine's treatment of marriage and a renewed interest in the place of marriage in relation both to the Fall and to the call to celibacy were the basis of the theology of marriage that flourished in the twelfth century. This eventually crystallized around the doctrine that marriage is one of the seven sacraments, the "sacred medicaments" that Christ, like the Good Samaritan, applies to human nature, the traveler whom Satan had left dying by the roadside.[98] Such was the nuptial theology of an elite clergy devoted to reform and high moral standards but overly preoccupied with the pastoral ideals and problems of their own celibate (ideally, ascetic) way of life. The rite of marriage in the Anglican *Book of Common Prayer* perfectly expresses this high-medieval, ascetical doctrine when it says that

---

[96] See Reynolds, *Marriage in the Western Church*, 259–79.

[97] Augustine, *De Genesi ad litteram* IX.7, CSEL 28/1, 275: "utriusque sexus infirmitas propendens in ruinam turpitudinis recte excipitur honestate nuptiarum, ut, quod sanis esse posset officium, sit aegrotis remedium."

[98] On marriage in twelfth-century theology, see Hans Zeimentz, *Ehe nach der Lehre der Frühscholastik* (Düsseldorf, 1973). On the moral and anthropological basis of this development, see Richard Heinzmann, *Die Unsterblichkeit des Seele und die Auferstehung des Leibes*, = *Beiträge zur Geschichte der Philosophie und Theologie des Mittelalters* 40.3 (Münster, 1965). On the sacraments as medicaments, see Reynolds, *Food and the Body* (Leiden, 1999), 128–30.

marriage "was ordeined for a remedy agaynste sinne and to avoide fornication, that suche persones as have not the gifte of continencie might mary, and kepe themselves undefiled members of Christes body."[99]

That way of construing marriage has no place at all in our sacred preambles, in which the view of marriage is closer to Ambrosiaster's than to Augustine's.[100] Needless to say, there is no mention of marriage as a sacrament, for that doctrine first appears in the early twelfth century. But our anonymous clerics posit no rupture, as Augustine did and as the schoolmen will do, between marriage before and after the Fall, or between marriage before and after Christ. On the contrary, not only is marriage as good today as it was in the beginning, but it is good today *for the same reasons* as it was in the beginning, chief among which is legitimate procreation and the perpetuation of the human race. They emphasize the continuity, not any rupture or discontinuity, between marriage as it is now and as it was in Eden. In this respect, they are in agreement with a remarkable statement in the nuptial rite of the eighth-century Gregorian sacramentary known as the *Hadrianum*, according to which marriage is the only (*sola*) institution the blessedness of which survived original sin and the Flood. Here, in the petitions for nuptial blessing, the priest addresses:

God through whom woman is joined to man and [through whom] the covenant ordained in the beginning is endowed with a blessing that alone was taken away neither through the penalty of original sin nor through the judgment of the Flood.[101]

The early sacred preambles see no need for a *new* justification of marriage, whereby marriage is still good despite the Fall but for modified, remedial reasons. Theirs is instead a robust, domestic, commonsensical theology of marriage, and one that is fully congruent with liturgical ministry among the laity and with the blessing of the chief moments of passage in human life: birth, marriage, and death.

Missing, too, is the other chief component of the doctrine of marriage as a sacrament: the premise that marriage symbolizes Christ's union with the Church. Ephesians 5:32 (the proof text for the doctrine of marriage as a sacrament) does not appear in any of them. (It appears only rarely in western marriage liturgies throughout the Middle Ages.) There is no particular reason why it should not have appeared, for the theme is perennial, but in fact the thoughts of our anonymous clerics are elsewhere. Only one of the preambles touches on the theme, namely, *Extr.* I 9 (Doc. 12), which appeals to Ephesians 5:25 for its pastoral message of peace: "Husbands, love your wives as Christ loves the Church." Interestingly, this Pauline

[99] Quoted from the 1559 rite in Searle and Stevenson, *Documents of the Marriage Liturgy*, 217.
[100] On Ambrosiaster's view of marriage, see Reynolds, *Marriage in the Western Church*, 242–43; and David H. Hunter, "*On the Sin of Adam and Eve:* A little-known defense of marriage and childbearing by Ambrosiaster," *Harvard Theological Review* 82 (1989): 283–99.
[101] Ritzer, *Le mariage*, 428, sect. 7: "deus per quem mulier iungitur uiro, et societas principaliter ordinata ea benedictione donatur, quae sola nec per originalis peccati poenam nec per diluuii est ablata sententiam."

text appears along with Genesis 2:24 and two other nuptial texts (Matt. 19:5 and Psalm 18:6) in the preamble to a royal act of King Henry I of France, issued in 1060, whereby Henry renovated the abbey of Saint-Martin des Champs. Here the theology of the mystical marriage is explicit, but it is used not to illumine literal marriage but to show how the king, by supporting the church and enriching her architecture, unites the church to Christ as his bride. Thus Henry can say, with the Psalmist, "I have loved the beauty of the Lord's house and the place of his habitation."[102]

For the most part, it is not obvious in the *Extravagantes* preambles that literal marriage is supposed to signify or to represent anything at all in an analogical way, by the logic of "just as ... so also. ... " Dimly, perhaps, they imply that marriage signifies the unity of God or his creativity, but not explicitly. They are symbolic, though, in another sense, for each quickly links a particular human marriage in the here-and-now to the institution of marriage in the beginning, and to the creation of the first parents and, indeed, of the angels and of the cosmos, and thus to God the Father, creator of heaven and earth. *This* marriage between *N.* and *N.* becomes universal through the primordial marriage, to which it is assimilated immediately, with no reference to the fall of human nature or to marriage as a remedy against the Fall. And the primordial marriage is mysterious and divine through its immediate association with the creation of all things in the beginning, and thus with God the Father almighty, the "supreme and ineffable" first principle. The cosmos itself, according to *Extr.* I 13, originated not from merely physical causes (the atoms and the void) but from God the Father and creator, who, in the beginning, made man and woman and joined them in matrimony. The preambles are witnesses to an inevitable, intuitively self-evident association between a marriage and the creation of the universe. Every wedding is a primordial event, putting the observers in touch with the origin of the world.

As important as the doctrinal content of the sacred preambles, therefore, is their rhetorical, quasi-liturgical trajectory, proceeding in giant steps from God as creator through the dawn of the world, and thus through the first, archetypal marriage (of those whom God the Father himself personally joined together) to this present marriage of two mere individuals, named *So-and-So* and *So-and-So*, who give and receive a dowry and are united in marriage before a priest.

One may wonder how much the laity who read or heard such charters would have understood or cared about what was said (not to mention how happy the fortunate brides would have really been, however substantial their dowries). Perhaps a priest would have translated or glossed the charters for them. Be that as it may, among the chief functions of the Christian religion is to set the particularities of human experience in much wider contexts, which belong to another order and which seem, by linking the here-and-now to things that are primordial

---

[102] See Parisse, "Préambules de chartes" (n. 52 earlier), at 154. I am grateful to Laurent Morelle for drawing my attention to the similarities between *Extr.* I 9 and the royal deed of 1060.

or divine, to transcend everyday life; and which therefore establish, in return, universal norms for the here-and-now, imposing absolute and eternal values. That is precisely what the *Extravagantes* preambles do, and with impressive and moving eloquence, notwithstanding their strangely ornate language.

APPENDIX: THE DOTAL FORMULAE IN ZEUMER'S COLLECTION

I have analyzed the dotal formulae by indicating the main components of each (as applicable) with capital letters, thus: (A) preamble, (B) exposition, (C) disposition, and (D) penalty clause. The symbol * means that a complete or partial translation is included. The symbol + means that the charter includes a sacred preamble.

FORMULAE ANDECAVENSES
(*And.* 1 c, 34, 40, & 54)

The *Formulae Andecavenses* is a Merovingian formulary composed at Angers, consisting of formulae for private (rather than royal) acts, drawn up mostly in the sixth and early seventh centuries. The four dotal formulae are all secular. Only *And.* 54 includes a preamble. *And.* 1 c* (p. 5), entitled *cessio* ("cession," "gift"), is part of the evidence presented by a woman seeking to obtain that part of her endowment due to come from her own parents.[1] The preamble to the record as a whole (*And.* 1 a, p. 4) states that the woman presented her suit during the fourth year of the reign of King Hildebert. *And.* 34* (p. 16), which is headed *Incipit dotis*, is dated in the same way. *And.* 40 (pp. 17–18), entitled *cessio*, is similar to *And.* 1 c. It has all the same elements, except that the *sponsus* mentions in the exposition that he has betrothed his *sponsa* according to Roman law (*secundum lege Romana*; cf. *Tur.* 15, p. 143). *And.* 54 (p. 23), which is also entitled *cessio*, is similar to *And.* 1 c and *And.* 40, but it has a legal preamble. It begins with an exultation: "How good and fortunate this is!" (*Quod bonum, faustum sit!*).

In *And.* 1 c, there are, in effect, three dispositions, the first (C1) being of immovable property (land and whatever belongs to it), the second (C2) of domestic items such as jewelry, and the third (C3) of domestic animals. Le Jan suggests that the second list is a vestige of the morning gift.[2] A similar division between real estate and domestic items occurs in *Lind.* 7 (p. 271), and there are perhaps signs of it in *Tur.* 14 (Doc. 4) and *Tur.* 15 (p. 143). The list is continuous in other dispositions, although with immovables such as land and buildings naturally coming first, and movables

---

[1] There is an English translation of this formula in Francis A. Laine, *The Angevin Formulae: A Translation with Linguistic Commentary, A Summary of a Thesis* (Nashville, 1951), 8–9.
[2] See Le Jan, "Aux origines," 59.

such as jewelry, clothes, and utensils last: cf. *And.* 40 (p. 17), *And.* 54 (p. 23), *Sen.* 25 (Doc. 7), and *Marc.* II 15 (p. 85). Some interpret the bedspread included in *And.* 1c as symbolic of marriage, but it is just as likely that such items were mentioned because they were precious. Cf. *Sen.* 25 (Doc. 7), where several bedspreads are included.

DOCUMENT 1 (*AND.* 1C, P. 5, COMPLETE):

[B] My dearest betrothed, to be cherished with all my love, daughter of *So-and-So*, name *So-and-So*, I *So-and-So*. And because, with the Lord's good favor, I have betrothed you according to custom and with the agreement of your parents, therefore I cede to you from the estate of my property,[3] both as a betrothal present and as a gift to you,[4] these things: [C1] A house [*casa*][5] with the surrounding enclosure, movable and immovable property, vineyards, woods, meadows, pastures, standing and running waters, things adjoining and bordering, and through this cession, my dearest betrothed, I entrust and transfer all the aforesaid things to you on the most happy day of our marriage, so that you shall receive them as yours by right. [C2] I cede to you a bracelet worth *so many* solidi, *so many* tunics, a bedspread worth *so many* solidi to cover the bed, gold earrings worth *so many* solidi, a ring worth *so many* solidi. [C3] I cede to you a horse with its saddle [*sambuca*][6] and all its trappings, *so many* oxen, *so many* cows with their calves, *so many* sheep, *so many* pigs. You are to receive as your estate all the things written here, as yours by right and under your control, and you may leave them to your children, if any shall have been begotten between us, excepting the right of [the monastery or church dedicated to] *such-and-such* a saint whose land it is found to be.[7] [D] And if at any time there shall be someone who wants to contest this cession, which I have asked to be written down for you in good

---

[3] I read *de rem proprietatis* instead of Zeumer's *de rem paupertatis*. Compare *Tur.* 14, pp. 142–43, lines 27–28: "re proprietatis mcae." I am grateful to David Bright for suggesting this correction.

[4] Zeumer, *Formulae*, p. 5, lines 4–5: "tam pro sponsaliciae quam pro largitate tuae...." This phrase is probably a rhetorical (and garbled) expansion of *sponsalitia largitas* ("betrothal gift," with *sponsalitia* as a feminine adjective), which occurs in *Cod. Theod.* III.5.2, interpr., and thus in Alaric's *Breviary* (*Lex Romana Visigothorum*, ibid.). It also occurs in two of the Visigothic dotal formulae (*Vis.* 14, p. 581, line 26, and *Vis.* 17, p. 582, line 21).

[5] Or perhaps something grander, such as "manor" or even "castle."

[6] Following Niermeyer et al., *Mediae Latinitatis Lexicon Minus*, I translate *sambuca* as "saddle," and not "chariot" (as Zeumer suggests), but one might make a good case for "harness" or "bridle" (cf. *bucca*: "cheek," "mouth"). There is, as far as I know, no etymological connection with the botanical class to which belongs the elder tree (*sambucus* or *sambuca nigra*), and from which a popular anise-flavored Italian liqueur gets its name.

[7] "salvi iure sancti illius, cuius terre esse videtur." Although the correct translation of *sancti* might be not "saint" but "sanctuary" or "sacred building," the phrase probably refers to the right of a monastery or church that was dedicated to Saint *So-and-So* (the patron saint), for it was customary to designate ecclesiastical establishments in this manner. Variants of the idiom (e.g., *terraturium sancti illius*) occur also in *And.* 4, 8, and 21 (pp. 6, 7, and 11). The point is that the woman's rights to the land are conditional on any such prior rights, which would take precedence.

faith, or who presumes to bring an action or a claim against it, whether it be I myself, or anyone from my heirs or my kinsfolk, or any man or a person who is an outsider or sent as an emissary, then before he undertakes the lawsuit, he shall pay double to you and as much again as this cession contains, or as much more as it is worth at that time, and his claim shall have no effect, and this cession and our will shall for all time remain firm.

Document 2 (*And.* 34, p. 16, complete):

[B] In the 4th year of the reign of our lord King Hildebert, I in the name of God *So-and-So* avow that I was to have this certificate of dowry [*libellum dote*] prepared, which has now been done accordingly, for my dearest betrothed named *So-and-So.* [C] Out of my fondest love for her, I give to you [*sic*] in this charter for the certificate of a dowry, a house [*casa*]. The aforesaid girl, my betrothed *So-and-So,* shall have, hold, and possess it, and may do with it what she wills. [D] And if anyone, be it I myself or any other person in opposition, shall presume to make an action against what I have willed here or against this certificate of dowry, he shall pay a fine of *so many* solidi, and if anyone makes such a claim, it shall be of no avail.

Marculfi Formulae
(*Marc.* II 15)

This Merovingian formulary was compiled by a monk called Marculf, who dedicated it to a certain Bishop Landri (probably the Landri who was Bishop of Paris 650–56). It is in two books, the first consisting of royal charters, and the second of charters for private *acta. Marc.* II 15 (p. 85), entitled *Libellum dotis* ("Certificate of dowry"), includes all the principal parts, including a legal preamble. Here, the father of the *sponsus* gives the dowry *in tanodono* to the *sponsa.* It begins with an exultation: "How good, fortunate, happy, and prosperous a thing has come to pass!" (*Quam bonum, faustum, filex prosperumve eveniat!*).

To be noted also is *Marc.* I 12* (pp. 50–51), an act of mutual exchange (*interdonatio*) between a childless husband and wife, which they enacted before the king. This royal charter begins with a preamble stating how God, the creator of heaven and earth, joined the first couple in matrimony. The opening words are almost the same as those of *Bit.* 15, a dotal charter (see below, Doc. 6).

+ Document 3 (*Marc.* I 12, pp. 50–51, preamble only):

Since the almighty God, creator of heaven and earth, as it is said in Scripture, permitted male and female to be joined together in union in the beginning, saying, "A man shall leave his father and mother and cleave unto this wife, and they shall be two in one flesh" [Gen. 2:24]....

FORMULAE TURONENSES
(*Tur.* 14 & 15, & *Tur.* app. 2 & 3)

Zeumer's text of this collection (composed at Tours) is based on two manuscripts, dating respectively from the ninth and tenth centuries. *Tur.* 14* (pp. 142–43), dating perhaps from the mid-eighth century, is a standard dotal charter with a secular preamble and a penalty clause. It is entitled *Donatio in sponsa facta*. *Tur.* 15* (p. 143), entitled *Traditio*, is a similar dotal charter (without preamble) except that it records that the *sponsus* has not only betrothed the *sponsa* but has already promised to give her a dowry "before the day of the marriage" (*ante die nuptiarum*), which he does now. In an appendix to the *Formulae Turonenses*, Zeumer adds four comparable formulae from another ninth-century manuscript. Included here is a similar pair: *Tur.* app. 2 (pp. 163–64), entitled *Donatio in sponsa facta*, is similar to *Tur.* 14, although it has a more elaborate preamble; and *Tur.* app. 3 (p. 164), entitled *Hic est traditio*, is similar to *Tur.* 15. In *Tur.* 15, the *sponsus* says that he makes the dotation "in accordance with Roman law" (*secundum legem Romanum*): cf. *And.* 54 (p. 23).

DOCUMENT 4 (*TUR.* 14, PP. 142–43, COMPLETE):

[A] Law and custom demand that whatever has been promised or bestowed between a betrothed man and woman for their forthcoming marriage, whether by the consent of their parents or their own if they are legally independent [*sui iuris*], should be solemnly confirmed in writing.[8] [B] Therefore I in the name of God So-and-So. Since it is well known to many that I have betrothed you So-and-So by your own free will and with the consent of our parents and kinsfolk, it has pleased me that I should give to you something from my estate, confirming it with this certificate of dowry [*libellum dotis*] before the day of our marriage, which I have done accordingly. [C] Therefore I give to you and I will to be given a plot of land from my estate, called So-and-So, situated in the district [*pagus*] So-and-So, with the lands, buildings, tenants,[9] serfs, freedmen, vineyards, woods, meadows, pastures, standing and running waters, things movable and immovable, with whatever is upon them or adjacent to them, both from my personal property [*alodis*] and from property purchased or acquired from elsewhere, whole and entire, whatever I am seen to possess at the present time; and *so much* gold jewelry, *so much* silver, tunics. All the things said above, by the title of this certificate of dowry, I shall fulfill and hand over at the time of our marriage, so that as long as you shall live, you shall have and hold it according to the order of the law, and bequeath it to our children, who will be begotten by us. [D] But if there shall

---

[8] Compare *Cod. Theod.* III.5.2, interpr.
[9] Or "tenures" (*accolae*).

be anyone, whether it be I myself or any other person, who presumes to make an action against this donation or to generate calumny against it, he shall not get what he claims, and moreover he shall compensate the one against whom he brought the claim with 100 solidi, and this gift, confirmed by my hands and by the hands of good men and established with this covenant, shall always remain firm.

DOCUMENT 5 (*TUR.* 15, P. 143, EXPOSITION ONLY):

Since it is known to many that I *So-and-So* betrothed a certain girl *So-and-So* with the consent of our parents and kinsfolk, and that I agreed to give her something from my estate before the day of our marriage, therefore it has pleased me....

FORMULAE BITURICENSES
(*Bit.* 15)

Formulae Bituricenses is the title given to a set of nineteen formulae assembled from different collections but all composed in Bourges. *Bit.* 15* (pp. 174–75) is a dotal formula from a ninth-century manuscript. The preamble includes sacred themes as well as references to Roman and secular law. The charter has all the standard elements, including a penalty clause (setting the fine at ten pounds of silver).

+ DOCUMENT 6 (*BIT.* 15, PP. 174, PREAMBLE ONLY):

Since the almighty God, creator of heaven and earth, as it is said in Scripture, joined male and female together in union in the beginning, for it is written: "It is not good for a man to be alone. Let us make a help for him like unto himself" [Gen. 2:18]; and God bestowed a blessing upon them, saying, "Increase and multiply and rule over all creeping things [*reptilia*] that are under heaven" [cf. Gen. 1:28].[10] And our Savior uttered these words: "For this reason, a man shall leave father and mother and cleave unto his wife, and they shall be two in one flesh" [Matt. 19:5, Mark 10:7–8]. And the Holy Spirit decreed through the sacred emperors that unions made to procreate human kind should not be entered into incestuously or illicitly.[11] Therefore it has been determined that if any free person should wish to confer something from the estate that belongs to him, this ought to be written down solemnly in a signed document,

[10] The term *reptilia* has crept in from Gen. 1:25.
[11] Compare *Cod. Theod.* III.12.

for such is required both by the manor and by the municipal rolls.[12] Therefore I in the name of God *So-and-So.* . . .

CARTAE SENONICAE
(*Sen.* 25)

The *Cartae Senonicae* is one of two formularies made at Sens and preserved in the same ninth-century codex. It consists of material composed during the reign of Charlemagne and before 775. *Sen.* 25* (p. 196), entitled *Libellum dotis*, is a sacred charter with most of the standard elements, including a penalty clause, although there is no record of the betrothal in the exposition (cf. *And.* 34). It includes an exultation.

+ DOCUMENT 7 (*SEN.* 25, P. 196, COMPLETE):

[A] Since almighty God permitted conjugal union and gave this command to men: that each one should be married to his own wife [cf. 1 Cor. 7:2], according to the custom of previous Christians; and again, since we read that our Lord himself, with his disciples, was invited to a wedding [John 2:1–11], and that "what God has joined, man should not separate" [Matt. 19:6, Mark 10:9]. How good, happy, and fortunate it is! [B] Therefore he *So-and-So* gives to the honest girl his betrothed by name *So-and-So*, with whom, if it pleases Christ, I [*sic*] intend to be joined in marriage, [C] and I will to be given in perpetuity, and I transcribe and transfer from my right to the right and control of this girl, the following from my own estate in the district *So-and-So*, in the place called *So-and-So*, including homesteads, houses, and dwellings, whole and in their entirety, with the undefined estate, and *so many* female servants with names *So-and-So* and *So-and-So*, and *so many* horses, *so many* oxen, *so many* cows with calves, *so many* head of sheep, *so many* head of pigs, bedspreads suitable for *so many* beds, jewelry in gold and silver worth *so many* solidi, utensils of bronze and iron, shirts – whatever is reasonably included in a house. All the things listed above, when the day of our most happy wedding arrives, my dearest betrothed *So-and-So*, at the present day you may have, hold, and possess, and you have the free and entirely firm power from the present day of doing whatever you may wish to do with it. [D] But if there is someone (which I cannot believe would happen), whether it be I myself or one of my heirs, or any other person in opposition, who attempts to make a claim against this certificate of dowry, he shall pay to you and for the benefit of the fisc a fine of *so many* ounces of gold, and the present certificate of dowry shall stand firm.

---

[12] "qui hac conditione et iurae postulat praeturium et gestis requirit municipalibus."

Formulae Salicae Bignonianae
(*Big.* 6)

The *Formulae Salicae Bignonianae* is named after its first editor, Jérôme Bignon. The formulae were composed for a region subject to Salic law toward the end of the Merovingian period or in the early Carolingian period. *Big.* 6* (p. 230), entitled *Tinado bono*, is a sacred but fairly simple dotal charter. It includes all the standard elements, including a truncated penalty clause, which simply says, "And if anyone...," leaving the details to be filled in. In recalling the betrothal, the *sponsus* calls the woman his wife (*coniux*); and he recalls that he betrothed her before witnesses with a solidus and a denarius in accordance with Salic law. The redactor picks up the sacred themes of the preamble in the confirmation, where he says that the estate will become hers "when God will have joined us together on the happy wedding day."

+ Document 8 (*Big.* 6, p. 230, preamble only):

Since the Lord conceded from the beginning and commanded in the Old Testament that "a man shall leave his father and mother and cleave unto his wife, and they shall be two in one flesh" [Gen. 2:24], and [in the New Testament that] "What God has joined, man should not separate" [Matt. 19:6, Mark. 10:9]. For I in the name of God *So-and-So*....

Formulae Salicae Merkelianae
(*Merk.* 15 & 17)

This collection is named after one of its editors, J. Merkel. The formulae are taken from a Vatican codex dating from the ninth or tenth century. The collection falls into four parts. The first part (*Merk.* 1–30 or 1–31) seems to be dependent both on Marculf's collection and on the *Formulae Turonenses*. It consists of formulae for private acts composed during the second half of the eighth century, and it includes two dotal formulae: *Merk.* 17 (pp. 247–48), entitled *Libellum dotis*, is a version of *Marc.* II 15 (see earlier); and *Merk.* 15* (pp. 246–47), entitled *Tandono*, is a sacred dotal charter of standard form (without a penalty clause). Here the *sponsus* recalls that he betrothed his *sponsa* with the traditional solidus and denarius of Salic law.

+ Document 9 (*Merk.* 15, pp. 246–47, complete):

[A] Since the Lord omnipotent, creator of heaven and earth, permitted spouses to be joined together in union, for as it is written in Scripture, "A man shall leave his father and mother and cleave unto his wife, and they shall be two in one flesh" [Gen. 2:24], [B] therefore I in the name of God *So-and-So*, the son of *So-and-So*, was to betroth this free [*ingenua*] girl, by name *So-and-So*, with a solidus and a denarius according to Salic law and ancient custom, which accordingly I have done. [C] Therefore I give to the said girl by name *So-and-So* through this dotal charter [*tandono*] my estate in the place called *So-and-So*, in the district [*pagus*] *So-and-So*, in the subdivision [*centena*] *So-and-So*, which I acquired formerly as my legitimate inheritance from my father, that is, the lands, houses, and the rest in the aforesaid estate. Through this dotal charter [*tandono*], I give and transfer the above to this girl, so that on the most happy day of our marriage, as God decrees, when I shall join myself to her in the union of marriage, she shall have, hold, and possess what has been written and named above, and she may bequeath it to her heirs, or to whomever she wishes, and she enjoys the free and entirely firm power in every way to do with it thereafter what she wills.

FORMULAE SALICAE LINDENBROGIANAE
(*Lind.* 7)

This collection is named after its first editor, Friedrich Lindenbruch (seventeenth century). It consists of formulae for private acts contained in two ninth-century codices and composed for a region subject to Salic law. *Lind.* 7 (pp. 271–72), entitled *Libellum dotis*, is a secular dotal charter – or rather a "mixed" one, for the sacred aspect of marriage appears in the confirmation, where the *sponsus* states that "all the aforesaid things, whenever the day of our marriage arrives, and God joins us together, you, my dearest spouse named *So-and-So*, shall from that day have, hold, and possess." It includes a penalty clause but no preamble. The *sponsus* recalls that he has betrothed his *sponsa* with the solidus and denarius of Salic law.

FORMULAE AUGIENSES
(*Aug.* B 24 & 25)

Zeumer includes under this title three different collections from the Abbey of Reichenau preserved in ninth-century manuscripts. Collection B is from the eighth and nineth centuries and consists of formulae for private *acta*. These two dotal formulae are essentially secular but include some sacred references. Both state that the woman will have the usufruct of the estate. *Aug.* B 24 (pp. 357–58), entitled *Libellum dotis*, is a standard secular charter without preamble. The donor calls the charter a dotal document (*epistola dotis*). In the exposition, the *sponsus* recalls that he has betrothed her in accordance with the law of the Alamanni. (Reichenau, like St. Gall, was in a region subject to Alamannian law.) In the confirmation, the *sponsus* says that when his wife dies, the dowry shall revert to him, or if he has died, to his children "if the Lord has willed to grant them," or otherwise to his nearest heirs. *Aug.* B 25 (pp. 358–59), entitled *Libellum dotis*, is a secular charter similar to *Aug.* B 24, although the *sponsus* begins by saying that he has betrothed her "through the will of our Lord Jesus Christ and with the consent of our kinsfolk [*per dispositionem domini nostri Iesu Christi et consensu amicorum nostrorum*]." The donor refers to the gift as her legitimate dowry ("tibi dotem legitimum decrevi"). The wife is to have the usufruct of the estate as long as she lives. If she dies first, the estate will revert to him. If he dies first, the estate will pass eventually to his "legitimate heirs." A reference in the conclusion implies that the original was signed in the year 843.[13]

FORMULAE SANGALLENSES MISCELLANEAE
(*Sang.* 12, 13, 16, 18, & 19)

This collection, from the Abbey of St. Gall, consists of twenty-five formulae dating from the mid-eighth to the late ninth centuries. (Again, the provenance implies that the formulae would have been intended for Alamanni.) It includes five dotal formulae, all of which call the gift a *dos*. All are entitled *Carta dotis* ("dowry charter") except *Sang.* 18, which is untitled. *Sang.* 16* (p. 387) is sacred; the others are secular. In *Sang.* 12 (p. 385), although the dowry (*dos*) is to come (as usual) from the *sponsus* to his *sponsa*, the girl's own father states the act. He begins by saying (A) that being mindful for the need to sustain the race of mortal human beings through procreation, (B) he has been pleased to give his daughter, *N.*, to a certain illustrious man, *N.* Next (C) come details of the gift. This charter might be construed as a wedding contract. It concludes with provision for subscription by the witnesses who are present. *Sang.* 13* (p. 385) and *Sang.* 19 (p. 388) are alike and unusually brief. *Sang.* 16* (p. 387) has a sacred preamble that is unusual in the Scriptural texts to which it alludes. There is no penalty clause, but there is provision at the end for several different specified relations to sign (father, brothers, uncles, cousins, and so on). *Sang.* 18 (p. 388) is a standard secular charter with no preamble but with a penalty clause and an elaborate subscription. *Sang.* 18 and 19 may be marriage contracts as well, but this is far from certain.

DOCUMENT 10 (*SANG.* 13, P. 385, COMPLETE):

It has pleased me, *N.*, that I should hand over to you, my betrothed *N.*, as your dowry [*dos*] and to be under your power, one village and three homesteads, to possess all the days of your life, *and so on*.

+ DOCUMENT 11 (*SANG.* 16, P. 387, PREAMBLE AND EXPOSITION ONLY):

[A] Since sacred Scripture says, "A wife will be prepared for the man by the Lord" [Prov. 19:4, Vetus Latina],[14] and again, "Increase and multiply, and I shall establish my covenant with you" [cf. Lev. 26:9, Gen. 1:28], [B] it pleased

---

[13] See Zeumer, *Forumulae*, p. 358, n. 3.

[14] Compare Prov. 19:4 in *Bibliorum Sacrorum Latinae Versiones Antiquae seu Italica* (1743; repr. Munich, 1976), vol. 2, 326: "A Deo autem praeparabitur viro uxor." This version of the text follows the Septuagint. Compare Gen. 24:44 (which is Zeumer's reference).

me, *N.*, to ask the noble and religious man *So-and-So* for his daughter, named *So-and-So*, to be betrothed to me and in due course to be received as my wife. And since, with the consent of his nearest kinsfolk, he agreed to my request, [C] I have given to her, the same betrothed and my future wife, as her dowry [*dos*]. . . .

COLLECTIO SANGALLENSIS SALOMONIS III TEMPORE CONSCRIPTA
(*C. Sang.* 12 & 18)

This collection is so called because it seems to have been compiled at the Abbey of St. Gall when Salomo III, the Bishop of Constance, was Abbot (i.e., 890–919/920). The compiler was supposedly Notker Balbulus ("the Stammerer"), an illustrious monk and musician of St. Gall who died in 912. The collection is preserved in several manuscripts from the tenth and eleventh centuries. The collection falls into four parts, the second of which (*C. Sang.* 6–21) consists of charters for private acts drawn up ca. 870, including two dotal instruments. *C. Sang.* 12 (p. 404), entitled *Carta dotalis* ("dotal charter"), is a secular charter that has no preamble but includes a penalty clause and a subscription. *C. Sang.* 18 (pp. 406–07), entitled *Carta dotis*, is a secular charter of standard form. The donor calls the charter *epistola dotis*. It has a penalty clause but no preamble.

FORMULARUM PITHOEI FRAGMENTA
(*Pith.* 55, 57, & 60)

The *Formularum Pithoei Fragmenta* consists of fragments that came originally from a manuscript loaned by Pithou to Du Cange when the latter was preparing his famous glossary of medieval Latin. Sadly, the manuscript, which included at least 108 formulae prepared in the eighth century for a territory subject to Salic law, later disappeared. Zeumer gathered the quotations from Du Cange's *Glossarium*. The fragments *Pith.* 55 and 60 (pp. 597–98) are probably from dotal charters. These fragments simply record the Salic betrothal gift of the solidus and denarius (which *Pith.* 60 refers to as an *arrha*). *Pith.* 57 (p. 597) is part of the disposition from a dotal charter.

EXTRAVAGANTES
(*Extr.* I 9–15)

Under the heading of *Extravagantes*, Zeumer gathered numerous formulae found isolated in manuscripts, rather than in medieval formularies or in systematic scholarly compilations. He sorted them into two collections, the first of which includes seven dotal charters (*Extr.* I 9–15, pp. 538–43).

Extr. I 9* and 10 come from the same Leiden codex. According to K. A. de Meyier, they were written in the first half of the eleventh century.[15] *Extr.* I 9* mentions the district of Orléans (*pagus Aurelianensis*). *Extr.* I 10 (which is probably the oldest in the set) mentions the district of Floriaco (*pagus Floriacensis*), which Zeumer suggests was probably named after the village of Floriaco near Orléans, where there was a Benedictine monastery. *Extr.* I 10 says that it was done in the reign of King Pippin: he must have been one of the two kings of Aquitaine with that name, i.e., Pippin I (814–38) or Pippin II (838–48). *Extr.* I 11* is from an eleventh-century Vatican codex, whereas *Extr.* I 12* is a Salic charter from a tenth- or eleventh-century Escorial codex.[16] *Extr.* I 13* and 14* are both from another Leiden codex, but written in two different hands.[17] According to Zeumer, they were written in the late tenth century, but K. A. de Meyier places them in the ninth century.[18] However, as noted previously, their style and content suggest that the mid-eleventh century would be a more likely date. *Extr.* I 15* is from a late–twelfth-century codex. All of these formulae have sacred preambles except *Extr.* I 10, which is a standard secular charter.

Extr. I 9* (pp. 538–39) is a standard dotal charter but with an extended sacred preamble. It concludes with names for seven signatures (including that of the *sponsus*), but with spaces for six more. In the subscription, the instrument uses the word *osculum* ("kiss") in a transferred sense to refer to the dowry or dotal charter (The word *osculum* is used in its proper sense earlier in the document.)

Although *Extr.* I 10 (p. 539) has no preamble, it is otherwise similar to *Extr.* I 9. This charter, too (but in the penalty clause), uses the term *osculum* in a transferred sense, to refer to the dotal agreement or the charter itself.

Extr. I 11* (p. 540) is a sacred charter that includes all the standard elements including a penalty clause and a final corroboration ("I *So-and-So*, who asked for this testament of dowry to be made and affirmed").

Extr. I 12* (pp. 540–41) must have been composed for Salic jurisdiction, for it refers to betrothal with the solidus and denarius. It includes an extensive sacred preamble, and one of the sacred themes is picked up in the penalty clause, where the *sponsus* says that God will have joined them together in matrimony (cf. *Lind.* 7, described earlier) and that the wrath of God will therefore descend on anyone who makes an action against the dowry.

Extr. I 13* (pp. 541–42), with the incipit *Summus et ineffabilis pater*, includes the most elaborate preamble in the collection. Indeed, there is not much else: the disposition is reduced to a few words, without specifics.

---

[15] Leiden, Universitatsbibliothek, Vossianus latinus, 8°, MS 15, 206r and 210r. See K. A. de Meyier, *Codices Vossiani Latini*, Part 3: Codices in Octavo (Leiden, 1977), 40, 41. According to Zeumer, they are written in two different tenth-century hands.

[16] MS Escorial L.III.8, from Real Biblioteca del monasterio de San Lorenzo de Escorial.

[17] Leiden, Voss., fol., MS 70, 81 v.

[18] K. A. de Meyier, *Codices Vossiani Latini*, Part 1: Codices in Folio (Leiden, 1973), 144.

Extr. I 14* (p. 542) includes the names of the spouses. There is a preamble touching on both sacred and secular themes. After the exposition, there is a lacuna of three lines where the details of the dowry (the matter of the disposition) would have been.

Extr. I 15* (pp. 542–43) is very similar to *Extr.* I 12* with regard to its content and the sequence of ideas, but the words are different and the language is much more ornate.

+ DOCUMENT 12 (*EXTR.* I 9, P. 538, PREAMBLE AND EXPOSITION ONLY):

[A] The almighty Creator of the universe, by whose powerful goodness the things that are began substantially to be, made man from the dust of the earth and breathed the breath of life into his face; and lest the man should seem to be without a help like unto him, he presented the man, who was alone, with a helper, a rib having been taken from his side as he slept. Help was given in this way so that the intention of love should originate in the number two. Paul the Apostle, teacher of the Gentiles, showing how such a union should be confirmed and inseparably maintained, said, "Husbands, love your wives, as Christ also loved the church," in confirmation of peace [Eph. 5:25, 2:17]. He alluded to this clearly when he said, "The man should not have power over his own body, but the wife, and in like manner the woman should not have power over her own body, but the husband" [1 Cor. 7:4]. Nor does he keep silent about the rendering of the debt: "The man," he says, "should render the debt to his wife, and likewise the wife to her husband" [1 Cor. 7:3]. With these admonitions in mind, therefore, and in order to obey the divine precept, for the Creator of all things said, "Increase and multiply and fill the earth" [Gen. 1:28], [B] for this reason, I in God's name N., whose father is by name N., and whose mother is by name N., have, as many persons already know, willed legally to betroth to myself a certain woman by name N., whose father was by name N., and mother by name N., with the consent of our parents and kinsfolk, and I am resolved, God willing, to come to the day of our marriage. [C] And I cede to her on the day of our marriage, once the kiss [*osculum*] has taken place and the ring has been put on, some things from my estate, which are as follows....

+ DOCUMENT 13 (*EXTR.* I 11, P. 540, PREAMBLE AND EXPOSITION ONLY):

[A] In the name of the holy, single, and undivided Trinity of eternal majesty, with good fortune [*feliciter*].[19] The authority of the Christian religion, and the

---

[19] The adverb *feliciter* ("happily," "fortunately") was traditionally added to the dating of a charter to mean "under good omens," but here, as well as evoking a diplomatic convention, it may echo wedding greetings (meaning roughly the same as our modern "congratulations!"). In any case, it functions here as an abbreviated exultation: cf. the dotal charter *Marc.* II 15 (p. 85), which begins: "Quod bonum, faustum, filex [*sic*] prosperumve eveniat!"

traditions of the Fathers who have gone before us, not to mention the civil laws, clearly teach us, and moreover the proclamations of the holy Scriptures of the Old and New Testaments through many and varied sayings instruct us, who seek to bring to their conclusion the proceedings of this worldly matter, about the union of husband and wife in matrimony, and they make quite clear how good it is to marry legitimately. The Lord too, Creator of all things, made this clear to us in Scripture when he said, "A man shall leave his father and mother and cleave unto his wife, and they shall be two in one flesh" [Gen. 2:24, Matt. 19:5, Mark. 10:7–8]; and in another place he says, "What God has joined, man should not separate" [Matt. 19:6, Mark. 10:9]. [B] Therefore I in God's name *So-and-So*, strengthened by the example of the witness of such authorities, and wishing to imitate the life of the holy Fathers who have gone before us, with the consent and will of noble men and of our parents, have been seen to betroth, in accordance with the custom of the law, a certain girl by name *So-and-So*, and I am determined through love of posterity alone, with God's help, to be united with her in human marriage. [C] Therefore to establish her title and to provide a monument to her honor, I give to my most beloved betrothed through this dotal testament [*dotis testamentum*]....

+ DOCUMENT 14 (*EXTR.* I 12, PP. 540–41, COMPLETE):

[A] At the beginning of human creation, God willed that man, whom he had created to his own image, should rule over the world and multiply, filling the earth with his offspring [Gen. 1:28]. And God decided, by his own counsel,[20] to present the man, who was alone when he made him, with a help like unto him [Gen. 2:18, 20–21]. Therefore he created a woman for the man from his rib, whom he united to the man in the bond of marriage, blessing them and saying, "Increase and multiply and fill the earth" [Gen. 1:28]. And it is written, "For this reason a man shall leave his father and mother and cleave unto this wife, and they shall be two in one flesh" [Gen. 2:24]. But we read too that an angel came from heaven to Tobias, to confirm his union of marriage [Tob. 9:8–11]. And our Lord Jesus Christ, who had granted marriage in the beginning, deigned to sanctify it by his own presence, honoring it with the first of his signs in the presence of the disciples, when he turned water into wine, gladdening the hearts of the guests [John 2:1–11]. [B] Instructed, therefore, by these and other lessons from the New and Old Testaments, I *So-and-So* have espoused with thirteen gold pennies [*per 13 aureos nummos*],[21] in accordance with Salic law, my dearest and most beloved betrothed, by name *So-and-So*, with the consent of our parents and kinsfolk on both sides, and it has pleased

[20] Because when God decided to create human beings, he said, "Let *us* create" (Gen. 1:26): the plural form implies some "conference," as it were, within the Godhead.
[21] Equivalent to a solidus and a denarius: compare the shillings and pence of the United Kingdom in pre-metric days.

me to honor her with something from my own estate in the title of her perpetual dowry [*dos perpetualis*]. [C] Therefore I *So-and-So*, O my most estimable and most beloved betrothed *So-and-So*, give and hand over to you as your own, in the district *So-and-So*, in the village called *So-and-So*, the manor belonging to the demesne, with the buildings upon it and the church and the mills, the cultivated and uncultivated land, meadows, woods, with standing and running waters, exits and entrances. Belonging to that manor are *so many* manors with the serfs of both sexes pertaining to them. All these things as listed above I give and hand over to you, my dearest and most beloved betrothed *So-and-So*, whole and entire, the undefined property, whatever is seen to be my possession there, with the understanding that from this day forth, you are to have, hold, and possess everything listed above, or thereafter may do whatever you will with it, having free and firm power of action in all things, with Christ's favor. [D] But if someone (which I can hardly believe would happen) should presume to act against this certificate of dowry or try to undo it, he shall know the wrath of him who joined the woman to the man and wished the earth to be filled, and he shall pay a fine of 100 pounds of gold and 1000 of silver, and his action will be without avail, while this present certificate of dowry shall remain firm, stable, and unshaken for all time with the attached stipulation.

+ DOCUMENT 15 (*EXTR.* I 13, PP. 541–42, COMPLETE):

[A] The supreme and ineffable Father, whose superessence precedes[22] by the excellence of its nature even the atoms and the void, which are said in the absurd doctrines of some ancient philosophers to have existed always, as if they were two ultimate and eternal principles, provided by means of that form of the total good which is begotten in him,[23] although not begotten in a temporal way, that is, through his coeternal and consubstantial wisdom, the resplendent abode of highest heaven for the ten orders of spiritual hosts who were created to the glory and honor of his name. It pleased God to endow the choirs of angels who were subtlest in nature (as well as the others, who had been assigned different natures and adorned with different gifts) with the power of choice. Thus they could either enjoy perpetual happiness by serving God, and so remain true to their inborn goodness, showing all due devotion, or they could lose this happiness irrevocably by their contempt. It should not be supposed that the fount of all good things wished to confer free choice upon them in order that some should be ruined through their criminal arrogance. On the contrary, he did this to ensure that he had with him beings who had

---

[22] Here I read *precurrit* instead of Zeumer's *percurrit*. I am grateful to Édouard Jeauneau for suggesting this correction.

[23] "per insitam sibi . . . totius boni formam": an echo of Boethius, *Consolation of Philosophy* III, m. 9, 5–6 (CCL 94, 52): "insita summi forma boni."

earned his reward by their zealous service, a service that was not coerced but free. But the angels of that choir which took the name of Lucifer ["Light Bearer"], because of the brilliance that they had received at the moment of creation from God's munificence, failed to respect the creator's excellence and to revere his majesty. Hence they were filled with self-admiration, and at once, stripped of the vestment of light, they fell headlong into the abyss, darkened with all manner of foulness. Then the other heavenly hosts, observing with consternation the judgment and ruin of these celestial beings, were frightened that the same would happen to them, and they therefore turned away from that imperfect and simple endowment which is constituted by free choice, to ensure that no tendency to sin should ever touch them. It was for this reason, therefore, that human kind came into being, namely, so that humankind was able, through obedience, to achieve that glory which [the fallen choir] had lost though pride and irremediable guilt. Now, the good creator and disposer of all things did not wish that men should achieve the multiplication of human kind by freely abusing whichever women they might choose. On the contrary, he wished marital fidelity to be observed between each man and his wife. Therefore he betrothed one woman, not several, to the first man, and while this man was still holy and wise he said through him, "A man shall leave his father and mother and cleave unto his wife, and they shall be two in one flesh [Gen. 2:24]." In this way, he who married the one virgin to one man, and who made them two in one flesh, implied that it was forbidden for either partner to be joined to a third after separation. But this is shown by so many statements of the New and Old Testaments that it does not need to be confirmed by any arguments on our part. Our Lord Jesus Christ showed clearly that legitimate marriage is a sacred compact and not a crime by deigning to be present at a wedding feast with his disciples, where he graced marriage with the first of his signs [i.e., miracles: John 2:11]. [B] Therefore I, by name ___, a knight of God, desiring to imitate the institutions of the holy Fathers [i.e., the Patriarchs], wish to take you, by name ___, as my wife because of the desire to beget offspring [*propter amorem generandae prolis*], and to abide faithfully by the conjugal rule in matrimony. [C] And I will to bestow upon you something from what I possess, so that, the union of marriage having been performed according to custom, you shall by my oath [*ex mea legione*][24] have these things as your rightful dowry [*dos*].

May you always render to your *sponsus*, who has done this,
Dutiful service and loving fidelity.[25]
Amen. Blessed be God!

---

[24] Compare the definition of *legio* in Charles Du Cange et al., *Glossarium Mediae et Infimae Latinitatis*, new edition, vol. 5 (Paris, 1938): "An oath by which something said or promised was confirmed and safeguarded, as if by a legion." (My translation.)

[25] An elegiac couplet: "Reddas ipsa diu sponso, qui talia fecit, / Servitium suplex et sub amore fidem."

+ Document 16 (*Extr.* I 14, p. 542, complete):

Reliant on the divine authority whereby God formed woman from the rib of the first parent, and supported by the strength of what the Gospel teaches, saying, "For this reason a man shall leave his father and mother and cleave unto this wife, and they shall be two in one flesh" [Matt. 19:5, Mark 10:7–8], and corroborated by the legal institution of my predecessors, [B] I, the knight Gauscelinus, with the consent of our parents and kinsfolk, choose to take you in marriage, O my most beloved betrothed, by name Ascelina, in the desire to procreate offspring [*procreandorum amore filiorum*], [C] and I wish to honor you from my possessions to the extent that I am able. – – –.[26] What more need be said? We also, by God's gift, shall remain undivided, and likewise our possessions, with God's blessing, shall remain firm, stable, and undivided[27] throughout our life together, by the same authorities[28] as we cited above. So be it!

+ Document 17 (*Extr.* I 15, pp. 542–43, complete):

[A] Many assertions of the sacred scriptures and writings of the expert doctors teach us quite plainly and in detail that God, the maker and governor of all things, created the angelic nobility to praise and glorify him. But some of the host, because of ruinous pride, were cast out from the heavenly seat in an irreparable fall. Lest their blessed station should become deserted, the same God, having formed the entire cosmic system [*tocius machina mundi*], made man from dirt as from matter, in the image of his own splendor. And having put the man to sleep at the bidding of his will and taken a rib from his side, he fashioned a woman for him. Next, confirming them by his blessing, he said, "Increase and multiply" [Gen. 1:28], and he added, "A man shall leave his father and mother and cleave unto his wife, and they shall be two in one flesh" [Gen. 2:24]. And eventually the Lord came in the flesh, and not refusing, with the presence of his body, to go to a wedding, he converted the waters[29] into wine and illumined marriage with his holy miracles. But the Apostle too commends the goodness of marriage for the avoidance of fornication when he says, amongst other things, "Let each one have [his own wife] because of fornication" [1 Cor. 7:2]. Accordingly, a custom has most beautifully taken root such that any man who wills to take a wife should take her in fidelity, with legitimate consent, and in the hope of offspring, not motivated by lust; and that he should make a legally constituted dotal charter

---

[26] Lacuna of three empty lines.
[27] "nostra ... firma et stabilita individuaque ... manebunt." Compare *Extr.* I 12, line 23 (p. 541): "hic libellus dotis firmus et stabilis inconvulsusque ... permaneat."
[28] That is, biblical quotations.
[29] Literally, "liquids" (*latices*): the Latin of this charter is extravagantly ornate!

[*osculum*] whereby he gives her something from his own estate; and that he should not proceed secretly, as do the gentiles who do not know God, but rather, having summoned kinsfolk to be present from both sides, he should establish a publicly celebrated marriage. [B] Being mindful, therefore, of these authorities, I, *N.*, choose to have you, my most beloved betrothed, *N.*, as my wife [*uxor*], not without the legitimate agreement both of my parents and of yours; and [C] from my estate in accordance with the rite of our predecessors I constitute a dotal agreement [*osculum*], giving you *such and such*.

CHAPTER FIVE

Marriage and Diplomatics: Five Dower Charters from the Regions of Laon and Soissons, 1163–1181

Laurent Morelle

One does not find many charters for the constitution of dowers in the archives of the tenth through twelfth centuries. The impressive series of *sponsalicia* from Cluny is unique in this respect, a precious exception confirming the rule of rarity that seems to prevail with acts of this sort, even when they pertain to persons of princely rank.[1] Yet in the course of an entirely different investigation, I had the good fortune to encounter a small group of five dower charters, most of which were

---

[1] For sources of this type, see Jean Verdon, "Les sources de l'histoire de la femme en Occident aux Xe–XIIIe siècles," *Cahiers de civilisation médiévale* 20 (1977): 219–51, at 242–44. André Lemaire's study, "Les origines de la communauté de biens entre époux dans le droit coutumier français," *Revue historique de droit français et étranger*, 4th ser., 7 (1928): 584–643, depends in part on the exploitation of the dower charters that he was able to assemble from the Frankish period to the beginning of the thirteenth century. Georges Duby has focused on the Cluny *sponsalicia* in his *La société aux XIe et XIIe siècles dans la région mâconnaise*, 2nd ed. (Paris, [1953] 1971), 65 and 217–18; and in idem, *Le chevalier, la femme et le prêtre: Le mariage dans la France féodale* (Paris, 1981), 103–10. See also André Vandenbossche, "La dot d'après les actes de la pratique," in idem, *Contribution à l'histoire des régimes matrimoniaux: La dos ex marito dans la Gaule franque* (Paris, 1953), 151–226. (In fact, this study runs to the end of the tenth century.) All these authors have stressed the general rarity of dower charters, especially from the eleventh and twelfth centuries. Among scholars who have studied the dowers of the Norman duchesses is Lucien Musset: see his "Actes inédits du XIe siècle. III: Les plus anciennes chartes de l'abbaye de Bourgueil," *Bulletin de la Société des antiquaires de Normandie* 54 (1957–58): 27–36, at 28 ff. Joseph Avril discusses a twelfth-century formula for nuptial charters in his *Le gouvernement des évêques et la vie religieuse dans le diocèse d'Angers (1148–1240)*, vol. 1 (Lille and Paris [1984]), 179–84.

What follows is a translation of Laurent Morelle, "Mariage et diplomatique: Autour de cinq chartes de douaire dans le Laonnois-Soissonnais 1163–1181," *Bibliothèque de l'École des chartes* [hereafter BEC] 146 (1988): 225–84, and it is included here with permission of BEC. The translation was done with the collaboration of the author, who had made some corrections and minor changes to the French text. The editors have omitted an appendix, entitled "Regarding the Laonnois formula of 1163/1176: Did the church preferentially favor marriage in the first non-prohibited degree?" (258–65). In place of Prof. Morelle's editions of the five dower charters (in Latin), this version includes English translations done by Prof. Joseph Goering. Where necessary, the editors refer the reader to the original text in BEC. Note that for the purposes of this chapter, the "dower" (*douaire*) is the *dos ex marito*, i.e., the principal assign that a man gives to his bride (or to her family) to confirm their betrothal or marriage.

unpublished.[2] It is a homogeneous corpus from two points of view: as regards the date of their composition, because these acts emerge during a short period of less than twenty years (1163–81); and as regards their district of origin, because they all derive from the ecclesiastical province of Reims. Four of them are from the diocese of Laon (Charters 1, 3, 4, and 5), and the other (2) is from the neighboring diocese of Soissons.[3]

The rarity of this diplomatic genre, the uniformity of the body of material, and the hitherto lukewarm interest in matrimonial questions among historians were all reasons inviting the preparation of a rather extensive commentary. It was desirable first to examine, as well as their internal characteristics, problems regarding the production of these documents. Two lines of approach then suggested themselves, which I have followed in turn: first, I have examined the manner in which most of the charters spoke of marriage; then, passing from the preamble to the disposition, I have focused on the description of the dower itself, attempting, insofar as the biographical data concerning the spouses permitted it, to determine the characteristics of the matrimonial unions documented therein.

ARCHIVAL AND DIPLOMATIC EXAMINATION

The Textual Tradition of the Charters

None of these acts is extant in the original. Instead, all the texts are known from copies made by scholars in the seventeenth and eighteenth centuries from the original or from a medieval cartulary that has now disappeared. They belonged to the archives of four religious establishments: the Benedictine abbeys of Nogent-sous-Coucy (Charters 1 and 4), Saint-Prix de Saint-Quentin (3), and Saint-Crépin-le-Grand de Soissons (2); and Saint-Martin de Laon, a community of Premonstraten-sian canons (5).

---

[2] The charters are appended at the end of this chapter. Only Charter 3 has been published before (by Dom Luc d'Achery in his *Spicilegium*). It is partly because of the curiosity of Dom Grenier that I was able to assemble these documents, for in the notice accompanying each copy of Charters 1, 2, and 4 that he sent to the Cabinet des chartes (copies of the Moreau collection), the famous Maurist had the good idea of mentioning the existence of the two other charters; and after finding Charter 2, it was easy for me to locate Charters 1 and 4. What brought my attention to Charter 3 (which Lemaire knew from the d'Achery edition) was Dominique Barthélemy, *Les deux âges de la seigneurie banale: Pouvoir et société dans la terre des sires de Coucy (milieu XIᵉ – milieu XIIIᵉ siècle)*, 2nd ed. (Paris, 2000), 208, n. 190. Barthélemy, who was not aware of the edition cited earlier, had discovered the only extant manuscript copy of the text. It was during research into the cartularies of the Laonnois and northern Soissonnais that I got hold of Charter 5. It is important to point out that I have not undertaken, within the scope of this article, a systematic investigation of the available documentary sources concerning the region and the period in question. What guided my work was mainly biographical research into the participants. May I acknowledge here the great assistance of my wife, Josiane Barbier, who gave me access to her dossiers on the Laonnois aristocracy of the twelfth century.

[3] The corpus looks homogeneous, too, from a third standpoint, that of the social level of the spouses. Apart from those in Charter 5, who cannot be identified, the spouses belonged to the lesser or middle aristocracy. On this point, see the section entitled "Three Case Studies," which follows, as well as the notes on the identification of the spouses that follow the texts of the charters in the appendix.

One may assume that in most cases, an abbey acquired the parchment at the same time as it acquired the dower goods listed in the charter. Deposited in the charter room and transcribed in a cartulary, the act would then have been evidence of a donation made by the couple or, perhaps more often, by the widow or her heirs.[4] But the cession of a charter to an ecclesiastical establishment was sometimes the result of a more complicated process. This is shown by the history of a charter (now lost) that Raoul d'Écry, a knight in the entourage of the Sire de Pierrepont, granted to his wife Émeline de Bosmont between 1174 and 1184.[5] Among the properties constituting the dower was a carucate of land that Raoul held in fee from his brother Jean, but improperly, for their father Foulque d'Écry had previously granted it to the canons of Saint-Martin de Laon. Acknowledging the rights of the canons, Raoul, with his wife's consent, restored the land to them, with the bishop acting as intermediary. Then Émeline, "because she did not wish the church to be troubled henceforth, rendered the charter of her dower to the abbot and brethren of St. Martin [*quia nolebat ecclesiam inde de caetero disturbari, reddidit abbati et fratribus Sancti Martini cartam dotis suae*]." In this case, the document was placed in the abbey's charter room without there being, in the proper sense, a cession of the dower done in the abbey's benefit. Moreover, the source specifies that the charter listed other betrothal gifts (*dona sponsalia*) besides the disputed curucate of land. This shows clearly that the preservation of a dower charter by an ecclesiastical establishment does not necessarily imply that the latter had acquired rights over the entirety of the properties listed by the document.[6]

It would be unjust to complain that the diplomatic dossier assembled here is meager. The existence, on average, of only one charter in every four years is

[4] The charter of 1170 that Dreu d'Allemant granted to his wife Brune (2) comes from the archives of Saint-Crépin-le-Grand. In 1152, Dreu, his mother, and his stepfather had concluded an agreement with the same establishment concerning the wood of Le Fruty, a place mentioned in the dower charter: see William M. Newman, *Les seigneurs de Nesle en Picardie (XIIᵉ–XIIIᵉ siècles): Leurs chartes et leur histoire*, Bibliothèque de la Société d'histoire du droit des pays flamands, picards et wallons 27, vol. 2 (Paris, 1971), p. 55, no. 20. It is possible, therefore, that Saint-Crépin received the nuptial charter at the same time as acquiring the dower lands at Le Fruty. On the charter of 1152, see also text of Charter 2. Note, too, that Mathilde d'Épagny, beneficiary of Charter 1, belonged to a family whose seat was at a short distance from the abbey of Nogent-sous-Coucy, where her dower charter was eventually preserved.

[5] The fortunes of Émeline's dower and of her charter are reported in a charter granted in 1184 by Roger, Bishop of Laon (Cartulary of Saint-Martin [Stein no. 1868], Arch. dép. Aisne, H 872, fol. 111; unless otherwise noted, all the shelf marks cited here are from the Arch. dép. Aisne). The charter carried the seal of this bishop, appointed in 1174 (see n. 9 later). On the spouses, see n. 94.

[6] One might ask, as Émeline's active role suggests, whether some wives entrusted their charters to religious houses chiefly to ensure their preservation, for we know that widows' dowers were often the subject of dispute. For a possible piece of evidence for this motive, see the dower charter (1159) that Philip of Alsace, count of Flanders, made in favor of his wife Élisabeth de Vermandois, which was placed and preserved in the abbey of Mont-Saint-Quentin: see Thérèse de Hemptinne and Adriaan Verhulst (eds.), *De oorkonden der graven van Vlaanderen (juli 1128 – september 1191)*, vol. 2.1: *Regering van Diederik van de Elzas (juli 1128 – januari 1168)*, Commission royale d'histoire, Recueil des actes des princes belges 6 (Brussels, 1988), no. 182; and cf. my review, BEC 150 (1992): 358–62, at 360.

understandable because these documents, normally retained by the wife, were intended to disappear with the dowager. Indeed, the number of dower charters preserved or merely attested[7] appears, in fact, to be rather large for such a restricted geographical and chronological range. This impression becomes even stronger when one considers that dower charters from earlier periods seem (as far as I have been able to ascertain) to be nonexistent in this region (although only very full research, which I have not been able to carry out, would permit a conclusion on the matter). One seems to be confronted here, therefore, with a "documentary upsurge" pertaining especially to the Laon region.[8]

How might one interpret this upsurge? Should one posit a lucky archival accident that lifts the veil over a hidden diplomatic practice? That is improbable, for the extant charters exceed the limits of a single cartulary. Moreover, on that assumption, mentions of lost charters should crop up more consistently. I believe, rather, that this upsurge indicates a real change, whether because a larger number of charters were composed around 1160–80, or because they were better preserved (being judged more valuable in this period or in the decades that followed), or because of a combination of factors. Let us nevertheless leave this question unresolved, for it requires us first to place the dower charters in the more general context of the intervention of the church in this field.

The Redaction of the Charters

The charters presented here take the form of acts, the author of which was the husband (whose name appears in the intitulation), but which were enacted under the seal of ecclesiastical authority. The charter from Soissons (Charter 2) had attached to it the seal of the cathedral chapter of Saint-Gervais-et-Saint-Protais, whereas the four acts from Laon bore the subscription of the episcopal chancellor and were certainly embellished with the bishop's seal (like the charter of Raoul d'Écry mentioned previously, which was sealed with the prelate's "image").[9] The striking consistency of the Laon examples suggests that the bishop's chancery played a

---

[7] Besides the charter of Émeline already cited, we may mention the *instrumentum* that Clérembaud de Berlancourt granted to his wife Agnès in 1171 (Aisne, arrondissement Vervins, canton Sains-Richaumont). This charter, now lost, which is known through an episcopal act of 1177 (Cartulary of Thenailles [Stein no. 3812], Bibliothèque nationale de France, lat. 5649, fol. 32v) that gives its contents, is cited by Barthélemy, *Les deux âges* (n. 2 earlier), 209, n. 191.

[8] Six of the seven documents recorded concern the diocese of Laon. We shall see that certain specific aspects of the Laonnois material invite us to regard the diffusion of dower charters in this diocese as a phenomenon that is somewhat peculiar in its character and scope.

[9] The episcopal charter through which we know this fact (for references, see n. 5 earlier) expresses it as follows: "[carrucatam terrae] quam et idem Radulphus Emelinae uxori suae dedit in dotem et per litteras nostra imagine sigillatas fecit confirmari." (What follows shows that these *litterae* were, in fact, the dower charter.) Moreover, we know from a charter of the same Bishop Roger (see references in n. 7 earlier) that the *instrumentum dotale* granted to his wife by Clérembaud de Berlancourt was enacted *sub testimonio* [*Galteri*] *episcopi*. This expression seemingly refers to the bishop's seal, and in any case, it attests to the guarantee that he provided for the dispositions directed.

preponderant and even monopolistic role in the composition of dower charters, at least those affecting the aristocracy of the *milites*. But the scarcity of material from Soissons prevents us from deciding whether the cathedral chapter played a comparable role in the neighboring diocese.

The chancery of Laon was not content with authenticating such charters: it also attended to their preparation, as the chancellor's subscription indicates.[10] Indeed, it seems to have applied a formulary, because we find the same preamble and the same beginning of the disposition in two marriage charters separated by thirteen years and apparently concerning entirely different lineages (Charters 1 and 3).[11] This is surely a clear sign that the activity of the chancery in matrimonial affairs had become standardized, and it is consequently an index of the intensity of that activity.

The Elements of the Diplomatic Discourse

In the absence of the originals, the external characteristics of these documents remain undiscoverable. Nevertheless, for the charter from Soissons (Charter 2), there is an eighteenth-century tracing that reproduces the first words of the original. This fragile facsimile displays a first line in large characters with very elegant handwriting: evidence of a quality of execution that is consistent with the solemn style of writing that this charter displays, as with the majority of similar ones.

Four of the five charters open with a simple invocation of the Trinity, whereas the charter of 1181 (5) begins with a brief *In nomine Domini*. The invocation may be followed by "amen" (1/3, 2). Then comes the preamble. This is extremely elaborate in 1163/1176 and in 1170 (120 words for Charters 1 and 3; 97 for Charter 2), but it is markedly shorter in 1177 (Charter 4, 44 words), and it is reduced to a brief sentence of fourteen words in 1181 (Charter 5). The preamble of this last charter is fundamentally different from the others in that it alone deals with the dower, whereas the only theme developed in the preambles to Charters 1/3, 2, and 4 concerns the benefits of the matrimonial state.

To the preamble is attached the subjective intitulation (the husband's name preceded by *ego*), introduced by a simple adverb meaning "therefore" (1/3: *igitur*; 5: *iccirco*) or by a causal subordinate clause introduced by *cum* ("since" or "because") and serving as a summary (2 and 4).[12] The intitulation is incorporated into the disposition, the structure of which (with the exception again of 5) is the same:

---

[10] "Angotus cancellarius relegit, scripsit et subscripsit" (1); "Ego Willelmus cancellarius scripsi" (3, 4, and 5). These formulas conform to those that may be seen in other contemporary charters produced by the Laonnois chancery. For Angot's signature, see Annie Dufour-Malbezin (ed.), *Actes des évêques de Laon: Des origines à 1151* (Paris, 2001), 30.

[11] For this reason, Charters 1 and 3 are often grouped together (1/3) in what follows.

[12] "Cum ad nuptiales celebrationes ipsius Domini simus instructi sententia..., ego..." (Charter 2); "Cum igitur hec et alia multa sacre Scripture testimonia in commendatione veniunt nuptiarum, ego..." (Charter 4).

the husband, addressing his *sponsa*,[13] whom he names and addresses with an affectionate adjective (1/3: *dilectissima*; 2: *karissima*),[14] tells her that he takes her as his wife[15] and gives her a certain amount of property specified in the text that follows.[16]

In comparison with this formula, Charter 5 shows two important variations: first, there is no verb indicating that the author of the act hereby takes the one named as his wife; second, the term *uxor* ("wife") replaces *sponsa* ("betrothed") in the address to his partner (*dilecta uxor mea Bertrea*). A third variation should be mentioned, although it is a formal one: the listing of the assigned goods, which is introduced by the verbs *dedi* ("I have given") and then *assignavi* ("I have assigned"), is preceded by an introductory clause stating that he has arranged for the following gift to be given to her for their marriage ("subscriptam tibi donationem propter nuptias ordinavi"), a statement that makes the patrimonial dispositions of the act stand out clearly.

Some further observations on the diplomatic elements described previously are in order here. The name of the husband, like that of the wife, is ordinarily devoid of a determinative, surname, or place reference. Yet Charter 3 seems to deviate from this rule, inasmuch as it has as the intitulation the phrase "I, Arnoul de Monceau." Perhaps someone using the document added this determinative ("de Monceau") to the original version, for in contrast, there is no such exception in the naming of his wife. We note finally that in 1163 (1), the disposition concludes with a clause specifying the rights of the bride: this is the only charter displaying such a formula.[17]

The corroborative clause is traditionally composed of two syntactic elements. The first element is a subordinate clause of purpose expressing the finality of the document. The three most recent charters (3, 4, and 5) use a positive expression, referring to the unchallenged possession of the property (3 and 4: *ut haec in pace possideas*)[18] or the permanence of the judicial act (5: *ut haec donatio firma tibi permaneat*). In contrast, the first two charters employ a negative formula that

---

[13] This term is missing in Charter 2.

[14] On adjectives of this type in diplomatic documents, see Jean Leclercq, *Le mariage vu par les moines au XIIe siècle* (Paris, 1983), 15–16.

[15] "Te michi uxorem conjungo" (Charters 1 and 3); "duxi te uxorem" (4); "religiosa... unione uniri tibi preeligens" (2).

[16] "Doque tibi jure dotativo optimam partem de his que possideo, scilicet..." (1 and 3); "et dedi tibi jure dotalicio..." (4); "in donationem propter nuptias...tibi concedo..." (2). The verbs in the disposition are in the present tense in the first three charters (1/3, 2), and in the perfect tense in the last two.

[17] "Hec omnia do tibi tenore juris quod amodo ea libere habeas [et] quiete possideas." On this disposition, see subsequent discussion toward the end of the section entitled "Three Case Studies."

[18] Charter 3 presents an inaccurate formula inasmuch as it states that the goods in the dower have been sealed: "Ut igitur haec in pace possideas, ea tibi feci sigillo... episcopi confirmari...." The poor wording probably comes from an imperfect adaptation of the type of formula that is correctly used in the corroboration to Charter 4. The resemblance between Charters 3 and 4 on this point suggests a common model.

applies to the written act (2: *et ne contra cartam alicui liceat malignari*) or that defines nothing in particular (1: *hoc autem ne possit... infringi vel immutari*). The second element is the main clause specifying the means of corroboration. All the acts except Charter 5 (which is again exceptional) mention the presence of the seal and of the witnesses. In Charter 5, the redactor has quite logically mentioned the putting of the grant in writing before mentioning its sealing, but he has not deemed it useful to mention the witnesses.

The presentation of the witnesses varies. Charters 1, 3, and 4 have subscriptions of the type "Sign of so-and-so" (*Signum talis*),[19] but the other two enumerate the names of witnesses in a continuous list. In 1170 (2), the list of names, in the genitive, is introduced by *videlicet* ("namely"), an adverb that organically combines the list with the corroboration (... *legitimorum virorum ... testimonio confirmo, videlicet Herberti.* ...). In 1181 (5), the names of the witnesses, in the nominative, are introduced by the usual expression in this form of presentation: *Testes sunt hujus rei* ("The witnesses of this [act] are...."). The number of witnesses or signatories is variable, and there is a noticeable decline between the beginning and the end of the period: fifteen in 1163 (1) and eighteen in 1170 (2), but ten in 1176 (3), and only seven in 1177 and 1181 (4 and 5). First appear the clerics and monks, if there are any. Then come the laymen, divided, it seems, into two more or less strictly separated groups: first the husband's witnesses, and then the wife's (apparently less numerous).[20] Oddly enough, the redactor of Charter 1 omitted to note the ties of kinship that bound the spouses to the witnesses and the witnesses to each other.[21]

All the charters are dated by the year of the Christian era, preceded by *actum* ("done" or "enacted": 1, 2, and 3) or by *scriptum* ("written": 4 and 5). Charter 5 is again distinct, this time by its mentioning, before the date, the *recognitio* of the act before the bishop. Besides the dating according to the Christian era, Charter 2 gives the years of the king's reign and the bishop's, whereas Charter 5 states what day it was (*in die Mathiae apostoli*).

In the Laon charters, as we have seen, the final protocol ends with the subscription of the chancellor, which the charter from Soissons omits.

---

[19] In Charter 4, the presence of a priest of the episcopal chapel is indicated thus: "Symon quoque presbiter ... hiis interfuit." The different treatment no doubt indicates that the priest (possibly the officiating priest) did not participate on the same basis as the other signatories. It seems to me that the adopted expression emphasizes his presence at the ceremony, whereas the signatures, emanating from the socio-familial entourage of the spouses, indicate consent to the stated dispositions.

[20] The division of the lay witnesses into two groups is striking at least in Charters 1 and 2 (see, in the appendix that follows, the corresponding notes on the identification of the spouses). It did not prevent the witnesses from a higher social level (who could intervene for one or the other or both of the spouses) from appearing at the head of the list of laymen. Such is the case with Gérard de Quierzy (2) and Hugues de Pierrepont (4).

[21] This omission may not have been innocent. For kinship bonds that are not mentioned, see the appendix, Charter 1, n. 22.

A Diplomatic Genre with Two Categories

Diplomatic analysis shows that although all these charters have a common architecture, inherited from the early Middle Ages,[22] they also display differences of
varying importance. The examination of these differences leads us above all to
regard Charter 5 as distinct. It contains three novelties that we have already noted.
First, the preamble of act, which is limited to a brief sentence, only discusses the
dower, whereas the other preambles praise the matrimonial state without saying
a word about the dower. Second, in the disposition of Charters 1–4, the husband
declares to his *sponsa* that he takes her as his wife and only then lists the goods with
which he endows her, whereas the declaration of marriage is omitted from Charter
5. Third, and also in the disposition, Charter 5 alone calls the beneficiary of the
dower the man's "wife" (*uxor*), whereas she is called his "betrothed" (*sponsa*) in the
other charters.[23] These peculiarities establish a distinction between two kinds of
instrument: the *nuptial* charter represented by Charters 1–4; and the purely *dotal*
charter, of which Charter 5 is an example.

Charter 5, then, seems to be an act of "regularization" drawn up after the marriage. The woman is no longer a *sponsa*, a term that characterizes a transitional state
before the consummation of the marriage.[24] Instead, she is an *uxor*: a woman fully
drawn into the married state. Therefore, it seems that Charter 5 took place *after* the
wedding. It is to be expected that this act does not include any announcement of the
marriage on the husband's part, which would be incongruous in such a document.
Moreover, one can understand how a preamble enlarging on the theme of the benefits of marriage would be inappropriate. Of strictly patrimonial import, the charter
of 1181 (5) is clear, sober, and precise,[25] making no sacrifice to ceremonial effect.

---

[22] Certain formal elements, such as the grouping preamble-intitulation-disposition, as well as the wife's
being addressed in the vocative case, are firmly entrenched in the Cluny *sponsalicia* of the tenth to
the beginning of the eleventh century, and one may observe their emergence in the Merovingian
formulas for *libelli* or *cartae dotis* that Karl Zeumer assembled in *Formulae merowingici et karolini
aevi*, MGH *Leges* V: *Formulae* (Hanover, 1882–86): see references given for the terms *sponsa* and *dos*
in Zeumer's index. [This material is discussed here in Chapter 4.]

[23] Nevertheless, Charter 2, as I have noted, gives no title of this sort to the wife.

[24] The terms *sponsus* and *sponsa* (like the word *desponsatio*), as used in twelfth-century sources, cannot
be translated unless one takes some account of the doctrinal controversies of the period regarding
the formation of the matrimonial bond. Were *sponsi* mere "fiancés," or were they already "spouses"?
On these debates, see for example Gabriel Le Bras, "Mariage: La doctrine du mariage chez les
théologiens et les canonistes depuis l'an mil," *Dictionnaire de théologie catholique*, vol. 9 (1927), 2139–
54; and Jean Gaudemet, *Le mariage en Occident, les mœurs et le droit* (Paris, 1987), 165–69 and 175–77.
It appears that the terms *sponsus* and *sponsa* designated persons who were mutually "engaged," but
that such terms applied to them only before the consummation of their marriage. These are the
terms characteristically employed in the matrimonial *ordines* of the twelfth century even after the
exchange of consent: see Jean-Baptiste Molin and Protais Mutembe, *Le rituel du mariage en France
du XIIe au XVIe siècle* (Paris, 1974), 284–93 (*ordines* I–VII). It seems that the consummation of the
marriage determined what terminology was applicable to the married couple in legal documents.

[25] We have noted previously certain formal elements illustrating this characteristic: the summarizing
introduction to the disposition, the mention of the *recognitio* before the bishop, and the inclusion
of the day in the dating of the act.

In contrast, all the other charters presented here have the air of having been prepared for the wedding. They were surely intended to be harmoniously inserted into the marriage ritual, in which they were to be read. The work of Jean-Baptiste Molin and Protais Mutembe has shown that in the marriage liturgy found through-out northern France from the end of the eleventh century, several phases of the ritual took place "before the doors of a church" (*ante januas ecclesiae*), notably the reading of the dower charter. And it is, in fact, this type of ceremonial for which we have evidence in the Laon region: it is found in a missal written in England around 1125/1135, which was brought to Laon "very shortly afterwards."[26] It is probable that during the period 1160–70, the reading of the dower charter often accompanied the "handing over" of the wife to her husband.

Considered in their proper context, then, the specific traits of Charters 1–4 take on a new significance. Their preambles are concerned not with justifying the customary institution of the dower but with proclaiming – indeed, with defending – the virtues of the sacrament of marriage. Thus it is not surprising that on the day of the wedding, the husband declares his union with his *sponsa* before listing the properties that he reserves for her.[27] The solemnity of the act, its deliberately oratorical tone, and its barely restrained structure accord well enough with a public reading done in the course of a ceremony.

It would be good to know how charters of this sort evolved after the period 1160–80. Unfortunately, there is a dearth of examples for comparison in the last decades of the twelfth century.[28] I have argued that by following the chronology of

---

[26] Molin and Mutembe, *Le rituel*, 36 and 289–91 (edition of the *ordo* in question, no. V). The missal is preserved in Laon (Bibl. mun., ms. 238).

[27] On this point, one should note the disparity between the Cluny *sponsalicia* of the tenth and eleventh centuries and the nuptial charters examined here. The former often use, in the disposition, a formula that in some sense defines the position of the donation in relation to the stages leading up to the wedding and the matrimonial state. See, for example, Auguste Bernard and Alexandre Bruel (eds.), *Recueil des chartes de l'abbaye de Cluny*, 6 vols. (Paris, 1876–1903), vol. 2, act no. 969 (January 955): "Dulcissima id est bene cupientissima esponsa mea, nomen Tetdrada, ego, in Dei nomen, Vulricus, ... tibi esponsavi, et, si Domini placuisset, ad legitimum conjugium tibi sociari volo; in pro eo [sic] dono tibi ...." Comparable formulae are found in numerous *sponsalicia* from the Cluny archives, but this concern is not restricted to Burgundian redactors of the tenth century. It appears in a more or less veiled form in several formulas included among Zeumer's *Formulae*; for example: "Quamobrem ego in Dei nomine N. ut multis habeatur percognitum, aliquam feminam nomine N. mihi una per consensum parentorum nostrorum et amicorum eam legibus sponsare decerno, et ad diem nuptiarum, Domino iubente, pervenire delibero. Et coedo ei ...." (*Form. extravagantes*, I, no. 9, p. 538 [from a tenth-century copy, probably originating in Orléans]). Here the donation is located as a prolongation of the betrothal (*desponsatio*) and as preliminary to the marriage. In contrast, our nuptial charters clearly combine the statement of the marriage with the dower and are silent about the ceremony of betrothal. Likewise, the statement of marriage emerges more clearly (as in the clear-cut formula of Charters 1 and 3) than in the older charters, and it takes the form of a decision made in the present. The development of the disposition seems rich with significance: in neglecting the stages contributing to matrimony, the act both sanctions the liturgical ceremony (in which the reading of the *dotalicium* occurred) and emphasizes the importance of the statement of voluntary consent in the formation of the marriage bond.

[28] It is difficult to explain this documentary lapse. I advance an hypothesis later, in n. 109.

the existing charters, one perceives a relative shortening of the preamble, a decrease
in the number of witnesses, and the replacement of bombastic negative formulas
with more direct positive expressions. Nevertheless, the small size of the assembled
dossier deprives such observations of any great value. Archival accident can give
an illusion of a tendency toward sobriety where, in fact, there is only a variation in
individual cases.

One may add a disconcerting example to this dossier: a dower charter with the
date 1204, enacted in the name of a certain Jean with possessions in the Ardennes,
but under the seal of Roger de Rozoy, Bishop of Laon (the same bishop as the one
who oversaw Charters 3, 4, and 5). This act displays the same characteristics as the
purely dotal charter of 1181 (5), except that the beneficiary is said to be a *sponsa*,
and not an *uxor*.[29] Without wishing to infer too much from a single example, one
may nevertheless ask whether, progressively in the course of the last decades of the
twelfth century, dower charters may have lost their "nuptial" character and become
limited to the judicial core that in the last analysis was their reason for existence.

THE PREAMBLES: A PASTORAL TEACHING ON MARRIAGE

Besides what is apparent in the disposition,[30] certain formal aspects of the dower
charters seem to reveal, in their own fashion, a particular conception of the union
of matrimony. For example, if the designation of the spouses by their names alone
is clearly a heritage from ancient times, its continuance in the twelfth century, when
the use of toponymic designations was becoming extensive, appears to be a way
of affirming that marriage is the affair of two individuals – of two acts of will –
and not of two kinships identified by an attached place name.[31] In this detail, one
may discern the struggle that the church undertook to rescue matrimonial consent
from the pressures of family strategy.

Yet it is in the preambles of these nuptial charters that a discourse develops on the
dignity of marriage and its sacramental value. Put into the mouth of the husband,
the words said in praise of marriage certainly express the voice of the church (and
more precisely that of the diocesan ordinary, given that the Laon charters were

[29] Godefroid Kurth (ed.), *Chartes de l'abbaye Saint-Hubert en Ardenne*, vol. 1 (Brussels, 1903), nos.
CXLVII–CXLVIII, p. 194 (charter partially reproduced in Lemaire, *Les origines*, 606). Just as in
Charter 5, there is a short preamble about the dower (here described as *precium pudicie*), there is
no statement of marriage, there is a summarizing sentence before the listing of properties ("Ego
Johannes... subscriptam donationem propter nuptias ordinavi"), and there is an analogous corroboration ("Ut igitur donum istud in pace possideas"). But in 1204, the apposition *karissima sponsa*
replaces the *dilecta uxor mea* of 1181.
[30] See n. 27 earlier.
[31] In Charter 1, the absence of indications of bonds of kinship among the witnesses (see Appendix,
Charter 1, n. 22) may arise from the same attitude. Note that in the nuptial charters in this collection,
the husband no longer recalls that the parents agreed to the marriage, as was the case in the Cluny
sponsalicia.

issued by the episcopal chancery, and that the act from Soissons probably came from the cathedral chapter). Preambles of this sort, devoted to the matrimonial state, were not an innovation of twelfth-century diplomatics. Indeed, one notes some charters furnished with preambles among the numerous Cluny *sponsalicia* of the tenth and early eleventh centuries.[32] These are usually limited to one or two biblical quotations, which spring suddenly upon the reader, but sometimes, "when those who are being married are the rich and the great," they are "long and pompous."[33]

Such solemnity reached its zenith in princely *acta*. The dower charters granted by the Norman dukes Richard II and Richard III to their spouses, respectively Judith and Adèle, display exceptionally extensive preambles.[34] It is true that their prolixity and the abundance of quotations were congruent with the sociopolitical rank of the partners, but it is also true that these texts, probably read by the husband[35] in the midst of a great concourse of vassals, kinsfolk, and friends, offered the church an ideal opportunity to disseminate its conception of marriage among the lay aristocracy. The relatively long preambles of the four nuptial charters presented here, from a century and a half later, in a period when this element of diplomatic discourse tended to lose amplitude and consistency, might pass as an insignificant survival, were it not that their unusual vitality is clearly linked to the role played by dotal charters in the henceforth better codified pattern of matrimonial rituals. Bearing a pastoral message, these texts exemplify the preoccupations of the episcopate and reveal indirectly the attitudes of the knightly society for which they were intended.

Between these two groups of preambles – those of the tenth to eleventh centuries and those done between 1160 and 1180 – there are marked differences, especially concerning the number and treatment of biblical quotations. In the *acta* done prior

---

[32] I have noted thirty *sponsalicia* in the *Recueil des chartes... de Cluny*: nos. 7, 75, 86, 189, 190, 229, 439, 496, 516, 659, 705, 725, 857, 969, 1211, 1242, 1331, 1390, 1392, 1412, 1415, 1426, 1427, 1777, 2265, 2618, 2628, 2633, 2659, and 2875. To these documents, one may add the dower charters granted after the wedding, although these are not always easy to distinguish from gifts between spouses. For partial lists of the Cluny *sponsalicia*, see Lemaire, *Les origines*, 593, n. 2, and 594, n. 2; and André Deléage, *La vie rurale en Bourgogne jusqu'au début du XIe siècle*, vol. 1 (Mâcon, 1941), 240, n. 7.

[33] I have found only twelve charters with preambles (*Recueil des chartes de... Cluny*, nos. 7, 86, 439, 496, 659, 705, 725, 857, 969, 1211, 1390, 2265). Seven of these preambles (nos. 439, 496, 659, 857, 969, 1211, 1390) are very short (two to four lines of text), and three contain six to nine lines (nos. 7, 86, and 705). Two of them (nos. 725 and 2265) are more extensive. The two quotations are from Duby, *Le chevalier*, 106, regarding act no. 2265 (the preamble of which he analyzes). This charter, drawn up in 994, concerns "Oury, master of the château of Bâgé en Bresse, the most powerful, with the Sire de Beaujeu, of the vassals of the count of Mâcon" (ibid.). The formulas extracted from the *libelli dotis* assembled by Zeumer (*Form. extravagantes*, I, nos. 9–15) contain extensive preambles, too, but unfortunately these texts are difficult to date, being known from copies of the tenth through twelfth centuries.

[34] For editions of the two acts, see Marie Fauroux, *Recueil des actes des ducs de Normandie de 911 à 1066*, Mémoires de la Société des Antiquaires de Normandie 36 (Caen, 1961), no. 11, pp. 82–85 (charter for Judith, 996–1008), and no. 58, pp. 180–82 (charter for Adèle, 1026–27).

[35] This at least is the opinion of Duby, *Le chevalier*, 106. One may presume that the officiating priest had the husband repeat the sentences of the text after him, translating as necessary.

to the twelfth century, biblical quotations form the basic framework of the preamble. At Cluny, the shortest preambles restrict themselves to reproducing all or part of Genesis 2:24 (probably quoted from Matthew 19:5 or Mark 10:7–8), and especially "What God has joined together, let man not separate [*Quod Deus conjunxit, homo non separet*]" from Matthew 19:6 (= Mark 10:9).[36] The more developed preambles supplement these two scriptural mainstays,[37] some with Genesis 9:1 ("Increase and multiply"), some with a version of 1 Corinthians 7:2 ("But because of fornication, let every man have his own wife, and every woman her own husband"), and some with Genesis 2:18 ("It is not good for man to be alone: let us make him a help like unto himself"), a text that is sometimes extended by the account of the creation (from Gen. 2:21 and 23). In addition, the miracle at Cana is evoked rather frequently.[38]

The taste for quotations was no less strong in the entourage of the Norman dukes. The preamble of the *dotalicium* for Judith rehearses six scriptural references,[39] and that granted to Adèle includes three.[40] Most of these quotations were already found in the Cluny corpus, but there are some new extracts, too, better fitted to emphasize the spiritual and sacramental value of marriage.[41]

In making a display of quotations, the redactors of these nuptial charters seem mainly to have wished to prove the legitimacy of ecclesiastical intervention in these profane affairs. But there is really no orderly exposition here: the references are all presented in the same way, often simply strung end to end and set out in the order of the sacred books, as is seen in the Norman *dotalicia*. If there is an embryonic commentary here, as in the Norman charters, a moral and disciplinary intention is always present: the object is to declare loudly and clearly that not every union is legitimate.[42]

---

[36] Gen. 2:24 ("Quamobrem relinquet homo patrem suum et matrem, et adhaerebit uxori suae et erunt duo in carne una"): *Recueil des chartes de... Cluny*, nos. 439, 659, 969 (in part), and 1390. Matt. 19:6: nos. 439, 496, 659, 969, 1211, and 1390. No. 857 gives no textual quotation but recalls the creation of man ("masculus et femina") and the establishment of marriage in view of fornication. For the references to these allusions, see subsequent discussion and n. 41.

[37] Only one of these charters (*Recueil des chartes de... Cluny*, no. 7) omits Gen. 2:24.

[38] For Gen. 9:1, see *Recueil des chartes de... Cluny*, no. 7. For 1 Cor. 7:2, see no. 725. For Gen. 2:18, see nos. 705 and 725. For Gen. 2:21 and 2:23, see no. 725 (and no. 86 includes an allusion to the creation). The wedding at Cana is mentioned in nos. 7, 725, and 2265.

[39] Gen. 1:27, 2:24, 9:1; Matt. 19:6 (= Mark 10:8); Eph. 5:25. Along with these references, there is a supporting allusion to the wedding at Cana.

[40] Gen. 2:24, Matt. 19:6 (= Mark 10:9), and Eph. 5:25. Here again, I do not count a reference to Cana.

[41] Matt. 19:6 (= Mark 10:8): "jam non sunt duo sed una caro"; Eph. 5:25: "Viri, diligite uxores vestras, sicut et Christus dilexit Ecclesiam." The use of Gen. 1:27, with contamination from Gen. 1:26 ("Creavit Deus hominem ad imaginem et similitudinem suam, masculum et feminam creavit eos"), is not entirely new (see n. 36 earlier).

[42] Charter for Adèle (act cited n. 34 above), where, having quoted Gen. 2:24, the author continues: "Unde patenter datur intelligi non quocunque modo vel fortuitu quasi ex libero animi arbitrio mulierem sociandam esse viro....."; and then at the end of the preamble: "His... et multis aliis dominicis preceptis habetur fixum viri et mulieris conjugium legitime in Domino semper celebrandum."

The preambles of the nuptial charters included in our corpus (Charters 1–4) are of a quite different construction. Here, scriptural references are reduced to a minimum. Among the three preambles,[43] only that of the act from Soissons (2) presents a true scriptural quotation, namely, Genesis 2:24. Admittedly, the preamble to Charters 1 and 3 unambiguously evokes the same passage from Genesis, but here the redactor has incorporated it into a sentence of his own, and he has changed the order of the propositions in the sacred text.[44] As for Charter 4, its preamble is distinguished by the absence of any quotation at all, reworked or otherwise.

The small number of quotations does not indicate any ignorance of the fundamental texts. The preambles refer more than ever to Christ's miracle at Cana, which is truly the central theme of the preambles. (Charter 2 is exemplary in this respect.) But the redactor no longer hides behind a wall of quotations. Instead, he merely invokes the scriptural passages to present a reflection or to build up a discourse. Quotation gives way to allusion as passive enumeration evolves into reasoned argument.

These changes, pertaining to the author's attitude to his texts of reference, are signs of a new maturity and depth in the pastoral message about marriage. The aim is no longer bluntly to drive the divine word into the people's minds, but rather to make them sharers in the theological conviction of the redactor: reasoning takes precedence over argument from authority. This desire to convince presupposes that there is some resistance to be overcome, and the adversary to be overthrown is heresy. These three preambles have a simple but precise end in view: to affirm and, indeed, to demonstrate the worthiness (*dignitas*) of marriage and its sacramental value, refuting the "execrable folly" (*execrabilis insania*: 1/3) or the *error* (2) of the heretics, those "detractors of marriage" (*detractores nuptiarum*) who deny that there is any good in matrimony.

Unanimity is not the same as uniformity. One may divide the nuptial preambles into two types: the first, which is of a *normative* character, is represented by the Laon formula found in 1163 and 1176 (1 and 3), and the second, which might be called *demonstrative*, brings together the charters of 1170 and 1177 (2 and 4).

The Laon formula of 1163/1176 forms a triptych. In the first panel, consisting of two dense sentences, the redactor recalls the progressive institution of the sacrament of marriage. Inaugurated by the union of Adam and Eve, whose example the patriarchs followed, and sanctioned by angelic marks of respect,[45] marriage was

---

[43] There are four nuptial charters in our set (1–4), but Charters 1 and 3 have the same preamble. Charter 5, as explained earlier, is purely a dower charter, rather than a nuptial charter.

[44] "In conjugali . . . copula verbis ipsius Domini, quibus *virum uxori sue adherere et propter hoc patrem et matrem relinquere* precepit . . . exhibetur obedientia."

[45] "Nuptiale sacramentum . . . angelorum obsequiis confirmatum." This phrase is probably an allusion to Gabriel, the angel of the Annunciation, and to the annunciation of the birth of John the Baptist to Zacharias; but it probably refers especially to Raphael, whom God sent to give Sarah to Tobias as his wife and to deliver her from the demon Asmodeus (Tob. 3:8, 3:25, 8:3, etc.). The preamble to a formula for a *carta dotis*, published among Zeumer's Formulae, includes an explicit allusion to

definitively consecrated and its dignity was confirmed by the miracle at Cana. Here the author evinces a real historical and theological sensibility in showing that Cana is the outcome in the last times (*in fine temporum*) of a process that began at the beginning of the world (*ab ipso mundi exordio*).

For the faithful, the argument continues (and here is the second "panel" of triptych), the lesson of Scripture is unequivocal: the prescription of Genesis 2:24 should be realized in conjugal union. The faithful should do nothing else in this respect but humbly obey the divine command. Moreover, it is a "perfidious and execrable folly" for the heretics to denigrate the goodness of marriage.[46]

The preamble might have ended there. But in a third panel, the redactor under-lines the proper value of the sacrament from a spiritual point of view. Herein lies the originality of the formula. Marriage, he says, serves to revive or restore love (*caritas*) between individuals, for on the one hand, the wedding "extends" the bond of charity between those who are not related (*inter extraneos*) and even between those who do not know each other (*ignotos etiam*), while on the other hand, the good (*bonum*) and the fidelity (*fides*) of marriage retrieve, as it were, that charity which escapes when the "bond of kinship" (*linea propinquitatis*) is no longer able to retain it. But this sentence, of Augustinian inspiration, does no more than state the mission of conjugal union, which consists in producing kinship, the natural source of the bond of charity among men, where it has been lacking. It is going too far to read into it, as some have done, any encouragement to choose one's spouse from the first degree of nonprohibited relationship.[47]

Thus, the Laon formula of 1163/1176 is characterized by its didactic, even dog-matic tone: it affirms and asserts, rather than seeking to demonstrate. But the preambles of Charters 2 and 4 are constructed on entirely different lines. Here the argument is less broad, being centered on the nonsinful character of marriage. The redactors wish to demonstrate, in opposition to the heretics, that there is no sin in decently and regularly celebrated marriages (2: *condigna reverentia et honore sibi debita celebratis*; 4: *recte factis*). The two texts develop an argument *a contrario*: if

---

Tobias's angel: "sed et angelum de caelo ad corroborandam nuptiarum copulam ad Tobin venisse legimus." This formula is known from a manuscript dating from the tenth or eleventh century (*Form. extravagantes*, I, *libelli dotis*, no. 12, p. 541).

[46] The Latin text here is of a very concise construction: "In conjugali enim copula *verbis ipsius Domini, quibus virum uxori sue adherere et propter hoc patrem et matrem relinquere precepit*, humilis exhibetur obedientia et hereticorum qui nuptiali bono conantur detrahere perfida et execrabilis confutatur insania." The passage "verbis ... precepit" can be understood either as a complement to *obedientia* alone (*verbis* being a dative) or to *confutatur* (*verbis* being in the ablative). In the first case, the passage would mean that heretical folly is refuted in conjugal union (i.e., one's conjugal union proves that one rejects heresy); in the second, there would be the additional idea that the words of Gen. 2:24 themselves refute the antimatrimonial heresy. The inversion of the statements of Gen. 2:24 (God told man to be united with his wife, and therefore to leave his father and mother) also legitimizes marriage.

[47] [Prof. Morelle discusses this hypothesis, proposed by Dominique Barthélemy, at length in an appendix to the original article: see BEC 146 (1988), at 258–65].

the conjugal state had been stained by sin, God would never have joined Adam and Eve in conjugal union (*conjugium*: 4), Christ would never have wished to attend a wedding and perform a miracle there (2 and 4), and God the Father would not have "prefigured" (*prefiguraret*), through the matrimonial "compact" (*foedus*), the sacrament of Christ and of the church (2).

The anti-heretical purpose of the demonstration is manifest in the charter of 1177 (4), the more concise of the two. Although the term "heretic" is not employed here, the preamble opens bluntly with a reference to the protests of those who oppose marriages by what they say (*qui nuptiis obloquuntur*). But the same purpose is still more vivid in the Soissons charter of 1170 (2), which constitutes an astonishing piece of rhetoric, in three phases that the author has clearly developed with some care. In the first place, the author announces what he is going to demonstrate: the episode at Cana "is a sufficient and cogent reason" to refute "the depraved doctrine of the heretics." The former expression (*valida satis est et cogens ratio*) is remarkable: it seems to appeal to the reasoning abilities of the author's imaginary interlocutors. Then follows the argument, properly so called, the architecture of which we have already seen. Here the author employs the weightiest rhetorical devices: verbal redundancy (*si macula vel noxa*), which he sometimes combines with oratorical repetition (*eis nullatenus Agnus immaculatus, Agnus innocens interesset*); use of specialist terminology (*reatus, infuscare*); and emphatic contrasts (*tam excellentem copulam / tenuis reatus*). The conclusion is worthy of classical perorations: in a bombastic denunciation, the author vows to silence the heresiarchs Marcion and Tatian, whose hostility to marriage Saint Jerome had denounced in his own time.[48] Then, in the subordinate clause that introduces the disposition, the author gives the only scriptural quotation of the preamble (Gen. 2:24), almost as though the structure of the text prevented him from finding another place in which to put it.

Because of the scantiness of the documentary material at our disposition and the narrowness of the chronological field covered, we cannot be sure that the second type of preamble replaced the first (albeit with some overlapping). Yet this is what the chronology of the examples suggests (the first type having appeared in Laon in 1163, and the second being found in Soissons in 1170 and Laon in 1177). If this was the case, the adoption of a preamble turning on the problem of the presence or absence of sin in marriage, and taking the form of a reasoned reply to the heretical objection, may indicate that the heretical challenge revived in the 1170s, or at least that there was a clearer perception then of the essential point on which the debate focused.

One needs to be careful here. Do these preambles, permeated by a preoccupation with heresy, really testify to a doctrinal opposition that was particularly disquieting

---

[48] *Adversus Jovinianum*, I, 3 (PL 23:223): "Neque nos Marcionis et Manichei dogma sectantes nuptiis detrahimus. Nec Tatiani principis Encratitarum errore decepti omnem coitum spurcum putamus." Like Saint Jerome, the author of the preamble uses the expression *detrahere nuptiis*. Does this represent a direct borrowing from the patristic text?

in the eyes of the local churches of Laon and Soissons? Or was there perhaps an element of rhetorical *topos* in these texts, which embroidered a theme that although certainly current was well suited to literary flights, as we have seen in the Soissons charter (2)? To answer this question, it would be necessary to examine the characteristics of the charters collected here in the light of contemporary *acta* of the same nature but coming from other regions. At this time, such a comparison is hardly possible. It is interesting to note, nevertheless, that the Soissons region was a hotbed of anti-matrimonial heresy in the first decades of the twelfth century. Guibert de Nogent records that in the time of Lisiard, Bishop of Soissons (1108–26), one of the leaders of the movement lived in Bucy, a village near the city where Dreu d'Allemant, the husband named in the charter of 1170 (2), had some property.[49] Memories of these heretical communities would have awakened the sensibility of the clergy to the matter, but one can also envisage the persistence of the heterodox movement fifty years after the manifestations described by Guibert.

However that may be, the preambles present a remarkable echo of the anti-heretical writings of the period (those of St. Bernard or of Egbert of Schönau, for example), which clearly had at heart the defense of the conjugal state and a demonstration that carnal union is not necessarily sinful.[50] Still more interesting is the possible connection with a treatise on the sacrament of marriage ascribed to Walter of Mortagne,[51] for its presumed author directed the cathedral school of Laon before governing the diocese (from 1155 to 1174),[52] and it was under the seal of this same bishop that the nuptial charter of 1163 was confirmed (1). One chapter of Walter's treatise, entitled *Quod bona res sit conjugium*, is specifically designed to refute the anti-matrimonial doctrine, and the miracle of Cana is prominent among the arguments adduced.[53] It is thus tempting to regard Walter as the more

---

[49] Guibert de Nogent, *Autobiographie*, in Edmond-René Labande (ed. and trans.), *Les classiques de l'histoire de France au Moyen Âge* 34 (Paris, 1981), 428–29. On the geography and chronology of the heretical movements of the twelfth century, see Jean-Pierre Poly and Eric Bournazel, *La mutation féodale: X^e–XIIe siècles*, Nouvelle Clio 16 (Paris, 1980), 383–95; or 2nd ed. (Paris, 1991), 384–403. It was from Soissons that Pierre de Bruys departed ca. 1115 for a peregrination of some twenty years. His disciple Henri, called "de Lausanne," may, in fact, have been from Laon, if one accepts the hypothesis of a confusion of *Lausanensis* with *Laudunensis* that Poly and Bournazel advanced with some reservation in the 1980 edition (394, n. 1); but they abandon this hypothesis in the second edition of 1991 (403–05).

[50] Leclercq, *Le mariage* (n. 14 earlier), 20–23.

[51] *De sacramento conjugii*, PL 176:153–74. On the ascription of this treatise (traditionally incorporated into the *Summa sententiarum*) to Walter of Mortagne, see the references given by Joseph de Ghellinck, *Le mouvement théologique du XIIe siècle*, 2nd ed. (Bruges, 1948), 198. See also Marcel Chossat, *La Somme des sentences, œuvre de Hugues de Mortagne vers 1155* (Louvain, 1923), 78 ff.

[52] On Walter of Mortagne, see François Petit, "Gauthier de Mortagne," *Analecta praemonstratensia* 50 (1974): 158–70.

[53] PL 176:155C: "Quia vero sunt quidam haeretici qui detestantur nuptias et judicant damnabilem viri et mulieris copulam conjugalem, ad praesens dicendum est utrum res bona an mala conjugium. Affirmamus igitur conjugium rem esse bonam.... Quod apparet ... per hoc quod Christus in Cana Galilaeae vino in aquam mutato nuptias miraculo commendavit."

or less direct inspiration of the formula of Charters 1 and 3. Indeed, one may go even further. Oddly enough, it was under the episcopate of Walter of Mortagne that the first examples of nuptial charters appeared in the Laon region, enacted under the bishop's seal.[54] This coincidence may indicate that Walter, being preoccupied with matrimonial questions,[55] was determined not only to encourage but also to control the drawing up of such charters, as would be suitable for spreading the church's teaching on the subject. The personality of Bishop Walter might then partly explain the documentary upsurge referred to in the first part of this chapter.

Be that as it may, other objects besides the pastoral function of nuptial charters aroused the interest of the ecclesiastical authorities. In controlling the production of these diplomatic instruments, the church granted herself the right to influence matrimonial strategies and watched over the lot of future widows: two points that involved the question of the dower, to which we now turn.

THE DOWER AS AN INDICATOR OF SOCIAL SITUATIONS AND MATRIMONIAL STRATEGIES

The central element of the dower charter naturally consists of the enumeration of the goods and rights conceded to the wife. This part of the diplomatic discourse presents the husband's fortune in a rather different light from that which one finds in the other legal transactions that too often constitute the ordinary fare of the medievalist. In place of equivocal, diachronic, and fragmentary sources, one finds here information that is definite, provided at a single instant, and organically grouped together. Yet although the dower certainly reflects a patrimony, the image is not necessarily faithful. What proportion of its resources does it reveal? What distortions does it contain? One might wish to reconstruct a patrimony from the dower, but that would undoubtedly be wishful thinking.

In fact, it is possible to work out only those factors that influenced the composition of the dower, the interaction of which resulted in the establishment of a mixture of goods and rights. Among these there were those "rules of the game" imposed by law or custom. But the dower was also, perhaps above all, the fruit of negotiations, the result of compromise. It was, in the fullest sense of the term, an *agreement*, which signifies willy-nilly that it bears the mark of the debaters' talents, that it takes account of the protagonists' idea of what a "good dower" was, that it expresses in its own way the price the husband attached to the union, and, finally,

---

[54] Besides Charter 1, we know of the existence of the nuptial charter (now lost) of Agnès, wife of Clérembaud de Berlancourt (see n. 7 earlier).

[55] Besides the treatise in question, three letters by Walter on the subject are preserved: see Edmond Martène and Ursin Durand (eds.), *Veterum scriptorum et monumentorum historicorum, dogmaticorum, moralium amplissima collectio*, vol. 1 (Paris, 1724), 833–37, 839–43.

that it shows the relative strength of the contracting parties. The configuration of the dower is closely linked to the choice of a wife and to the husband's status. It is therefore inseparable from a particular matrimonial strategy.

A complex indicator, the dower does not become intelligible unless it is supported with information drawn from a relatively rich genealogical dossier. It then converges with a better understanding of political alliances. Lacking evidence or adequate analyses, I have succeeded in fully investigating only those alliances established by Charters 1, 2, and 4, and even these attempts illustrate the difficulty of interpreting matrimonial practices.

The Rules of the Game

The dowers described here are ordinarily made up of two parts: first, the portion of the husband's property granted at the time of the marriage, which is precisely stated in the charter; and second, half of the husband's future acquisitions.

In regard to the share of the existing goods, the charters give no indication as to what it represents in relation to the husband's patrimony. Is it the same proportion as for subsequently acquired property, or the equivalent of the dowry contributed by the wife?[56] The silence of the charters on this point may be evidence either of a consensus or of a great latitude granted to the contracting parties in fixing the amount. In this respect, the expression that the Laon formula of 1163/1176 uses to introduce the list of goods and to give it a gracious character (Charter 1/3) is particularly interesting: "the best part of the things that I possess [*optimam partem de his quas possideo*]." The phrasing is mainly qualitative, which says much about the absence or weakness of the rules in matters of division.[57]

In regard to the categories of goods that might enter into the composition of a dower, the diversity that one finds when merely reading over the lists seems to show that no type of goods (land, revenues from rights, money in coins), however held (whether as a fief or an allodium), was excluded *a priori*. In regard to fiefs,

---

[56] On these two competing or successive principles, see for example the investigation by Pierre Toubert, *Les structures du Latium médiéval: Le Latium méridional et la Sabine du IXe siècle à la fin du XIIe siècle*, Bibliothèque des Écoles françaises d'Athènes et de Rome 221 (Rome, 1973), 757–60. Lemaire (*Les origines*, 590 ff.) gives several French examples from the eleventh and twelfth centuries of the application of the principle of an equal share of the property for the dower and of that covering acquisitions.

[57] I do not believe that one may use this expression, as D. Barthélemy is inclined to do (*Les deux âges* [n. 2 earlier], 174), to clarify the scale of economic values of a knight (*miles*) in 1175. Because this expression is an integral part of a formula drawn up by the episcopal chancery, there would seem to be nothing personal in the sentiment. By the same token, the expression may express the church's effort to "spiritualize" the gift given by one spouse to the other. Moreover, it is by no means impossible that the term *optimam partem* is a reminiscence of Luke 10:42 ("Mariam optimam partem elegit, quae non auferatur ab ea"). The apparent echo may be merely verbal and unconscious, but if it refers to the Gospel passage, it may indicate that in comparing the wife's dowry to the *optima pars* chosen by Martha's sister, the author wished to recall discreetly that the dowry, which, in a sense, the wife chose, should not be taken from her.

Charter 1 (dated 1163) is surprising. The husband assesses his wife's dower in a lump from all that he holds in fee from two Soissons abbeys and from the count of Soissons. Nothing more is said about the composition of these fiefs. Moreover, the act does not breathe a word about the consent of the lords of these fiefs, which seems strange. Should we understand that because there was no real transfer, the action of burdening a fief with dower obligations did not require the consent of the lord to whom the lands belonged? Or should we hold rather that the consent was implicit? It is difficult to answer.[58]

With one exception (Charter 1), all the charters add half of the husband's future acquisitions to the goods granted at the time of the marriage. André Lemaire has observed that this practice was widespread in the customary law region of France, notably in the north and northeast.[59] Such is the form that the wife's sharing in the acquisitions of the household took in the pre-community property system. In the absence of common property, the husband thus naturally speaks of *his* acquisitions,[60] for it is taken for granted that the husband manages the household, even if dower rights over acquisitions were justified by the idea of *collaboratio* between the spouses.[61] Nevertheless, the husband refers to "our acquisitions" in the charter of 1170 (2), and the word "our" seems indeed to refer to both spouses, manifesting a certain communitarian spirit.

Only Charter 1, then, omits dower rights over acquisitions, which is puzzling when one considers the homogeneity of the group of documents and the fact that the charter was prepared according to the same formula as Charter 3. This anomaly does not appear to be an accident of textual tradition because the charter also displays another oddity, possibly connected with the first, as we shall shortly see.

Among the elements of the dower, one that recurs frequently is the husband's residence: the *domus* or *mansio*. The wife receives either a dwelling that has already been built[62] or one that the husband commits himself to build for her.[63] In the latter case, the charter specifies the sum of money dedicated to this purpose. It is probably in this house that the wife will reside during her widowhood, and where

---

[58] For another, less legal interpretation, see n. 84, later.

[59] Lemaire, *Les origines*.

[60] Charter 3: "medietatem omnium quae acquisiero"; Charter 4: "m. omnium acquisitionum mearum"; Charter 5: "m. acquisitionum mearum"; wording of the lost charter of 1171 (see n. 7 earlier): "m. omnium que acquiret."

[61] The idea of a *collaboratio* of the spouses was present from the very early Middle Ages. Compare the Frankish *tertia collaborationis* (on this institution, see Vandenbossche, *Contribution à l'histoire des régimes matrimoniaux*, 93–101).

[62] Charter 1: "Ad hec do tibi domum meam apud Sessoniam ....."; lost charter of 1171 (for references, see n. 7 earlier, and for contents, see n. 68 subsequently).

[63] Charter 3: "doque tibi ... quinquaginta libras suessionensis monetae, triginta videlicet pro quadam domo, amicorum tam meorum quam tuorum consilio, loco tibi congruo facienda ...."; Charter 5: "Dedi tibi ... mansionem quam faciam, et si nullam fecero, assignavi tibi nomine mansionis quadraginta libras bonae monetae ...."

she can also find refuge in case of conflict during their life together. Because it was seemingly a place of security for her, one may understand the importance the wife's family attached to it. Charter 3 stipulates that the wife's house will be built in a place chosen by her with the advice of the kinsfolk (*amici*) of the two spouses.[64]

The charters in our corpus display a depressing silence on the subject of the bride's rights over the goods granted to her. In most cases, they are content to wish the bride peaceful possession of her goods for the future (3 and 4). As for the present indicative form of the verbs expressing the cession: this shows the immediacy of the grant itself, and not that of its effects.[65]

One would interrogate our dower charters in vain, in my view, if one's aim were to determine what this *possessio* signified, what the wife's rights were at the dissolution of the marriage (probably a right of survivorship), or what room to maneuver she had during the cohabitation, when her rights were "latent." Nevertheless, Charter 1 may give us a basis for investigation. I have already drawn attention to the peculiarity of this document, in discussing the elements of diplomatic discourse. It is the only one that contains, at the end of the listing of the dower, the following sentence: "All these things I give to you with the legal right to have them freely and to possess them peacefully henceforth [*Haec omnia do tibi tenore juris quod amodo ea libere habeas [et] quiete possideas*]." The exegesis of such a formula is risky, but apparently the act confers upon the wife the immediate possession of her dower. (The term *amodo* means "henceforth" or "from now.") Far from being a simple right of survivorship, as we usually assume for this period, the dower enumerated here was actually put in the hands of the wife (or of her family) during their life together. The husband thus seems to have voluntarily restricted his freedom of action. It is tempting to connect this unique disposition with the absence, also unusual, of a dower right over acquisitions in the same charter. Did the former compensate for the latter? or vice versa? There is some difficulty in judging the reasons for this combination, which certainly shows a very slight regard for community property.[66]

The exception of the act of 1163 (1) shows the relative flexibility of the practices followed in establishing dowers, and it suggests how weighty were the negotiations that resulted in the dowers defined in the charters. We shall now attempt to interrogate our charters on this point.

---

[64] See the previous note. Regarding Clérembaud de Berlancourt's giving as a dower the house that he possessed in Berlancourt (see n. 62 earlier), Barthélemy (*Les deux âges*, 209, n. 191) concludes plausibly that "the wife is thus made mistress of the household." But I do not think that this interpretation applies to all the recorded examples.

[65] This point is especially clear in Charter 3, where the husband gives (in the present tense) fifty pounds (*librae*) while immediately suggesting that he might die before paying the sum: he is clearly referring to the distant future.

[66] The linking of these two facts, if it is valid, may indicate that the wife's family entertained few illusions about the real possibility of acquisitions on her husband's part, since he was a younger son. See also n. 84 later.

Negotiations and Strategies

Within a framework of rules and practices that seems not to have been very restrictive, bargaining and self-interest could have a free hand. In the act from 1163 (Charter 1), one reads a long and detailed list of diverse revenues, some of which are rather modest, as though the husband, Barthélemy de Sissonne, had had to carry on a close struggle with the other contracting party.[67] Beyond the simple statement, one might wish to find in the final product traces of the possibly divergent interests that contributed to its composition. To do that, one should distinguish the wife's point of view from her husband's.

First, the dower is designed to take care of the needs of the widow. From this standpoint, the terms of the dower do not show only the greater or smaller diversity of the husband's patrimony. The terms are not only a reflection of wealth: they also reveal the economic preoccupations of the wife's family. As evidence of the presence of this theme, we may cite the impression of balanced composition given by certain dowers. Thus, on the one hand, a maximum geographical concentration (doubtless motivated by a restricted range of possibilities)[68] is counterbalanced by a diversity of revenues (*in commodis universis*). On the other hand, where only one type of revenue is found, or nearly so (2), we observe a maximum geographical dispersal. The dower having been selected, in theory, a long time before its *ad hoc* use, the wife's family ought take care that the goods granted suffer as little as possible from depreciation. Revenues are needed that are reliable and lucrative, or thought to be so; the revenues of a toll (*guionage*) (3) or of a mill (4), a rent in grain (1), or part of a tithe (5) could offer the desired stability. At the same time, this concern may come up against that of the husband, for whom such sources of revenue do not have the character of a "heritage."

In addition, there is the attention given to the geographical location of the property. This is naturally important in marriages allying lineages whose anchor points appear relatively far apart. Such is the case with the marriage of Barthélemy de Sissonne (Charter 1). His wife, Mathilde d'Épagny, belonged to a family whose dominant attachment to a castellany was not that of the husband, and the goods granted by the latter were in the same regions as those in which the activities of the Épagny family were centered. (I shall discuss this union later.) We may conclude that the wife's family was not indifferent to this manner of locating the dower.

Second, seen from the husband's point of view, the dower that he bestowed expressed, as we have said, the value that he attached to the marriage. The price to be paid will be all the higher, with respect to the resources possessed by the future husband, when the latter finds himself in the position of a suitor, a weakness that makes him more exposed to the demands of the other contracting party. But this interaction of forces is complex. To the respective position of the families in

---

[67] What has just been said about the rights granted to his wife is congruent with this impression.

[68] Charter 4; contents of the lost charter of 1171 (reference given earlier, n. 7): "dedit Agneti uxori sue jure dotalicio medietatem de Berleincurt et domum suam quam ibi habebat totam...."

a sociopolitical sense must be added the personal position of the future spouses (that of an heir or cadet, and so on). All this is but barely discernible, and with much uncertainty, except in concrete cases.

Finally, we cannot neglect, in the configuration of the dower, the importance of practices that tended to derive the wife's dower by preference from property that supplied the mother's dower, or from acquisitions.[69]

Three Case Studies

1. A Family Strategy on a Regional Scale (Barthélemy de Sissonne, Charter 1)

Barthélemy de Sissonne[70] was a younger son of Pierre de Sissonne, an important person who appears in our sources in 1117,[71] and whom a charter of Barthélemy, Bishop of Laon, described, as early as 1130, as "a knight and lord of the same town" (*miles et dominus ejusdem ville*), that is, of Soissons.[72] Precociously employed, this form of designation (*dominus* followed by a place name) indicates an elevated sociopolitical rank. We know of five children of Pierre and his wife Guiburge: two sons, Guillaume (cited from 1133 onward, and always first in lists)[73] and our Barthélemy (who does not appear until 1149);[74] and three daughters, Liduide, Beuza,

---

[69] The maternal dower, like the maternal inheritance, went by preference to the younger son and provided for a new dower: see Dominique Barthélemy, *Histoire de la vie privée*, vol. 2: *De l'Europe féodale à la Renaissance* (Paris, 1985), 157; and Robert Fossier, *Enfance de l'Europe, aspects économiques et sociaux*, Nouvelle Clio 17 (Paris, 1982), 918. Charter 1 may be an example of a dower transmitted from mother-in-law to daughter-in-law (see n. 83 subsequently); and one may say with greater certainty that the dower described in Charter 2 was supplied from the acquisitions of the husband's parents (see case study 2).

[70] For the identification of the spouses in Charter 1, see the note that follows the translation of this charter in the Appendix.

[71] Cartulary of Saint-Martin de Laon, H 871, fol. 207r (charter of Bishop Barthélemy).

[72] Cartulary of Saint-Michel-en-Thiérache (Stein no. 3497): Bibl. nat., lat. 18375, 115–16.

[73] On Guillaume de Sissonne, especially his marriage and descent, see the note by Newman, *Les seigneurs de Nesle* (n. 4 earlier), vol. 1, 171, note b. Episcopal act of 1133, cartulary of Saint-Martin de Laon, H 872, fol. 133. Guillaume de Sissonne died at the latest in 1189 (cartulary of Saint-Michel-en-Thiérache, Bibl. nat., lat. 18375, pp. 116–17, episcopal act: "Post obitum supradicti Willelmi, Ermengardis uxor ejus in extremis posita dedit . . . ."). In 1180, Guillaume was probably alive (cf. the "neutral" mention in cartulary of Foigny [Stein no. 1371], Bibl. nat., lat. 18374, fol. 149, episcopal act). Other mentions of Guillaume noted (all episcopal or archiepiscopal acts): cartulary of Foigny (Stein no. 1369), Bibl. nat., lat. 18373, fol. 11 (n.d., but before 1151), 20v (1141), 22v (1144), 48 (1153); lat. 18374, fol. 149 (1180); cartulary of Saint-Martin de Laon, H 872, fol. 6v (1141); H 871, fol. 207v (1149); H 872, fol. 134 (1153), 169v (1155), 84v (1160), 110 (1178); cartulary of Saint-Médard de Soissons (Stein no. 3723), H 477, fol. 48v (1162); cartulary of Saint-Yved de Braine (Stein no. 617), Arch. nat., LL 1583, p. 119 (1166). In the subsequent discussion, the acts mentioned in the present note are cited simply by their dates.

[74] Barthélemy is mentioned from 1149 onward in the acts cited in the previous note, except in those of 1155, 1162, 1178, and 1189. He also appears in several charters in the cartulary of Saint-Crépin-en-Chaye (Stein no. 3350), Bibl. nat., lat. 18372, fol. 25v (1183, act of Nivelon, Bishop of Soissons), 26v (1184, act of the same), 12v (1184, act of Pope Lucius III [Jaffé no. 15138]; Johannes Ramackers (ed.), *Papsturkunden in Frankreich*, N.F., vol. 4: *Picardie* [Göttingen, 1942, no. 278]), 24v (1192, act of the

and Marguerite, the first two being mentioned from 1133[75] and before Barthélemy, who was certainly their junior (and thus comes in fourth place among the known children of Pierre de Sissonne).

At the time when his son Barthélemy took a wife, Pierre de Sissonne had been dead for fully fifteen years.[76] It was Guillaume, the oldest of his sons, who led the family. The redactor of the nuptial charter placed Guillaume's name at the head of the list of the husband's witnesses, showing thereby his preeminence in the family as well as in the aristocratic network woven around the Sissonnes.

We cannot understand Barthélemy's marriage without examining Guillaume's. In 1153 or before, Guillaume married Ermengarde, the widow of Éble de Blanzy.[77] This woman belonged to the powerful family of the Sires de Quierzy. The daughter of Sire Gérard II, she was the sister of Gérard III, who was a boy (*puer*) in 1135 and bore the title of "lord" (*dominus*) in 1166. Her other brother, Nivelon, was provost of the cathedral chapter of Soissons before becoming the bishop of that city in 1176.[78] Located within the diocese of Soissons, Quierzy was on the border of the region of Laon. Moreover, its lords held their eponymous castle from the bishop of Noyon but moved mainly within the orbit of the religious establishments of the Soissonnais. Their holdings, particularly strong to the northeast of the episcopal city, extended as far as the eastern limits of the diocese, near Blanzy.[79] This Soissons orientation doubtless explains the marriages of Ermengarde, the youngest daughter

---

bishop cited earlier); and in an episcopal act in the cartulary of Saint-Vincent de Laon (Stein no. 1870): Bibl. nat., nouv. acq. lat. 1927, fol. 350v (1168).

[75] Marguerite does not appear before 1153 (charter for Saint-Martin).

[76] Charter for Saint-Martin of Bishop Barthélemy (1149): "Guillelmus de Sessonia, assensu matris sue et fratris sui Bartholomei, concessit." The absence of any reference to Pierre seems to imply that the latter was dead at the time of the reported grant, and all the more at the time of the bishop's confirmation of it. In 1153 (charter for Saint-Martin), we learn that Guillaume had confirmed in general all the grants made to the institution by his father (see n. 89). Guillaume evidently served as head of the family.

[77] Ermengarde is mentioned for the first time in 1153 (charter for Saint-Martin). This mention, unknown to Newman, moves back by at least thirteen years the beginning of Ermengarde's widowhood, which Newman dated to before 1166 (charter for Saint-Yved, cited earlier in n. 73). Ermengarde had at least one son by her previous husband, also called Éble, and one daughter, called Aelis, as shown by the same charter of 1166.

[78] For the genealogy of the Sires de Quierzy, see Newman, *Les seigneurs de Nesle*, vol. 1, 155–69.

[79] For the multiple engagements of the Sires de Quierzy and their connections in the Soissonnais, see Olivier Guyotjeannin, *Episcopus et comes: Affirmation et déclin de la seigneurie épiscopale au nord du royaume de France (Beauvais-Noyon, X^e – début XIIIe siècle)*, Mémoires et documents (Société de l'École des chartes) 30 (Geneva, 1987), 222–24; see also the numerous Soissonnais references given by Newman (as in previous note). Other evidence on the position of the Quierzys in Soissonnais: Bibl. nat., coll. de Picardie 295, nos. 2 and 4 (originals from Notre-Dame de Soissons, royal act, 1146, episcopal act, 1183); cartulary of Saint-Crépin-en-Chaye: Bibl. nat., lat. 18372, fol. 25v (1183, episcopal act cited in n. 74). The Sire de Quierzy was lord of the fief at Blanzy (Blanzy-les-Fismes: Aisne, arr. Soissons, cant. Braine; charter of 1166 for Saint-Yved). In 1135 (cartulary of Saint-Yved de Braine, Arch. nat., LL 1583, 117–19, charter of Bishop Josselin), Gérard II de Quierzy affirmed, on the occasion of a contested grant, that the great tithe of Blanzy granted to Saint-Yved was in his *dominium*, a point that no one contested.

of a lord. Indeed, one gets the impression that the object was to choose for her the husbands best suited to increasing or maintaining the family's influence in one of the directions taken by its patrimony. In fact, an "eastern marriage" was sought twice in succession: with Éble de Blanzy (undoubtedly a vassal of the lord), who died prematurely;[80] and then with Guillaume de Sissonne. These were both in the same district, a little east of the center of the Soissonnais, on the borders of the three dioceses of Laon, Reims, and Soissons.

For the Sissonnes, the situation was a little different because the family was of a lower rank than the Quierzys, and Guillaume was the eldest son: his marriage was more vital to the future of the family. Therefore, one is confronted with a classic case of masculine hypergamy, tempered, to be sure (and this is perhaps what made it possible), by the circumstance that the husband had a greater hope of inheritance than his wife. It appears that in Guillaume's marriage, geographical strategy had less importance than the hope of raising and expanding the kinship of the Sissonnes.[81] It seems, in fact, that Guillaume succeeded in his effort, for one of his sons, Jean, became archdeacon of Soissons from 1188 to 1226, a promotion attributable, at least in part, to the advantage of his avuncular connection with the bishop, Nivelon.

The marriage of Barthélemy, Guillaume's brother, followed the direction set by his senior. This might seem odd, for we know from the work of Georges Duby that we should expect celibacy to be imposed on youngest sons. But the male offspring of Pierre de Sissonne, being reduced to two individuals, were not forced into compulsory celibacy. By and large, Barthélemy's marriage served the interests of the family.

Mathilde, Barthélemy's wife, belonged to a lineage whose social and political rank was much lower than that of the Quierzys, but which is difficult to assess. Mathilde's father, Itier d'Épagny, appeared in the entourage of the Sires de Coucy, and Gui de Guny (one of those named in the act, whose family was raised in the middle of the century to a point just below the castellans)[82] held a fief from Itier. Gui de Guny belonged to the entourage of the Épagnys, and the name "Itier," borne by several scions of this stock, suggests close ties of kinship. As with the Gunys, the interests of the Épagnys were not limited to the single association with Coucy: the location of their eponymous holding, on the road between Coucy and Soissons,

---

[80] This follows from the charter of 1166 already cited (see next note).

[81] The documentation assembled sheds little light on the patrimonial interests of Guillaume in the Soissonnais. All the evidence suggests that the lands at Blanzy that he gave to Saint-Yved de Braine in 1166 were among the possessions held in right of his wife Ermengarde, widow of Éble de Blanzy, and therefore they probably derived from her deceased husband. Given that his lands "descended from the fief" of the Sire de Quierzy ("Ratum habuit hoc [i.e., concessionem] Gerardus de Cherisi, de cujus feodo hec omnia descendebant"), we may conclude, on the one hand, that Éble was a vassal of the Sire de Quierzy, and on the other hand, that Guillaume had become a vassal of the sire for his possessions.

[82] On Itier and Gui de Guny, see Appendix, Charter 1, nn. 12 and 13.

connected them with the diocese of the latter, and their entourage, through the Gunys and Gilles de Chauny, implies an orientation toward the Oise. Doubtless, the Épagnys were among those lords of villages who owed their success to their belonging to more than one circle of influence.

The social level of the union contracted by Barthélemy, which was lower than that of his older brother's marriage, seems to have reflected the difference imposed by their order of birth, although the disparity should not be exaggerated, for Mathilde may have been an heiress. In any case, his matrimonial choice seems to have been coordinated with his brother's, which it reiterated in a minor key. The object of this marriage may have been a multiplication of partners to reinforce the gain from the first venture.

It is necessary to distinguish between two sorts of property in Mathilde's dower: on the one hand, the fiefs held from the count of Soissons and two religious establishments (unspecified property) in the Soissons region; and on the other hand, the property and revenues located in Sissonne itself and in the two villages of Arrancy and Ployart, which are scrupulously described. The difference shown in how the properties are listed certainly reflects a difference in character, for alongside the fiefs is found an allodial domain that represents the heritage, the ancestral share that returns to Barthélemy.[83] The latter is more minutely described because it is of more importance than the first category, the acquisition of which was probably more recent: it was possibly obtained after his older brother's marriage through the influence of the Sire de Quierzy in the Soissons region.[84]

---

[83] It is possible that the lands in Arrancy and Ployart had already served to supply a dower, namely, that of Guiburge, mother of Barthélemy. In 1153, after Pierre de Sissonne had died, an episcopal act in favor of Foigny recounts the confirmation by his widow Guiburge and his two sons Guillaume and Barthélemy of the grant previously made by Pierre ("their" father) of the tithe of Arançot (now a farm situated in the commune of Arrancy) and in Ployart. Oddly enough, Guiburge is named first ("quod Guiburgis uxor Petri de Sessonia et Guillelmus et Bartholomeus filii eorum . . . dederunt et concesserunt totam decimam quam possidebant in territorio de Erenzoth, quam etiam pater eorum . . . prius contulerat . . . ."). Four years before, in 1149, it was Guillaume who took his father's place in expanding an earlier gift of his father's, and in 1153, too, the general confirmation of the paternal gifts to Saint-Martin de Laon was enacted: "assensu fratris sui Bartholomei et matris suae Wiburgis necnon etiam uxoris suae Ermengardis et sororum suarum Lidvidis, Beuzae et Margaritae . . . ." The precedence of Guiburge in the case of Arançot and Ployart may mean that she had specific rights (dower rights, for example) over these lands. If that is so, we cannot say that Arançot and Arrancy were among the recent acquisitions, because Pierre de Sissonne possessed, among other properties, an alodium and the *casa altaris* in one, and the other half of the *casa* [*altaris*] in the other (charters cited of 1141 and 1144 for Foigny). Besides, even under the hypothesis that Guiburge's dower was located in Arrancy and Ployart, it is not entirely certain that the lands of the dower passed to Barthélemy rather than to his older brother, because the latter also held property in Arrancy (cited charter of 1180 for Foigny; for text, see Appendix, Charter 1, n. 21).

[84] We have seen previously that Barthélemy probably left to Mathilde, and thence to her family, the immediate disposition of her dower. This clause therefore caused certain of the Épagnys to be the titularies of Soissonnais fiefs. This may have been the main stake in Barthélemy's marriage. One might transmit a fief under the cover of a dower, doing the negotiations beforehand and in concert with the lords of the fiefs. A long description would perhaps not have been more useful.

2. A Marriage of a Younger Brother in the context of a Castellany's Sphere of Influence (Renier de Rary, Charter 4)

Renier and his three brothers, Aubri, Clérembaud, and Gui, were sons of Barthélemy de Bosmont, mentioned in the sources between 1138 and 1163. Barthélemy himself was the son of Aubri I (called "de Bosmont" or "de Monchâlons" in different sources), who comes to light around 1098–1104, and who is known to have died before 1144.[85]

Renier appears between 1152 and 1186. He was evidently Barthélemy's third son. His brother Aubri II, who is mentioned between 1144 and 1190, was surely the oldest, and primogeniture gave him an indisputable preeminence over his younger brothers.[86] Renier was younger, too, than Clérembaud, mentioned in various documents covering the years 1152–86.[87] As for Gui, Renier's third known brother: he does not appear before 1162, when he is described as a *clericus*; but that designation is strangely lacking thereafter, and the redactors of charters do not attribute any particular status to him, always citing him last.[88] It is likely, therefore, that Gui was the youngest.

Renier's situation, with two older brothers, seems to have been hardly propitious for contracting marriage. The distribution of Barthélemy de Bosmont's property was apparently unequal, although each of the three older brothers received some stronghold of the paternal power.[89] Renier's nuptial charter reveals on his part a relatively constricted position, lacking a wide range of choice – at least if we may

---

[85] For the genealogy of the seigneurs de Bosmont, see Barthélemy, *Les deux âges* (n. 2 earlier), 516–19 (although several complementary points would need to be added, for Renier's nuptial charter was not known to the author).

[86] Aubri is the only son mentioned in 1144 (cartulary of Thenailles, Bibl. nat., lat. 5649, fol. 15v); his brothers do not appear until 1152 (cartulary of Saint-Martin, H 873, fol. 239v). Always mentioned before his brothers, he is the only one to carry the paternal eponym "de Bosmont," and also the only one to whom Hugues de Pierrepont (a witness to Charter 4) gives the title of *dominus* in 1177 (cartulary of Thenailles, Bibl. nat., lat. 5649, fol. 40v: "Dominumque Albricum de Bomont cum fratribus suis Renero, Clarembaldo. . . ."). We shall see that Renier held fiefs from his brother.

[87] Clérembaud, attested from 1152 to 1186 (cartulary of Saint-Martin de Laon, H 872, fol. 111v; mention not noted by D. Barthélemy, who does not notice him after 1177), is named before Renier in 1152 (ibid., H 873, fol. 239v), a charter that lists in order the sons (Gui does not appear) and the daughters (three in number) of Barthélemy; likewise in 1171 (cartulary of Thenailles, Bibl. nat., lat. 5649, fol. 32v) and in 1178 (cartulary of Saint-Vincent de Laon, Bibl. nat., nouv. acq. lat. 1927, fol. 352). The charter of 1177 cited in the previous note, however, mentions Renier before Clérembaud.

[88] The qualification disappears in 1168 (cartulary of Saint-Vincent de Laon, Bibl. nat., nouv. acq. lat. 1927, fol. 350v); Gui is mentioned for the last time in the nuptial charter. This may be a case of a "return to the world" by a younger son who had initially taken clerical vows. I am inclined to think, however, that the term *clericus* was a sobriquet given to any son who was destined (albeit perhaps only provisionally) to hold a position in the church because of his low family rank.

[89] Clérembaud received Cilly (adjoining Bosmont) and Renier in Rary (today in the commune of Saint-Pierremont, contiguous with Bosmont), whereas the father's eponymous seat fell to Aubri. The contiguity of the three places that served as geographical anchor points is remarkable. If this shows the area of concentration of the family patrimony, one has the impression that it reflects a wish for a personal identification that does not overlook the district of origin.

thus interpret the fact that Renier drew his wife's dower from what he held in Rary, the heart of his patrimony. Another indication of the unequal division of the family inheritance is the introduction of the system of *frérage* into the relations between the eldest brother and his cadets.[90] Thus Renier de Rary, in 1185, granted the Premonstratensians of Thenailles an annual *muid* of wheat to carry to Sainte-Geneviève with the consent of the older brother, to whose fief he was subordinate ("assensu Albrici fratris sui de cujus feodo descendebat").[91]

The sons of Barthélemy de Bosmont appeared in association with the Sire de Coucy, but they belonged primarily to the entourage of the major castle of Pierrepont.[92] This connection is also evident in the nuptial charter, because it is Sire Hugues de Pierrepont who heads the list of witnesses, before Renier's own brothers. Also in 1177, we see this same Hugues make Aubri (whom he calls *dominus* for the occasion) and his brothers Renier and Clérembaud guarantors of the agreement that he has just concluded with the religious of Thenailles.[93]

In a remarkable manner, the castellany of Pierrepont provided the context for many matrimonial alliances arranged by the Bosmonts. One example is particularly striking: Émeline and Ode, two sisters of Aubri II de Bosmont, married two sons of Foulque d'Écry, respectively Jean de Bucy[-lès-Pierrepont] and Raoul *Clericus*, who came from the same network of families.[94] This close alliance between families

---

[90] As understood here, *frérage* (a method of "feudalizing" the relationship of preeminence already existing among brothers) is best understood in relation to *parage*. In *parage*, the eldest brother, who was entitled to all the fiefs included in the succession, was the only one who paid homage to the lord. He was guarantor for his brothers, but they owed no homage to him, for they were linked to him not by dependence but only by association. *Frérage* is *parage* with homage, as it were: the younger brothers paid homage to the elder. On this definition, see Paul Ourliac and Jean-Louis Gazzaniga, *Histoire du droit privé français de l'an mil au Code Civil* (Paris, 1985), 328–29.

[91] Cartulary of Thenailles, Bibl. nat., lat. 5649, fol. 8v and 16. *Frérage* might offer the younger sons the opportunity to better their lot, thus defusing many family conflicts, and yet without entirely negating the advantage that the cohesion of inherited lands drew from an unequal system of inheritance. For the socio-political significance and the consequences of the introduction of *frérage*, see the extensive and original reflections of Barthélemy in *Les deux âges* (n. 2 earlier), 180–88, and especially idem, "L'État contre le 'lignage': Un thème à développer dans l'histoire des pouvoirs en France aux XIᵉ, XIIᵉ et XIIIᵉ siècles," *Médiévales* 10 (1986): 37–50, at 43–45.

[92] For this reason, it seems to me excessive to affirm (as Barthélemy does in *Les deux âges*, 150) that the separation of the two branches derived from Aubri I (Barthélemy to Bosmont; Hugues, his brother, to Monchâlons) occurred as a response to the respective spheres of influence of different castellanies (Marle for Barthélemy, Pierrepont for Hugues).

[93] See n. 86 earlier.

[94] Dominique Barthélemy reports the names of three sisters of Aubri II: Ide, Isabelle, and Gode. (Ode, mentioned in 1156 as a daughter of Barthélemy de Bosmont [cartulary of Saint-Martin, H 873, fol. 23], is probably the same person as Gode.) Émeline, regarding whom a charter of 1184 (ibid., H 872, fol. 111) states explicitly that Aubri de Bosmont is her brother, should be considered a fourth daughter of Barthélemy; unless perhaps there was a change of name, but this is unlikely. The previously cited charter of 1184 attests that Émeline is the wife of Raoul *Clericus*, and we have noticed previously the adventures of Émeline's nuptial charter (see n. 5 earlier, and the corresponding discussion). The evidence of the marriage of Ode with Jean de Bucy is less clear. Nevertheless, in 1156 (ibid., H 873, fol. 23) Barthélemy de Bosmont and his daughter Ode strangely gave their consent to a grant of Foulque

who were connected with the same lord appears clearly in the legal documents. Thus Aubri de Bosmont figures with Hugues de Pierrepont among the witnesses of a donation by Foulque d'Écry to the Premonstratensian abbey of Saint-Martin de Laon, cited in an episcopal charter of 1156;[95] and Jean de Bucy is found beside the same Aubri in 1183 as a guarantor of the agreement made between Hugues and Saint-Martin de Laon in reparation for the injuries done to the canons by the lord's older son.[96] The relations of the Écrys and Bucys with the Bosmonts seem to me to illustrate a form of alliance based on solidarity among knightly houses having interests in common because of their association with the same castellany.

The marriage of Renier and Brune fits well into this perspective. Brune was the eldest daughter of Guillaume de Monceau,[97] who was the husband of a certain Élisabeth, the son of Eudes *de Abbatia,* and the brother of Clérembaud *de Abbatia.*[98] Now, Clérembaud, Brune's uncle, was associated with the Pierreponts because he also appears as a guarantor of the agreement of 1183 just mentioned.[99] Renier's wedding manifestly belongs to a matrimonial strategy dominated by the major castle of Pierrepont.

Brune's marriage with Renier was a remarriage on her part, as we learn from a very precise document of 1178 stating that Renier's wife (who is not named) has a son named Éble *(Ebalus),* whom the redactor takes care not to describe by any formula leading us to believe that Renier was his father.[100] One wonders whether Brune's widowhood and the presence of an orphan was not a stroke of good luck for Renier, making it easier for Guillaume to accept his eldest daughter's "misalliance" with a younger son of the family.

3. A Reflection of Family Dynamics (Dreu d'Allemant, Charter 2)

There is less to be said about the marriage of Dreu d'Allemant. Because we have not succeeded in identifying the mysterious Mateline whom Dreu took for his

---

d'Écry. This formula indicates a special bond between the family of Foulque on the one hand and Barthélemy and his daughter on the other. An Ode is mentioned later (1184, ibid., H 872, fol. 111; 1189, ibid., H 873, fol. 112) as the wife of Jean de Bucy. It is likely that this is the same person, all the more so because the oldest son of Jean and Ode was named Barthélemy, which was the name, under this hypothesis, of his maternal grandfather (ibid., H 873, fol. 28); and his fourth son, Aubri, would revive the name of the brother-in-law and head of the family of Bosmont after the disappearance of Barthélemy (ibid., H 872, fol. 111). On Foulque d'Écry, see Appendix, Charter 1, n. 6.

[95] Cartulary of Saint-Martin, H 873, fol. 23.

[96] Cartulary of Saint-Martin, H 873, fol. 28.

[97] Probably Monceau-le-Waast, six kilometers from Pierrepont.

[98] Cartulary of Saint-Vincent de Laon, Bibl. nat., nouv. acq. lat. 1927, fol. 205v, charter of Bishop Roger (1178) recognizing the grant by which Guillaume *de Moncellis,* son of Eudes *de Abbatia,* ceded to Saint-Vincent the share of the tithe he held at Bucy and everything he possessed there "assensu fratrum suorum Clarembaldi et Ingelranni et uxoris sue Elizabeth necnon et filiarum suarum et Ebali primogenite filie sue liberi et eciam Raineri de Boomont qui ipsam primogenitam filiam in uxorem duxerat."

[99] Cited n. 96 earlier.

[100] Charter cited n. 98 earlier.

wife,[101] the strategy underlying their union remains undiscoverable. And yet the structure of the dower, clarified by some meager complementary sources, permits us to sketch out a commentary on the social situation of this knight.

Mateline's dower was remarkable in two respects. First, its largest part was composed of lands situated in several places comprising a limited area around the eponymous village of Allemant.[102] Second, in each of these scattered lands, the property assigned to the dower was, in fact, only Dreu's portion of a property possessed jointly by him and his mother, the widow of Payen *de Novo Vico* (Dreu's father), who had remarried a certain Robert *de Baisi*.

This second characteristic seems to imply that Dreu's mother possessed, by dower right, part of the lands in question, the other part having come to Dreu as the heir of his father, Payen. It seems reasonable to suppose (although the formula leaves this point in doubt)[103] that in each case, the division of rights was equal as regards Dreu and his mother. In other words, Dreu's mother probably received as a dower half of each piece of land considered.[104] Such a dower allotment displays the situation that would result from the application of the clause of our documents granting the dowager half the couple's acquisitions. If that reasoning is correct, the lands in question belonged to Payen's acquisitions.

Against this interpretation, one might object that the documentation concerning Payen shows evidence of an ancient holding in places where Dreu and his mother were sharing lands, a holding going back to Dreu's paternal grandfather.[105] It is possible to resolve this objection, I believe, if we assume that the lands in question, which were listed in the nuptial charter, did not represent everything that Dreu possessed in these places. The same assumption would also explain the subtle turn of the expressions describing the lands: the redactor would have preferred a ponderous but precise expression to one that is more spirited but ambiguous. In short, I wonder whether Mateline's dower may reflect, in regard to this category of lands (the local concentration of which has been described previously), Dreu's father's efforts to round out his patrimony in the neighborhood of Allemant, Dreu's eponymous village.

[101] For references to the biographical items concerning Dreu and his entourage, see the notes to Charter 2 in the Appendix at the end of this chapter.

[102] See Map 2.

[103] The poor tradition of the text adds to the contorted style of the formulae. The standard expression is this: "totam partem meam terre quam ego similiter et ipsa habemus apud...."

[104] The sources mention neither brother nor sister for Dreu, which would explain, under this theory of the dower, why there was no third party taking from each parcel cited in the charter. The expressions used to describe the property possessed by Dreu and his mother nevertheless seem to emphasize the undivided character of their rights.

[105] Cartulary of Saint-Crépin-en-Chaye, Bibl. nat., lat. 18372, fol. 23 (charter of Josselin, Bishop of Soissons, between 1137 and 1152). Among the properties confirmed to Saint-Crépin was the *curtis* of Vaurains; in the piece of land, adjoining Vaudesson and the wood of Le Fruty, that belonged to this *curtis*, Payen disposed of a half-*terrage* [rent in kind]; nevertheless, one parcel granted by Payen's father was exempt from this.

Now, this local connection was not that of Payen, who was designated as being from another village (*de Novo Vico*). The development may reflect a drifting of the center of power from one generation to another. Under that hypothesis, it is perhaps not insignificant that the second group of properties granted to Mateline, which was not burdened with the rights of her mother-in-law, was located apart from the first group, in Soissons itself and in its suburban villages. May one assume that these properties preserve the traces of a second patrimonial center, possibly older than the center around Allemant?

If that argument deserves any credence, Mateline's dower would permit us to glimpse the dynamics of a generation of minor knights concerned with consolidating their village connections[106] under the shadow of the lords to whom they were affiliated.[107] It would be very useful here to know what Mateline's origin was. I would cautiously advance the hypothesis that she may have belonged to a family associated with Pierrefonds,[108] and if that were so, the union would testify to an enlargement of Dreu's horizon.

CONCLUSION

If dower charters from this period deserve attention, they certainly owe this partly to their rarity, but they owe it even more to the density of information that they contain, especially the *nuptial* charters among them. By approaching the material from various angles, yet without pretending to have exhausted the range of possibilities, I have tried to show how one may use such diplomatic sources, which unfortunately require many complementary investigations and prove reticent unless one gathers a rather extensive biographical dossier for the couples concerned.

When supported by other information, the documents "speak" to us. The configuration of a dower, which was the fruit of negotiations the importance of which has been emphasized, helps us understand the strategy behind a union (as in Charter 1), or gives the measure of a social situation (4), or even suggests the evolution of a patrimony (2). Thus, the legal documents permit, as a result of a "monographic" approach, the testing of the indispensable analytical models of the matrimonial system of the twelfth century.

Nevertheless, the interest of dower charters, and especially of nuptial charters, is no less if we examine the diplomatic genre itself and, still more precisely, consider how these documents were produced and elaborated. From this point of view, the diocese of Laon proves to have been quite remarkable. For one thing, the

---

[106] D. Barthélemy's thesis (in *Les deux âges*) shows very well, as regards the region near Coucy, how the *milites* shifted during the mid-century from a society centered on castellanies to one rooted in villages.

[107] At the head of the lay witnesses to the nuptial charter stands the Sire de Quierzy, who belonged firmly among the Soissonnais (see n. 79 earlier). It is very likely that Dreu d'Allemant held some fief from him. A little farther on, we note the presence of Raoul Revel, seneschal of the count of Soissons (see Appendix, Charter 2, n. 39). Dreu was probably a vassal either of Raoul or of the count.

[108] See subsequent note on the identification of the spouses in Charter 2.

"documentary upsurge" that we have noted in this jurisdiction[109] coincides with the accession to the episcopal seat of Walter de Mortagne (1155–74), a prelate known to have been very concerned about doctrinal issues regarding marriage. Similarly, it looks as though the episcopal chancery exercised a kind of monopoly over the copying of these documents.[110] This shows, in my view, that the diocesan church, far from being indifferent to these documents, saw in them a significant means of intervening in matrimonial practices. Dower charters permitted the clergy to control alliances and to watch over the rights of widows, and also to disseminate the canonical doctrine on marriage. As vehicles of pastoral admonition, nuptial charters, in fact, bear the traces of a doctrinal evolution pertaining to the conception of the conjugal bond. Permeated by the obsession with anti-matrimonial heresies, they reveal concretely the considerable anxiety of the prelates in charge of souls, and they seem to testify to a real heretical challenge.

In short, dower charters appear as one of the instruments through which the diocesan authorities could intervene in the religious and social life of the laity. In these legal documents, we possess "a precious observation post"[111] for the history not only of marriage but also of diocesan government.

Appendix: The Charters and the Persons Named in Them*

Charter 1
1163

Barthélemy [de Sissonne] takes as his wife Mathilde [d'Épagny] and grants her as her dower all that he holds in fief from the abbess of Notre-Dame de Soissons, from the abbot of Saint-Médard de Soissons, and from the count of Soissons; various goods and revenues

---

[109] As noted earlier, the causes of this documentary upsurge were probably diverse. Along with an increase in the number of charters, one must also reckon with an increased attention by the archivists to this type of act. This last element might mean that in the years 1160–1180/90, more than in the past, wives' or widows' dowers were the subject of disputes or were coveted by husbands, brothers, sons, or brothers-in-law; and this increased tension might be connected with the development of an unequal pattern of inheritance. It should be added that in such a context, the episcopal sanction given to the charters increased their value in case of litigation over the lands they described. If one accepts this theory, the documentary decline in the following period would not indicate the end of a documentary practice or a decline in donations supported by dower goods, but rather the effect of solutions (such as *frérage*) introduced to alleviate such tensions in aristocratic families.

[110] Needless to say, one cannot confirm this monopolistic character. It is clear at least that the bishop of Laon could reserve to himself the preparation of these charters when they concerned vassals of the *episcopium* or families most closely frequenting the episcopal court.

[111] I have borrowed the expression from Marcel David, "Le mariage dans la société féodale" (note critique), *Annales ESC* 26 (1981): 1050–55, at 1050.

* [English translations of the five charters are by Prof. Joseph Goering. For Prof. Laurent Morelle's editions of the original Latin texts (with critical apparatus) and for identification of the sources, see the original article, BEC 146 (1988), at 266–84.]

in Sissonne, including his house; and finally all his possessions in Arrancy and Ployart. Charter enacted under the seal of Walter [of Mortagne], Bishop of Laon.

(See Map 1.)

In the name of the holy and undivided Trinity, amen.

The marriage sacrament, instituted by God's authoritative precept for our first parents at the beginning of the world [cf. Gen. 2:18–24] and confirmed by the imitation of the patriarchs [cf. Gen. 12:5, 24:51, 29:28] and by the observances of angels [cf. Tob. 6:10–22, Luke 1:5–38], leaves to future generations no mean example of human social relations. Now at the end of time our Savior, by attending a wedding [cf. John 2:1–11], has commended marriage most highly by his presence and has hallowed it with a lasting dignity, as attested by his miraculous changing of water into wine. In the Lord's own words regarding conjugal coupling, by which he urges a man to leave his mother and father and to adhere to his wife [cf. Matt. 19:5], one finds an example of humble obedience and a refutation of the perfidious and execrable folly of the heretics who attempt to disparage the goodness of marriage. Moreover, the bond of this love is spread abroad through marriage to embrace non-kin and even strangers, and where this love could not be conserved by the bond of kinship, it is called back, as it were, like a fugitive, by the blessing [*bonum*] and the fidelity [*fides*] of marriage.

Therefore I, Barthélemy, taught by the example of the holy fathers, and attracted by such great privileges of marriage, join you, Mathilde, my dearest betrothed, to me as my wife in legal and lasting matrimony, and I give to you as your rightful dower [*jure dotalicio*] the best part of what I possess, namely, whatever I hold in fee from the abbess of the church of St. Mary in Soissons. In addition, my dearest betrothed, I grant to you in the same right whatever I hold in fee from the abbot of St. Médard and from the Count of Soissons. To these things I add my house at Sissonne and ten measures of grain according to the measure of Sissonne as rent,[1] namely, five measures of rye and five of oats, as well as one carucate of land there, along with a small hospice and its family, and whatever I possess at Arrancy[2] and at Ployart.[3]

All these things I give to you with the legal right to have them freely and to possess them peacefully henceforth. So that no one may infringe upon or alter this, I have had it confirmed by the seal of the lord Walter Bishop of Laon,[4] and by the signatures of witnesses.

---

[1] Sissonne: Aisne, arrondissement Laon, chief town of the canton.

[2] Arrancy: Aisne, arr. and cant. Laon.

[3] Ployart: Aisne, arr. and cant. Laon, comm. Ployart-et-Vaurseine (adjoining Arrancy).

[4] Walter of Mortagne, Bishop of Laon from 1155 to 1174 (see n. 52 earlier).

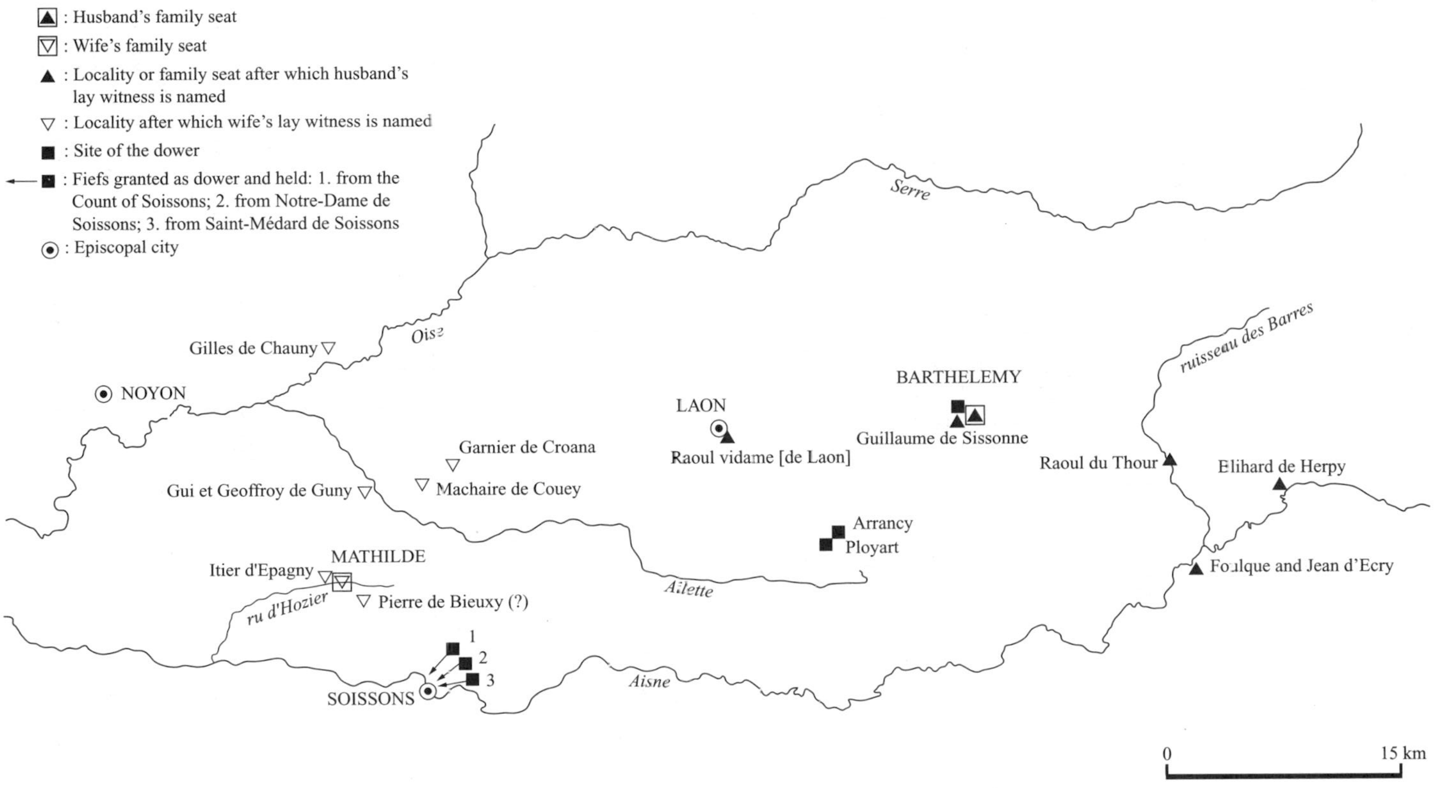
: Husband's family seat
: Wife's family seat
: Locality or family seat after which husband's lay witness is named
: Locality after which wife's lay witness is named
: Site of the dower
: Fiefs granted as dower and held: 1. from the Count of Soissons; 2. from Notre-Dame de Soissons; 3. from Saint-Médard de Soissons
: Episcopal city
Serre
Oise
Gilles de Chauny
NOYON
Gui et Geoffroy de Guny
Garnier de Croana
Machaire de Couey
LAON
Raoul vidame [de Laon]
BARTHELEMY
Guillaume de Sissonne
ruisseau des Barres
Raoul du Thour
Elihard de Herpy
Foulque and Jean d'Ecry
Arrancy
Ployart
Ailette
MATHILDE
Itier d'Epagny
ru d'Hozier
Pierre de Bieuxy (?)
1
2
3
SOISSONS
Aisne
0
15 km

Map 1. 1163 – Marriage of Barthélemy de Sissonne and Mathilde d'Épagny

Sign of Guillaume de Sissonne.[5] Sign of Foulque d'Écry.[6] Sign of Raoul the Vidame [of Laon].[7] Sign of Raoul de Thour.[8] Sign of Gui Piedeloup.[9] Sign of Blihard de Herpy.[10] Sign of Jean d'Écry.[11] Sign of Hugues de Montemont. Sign of Itier d'Épagny.[12] Sign of Gui de Guny.[13] Sign of Geoffroi de Guny.[14] Sign of Gilles

[5] On Guillaume, see n. 73 earlier.

[6] Foulque d'Écry (today Asfeld: Ardennes, arr. Rethel, chief town of the canton) appears from 1149 to 1173 in numerous documents, especially for Saint-Martin de Laon: cartulary of Saint-Martin, H 871, fol. 207v (1149); H 873, fol. 23 (1156); H 871, fol. 255v (1159), fol. 209v (1165); H 872, fol. 108v (1168); another cartulary (Stein no. 1869), Bibl. mun. Laon, ms. 532, fol. 278 (1173). In 1184 (H 872, fol. 111) he is stated to be deceased. Four brothers of Foulque are known, including Boson, archdeacon of Reims, and three sons, Jean de Bucy, Blihard, and Raoul, called *Clericus* (on the connection of Jean and Raoul with the Bosmonts, see n. 94 earlier and the corresponding discussion). Foulque d'Écry held fiefs from the Sire de Pierrepont, for whom he testified (for example in the cited charters of 1149, 1165, and 1168), and in 1162 he signed, among the members of the entourage of Pierrepont and Rozoy-sur-Serre, just after Guillaume de Sissonne, an agreement made between Henri, lord of Marle, and Saint-Médard de Soissons (cartulary of Saint-Médard, H 477, fol. 48v). On Henri de Marle, with possessions in the spheres of influence of several castles, see notes by Barthélemy (*Les deux âges*, 147–48).

[7] Raoul, Vidame of Laon, son of Hector, appeared in 1158 and 1165 (Maxime de Sars, *Le Laonnois féodal*, vol. 2 [Paris, 1926], 203). His father signed the charter of 1162 mentioned in the previous note just after Foulque d'Écry.

[8] Raoul du Thour (Ardennes, arr. Rethel, cant. Asfeld) was a witness of the general confirmation by Guillaume de Sissonne of the grants made by his father to Saint-Martin de Laon (episcopal act of 1153, reference earlier, n. 73). Reciprocally, Guillaume de Sissonne was among the witnesses of a donation of Raoul du Thour to Saint-Martin, mentioned in 1155 (reference ibid.).

[9] This person was also among the witnesses of the two donations mentioned in the previous note.

[10] Blihard de Herpy (Herpy-l'Arlésienne: Ardennes, arr. Rethel, cant. Château-Porcien) was a witness to a donation of Guillaume de Sissonne mentioned in 1178 (for reference, see n. 73 earlier).

[11] This is certainly the son of Foulque d'Écry mentioned earlier (on the absence of any indication of relationship see n. 22 to Charter 1).

[12] On Itier d'Épagny (Aisne, arr. Soissons, cant. Vic-sur-Aisne), see Barthélemy, *Les deux âges*, 239 and 242, n. 32; Newman, *Les seigneurs de Nesle*, vol. 2, 120, n. 2. He is noted in 1158 (charter of Ansculf, Bishop of Soissons: cartulary of Saint-Martin de Laon, H 872, fol. 219), in 1164 (Newman, *Les seigneurs de Nesle*: grant for Prémontré), and in an undated charter (ca. 1160) of Raoul, Sire de Coucy (Bibl. nat., nouv. acq. lat. 2096, pièce originale no. 5). A son of Gérard Dollez, Itier had two brothers, Jean Dollez and Gérard. No children of his are known except his two daughters Mathilde and Ade (see subsequent note on the identification of the spouses).

[13] For the genealogy of the family of Guny (Aisne, arr. Laon, cant. Coucy-le-Château), see Newman, *Les seigneurs de Nesle*, vol. 2, 95–100; on the activities and the sphere of influence of the Gunys, see Barthélemy, *Les deux âges*, 150–51. Gui [II], son of Adon de Guny, appears between 1147 and 1192. A grant he made to Saint-Martin de Laon was completed "annuente domino suo Itero de Spanni de cujus feodo terram hanc tenebat" (charter of 1158 cited in previous note). An episcopal charter of 1168 for Saint-Vincent de Laon (reference earlier in n. 74), recording a gift of Clérembaud de Cilly (brother of Renier de Ray, author of Charter 4), mentions among the witnesses Gui de Guny, and with him Gui d'Arblincourt (see subsequent, Charter 2, n. 38) and Barthélemy de Sissonne.

[14] Geoffroi, brother of the preceding, attested in 1158 and 1161. For the absence of any indication of kinship see n. 22 later.

de Chauny.[15] Sign of Pierre de Vinci [Bieuxy?].[16] Sign of Machaire de Coucy.[17] Sign of Garnier de Crasne.[18]

Done in the year of the Incarnation of the Word 1163. Angot the chancellor devised, copied, and signed this.

A Note on the Identification of the Spouses in Charter 1

I propose that Barthélemy was the brother of the Guillaume de Sissonne who signed the document first, and that Mathilde was the daughter of Itier d'Épagny, who also appears among the witnesses.

Guillaume is at the head of the list, a position which, in a layman, is evidence of a privileged relation to the husband (the author of the act), and which implies the recognition of his social and familial preeminence. Now, Guillaume had a younger brother named Barthélemy, who may very well have been Mathilde's husband.[19] An examination of how the dower was composed strengthens this hypothesis. First, the charter tells us that Mathilde's husband disposes of various lands and revenues in Sissonne (notably a house), a situation that is perfectly normal if it applies to Barthélemy de Sissonne. Second, part of the dower comprises what he holds in fee from two Soissonnais abbeys and from the count of Soissons. The same geographical orientation can be observed in Barthélemy's activities, given that before 1184 he gave the canons of Saint-Crépin-en-Chaye certain revenues from a house located in Soissons.[20] Finally, Barthélemy grants as dower what he possesses in Arrancy, where we know that the Sissonnes held property; and in 1180, Barthélemy approved (having hitherto opposed) the donation by his brother Guillaume to the Cistercians of Foigny of lands located in Arrancy.[21] All these

---

[15] Gilles de Chauny (Aisne, arr. Laon, chief town of canton) and Pierre his brother were witnesses of two charters of Raoul, Sire de Coucy (charter cited earlier in n. 12 to Charter 1; charter of 1170: cartulary of Saint-Martin de Laon, H 873, fol. 129).

[16] In 1183 (cartulary of Saint-Crépin-en-Chaye, Bibl. nat., lat. 18372, fol. 25v) Nivelon, Bishop of Soissons, confirmed to the canons of Saint-Crépin a donation of one Pierre *de Biuci* (= Bieuxy: Aisne, arr. Soissons, cant. Vic-sur-Aisne). Was Pierre *de Vinci* in fact this other Pierre? Such an error in reading is not improbable.

[17] Barthélemy (*Les deux âges*, index) does not note any Machaire near the château of Coucy.

[18] Garnier de Croana was a witness, among other persons very close to the château of Coucy, of a charter of 1176 of Ives de Coucy, son of Gui, the lord of the château, in favor of Saint-Crépin-en-Chaye (cartulary of Saint-Crépin-en-Chaye, Bibl. nat., lat. 18372, fol. 45). Croana is definitely not Craonne (Aisne, arr. Laon, chief town of the canton), but Crasne, a name now borne by a farm about two kilometers northeast of Coucy-le-Château.

[19] On Barthélemy, see n. 74 earlier, and the whole corresponding discussion.

[20] Donation reported in three charters in the cartulary of Saint-Crépin, two in 1184 and the last in 1192 (reference earlier, n. 74); and see subsequent material, *in fine*.

[21] Cartulary of Foigny: Bibl. nat., lat. 18374, fol. 149, charter of Roger, Bishop of Laon: "Bartholomeus similiter de Sessonia, qui ecclesiam memoratam diu vexerat super quibusdam terris in territorio de Arenci sitis quas Willelmus de Sessona, frater ejus, dederat eidem ecclesie in perpetuum ad terragium excolendas, venit ante nos...."

factors weigh in favor of the proposed identification.[22] There is another argument that one should advance, but because it involves both Barthélemy and his wife Mathilde, we shall come to it later.

The identification of Mathilde as the daughter of Itier d'Épagny depends entirely upon the examination of the subscriptions. The list of witnesses reveals very clearly the existence of two groups, which one would naturally attribute to each of the two spouses respectively. With Barthélemy one finds not only Guillaume de Sissonne but also Foulque and Jean d'Écry, Raoul, Vidame of Laon, Raoul du Thour, Gui Piedeloup, and Blihard de Herpy. Their eponymous villages define a large area to the northeast and east of Laon, and we find evidence of the relations between these people and the Sissonnes. Around Itier d'Épagny are collected the brothers Gui and Geoffroy de Guny and Gilles de Chauny.[23] The latter group returns us to the borders of the Laonnois and the Noyonnais, to the west and southwest of the castle of Coucy, which seems to be a common denominator for the members of the circle. This was certainly the entourage of the *sponsa*, among whom one must look for a Mathilde who might have contracted marriage with Barthélemy in 1163.

Mathilde is unfortunately a common name in this region during the twelfth century, and in the families of d'Épagny and de Guny, one finds at least three persons called Mathilde living at this time. One, a daughter of Itier de Guny, is mentioned from 1122 to 1163. She is also mentioned with her father and her brother Itier in a document that William M. Newman dates to 1141/1146. Her matrimonial destiny is unknown.[24] Another Mathilde is the daughter of Oilard de Guny, brother of the same Itier de Guny mentioned previously. Oilard was a witness in 1131 and appears for the last time in 1169. This Mathilde is mentioned in 1163, among six brothers and three sisters. Nothing else is known about her.[25] The third Mathilde is the daughter of Itier d'Épagny and Élisabeth. Her sister was a certain Ade. All this information comes from a charter of 1208 by Jean de Truegny, grandson of Itier and son of Ade, and therefore nephew of Mathilde.[26]

Of these three Mathildes, the last is best suited in this case. On the one hand, the only members of the Guny family who appear among the witnesses do not belong

---

[22] It will, no doubt, be objected that if Barthélemy and Guillaume were brothers the redactor of the charter would have indicated this connection in Guillaume's signature. The obstacle is not insurmountable: on closely examining the list of witnesses, one sees that no bonds of kinship are specified, even when they are hardly doubtful (between Foulque d'Écry and his son Jean, and between Gui de Guny and his brother Geoffroi). The absence of descriptions such as *fratris Bartholomei* or *fratris mei* accompanying the signature of Guillaume de Sissonne should be taken for a particular application of a general principle of systematically omitting such indications. Doctrinal considerations might explain this practice (see earlier, n. 31).

[23] The mysterious Pierre *de Vinci* (or rather de Bieuxy) and Garnier de Craonne also probably belonged to the wife's entourage.

[24] Newman, *Les seigneurs de Nesle*, vol. 2, 97, n. c.

[25] Ibid., n. f.

[26] Ibid., 120, n. 2.

to the branches from which the daughters of Itier and of Oilard de Guny came: Gui and Geoffroy were sons of Adon de Guny, who was brother of Itier and Oilard. On the other hand, if we opt for the daughter of Itier d'Épagny, the presence of the latter among the signers, and moreover apparently at the head of the wife's group, is easily explained.

Last but not least, two documents from the archives of Saint-Crépin-en-Chaye, from 1184 and 1192 respectively, tell us that Barthélemy de Sissonne had a son named Itier.[27] This name was not very common, and for the region and the period that interest us, its occurrences are concentrated in the families of d'Épagny and de Guny,[28] which implies that the name of Barthélemy's son came from his maternal ancestors. Indeed, I suggest that he was named after his maternal grandfather.[29] With this miraculous Itier, who adds a decisive element to the argument, I think we may regard as established the identification of the couple Barthélemy and Mathilde with Barthélemy de Sissonne and Mathilde d'Épagny.

CHARTER 2
1170 (after July 31), Soissons

Dreu [d'Allemant], in choosing to be united with Mateline in bonds conforming to religion (religiosa quam docet [Dominus] unione uniri te preeligens), gives her as her dower a piece of land that he has held for a short time and whose location he will specify [later], his house in Soissons, his vineyards of Pommiers and Bucy[-le-Long], his portion of the lands that he and his mother hold in Nanteuil[-la-Fosse], Jouy, and Aizy, in Le Fruty, in Vaurains, in Vaudesson, and in Allemant, all that he holds in Marcilly, all his lands of Feria, as well as half of the couple's future acquisitions. Charter enacted under the seal of the [cathedral] chapter of Saints-Gervais-et-Protais de Soissons.

(See Map 2.)

In the name of the holy and undivided Trinity, amen.

That the Lord Jesus not only accepted an invitation to a wedding in Cana of Galilee and attended the celebration but also deigned to gladden it by performing there the first of his miracles [cf. John 2:1–11] is a sufficient and

---

[27] Privilege of Pope Lucius III of December 17, 1184 (document cited earlier, n. 80): "domum quam Bartholomeus de Suessona et filius ejus Itarius dederunt vobis in elemosinam sub censu....";the charter of the bishop of Soissons (1192, charter cited earlier, n. 74) is more precise about the manner of the donation, but adds nothing about the donors; the absence of any mention of Mathilde may mean that she was dead at the time of the gift.

[28] Nevertheless, in 1161 Ives de Nesle, count of Soissons, confirmed a grant made by Itier, lord of Chauny, of half the mill of Épagny. Was this Itier d'Épagny?

[29] Barthélemy (*Histoire de la vie privée*, 107) observes that "first names ... were transmitted as hereditary attributes from father to son, uncle to nephew, but also (and possibly above all) from maternal grandfather or granduncle to grandson or grandnephew."

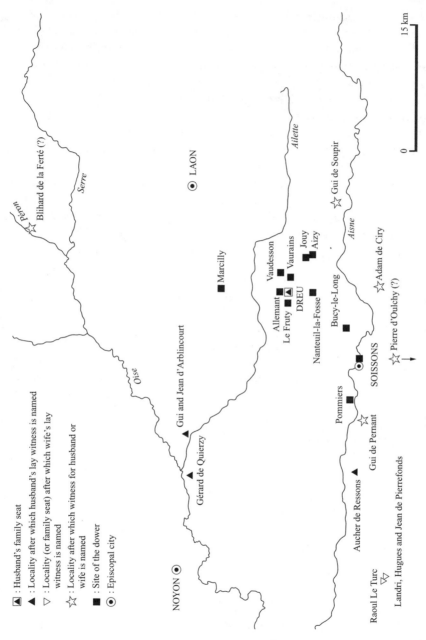

Map 2. 1170 – Marriage of Dreu d'Allemant and Mateline.

◀ : Husband's family seat

▲ : Locality after which husband's lay witness is named

▽ : Locality (or family seat) after which wife's lay witness is named

☆ : Locality after which witness for husband or wife is named

■ : Site of the dower

◉ : Episcopal city

NOYON ◉

Gérard de Quierzy ◀

Gui and Jean d'Arblincourt ▲

Oise

Aucher de Ressons ◀

Gui de Pernant ☆

Raoul Le Turc ▽

Landri, Hugues and Jean de Pierrefonds

Pommiers ■

SOISSONS ◉

Pierre d'Oulchy (?) ☆

Adam de Ciry ☆

Bucy-le-Long ■

Nanteuil-la-Fosse ■

DREU ◀ ■

Le Fruty ■

Allemant ■

Vaudesson ■

Vaurains ◀

Jouy ■
Aizy ■

Aisne

Gui de Soupir ☆

Ailette

Marcilly ■

LAON ◉

Serre

Péron

Blihard de la Ferté (?) ☆

0   15 km

cogent reason for refuting the depraved doctrine of the heretics who belittle marriage. For if there were something unseemly or harmful [*macula vel noxa*] in celebrating marriages with due reverence and honor, in no way would the spotless Lamb, the innocent Lamb, have been present. Still less would he have distinguished the proceedings further with the first fruits of his miracles. If such an excellent union were sullied by even the slightest suspicion [*si tam excellentem copulam vel etiam tenuis reatus infuscaret*], God the Father would in no way have prefigured by the marriage compact [*foedus*] the most praiseworthy mystery of Christ and the church [cf. Eph. 5:32]. Let the detractors of marriage, Marcion and Tatian,[30] hold their tongues, censuring their error by silence.

Since we have been instructed by the Lord himself concerning these nuptials, who said: "For this reason a man shall leave his father and mother and be joined to his wife, and the two shall be one flesh" [Gen. 2:24, Matt. 19:5], I, Dreu, relying on such a great and sure saying of the Lord, and choosing to be joined to you, my dearest Mateline, by the religious union that the Lord recommends, give to you as a marriage gift [*donatio propter nuptias*] according to the practices of holy church the land that I currently hold in the places that I shall now declare. I give to you my house in Soissons, my vineyard in Pommiers,[31] my vineyard in Bucy,[32] [my share] of the land that my mother and I have at Nanteuil, all of my share of the land that she and I have at Jouy and Aizy, all of my share of the land that she and I have at Fruty, all of my share of the land that she and I have at Vaurains, all of my share of the land she and I have at Vaudesson,[33] all of my share of the land that we have at Allemant, and all that I have at Marcellianum,[34] and all of my land of Feria,[35] and one half of all of our acquisitions.

So that no one may impugn this record of my provision, I confirm it to you by the seal of the [church of the] blessed martyrs Gervase and Prothasius, and by the incontrovertible testimony of lawful witnesses, namely, Herbert a canon of Paris,[36] Gérard de Quierzy,[37] Gui de Arblincourt, Jean his

---

[30] Compare Jerome, *Adversus Jovinianum*, I, 3 (PL 23:223).

[31] Pommiers: Aisne, arr. and cant. Soissons.

[32] Bucy-le-Long: Aisne, arr. Soissons, cant. Vailly.

[33] Nanteuil-la-Fosse, Aizy, Jouy, Le Fruty (a village in Allemant), Vaurains (now a farm in Vaudesson), and Vaudesson are all in the same location as Bucy-le-Long (see earlier).

[34] Probably Marcilly: Aisne, arr. Laon, cant. Anizy-le-Château, comm. Faucoucourt.

[35] Place not identified.

[36] Herbert de Paris (*de Parisius*) is mentioned in the charter of archdeacon Nivelon of Soissons (reference subsequently, n. 53) as a witness of Dreu's promise not to be prejudiced against the Premonstratensians of Laon because of the donations of his mother and stepfather he had just approved.

[37] On Gérard III de Quierzy (Aisne, arr. Laon, cant. Coucy-le-Château) see earlier, n. 78 and the corresponding discussion.

brother,[38] Raoul Revel,[39] Guillaume Senis,[40] Robert my stepfather,[41] Gérard de Castello,[42] Aucher de Ressons,[43] Gui de Pernant,[44] Raoul le Turc,[45] Gui de Soupir,[46] Landri de Pierrefonds, Hugues and Jean his sons,[47] Adam de Ciry, Blihard de Ferietas [i.e., La Ferté-Chevresis?],[48] Pierre de Oulchy.[49]

Done at Soissons in the year of the incarnation of the Word of God 1170, the thirty-fourth year of the reign of Louis the younger as king of the Franks following the death of Louis his father, by Hugues the chancellor,[50] in the twelfth year of the bishop's episcopacy in Soissons.

---

[38] For the genealogy of the seigneurs d'Arblincourt (Bac-Arblincourt: Aisne, arr. Laon, cant. Coucy-le-Château, comm. Bichancourt), see Barthélemy, *Les deux ages*, 513–16. Gui I appears beside Dreu d'Allemant among the witnesses of a charter of 1170 granted by Ives de Nesle, count of Soissons (references later, n. 55). He appears in the entourage of the Sire de Coucy between 1163 and 1174; he died in 1179 in the Cistercian habit he took up at Ourscamp. His brother Jean is mentioned between 1161 and 1174 in the charters of the Sire de Coucy and the count of Soissons.

[39] Raoul Revel, seneschal of Ives de Nesle, count of Soissons in 1155, died after 1178 (genealogical outlines in Newman, *Les seigneurs de Nesle*, vol. 2, p. 160, n. 5).

[40] In 1152 (charter cited subsequently in n. 50), Guillaume l'Ancien was a guarantor for Dreu, his mother, and his stepfather; in 1166 he signed a charter of the count of Soissons (Newman, *Les seigneurs de Nesle*, vol. 2, no. 41, p. 108). He gave his consent to the *laudatio* granted by Dreu to the gifts made to Saint-Martin de Laon during his minority by his mother and father-in-law (undated charter, before 1184, mentioned later in n. 53).

[41] On Robert, see later, "Note on the Identification of the Spouses in Charter 2."

[42] Gérard *de Castello*, mentioned beside Payen *de Novo Rure* in a false charter of the count of Soissons (see n. 54 below), figures with Guillaume l'Ancien and under the same titles as he in the charters already mentioned (see n. 40 earlier) of 1152 and before 1184. He also witnessed the charter of 1170 already cited (n. 38 earlier).

[43] Aucher de Ressons (Ressons-le-Long: Aisne, arr. Soissons, cant. Vic-sur-Aisne) also gave his consent to the *laudatio* mentioned earlier (n. 40). In 1173, the count of Soissons confirmed a grant by Helvide, Aucher's mother, to Saint-Jean-des-Vignes de Soissons (Newman, *Les seigneurs de Nesle*, vol. 2, no. 59, p. 134); Jean d'Arblincourt was a witness, and Aucher and his brother Pierre *laudaverunt*.

[44] Gui, viscount of Pernant (Aisne, arr. Soissons, cant. Vic-sur-Aisne), appeared in 1176 (Newman, *Les seigneurs de Nesle*, vol. 2, no. 72, p. 151; charter of the count signed by Raoul Le Turc).

[45] For the genealogy of the Le Turc family, see Newman, *Les seigneurs de Nesle*, vol. 1, 175–77. Raoul, son of Jean Le Turc of Pierrefonds, appears from 1144 to 1189.

[46] Soupir: Aisne, arr. Soissons, cant. Vailly.

[47] Landri de Pierrefonds (Oise, cant. Attichy) and his son Hugues appear as witnesses of two charters of Conon, seigneur de Pierrefonds, in 1168 (collection of titles relating to Longpont [Stein n° 2216]: Bibl. nat., lat. 5470, fol. 189) and in 1172 (cartulary of Saint-Martin de Laon: H 872, fol. 219v). In 1180, Hugues signed a charter of the same Conon (now also count of Soissons) confirming the donation of Hervé, son of Hugues, to Longpont (Newman, *Les seigneurs de Nesle*, vol. 2, no. 86, p. 171). In 1176, Jean witnessed a charter of the same Conon in favor of Ourscamp (ibid., no. 73, p. 154).

[48] The identification of this Blihard *de Ferietate* with Blihard de La Ferté-Chevresis (Aisne, arr. Saint-Quentin, cant. Ribemont) is very uncertain. For one thing, we would here expect *Firmitate* and not *Ferietate* (but an error in reading is possible); for another, the social rank of the Sire de La Ferté, master of an important château, was much higher than that of the persons who surround him. On Blihard de La Ferté see especially D. Barthélemy, *Les deux âges*, 112 (see also index).

[49] Possibly Oulchy-le-Château: Aisne, arr. Soissons, chief town of the canton.

[50] Hugues de Champfleury, chancellor of Louis VII and Bishop of Noyon (1159–75).

Note on the Identification of the Spouses in Charter 2

Of the two partners in the act, only the husband, Dreu, is identified. I have not succeeded in placing his wife Mateline in any known family. With respect to her, therefore, I shall content myself with proposing a hypothesis.

For Dreu's identity, the list of witnesses is our basic evidence. It includes one Robert, who is said to be Dreu's stepfather (*testimonio...Roberti victrici mei*). Now, an act of Ives de Nesle, count of Soissons, dated 1152 by its editor, records an agreement concluded in the count's presence between the monks of Saint-Crépin-le-Grand de Soissons on the one hand, and *Robertum de Baisi et Ydam uxorem ejus et Drogonem, ejusdem Yde filium* on the other, an agreement by the terms of which the abbey received the wood of Le Fruty from the other party for clearance.[51]

There can be no doubt that the Robert and Dreu of the dower charter are the same as those in the count's charter. Besides the same connection of parenthood, we have two further pieces of evidence: first, the charter of 1152 concerns the wood of Le Fruty, a place mentioned in the listing of the dower granted to Mateline; and second, the guarantors of the agreement of 1152, Guillaume l'Ancien and Gérard de Castello, are among the witnesses who attest to Dreu's marriage.[52]

The documentation for Ide, Dreu's mother, and for Robert, his stepfather, is sparse. The chief item is a charter of the bishop of Soissons granted in 1184 to the Premonstratensians of Saint-Martin de Laon,[53] from which we learn that Robert and Ide, then deceased, had two children named Adam and Hugues. Dreu's father, dead by 1152 at the latest, was named Payen *de Novo Vico*.[54]

Still a minor in 1152, Dreu appears in 1170, the year of his marriage, among the knights (*milites*) who testified to the agreement concluded between the monks of Corbie and the Seigneur d'Oisel,[55] where he is called "Dreu d'Allemant." He died between 1170 and 1184, apparently without issue, for the charter of 1184 tells us that it was to a certain Pierre Cot (*Petrus Costius*), whose connection with

---

[51] Newman, *Les seigneurs de Nesle*, vol. 2, no. 20, p. 55.

[52] For these witnesses, see earlier, notes 11 and 13. Note that the agreement of 1152 was made on the establishment of, or led to, Mateline's dower charter.

[53] Cartulary of Saint-Martin de Laon, H 871, fol. 188. This charter recalls the eventful history of the donation of the right to pasturage granted to Saint-Martin by Robert, Ide, and Dreu over all their lands, and its later confirmation by Dreu. Two other older charters also mention these facts (undated Soissonnais charters of Bishop Josselin and archdeacon Nivelon: ibid., fol. 371 and 372); this collection of charters was exploited, with respect to Robert, by Newman, *Les seigneurs de Nesle*, vol. 2, p. 56, n. 3.

[54] The episcopal act of 1184 states that Dreu had granted Saint-Martin "easements for pasture" (*aisentias pasturarum*) on all his lands in Allemant, Vaudesson, Rohain, and Algival for the soul of his father Payen *de Novo Vico*. A *Paganus de Novo Rure*, named after Gérard *de Castello*, figures among the witnesses of a charter in the name of Ives, count of Soissons (Newman, *Les seigneurs de Nesle*, vol. 2, no. 7 bis, p. 35), which is undoubtedly false, as its editor has shown, but the list of witnesses in which may have been borrowed from a true charter of Bishop Josselin (1126–52). In my opinion, this Payen *de Novo Rure*, unknown to Newman, is none other than Payen *de Novo Vico*.

[55] Newman, *Les seigneurs de Nesle*, vol. 2, no. 47, p. 116.

Dreu is not explained, that the latter's lands passed by right of inheritance (*jure hereditario*).[56]

For the discovery of Mateline's identity, our only resource is to try to divide the witnesses into two groups corresponding to the two spouses. Unfortunately, it is impossible to make a strict separation. The first few names (Gérard de Quierzy, Gui and Jean d'Arblincourt, and Raoul Revel) owe their presence as much to their social eminence and their strong connection with Soissons as to their relations with the husband; and the next names (Guillaume l'Ancien, Gérard *de Castello*, and Aucher de Ressons) form a group around Robert, his stepfather, the nucleus of Dreu's kin. One hesitates to assign the names that follow these to Dreu or to Mateline. Nevertheless, one seems to reach firmer ground in this onomastic swamp when one gets to the name of Raoul Le Turc and that of Landri de Pierrefonds, who is accompanied by his two sons, Hugues and Jean: these four names are all associated with the castle of Pierrefonds. Still more remarkable, Landri is accompanied by two of his sons. Such strong representation by one family may indicate that Mateline belonged to that lineage. In any case, it seems likely that the castle of Pierrefonds is the pole around which the wife of Dreu d'Allemant revolved.

CHARTER 3

1176

Arnoul de Monceau[-sur-Péron] takes Agnès as his wife and grants her as a dower, besides half of his acquisitions, his "wionage" (wionagium) of Laon,[57] along with fifty Soissons pounds, of which thirty are reserved for the construction of a house and the rest are to be "multiplied" in lands. If Arnoul dies before the sum is paid, the debt will be imposed on his wionage of Monceau. Charter enacted under the seal of Roger [de Rozoy], Bishop of Laon.

(See Map 3.)

In the name of the holy and undivided Trinity, amen.

The marriage sacrament, instituted by God's authoritative precept for our first parents at the beginning of the world [cf. Gen. 2:18–24] and confirmed by the imitation of the patriarchs [cf. Gen. 12:5, 24:51, 29:28] and by the observances of angels [cf. Tob. 6:10–22, Luke 1:5–38], leaves to future generations no mean example of human social relations. Now at the end of time our Savior,

---

[56] Charter cited: "Post obitum vero Drogonis, Petrus Costius ad quem terra ipsius hereditario jure descendit ... predictam elemosinam [i.e., the donation of "easements for pasture" made by Dreu; see above, n. 34] ... laudavit."

[57] That is, Arnoul's share of the *wionage* of Laon.

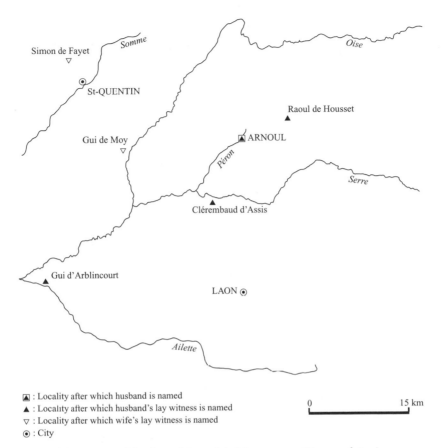

Simon de Fayet
▽

Somme

Oise

St-QUENTIN

Raoul de Housset
▲

Gui de Moy
▽

◪ ARNOUL

Péron

Serre

▲
Clérembaud d'Assis

Gui d'Arblincourt
▲

LAON ⊙

Ailette

◪ : Locality after which husband is named
▲ : Locality after which husband's lay witness is named
▽ : Locality after which wife's lay witness is named
⊙ : City

0   15 km

Map 3. 1176 – Marriage of Arnoul de Monceau-sur-Péron and Agnès.

by attending a wedding [cf. John 2:1–11], has commended marriage most
highly by his presence and has hallowed it with a lasting dignity, as attested
by his miraculous changing of water into wine. In the Lord's own words
regarding conjugal coupling, by which he urges a man to leave his mother
and father and to adhere to his wife [cf. Matt. 19:5], one finds an example of
humble obedience and a refutation of the perfidious and execrable folly of
the heretics who attempt to disparage the goodness of marriage. Moreover,
the bond of this love is spread abroad through marriage to embrace non-kin
and even strangers, and where this love could not be conserved by the bond
of kinship, it is called back, as it were, like a fugitive, by the blessing [*bonum*]
and the fidelity [*fides*] of marriage.

Therefore I, Arnoul de Monceau, taught by the example of the holy fathers,
and attracted by such great privileges of marriage, join you, Agnès, my dearest
betrothed, to me as my wife in legal and lasting matrimony, and I give to you

as your rightful dower the best part of what I possess, namely, my *guionage*[58] from Laon and fifty pounds of Soissons money divided thus: thirty pounds for building a house in a place amenable to you, according to the advice of both your kinsfolk and mine, and the rest to be invested in land. If I should die before paying this money in full, you shall draw on my gainage from Monceau until the aforesaid sum is fully paid. In addition, I give to you one half of everything that I shall acquire.

So that you may possess these things peacefully, I have caused them to be confirmed to you by the seal of our lord Roger Bishop of Laon,[59] and by the testimony of the undersigned.

Sign of Gautier the archdeacon of Laon. Sign of Baldwin the archdeacon. Sign of Foulque the chanter. Sign of Master Bruno. Sign of Rainer the archpriest. Sign of Raoul de Housset.[60] Sign of Gui de Arblincourt.[61] Sign of Clarembald de Assis.[62] Sign of Simon de Fayel.[63] Sign of Gui de Moy.[64]

Done in the year of the Lord's incarnation 1176. I, Guillaume the Chancellor, wrote this.

Note on the Identification of the Spouses in Charter 3

The uncertainty of the subscription does not put in doubt the identification of the husband with Arnoul de Monceau-sur-Péron,[65] a nephew of Blihard, Sire *de*

---

[58] The term *wionage* (or *guionage*) was frequently employed in the Laonnois and in the Vermandois to designate the *conduit des marchands* (the right to collect a fee for giving merchants safe conduct across one's territory). On the exercise of this right in the Laonnois and, more precisely, in the lordship of Coucy, see Barthélemy, *Les deux âges*, 377–87.

[59] Roger de Rozoy-sur-Serre, Bishop of Laon from 1174 and until at least 1204 (Barthélemy, *Les deux âges*, 312) was dead by 1207. One should correct Pius Bonifacius Gams, *Series episcoporum* (Regensburg, 1873), 559, who gives 1201 as the end of Roger's episcopate.

[60] For the genealogy of the Seigneurs de Housset (Aisne, arr. Vervins, cant. Sains-Richaumont), see Barthélemy, *Les deux âges*, 519–22: "Raoul I de Housset was a signatory for the Sires de Coucy eleven times between 1147 and 1187, but he also appeared with the Sires de La Ferté-Chevresis in 1159, Ives de Nesle, and Clérambaud de Berlancourt" (ibid., 519). In 1168 (Édouard de Barthélemy, *Analyse du cartulaire de l'abbaye de Foigny* [Vervins, 1879], 37), Raoul de Housset and Arnoul de Monceau were both mentioned as guarantors of an agreement concluded between the monks of Foigny and Scot de Lehérie (a knight of the Guise faction who would later be the testamentary executor of Raoul I: see Barthélemy, *Les deux âges*, 219).

[61] On Gui d'Arblincourt, see Charter 2, n. 16.

[62] Probably Clérembaud d'Assis (Assis-sur-Serre: Aisne, arr. Laon, cant. Crécy-sur-Serre), whose village lordship was under a fief of the Sire de Coucy in 1188 (Barthélemy, *Les deux âges*, 189).

[63] On the Fayel family (now Fayet: Aisne, arr. Saint-Quentin, cant. Vermand), see W. M. Newman, *Les seigneurs de Nesle*, vol. 2, 101–03. See also O. Guyotjeannin, *Episcopus et comes*, 220. The Sires de Fayel belonged to the entourage of the counts of Vermandois; Simon, brother of Rorgon and son of Ode, Dame de Fayel, appears from 1144 to 1186.

[64] Moy-de-l'Aisne: Aisne, arr. Saint-Quentin, chief town of canton. On Gui de Moy, see W. M. Newman, G. Constable, and Th. Evergates (eds.), *The Cartulary and Charters of Notre-Dame of Homblières*, Medieval Academy Books 97 (Cambridge, Mass., 1990), no. 48, p. 109.

[65] On the seigneurs de Monceau-sur-Péron (Aisne, arr. Vervins, cant. Sains-Richaumont, comm. Monceau-le-Neuf-et-Faucouzy), see the genealogical study by D. Barthélemy, *Les deux âges*, 523–25.

Ferietate (La Ferté-Chevresis?),[66] who appears between 1163 and 1190 in seven subscriptions to the charters of Raoul, Sire de Coucy.

His wife Agnès was, in fact, his second wife. Arnoul had first married the widow of Anselme de Marle, Adélaïde, whom D. Barthélemy considers to be a daughter of Sire Bouchard de Guise. I have not succeeded in identifying Agnès, who should probably be associated with a family from the Vermandois, possibly that of Simon de Fayel or of Gui de Moy, witnesses who certainly belong to the bride's group.[67]

CHARTER 4
1177

Renier[de Rary] takes as his wife Brune [de Monceau-le-Waast] and grants to her as her dower all that he holds in Rary, all the mills that he owns, and half of his future acquisitions. Charter enacted under the seal of Roger [de Rozoy], Bishop of Laon.

(See Map 4.)

In the name of the holy and undivided Trinity.

Despite the prating of those who denigrate marriage, matrimony is good and respectable when it is legitimately formed and dutifully maintained.[68] By no means would the Creator of all things have joined our first parents in marriage [cf. Gen. 2:18–24], by no means would he have wished to be bodily present at the celebration of nuptials [cf. John 2:1–11], nor to have honored them with the first of his miraculous signs, if he knew that there was sin in a properly constituted marriage.

Since, therefore, these and many other testimonies of sacred Scripture praise marriage, I, Renier, wishing legitimately to beget children, have taken you, Brune, my dearest betrothed, as my wife, and I have given to you as your rightful dower possession of all that I have in general profits at Rary,[69] and whatever I have in mills, and one half of all of my acquisitions.

So that you may possess these things peacefully, I have confirmed them to you solemnly through this dotal instrument by the seal of our lord Roger, Bishop of Laon,[70] and further corroborated by the witness of those who are inscribed below.

---

[66] On Blihard, see earlier, Charter 2, n. 48.

[67] The Vermandois connections of these two witnesses appear in Map 3.

[68] The tradition of the text here is poor, but some corrections permit us at least to restore the probable meaning of the sentence.

[69] Rary: Aisne, cant. Marle, comm. Saint-Pierremont.

[70] See Charter 3, n. 59.

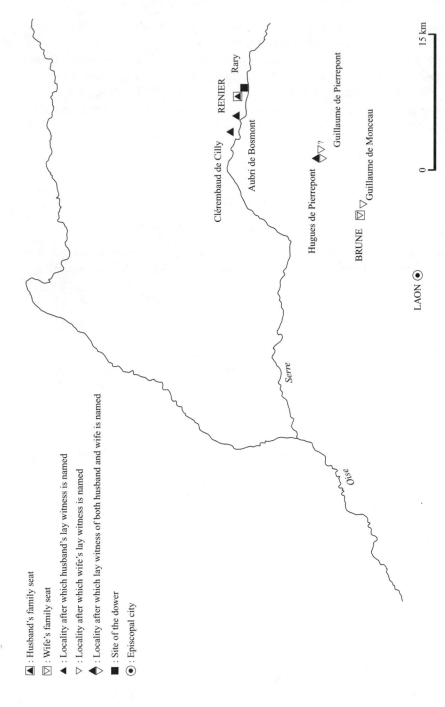

Map 4. 1177 – Marriage of Renier de Rary and Brune de Monceau-le-Waast.

◀ : Husband's family seat

▽ (boxed) : Wife's family seat

▲ : Locality after which husband's lay witness is named

▽ : Locality after which wife's lay witness is named

◆ : Locality after which lay witness of both husband and wife is named

■ : Site of the dower

⊙ : Episcopal city

15 km

0

Clérembaud de Cilly

RENIER

Rary

Aubri de Bosmont

Serre

Oise

Hugues de Pierrepont

Guillaume de Pierrepont

BRUNE

Guillaume de Monceau

LAON ⊙

Sign of Hugues de Pierrepont.[71] Signs of Aubri de Bosmont[72] and Clarembald and Gui our brothers. Signs of Guillaume de Pierrepont[73] and Gui[74] and Guillaume your father.[75] Simon the priest of the bishop's chapel was present along with these.

Written in the year of the Lord's incarnation 1177. I, Guillaume the Chancellor, wrote this.

Note on the Identification of the Spouses in Charter 4

The identification of the spouses does not raise any difficulty. The bonds of kinship indicated by the subscriptions place Renier in the family of the Bosmonts.[76] Moreover, the wife's name and the location of her dower permits us to affirm that the Renier de Rary whom we see acting by consent of his wife Brune in two charters of 1178[77] and 1185[78] is indeed the brother of Aubri de Bosmont.[79] For the identification of Brune see earlier discussion, note 98.

CHARTER 5
1181 or 1182,[80] February 24 [Laon]

*Eudes grants as a dower to his wife Bertrea, first, all that he has from the tithe of Thierny and his large vineyard located in Ruespoourouse; second, a house (*mansio*) that he will*

---

[71] Masters of an important castle, the Sires de Pierrepont (Aisne, cant. Marle) belonged to the high aristocracy of the Laonnois. On Hugues, called *de Wasnoe*, see M. de Sars, *Le Laonnois feudal*, vol. 3 (Paris, 1929), 122–23. Hugues appeared in 1145 and died a little after 1188. His wife Clémence (younger daughter of Itier, count of Rethel) found herself the aunt of Emperor Henry VI. The eldest son of Hugues, Guillaume, mentioned from 1161 onward, died in the Holy Land during the Third Crusade. A younger son, Hugues, had a brilliant ecclesiastical career in the diocese of Liège, of which he became bishop in 1200.

[72] Bosmont, same locality as Pierrepont.

[73] This may be Guillaume, son of Sire Hugues de Pierrepont.

[74] No known son of Hugues de Pierrepont was named Gui.

[75] That is, Guillaume de Monceau (see earlier discussion, case study 2, at n. 97). This Monceau is more likely to be Monceau-le-Waast (in same locality as Pierrepont and Bosmont) than Monceau-les-Leups (Aisne, arr. Lanon, cant. La Fère), which is farther west by a good ten kilometers and much farther from Guillaume's seat (see earlier, n. 108; gift to Bucy-les-Pierrepont).

[76] See the earlier discussion, under "Three Case Studies," no. 2.

[77] Cartulary of Saint-Michel-en-Thiérache: Bibl. nat., lat. 18375, p. 104, episcopal charter.

[78] Cartulary of Thenailles: Bibl. nat., lat. 5649, fol. 8v, episcopal charter; note that the act takes into account the consent not only of Brune but even of Renier's children, apparently still very young if they were, as it is reasonable to think, children by Brune.

[79] D. Barthélemy does not make this connection in his monographic study of the seigneurs de Bosmont (*Les deux âges*, 517, n. B).

[80] The document is dated on Saint Matthias' day (February 24), 1181. Because of the time of year, the date 1181 should read 1182 if the episcopal chancery of Laon followed the Florentine or paschal style. To my knowledge, the style then in use has not been determined with certainty. Nevertheless, "the style used seems to have been that of Christmas" in the first half of the century, according to Annie

build for her, or if he does not build it, 40 pounds of good money assigned on the lands of Montbérault; and finally, half of his acquisitions. Charter acknowledged and confirmed before Roger [de Rozoy], Bishop of Laon.

In the name of the Lord.

It is an approved custom that a man should give a wedding gift [*donatio nuptialis*] to the woman whom he takes as wife. Therefore I, Eudes, have drawn up for you, my beloved wife [*uxor*] Bertrea, the marriage gift [*donatio propter nuptias*] described below. I have given to you for that purpose whatever I have in tithes from Thierny,[81] and the large vineyard situated at the place called Ruespoourouse,[82] and a house that I shall build (and should I fail to build it, I have assigned to you forty pounds of good money against the land at Montbérault),[83] and one half of my acquisitions.

So that this gift may remain firm in your hands, I have caused it to be faithfully recorded here, and to be confirmed by the authority of our lord Roger Bishop of Laon.[84] The witnesses of this act are Hugues the abbot of St. Vincent [of Laon][85] and two of his monks, Renaud the almoner and Gautier d'Orchies,[86] Pierre de Laon, Jean de Monampteuil,[87] Raoul de Chevregny,[88] and Jean Cignus.

The aforesaid was solemnly recognized before the bishop, and written in the year of the Lord 1181, on the feast of Matthias the Apostle. I, Guillaume the Chancellor, wrote this.

Note on the Identification of the Spouses in Charter 5

I have been unable to identify either the husband or the wife in this charter. The two places in which Bertrea's dower is located (Thierny and Montbérault) are almost adjoining, as are Monampteuil and Chevregny, the places attached to the names of two lay witnesses. These two groups of villages of the southern Laonnois, not far from each other, define a narrow perimeter within which one should probably

Dufour-Malbezin ("Catalogue des actes des évêques de Laon antérieurs à 1151," *École nationale des chartes: Positions des theses*, 1969, p. 39). The date stated here takes account of these two possibilities, but for the sake of simplicity, the act is stated in the body of the article to be from 1181 (the date indicated in the document).

[81] Thierny: Aisne, cant. Laon-nord, comm. Preles-et-Thierny.

[82] Place not identified (in the Thierny district?).

[83] Montbérault: Aisne, cant. Laon-nord, comm. Bruyères-et-Montbérault.

[84] See Charter 3, n. 59.

[85] Hugues, abbot of Saint-Vincent de Laon from 1174 to 1205 (see *Gallia christiana*, vol. 9 [Paris, 1751], col. 579–81).

[86] Possibly Orchies: Nord, chief town of canton.

[87] A Jean de Monampteuil (Aisne, arr. Laon, cant. Anizy-le-Château) is mentioned in an undated charter of Hugues, abbot of Saint-Martin de Laon (cartulary of Saint-Martin: Bibl. mun. Laon, ms. 532, fol. 65va); Hugues was abbot from 1193 to 1197 (Dom Norbert Backmund, *Monasticon Praemonstratense*, vol. 2 [Straubing, 1952], 512).

[88] Chevregny, same locality as Monampteuil.

look for the places to which both husband and wife were attached. The presence of the abbot and two monks of Saint-Vincent de Laon seems to indicate that Eudes was a member of the *familia* of that establishment, either as a mayor (i.e., rural provost) or as a minor knight of the abbey's entourage.

Addendum to the English Version of the Article

Since the completion of the foregoing study in the spring of 1988, many works have appeared addressing more or less closely both the themes with which the study deals (such as the outlines of the *dos ex marito*, the wife's rights to this *dos*, the matrimonial strategies of the aristocracy, the discourse on marriage, and the place of such documents in the wedding ritual) and the diplomatic material that it exploits (i.e., *dotalicia* and "nuptial charters"). It seems that such research has focused chiefly on periods prior to the twelfth century, and especially before 1000, with special attention to patrimonial transfers between the spouses and to the status and rights of married women and widows. Ample material for reflection is found in the proceedings of two important colloquies: Michel Parisse (ed.), *Veuves et veuvage dans le haut Moyen Âge, [actes de la] table ronde organisée à Göttingen par la Mission historique française en Allemagne* (Paris, 1993) (round table of 1991); and François Bougard, Laurent Feller, and Régine Le Jan (eds.), *Dots et douaires dans le haut Moyen Âge*, Collection de l'École française de Rome 295 (Rome, 2002) (round table of Lille and Valenciennes, March 2000). The latter volume contains a useful bibliography on the subject. See also Emmanuelle Santinelli, *Des femmes éplorées? Les veuves dans la société aristocratique du haut Moyen Âge* (Villeneuve-d'Ascq, 2003).

Dower charters have been exploited, too, in a range of *thèses* on regional social history. For the nearest northern regions, we cite the monumental work of Dominique Barthélemy, *La société dans le comté de Vendôme de l'an mil au XIVᵉ siècle* (Paris, 1993), 541–53. See also Bruno Lemesle, *La société aristocratique dans le Haut-Maine (XIᵉ–XIIᵉ siècles)* (Rennes, 1999), 124–26.

My essay cites a large number of charters of the bishops of Laon, but only from manuscript sources. Henceforth, these charters (albeit only up to 1151) will be easily accessible in Annie Dufour-Malbezin (ed.), *Actes des évêques de Laon des origines à 1151*, Documents, études et répertoires publiés par l'Institut de recherche et d'histoire des textes 65 (Paris, 2001). This edition contains several charters cited in nn. 72, 73, and 83 (as well as in the comment in n. 10). One notes, too, that the charters of Saint-Yved de Braine (see nn. 73, 77, and 79) now have the benefit of an edition: *Le chartrier de l'abbaye prémontrée de Saint-Yves de Braine*, Mémoires et documents de l'École des chartes 49, edited by the students of the École nationale des chartes under the direction of Olivier Guyotjeannin (Paris, 2000).

Finally, it seems to me that my commentary on the preambles of the nuptial charters would have benefited from situating these literary fragments in a larger context. To appreciate correctly the originality of the long prologues and to assess their debt to a certain rhetorical tradition, it is necessary, I think, to keep in mind that the taste for long preambles, sometimes excessive and turning to dogmatic or pastoral argument, seems to have undergone a development (for certain types of charters) that began at the end of the tenth century and continued through the course of the eleventh, after which preambles waned during the twelfth century. On this subject, see especially Michel Parisse, "Préambules de chartes," in Jacqueline Hamesse (ed.), *Les prologues médiévaux: Actes du colloque international . . . Rome, 26–28 mars 1998*, Fédération internationale des instituts d'études médiévales, Textes et études du Moyen Âge 15 (Turnhout, 2000), 141–69; and idem, "Arenga et pouvoir royal en France du Xᵉ au XIIᵉ siècle," in Jürgen Petersohn (ed.) *Mediaevalia Augiensia: Forschungen zur Geschichte des Mittelalters*, Vorträge und Forschungen 54 (Stuttgart, 2001), 13–27. Also, one should place the reading of nuptial charters during the marriage ceremony in the context of more general practices of the public reading of legal documents (*recitatio*), as, for example, when they were promulgated or when they were presented to a judicial authority.

CHAPTER SIX

MARRIAGE AGREEMENTS FROM TWELFTH-CENTURY
SOUTHERN FRANCE

Cynthia Johnson

Situated geographically and chronologically between the two focal points of
research on premodern family life – that of medieval England and northern France
on the one hand, and that of Renaissance Italy on the other – twelfth-century
southern France presents a privileged context within which to examine medieval
marriage.[1] As both a Mediterranean society and a medieval one, southern France
(which, following Fredric Cheyette, I shall call Occitania) was located at the cross-
roads between these two regions and shared features of both.[2]

[1] The following abbreviations are used throughout the chapter and the appendix: ADA — Archives
départementales de l'Aude; ADHG = Archives départementales de la Haute-Garonne; Amado,
Thèse = Claudie Duhamel-Amado, "La famille aristocratique languedocienne: Parenté et patrimoine
dans les vicomtés de Béziers et d'Agde (900–1170)" (Thèse d'Etat, Université de Paris IV, 1994); HGL =
Claude Devic and Joseph Vaissette (eds.), Histoire générale du Languedoc, 2nd ed., 15 vols. (Toulouse,
1872–92); Johnson, Marrying = Cynthia Johnson, "Marrying and Dying in Medieval Occitania: A
Case-Study Approach to Dowries, Disputes, and Devolution in Twelfth-Century Southern France"
(Ph.D. diss., Emory University, 2005); LIM = A. Germain and C. Chabanneau (eds.), Liber Instrumentum Memorialium: Cartulaire des Guillems de Montpellier (Montpellier, 1884–86); and Annales
ESC = Annales: Économies, sociétés, civilisations (Paris), a serial publication that many American
libraries list simply as Annales. All monetary values, unless otherwise indicated, are the solidi produced at the mint in Mauguio. I should like to thank Christopher Gardner, R. H. Helmholz, Philip
Reynolds, and Stephen D. White for their comments on earlier drafts of this chapter, David Bright
and Mireille Mousnier for assistance with the translation of specific terms, and Diana Hunt for
expert editing. Research for this project was materially supported by grants from the French Minister of Foreign Affairs (Bourse Chateaubriand), Emory University, and the CNRS research team
FRAMESPA in Toulouse.

[2] The dominant model of medieval marriage and family, in which family structure completed the
shift from a bilateral to a patrilineal kinship system in the twelfth century, has been based largely on
sources from northern France and England and was developed primarily by Georges Duby. See idem,
The Chivalrous Society, translated by Cynthia Postan (Berkeley, 1977); idem, "Lignage, noblesse, et
chevalrie au XIIᵉ siècle dans la région mâconnaise: Une révision," Annales ESC nos. 4–5 (1972);
and idem, The Knight, the Lady, and the Priest: The Making of Modern Marriage in Medieval France,
translated by Barbara Bray (New York, 1984). For a fuller historiographical review and critique of this
model, see Johnson, Marrying, 5–34. For the bibliography on marriage and family in Renaissance
Tuscany, refer to Thomas Kuehn's chapter in this volume. See also Guido Ruggiero, Binding Passions:

Our chief evidence regarding the practice of getting married in twelfth-century Occitania consists of documents that were drawn up to record the transfer of marriage gifts. Of the thousands or perhaps hundreds of thousands of marriage agreements that must have been written during the twelfth century, only a tiny sample remains for us to examine. This chapter is based on a close reading of seven such agreements, selected from a database I have compiled of the nearly eighty extant documents describing marriage arrangements from the period 1095–1210.[3]

INTRODUCTION

Before I analyze these seven documents in detail, some remarks are necessary to situate the discussion. This general introduction is in five sections. The first provides a very brief overview of the historical setting of Occitania during this period. The second section introduces the documents used for the study of marriage. Summaries of the findings about the gifts exchanged at marriage and about the legal culture surrounding their transfer are presented in the third section. In the fourth section, I consider the timing of the process of getting married and the evidence about the persons represented in the documents as giving away the spouses or as contributing wealth. The fifth and final section discusses what these marriage agreements reveal about the role of the church in getting married.

The Historical Context
Situated along the Mediterranean coastal plain, from Toulouse to the Rhone, Occitania had more in common with its Catalonian and Italian neighbors than it did with Paris or England in the twelfth century.[4] Cities marked by their Roman heritage and linked together by the Via Domitia were the focal points of social life, and Occitanians identified themselves by the city or fortified village from which they came, rather than by their region or county.[5] Commercial life and trade were thriving by the eleventh century, and during the twelfth century, the city consulate was introduced in major towns. The documentation that records the financial

---

Tales of Magic, Marriage, and Power at the End of the Renaissance (Oxford, 1993) for an excellent example of a microhistorical approach to the study of marriage.

[3] For a more in-depth treatment of Occitanian marriage, as well as the relevant historiography and bibliography, see Johnson, *Marrying*, Part I. The extant marriage documents are presented in ibid., appendix 1.

[4] The literature on the history of Occitania is vast. The best introduction to the subject in English is Fredric L. Cheyette, *Ermengard of Narbonne and the World of the Troubadours* (Ithaca, 2001), which includes an extensive bibliography. My introductory comments are largely dependent on this work.

[5] The Latin term for such a fortified village is *castrum*. Because the English term "castle" brings to mind only the actual castle building, not the village, and because the phrase "fortified village" is cumbersome, I have retained the original Latin term. For more information on Occitanian villages, see Monique Bourin-Derruau, *Villages médiévaux en Bas-Languedoc: Genèse d'une sociabilité* (Paris, 1987).

affairs of Occitanians reveals that their wealth came not only from agriculture, but also from mills, rights to salt flats, fishing, tithes, road tolls, and, increasingly over the twelfth century, a thriving credit market involving land speculation.[6] Such commercial activity was not limited to wealthy elites: a glance at most cartularies from the region quickly reveals a complex variety of property transactions and financial know-how even among those of relatively modest means. Moreover, the preparation or redaction of these documents was not a privilege restricted to a clerical or monastic elite, as it was in northern France, for they were often written by lay notaries. Even peasants kept charters in their homes.[7] There were workshops for the writing of documents in Occitanian cities and castles from at least the twelfth century, although the earliest extant notarial register dates from 1248, in Marseilles.

Occitanian women enjoyed a more privileged status in comparison with their northern counterparts, partly because of the influence of Visigothic law on the region.[8] Here, in the twelfth century at least, women were often lords, holding *castra*, creating political alliances, approving documents with their own seals, giving castles to their men, receiving oaths of loyalty in return, and sometimes even leading their armies into battle.[9] This was also the world in which troubadour poetry was born.[10] While men and women troubadours sang with enthusiasm about romance and sexual adventures (and occasionally about extramarital affairs), the dualist Cathars preached about the evils of procreation and promoted sexual abstinence for all good Christians.[11]

---

[6] For the variety of goods that could constitute someone's wealth, see Cheyette, *Ermengard of Narbonne* (n. 4 earlier), 60–61, and ch. 3 in general.

[7] See Fredric L. Cheyette, "The invention of the state," in Bede Lachner (ed.), *The Walter Prescott Webb Memorial Lectures: Essays on Medieval Civilization* (Austin, 1978), 143–78, at 152–53. See also Amado, *Thèse*, vol. 2, 406–07: Amado discusses a group of villagers who, when called to testify as to the marriageable age of two young girls, traveled for several days with their charters to the proceedings. The charter of witness testimony is in LIM, no. 564.

[8] I discuss the relatively privileged status of Occitanian women throughout Johnson, *Marrying*. Pierre Bonnassie argues that this favorable position was attributable to Visigothic influence in his *La Catalogne du milieu du Xe à la fin du XIe siècle* (Toulouse, 1976), vol. 1, ch. 4. See also the references that follow, n. 9.

[9] For women, castles, and oath taking, see Cheyette, *Ermengard of Narbonne* (n. 4 earlier), 237–38, and more generally chs. 10 and 13; and on women warriors, ibid., p. 13. For a general overview of the powerful roles of Occitanian women, see ibid., 25–34 and the references given there, as well as Fredric L. Cheyette, "Women, poets, and politics in Occitania," in Theodore Evergates (ed.), *Aristocratic Women in Medieval France* (Philadelphia, 1999), 138–77. For detailed information about women's holding *castra*, naming patterns privileging the female line, and female-to-female lines of transmission of inheritances, see also Claudie Duhamel-Amado, *Genèse des lignages méridionaux*, vol. 1: *L'aristocratie languedocienne du Xe au XIIe siècle* (Toulouse, 2001).

[10] See Cheyette, *Ermengard of Narbonne*, ch. 13, on the relationships among troubadour poetry, lordship, and relations between the sexes. See also Cheyette, "Women, poets, and politics."

[11] For a reliable introduction to the Cathars, see R. I. Moore, *The Formation of a Persecuting Society: Power and Deviance in Western Europe, 950–1250* (Oxford, 1987), ch. 1, especially 11–26. See also Cheyette, *Ermengard of Narbonne*, ch. 16.

Twelfth-century Occitania possessed no clearly articulated system of law; rather, Visigothic, Roman, Frankish, and customary traditions overlapped.[12] There was no court system with clear jurisdiction to enforce authoritative, impersonal decisions. Instead, disputants chose groups of arbiters (often friends) to find a compromise that the parties could accept, and the arbiters freely modified legal traditions, customs, or written agreements to achieve that end. Although phrases from rediscovered Roman law (*ius civilis*) began to appear in Occitanian documents in the twelfth century, actual Roman practices would take another century or two to become established.[13] The "notariate" was not yet the professional class that it would become in the southern Europe in the late Middle Ages (especially in Renaissance Italy, where notaries were the official recorders of legal documents in official registers).[14]

Although Occitania had a long tradition of writing down important property transfers, especially at marriage and death, it remained a largely oral culture. Norms governing behavior were retained and transmitted in forms that were oral and easily memorized, such as oaths, gestures, or the poetic narratives of troubadour poetry. These narrative and didactic forms of discourse were concerned with individuals and their actions within their social network, not with abstract categories of persons: as Cheyette puts it, "most notions of law, ideals of behavior, political rules, and social mores were remembered in the form of statements about particular persons... *doing* things... statements about actions that were visible and had visible consequences."[15] When Occitanians such as those in the marriage documents appended at the end of this chapter were engaged in transactions, they were acting not as representatives of abstract legal categories (husband, wife, father), but rather individuals who were members of certain families, parishes, and neighborhoods, acting within a complex web of social relationships.[16]

[12] The bibliography on Roman law during this period is vast. For an introduction, see the articles by André Gouron reprinted in *La science du droit dans le Midi de la France au Moyen Age* (London, 1984); idem, "Les étapes de la pénétration du droit romain au XIIe siècle dans l'ancienne Septimanie," *Annales du Midi* 69 (1957): 103–120; Marie-Louise Carlin, *La pénétration du droit romain dans les actes de la pratique provençale (XIe–XIIIe siècle)* (Paris, 1967); and the introduction to John H. Pryor, *Business Contracts of Medieval Provence: Selected Notulae from the Cartulary of Giraud Amalric of Marseilles, 1248* (Toronto, 1981). For a revisionist study of law, which reveals the ways in which judges and disputants adapted legal traditions to suit their needs, see Jeffrey Bowman, *Shifting Landmarks: Property, Proof, and Dispute in Catalonia around the Year 1000* (Ithaca, 2004).

[13] See Roger Aubenas, *Cours d'histoire du droit privé: Anciens pays de droit écrit XIIIe–XVIe siècles*, vol. 2: *Aspects du mariage et du droit des gens mariés* (Aix-en-Provence, 1954), 33–34.

[14] For an introduction to documentary forms in southern France, the influence of Germanic and Roman traditions, and the medieval notariate from a juridical perspective, see Pryor, *Business Contracts* (n. 12 earlier), 8–24. For a social historian's analysis of the production, meaning, and use of written documents in Occitania, see Cheyette, "The invention of the state" (n. 7 earlier), 152–56.

[15] Cheyette, "The invention of the state," 161.

[16] The preceding paragraph has closely followed ibid., 158–61. For a fine critique of the problems that result when historians use abstract categories to analyze a population to whom such abstract thinking was entirely foreign, see Fredric Cheyette, "Georges Duby's *Mâconnais* after fifty years: Reading it then and now," *Journal of Medieval History* 28 (2002): 291–317, especially 315–17.

Given the context, therefore, I would argue that it would be a mistake to read the marriage documents discussed subsequently as written contracts or legal records. In fact, nineteenth-century archivists did not classify many of them as "marriage contracts," but rather as "donations," "agreements," "quitclaims," and so on. It is difficult to dissociate the term "contract" from its modern connotations, whereby it refers to a legally binding agreement that follows a set formula and is regulated by clear and enforceable rules of secular contract law.[17] Such a system did not exist in medieval Occitania (or for that matter in any other region of France) until the mid-thirteenth century. Before that time, when people were in conflict over property (including marital property), they did not appeal to courts that would judge by impersonal norms, but rather to a group of arbiters whose job was to assuage anger and to find a compromise that would reestablish the peace.[18] Such disputes over marital or other property were settled, as Cheyette puts it, "not by considering the parties as vendors and purchasers, donors and recipients, and applying rules appropriate to those categories, but rather by the search for a resolution in which the status and self-esteem of both parties would be saved and a continuing social relationship created or renewed."[19] Although someone involved in such arbitration might produce documents that supported his or her claim, some sort of compensation would still be paid to the other party even if the claim were upheld. Charters could lend weight to someone's claim, but witness testimony and the claimant's social status, friends, and local influence counted for more. In fact, there is evidence that written records, in this society at least, served primarily to record who witnessed the event.[20]

Marriage Documents

The documents that can be profitably used for the study of marriage fall into three main categories. The first category consists of the documents commonly referred to as "marriage contracts," although (as mentioned earlier) that term can be misleading for a number of reasons, not the least of which is that, as far as we know, they did not establish the legal validity of a marriage. These documents provide information about the exchange of goods at marriage and the intended devolution of that property after the marriage ended. The second category includes testaments, in which the testator left certain goods to endow his or her children when they married. It also includes receipts of payment of the marriage gifts, which were sometimes written down because there could be significant lapses of time

---

[17] For a critique of *juridisme* in studies of kinship and marriage, see Pierre Bourdieu, *Outline of a Theory of Practice*, translated by Richard Nice (Cambridge, 1977), 22–38. See also idem, "Norms et déviances: Les stratégies matrimoniales dans le système de reproduction," *Annales ESC* 27, nos. 4–5 (1972): 1105–25.

[18] See Cheyette, "The invention of the state" (n. 7 earlier); and idem, "Suum cuique tribuere," *French Historical Studies* 6/3 (1970): 287–99.

[19] Cheyette, "The invention of the state," 161.

[20] Ibid., 159.

between the writing of the marriage act and the marriage ritual itself, and between the latter and the actual payment of the marriage gifts. The third category includes sales, donations to religious communities, mortgage documents, quitclaims, and disputes, for these sometimes mention that the lands involved were marriage gifts, but in such cases, the scholar is dependent on the chance mentions by notaries.

It is documents of the first category, which I shall call "marriage agreements," that are the subject of this chapter.[21] Most of the extant marriage agreements are copies, transcribed into ecclesiastical cartularies (usually those of military orders or cathedral chapters) when the churches had an interest in the properties involved, or into the seigneurial cartularies of the lords of Montpellier and the Trencavel family when their families were involved. Some were originally written by notaries and were later transcribed into ecclesiastical cartularies, which the city notary public would then authenticate. Some are extant only in *Ancien Régime* collections of transcribed medieval documents. Several original manuscripts, including some chirographs, exist in the Departmental Archives in Toulouse.[22] These documents are our chief evidence regarding how Occitanians got married during the twelfth century and what they considered important in marriage, but as noted previously, they are concerned almost exclusively with the transfer of property. In later centuries, bishops heard cases about the validity of a marriage, but no registers from bishops' courts survive from the twelfth century.[23] We have no chronicles or eye-witness accounts; no family records, or *ricordanze*, for Renaissance Florence; nor any civic archives similar to those of the city of Douai that Martha Howell analyzes in this volume. No official court records, such as those from England that R. H. Helmholz ably exploits, are extant. Documents containing disputes over marital property are extant for Occitania, but they generally record only the resolution and neither the claims made by the parties nor the process of negotiation.

As Thomas Kuehn points out in his chapter, marriage agreements recorded only the end point of what was certainly a long process of negotiation involving many persons who were not mentioned in the final charter. As Pierre Bourdieu has shown in another context, preliminary negotiations for marriages tended to be carried out by women, common friends, or lower-level people who acted as go-betweens, so that no honor was lost in the event that the negotiations did not succeed.[24] Only after the negotiations appeared to be successful did the main representatives of the family meet to officialize and make the agreement public. When a father is

---

[21] The medieval authors used no single term consistently to identify such documents as a category.

[22] Chirographs were pieces of parchment on which two copies of the same act were written, one for each of the parties. The parchment was then cut into two pieces through a word, so that the original document could be verified by matching the two halves.

[23] The earliest known registers from a French bishop's court date from late–fourteenth-century Paris. See Charles Donahue, Jr., "English and French marriage cases in the later Middle Ages: Might the differences be explained by differences in property systems?" in Lloyd Bonfield (ed.), *Marriage, Property, and Succession* (Berlin, 1992), 339–66, at 342–43.

[24] Bourdieu, *Outline* (n. 17 earlier), 34–35.

represented as arranging his child's marriage, either in a charter or in a medieval romance, Bourdieu would remind us that we are dealing in that case with the official side of family life – the public image of itself that it wants to portray – and not necessarily the way in which the actual negotiations occurred. In view of what we know about Occitanian society, the mobility of its people, the life of its courts, and its bustling cities, it seems very likely that the unofficial kinds of marriage negotiations that Bourdieu describes would have been carried out here, too, even though they were not recorded in our official marriage agreements.

Although the surviving evidence about Occitanian marital property is fairly abundant, only five marriage agreements indicate where they were written.[25] The bishop of Béziers claimed the right to a few *deniers* at the writing of each marriage charter written in his *scriptoria*, although there are virtually no marriage agreements extant in Occitanian bishops' cartularies.[26] Later copyists would have had little reason to preserve the marital documents of people long dead, and in addition, the clerics faced stiff competition from notaries, both private ones and those working for city consulary. Although most authors of marriage agreements are simply identified by name, three of them are labeled with religious identifiers, and four from the very end of our period, 1197–1207, as notaries.[27] The extant marriage documents show a slight tendency to be written in secular rather than ecclesiastical quarters. Because lay archives had a much poorer rate of survival than ecclesiastical ones, the percentage of secular marriage agreements, in reality, was probably much greater than the extant records would suggest.

Marriage Gifts and the Legal Context

Legal historians have treated the nature, origin, and rights related to marriage goods in great detail as part of an attempt to narrate the history of successive marital "regimes" and systems of property law. A great deal of this work has focused on tracking changes in the terminology used in documents, with special attention to the terms used for marriage gifts (*morgengabe* and its cognates, *pretium*, *dos*, *donatio ante nuptias*, and so on). Legal historians reason that by identifying the gift (for example, as brideprice, morning gift, dowry, or dower), one can identify

---

[25] Thus: "acta sunt hec … apud Omellacium in ecclesia Sancti Salvatoris" (Doc. 3); "factum est in domo Guillelmi de Nempse, in foro" (Doc. 4); "factum est apud Montepessulanum in domo seu stari Sancti Firmini" (LIM no. 129); "laudata fuit … apud Agathen ante ostium camere episcopi in manu domini Villelmi Agathensis episcopi" (Foreville, *Le cartulaire*, no. 96); "scripsit in castello de Cerviano, in operatorio magistri petri" (Doc. 7). One other document, from 1170, states that the act "fuit factum in manu Ugonis abbatis Sancti Saturnini" (ADHG H598) but does not state where the redaction was done.

[26] Duhamel-Amado, *Genèse des lignages méridionaux* (n. 9 above), vol. 1, 125 and n. 38. The charter containing the bishop's recognition of his rights is found in J. Rouquette (ed.), *Cartulaire de Béziers (Livre Noir)* (Paris, 1918), no. 140.

[27] See Johnson, *Marrying*, appendix 1, table 1, nos. 4 (*canonicus*), 25 (*clericus*), 26 (*deaconus*), 31 (*notarius publicus*), 35 (*notarius publicus*), 36 (*deaconus* at the order of the *tabellio publicus*), 41 (*tabellio publicus*).

marriage practices at a given time as "Germanic," "Roman," or "Christian."[28] However the documentary and historical context may be more informative than precisely what the gift is called. The terminology used to describe the gifts in Occitania varied considerably during the period studied here. Several terms for the marriage gift from the husband's side – including *sponsalicium, dotalicium,* and, by the late twelfth century, *donatio propter nuptias* – were used interchangeably. The notaries often gave no name at all to the wife's contribution, but when they did so, they used the term *dos* (or one of its variants). Yet although the terms *donatio propter nuptias* and *dotalicium* were applied almost exclusively to the husband's gift, the term *sponsalicium* was sometimes used for the wife's contribution, and the term *dos* might denote the husband's gift as well as his wife's. In practice, the terminology was immaterial. For example, everyone would have known that a wife had a customary right to a portion of her husband's property, and it would not have mattered what the gift was called in the document. Because the terms referring to marriage gifts in the agreements varied greatly and were sometimes absent, I have chosen (somewhat arbitrarily, but in line with current scholarly practice) to use the word dowry for any properties coming from the bride's side, and dower for any properties coming from the husband's side.

Because there are extensive treatments of these terminological questions in the literature by legal and social historians, I shall not discuss them further here, but a general overview of the findings of legal historians will be useful to situate the discussion of the documents. Before the renaissance of Roman law that began in the mid-twelfth century, a mixture of Visigothic, Frankish, Christian, and customary traditions influenced the management of marriage goods in Occitania and resulted in what legal historians call a "communitarian" regime, in which the spouses jointly managed their properties.[29] In addition to possessing their own individual goods

---

[28] The literature treating the precise definitions of these terms and their meaning at given points in time is extensive. For a review of the anthropological literature (and potent critiques of the structuralist, Marxist, and structuralist-functionalist influences on the study of marriage gifts), see John L. Comaroff, "Introduction," in idem (ed.), *The Meaning of Marriage Payments* (London, 1980), 1–44. A recent article has revisited the influence of Mauss's ideas and applied the results to marriage gifts in Renaissance Italy: Jane Bestor, "Marriage transactions in Renaissance Italy and Mauss's essay on the gift," *Past and Present* 164 (1999): 6–46. Jack Goody presents an important critique of historians' use of these terms in idem, *The Development of the Family and Marriage in Europe* (Cambridge, 1983), appendices 1 and 2. He was responding to a seminal article tracing the change in Europe to a dowry regime by Diane Owen Hughes, "From brideprice to dowry in Mediterranean Europe," *Journal of Family History* 3 (1978): 266–96. Legal historians have also analyzed the terms for marriage gifts in order to define the marriage regime for each region of France. For Occitania, see subsequent n. 29. See also François Bougard, Laurent Feller, and Régine Le Jan (eds.), *Dots et douaires dans le haut Moyen Âge* (Rome, 2002); and Michel Parisse (ed.), *Veuves et veuvage dans le haut Moyen Âge* (Paris, 1993).

[29] The classic studies of Occitania's marriage regime from the perspective of a legal historian are Jean Hilaire, "Les régimes matrimoniaux aux XIᵉ et XIIᵉ siècles dans la région de Montpellier," *Recueils de mémoires et travaux publiés par la Société d'histoire du droit et des institutions des anciens pays du droit écrit*, vol. 3 (Montpellier, 1955); and idem, *Le régime des biens entre époux dans la région de*

and the goods that they acquired together, the couple had the marriage gift from
the husband's side (*sponsalicium, dotalicium, donatio ante,* or *propter nuptias*) and
a contribution from the wife's side (the *dos,* or what she contributed *in dotem*). If
the husband pre-deceased his wife, she would have the marriage gifts that he had
given to her and also his goods in usufruct; he could also bequeath them to her
outright. If the wife pre-deceased her husband, he would hold their joint properties
in usufruct. Marital properties could only be alienated with the approval of both
spouses. Although these practices were the most common, the parties could modify
the provisions according to their wishes.

With the arrival of Romanized law (beginning in the mid-twelfth century), a
change supposedly occurred, although its chronology and extent have been much
debated. The communitarian norm turned into an individualistic one, which
legal historians characterize as a "dotal regime." Several changes were purport-
edly involved. First, the dowry was given directly from the bride's father to the
husband. Most often, the theory goes, this gift was in cash. Moreover, the dowry
became inalienable, and therefore the wife had to intervene in documents recording her husband's transactions to promise that the properties alienated did not
form part of her dowry. Because the dowry was most often in cash, the husband
possessed the cash to do with as he wished, but at the end of the marriage the cash
dowry had to be fully returned to his wife. (In practice, the wife often received a
portion of her husband's goods in addition to the return of her dowry.) Hence the
husband had to provide guarantees of various sorts or collateral to protect the wife
against the loss of her dowry.

Historians have regarded this transformation to a "Romanized" dotal regime
as a crucial factor to be considered in the larger debate over marriage and gender
relations. That debate has often depended on determining the nature of marriage
goods and how they were managed between the spouses. Moreover, a good deal
of historiography on medieval women has been devoted to tracing their relative
freedom (or constraint) in regard to the alienation of property, a capacity that
is presumed to be a direct indicator of their status. As the argument goes, one
result of the change to a dotal regime was that the contribution from the wife's
family was received by the husband instead of passing directly to her: in other
words, the husband alone administered the couple's property, and women lost their

---

*Montpellier du début du XIIIe siècle à la fin du XVIe siècle: Contributions aux études d'histoire du droit
écrit* (Montpellier, 1957). The marriage regime for all of southern France is described in Aubenas,
Cours d'histoire du droit privé (n. 13 earlier), vol. 2, 35–53. For an earlier period in Occitania and
the influence of Visigothic law, see Claudie Duhamel-Amado, "Donation maritale et dot parentale:
Pratiques aristocratiques Languedociennes aux Xe–XIe siècles," in Bougard, Feller, and Le Jan (eds.),
Dots et douaires (n. 28 earlier), 153–70. On the communitarian regime of goods between spouses,
see Roger Aubenas, "La communauté entre époux en Languedoc au Moyen-Âge," *Annales de la
Faculté de Montpellier* (1944). Hilaire also noted the communal holding of property, although he
reasoned that it went against the "natural" dominance of the husband in conjugal life. See Hilaire,
"Les régimes matrimoniaux," 22–23.

juridical capacity to manage their own goods. In addition (the argument goes), the wife was excluded from further inheritance of her parents' goods. Central to this argument is the premise that the nature of goods conferred as dowries changed from contributions of land to contributions in cash. In sum, historians have regarded all of these transformations in property management as evidence of a loss in status for women.[30]

Much of this reasoning is questionable. The primary evidence for such changes has been the appearance of Romanized legal phrases in the marriage agreements. Yet, as legal historians have long known (but social historians have tended to overlook), the actual changes resulting from the renaissance of Roman law took centuries to filter down to the level of practice, and varied greatly from region to region.[31] Furthermore, systematic analysis of marriage documents for twelfth-century Occitania challenges this theory by revealing a more complex picture of marriage gifts. Although cash contributions did become more frequent after 1150, it is important to note that they were often *accompanied* by gifts of land or of rents from land; it seems that they did not *replace* contributions of land. As we shall see, an apparently endless variety of goods constituted the marriage gifts: landed properties, towns or *castra*, cash, servants, mortgages, tenants with their holdings (see Doc. 3), knights, vineyards, taxes or other land rights, minting rights (see Doc. 4), churches, and even properties that one did not yet possess, such as future inheritances (see Doc. 5). In sum, in three-quarters of the documents mentioning dowries, the dowry was composed of goods or properties of several sorts, and not cash alone. Furthermore, when dowries were given in cash, landed property or rights were often sold to obtain that cash. Thus, real properties were still alienated in order to give the cash obtained as a dowry. The net effect was the same.

Rather than revealing a change in marital practices, the increasing presence of coin was part of larger processes of monetization, expanding trade, and land speculation taking place in twelfth-century Occitania. It was also a practical response

---

[30] The fundamental article on this topic is Hughes, "From Brideprice to Dowry." See Goody's critique of her article in idem, *The Development of the Family and Marriage in Europe*, appendix 2. (There are full citations to both in n. 28 earlier). The debate is continued in Christiane Klapisch-Zuber, *Women, Family, and Ritual in Renaissance Italy*, translated by Lydia Cochrane (Chicago, 1985). The correlation of property with status, and the argument that the status of women deteriorated dramatically with the shift to a narrow patrilineal structure and dowry regime, all form part of the dominant paradigm of medieval family structures known to Anglophone audiences primarily through the work of Georges Duby (for references, see n. 2 earlier). For Provence, this theory has been developed in Martin Aurell i Cardona, "La détérioration du statut de la femme aristocratique en Provence (X^e–XIIIe siècles)," *Moyen Âge* 40 (1985): 5–32. Claudie Duhamel-Amado responds to that article in eadem, "Femmes entre elles: Filles et épouses Languedociennes (XIe–XIIe siècles)," in *Femmes, mariages, lignages: XIIe–XIVe siècles: Mélanges offerts à Georges Duby* (Brussels, 1992), 125–55. Recently, more detailed empirical studies have shown that French women were not prevented from holding property, managing fiefs, and, in short, that they experienced no loss of status: see Cheyette, *Ermengard of Narbonne* (n. 4 earlier); Evergates (ed.), *Aristocratic Women in Medieval France* (n. 9 earlier) and Johnson, *Marrying*.

[31] See Aubenas, *Cours d'histoire du droit privé* (n. 13 earlier), vol. 2, 33–53.

to the need to define values in numeric equivalents.[32] Moreover, one should not assume that numeric values for loans, sales, or marriage gifts were always paid in coin. (One document states that a debtor owed 1000 solidi to be paid in cows and 2000 solidi to be paid in coin.)[33] In all types of transactions over the course of the twelfth century, land was increasingly sold to obtain cash. Although scholars have tended to view dowries in coin as inferior to landed properties from the woman's point of view, it is clear that, in general, most Occitanians in the second half of the twelfth century preferred cash to land. There were several advantages to having cash in this society: it could be easily divided among heirs or among those with multiple claims to a property; it was easily portable, a feature that could be useful in this relatively mobile society; and finally, it could be invested in the booming market in mortgages, yielding substantial profits for investors.

The purposes of marriage gifts were multiple and overlapping. They functioned as the joint property of the spouses, as insurance for the wife in case of widowhood or separation, and as patrimony for the children of the couple. The most common way in which Occitanian spouses obtained the goods that they transferred to each other at marriage was through inheritance from their parents or, if their parents had died, from their siblings. In many cases, these gifts were specifically labeled as an inheritance, a fact that supports Jack Goody's theory that marital assigns were a form of premortem devolution.[34] In fact, one of the most important conclusions to be drawn from the study of these documents has to do with the ways in which dowry, dower, and inheritance overlapped. Although the transfer of property at marriage and at death was essentially the same, inasmuch as part of the couple's goods passed to the children, what differentiated the two types was the timing of the transference, which resulted in a different set of circumstances.

In addition to inheritance and sale, another way of securing goods to be used as marriage gifts was for spouses to provide them out of their own property. In general, this option seems to have been preferred for second (or third) marriages and for people from middle to lower social groups. In about one third of the texts mentioning dowry arrangements, it was the wife herself who is represented as having given the dowry to her husband, and this tendency increased over the century.[35] It is important to note, then, that some women held properties in their own right even before marrying, in addition to what they would receive through marriage. Furthermore, in most of these cases, the bride is said to have given the dowry on her own, with no mention of the involvement or approval of other kin. This fact was probably a result of the particular demographic circumstances

---

[32] See Johnson, *Marrying*, ch. 1.

[33] HGL V, col. 682.

[34] Goody, *The Development of the Family and Marriage* (n. 28 earlier), 222–39; and idem, "Introduction," in Jack Goody, Joan Thirsk, and E. P. Thompson (eds.), *The Family and Inheritance: Rural Society in Western Europe, 1200–1800* (Cambridge, 1976), 1–9, at 1–2.

[35] See Johnson, *Marrying*, appendix 1, tables 1 and 2, nos. 8, 10, 12, 16, 24, 25, 29, 30, 36, 42, 43, 51, 52, 54, 56, and 58.

at a given moment in the family's life cycle. For example, it is likely that if a woman married after the death of her parents, she would have already received her inheritance and thus could give her own properties as a dowry, without requiring the approval of her siblings or kin.

Although the marriage documents always specify what the dowry properties were, either by assigning a numeric value to them or by providing a detailed listing of the properties, the groom gave specified gifts and then, in addition, an unspecified gift such as "half of all my goods." The reference to a quantified but unspecified portion of the husband's goods served as a guarantee to protect his spouse's dowry as mentioned earlier, so that if he mismanaged or lost it, she could claim an exchange of equivalent value from any of his remaining properties (see Doc. 5). Thus it was important to define the value of the dowry in the document so that the wife could be sure to recover it at the end of the marriage. This was also a good reason to define the value of the dowry in numeric terms rather than as landed holdings. But it is worth noting that the wife did not have to wait until widowhood to receive marital gifts; as most of the documents discussed here show, the wife entered into possession of her marital gifts once the marriage was finalized.

Regardless of how spouses obtained the goods to be transferred at marriage, the writing up of a document detailing the properties was one thing, whereas actually getting hold of the properties was another. The extant documentation shows that even in cases in which the parties claimed to have been fully paid and satisfied, actual receipt of the gifts could take years after the marriage itself had been concluded (see Doc. 7). In the twelfth century, Occitanians were aware of the problem of delayed marital payments, and they took measures to limit such potential for conflict, notably by adding provisions to marriage acts or by writing receipts of payment.

The Marriage Process

The extant marital agreements, as records of transfers of property, did not usually record the processes of negotiation or the rituals involved in marrying. For these aspects of marrying in France, scholars have relied on prescriptive or normative sources such as liturgical manuals,[36] and this reliance severely limits the kinds of conclusions that one may safely draw about actual practice. Nevertheless, the marriage agreements do indicate who was represented as giving the assigns to the couple, an aspect of the marriage process that scholars have interpreted as an important indicator of the parties' relative status. The extant documents do not support the conventional view that it was the bride's father who normally gave the dowry to his son-in-law. In roughly one third of the documented cases from twelfth-century Occitania, the bride herself gave her dowry to her husband, whereas

[36] The chief scholarly works that have established the paradigm for medieval France are Jean-Baptiste Molin and Protais Mutembe, *Le rituel du mariage en France du XIIe au XVIe siècle* (Paris, 1974); and Korbinian Ritzer, *Le mariage dans les églises chretiennes du Ier au XIe siècle* (Paris, 1970).

in another one-third either both of her parents or her mother alone gave the dowry. In only one third of the cases did the father alone bestow the dowry.[37]

At what moment was a marriage considered to have been completed? Was it when the couple exchanged the gifts? (That would be consistent with the maxim that there could be no marriage without a dowry.) Or was it when they exchanged words of present consent (the point at which the alliance would have become a marriage in contemporaneous canon law)? Whereas medieval theologians and canonists focused on defining the actual moment at which the sacrament of marriage was completed (usually to resolve cases of validity, prior contract, and so on),[38] for the laity, it was less important to determine when a marriage became valid than it was make sure that the marriage was a visible, public process. As Mia Korpiola confirms, getting married was a social process composed of several phases through which the couple progressively became perceived as married by their society, as opposed to a discrete act dividing the status of unmarried from that of married. The precise *terminus ad quem* of the process was not usually a matter of much concern for those directly involved.[39]

Nevertheless, it seems that in Occitania (and probably in most other medieval societies), it was the act of being "led" that made the marriage complete in the eyes of the couple and of their circle of friends and family (see Doc. 5). The husband was said to lead (*ducere*) his bride to their new home, at which there was a feast and consummation was presumed to take place. There is some foundation in late Roman law for the idea that the handing over of the bride (*traditio*) was the moment at which a marriage came into effect, and at least one medieval legal scholar formally proposed this thesis in the twelfth century.[40]

Yet the documents show considerable variety regarding who took or gave whom in marriage. Although we cannot assume that scribes directly transcribed social reality into their texts, they must have had reasons for such variations, even if those reasons are lost to us now. The documents represent various people as giving away the spouses in marriage. One quarter of the texts represent the bride's father as giving her to her husband, and another one quarter represent both parents as giving

[37] Johnson, *Marrying*, 142–43.

[38] For an important article outlining the development of the church's theory of consent, see Michael Sheehan, "Choice of marriage partner in the Middle Ages: Development and mode of application of a theory of marriage," *Studies in Medieval and Renaissance History* n.s. 1 (1978): 1–33; reprinted in James K. Farge (ed.), *Marriage, Family, and Law in Medieval Europe: The Collected Studies of Michael Sheehan* (Toronto, 1978), 87–117. The fundamental works on canon law are still relevant: Jean Dauvillier, *Le mariage dans le droit classique de l'église* (Paris, 1933); and Adhémar Esmein, *Le mariage en droit canonique*, 2 vols. (Paris, 1891).

[39] Mia Korpiola, "An act or a process? Competing views on marriage formation and legitimacy in medieval Europe," in Lars Ivar Hansen (ed.), *Family, Marriage and Property Devolution in the Middle Ages* (Tromsø, 2000), 31–54. See also Philip L. Reynolds, *Marriage in the Western Church* (Leiden, 1994), Part IV, 315 ff.

[40] See James A. Brundage, *Law, Sex, and Christian Society in Medieval Europe* (Chicago, 1987), 262, 266–67.

the bride to her husband. In fully half of the cases, the partners are represented as taking each other as man and wife. (Such passages appear more frequently in marriage acts in the latter half of the twelfth century.)[41]

From the perspective of theology and canon law, it was the exchange of present consent (or of future consent followed by consummation) that defined a valid marriage. One might expect to find evidence of such consent in phrases such as "I take you as my husband/wife," which notaries occasionally inserted into marriage documents. These references to the spouses' "taking" each other might plausibly be interpreted as records of *consensus de praesenti*, because although the documents were largely concerned with property exchange and devolution, they were not exclusively so. If marriage documents had been written to record only property and nothing else, the parties could have simply written up a receipt of payment (as some couples did). There is, in fact, no obvious reason why the words about "taking" should have been included in these marriage documents. It is possible that the parties wanted to express some idea of intention or consent, but it is equally possible that such phrases were merely another example of the increasingly formal and legalistic rhetoric employed by notaries at the end of the century.

Yet an example from the cartulary of the lords of Montpellier shows that we should not confuse the occasion of the spouses' "taking" each other, as recorded in the marriage documents, with the date of a completed marriage as understood by those involved. In the marital agreement of Guillaume VI of Montpellier and Sybille (dated 1129), Guillaume states, "I take you, my dearest fiancée, as my wife [*duco te karissimam sponsam in uxorem*]." Although one could argue that these words implied present consent and therefore that the couple was already married, a later document specified that Guillaume was actually to "lead" her on the feast of St. Michael, five months later.[42] Furthermore, those who held the *castra* and *villa* that he had given to her as marriage gifts would have to do homage to her within a month after the leading ceremony. Here is another indication that people considered the ceremony of leading to mark the actual moment of marriage, and it seems that there could be some considerable gap of time between the writing of the marriage agreement and the groom's leading of his bride.

Although the sources are not as revealing as one might like, they show that the marriage process could include separate occasions for betrothal, for written agreements, and for ceremonies of leading, depending on the circumstances and the wishes of the parties involved. Writing a document about the properties exchanged at some point in the process seems to have been standard practice even among people from modest levels of society, although it was probably not strictly obligatory. These several events were not required for a marriage to be regarded as valid

[41] Johnson, *Marrying*, 143–145.
[42] LIM: the marital agreement is no. 128, the text indicating "leading" on the feast of St. Michael, no. 136.

and complete either canonically or socially. All we can say with certainty is that the ceremony of "leading" was the moment at which the transfer of marriage gifts became irrevocable.

The Role of the Church

Georges Duby's theory of medieval family structures described two clearly defined models of marriage: one ecclesiastical, based on consent, exogamy, and indivisibility; one lay, based on arranged marriages, endogamy, and informal separation. According to this theory, these models competed for supremacy, and the church's model eventually took over as the dominant one.[43] But there is so little evidence of such topics in the documents of practice considered here that there is no way of knowing whether Duby's competing theoretical models of lay and ecclesiastical marriage ever influenced the marriages of actual people in medieval Occitania.

The documents of practice recording medieval marriages in Occitania do not discuss whether people married at a church, whether their marriage involved a priest, or whether they professed any words of present or future consent. (This finding is congruent with Helmholz's findings for late-medieval England and Kuehn's for Renaissance Florence.) Apart from standard invocations such as "In the Name of the Lord" and some rare biblical citations (see Doc. 4), there is nothing ecclesiastical about the texts themselves. Bishops or abbots sometimes appeared as witnesses to marriage documents along with counts or other lords, but they seem to have been present only as important temporal lords and not to officiate as clerics or priests. Needless to say, it does not follow from such silence that religion was unimportant.

COMMENTARY ON THE DOCUMENTS

For this chapter, I have selected seven marriage agreements from a database of the nearly eighty extant documents concerning marriage from twelfth-century Occitania. To distinguish marriage agreements from other sorts of transfers that could occur between marital partners, I have included only texts in which at least one word associated with marriage appears.[44] I have chosen the seven documents appended to this discussion both because they give a fair idea of the range of possible contents in marriage documents and also because they illustrate the most significant developments that occurred during the twelfth century. I have intentionally focused on

---

[43] Duby, *The Knight, the Lady, and the Priest* (n. 2 earlier).

[44] Scholars studying marriage documents for the south of France have often noted the lack of marital terminology in acts that were surely transfers of marital property. See Eliana Magnani Soares-Christen, "Alliances matrimoniales et circulation des biens à travers les chartes provençales (X^e–début du XIIe siècle)," in Bougard, Feller, and Le Jan, *Dots et douaires* (n. 28 earlier), 131–52; Hilaire, "Les régimes matrimoniaux" (n. 29 earlier); and Duhamel-Amado, "Donation maritale et dot parentale" (n. 29 earlier).

texts from middle to lower social groups to complement work on medieval marriage
that is concerned almost exclusively with the marriages of counts and princes.

Document 1
Petronilla Gives Her Daughter a Dowry (1127 n.st.)

The first document is clear and to the point.[45] It states that Petronilla gives her
daughter, also named Petronilla, to Bernard, and that she gives half of a house and
half of a vineyard as her daughter's dowry.[46] The simplicity of this text, the small-
ness of the dowry, and the relative anonymity of the actors are good indications,
considered together, that the socio-economic status of the family was below that
of the local aristocracy and even of the urban elites. I have included it to illustrate
marriage among people of modest means.

The text illustrates what elements needed, at a minimum, to be recorded in
writing at the beginning of the twelfth century. The scribe or notary devotes the
greatest number of lines to describing the location of the properties. The text
concludes with a short phrase indicating that the partners will have the properties
as long as they live, and their children after them. The signatures of three witnesses
follow, but none of the principal actors signs. Noticeably absent from the document
are formal or technical terms relating to marriage or marriage gifts; in fact, if the
scribe had not used the phrase "as a wife," it would have been difficult to identify this
document as a marriage agreement rather than an ordinary donation or exchange.
The sole purpose of this document, it seems, was to record the transfer of property
related to a marriage, probably because the properties were located in an area under
the bishop of Maguelone's lordship.

When Petronilla gives half of a house, the scribe calls it an *honor*. The word
honor is not easily rendered into English, for although it was used frequently in
twelfth-century Occitania, its meaning was fluid. It usually designated real property, but it could also refer to moveable goods, to cash, or to all three types of
goods at once.[47] In general, an *honor* represented something like a patrimony:
an ensemble of goods, rights, or privileges. Some idea of devolution or inheritance is often implicit, inasmuch as the term was often used for properties handed
down to successive generations but not usually for acquired properties. Because no
accurately equivalent term exists in English, I have preferred to leave the word
honor untranslated.

---

[45] The text is found in the cartulary of the Guillaumes of Montpellier (LIM, no. 52) in the section
containing agreements between the lords of Montpellier and the bishops of Maguelone.

[46] Note the transmission of female names from mother to daughter. See Amado, *Genèse des lignages
méridionaux* (n. 9 earlier), vol. 1, 285–92; eadem, "Femmes entre elles," (n. 30 earlier), 143–46.

[47] Niermeyer's Latin dictionary provides twenty-six possible meanings for *honor*, none of which is
applicable here.

Finally, it is worth noting that it is the mother who gives a dowry to her daughter. It is reasonable to assume that the mother is a widow, but even so, it is interesting that it is she herself, and not an uncle or a brother, who gives the dowry. In cases such as that of the young Petronilla, the responsibility to provide marriage gifts fell to parents, including mothers, in preference to other male kin of the family. Furthermore, this case is not an isolated example; other Occitanian marital agreements show mothers giving marriage gifts to their daughters or sons, as mentioned earlier.

Document 2
Pierre and Pontia Bestow Gifts on their Daughter and her Husband (1132)

In our second text, Pierre Matfred and his wife Pontia, together with their children, give vineyards to their daughter, Aicelene, and to her husband, Pierre Andre, for their marriage. Here too, as in the previous document, there is no reference to the spouses' "taking" each other; instead, the partners are represented as already married. There are the standard devolution clauses: the spouses will possess the lands until their death, when they will pass to their children; or, if there are no children, the properties will pass to the nearest relatives. It is worth noting that instead of representing the father alone as giving his daughter to her husband in marriage, as the standard models of medieval marriage might lead one to expect, the document records that both mother and father give the property to the couple. Like Document 1, this text is largely devoted to a description of the location of the property. The marriage gift itself is composed of two vineyards or sets of vines, both located in the *honors* of other persons. As with the first document, the relatively small size of the marriage gift probably indicates that the family was not wealthy, being at most town or village notables.

As is the case with nearly half of the extant marriage agreements, Aicelene received her marriage gifts from her parents as her inheritance.[48] At first, the scribe notes that the parents give vineyards to their daughter *in hereditate*. Yet afterwards, the

---

[48] Some scholars have argued that a daughter, once she received a dowry, was then excluded from making any further claims on the property of her natal family because the dowry was supposed to serve as her inheritance. This argument has been developed by legal historians such as Hilaire, "Les régimes matrimoniaux" (n. 29 earlier), 26–27. See also Martí Aurell i Cardona, "La détérioration" (n. 30 earlier), 11–12, 24; Eliana Magnani Soares-Christen, "Douaire, dot, héritage: La femme aristocratique et le patrimoine familiale en Provence (fin X^e–début XIIe siècle)," *Provence Historique* 46 (1996): 193–209, at 204–08; eadem, "Alliances matrimoniales" (n. 44 earlier), especially 137–38; and Jean Yver, *Egalité entre héritiers et exclusion des enfants dotés* (Paris, 1966). Yet it is not as clear as it might at first seem that a daughter's receipt of a dowry excluded her from further inheritance. Because of the revival of Romanized law, such a provision for exclusion was inserted into the custumals of Arles and Avignon, yet the provision did not begin to be applied in practice until the middle of the thirteenth century. To complicate matters further, the form of Roman law compiled in the *lo Codi* at Arles (ca. 1150) insisted on the equal rights of sons and daughters – even dowered daughters – to inherit. In actual practice, dowered and married daughters could and did inherit in twelfth-century Occitania, despite legal pronouncements to the contrary. See Johnson, *Marrying*, chs. 3 and 4.

parents give the same vines to the husband *de sponsalicio*.[49] Later in the text, when the scribe describes the devolution of the marital goods to future children, the gift to the couple is called an *honor*. Thus, in the same document, these same two pieces of vineyards were alternately labeled as an inheritance, as a marriage gift, and as something similar to patrimony.

As mentioned previously, such variation in terminology is common in medieval Occitanian marriage documents. Scholars have interpreted this fluidity of vocabulary as a result either of a decline in the use of Latin or of confusion as to the proper (i.e., Roman) senses of the terms.[50] Yet the scribe did not use the terms carelessly or in a way indicating that they were interchangeable. He used the term for inheritance only when the parents gave property to their daughter, indicating that the gifts she received for her marriage counted as part of her inheritance. But when they gave the same properties to her husband, he was not inheriting them, and therefore the term for a marriage gift was used. Only afterwards, when the text outlines the various clauses of devolution of the goods to the children, was the term *honor*, denoting a sort of patrimony, used. This use of terms suggests that one purpose of marriage gifts (perhaps the main one) was to create, for the benefit of the children of the marriage, a new patrimony constituted out of marriage gifts from both the wife's and husband's kin (see also Doc. 4). Given the fact that the same properties were labeled with three different terms and served at least three different functions simultaneously, how can one decide whether these vines fell into juridical categories of dowry, dower, or inheritance? These properties were many things at once, and their function depended on the relationship of the giver to the recipient. This case, therefore, provides good reason to adopt Goody's concept of devolution, so that all forms of transmission between generations can be taken into account and considered together.

The other main portion of Aicelene's and Pierre's marriage document concerns the conditions under which her parents give the land. The writer not only mentions that the couple and their children after them will have the *honor*, but he also specifies that the children who inherit must be the progeny of the wife and her husband. In theory, this clause would exclude not only illegitimate children from inheriting the *honor* but also those born from previous or subsequent marriages. Such clauses became standard over the course of the twelfth century.

In this, as in other texts we shall consider, we notice a change in wording that occurred during the twelfth century: the addition of the qualifier "legitimate" to the term designating the spouse, as in contemporaneous canon law (e.g., "I take you as my legitimate wife [or husband])." One might interpret this adjective in several ways. It may have been no more than a legal flourish resulting from the

---

[49] *Sponsalicium* is usually understood as the husband's marriage gift to his bride, but here the term denotes what we should call the dowry, i.e., the marriage gift that came from the wife's side to the husband.

[50] Jean Hilaire, "Les régimes matrimoniaux" (n. 29 earlier), 19.

new education of scribes in Roman law traditions. Because there is no extant documentation from twelfth-century bishops' *curia* (which presumably would have heard cases about legitimacy of a marriage), it is impossible to know whether the addition of the adjective "legitimate" had any substantive meaning. In view of the prevalence of multiple marriages, informal unions, and mistresses during the period, one might regard the change as a response to a real social problem that arose when illegitimate offspring, half-siblings, or concubines claimed the rights and properties given as marriage gifts.[51] Yet while cases of disputes over marital property involving children, siblings, or surviving spouses are extant, to my knowledge there is none in which illegitimate children or concubines claimed marital property.[52]

DOCUMENT 3

The Marriage of Tiburgueta of Aumelas and Adémar
of Murviel (1150 n.st.)

Our third document is an example of a marriage settlement between two families from the upper levels of the regional aristocracy. It illustrates the various political and economic consequences at stake. It pertains to the marriage, in 1150, of Tiburgueta (or Tiburge), daughter of Guillaume d'Aumelas (a younger brother of Guillaume VI of Montpellier), to Adémar de Murviel, a man from an aristocratic family in the Béziers region. This document is considerably more complex than the first two, which pertained to the marriages of people of lower status and lesser wealth.

We have more information about the context of this marriage and the persons involved than we do for any of the other marriages presented here. In the twelfth century, the Murviels were a family of important castellans, and members of this family were often in the company of the counts and barons from the Béziers region. According to one plausible hypothesis, one of these barons was the go-between who arranged this marriage between the Murviels (a family not well known outside the Béziers region) and the Guillaumes, lords of Montpellier, a family with ties throughout the south of France and Spain.[53] The parties gathered for the writing of the marriage agreement in the Church of the Holy Savior at the main *castrum* of the bride's family in Aumelas. The act was written in the presence of the lord of Montpellier, Guillaume VII, a cousin of the bride Tiburgueta. Raymond Trencavel,

---

[51] The extant evidence for concubinage and illicit affairs dates from the early thirteenth century and is analyzed in John H. Mundy, *Men and Women at Toulouse in the Age of the Cathars* (Toronto, 1990). Although there is little documentation for the twelfth century, in all likelihood these practices were not new when they first appear in our thirteenth-century sources. Evidence of multiple marriages is abundant for the twelfth century. See Johnson, *Marrying*, chs. 1 and 2.

[52] The extant disputes over marital property are analyzed in Johnson, *Marrying*, chs. 2 and 4.

[53] Amado, *Thèse*, vol. 2, Monographs: Murviel, 98.

viscount of Béziers and Agde, was also present as guarantor (*fidejussor*) for Adémar and of Adémar's obligations toward Tiburgueta. In all, fifteen men were listed as guarantor-hostages for Adémar (see the discussion of this term subsequently), and twenty-eight other people, in addition to the scribe, were witnesses to the act.

By following the family over the course of three generations, one can understand some of the consequences that the marriage practices could have both for politics and for the holding of property among the upper levels of the aristocracy. The marriage of Adémar and Tiburgueta was a minor matter at the time, involving second sons and modest nobles, and it involved properties peripheral to the families' main holdings. The marriage was probably intended to reinforce ties of kinship and friendship among people who were already closely associated with each other. But as a result of the hazards of chance and the death of other heirs, secondary family lines became the principal ones, and those who had never expected to inherit lordships and power suddenly did so. This is what happened when the lordship of Aumelas, formerly part of the lordship of Montpellier, ended up in the hands of Adémar, who, though originally from a second-ranking aristocratic family, effectively became the lord of Aumelas.[54]

The text itself includes many of the features that are common in twelfth-century Occitanian marriage acts, such as references in the same document to the marriage gifts from both sides (an inclusion that became increasingly common during the second half of the twelfth century) and standard clauses about the devolution of goods for children who might be born of the marriage, and about the return of these goods to close relations if there were no children.

Furthermore, the marriage agreement also gives us a sense of the variety of goods that could constitute marriage gifts in Occitania, as discussed earlier. Tiburgueta's father gives her, as her dowry, three manses, three *castra*, a *villa*, everything that he owned in the region of Narbonne, and 1000 sous. As usual, Adémar, the groom, gives half of all his real and moveable property (including his coinage) as the dower. In addition to the undefined half of all his goods, Adémar gives to his wife a dwelling inside the *castrum* of Murviel, a village woman with her children and their tenure, and a man called Bernard Raymond de Murviel (who was probably a knight of the *castrum*; he may have been a kinsman).[55] As often happened, Adémar adapted the standard gift to his wishes or circumstances: the family *castrum* of Murviel is to pass directly to the couple's children; only if there are no children will Tiburgueta receive half of that property. It is important to underline that these gifts did not serve as a widow's portion for Tiburgueta; she entered into possession of them at the marriage.

In order to guarantee the marriage gift from Adémar to Tiburgueta, fifteen men are listed as guarantor-hostages. If her marriage gifts were damaged or seized by

---

[54] For the full story, see Amado, "Les Guillems de Montpellier à la fin du XIIᵉ: Un lignage en péril," *Revue des langues romanes* 89/1 (1985): 13–29.

[55] Amado, *Thèse*, vol. 2, Monographs: Murviel, 93.

Adémar's heirs, these guarantors were to go to Montpellier and remain there as hostages as long as necessary, until all the property was restored to her. Although the naming of guarantor-hostages was a fairly widespread practice in agreements among the highest levels of Occitanian aristocracy, this was normally only for the purpose of guaranteeing peace accords. The adaptation of the practice to secure marital settlements was rare.[56] Not wanting to be detained as hostages, the guarantors would have tried to ensure that the parties kept their agreement. It is one example, which could be multiplied many times over, of how it was not so much legal rules or documents that restrained people's behavior as the interests of individuals within a complex web of social relationships.

Document 4
Guillaume of Tortosa Gives his Wife Ermessende a Dower (1153)

This act is rather short, even though, like the previous agreement, it concerns the higher levels of the aristocracy. It defines the marriage gift or dower that Guillaume of Tortosa, younger brother of the lord of Montpellier, gives to his spouse, Ermessende. Like most of the marriage documents conserved in the cartulary of the lords of Montpellier, the document mentions only the marriage gifts from the husband's side and says nothing about the dowry that he must have received with his bride.[57]

Guillaume's document begins: "It is the order of law and ancient custom that marriage is not made without a marriage gift, on account of the [financial] benefit of the children."[58] The first part of the sentence is a reformulation of the famous maxim, "There can be no marriage without a marriage gift [*Nullum sine dote fiat conjugium*]."[59] The use of some version of this maxim to introduce marriage documents began to occur in Occitania during the late twelfth century, with the influence of the new law schools and rediscovered Roman law. Although the maxim is generally thought to refer to the *dos ex marito* (in our terms, a dower), some of

---

[56] I have found two other examples of this practice, which was limited to the highest level of the regional aristocracy: see LIM, no.129, and HGL V, col. 682–83.

[57] Henri Vidal, "Les mariages dans la famille des Guillems, seigneurs de Montpellier," *Revue historique de droit français et étranger* 62 (1984): 231–45, at 233–34.

[58] LIM, no. 145. "Legalis est ordo et antiqua consuetudo ut coniugium sine dote non fiat propter filiorum honestatem." I have found five other marriage documents that refer to custom or law, in addition to those mentioned below in n. 60. Only one mentions Roman law explicitly: see Raymonde Foreville (ed.), *Le Cartulaire du chapitre cathédral Saint-Étienne d'Agde* (Paris, 1995), no. 297. The other four refer to either the custom of the region or refer vaguely to ancient custom: ADA, G13, 1 and 2; ADHG E253; and Foreville, *Le Cartulaire*, no. 389.

[59] This maxim, probably Frankish in origin, first appears during the Carolingian era and later becomes standard in canon law. See André Lemaire, "La *dotatio* de l'épouse de l'époque Mérovingienne au XIIIᵉ siècle," *Revue Historique de droit français et étranger*, 4th series, 8 (1929): 569–80; and idem, "Origine de la règle, 'Nullum sine dote fiat coniugium,'" in Gabriel Le Bras (ed.), *Mélanges Paul Fournier* (Paris, 1929), 415–24.

the reformulations in southern French sources appear to refer to gifts from either or both sides.[60]

Were gifts of some kind required to constitute a valid marriage in twelfth-century Occitania? Although canon lawyers and theologians might not have thought so, Occitanian marriage agreements seem to be based on that assumption. An exchange of marital gifts (with or without documentation) was the expected norm. Moreover, a woman's right to receive or recover her dowry in property disputes was invariably upheld, as if it were the card that trumped other claims and all other creditors.[61] Disputes occurred over whether the dowry had been paid or whether marital property could be alienated by one of the spouses, and there were attempts by the surviving spouse to reclaim marital property from a deceased spouse's kin. Yet not once in the extant texts did anyone challenge a married woman's right to a dowry. The evidence of practice from twelfth-century Occitania also shows that married and dowered women continued to take an active role in their natal families, managing property, inheriting, and making successful claims on their father's or natal family's property.[62]

The most interesting part of the opening preamble in Guillaume's document for present purposes is the premise that marital assigns are given for the sake of the children. Although some version of the maxim that marriage required a gift or *dos* appeared occasionally in marriage documents, this document, as far as I know, is the only one that explains *why* the gift was necessary: to provide for the future offspring. This reason should make us reconsider the idea that the dowry was intended solely for the wife. Scholars have generally studied marriage gifts from the perspective of the spouses, or of the spouses and their parents. But this statement indicates that people may have exchanged marriage gifts with their future descendants in mind.

It stands to reason that on the occasion of a marriage, the spouses' families would assemble a new patrimony from their respective goods to provide for the future grandchildren. The extant charters support this hypothesis (see Doc. 2). As noted earlier, one of the few features that all extant Occitanian marriage acts have in common is the provision for the children that outlines the devolution of the new

---

[60] The fact that authors often referred both to a *dos* and to a *donatio* when citing the maxim may imply that, in Occitania at least, the phrase was supposed to cover marriage gifts from both sides. See the following examples from MSS in the ADHG, quoted here from Mundy, *Men and Women at Toulouse* (n. 51 earlier), appendix 1: "Legalis est ordo et eterna de iure tenetur ut coniugium cum dote et donatione procedat, et dos sine matrimonio nullum effectum habeat" (no. 12); "Legalis est ordo et antiqua consuetudo et de iure tenetur secundum institutiones antiquorum patrum et coniugium cum dote vel donatione fiat" (no. 18); "Legalis est ordo et etiam de iure tenetur secundum institutiones antiquorum patrum ut coniugium cum dote vel donatione semper fiat et dos sine matriminio nullum effectum habeat" (no. 38).

[61] On widows' rights to their dowries in Occitania, see Johnson, *Marrying*, chs. 1 and 2; and Mundy, *Men and Women at Toulouse*, 97–98.

[62] For some recent work on the active role of medieval French women, see the references listed in n. 9 earlier.

family's goods to them. Furthermore, the documents specify that the marriage gifts should pass only to the children born of the couple, and thus not to children born from other marriages. This provision suggests that the marriage gifts did not simply merge indistinguishably with the spouses' other properties, nor form a sort of common familial holding, but were, at the moment of marriage, already reserved specifically for the children of the couple. When a spouse remarried, children from the second marriage did not, in theory, have any rights to the marriage gifts from the previous marriage (although in practice, a surviving spouse or children from subsequent marriages sometimes kept marital goods from a previous marriage).

After this opening phrase, Guillaume and Ermessende's agreement contains some quotations about marriage taken from the Bible. There are several similar preambles in Zeumer's collection of Frankish formulae, and they are not uncommon in northern French dower charters.[63] Yet I have found only four marriage agreements from twelfth-century Occitania with biblical references in the preambles, including Guillaume's, and all of them concerned the family of the lords of Montpellier.[64]

The preamble to Guillaume of Tortosa's charter includes three biblical quotations. Two occur in the other documents with similar preambles, namely, the verse from the creation narrative saying that a man shall leave his father and mother to be joined to his wife, when they shall be two in one flesh (Gen. 2:24), and the Apostle Paul's exhortation that men should love their wives as Christ loved the church (Eph. 5:25). But this document alone includes Jesus' dictum, "What God has joined, man shall not separate" (Matt. 19:6). Should we see here evidence of the growing influence of the clergy regarding the indissolubility of marriage? Perhaps, but in the mid-twelfth century nothing prevented elite Occitanians (nor those of more modest status) from separating from their spouses.[65] There are a handful of papal letters from earlier in the century encouraging certain Occitanian nobles not to repudiate their spouses, but the noblemen paid little heed to such counsel. In most cases, Occitanians separated from their spouses without formal, documented processes invoking canonical principles, and without requesting a bishop's

---

[63] See the chapters by Philip Reynolds and Laurent Morelle in this volume.

[64] LIM, nos. 128, 129, 145, and 561. An additional, late–eleventh-century marriage agreement concerned another family of the highest aristocracy: HGL V, cols. 738–39. Two other preambles in the database make a vague reference to divine precepts, although both were written by Guillaume Raimond, *notarius publicus* of Montpellier: see LIM, nos. 204 and 561.

[65] There is one famous exception from the very end of the twelfth century, when the Pope refused to recognize the second marriage of Guillaume VIII of Montpellier as legitimate. Even then, the Pope did not object to the separation of Guillaume VIII's daughter, Marie, and her subsequent remarriage to the King of Aragon. See Claudie Duhamel-Amado, "Guillaume VIII de Montpellier, Marie et Pierre d'Aragon," in *Majorque, Languedoc, et Roussillon de l'Antiquité à nos jours: Actes du LIIIème congrès de la Féderation historique du Languedoc méditerranéen et du Roussillon* (Montpellier, 1980), 35–45. See also the reference in n. 54 earlier.

consent to separate.[66] Moreover, while in theory one might annul a betrothal or a marriage by invoking the church's prohibition on incest, in practice the ecclesiastical prohibition of marriage between close relations did not stop the members of the Occitanian nobility from marrying whomever they wished throughout the twelfth century.[67] It would be going too far, therefore, to interpret the inclusion of Matthew 19:6 in the preamble to Guillaume's document as a sign of the clergy's increasing influence over marriage, although it might conceivably be a sign of Guillaume's own piety. Unfortunately, God did, in fact, separate Guillaume of Tortosa from his wife not long after the marriage: she died in childbirth and left all her properties to her husband. Guillaume, perhaps distraught, chose to join the Templars rather than remarry, and he departed for the Holy Land. He wrote a will before he left in which he named his brother as his heir.[68]

The question remains: if these were documents of property exchange, why add biblical citations about marriage? Some scholars have proposed (with reference especially to Anglo-Norman practice) that because marriage documents were sometimes read aloud on the steps of the church as part of the marriage ritual,[69] biblical preambles served to promulgate the church's growing insistence on the Christian doctrine or sacramentality of marriage. Others note the heretical challenge to marriage in the twelfth century and speculate that such passages were included to counter heretical teachings.[70] Given that the occurrence of biblical citations in marriage agreements from twelfth-century Occitania, the home of the Cathar heresy, was rare – they appear in only four out of nearly eighty marriage agreements – and because their use was restricted to documents concerning the lords of Montpellier that were written by lay scribes, it would be difficult to argue that such citations served as a conduit by which the clergy taught the laity about the Christian doctrine on marriage.

---

[66] I have found only one "official" divorce decree from this period: that of 1197 for the count of Comminges (LIM, no. 195). The decree claimed that there was an impediment of consanguinity and traced the genealogy of the two spouses to prove that claim. The count had previously separated from another wife (and was left as a widower by a third), but only in this case was an official document drawn up, probably because he intended to marry Marie of Montpellier: in view of the close connection between the lords of Montpellier and the Papacy, he needed to make the separation official. See Martin Aurell, *Les Noces du Comte: Mariage et pouvoir en Catalogne (785–1213)* (Paris, 1995), 430–31; and Paul Amargier, "La politique matrimoniale du comte Bernard de Comminges," *Revue du Comminges* 92 (1979): 174–78.

[67] Again, the one famous exception to common practice concerns the family of the lords of Montpellier. When Tiburge of Aumelas (granddaughter of the Tiburge in Doc. 3) broke the promise of marriage between herself and her cousin Guillaume IX of Montpellier, she invoked their kinship, most probably to avoid paying the hefty penalty of 10,000 sous outlined in the betrothal document for breaking the marriage promise. For the references, see n. 54 earlier.

[68] Guillaume of Tortosa's will is printed in Luc d'Achery and Louis François Joseph de la Barre, *Spicilegium*, vol. 3 (Paris, 1723), 526.

[69] Molin and Mutembe, *Le rituel du mariage en France* (n. 36 earlier), 36, 289–91.

[70] See Laurent Morelle, "Mariage et diplomatique: Autour de cinq chartes de douaire dans le Laonnois-Soissonnais 1163–1181," *Bibliothèque de l'École de chartes* 146 (1988): 225–84, at 238–40.

Attention to the socio-political context of the marriage agreement may better explain why the scribes included biblical preambles in these cases. It is worth noting that none of the other Occitanian counts or viscounts of the twelfth century included biblical preambles in their marriage agreements. The family of the Guillaumes of Montpellier were newcomers to lordship in Occitanian politics, without a Roman city or a Carolingian comital title to give them legitimacy, as the other Occitanian rulers had. It was probably for that reason that the lords of Montpellier had linked themselves to the Papacy by doing homage to the Pope and placing their lands under his direct protection. It is likely, therefore, that such rhetorical flourishes were intended to emphasize the family's increasing power and their privileged status as the Pope's representatives rather than their devout faith.

DOCUMENT 5
A Marriage Among the Lower Levels of the Aristocracy (1165)

The fifth document records that Bernard Jordan gives his daughter, Ermessende, in marriage to Pierre Bernard. As another example of the variety of goods that composed Occitanian marriage gifts, he gives, as a dowry, an *honor*, a quarter of the tithe in Pouzols and its region, and 2000 sous. This marriage agreement is a fairly representative example of marriage agreements among the lower levels of the nobility in the second half of the twelfth century: the financial arrangements become more complex, the husband has to offer gifts and assurances to guarantee the wife's dowry, and marriage gifts from both sides are included in the same text.[71]

Moreover, this text illustrates the increasingly *legalistic* discourse that began to infiltrate marriage agreements in the mid-twelfth century. In fact, documents recording all kinds of property transfers from late–twelfth-century Occitania show a similar shift in rhetoric, which scholars usually attribute to the revival of Roman law. Whether it represents a change in the way that people thought about marriage or was merely on the level of rhetoric remains debated. Perhaps, as one scholar has argued, the new expressions appeared in the documents so that scribes could show off their knowledge of legal formulae, lengthen the contract, and thereby demand higher fees from their clients.[72]

Increasing complexity can be seen also in the financial arrangements. In this case, the property descriptions are rather detailed, and the devolution clauses are complicated and seemingly designed to anticipate any eventuality. The bride's father bestows properties and 2000 sous as dowry with the condition that the couple possesses it jointly. If there are no children, or if they have died before the

---

[71] According to Amado, this text is the first example in the region around Béziers to include both gifts (the *dos* and *sponsalicium*) in the same act: see eadem, *Genèse des lignages méridionaux* (n. 9 earlier), vol. 1, 435–36. See also Jean Hilaire, "Les régimes matrimoniaux" (n. 29 earlier), 24–25.

[72] Arthur Giry, *Manuel de diplomatique* (Paris, 1894), 560–61.

age of majority, the goods will revert to the wife's father or to her father's heirs. The husband Pierre shall have it if his wife Ermessende dies first, and Pierre may keep the remaining 500 sous, and then when Pierre dies, any surviving children will receive the *honor* and 1500 sous. This provision required Pierre to keep the *honor* and 1500 sous intact so as to pass this estate on to their children: here we see the dowry functioning as patrimony. If Ermessende outlives Pierre, she will keep the *honor* and the 1500 sous, whether there were children or not: here is evidence that the dowry was supposed to provide for the wife. Whatever happens, Pierre may do as he wishes with the 500 sous: in this respect, part of the dowry is for the husband's benefit. Like Document 2, then, this text shows the ways in which marital gifts served multiple functions simultaneously.

As further evidence of the impossibility of neatly categorizing "marriage gifts" and "inheritances," when Pierre guarantees Ermessende's dowry by pledging his goods, some of those goods are ones that he does not yet possess but will inherit at his mother's death. Indeed, he states that if he dies before his wife, she will inherit on his behalf, and the goods will come to her as they would have to him if he were alive, by right of marriage gift and guarantee (*ratione sponsalicii et pignoris*). Because he had at least three other brothers who were alive when this document was drawn up, the provision meant that his portion of the maternal inheritance would pass to his wife rather than reverting to his brothers: He had already given away his future inheritance to his wife as a marriage gift and as security for her dowry and inheritance.

Pierre's mother then makes an appearance in the deed, acknowledging and consenting to the marriage gift. She also gives Pierre his part of the inheritance from his father's *honor* and moveable goods, and she confirms that he will receive his share of her *honor* when she dies. Even after years of marriage, therefore, Pierre's mother could still distinguish clearly which properties came from her husband's side and which from her own. And yet, as most of our texts indicate (with adverbs such as *communiter* and *pariter*), the spouses possessed the properties jointly, even if they remembered the separate origin of the goods. In Pierre's case, his marriage gifts were also his inheritance from both his mother's side and his father's. Thus it seems that not only daughters' but also sons' marriage gifts were understood as a form of premortem devolution.

Whereas the property Pierre gave at marriage was part of his own inheritance, the agreement also states that his marriage gift served as security to guarantee against the loss of his wife's dowry. Such provisions were common in this region, especially during the latter half of the twelfth century. If necessary, a widow in disputed cases could sell or claim her husband's goods (to which she might otherwise have had only usufruct rights) in order to reclaim her dowry. In a growing money economy, it seems that husbands had begun to use the cash part of the dowry for investments and speculation and hence sometimes lost it. Furthermore, Pierre reinforces the guarantee of his wife's dowry and inheritance, stating that if he uses her 1500 sous to acquire an *honor*, that *honor* would be returned to her or to her heirs. From this it follows that even if there are no children, his natal family cannot inherit the *honor* acquired with her money. The provision suggests that people were aware that intrafamilial conflicts occurred and tried to offset them.

The addition of clauses and conditions about what would happen if one of the parties died before the marriage took place (wherein the increasing legalism of the texts is evident) raises questions about the timing of the marriage process. In the beginning of the document, the father gives his daughter (in the present tense) to her husband as his legitimate wife, and with that he bestows the dowry (with all its various conditions). Later, the husband states that he gives his gift to his wife Ermessende (again in the present tense). It would seem logical to conclude that at least by this point, they were already married. Scholars generally assume, in fact, that the date of the agreement is the same as that of the marriage.

Yet toward the end of the document, there is a condition stating that if Ermessende dies before Pierre has taken her as his wife, he cannot claim or seek anything from the properties given as dowry, and that Ermessende or her father cannot claim anything from Pierre's goods if he dies before the marriage. Clearly, the partners were not yet completely married in the eyes of their kin and friends. This document provides further evidence that it was the "leading" that completed the marriage, as discussed earlier, for it specifies that if one of the parties dies before the ceremony of leading, then no one can claim the properties given in the marriage agreement. Even though the document had been written, the gifts had been exchanged (or at least promised),[73] and Pierre already called Ermessende his wife, the claims of both partners on the marital property were not valid until the "leading" had occurred. It follows, then, that the marriage agreement could not have served as proof that they were already married.

DOCUMENT 6
A Man and a Woman Give Each Other Marriage Gifts (1195)

Document 6 is an example of a fairly simple exchange of marriage gifts from the end of the twelfth century. The same scribe has recorded the gifts from the husband and from the wife as two separate acts on the same parchment (which appears

---

[73] It is important to distinguish between *promising* to bestow marital gifts and actually *receiving* them. Part or all of the marriage gifts sometimes remained unpaid many years after the spouses married or were still unpaid when one of them died, even if both parties swore in the marriage agreement they had received the entire sum (cf. Doc. 7). Amado has found a Provençal document from 1083 whereby the dowry of 5000 sous was to be paid over a period of five years: see "Donation maritale" (n. 29 earlier), 161, n. 23. See also Francine Michaud, *Un signe de temps: Accroissement des crises familiales autour du patrimoine à la fin du XIIIe siècle* (Toronto, 1994). Michaud finds that, in late-medieval Marseilles, most intrafamilial disputes involved marital property and, in particular, the delayed payment of marriage gifts.

to be the original manuscript). I have included it partly because it is one of the few extant examples of marriage agreements among persons at the middling levels of society from this period and partly for comparison with Document 1 (from the early twelfth century). Moreover, the text provides evidence about the social networks surrounding the marrying couple, as well as about the characteristic agency of Occitanian women.

In the first of the two acts, Ricsenda gives herself and her dowry to Eichard. In the second, Eichard gives himself as her husband, and he gives all the rights that he has or may acquire as the dower. Both acts include the standard clauses about usufruct and devolution to the children. Unlike the other documents, there is no detailed description of property in land. Instead, they give each other any rights (*iura*) that they may have, and she gives him two hundred sous and an *honor* that she will later inherit. (These gifts should be compared with Pierre's gift to Ermessende in Doc. 5, described earlier.) The size of Ricsenda's gift indicates that her socio-economic status was on par with that of an important villager.[74]

Although the two acts are simple and straightforward, containing the common features of marriage documents, the document shows that by the end of the twelfth century, the fashion for elaborate legal rhetoric had reached down to more modest levels of society. For example, the scribe says that they take each other as "legal" (i.e., legitimate) husband and wife (*in legalem uxorem / maritum*), and that they marry from a desire to beget legitimate children (*affectans ex te habere legitimes infantes*). The property will devolve to the children "generated from us [*ex nobis generati*]." There is also greater specificity in the financial conditions of the gifts. The scribe states that the husband gives not only what he currently owns, but also whatever he will acquire in the future (a stipulation occurring with increasing frequency in marriage agreements drawn up during the second half of the twelfth century).

Although Ricsenda and Eichard seem to marry each other in their own right – for they are said to take each other as husband and wife and to give each other marital gifts in the first person (*ego*) – they do so "with the counsel of my *amici*."[75] Moreover, Ricsenda states that any alienation of half of the *honor* that she gives to Eichard would require her counsel and that of the *amici* on both sides. The term *amici* is usually translated as "kin" or "kinsfolk," but it can also refer to

---

[74] In a study of the nobility in the regions of Béziers and Agde, Amado identified the following levels of dowry: 10,000–20,000 sous for members of comital families; around 3,000 sous for local aristocratic families (castellans); 500–1,000 sous for the lesser (*petite*) aristocracy; and around 100 sous for important villagers: see Duhamel-Amado, "Femmes entre elles" (n. 30 earlier), 134–37. As with testaments, however, there is a risk of circular logic in using the amount of a dowry as an indicator of a family's socio-economic status, for without complementary documentation, one cannot know whether the amount represents a small or a large proportion of the person's total wealth.

[75] The bride also has the counsel of her brother Jean and her sisters.

an undifferentiated mix of friends, kin, or supporters.[76] Later in both acts, when outlining the future devolution of the marital property, the scribe uses the word *propinqui*, which usually denotes relatives. Yet, as is the case with the terms for the marriage gifts, the scribe does not use the terms haphazardly or treat them as interchangeable: he uses *amici* when referring to the supporters (kin, friends, and others) who were there to advise Ricsenda or Eichard, keeping their best interests at heart, and he uses *propinqui* to designate those kinsfolk who might make claims to the marital goods as their own family property. The *propinqui* might or might not be supporters; they might, indeed, even be hostile. Even though Ricsenda had siblings who were alive when the document was written, she states in the act that her *amici* generally would have a say in matters of marital property; the *propinqui* have a much smaller role.

In general, texts from the end of the twelfth century seem to represent a greater freedom of individual action on the part of the spouses themselves. Spouses are increasingly said to "take" each other in marriage, without the involvement of kin, and some spouses, as Eichard does here, outline the devolution of their property to their *propinqui* or to "whomever else [they] may choose." Should we interpret this development as indicating a weakening of kinship ties at the end of the twelfth century, to the benefit of friends and individuals? Although this hypothesis is plausible, the apparent development could also be a reflection of low status combined with a change in document survival rates. Ordinary people like Ricsenda and Eichard, who did not have titles, *castra*, or vassals, probably had a greater freedom to act individually than their noble counterparts would have had because less was at stake. Furthermore, from the last quarter of the twelfth century, the percentage of extant documents concerning those of middle to lower status increases significantly. These two phenomena, taken together, could explain why the body of extant documents gives the impression of a greater range of individual action at the end of the twelfth century.

DOCUMENT 7
Brothers Give an Inheritance to their Sister, and She Takes a Husband (1197)

In our last document, from 1197, two brothers, Jordan and Bernard, give their sister Rixende 3000 sous as her inheritance, which she, in turn, gives as a dowry to Pons Moine, whom she takes as her husband. The social status of this family was that of the lower-level, castle-holding aristocracy, and there are some indications that the bride in Document 7, Rixende, was a child of the marriage discussed in

---

[76] See Benoît Cursente, "Entre parenté et fidelité: Les 'amis' dans le Gascogne des XIe et XIIe siècles," in Hélène Débax (ed.), *Les sociétés méridionales à l'âge féodale: Hommage à Pierre Bonnassie* (Toulouse, 1999), 285–92.

Document 5.[77] As in the previous examples, Document 7 includes certain features that are usual in marriage agreements of this region and period, namely, the overlap between inheritance and marriage gifts, increasing complexity of the legal and financial conditions, the inclusion of marriage gifts from both sides in the same document, and stipulations regarding the devolution of patrimony to the children. The text also provides some interesting evidence about the ways in which Occitanians modified and adapted customary marital arrangements to reflect their personal circumstances.

At the beginning of the text, Rixende's brothers give 3000 sous to their sister "as her inheritance since she wishes to marry."[78] Rixende accepts the money and declares she will not claim anything further from her father's goods or from the goods of her brothers.[79] She then takes Pons Moine de Monte Albo as her husband, giving him the 3000 sous as a dowry. (The name Moine [*monachus*] is odd, but it is clear he was not a monk.) As in Documents 2 and 5, notions of inheritance and marriage gifts were inextricably woven together: how could one classify these 3000 solidi exclusively as inheritance or as dowry? This case, like many others from Occitania, confirms Goody's assertion that dowry was, in effect, a premortem form of inheritance, and the analysis of Rixende's dowry in terms of the overall devolution of family goods implies that she was not excluded from inheritance but rather received her share earlier.

Moreover, it is clear from the text that Rixende's father was already deceased, and her mother was probably no longer alive either. Probably because her parents had died, it was Rixende's siblings who gave her the inheritance. It was not unusual for siblings to be involved in marriage arrangements when their parents had died. In all, four marriage agreements in the database represent siblings as dowering their sister, a bride's siblings confirm the bestowal of a dowry in seven others, and in five acts, the groom's siblings approve his marriage gift to his bride.[80] Who gave the spouses or the gifts was something determined rather by the particular timing of the marriage and the demographic composition of the family at that time than by any clearly articulated set of marital rules.

Although her brothers give the inheritance, it is Rixende herself (speaking in the first person) who takes Pons in marriage. And it is she alone who gives him the dowry of 3000 sous. As in the previous agreement between Ricsenda and Eichard, Rixende is represented as acting for herself. Scholars have often regarded medieval

---

[77] Amado, *Thèse*, vol. 2, Monographs: Servian.

[78] " . . . donamus tibi sorori nostre Rixendi tria milia solidorum melgoriensium pro tua hereditate cum vis nubere viro."

[79] It is important to note that even when the agreement included a clause promising that there would be no further claims, this did not prevent anyone from actually bringing a lawsuit. See the intrafamilial disputes discussed in Johnson, *Marrying*, chs. 2 and 5.

[80] The documents are listed in Johnson, *Marrying*, appendix 1, thus: brothers dowering: table 1, nos. 10, 32, and 45, and table 4, no. 1; the bride's siblings confirming: table 1, nos. 4, 16, 26, 29, 30, 35, and 40; the groom's siblings confirming: table 1, nos. 2, 20, 29, 35, and 50.

and early modern marriage as an exchange of a woman between the woman's father and her husband (or between her brothers and her husband if her father had died). In this view, women were objects of exchange or pawns in political arrangements. But Rixende's marriage is one of many examples from the south of France in which the woman herself has an active role in marrying and in managing property.

As well as the cash that she inherits, Rixende had already received gardens in the district of Servian from her mother, which she gives to her husband as part of the dowry. Here we see rare evidence of separate lines of female devolution, which (it is important to note) were not documented at the time of the transfer. Such evidence reminds us that marriage agreements (and testaments) reveal only a fraction of the parental goods that devolved to the children, and not the sum total. We must be careful, therefore, in drawing conclusions about the relative status of children, wives, or husbands that are based solely on the properties that they are said to receive in such documents. Finally, it is worth noting that the gardens that Rixende received from her mother bordered the lands of a certain Pons de Monte Albo. Given the uniqueness of the name, we may infer that this was surely the same Pons de Monte Albo as the one whom she was marrying. In that case, Rixende and her husband not only came from the same locality but had probably also known each other for a long time.

In addition to the overlap between marriage and inheritance gifts and the relative agency of Rixende, this document reveals the increasing complexity of the Occitanian economy at the end of the twelfth century, as well as the knowledge of financial management that people applied in adapting practices to suit their personal needs. First, when Pons gives half of all the *honor*s that he possesses or will possess in the future, he also stipulates that the gift does not include his moveable goods: these are the goods "in which I give you nothing." We can only guess as to why Pons wanted to make this restriction. He added further stipulations about the financial agreement: he would guarantee her dowry with his *honor* (compare this guarantee with that of Pierre and Ermessende in Doc. 5), but any profits that might result would not be counted in the principal. This meant that he guaranteed the original amount (the "principal" of the dowry), but that his *honor* was not to be used to guarantee any profits, which would be his alone. Pons adds that regardless of whatever he might acquire with Rixende's money, she would eventually recover the original amount that he had spent. Thus she would not lose any of the principal, but neither would she make any profit.

Although more complicated than most marriage agreements, the agreement of Rixende and Pons documents a common practice in which a husband's marriage gifts were used as a sort of guarantee for the wife's dowry.[81] As noted earlier, this meant in theory that if the husband lost or wasted the wife's dowry, she could

---

[81] See J. Burgues, "Les garanties de restitution de la dot en Languedoc: Des invasions barbares à la fin de l'Ancien Régime" (Thèse de Droit, Université de Montpellier, 1937).

reclaim the value on any of his goods. These guarantees, which were included in documents with increasing frequency during the latter part of the twelfth century, may seem to be purely formulaic; yet their appearance was most likely a result of the expanding economy and the growth of investment opportunities. The provision was often activated when widows reclaimed their dowries from their deceased husbands' estates. In the case of Pons and Rixende, as was common, Pons had to guarantee her dowry with his goods even though he had not yet received the dowry. It seems that he added this provision so that he or his heirs would not be caught having to reimburse a dowry that had never been fully paid.

Furthermore, Pons added another condition: if, by the day of Rixende's death, her family has fully paid the dowry of 3000 sous, she may have half of his *honor* during her lifetime; but at her death, it will return to his nearest relatives or to whomever he designates. If the 3000 sous have not been completely paid by the day of her death, his *honor* will be mortgaged to her heirs under the same conditions, namely, that the profits are not to be added to the principal. Even though Rixende stated that she had received the 3000 sous from her brothers and was satisfied, it is clear that she had not, in fact, received the money. Thus, not only had she not received the inheritance and dowry when the document was drawn up, but there must have been some possibility that the dowry might still not have been paid by the day of her death. This document shows that the actual payment of the marriage gifts must have been delayed frequently enough for Pons to think it necessary to add a provision for such an eventuality. As we have seen, assigning marital gifts was a complex process because several competing interests were involved: the bride or groom had to be properly endowed with gifts from the family's patrimony, yet a fair share had to be reserved for their siblings, while (for first marriages) the parents were usually still living and would need the properties to maintain themselves for conceivably twenty to forty more years. If we admit a close connection between inheritance and dowry, as the majority of our documents suggest we should, then it would stand to reason that the actual payment of the dowry could often be made much later – even after the death of the person holding the properties, as we saw, for example, in Document 5, in which a future inheritance was given as *sponsalicium*.

Finally, Rixende and Pons's charter is one of the few that tell us something about how such marriage documents were prepared. We are told that it was written at the request of Rixende's brothers Jordan and Bernard, as well as of Rixende and Pons themselves and of the other witnesses. Furthermore, it was written in the main castle of the principal line of the Servian family, in the workshop of Master Pierre. This is rare evidence of a secular *scriptorium* or notarial office of some sort located within the castle of a baron of the regional aristocracy. The workshop was apparently important enough for at least one other scribe to be working there, as well as Master Pierre.[82] Because the branch of the family to which Rixende

---

[82] See n. 25 earlier for references to other Occitanian documents that indicate where they were written.

and her brothers belonged had connections with the cathedral chapter at Béziers and with the priory of Cassan,[83] they could have had their marriage document drawn up by a cleric, and a canon or the prior of the chapter at Béziers might have presided. Yet Rixende and her family chose to have their marriage acts written in a "secular" context. Might one interpret this choice as evidence that marriage was still considered a secular, familial affair? Perhaps, but these marriage documents are, after all, solely concerned with the exchange of family property and the devolution of that property, and therefore a family environment was fitting. Needless to say, the fact that the document was prepared in a nonecclesiastical context does not exclude the possibility that some sort of church ritual or ceremony would have occurred at another time.

CONCLUSION

This discussion of selected Occitanian marriage agreements brings to light certain general features of marriage in the twelfth century. First, it is clear that these documents were concerned, above all, with the properties given in marriage and with their devolution to future offspring. Most of the lines in these texts specify the conditions surrounding the gifts and who would inherit the properties after the spouses' deaths. It is also clear that a woman's right to her dowry had a strong social force; whatever else may have come into a woman's rights to their dowries were always upheld. In addition, whether because of a change in legal rhetoric influenced by the revival of Roman law or because of a real change in marriage practices, the documents show an increasing concern throughout the course of the twelfth century to specify that the children who inherit should be legitimately born from both parents (a provision that excluded, at least in theory, children born from previous or future marriages as well as illegitimate offspring). Finally, over the course of the twelfth century, the marriage agreements for all social levels became more detailed and complex, both in regard to the financial terms and conditions recorded in them and in regard to the legalistic rhetoric of restriction clauses and the anticipation of all sorts of eventualities.

Most of the extant evidence concerns the gifts exchanged at marriage. As we have seen, they functioned as a form of premortem inheritance and as such they should be considered within the framework of all types of devolution of familial property among generations. It is also strikingly clear that the variety of goods given at marriage was much greater than our current models of marriage can account for or explain. The same is true of the manner in which those gifts were obtained and the persons who were represented as giving them. Although fathers often played a role in marrying their children, they were not the only ones who could do so. In fact, fathers are represented as giving away the spouses or marital

[83] Amado, *Thèse*, vol. 2, 110, 117 bis.

properties in only half the cases. When the parents were alive and the spouses
were young, the parents naturally had a larger role. Yet in marriages between
older children or in those that took place after the death of the parents, the spouses
themselves or occasionally their siblings were responsible for bestowing the marital
gifts.

In regard to the much-debated shift to cash dowries during the twelfth century,
the Occitanian evidence demonstrates the need to rethink this supposed transition.
First, the changes in the rhetoric and provisions of the documents must be resituated
within the larger economic context of twelfth-century southern France. We should
not be fooled by the fact that values were increasingly specified in numeric terms, for
their actual payment could have been either in coin or in kind. Furthermore, as cash
was essential for investment in the growing speculation in credit (the mortgages
in pignora), the marriage agreements are further evidence of preference for cash
among Occitanians. This preference is evident in transactions of all types, and not
only in marriage agreements. Because coinage offered significant possibilities for
investment and wealth, cash dowries for daughters could have been a useful and
preferred type of gift, and not necessarily a mark of women's lower status. Finally,
the actual payment of the dowry was not a simple affair, and it might be delayed
for many years, even until after the death of one of the spouses.

Because the extant marriage agreements are concerned largely with issues of
property, they reveal little about the role of the church or about the ritual processes of marrying. Therefore, it is not possible to conclude from this evidence
whether there were competing models of marriage in twelfth-century Occitania, as
Georges Duby has proposed for northern France. The texts suggest that people
considered the spouses to be completely married only after the ceremony of
"leading" had taken place, and apparently without any regard for whether the
spouses had pronounced words of present or future consent. Other than some rare
biblical citations in a few preambles, there is little evidence of any ecclesiastical
presence. Lay notaries tended to draw up the documents, both in secular homes
and in family chapels.

Above all, the extant twelfth-century marriage agreements reveal the significant level of personal agency among Occitanians, including women. Rather than
blindly following the rules of a marriage regime, they modified their marriage
arrangements according to their circumstances, while working within the boundaries of what was considered acceptable. Multiple legal and customary traditions
overlapped, which Occitanians (or their notaries) borrowed from or adapted as
needed. Evidence from dispute resolution as well as certain provisions in the
texts themselves (such as the emphasis on the "leading" ceremony) indicates that
these agreements did not, in themselves, serve as proof of a marriage. Although
these documents might be produced to support one's claim in a dispute, witness
testimony (or the giving of guarantor-hostages for the aristocracy) counted for
as much, if not more. In sum, the considerable variation found in Occitanian

marriage practices was not random or haphazard but rather was linked to various conditions such as the timing of the marriage, the moment in the family life cycle, the economic conditions, or the micropolitical situation within the couple's social networks.

∾

APPENDIX: SEVEN MARRIAGE AGREEMENTS

In the following translations, I have used modern French equivalents for the names of places and persons as much as possible, although I have not searched all the family names to see whether they might correspond to modern French places. I have not generally translated *de* in compound family names as "of," because naming patterns were undergoing various transformations during this period, and it is not always clear whether the combination of *de* with a place name, in fact, referred to a place or had already become part of the family name itself. Throughout the translations, the phrase "marriage gift," unless otherwise noted, translates the Latin term *sponsalitium* (or *sponsalicium*), which usually denoted the husband's gift to his wife but sometimes denoted the wife's gift to her husband.

I have made all the translations from printed editions except Document 6, which I transcribed from manuscript. (The transcription is included subsequently.)

DOCUMENT 1: *Petronilla Gives Her Daughter a Dowry (January 1126) (1127 n.st.)*[1]

In the year of the incarnation of the Lord 1126, in the month of January, on Saturday, the eighth, *epacta* six, *concurrens* five,[2] with King Louis reigning in France. This charter having been made in the name of God,[3] that I Petronilla, mother, give my daughter named Petronilla to Bernard as his wife; and I give to him with her this *honor*, namely, half of a certain house that is in Montpellier, at the main part [*in capite*] of the village [*vicus*] that is called Flocaria[4]

---

[1] LIM, no. 52.

[2] I have modernized all the dates following Arthur Giry, *Manuel de Diplomatique* (Paris, 1894). The *epacta* and *concurrens* are additional ways of dating that indicate the year 1127 n.st. The abbreviation "n.st." signifies the "new style," that is, the year according to our modern dating system whereby the new year begins on January 1. In the Middle Ages, different regions followed different traditions of dating, with the new year beginning, for example, at the Incarnation or the Annunciation. Occitanian texts generally are dated from the Incarnation.

[3] See n. 27 below.

[4] Flocaria was located to the east of Montpellier, and it is thought to have been a center of the wool trade. Petronilla and her family may therefore have been involved in the wool industry, perhaps as artisans or traders. Saint-Marie was one of two main churches in the city.

and is near the gate that is called d'Obilion and is on the road which goes to Centrayrargues; and whatever belongs to the aforementioned half of the house, I give likewise to him. In addition, I give to him half of a certain vineyard that is at the main part [*in capite*] of the vines of Sainte-Marie Belle. All these aforementioned things we give and we grant to them, that is, I the aforesaid mother and my son Guillaume, on the following terms: that they as long as they live and the children who will be born from them possess it by perpetual right without any contradiction.

Guillaume Bellin, Jean Adémari, and Pierre Adalguer were present at this [proceeding].

DOCUMENT 2: *Pierre and Pontia Bestow Gifts on Their Daughter and Her Husband, March 1132*[5]

In the name of the Lord. I Pierre Matfred and my wife Pontia and our children, we, together, with good will, give to you our daughter Aicelene as an inheritance [*in hereditate*] and to your husband Pierre Andre as a marriage gift [*de sponsalitio*], in the district of Le Viala, in the *honor* of Étienne d'Aviatio and his brother Pierre, one measure[6] of vines that borders the *honor* of Rostagn on the east, and that fronts and borders the *honor* of that same Étienne and his brother Pierre on the north and south and west. Furthermore, we give to you the aforesaid couple, in the district of Bessan, in the *honor* of Jordan, in the place that is called Montadhol, one measure of vines, which on the west and north and on the east and south fronts and borders the *honor* of that same Jordan. Indeed, we give you this *honor* under the following condition: that you should have and hold and possess it; and if you will have children procreated from you Pierre and born from you Aicelena our daughter, they may have [the properties]. But if not, you Pierre Andre may have that whole aforementioned *honor* during your life, but after your death and that of our daughter Aicelina the aforesaid *honor* should revert to our nearest relatives [*propinqui*]. The charter of this gift was made on the fifth of March,[7] King Louis reigning. Signed Pierre Matfred and Pontia his wife and their children, who had this document written and who sign it with their own hands and asked the witnesses to sign it. Signed Guillaume de Villare. Signed Raimond Rossenoli. Signed Guillaume Textoris. Severus wrote this.

---

[5] Raymonde Foreville (ed.), *Le cartulaire du chapitre Cathédral Saint-Étienne d'Agde* (Paris, 1995), no. 201.

[6] The term used here – *semodiata* – was commonly used in the south of France. According to Niermeyer, it was the amount of land that would be sown with half a muid of seed-grain.

[7] The editor assigns the date of 1132 to this deed and states that the scribe used the Pisan style. The date given in the text is "III nonas marcii, luna XIIII," which corresponds to 1132 (n.st.) according to Giry's tables. If the document was indeed written in 1132, the fifth of March was a Saturday.

DOCUMENT 3: *The Marriage of Tiburgueta of Aumelas and Admar of Murviel February 7, 1149 (1150 n.st.)*[8]

In the name of our Lord Jesus Christ. In the year of his incarnation 1149, in the month of February. I Guillaume d'Aumelas handing over my daughter Tiburgueta in matrimony to you Adémar de Murviel give to you on her behalf as a dowry all that I (or man or woman through me) have in the villa of Saint Jory and in its district, and in the manse of Carascause, and [in the manse] of la Fosse, and [in the manse] of Fan; and all that I (or man or woman through me) have in the *castrum*[9] of Cournonsec[10] and in its district; and all that I (or man or woman through me) have in the *castrum* of Maderns and in its district; and all that I (or man or woman through me) have in the *castra* of Montady and in their districts; and all that I (or man or woman through me) have or ought to have in Narbonne and in the Narbonnais. This whole aforesaid *honor* and in addition 1000 sous of Mauguio[11] that I include in the same dowry I give to you Adémar de Murviel as a dowry on the following terms [*tali tenore*]:[12] that you should have and hold and use and enjoy it throughout your life, and after your death, if you have survived my daughter, namely, your wife Tiburgueta, everything shall revert to the child or children whom you will have from her, but if not,[13] it should revert to me or to my closest relatives [*propinqui*].

And I Adémar de Murviel, in the name of God, taking[14] you Tiburgueta as my wife, give to you as a *donatio propter nuptias*[15] and bestow upon you as a marriage gift half of all my goods, of *honor* and of money, excepting only the *castrum* of Murviel, from its outer gates and within [them], which I keep for the child or children whom I shall have from you, to whom I give and grant that *castrum*. And I give to you in that same *castrum* as a marriage gift the entire dwelling, with all that belongs to it, that is next to the ditch and to the manse of Deodat de Brazad, and likewise [I give] Guillelma de Laurag with her children and all her tenury. And if we shall not have a child or children together who survive you, I give to you as a marriage gift an entire half of the entire *castrum* of Murviel, just as with all my other properties and goods that

---

[8] LIM, no. 551.

[9] That is, a fortified village.

[10] Today, a city in the *canton* of Pignan. The first indications of a *castrum* there date from 1063.

[11] Coinage of several kinds circulated in twelfth-century Occitania, with values and exchange rates that changed frequently over the course of the century. The most common variety was the one mentioned here: the *solidus* produced at Mauguio (*Melgorio*).

[12] *Tenor* was a term borrowed or adapted from Roman law, usually meaning "content, text, import of some legal document." Here, the writer clearly refers to the condition of entitlement that follows.

[13] That is, if there are no children.

[14] Literally, "leading" (*ducens*).

[15] The term *donatio propter nuptias* almost always denoted the husband's gift to his wife.

I now have and whatever I am going to have. And thus the entire half of all my *honor* and money, and half of all of my goods that I have and whatever I am going to have, just as it is written above, on the following terms and by this agreement I the same Adémar de Murviel give and bestow as a marriage gift or as *donatio propter nuptias* upon you Tiburgueta my wife: that after my death, if you will have survived me, you shall have and hold and use and enjoy it throughout your life, and after your death it shall revert to any child or children whom we may have together; otherwise, to my nearest relatives. I add also to this that I give to you as a marriage gift Bernard Raimond de Murviel.

The [persons named below] swore on the Holy Gospels of God that this marriage gift, as written above, should be held and honored for the aforesaid Tiburgueta thus: That if it be diminished or violated in any way, or if later anything be removed from it by the heirs of Adémar de Murviel or through some allegation brought by them, then [the persons named below] should hold themselves as hostages for her at Montpellier, without any fraud, however often it was done, until everything be restored to her, namely, Pierre Raimond de Zaveneira, Bernard de Murviel, Armand de Murviel, Sicard de Murviel, Pons de Ceda....[16] Moreover, lord Trinvavillus was present as guarantor[17] to the aforesaid Tiburgueta and to Guillaume d'Aumelas and to Guillaume of Montpellier of all the things written above, and he [lord Trinvavillus] accepted in his faith the same Tiburgueta and Guillaume d'Aumelas, her father, concerning the marriage gift as well as this whole agreement.

These things were done, in the year stated above, the seventh of February, in the home of Les Aumelas, in the church of the Holy Savior, in the presence and witnessing of Guillaume of Montpellier, Guillaume Airadi, Berengar Airadi, Bernard Airadi, Berengar de Vallauques and Bertrand his son, Arman de Aumelas, Guirald de Aumelas, Pons de Mesoa, Rostagn de Popian ... [eighteen other witnesses follow] and Durantus, notary.

Document 4: *Guillaume de Tortosa Gives His Wife Ermessens a Dower (July 1153)*[18]

It is the order of law and of ancient custom that a marriage should not be made without a marriage gift [*dos*], for the sake of the advantage [*honestas*] of the children.[19] For this reason a man shall leave his father and mother, and shall be joined to his wife, and they shall be two in one flesh [Gen. 2:24]. And what

---

[16] The document lists ten other hostage-guarantors.

[17] The Latin term here is *fidejussor*, denoting someone who guarantees the fulfillment of financial liability. Amado identifies Trinvavillus as Raimon Trencavel, viscount of Béziers and Agde: see eadem, *Thèse*, vol. 2, Les Murviel, 98.

[18] LIM, no. 145.

[19] I presume the latter clause refers to wealth or financial advantage.

God has joined, man may not separate [Matt. 19:6]. And the Apostle Paul said: Husbands, love your wives as Christ loved the Church [Eph. 5:25].

And therefore in the name of God, I Guillaume de Tortosa give to you, my wife named Ermessens, as a marriage gift half of the three *denarii* that I have in [the minting rights at] the mint of Mauguio, and half of my entire *honor* that I have in Substantion. All of this as stated above I give to you Ermessens as your marriage gift under the following terms, that if we have children who will be generated from me and born from you, you shall have [this property] during your life, and after your death they will revert to our children. If, however, we shall not have children, you may likewise have [the property] during your life and after your death it shall revert to my closest relatives [*propinqui*].

This charter was made in the month of July, in the year of the incarnation of the Lord 1153. Signed by Guillaume, who ordered this charter to be written and asked the witnesses to sign it. Signed Bernard, count. Signed Guillaume de Mairois. Signed Raimond de Levedon.

The witnesses are Guillaume de Sobeiras, Guillaume Siguini, Guillaume de Sobeiras, the son of Guillaume de Sobeiratz, Pierre de Brugeiras, Guillaume de Nempse, Bertran de Castrias, Raimond de Lairanicis. It was made in home of Guillaume de Nempse, in the market square [*in foro*].

DOCUMENT 5: *The Marriage Gifts Between Pierre Bernard and Ermessende (August 1165)*[20]

In the year of the incarnation of the Lord 1165, I Bernard Jordan give Ermessende my daughter to you Pierre Bernard as your legitimate wife. And I give to you with her as a dowry [*in dote*] and to her as her inheritance [*in hereditate*] that entire *honor* which I have at Abeilhan and in its districts which Gerard de Pouzols has released, and a fourth part of the taxes [*decimae*] of the village of Pouzols and of its districts, which the same aforesaid Gerard has released, and 2000 sous of Mauguio. The entire aforesaid *honor* and aforesaid moveable goods [*avere*] I Bernard Jordan give to you Pierre Bernard with Ermessende as dowry, namely, under the following agreement: that you and she together shall have and hold this dowry during your entire lives. And if you survive her, you may have this dowry during your entire life. After your death, the whole aforesaid *honor* and 1500 sous of the aforesaid 2000 should remain with the child or children, the one or ones that you will have had from her, if at that time they will have survived; you may do as you wish with [the remaining] 500 sous. But if a child has not survived at that time, or if he [or she] survives and dies while still a minor, the entire aforesaid *honor* and 1500 sous of the 2000 aforementioned sous shall revert to me Bernard Jordan or to my heirs; you may do as you wish with the remaining 500 sous, as is stated

---

[20] J. Rouquette (ed.), *Cartulaire de Béziers (Livre Noir)* (Paris, 1918), no. 213.

above. But if she survives you, with or without a child, the entire aforesaid honor and the 1500 sous of the 2000 aforesaid shall remain with her; you may do as you wish with the 500 sous.

And I Pierre Bernard, with the counsel, consent, and will of my mother and my brothers, namely, Guillaume and Miron and Bernard, give to you my wife Ermessende as a marriage gift half of all my entire *honor* and moveable goods [*avere*] and of all of my goods, whatever I now have and am to have or in the future shall have or ought to revert to me after my mother has died. And I do this on the following terms: that you and I together shall have and hold this marriage gift during our lives, and if you survive me, you shall have the aforesaid marriage gift during your life; after your death the aforesaid *honor* remains with the child or children whom you will have from me, if at the time they have survived; you may do as you wish with the moveable goods [*avere*]. But if a child from me has not survived, or also if he [or she] survives and dies while still a minor, the aforesaid *honor* shall revert to my heirs. But the entire *honor* of this marriage gift I give and approve and grant to you Ermessende as surety for the 1500 sous that belong to your inheritance and must remain preserved and entire as has been stated. And if I shall die before my mother Saura, the entire right of recovery [of inheritance] that ought to revert to me after death of my mother shall instead revert to you, just as [it would have reverted] to me if I were alive, by right of a marriage gift and surety.[21]

And I Saura consent to, approve, and grant the entire aforesaid marriage gift, and I give and release and relinquish to you Pierre Bernard, now at the present time, your share of inheritance [*tua frairesca*][22] that comes to you from the *honor* of your father Raimond my husband and likewise your share of inheritance from movable goods [*avere*]. And from my own *honor* I consent to, grant, and approve for you your share of inheritance after my death.

And if I Pierre Bernard acquire an *honor* by mortgage or purchase with the aforesaid 1500 sous that are your inheritance, that entire *honor* shall revert to you Ermessende or to your heirs.

Moreover, let it be known that if Ermessende my daughter dies before you Pierre Bernard have taken her as your wife [*in uxorem ductam habeas*], you

---

[21] That is, they would revert to her according to the customary rights pertaining to marriage gifts and sureties of mortgages.

[22] The term *frairesca* refers here to a practice peculiar to Occitania. A testator could choose to bequeath his or her properties to a group of people, usually siblings (male and female), in an undivided bloc. This group of people would then possess and manage the properties communally for an unspecified amount of time. When, at a certain point, they chose to divide the properties, the term *frairesca* denotes the alienable part that each participant received, the only imperative being that each person received an equal share. Many variant spellings of this word exist, including *fratresca*, but note that Niermeyer's definition of *fratresca* ("a younger brother's share of an inheritance") is incorrect for southern France. See Amado, *Genèse des lignages méridionaux*, vol. 1: *L'aristocratie languedocienne du Xe au XIIe siècle* (Toulouse, 2001), 344–45.

may not seek anything in the *honor* that I Bernard Jordan give to you Pierre Bernard with Ermessende my daughter as a dowry, nor in the aforesaid money nor in the use made of it, because of that which I Bernard Jordan agree upon with you. And if you Pierre Bernard die before you have taken Ermessende as your wife [*in uxorem ductam habeas*], we are not able, neither I Bernard Jordan nor Ermessende my daughter, to seek or ask for anything in the aforesaid marriage gift.

The witnesses and observers of this proceeding were Ermengaud, Bernard de Servian, Pierre Jordanus, Bernard Petri, Guillaume de Servian, Etienne de Montros, Pierre Ugo.

This charter was made in the month of August on Tuesday, King Louis reigning. Pierre wrote it.

Pons de Genetras copied this document [into the cartulary] from the authentic text, neither adding nor removing anything, by the order of Bernard Martin, public notary of Béziers, in the year from the birth of Christ 1200, the month of May. Present and reading [the text were] Engelbert, canon of Saint-Nazaire, Bertrand de Servian, Bernard de Narbonne, Raimond de Caliano. I the same Bernard Martin sign it.

Document 6: *Ricsenda Maurina and Eichard de Saint-Pons Give Each Other Marriage Gifts (October 1195?)*[23]

(A) In the year of the incarnation of Christ 1125 [*sic*],[24] King Phillip reigning, and on the 28th of October. In the name of the Lord. Let it be known to all people hearing these things that I Ricsenda Maurina with the advice of my brother Jean and my sisters and other supporters [*amici*][25] of mine give and commend my body as legal wife to you Eichard de Saint-Pons, wishing to have legitimate children from you. And I give to you as dowry 200 of the good sous of Mauguio; and you can do what you wish with half, and the other half shall always remain *in honore* by my counsel and that of my supporters [*amici*] and yours. Furthermore I give to you as dowry all my part of the entire honor that comes to me or ought to come in any way or is able to do so, and also my portion of inheritance [*fraternitas*] and whatever by right I shall have or ought to have in any way whatever, wherever it be. I do this under the following condition: that while we live, both of us should have and possess it equally during all our life, and our children [should have and possess it] after us. But if the child or children generated from us do not survive and you Eichard my husband survive me, you shall have and hold all the aforesaid things during all

---

[23] ADHG, H Malte Caignac 59, no. 4 (2 Mi 98, no. 181).

[24] The two acts recorded in this charter are clearly dated thus: (A) *mcxxv* [1125]; (B) *mcxcv* [1195]. Because the handwritten signs are quite similar, a scribe might easily have read *xc* as *xx* (or vice versa). Several features of the document lead me to conclude that 1195 is the more likely date.

[25] Literally, "friends." See the discussion of this term in the commentary earlier.

your life. After your death the aforesaid 100 sous of Mauguio that are *in honore* and my other *honor* likewise shall revert to my nearest relatives [*propinqui*] or to those whom I shall have ordered. By order the witnesses of all of these statements are Pierre Martin, Guillaume Guiraud, Pons Guifre, Guillaume de Saint-Pons.

    Raimond de Bualacho wrote this.

(B) In the year of the incarnation of Christ 1195, King Phillip reigning, and on the 28th of October. In the name of the Lord. Let it be known to all people hearing these things that I Eichard de Saint-Pons with the advice of my supporters [*amici*] give and commend my body as legal husband to you Ricsenda Maurina my wife, wishing to have legitimate children from you. And I give to you as a gift [*in donacionem*] all my rights, moveable and immoveable,[26] that I now have and henceforth may in any way acquire with you and profit from in any way. I do this under the following condition: that while we both live, we hold and possess them together during all our life, and our children [shall hold and possess them] after us. And if the child or children generated from us do not survive and you Ricsenda survive me, you shall have and hold all the aforesaid things during all your life. After your death it shall revert to my nearest relatives [*propinquis*] or to those whom I shall have ordered. By order the witnesses of all of these statements are Pierre Martin, Guillaume Guiraud, Pons Guifre, Guillaume de Saint-Pons.

    Raimond de Bualacho wrote this.

Latin Transcription of Document 6

(A) Anno ab incarnatione Christi M.C.XX.V [*sic*]. Regnante Filippo rege et in quinto kalendas Novembris. In domini[27] nomine. Notum sit omnibus hominibus haec audientibus quod ego Ricsenda Maurina, consilio fratris mei Johanis et sororum meorum et aliorum amicorum meorum, dono et laudo corpus meum in legalem uxorem tibi Eichardo de Sancto Poncio affectans ex te habere legitimos infantes. Et dono tibi in dotem[28] CC solidos bonorum Melgoriensium; et medietatem ad faciendam inde omnem voluntatem tuam et, altera medietas maneat semper in honore consilio mei meorumque amicorum atque tuorum. Itemque dono tibi in dotem omnem partem meam tocius honoris qui mihi advenit et advenire debet ullo modo vel potest atque fraternitatem meam, et quicquid iuris habeo et habere debeo quoquomodo

[26] That is, the rights in both moveable and real property.
[27] Or *dei*. Although the latter is the usual expansion (in other regions or in texts of other kinds) of the abbreviation occurring here, Occitanian charters begin with the invocation "In nomine Domini," as is clear from many charters in which the phrase is not abbreviated. This observation may apply to the phrase "in nomine Dei" in the edited documents translated here, but I have not attempted to amend these editions.
[28] Or *in dote*.

ubicumque sit. Hoc autem sub tali condicione quod dum simul vixerimus, ambo pariter habeamus et possideamus in omni vita nostra, et infantes nostri post nos. Quod si infans vel infantes ex nobis generati non superstites fuerint, et tu Eichardus vir meus supervixeris me habeas et teneas omnia predicta in omni vita tua. Post obitum tuum meis propinquis revertatur vel cui iussero predicti C sol. Melg. qui sunt pro honore et alius honor meus similiter. Iussu iam dictorum omnium horum testes sunt : Petrus Martinus. Guillelmus Guiraudus. Poncius Guifre. Guillelmus de Santo Poncio.

Raimundus de Bualacho scripsit.

(B) Anno ab incarnatione Christi M.C.XC.V. Regnante Filippo rege et in quinto kalendas Novembris. In domini[29] nomine. Notum sit omnibus hominibus haec audientibus quod ego Eichardus de Sancto Poncio, consilio amicorum meorum, dono et laudo corpus meum in legalem maritum tibi Ricsende Maurine uxori meae, affectans ex te habere legitimos infantes. Et dono tibi in donacione omnia iura mea mobilia et immobilia que nunc habeo et amodo tecum adquirere et lucrari potero ullo modo. Hoc autem sub tali condicione quod dum simul vixerimus ambo teneamus et possideamus in omni vita nostra et infantes nostri post nos. Et si infans vel infantes ex nobis generati non superstites fuerint, et tu Ricsenda supervixeris me, habeas et teneas omnia predicta in omni vita tua. Post obitum tuum revertatur propinquis meis vel quibus iussero. Iussu iam dictorum omnium horum, testes sunt: Petrus Martinus. Guillelmus Guiraudus. Poncius Guifre. Guillelmus de Santo Poncio.

Raimundus de Bualacho scripsit.

DOCUMENT 7: *Brothers Give an Inheritance to Their Sister Rixende, and She Takes Pons Moine de Monte Albo as Her Husband (September 1197)*[30]

In the name of the Lord. In the year of his incarnation 1197, the month of September, King Philip reigning. Let it be known to all those hearing this charter that I Jordan de Servian and I Bernard his brother both together freely and with sound mind give to you our sister Rixende 3000 sous of Mauguio for your inheritance [*pro sua hereditate*] when you wish to be married to a husband.

And I Rixende receive from you my brothers those aforementioned 3000 sous of Mauguio, on account of which I consider myself paid in respect of all of our goods and of those which were my father's and I am thereafter satisfied. And I promise to you by this agreement that I shall not claim or demand anything from what remains in my father's goods or in yours, nor have someone

---

[29] Or *dei*: see note earlier.
[30] Rouquette (ed.), *Cartulaire de Béziers* no. 329.

else make such a claim or demand. And thus having been coerced by no one but acting by my own free will, I swear to you on these holy four Gospels of God, which I touch bodily.

Next, in the name of God, I Rixende freely and with sound mind and with the counsel and consent of my two aforesaid brothers receive you Pons Moine de Monte Albo as my legitimate husband, and I give myself to you as your legitimate wife. And I bestow upon you as a dowry 3000 sous of Mauguio, yet on this condition: that as long as we both shall live we have and hold them together; and if we shall have a child or children that will be born from me and procreated from you, they shall have them [the sous] after us; but if not, and you survive me, you shall have and hold the aforesaid 3000 sous of Mauguio during your whole life, but after your death the aforementioned 3000 sous of Mauguio shall revert peacefully and quietly to my closest relatives [*propinqui*], or to whomever I shall have wished. In addition, I bestow upon you as a dowry those gardens which my mother bequeathed to me as an inheritance in the district of Servian, which border on the north the river Lène, on the east the road to Béziers, and on the west the *honor* of Pons de Monte Albo, which I grant to you with the aforementioned conditions.

I also Pons Moine receive you the aforesaid Rixende as my legitimate wife and give myself to you as your legitimate husband, and freely and with sound mind I give to you as a *donatio propter nuptias* half of my entire *honor*, as much as I now have or ought to have or shall in time, God willing, have acquired with you, except for moveable goods, in respect of which I grant you nothing. But I grant the aforesaid gift to you on this condition: that as long as we both shall live, we should have and hold it together, and if we shall have a child or children who have been born from me and procreated from you,[31] they may have it after us; but if [not], and you survive me, you may have and hold the aforesaid gift for your entire life. I the aforesaid Pons Moine pledge the aforesaid gift to you the aforesaid Rixende in respect of the aforesaid dowry [*pro predicta dote*], and in accordance with property rights and as a surety [*juri boni et rati pignoris*] I grant it to you in such manner that henceforth any resulting profits not be counted with the principal of the aforesaid money. But if the aforesaid 3000 sous of Mauguio have been paid out by you [the brothers] or by your [representatives] to you [Rixende] or to your [representatives],[32] you may afterwards have and hold the aforesaid half of my entire honor for your entire life, but after your death it shall revert freely to my close relatives [*propinqui*] or whomever I wish. But if by the day of your death the aforesaid

---

[31] Children are usually said to be "born" from the mother, and not, as here, from the father. The Latin in the printed edition is as follows: "et si infantem vel infantes habuerimus qui de me sunt nati et de te procreati, post nos habeant illi. . . . " If the edition is correct (I have not been able to consult the original), then the scribe has mistakenly inverted the standard formula.

[32] "a vobis vel a vestris . . . tibi vel tuis. . . . "

3000 sous of Mauguio have not been paid to you or to your [representatives], the aforesaid gift is pledged to your heirs under the same conditions as it is to you, such that the resulting profits should not be counted with the principal.

Furthermore, let it be certain to all hearing these things that I the aforesaid Rixende approve and grant all the things written above; and if some right or claim on the other half of the *honor* or on all the other moveable goods comes to me, I renounce that right and claim entirely.

Furthermore I the aforesaid Pons give, approve, and grant to you the aforesaid Rixende whatever I shall have acquired with your money by purchase or mortgage: you may have and receive it for the same price for which I acquired it. You may have the remainder of the aforesaid money and likewise half of my *honor*, as stated above. And let it be known that I Pons Moine consider myself duly paid the 3000 aforesaid sous so that nothing henceforth remains to be paid by your people.

The witnesses and observers of this proceeding were Guillaume de Montblanc, Pierre Augerius, Raimond Augerius, Pierre Capellanus . . . [nine other witnesses follow].

By the order of the aforesaid Jordan and of Bernard his brother and of Rixende their sister and of Pons Moine and of all the aforesaid witnesses, Berengar Olericus de Magalatio wrote this in the castle[33] of Servian, in the office of Master Pierre.

Pons de Genestars copied this document from the authentic document, neither adding nor removing anything, by the order of Bernard Martin, public notary of Béziers, in the year from the birth of Christ 1200, in the month of May. Those present and reading were Engilbert, canon of Saint-Nazaire, Bertrand de Servian, Bernard de Narbonne, Bernard de Calveto. I the same Bernard Martin sign it.

---

[33] Here the Latin term is *castellum*, which properly denotes a castle, as distinct from a *castrum*, a fortified village.

CHAPTER SEVEN

MARRIAGE CONTRACTS IN MEDIEVAL ENGLAND

R. H. Helmholz

Historians who have written about law and the institution of marriage in England can be divided into two camps. In the one stand those whose interests center in the history of the canon law on the formation of marriage, the predecessor of modern family law.[1] In the other are historians whose principal concerns lie with the process of wealth transmission from one generation to another, the law of estates, and familial control of property.[2] Little common ground, except the obvious factual connection created by the event of marriage, has existed between these two groups, although there has never been actual enmity or even

---

[1] See Eric J. Carlson, *Marriage and the English Reformation* (Oxford, 1994); David Cressy, *Birth, Marriage, and Death: Ritual, Religion, and Life-Cycle in Tudor and Stuart England* (Oxford, 1997), 233–376; P. J. P. Goldberg, *Women, Work, and Life Cycle in a Medieval Economy: Women in York and Yorkshire c. 1300–1520* (Oxford, 1992), 203–66; R. H. Helmholz, *Marriage Litigation in Medieval England* (London, 1974); Ralph A. Houlbrooke, *Church Courts and the People during the English Reformation, 1520–1570* (Oxford, 1979), 55–88; Martin Ingram, *Church Courts, Sex and Marriage in England, 1570–1640* (Cambridge, 1987); Diana O'Hara, *Courtship and Constraint: Rethinking the Making of Marriage in Tudor England* (Manchester, 2000); Frederik Pedersen, *Marriage Disputes in Medieval England* (London, 2000); Michael M. Sheehan, *Marriage, Family and Law in Medieval Europe: Collected Studies*, edited by James Farge (Toronto, 1996). For the broader history of the subject, see Christopher N. L. Brooke, *The Medieval Idea of Marriage* (Oxford, 1989); James A. Brundage, *Law, Sex, and Christian Society in Medieval Europe* (Chicago, 1987); John Witte, Jr., *From Sacrament to Contract: Marriage, Religion, and Law in the Western Tradition* (Louisville, 1997); David L. D'Avray, *Medieval Marriage: Symbolism and Society* (Oxford, 2005).

[2] See H. J. Habakkuk, *Marriage, Debt, and the Estates System: English Landownership, 1650–1950* (Oxford, 1994); J. M. W. Bean, *The Decline of English Feudalism, 1215–1540* (Manchester, 1968); Joseph Biancalana, *The Fee Tail and the Common Recovery in Medieval England, 1176–1502* (Cambridge, 2001); Lloyd Bonfield, *Marriage Settlements, 1601–1740: The Adoption of the Strict Settlement* (Cambridge, 1983); Amy Louise Erickson, *Women and Property in Early Modern England* (London and New York, 1993 and 1995), 102–51; Eileen Spring, *Law, Land & Family: Aristocratic Inheritance in England, 1300 to 1800* (Chapel Hill, 1994); Simon Payling, "The politics of family: Late medieval marriage contracts," in R. H. Britnell and A. J. Pollard (eds.), *The McFarlane Legacy: Studies in Late Medieval Politics and Society* (New York, 1995), 21–45; R. B. Outhwaite, "Marriage as business: Opinions on the rise of aristocratic bridal portions in early modern England," in Neil McKendrick and R. B. Outhwaite (eds.), *Business Life and Public Policy: Essays in Honour of D. C. Coleman* (Cambridge, 1986), 21–37.

profound disagreement. They have simply been concerned with different facets of marriage.

Besides this difference in focus, these two groups have also been separated in several ways: by the nature of the records that they examine, by the formal law to which they refer, and even by the class of the men and women that they study. For example, most historians of the canon law have devoted their primary attention to quite ordinary people: men and women whose station in society was below that of the gentry. The historians of family property, by contrast, have paid particular attention to the aristocracy and the upper gentry. Although the same formal law applied to all, practice differed in some measure depending on who the people were. The surviving evidence suggests that their concerns called for examination of different aspects of the law. Thus, it appears that what I have called secular marriage contracts involved the upper classes, whereas what I have called spiritual marriage contracts involved men and women a little lower down the social pecking order. The difference is evident in the evidence to be discussed. Yet it was never a categorical difference, and it may have as much to do with the state of record survival as it does with social reality. Poor people, too, worried about their property, and rich people cared about whom they married.

This chapter makes a connection between these two approaches to the law of marriage by examining secular marriage contracts (of which ten examples are given in the appendix) and comparing them with the marriage contracts that came before and were enforced in the English ecclesiastical courts. Another way to put it is to say that marriage settlements and the agreements by which marriage itself was contracted are to be compared and contrasted. So far as I know, no one has attempted this comparison.[3] It seems nonetheless to be a natural subject for study, and one that holds a promise of shedding some new light on several aspects of the attitudes toward marriage of medieval men and women. The comparison of the two kinds of contracts may tell us something about the decisions that people made in earlier centuries in selecting marriage partners. It may also help us trace the history of freedom of choice in marriage. This has been a controversial subject among historians,[4] and what information we can glean from comparing these agreements may be relevant to it.

---

[3] Surprisingly, one of the few attempts to consider both aspects is a literary study: Kathryn E. Jacobs, *Marriage Contracts from Chaucer to the Renaissance Stage* (Gainesville, Fla., 2001). There is now a considerable body of scholarship connecting contemporary ideas about marriage with their portrayal in literature: see Ann J. Cook, *Making a Match: Courtship in Shakespeare and his Society* (Princeton, N.J., 1991); and Conor McCarthy, *Marriage in Medieval England: Law, Literature and Practice* (Woodbridge and Rochester, N.Y., 2004). It has also been of interest to historians of gender. Only a few historians have examined the subject from a liturgical perspective; see, e.g., Kenneth W. Stevenson, *Nuptial Blessing: A Study of Christian Marriage Rites* (New York, 1983).

[4] See, e.g., Alan Macfarlane, *Marriage and Love in England: Modes of Reproduction 1300–1840* (Oxford, 1986), 119–47 (chapter entitled "Who controls the marriage decision"). Macfarlane takes the view that in England, the couple, not the family, held the dominant position.

The Problem of Definition

What was a marriage contract? It is a simple question, but the answer is not obvious. Others in this volume have faced the same quandary. For comparative purposes, I have adopted a straightforward and a designedly legal definition. In order to qualify as a marriage contract within the meaning adopted here, an agreement must include a statement in which an obligation to marry is expressed, or is at least stated as one object of the contract. The contract may include other things, but it must include an agreement to marry. This definition has the effect of excluding some acts obviously connected with marriage. It excludes, first, many of the grants made in consideration of marriage that are often called marriage settlements.[5] In a large number of these settlements, marriage was the *occasion* for a grant of land or chattels, but the actual agreement to marry was made separately and not mentioned in the settlement itself. The definition excludes, second, grants of the right to control the marriage of a minor: sales of wardship, as they were usually called. In these grants, marriage was the subject of the formal instrument, but usually no specific marriage was being contracted. It excludes, third, negotiations about marriage. The question often brought into litigation before the ecclesiastical courts in medieval England was whether a couple had entered into an enforceable contract of marriage or instead had merely discussed the terms under which they might possibly join together in marriage, then or later. Agreements and documents under this second category – marriage negotiations – have also been excluded from coverage.

What, then, does the category include? Is this definition limited to the exchange of what we should call matrimonial vows, that is, what the medieval jurists called the exchange of mutual consent to take the other as spouse, an exchange entered into by *verba de praesenti*? No, I do not define it so narrowly. The working definition includes not only agreements intended to create an obligation to marry but also those merely stating that a marriage was being made at the same time a transfer of property took place. And the agreement might be future or present in its effect. To it, the parties might add conditions and agreements about the terms of entry into marriage. Gifts or tokens could be, and often were, exchanged at the same time as part of the same transaction.[6] To qualify, the obligation need not even have been made by the man and woman themselves who were getting married: the agreement between parents or guardians that their children should be (or were being) married

---

[5] The distinction has very old roots in Christian history: see David Hunter's chapter in this volume.

[6] See, e.g., Ex officio c. Sever (London 1513), Guildhall Library, London, MS. 9065/11, f. 119v, in which one party alleged a matrimonial contract and a gift of 20li. made at the same time, his apparent purpose being to show the seriousness of the intent to contract a marriage. See also Laura Gowing, *Domestic Dangers: Women, Words, and Sex in Early Modern London* (Oxford, 1996), 142, 177; Peter Rushton, "The testament of gifts: Marriage tokens and disputed contracts in North-East England, 1560–1630," *Folk Life: A Journal of Ethnological Studies* 24 (1985): 25–31.

also qualifies.[7] So does a marriage entered into by proxy. All that the criteria of this paper exclude are matters that were purely ancillary to marriage itself. The justification for adopting this limited definition is the desire to compare like with like, to focus on marriage rather than dynasties and the accumulation of land by families. I recognize that this definition excludes some important transactions connected with marriage.

Under the definition that I have adopted, written marriage contracts are not numerous for England.[8] Ten examples are given in the appendix, and more could be given, but they have not survived in large numbers. And none of those that do survive comes from "official" record repositories, either ecclesiastical or secular. Most seem to have been preserved among family muniments. Many must have been lost for that reason: they ceased to have any relevance after a few generations, and their private owners discarded them.

The absence of a strong notarial tradition in England must also have made a difference in practice. The lack of written agreements to marry, such as might naturally have been prepared by a notary public, is particularly noteworthy for the English ecclesiastical courts. Virtually all the marriages encountered in their records were contracted orally. Written contracts involving marriage do appear very occasionally in the ecclesiastical archives,[9] but written contracts between the young men and women themselves in contracting marriage, if they were made at all, were rarely put before the ecclesiastical courts.

On the common law side, the contracts were written, although notaries public did not prepare them, as seems usually to have been the case on the Continent. The English agreements have not been preserved in large numbers, as just noted. Perhaps they were not made with great frequency in fact. In contrast, written marriage settlements of other sorts – that is, grants of land and chattels on the occasion of marriage that are not strictly marriage contracts – are easy to find in the archives. Indeed, there is reason for thinking that a written marriage contract properly speaking was most often made when the partners themselves were incapable of

---

[7] This was, in fact, the norm in some places; see Jean-François Poudret, *Coutumes et coutumiers: Histoire comparative des droits des pays romands du XIIIe à la fin du XVIe siècle* (Berne, 2002), 3:65–103.

[8] A similar situation existed for the northern part of what has become France (in contrast with the southern part of the same land); see Martha C. Howell, "Documenting the ordinary: The *Actes de la Pratique* of late medieval Douai," in Adam Kosto and Anders Winroth (eds.), *Charters, Cartularies, and Archives: The Preservation and Transmission of Documents in the Medieval West* (Toronto, 2002), 151–73, at 152; Monique Mestayer, "Les contrats de mariage à Douai du XIIIème au XVème siècle," *Revue du Nord* 41 (1979): 353–80.

[9] See Charles Donahue, Jr., and Norma Adams, *Select Cases from the Ecclesiastical Courts of the Province of Canterbury, c. 1200–1301*, Selden Society 95 (London, 1981), Introduction, 81–88, which seems to have reached this same conclusion. In a response made while this volume was in preparation, Frederik Pedersen pointed out an ecclesiastical cause in which a disputed agreement about gifts in consideration of marriage came before the court: Percy c. Colvyle (York, 1323), Borthwick Institute of Historical Research, York (hereafter abbreviated as BI), CP E 12. See also D. M. Smith, *Ecclesiastical Cause Papers at York: The Court of York 1301–1399* (York, 1988), 5.

entering into a marriage at the time the contract was written, usually because they were too young. Planning for future contingencies was one reason for resorting to a written marriage contract in medieval England.

English Marriage Contracts

The only attempt known to me that deals both with common law contracts relating to marriage and marriage contracts enforced in the ecclesiastical forum comes from the pages of Lawrence Stone's famous work, *The Family, Sex and Marriage*.[10] Stone separated the various agreements by time. First in time came the agreement of the two families involved, including, most importantly, the gifts and conveyances of land to be made as part of the marriage settlement. Once the bargaining had been concluded, the terms could be written down to avoid future dispute. This was the family's part. For the sake of convenience, I refer to such agreements as secular contracts. Next in time came the agreement to marry between the man and woman involved: spousals as they were called at the time, but more accurately described as actual marriages under the law of the medieval church. The partners exchanged words of future or present consent to take each other in marriage. This was the ecclesiastical part. For similar reasons of convenience, I call such agreements spiritual contracts, although very often there was nothing particularly spiritual or "other-worldly" about them. Partners might even contract into a binding marriage in a tavern.[11]

It is important to notice the order and the distinction between the two types of agreements. The spiritual contract expressed with present intent (*per verba de praesenti*), once made, would not admit further hesitation or bargaining, for in the eyes of the church it constituted a binding marriage. But it was also part of a process, one that might turn out to be quite lengthy.[12] After these two steps had been taken, in Stone's depiction, the publication of banns and solemnization in church then followed as a matter of course. What we think of as "a wedding" was the end of the process.

Further research into practice during the Middle Ages has supported this understanding of the way people entered marriage.[13] But a little refinement has been necessary. The two first steps clearly existed during the Middle Ages, but the evidence also shows that the secular and spiritual aspects of marriage were not

---

[10] Oxford, 1977. See especially p. 31.

[11] For example, Laurens c. Gell (York, 1472), BI, CP F 252. As was true with several other areas of practice, this was not limited to England: see Silvana Seidel Menchi, "Percorsi variegati, percorsi obbligati," in *Matrimoni in dubbio: Unioni controverse e nozze clandestine in Italia dal XIV al XVIII secolo* (Bologna, 2001), 17–60, at 18–19.

[12] This was not a new phenomenon: see Philip L. Reynolds, *Marriage in the Western Church: The Christianization of Marriage during the Patristic and Early Medieval Periods* (Leiden, 1994), 315–412.

[13] See Henry A. Kelly, *Love and Marriage in the Age of Chaucer* (Ithaca, N.Y., 1975), 173–76.

always so neatly distinguished as Stone's schema indicates. Protracted and difficult negotiation might intervene at several points, and this might concern both the transfer of property and the marriage itself. There might, for example, be uncertainty even about the spiritual contract: about its terms and about proving it in a court of law. Stone's observation remains an acute one all the same. It captures the most common and salient characteristic of contracting marriage during these centuries. As Robert Palmer has found in examining the plea rolls of the royal courts, marriage was "a time of bargaining" in medieval England.[14] That being so, it is instructive but hardly surprising to find that the two types of agreement had both similarities and dissimilarities.

SIMILARITIES BETWEEN SECULAR AND SPIRITUAL CONTRACTS

From a lawyer's perspective, several similarities stand out. First, contracts of both types contained an explicit agreement to marry; it was not simply understood. For the ecclesiastical forum, this is beyond doubt. Witnesses described a typical scene: William said to Alice, "Here I take thee Alice as my lawful wife, to have and to hold until the end of my life if Holy Church permits it. And of this I pledge my faith." Alice replied in the same fashion.[15] That is what made a marriage under the law of the church: an exchange of consent (in this case present consent). Yet the secular agreements contained an agreement to marry as well (usually an agreement to marry in the future). Consider Document 6 in the appendix, for example: "It is agreed ... that Henry, son and heir of Elias, shall take as his wife Sybill, daughter of Simon." Here the consent referred to a future event and the fathers of the couple gave it, but the agreement was more than a promise to give land if and when Henry and Sybill decided to get married. The words apparently were thought to impose some kind of an obligation to marry on the children. This was not true of all English marriage settlements, but it was true of some.[16]

Second, contracts of both sorts sometimes placed express conditions upon the marriage. Marriage contracts brought before the ecclesiastical courts, no less than

[14] Robert C. Palmer, "Contexts of marriage in medieval England: Evidence from the King's Court circa 1300," *Speculum* 59 (1984): 42–67, at 43; see also Judith M. Bennett, *Women in the Medieval English Countryside: Gender and Household in Brigstock before the Plague* (New York, 1987), 92–99; Christine Carpenter, *Locality and Polity: A Study of Warwickshire Landed Society, 1401–1409* (Cambridge, 1992), 112–16; K. B. McFarlane, *The Nobility of Later Medieval England* (Oxford, 1973), 84–87.

[15] Taken from Draycote c. Crane (Nottingham and York 1332–33), BI, CP E 23. The cause is discussed in Charles Donahue, Jr., "The policy of Alexander III's consent theory of marriage," in Stephan Kuttner (ed.), *Proceedings of the Fourth International Congress of Medieval Canon Law* (Vatican City, 1976), 251–91, at 264.

[16] For example, BL, Add. Ch. 13,065 (1472): "... it is agreyd and apoynted bytwene them [Walter Reynell and John Halegewille] by the avyse of their counsel and friends of both parties that John Reynell heir apparent to Walter Reynold shall marie and take to wiff Jane daughter to the said John Haleghewyll, and if the same John Reynell dye within the age of xiii yere that then the next heir of the said John Reynell shall marie and take to wyff the said Jane...."

the secular agreements, routinely contained conditions upon which their validity depended. The canon law envisioned the possible addition of conditions to
agreements of marriage, although it limited their potential scope. A title of the
Gregorian Decretals sanctioned and regulated them (X 4.5.1–7), and the subject
became something of a favorite among the canonists.[17] Likewise, the English common law admitted the possibility of adding conditions to contracts.[18] It was thus
no stretch of existing law for parties to secular marriage contracts to make them
expressly conditional upon an event or an exchange.

It is true that canon lawyers regarded some conditions as impertinent, dishonest,
or invalid. "I take you if I decide not to marry someone else," or "if you continue
to please me," were examples of conditions that the canon law treated as void
(although the marriage was still binding despite their addition). Yet many suspen-
sive conditions were admissible. The learning on the subject was intricate, and it is
easy to doubt its relevance to practice.[19] But, in fact, we do find added to spiritual
contracts such conditions as "I take you if you give me your lands," or "if you are
skilled in baking, brewing, and weaving." By far the most frequent of the conditions
were those requiring the assent of parents or guardians: "if my parents, friends, or
relatives consent," or some variant of these words.[20] Some partners also entered
into contracts of marriage that were conditional upon payment of the gifts in consideration of marriage, such as those commonly found in marriage settlements.

In the secular marriage contracts entered into between families, we likewise find
added conditions. The most frequent was "if the parties survived to a certain date,"
which was thought necessary to provide for the sensible passage of property within
a family. Document 5 in the appendix is a particularly noteworthy example of a
conditional contract: here, a younger child was substituted for the elder child in
case the elder should die before coming to marriageable age. People also made
contracts that were conditional upon furnishing a certain gift to the bride or
groom.[21] Conditions were means by which the parties made bargains and put
them into effect.

---

[17] See Thomas Sanchez (d. 1610), *De sancto matrimonii sacramento disputationum* (Lyons, 1739), lib. V
(one of his ten books is devoted to the subject). The author was at pains to justify his traditional
treatment, although, at Disp. 1 no. 1, he recognized that the Council of Trent's decree, *Tametsi*,
requiring the presence of the parish priest for validity, diminished its importance in practice. See
generally Rudolf Weigand, *Die bedingte Eheschliessung im kanonischen Recht* (Munich, 1963); Mario
Ferraboschi, *Il matrimonio sotto condizione* (Padua, 1937); Thomas Timlin, *Conditional Matrimonial
Consent: An Historical Synopsis and Commentary* (Washington, DC, 1934).

[18] John H. Baker, *An Introduction to English Legal History*, 4th ed. (London, 2002), 272–73; A. W. B.
Simpson, *A History of the Common Law of Contract* (Oxford, 1975), 90–95; William S. Holdsworth,
A History of English Law, vol. 8 (London, 1973), 71–75.

[19] Henry Swinburne (d. 1624), *A Treatise of Spousals or Matrimonial Contracts* (London, 1686), Sec. 12,
presents the law on the subject in detail.

[20] Shannon McSheffrey (ed.), *Love and Marriage in Late Medieval London* (Kalamazoo, 1995), 50–54.

[21] For example, BL, Add. Ch. 19,298 (1299), a temporary grant of land made "quousque rationabile et
competens maritagium" could be provided.

Third, and somewhat surprisingly, neither of the two types of marriage contract made direct reference to the institutional church or to spiritual matters more generally. Apart from formal invocation of the name of God, little of what we like to think of as religious solemnity or sentiment surrounded either form of agreement.[22] It might be said that both agreements were being made – to take now fashionable terminology – "in the shadow" of the law. That is, people intended the contracts to be valid and enforceable in an ecclesiastical court or a temporal tribunal, and they composed them accordingly. Yet neither was normally made in a specifically ecclesiastical setting, and neither had much to say about religion. The invocation of religious sanctions was not necessary for validity under the canon law as it then stood, and although the couples probably intended to solemnize their union formally later, these marriage contracts were not, themselves, made in churches. Even the famous endowment at the church door was rarely, if ever, mentioned in the agreements.

It is notable, moreover, that except for the early Anglo-Saxon contracts, few clerics were recorded as having been present at either form of contract. Nothing disqualified the clergy from acting as witnesses, and they would have done so in marriages celebrated *in facie ecclesiae*. Nevertheless, in the secular contracts and in the informal spiritual contracts that came before the ecclesiastical courts, they usually did not. As to the reason for their absence, one can only hazard a guess. In the case of ecclesiastical contracts, any cleric present might have been taking part in a clandestine marriage, something punished (but not by invalidity) under the medieval canon law. In the case of secular contracts, the clergy would have brought no special legal expertise to the table, and the status of the contracts by which parents arranged the financial future of their children might have been at best questionable under the church's law. Still, the entire absence of the clergy from the latter and their only occasional presence in the former remain points to consider in weighing up the nature of medieval marriage contracts and even the popular attitude toward marriage. It appears that friends and family members were regarded as the natural and suitable persons to witness a marriage contract.

Fourth, both types of agreement dealt with property as well as marriage. The two evidently went naturally together in the minds of the participants. For the secular contracts, this goes almost without saying. Every one of the examples in the appendix deals with a transfer of property to the couple involved. Indeed, although they all contain an agreement about the marriage itself, their primary purpose seems to have been to settle the terms that would govern matrimonial property. Thus we find the sometimes elaborate provisions for what would happen to land if one party died, or even (as in the case of Doc. 9) what would happen if the spouses were subsequently divorced.

---

[22] Compare the opposite finding about earlier medieval marriage agreements in France: see Philip L. Reynolds, "The dotal charter as theological treatise," *Recherches de théologie ancienne et médiévale* 61 (1994): 54–68, and the articles by Reynolds and Laurent Morelle in this volume.

For the ecclesiastical contracts, the conjunction of property with marriage was present, too, but in most cases, it was less important than the exchange of consent. The *legal* relevance of the former in the spiritual forum was limited to its utility in discovering whether the parties had intended to contract marriage. Thus the mutual giving of gifts by the partners would tend to show that they had intended to be man and wife, whereas the absence of gifts would tend to show the reverse. Witnesses in church courts often testified about the transfer of goods, and embarrassed defendants in matrimonial litigation were sometimes faced with the problem of explaining that gifts they had made or received had stemmed from some motive *different* from a matrimonial one. It was hard to "explain away" the receipt of property as being consistent with an intent other than one aimed at marriage.

Fifth – and probably the most surprising – each type of marriage contract almost never mentioned the other. The closest the secular contracts came was to note occasionally that due solemnization was something that would take place in the future, or within a limited time after the date of the contract.[23] But at least so far as I have discovered to this point, secular contracts did not make any mention of the couple's having entered into a specific contract of marriage by *verba de futuro* or *verba de praesenti*. Nor have I found an ecclesiastical contract made expressly conditional upon the observance of a contract such as the ones that appear in the appendix.[24] Although the two types dealt with many of the same things – agreements to marry, conditions attached to marriage, and property settlements – they seem almost to have existed in separate worlds. Ecclesiastical formularies do not mention marriage settlements as one way of proving the existence of a marriage.[25] Why this should have been, I am not sure. Perhaps the habit of placing spiritual and secular matters, such as ecclesiastical law and common law, into distinct categories may partially explain it. At any rate, the fact of separation is clear enough, and it is something that one should recognize in assessing the significance of the documents for the history of the law of marriage.

Sixth, both types of matrimonial contracts envisioned the possibility of arbitration or some other out-of-court means of settling disputed questions. In the case of the secular contracts this was normally explicit. For example, in Document 4, two friends of each party would determine when the agreed-upon 20 marks revenue had been paid. The contracts were carefully drafted, but they could not take care of every eventuality, and the parties to them were aware of the need for what we would

---

[23] For example, BL, Add. Ch. 5,467 (1408).

[24] In Hulse c. Felston (Chester, 1513), Cheshire Record Office, EDC 1/1, f. 52v, one of the witnesses mentioned the existence of a dispute over the *maritagium* at the time the parties contracted marriage by words of present consent, but no mention was made of any document.

[25] For example, Clement Colmore's Book (c. 1600), Durham University Library, DDR XVIII/3, f. 114v, listing *Contractus, Tractatus, Recognitio, Intersigna, Banna,* and *Fama* as among the elements subject to proof and relevant in matrimonial litigation, but nothing about *donationes* or dotal contracts.

call "alternative dispute resolution." Hence came the provisions for the settlement of future disputes in the secular agreements. In the case of spiritual contracts, the possibility was usually understood rather than stated. But it was *commonly* understood, as Frederik Pedersen has shown.[26] The families involved put their disputes before a group of neighbors and responsible people for discussion and (they hoped) resolution before going to an ecclesiastical court. Although this skated close to the edge of disobedience to the canon law,[27] it is what happened repeatedly in practice.

Seventh and finally, neither secular nor spiritual contracts made any provision for regulating the conduct of the man and woman during the course of their marriage; at least, I have found none. This excludes the trendy modern forms: agreements about who will do the dishes, where the couple will live, how long their vacations will be, and so on. Marriage was an adhesion contract, and matters such as these (had people thought of them at all) might have seemed to deny the husband's legitimate authority.[28] The contracts also overlooked something that it would have been possible and useful to consider, namely, the treatment of children from prior marriages. Death and remarriage was frequent in medieval England, and it would have been appropriate to deal with the fate of children in these agreements. But so far as I have been able to gather, such was not the case.

DIFFERENCES BETWEEN SECULAR AND SPIRITUAL CONTRACTS

I have already mentioned in passing some of the dissimilarities between the two types of contracts, but it seems sensible to state them explicitly. Three stand out in the records. First, the secular contracts were most often made between the families. The parents contracted for the children,[29] or perhaps it would be fairer to say that the fathers did. They provided for their daughters and sons, and the contracts were normally made in their name.[30] The spiritual contracts, by contrast, were made between the man and woman who were to be married. Where the parents appear in the ecclesiastical court records, usually it was as objectors to a union, not as contracting parties. Contracts of both kinds, in other words, agreed that a

---

[26] Pedersen, *Marriage Disputes*, 105–38; see also Barbara Hanawalt, "The power of word and symbol: Conflict resolution in late medieval London," in eadem, *Of Good and Ill Repute: Gender and Social Control in Medieval England* (Oxford, 1998), 35–52.

[27] The formal canon law did not permit compromise of disputes about the existence of marriage. See X.1.36.11.

[28] See generally Steven Ozment, *When Fathers Ruled: Family Life in Reformation Europe* (Cambridge, Mass., 1983).

[29] Although, in some cases, one of the partners might contract with the parent of the other; e.g., BL, Eger. Ch. 608 (1448), an agreement between John Blount and Thomas Corbet, father of Katherine. They agreed "that the said John Blount shall wed and take to his wife Katherine the younger daughter of the said Thomas between this and the feast of Michaelmas next coming after the date of this indenture." There follows an agreement about settlement of land and an annuity.

[30] For example, J. Horace Round, "A great marriage settlement," *The Ancestor* 11 (1904): 153–57.

marital union was to come into being, but the people who did the agreeing were not identical.

Second, the substance of the conditions added to the contracts was normally different. Although there was some overlap, the added conditions in the secular contracts were usually related to the fulfillment of the marriage's purpose: the continued life of the parties, the birth of children, and so forth. In the spiritual contracts, the most frequent conditions concerned the agreement of someone else besides the couple, typically the parents or other relatives. The conditions in them also occasionally embraced aspects of personal conduct of the parties, "if you are a virgin" being the most famous. The large exception to this difference is that both types included conditions relating to the exchange of land or personal property, but for the most part the added conditions were quite different.

Third, the secular contracts were written, whereas the spiritual contracts were oral. The former were not the notarial documents used in very many places across the Channel, but they were carefully drafted (although probably not copied out of a form book; they contain too much variation in substance and form for that). They were put into written form, just as the charters, grants, and other forms of agreements controlling the devolution of land were. The documents we have were sealed instruments, and most of them were made in the form of indentures or chirographs.[31] By contrast, the spiritual contracts were oral, and therefore they had to be proved by the recollection of the witnesses whom an ecclesiastical court cited to give evidence. This difference will appear unexceptional, even obvious, to historians familiar with the subject, but it is worth pointing out nonetheless. Although there may be examples yet to be discovered, so far, no causes in the ecclesiastical archives have been found in which one party was attempting to enforce a *written* contract to marry. Moreover, the expressed wishes of the partners were what counted in matrimonial litigation in England, not the agreement of the parents, and this shows up in the evidence of the oral agreements that was put before the courts. We cannot be quite so sure on the secular side, because the nature of the surviving evidence inevitably excludes oral agreements. Still, it is a matter of note that the secular agreements that we do have were all written documents, whereas the ecclesiastical archives provide evidence only of oral contracts.

Changes Over Time

These are the principal similarities and differences between the two types of matrimonial contracts. At least they are from one lawyer's point of view. Before attempting to draw out the broader lessons of the comparison, it seems right to say just a word (or two) about change. The documents in the appendix range from

---

[31] See M. T. Clanchy, *From Memory to Written Record, England 1066–1307*, 2nd ed. (Oxford, 1993), 87–88.

the eleventh through the fifteenth centuries, and it is only to be expected that there should have been change, if not indeed a transformation, taking place over this long period of some five centuries. The period witnessed dramatic change in some of the most basic ideas about law and government. One might expect matrimonial contracts to reveal change as well.

I perceive two changes in such documents during the medieval period. First (and most obvious), the secular contracts became more sophisticated from a lawyer's perspective over the centuries. Compared with the detailed provisions and conditions relating to the passage of land titles in gifts made in consideration of marriage found in the later documents, the Anglo-Saxon agreements appear primitive in the extreme. The nature of agreement about entering into marriage itself remained basically the same, but the ancillary transactions involving land mirrored the growth in complexity of the land law. This is exactly what one would expect. It need signal no new view about marriage itself.

Second, there was progress towards implementation of the church's understanding of marriage over these five centuries. This is evident in the spiritual contracts. A gradual acceptance by the laity of the canonical admonitions about the nature of marriage occurred between the twelfth century and the sixteenth. Fewer disputes over contracts came before the courts, probably reflecting greater compliance with the church's rules against clandestinity. More often, contracts that were made clandestinely followed the canonical forms, although this feature was not as pronounced as it would become after the adoption of the *Book of Common Prayer* in the sixteenth century had made the laity familiar with the "correct" way of exchanging wedding vows.[32] It was upon such gradual acceptance by the laity of the church's rules about contracting marriage *in facie ecclesiae* that matrimonial law could be tightened up, most famously by the Council of Trent's decree *Tametsi*, and (less famously) by subjecting clandestine marriages to greater discipline and higher standards of proof to obviate the need to enforce such marriages in the English ecclesiastical courts.[33]

When one has recognized these two changes and given them their due, one finds that in their most basic features the two types of marriage contracts changed relatively little over the course of five centuries. On the secular side, there was always an agreement usually involving the parents or guardians, to the effect that their children would be wed and that property would change hands and be put into the hands of the couple once the marriage had taken place. In the contracts

---

[32] See Ronald Marchant, *The Church under the Law* (Cambridge, 1969), 61; Martin Ingram, "Spousals litigation in the English ecclesiastical courts, c.1350–c.1640," in R. B. Outhwaite (ed.), *Marriage and Society: Studies in the Social History of Marriage* (London, 1981), 54–55; Ralph A. Houlbrooke, "The making of marriage in mid-Tudor England: Evidence from the records of matrimonial contract litigation," *Journal of Family History* 10 (1985): 339–351, at 351; Helmholz, *Marriage Litigation*, 72–73.

[33] See Ingram, *Church Courts*, 221; Carlson, *Marriage and the English Reformation*, 531; R. H. Helmholz, *Roman Canon Law in Reformation England* (Cambridge, 1990), 70–71.

made toward the close of the Middle Ages, that property might be taken back or else diverted from one channel to another if things did not work out as planned. Yet the substance of the earlier contracts was remarkably similar to that of the later ones. Only the details of the bargains changed, according to individual circumstance.

On the spiritual side, the greatest change came early, during the twelfth century. It was the result of Pope Alexander III's acceptance of the legal rule that words of present consent alone made a valid and indissoluble marriage. In a real sense, that defined the nature of the contracts that would come before the ecclesiastical courts. The judge's task would be to decide on the intention of the parties from the words that they had spoken and the circumstances surrounding their utterance. That task remained pretty much the same from the thirteenth century to the sixteenth. Thomas Sanchez discussed the same problems of interpretation in his great treatise on the subject in the sixteenth century, as did Hostiensis in the thirteenth, and with much the same resources. Henry Swinburne (d.1624), the English civilian and author of *A Treatise of Spousals or Matrimonial Contracts*, provided the same basic information, although more compactly. There *were* developments in the canon law of marriage between 1200 and 1500, even variations within court practice, but few that had any significant effect on the nature of the marriage contracts themselves.

Conclusions

Several conclusions emerge from the comparison of secular and spiritual marriage contracts, conclusions about the subject of marriage and the people's attitude toward the law that regulated it. Most striking is an apparent contradiction in the assumptions that lay behind the two types of contracts examined above. The secular agreements seem to have assumed that the family, in particular the fathers, of the man and woman who were to be wed had the right to arrange the match. Very occasionally, there was hesitation. Future agreement of one of the parties to the marriage itself might be made a condition for performance of the contract to transfer lands and chattels. But that did not happen often. For the most part, the operative assumption appears to have been that the family controlled marriage.

The spiritual agreements, by contrast, have little to say about family or fathers. The man and woman involved – their words, their consent, and their intention – were what counted in the ecclesiastical courts. As Michael Sheehan once wrote, the church was "pushing men and women towards the more individualistic view of marriage."[34] Lay society, it would seem from the secular contracts, was pushing back. Or to put this into more fashionable terms, the medieval church adopted

---

[34] Michael M. Sheehan, "The formation and stability of marriage in fourteenth-century England: Evidence of an Ely register," in idem, *Marriage, Family and Law*, 76 (article originally published in *Mediaeval Studies* 33 [1971]: 228–63).

one "model" of marriage. It is found in the spiritual contracts. The laity adopted another "model." It is found in the secular contracts. The two were at odds, and they competed against each other, apparently for centuries.

The natural and customary way of dealing with this competition is to ask which "model" was prevailing at any one time: to see a competition for societal assent being waged between two opposed conceptions about marriage.[35] Perhaps that is right. But the persistence of both "models" alongside each other for a very long period, with neither changing very much or referring to the other very often, does give one pause. It is true, I think, that some of the apparent opposition between these two forms of contracts is illusory. Not everything relevant is put into a contract. On the one hand, the friends and relatives of the parties to a spiritual contract may have had a great deal to do with its formation, even though the partners of the contract alone performed the legally relevant act. On the other hand, the partners themselves may have given their agreement to the secular contracts, at least in a general way, even though there was no reference to it in the provisions about the transfer of lands and chattels.[36] Nevertheless, I do think that our ideas about marriage must be large enough to encompass both these types of agreements. It may be that to ask which of the two "models" of marriage was winning the contest is a *question mal posée*.

Some of the evidence from the ecclesiastical court records does suggest that it is, in fact, not the right question. In litigation, we see cases in which fathers put pressure on their children to marry a particular person, or else pressure to withdraw from an unsuitable marriage that one of their children had contracted. Litigation ensued. But litigation occurs when things have gone wrong. These were extreme cases, occurring when a breakdown in the normal pattern of marriage occurred. More often, the choice of a marriage partner was circumscribed by factors other than the parties' desires.[37] To press modern ideas of young people's freedom back into the Middle Ages is to make the exceptional case into the normal one. Potential for generational conflict is undoubtedly present in the medieval canon law, and it sometimes broke into reality.[38] Yet to take the step of assuming from

---

[35] Georges Duby, *Medieval Marriage: Two Models from Twelfth Century France*, translated by Elborg Forster (Baltimore, Md., 1978); Peter Biller, *The Measure of Multitude: Population in Medieval Thought* (Oxford, 2000), 21–23, and the authorities therein cited.

[36] See the evidence on the first of these points in Diana O'Hara, "'Ruled by my friends': Aspects of marriage in the diocese of Canterbury, c. 1540–1570," *Continuity and Change* 6 (1991): 9–41, and eadem, *Courtship and Constraint*.

[37] McSheffrey, *Love and Marriage* (n. 20 above), 15. From a slightly later period, see Peter Rushton, "Property, power and family networks: The problem of disputed marriage in early modern England," *Journal of Family History* 11 (1986): 205–19; Alison Wall, "For love, money, or politics? A clandestine marriage and the Elizabethan Court of Arches," *Historical Journal* 38 (1995): 511–33; Thomas M. Safley, "Families unformed and reformed: Protestant divorce and its domestic consequences," in Jerome Friedman (ed.), *Regnum, Religio et Ratio: Essays Presented to Robert M. Kingdon* (Kirksville, Mo., 1987), 153–60.

[38] See Charles Reid, Jr., *Power over the Body, Equality in the Family: Rights and Domestic Relations in Medieval Canon Law* (Grand Rapids, Mich., 2004), 25–63.

spiritual marriage contracts that this potential was regarded as what *should* happen in practice is to ignore the evidence of the secular marriage contracts. Resistance to marriages arranged by families was a very old theme in the European tradition.[39] It was not an invention of the canon law in the twelfth century. For me, at least, recognizing this persistence of old patterns has been one benefit of comparing the two different forms of agreement.

Making the comparison has also underlined the lesson that marriage was not then, and is still not, simply a matter of the agreement of two individuals. Marriage had broader social goals. It did more than promote the current wishes of the spouses involved.[40] The consequences of ignoring this broader aspect of marriage are evident in our own society, and the history of marriage contracts from medieval England also stands as a reminder of that fact.

ᓚ

Appendix: Selected English Marriage Contracts, Eleventh–Fifteenth Centuries

DOCUMENT 1: *Anglo-Saxon Marriage Agreement* (1014 × 1116)[1]

Here in this document is stated the agreement which Wulfric and the archbishop made when he obtained the archbishop's sister as his wife, namely he promised her the estates at Orleton and Ribbesford for her lifetime, and promised her that he would obtain the estate at Knightwick for her for three livres from the community at Winchcombe, and he gave her the estate at Alton to grant and bestow upon whomsoever she pleased during her lifetime or at her death, as she preferred, and promised her 50 mancuses of gold and 30 men and 30 horses.

The witnesses that this agreement was made as stated were Archbishop Wulfstan and Earl Leofwine and Bishop Æthelstan and Abbot Ælfweard and the monk Brihthead and many good men in addition to them, both ecclesiastics and laymen. There are two copies of this agreement, one in the possession of the archbishop at Worcester and the other in the possession of Bishop Æthelstan at Hereford.

[39] For example, Karine Ugé, "The legend of Saint Rictrude," *Anglo-Norman Studies* 23 (2000): 281–97, at 289; C. H. Talbot (ed.), *The Life of Christina of Markyate, a Twelfth Century Recluse* (Oxford, 1959), 45–55.

[40] John Wall and Don S. Browning (eds.), *Marriage, Health, and the Professions* (Grand Rapids, 2002), 6; John Witte, Jr., *An Apt and Cheerful Conversation on Marriage* (Atlanta, 2001), 23–28.

[1] Agnes J. Robertson (ed.), *Anglo-Saxon Charters*, 2nd edition (Cambridge, 1956), no. 76.

DOCUMENT 2: *Anglo-Saxon Marriage Contract* (1016 × 1020)[2]

Here in this document is made known the agreement which Godwine made with Brihtric when he wooed his daughter; first, namely, that he gave her a pound's weight of gold in return for her acceptance of his suit, and he granted her the land at Street with everything that belongs to it, and 150 acres at Burmarsh and in addition 30 oxen, and 20 cows, and 10 horses and 10 slaves.

This was agreed at Kingston in King Cnut's presence in the witness of Archbishop Lifing and of the community of Christ Church, and of Abbot Ælfmær and the community of St. Augustine's, and of Æthelwine the sheriff, and Sigered the Old, and Godwine, Wulfheah's son, and Ælfsige Child, and Eadmær of Burham, and Godwine, Wulfstan's son, and Karl the king's retainer.

And when the maiden was fetched from Brightling, there acted as surety for all this Ælfgar, Sigered's son, and Frerth, the priest of Folkestone, and Leofwine the priest of Dover, and Wulfsige the priest, and Eadred, Eadhelm's son, and Leofwine, Wærhelm's son, and Cenwold Rust, and Leofwine, son of Godwine of Horton, and Leofwine the Red, and Godwine, Eadgifu's son, and Leofsunu his brother; and whichever of them shall live the longer is to succeed to all the possessions both in land which I have given them and in all things. Every trustworthy man in Kent and Sussex, thegn or *ceorl*, is aware of these terms.

And there are three of these documents; one is at Christ Church, the second at St. Augustine's, the third Brihtric has himself.

DOCUMENT 3: *Marriage Settlement by Roger, Earl of Warwick* (1123 × 1156)[3]

Roger, Earl of Warwick, to all his barons and his faithful friends, both present and to come, greetings. Know that I have given Agnes, my daughter, in marriage to Geoffrey the chamberlain, with the counsel of the king and of the bishop of Winchester and of Earl Warenne and of Robert, my brother, and of my other brothers and of my men; and with her I have given 10 knights for service out of the 17 which he holds from me in fee, that these 10 knights may be quit and free of all service which pertains [to me] and may perform their guards at [the castle of] Brandon. Besides this I have given the service of Henry, son of Voster. And if the king shall take a common aid from all his kingdom, Geoffrey shall contribute as much as falls on 10 knights. And if the king shall go on a military expedition within England, then these 10 knights shall go with him at my cost. But if I shall have pardon or quittance or abatement of service from the king, then Geoffrey shall have such pardon or quittance or abatement of service in respect of these 10 knights. And if I exact an aid from my knights, Geoffrey may exact the same if he wishes. And besides this I grant

---

[2] David C. Douglas (ed.), *English Historical Documents*, vol. 1 (New York, 1955), no. 129.
[3] Emma Mason (ed.), *Beauchamp Cartulary Charters 1100–1268* (Pipe Roll Soc., n.s. vol. 43, no. 285).

to Geoffrey and his heir to hold the county of Warwick from me and from my heirs in the same manner as I hold and may hold it from the king. These are the witnesses. On my part: the Earl Warenne; Robert, my brother, and Geoffrey and Henry; Siward, son of Turi; Hastecill "de Haruc"; Hugh, son of Richard; Thurstan "de Munst"; Walter, son of Hugh; Henry Drap; William Giffard; Hugh Abidon. On the part of Geoffrey: William "de Clinton"; William, son of Ralph; Hugh "de Clinton" and Maurice, his brother; Richard Turn; Robert, son of Geoffrey, and Elias, his brother; Stephen, son of Ralph, and Richard, his brother; Roger "de Frevilla"; Ralph "de Martinmast"; "Mig." of Northampton; Payn of Barford; William, son of Odo; Ralph of Drayton.

Rogerus comes Warr' omnibus suis baronibus et amicis suis fidelibus, tam presentibus quam futuris salutem. Sciatis me dedisse Agnetem filiam meam in uxorem Gaufrido camerario, consilio regis et episcopi Wynton', et comitis Warr', et Roberti fratis mei, et aliorum meorum fratrum et meorum hominum, in maritagium, et cum ea in servitium x milites de xvii quos tenet de me [in] feudo. Ita quod illi x milites quieti et liberi erunt de omni servitio quod adpertinet, et hii x facient suam custodiam de Brandun'; et preter hoc servitium Henrici filii Vosteri. Et si rex acciperit commune auxilium per suum regnum de hiis x, Gaufridus dederit mihi quantum pertinebit x militibus, et si rex gerrit in expeditionem infra Angliam, hii x milites ibunt ad castra mea in expeditione. Si ego vero perdonum vel acquietationem vel aliquam admensurationem a rege habuero, illud idem perdonum et acquietationem et admensurationem habebit Gaufridus quantum ad hos x milites pertinebit. Et si accipero auxilium de meis militibus, Gaufridus accipiat ad opus suum, si voluerit. Et pretera ego concedo Gaufrido et heredi suo tenere comitatum de Warr' hereditarie de me et meis heredibus, eodem modo quod de rege habeo vel habere potero. Huius rei sunt testes ex parte mea: comes Waren', Robertus frater meus et Gaufridus et Henricus, Siwardus filius Tur[kill]I, Hascetill de Haruc, Hugo filius Ricardi, Turstinus de Munft', Walterus filius Hugonis, Henricus Drap', Willelmus Giffard; Hugo Abidon'. Ex parte Gaufridi; Willelmus de Clint' (filius), Willelmus filius Radulfi, Hugo de Clint' et Mauritius frater eius, Ricardus Turn', Robertus filius Gaufridi et Helias frater eius, Stephanus filius Fadulfi et Ricardus frater eius, Rogerus de Freivilla', Radulfus de Martinmast', Nigellus de Norhampton', Paganus de Beref', Willelmus filius Odonis, Radulfus de Drait'.

DOCUMENT 4: *Marriage Contract between Gregory of Dina and William "of Martineio" (1154 × 1189)*[4]

Let it be known to all present and future men that this agreement has been made between Gregory of Dina and William of Martineio: that Ligerius son

---

[4] British Library, Add. Ch. 21,516.

of Gregory of Dina or another of his sons if Ligerius should die beforehand, shall take in marriage a daughter of William of Martineio, or will be married according to his counsel; under this condition, that William of Martineio shall redeem from pledge to Samuel the Jew of Northampton land of Ashby worth 20 silver marks. And if the sons of Gregory do not abide by this pact, the aforesaid William shall have all the land of Ashby until 20 marks and other expenses he incurred in this matter shall have been returned to him. And this by the view of two of the friends of Gregory and two of the friends of William of Martineio. And they have given faith that this agreement is to be kept. Witnesses: Sello of Gretton, William fitz Vakelino and William of Horne and Hugh of Alie and Geoffrey of Cort, William Berton, Reginald de Lisle.

Sciant tam presentes quam futuri quod hec conventio est inter Gregorium de Dina et Willelmum de Martineio, quod Ligerius filius Gregorii de Dina vel alter filius eiusdem si Ligerus prius decesserit ducet in uxorem filiam Willelmi de Martineio vel per consilium eius maritabit, hac tali condicione quod Willelmus de Martineio disvadiavit terram Gregorii de xx marchis argenti de Assebi a Samuello judeo de Norhamtuna. Et si filii Gregorii hoc pactum non tenuerint, predictus Willelmus totam terram de Assebi habeat donec reddatur ei xx marche et expensa alia quam in eodem negocio posuerit et per visum duorum amicorum Gregorii et duorum amicorum Willelmi de Martineio. Et hanc convencionem affidaverunt ipsi tenendam. Testibus Sellone de Gratton, Willelmo filio Vakelino et Willelmo de Horne et Hugone de Alie et Gaufrido de Cort, Willelmo Berton, Reignero de Lisla.

DOCUMENT 5: *Marriage Contract between Humphrey, Earl of Warwick and Ralph Thosney (1236) [Précis only]*[5]

This is the agreement made between Sir Humphrey, Earl of Warwick, of Hereford, on the one part, and Sir Ralph of Thosney, on the other, namely that the said Earl Humphrey has given in free marriage 40 pounds worth of land in the village of Newenton, in Wiltshire, to Roger, eldest and first born son of Sir Ralph of Thosney, with Alice his daughter. [It is agreed] that if the land in Newenton shall not suffice to produce 40 pounds, the said Earl Humphrey shall make it good to him from a suitable location in the same county. And if it should happen that the aforesaid Roger, son of Ralph of Thosney should die before coming to a proper age for contracting [marriage], the said Earl Humphrey shall grant and concede the aforesaid 40 pounds in land to Ralph, son of the said Ralph of Thosney with the aforesaid Alice, daughter of Earl Humphrey, in free marriage. And if the said Alice shall die

[5] *Beauchamp Cartulary Charters 1100–1268* (Pipe Roll Soc., n.s. vol. 43, no. 379).

before the contracting of marriage, the younger daughter of the said Earl
Humphrey born in legitimate marriage shall succeed in place of the said Alice
in marriage together with the aforesaid land. And the said Humphrey shall
hold the said 40 pounds worth of land in his hand until Roger or Ralph,
sons of the said Ralph of Thosney, shall legitimately contract with the daughter of the said Earl Humphrey. And the said Ralph of Thosney has given
and granted to Roger, his eldest son and heir, 40 pounds worth of land in
Carleton and Helland in Cornwall to endow the said Alice, daughter of the
said Earl Humphrey, in this manner, namely, that if the said land in Carleton
and Helland shall not suffice to produce 40 pounds, the aforesaid Ralph of
Thosney shall make it good to him from a suitable location in the same county.
And if it should happen that the said Roger should die before coming to a
proper age for contracting [marriage], the said Ralph of Thosney has given
and granted the said 40 pounds worth of land to Ralph, his younger son,
to endow the aforesaid Alice or another younger daughter born legitimately
to the said Earl Humphrey, if it should happen that the said Alice shall die
before coming to proper age for contracting [marriage]. And the said Ralph
of Thosney shall hold the said 40 pounds worth of land in his hand until the
said Roger or Ralph shall legitimately join together with the daughter of the
said Earl Humphrey. And if it should happen that the said land in Cornwall
is so held that it cannot be granted to endow the daughter of the said Earl
Humphrey, 40 pounds worth of land in the manor of Taunton shall constitute the dower and be granted to the daughter of the said Earl Humphrey at
the time she can lawfully contract [marriage]. And the said Earl Humphrey
and Ralph of Thosney are agreed that when the son of the said Ralph of
Thosney and the daughter of the said Earl Humphrey shall come to an age
when they may lawfully contract [marriage], they shall contract it at once,
and that immediately after the contract of marriage the said Earl Humphrey
and Ralph of Thosney shall put the son of the said Ralph and the daughter
of the said Earl Humphrey in lawful seisin of the aforesaid lands. Moreover,
for this agreement and grant, the said Earl Humphrey has given 200 marks to
the said Ralph of Thosney paid in hand. Each of them has sworn to keep this
agreement faithfully and without fraud. And for greater security, each has set
his seal to the present charter in the manner of a chirograph. These witnesses:
Sir Roger de Lacy, Earl of Lincoln, Sir John Biset, Sirs John son of Galfrid,
Emory of Saint Amand, Egidius of Clifford, John of Saint Laud, William of
Mown, John of Cheveron, and many others.

Hec est conventio facta inter dominum Humfredum comitem (Warr')
Her[e]ford' ex una parte, et dominum Radulfum de Thony ex altera, scilicet quod dictus Humfredus comes dedit in liberum maritagium xl^{ta} libratas
terre in villade Newenton' in Wilts' Rogero filio domini Radulfi de Thony,

primogenito etheredi, cum Alicia filia sua. Ita scilicet quod si terra de Newenton' non sufficeret ad quadraginta libratas terre perficiendas, dictus Humfredus comes perficiet eidem in loco competente in eodem comitatu, et si predictus Rogerus filius Radulfi de Thony in fata cesserit antequam ad maturam etatem contrahendi pervenerit, dictus Humfredus comes dat et concedit dictas quadragintas libratas terre Radulfo filio dicti Radulfi de Thony cum predicta Alicia, filia dicti Humfredi comitis, in liberum maritagium, et si de dicta Alicia ante contractionem matrimonii humanitas contigerit, filia dicti Humfredi comitis junior de legitimo thoro proveniens loco dicte Alicie succederit in matrimonio cum predicta terra. Et dictus Humfredus dictas xl libratas terre in manu sua teneat donec Rogerus vel Radulfus, filii dicti Radulfi de Thony, cum filia dicti Humfredi comitis legitime contraxerit. Et dictus Radulfus de Thony dedit et concessit Rogero filio suo primogenito et heredi xl libratas terre in Karleston' et Helleston' in Cornub' ad dotandam dictam Aliciam filiam dicti Humfredi comitis. Ita scilicet quod si dicta terra de Karleston' et de Helleston' non sufficeret ad xl libratas terre perficiendas, predictus Radulfus de Thony illas sibi perficiet in loco competente in eodem comitatu. Et si de dicto Rogero antequam ad maturam etatem contrahendi pervenerit humanitus contigerit, dictus Radulfus de Thony dat et concedit dictas xl libratas terre Radulfo filio suo juniori ad dotandam prefatam Aliciam, vel aliam filiam dicti Humfredi comitis juniorem de thoro legitime provenientem, si de dicta Alicia antequam ad plenam etatem contrahendi pervenerit humanitus contigerit. Et dictus Radulfus de Thony dictas xl libratas terre in manu sua teneat donec dictus Rogerus vel Radulfus cum filia dicti Humfredi comitis legitime conduxerit. Et si ita contigerit quod dicta terra de Cornub' impedita fuerit, quod in dotem filie dicti Humfredi comitis cedere non possit, xl librate terre eidem in manerio de Tauton' in dotem perficientur, et filie dicti Humfredi comitis ad tempus quo rationabiliter contrahere concesserit. Et adnuunt dicti Humfredus comes et Radulfus de Tony quod cum filius dicti Radulfi de Thoney et filia dicti Humfredi comitis ad tempus quo rationabiliter contrahere possint pervenerit, statim contrahant et statim post matrimonii contractum, dicti Humfredus comes et Radulfus de Thoney [cum de] omnibus terris predictis filio dicti Radulfi et filie dicti Humfredi comitis plenam seisinam facient. Pro hac autem conventione et concessione [dedit] dictus Humfredus comes dicto Radulfo de Thony ducentas marcas argenti premanibus. Hanc autem conventionem fideliter et sine dolo tenendam utraque illorum affidavit. Et ad maiorem securitatem habendam, presenti carte in modum cirographi confecte sigilla sua vicissim apposuerunt. Hiis testibus: domino Rogero de Lacy, comite Lincoln', domino Johanne Biset, dominis Johanne filio Galfridi, Amaurico de Sancto Amando, Egidio de Clifford', Johanne de Sancto Laudo, Willelmo de Mown', Johanne de Cheveron' et multis aliis.

DOCUMENT 6: *Marriage Agreement between Simon "of Leuekener"*
and Elias "of Witteford" (1243)[6]

Thus it is agreed between Simon "of Leuekener" and Elias "of Wytteford,"
that Henry, son and heir of the aforesaid Elias, shall take as his wife Sybill,
daughter of the aforesaid Simon. With the will and license of the aforesaid
Elias his father, he shall endow the aforesaid Sybill his [Henry's] wife with the
manor of Ropeford with its appurtenances, which the aforesaid Elias has given
to Henry his son to have and to hold to him and his heirs born of the aforesaid
Sybill, whether he shall survive his father or not, which manor shall remain
in the possession of the aforesaid Simon until the coming to full age of the
aforesaid Henry [to be used] for the sustenance of him and the aforesaid wife.
And when he shall come to full age, he shall restore it to the aforesaid Henry
without any impediment. Moreover, the aforesaid Elias has granted and by
this writing does oblige [himself] that from henceforth he shall not give or
pledge any land to the Jews or in any other way alienate it to the disinheritance
of the aforesaid Henry his son and his heirs, and of this he shall provide every
surety to the aforesaid son of which the aforesaid Simon and his counsel can
provide in the court of the Lord King or elsewhere. The aforesaid Elias has
granted also that the children of the aforesaid Henry his [Elias's] son born
of the aforesaid Sybill shall inherit all the lands and tenements that he now
possesses or shall possess, either by escheat or in any other manner, with the
exception of the annual rent of 40s. which he gave to Robert his son to be
levied from William Selwyn to support himself in the schools, until he shall
obtain that amount of revenue, and with the exception of the land of La Penne,
which he gave to Ralph "of Wilinton". For this, however, the aforesaid Simon
has given 140 marks to the aforesaid Elias. And that this agreement etc.

Oxon'. Ita convenit inter Simonem de Leuekener' et Eliam de Wyttefeud'
quod Henricus filius et heres prefati Elie ducet in uxorem Sibillam filiam
prefati Simonis, qui de voluntate et licencia prefati Elye patris sui predictam Sibillam uxorem suam dotabit de manerio de Roppeford' cum pertinenciis, quod prefatus Elyas ipsi Henrico filio suo dedit habendum et tenendum sibi et heredibus suis qui de predicta Sibilla exibunt, sive ipse patrem
suum supervixerit sive non, quod qu[idem] manerium remanebit in custo-
dia prefati Simonis usque ad legitimam etatem prefati Henrici ad suam et
prefate uxoris sustentacionem; et cum ad plenam etatem pervenerit, illud
prefato Henrico sine omni d[ifficultate] restituet. Prefatus [e]ciam Elyas
concessit et hoc scripto obligavit quod decetero nullam terram dabit inva-
diabit in Judeasmo vel aliquo alio modo alienabit ad exheredacionem prefati Henrici filii sui et heredum suorum; et inde omnimodam securitatem

[6] *Curia Regis Rolls*, 26–27 Henry III, no. 1514.

faciet prefato filio suo quam prefatus Simon et consilium [suum] poterunt providere in curia domini regis vel alibi. Concessit eciam prefatus Elyas quod pueri predicti Henrici filii sui ex predicta Sibilla procreati heredes ejus sint de omnibus terris et tenementis que ad presens possidet, sive per escaetam sive aliquo alio modo sit habiturus, exceptis xl. solidatis redditus quas tradidit Roberto filio suo annuatim percipiendas de Willelmo Selveyn ad se sustentandum in scola, donec tantum modo redditum habuerit, et excepta terra de la Penne, quam dedit Radulfo de Wilinton'. Pro hac autem etc., dedit prefatus Simon predicto Elye septies xx marcas. Et ut hec convencio etc.

DOCUMENT 7: *Marriage Contract between Roger "of Dikeleigh" and Richard Spencer (1342)*[7]

This indenture attests to the agreements made between Roger Dykelegh, on the one part, and Richard le Spenser of Bergholt, on the other, namely that John the son of the said Roger shall take as his wife Agnes, the daughter of the said Richard, and the said Roger shall take from the aforesaid Richard as a marriage portion twenty gold pounds upon a certain day contained in a certain written obligation made thereupon. And furthermore, the said Richard shall provide for the said Agnes for her chamber, two robes for her apparel, two beds for her retinue, one for her men of office the other for her serving boys, two linen towels and cloths, and other things as shall be appropriate for her status. And the said Roger shall provide for the aforesaid John and Agnes his wife and their sons and daughters to be born of their bodies, all things necessary for their nourishment and apparel and all other things connected thereunto as their status dictates, during the lifetime of the aforesaid Roger while the aforesaid Roger, John and Agnes shall desire to live together. And if either party refuse to consent to this living together, the aforesaid Roger shall give to John and Agnes all [his] lands and tenements in the vill of Little Bentlegh, to be held for the life of the aforesaid Roger in payment of the sustenance of the aforesaid John and Agnes and their issue. And the aforesaid Roger has agreed to enfeoff two suitable persons with all [his] lands and tenements in the vills of Mistelegh, Dykelegh and Little Brumlegh, so that having [taken] seisin therein, they should re-enfeoff the aforesaid Roger of all the aforesaid lands and tenements, to be held for his lifetime, and after the death of the said Roger, the lands and tenements shall remain to the aforesaid John and Agnes and the heirs procreated by them, and if they should die without heirs of their bodies, then the aforesaid tenements with appurtenances shall remain to the right heirs of the aforesaid Roger in perpetuity. And that all these things may be done and completed the aforesaid Roger shall come into the court of the

---

[7] British Library, Add. Ch. 58,445.

Lord King to make a fine, and [this] at the expense of the aforesaid Richard,
who shall be given notice. And each of the aforesaid parties obliges himself by
all his lands and tenements to hold and observe all the aforesaid provisions. In
testimony of which the parties aforesaid have set their seals to this indenture.
Witnesses: John Bromlegh, William Adam, John Gubroun, John Gernoun,
William Magge the younger, John Rogger, John Boyton, and others. Given at
Bergholt, Tuesday the feast of Saint Barnabas the Apostle, in the sixteenth year
of the reign of King Edward the Third after the Conquest.

Hec indentura testatur conventiones factas inter Rogerum de Dykelgh ex
parte una et Ricardum le Spenser de Bergholt ex altera, videlicet quod
Johannes filius dicti Rogeri capiet in uxorem Agnetem filiam dicti Ricardi,
et predictus Rogerus capiet de predicto Ricardo pro maritagio predicto vig-
inti libras argenti ad certos dies in quodam scripto obligatorio inde confecto
contento. Et preter hoc dictus Ricardus inveniet predicte Agneti pro camera sua duas robas pro corpore suo, duos lectos pro gentilibus, unum lectum pro hominibus de officio unum lectum pro garcionibus, duas mappas
cum tuell' et manutergo et alia sicut pro suo statu competit. Et predictus
Rogerus inveniet predictis Johanni et Agneti uxori eius et filiis et filiabus suis
de corporibus eorum procreandis omnia eis necessaria in victu et vestitu
et omnibus aliis eisdem contingentibus prout eorum statui decet tota vita
predicti Rogeri, dummodo predicti Rogerus Johannes et Agnes in una soci-
etate commorare voluerint. Et si altera pars eorum ad talem moram facere
consentire noluerit, predictus Rogerus dabit Johanni et Agneti omnia terra
et tenementa sua in villa de parva Bentlegh tenenda ad totam vitam predicti Rogeri in allocatione sustentacionis predictorum Johannis et Agnetis et
eorum exitus. Et predictus Rogerus concessit feoffare duas personas ydoneas
de omnibus terris et tenementis suis in villis de Misterlegh, Bykelegh, et
Parva Brumleth ita quod habita inde seisina refeoffaare debent predictum
Rogerum de omnibus terris et tenementis predictis tenendis ad totam vitam
suam. Et post decessum dicti Rogeri predicti tenementa cum pertinenciis
remanebunt predictis Johanni et Agneti et heredibus eorum procreatis. Et
si obierunt sine heredibus de corporibus suis exeuntis, tunc predicta tenementa cum pertinenciis rectis heredibus predicti Rogeri remanebunt in
perpetuum. Et ad omnia ista facienda et exequenda predictus Rogerus veniet
in curia domini Regis ad finem inde levandum [illegible] per predictum
Ricardum premunitus fuerit sumptibus predicti Ricardi. Et ad omnia premissa ex utraque parte tenenda et observanda utraque pars partium predictarum obligat se omnes terras et tenementa sua predicta per presentes.
In cuius rei testimonium huic indenture partes predicte sigilla sua alter-
natim apposuerunt. His testibus Johannes de Bromlegh, Willelmus Adam,
Johannes Gubroun, Johannes Gernoun, Willelmus Magge iunior, Johannes
Roger, Johannes de Boyton et aliis. Datum apud Bergholt die martis in festo

sancti Barnabe apostoli anno regni Regis Edwardi tercii post conquestum sexdecimo.

DOCUMENT 8: *Marriage Contract between Baldwin Malet et ux. and John Hylle (1380)*[8]

Indenture (in French) between Baldwin Malet, knight, and Lady Elizabeth his wife, on the one part, and John Hylle on the other, on Friday in Easter week, 3 Richard II, witnessing an agreement that John, son of Baldwin and Elizabeth, Baldwin's heir apparent, shall marry Joan, daughter of John Hylle. Baldwin and Elizabeth shall grant by fine in the king's court that half the manor of Contockeshede and half the advowson of the same which William de Lucy and Margaret his wife hold for their lives, and which ought to revert to Baldwin and Elizabeth and the heirs of Baldwin, shall revert to John Malet and Joan and their heirs after the deaths of William and Margaret. And if John and Joan die without heirs, reversion to Baldwin and Elizabeth and the heirs of Baldwin for ever. Also Baldwin, within nine years after the date of these presents, if he is still alive, will purchase the reversion of the manor of Oake, formerly of his inheritance, after the death of Sir John Tryvet, which shall be entailed within six months to John Malet and Joan and the heirs of their bodies, remainder, failing heirs, to the right heirs of Baldwin. Further, Baldwin and Elizabeth will take full possession of the manors of Lydyard, Enmore and Sutton and all other possessions which Baldwin granted, released and quitclaimed to certain persons; and then Baldwin and Elizabeth will grant by fine the manor of Lydeard (Lediard) to Thomas Fichet, knight, Hugh Durburgh, knight, Thomas Coote, parson of Enmore, Richard Lorgh, vicar of Bishop's Lydeard, Robert Hylle, the elder, and Robert Hylle the younger, his son, to hold to them and the heirs of Hugh. Within three months afterwards the feoffees will regrant the same to Baldwin and Elizabeth for their lives, with reversion to John Malet and Joan, and remainder, failing heirs, to the right heirs of Baldwin. The grants and reversions of Cauntakeshed and Lydeard shall be made by the quindene of St. Martin next.... After the said marriage has been accomplished Baldwin and Elizabeth shall have the charge of John and Joan and shall support them suitably according to their estate, until the reversions of Cauntakeshede and Oake are purchased and John and Joan are in possession after the deaths of the life tenants. Baldwin will grant the manors of Sutton and Enmore to the feoffees as abovesaid, on condition that if John Malet should survive during his father's lifetime, then the feoffees are obliged to make grant to Baldwin, and are bound to allow him to re-enter as in his first estate. If John Malet survives his father, then the feoffees are to grant the same to Elizabeth for her life, with reversion to John Malet and the heirs of his

[8] Robert W. Dunning (ed.), *The Hylle Cartulary* (Yeovil, Somerset, 1968), no. 305.

body, failing whom to the right heirs of Baldwin. And the said John Hylle will pay to Baldwin at Exeter £100 for the marriage and nurture of Joan, namely £50 at Midsummer next, at Michaelmas then following £20, and £30 at the following Easter. Mutual obligations in £200 for the proper execution of the agreement. Baldwin gives an annuity of £40 to John and Robert Hylle from the manors of Sutton, Enmore and Lydeard at Michaelmas and Easter equally, and John Hylle will provide a like annuity for Baldwin and Elizabeth from his lands in Devon for greater surety. These annuities will be bailed in the hand of Sir Hugh Durburgh. Seals of both parties.

DOCUMENT 9: *Marriage Contract of the Norreis Family (1441)*[9]

This indenture made between William Norreis of Speike, one partie, and Thomas Norreis, sumtyme of Derby, on that other part, here witness that the said parties by the assent and good will of Thomas, son and heire apparent to the said William, and Letice, doghter and heyre apparent to the sayde Thomas Norreis, ben agreet accordet and fully condiscendant in the form that follows: that is to say, that the said William shall ordeigne and make the said Thomas his son to take to wife and wedd the said Letice bitwene this and the fest of seynt Peter callet Lammas next comyng, if the said Letice be redy to be wedded to the said Thomas son of William. And the said Thomas Norreis sumtyme of Derby shall ordeine and make the said Letice to take to husband the said Thomas son of William and to hym to be weddid before the said fest if the said Thomas son of William be redy to wedd the said Letice. And the said William Norreis shall make a sufficient estate of londes and tenementes that he is now seiset of in fee simple other (or) fee taill to the yerely valew of C. s. over annual charges and reprises to the said Letice [for the] terme of hir lyve, the remainder after her discess to the said Thomas son of William and to the heyre of his bodye gotten bitwene hym and the said Letice, remainder over therof at the will of the said William in xl daies next after the said weddyng without any alienacion other (or) encumbraunce to be made bi the said William, other (or) inne the said londes and tenementes or any parcel of them before the said estate so to be made, and the saide William shall suffer all the londes and tenementes that come to hym bi dissent bi the dethe of his fader and of all other landes and tenementes that to the said William shall reverte or remayne bi the dethe of his moder or of any other if hit happen the said William his saide moder to survive, for to discende to the said Thomas his son and to his heres in fee simple other (or) fee taille without any alienacion charge other incumbraunce of other (or) inne the said londes and tenementes or any parcel of them to be made, bot suche as shall seace or be determynt bi the dethe of the said William titles of

[9] British Library, Add. Ch. 52,293.

dower and reconyusshaunce of severties of the peas and of aparaunce that the said William shall be bounden in to the kyng for himselfe or any of his fryndes in the caes, except and yif hit so happen that any devorse be made in tyme coming bitwene the sayd Thomas sone of William and Letice at the suite of the said Thomas son of William, then the said William shall pay or make to be paid to the sayd Thomas Norreis sumtyme of Derby his heyres other (or) his executors C. markes within ii yeres after the same devorse so made ... [some details of land transactions omitted] and the said William Norreis ys suret also that all the londes that come to hym bi discent bi the dethe of his fader ben now in his owen possession soule and as well the said William Norreis as Thomas Norreis sumtyme of Derby severally ben insuret by ther trothes that if ther be any thing in this indenture that of reson faithe and good conciouns shold be addit or diminyt after the true intent of the sayd parties that they shall abyde the reformacion advice and ordinaunce [blank in MS.]. In wittenesse of whiche thinge to the present indenture the parties aforesaid entour chaungeth have sette theyre sealles and written the xxiiii[ti] day of June in the yer of the reign of King Henry the sixt after the Conquest of Englond the xviiii.

DOCUMENT 10: *Marriage Contract between John Willingby and Thomas Kyme (1452)*[10]

This indenture made atte Boston the Thursday next aftyr the feast of Saint Michell tharchanungle the yere of the reign of King Henry the sixth aftyr the conquest of England the xxxi[th] between John Willinghby squyer, of the one part, and Thomas Kyme, of the othir part, bereth wytness that the said John and Thomas are agreed that John Kyme sone and heir to the said Thomas Kyme wiyth the grace of God shall wedde and take to wyffe Johanne Willinghby, systour to the said John Willinghby, before the feste of Pasche next coming after the date of this present writing, before which feste of Pasche the said John grantyth to make or do to make a lawful estate of landes and tenements in Kirketon Alberkirk and Soterton of the value of x li. yerely to have and to hold to the said John Kyme and Johanne Willinghby and to ther heires of ther bodyes lawfully begotyn and for defaute of such issue the remainder of the said landes and tenements to the said Thomas Kyme his heirs and his assigns for evermore, provided allway that theis estates aforerehersed shall be made aftyr the intent ensuant, that is to say, that yf yt fortuneth the said Johanne Willinghby to dye aftyr the said expouselx hadd none issue had between hir and the said John Kyme that thane yt shall be lefaull and lewfull to the said John Willinghby and his heires to reenter in to the half of the said landes and tenements afore bi the said John Willinghby assign, and the said John Kyme to reteyn the other half of thos landes and tenements during the terme of his

[10] British Library, Egerton Ch. 1,232.

lyffe and ... [similar provision if John Kyme died without issue]. Also yt is appointed between the parties aforesaid that nothir the wyffe of the said John W. nor the wyff of the said Thomas Kyme shall clayme any endowment of the said landes and tenements aforerehersed, and theruppon both parties shall be boundyn ether to other in C. li. Wherof the parties aforesaid to theis present indentures hath severeally sett their seale. Writtyn the day and yere abovesaid.

CHAPTER EIGHT

Marriage Contracts and the Church Courts of Fourteenth-Century England

Frederik Pedersen

We depend on documentary records for most of what we know about the conduct of marriages during the later middle ages, and for all that we know about marriage litigation during that period. This situation presents the historian with a problem: the survival of a document depends on medieval criteria for archiving, and we know that the vast majority of documentary evidence has not survived. Hence the material on which we must base our analysis is peculiar in two respects: first, it was written down under certain special conditions, and second, it managed to survive. Verbatim oral evidence has not survived at all from this period, when there were no court stenographers or tape recorders. Depositions record oral evidence only selectively and in a somewhat stylized, stereotypical form. Nevertheless, we can sometimes reconstruct both oral evidence and lost documents on the basis of the documents that remain.

In this chapter, by performing just such a reconstruction, I consider what kinds of negotiation preceded marriage in late-medieval England and what kinds of contracts were involved. I also try to ascertain whether or not people in the Middle Ages drew a sharp jurisdictional distinction between the "secular" and "spiritual" contracts made during marriage negotiations. The method chosen is to examine in detail the evidence of five fourteenth-century cases. One case was brought before Parliament, whereas the other four belong to the cause papers of the consistory court in York. These cases suffice at least to give some impression of the range of concerns expressed in marriage contracts. I also comment on the role of legal experts in the wider run of York cases.

Before considering particular cases, I provide some background information about the ecclesiastical courts and comment on the kinds of contracts involved in marriage.

Marriage Litigation in the Consistory Courts

The medieval consistory courts were a part of the jurisdiction of every bishop. As such, they were ubiquitous across Europe: every diocese had one. Their function was to enforce the discipline of the church. From the laity's point of view, therefore, the consistory courts were above all where they took their disputes about marriage.[1] In rare cases, they also provided the legal framework surrounding a breakdown in marital relations.[2] The plaintiff was usually, although not always, one of the two parties supposedly contracted in marriage. Plaintiffs could represent themselves in court, but they would normally choose to be represented by members of the court known as proctors, and neither the litigants nor their witnesses were obliged to attend the court themselves (although they often did). Instead, witnesses would be interviewed separately by examiners of the court, who usually had no other knowledge of the case apart from what they found in the interrogatory (a written list, to which the litigants or their proctors had agreed, of the questions under dispute). The proctors recorded the witnesses' responses to the interrogatory. The interrogatories and the written record of the depositions have sometimes survived, together with other procedural documents of the court, and historians can use these rare documents to construct some idea of how English people contracted marriages during the later Middle Ages.

The material surviving in the archdioceses of York and Canterbury is particularly detailed. In both jurisdictions, diocesan archives contain complete records of certain individual cases. The York material seems to be a random survival of the total business of the courts, whereas the Canterbury material appears to have been selected to demonstrate that the court had a particular jurisdiction during specific times of its existence.[3]

---

[1] For a magisterial analysis of how the law of marriage developed, see James A. Brundage, *Law, Sex, and Christian Society in Medieval Europe* (Chicago, 1987). Brundage's study has largely superseded such works as Adhémar Esmein and Robert Génestal, *Le marriage en droit canonique* (Paris, 1929); John A. Alessandro, *Gratian's Notion of Marital Consummation* (Vatican City, 1971); and Gérard Fransen, "La formation du lien matrimonial au moyen âge," *Revue de Droit Canonique* 21 (1971): 106–26. This chapter has benefited enormously from the editorial labors and eagle editorial eyes both of my wife, Sarah, and of Philip Reynolds. I should like to acknowledge their considerable input and the clarity, wit, and good humor of our discussions.

[2] The law of divorce did not allow for the dissolution of an existing bond that left the parties free to contract another marriage. It only regulated how the parties might set up separate households. As a consequence, litigants overwhelmingly presented cases that called for the annulment of a marriage (and often chose to perjure themselves to achieve that aim).

[3] For an elaboration of this point, see the introduction to Norma Adams and Charles Donahue, Jr. (eds.), *Select Cases from the Ecclesiastical Courts of the Province of Canterbury, c. 1200–1301* (London, 1981), 1–120. For York, see my *Marriage Disputes in Medieval England* (London, 2000), and P. J. P. Goldberg, *Women, Work, and Life Cycle in a Medieval Economy: Women in York and Yorkshire c. 1300–1520* (Oxford, 1992). Goldberg and I disagree over whether social historians can use these records (which necessarily focus on the upper echelons of society in the York region) as a window onto society as a whole: see Frederik Pedersen, "Demography in the archives: Social and geographical variables in fourteenth-century York cause paper marriage litigation," *Continuity and Change* 10 (1995): 405–36; P. J. P. Goldberg, "Fiction in the archives: The York cause papers as a source for medieval social history," *Continuity and Change* 12 (1998): 425–46; and Frederik Pedersen, "The York cause papers: A reply to Jeremy Goldberg," *Continuity and Change* 12 (1997): 447–55.

No written marriage contract has survived among the documents preserved by English ecclesiastical courts, yet we read about them in the evidence taken down from the witnesses. The act that constituted a canonically binding marriage was the speaking of words of consent in the present tense. In fact, the church's rules for the establishment of marriage *required* the marriage to be contracted by the exchange of spoken words (or by unequivocal gestures if one of the contracting parties could not speak). The constituting act was therefore purely oral. It might occur during marriage negotiations or quite informally and haphazardly. What we might loosely characterize as love talk could be the constituent act in the contracting of a valid marriage, at least in the period after the publication of Pope Alexander III's undated decretal *Veniens ad nos*.[4]

What the medieval consistory courts set out to discover when faced with a disputed marriage was this: Had a given exchange of words (or in some rare cases, of actions) established a canonically valid marriage? In order to answer this question, the courts focused their attention on establishing the exact words that the contracting parties had exchanged, or, in cases of doubt, on establishing whether the parties had consummated their marriage after a *de futuro* agreement to marry or after a conditional or unclear exchange of vows. Thus, the surviving evidence focuses very narrowly on whether an oral exchange of words that would have created a binding marriage had actually taken place. Yet it is evident from hints and fragments in the surviving documents that these exchanges of vows were often part of much more complex negotiations and arrangements, and that many marriages involved contracts whereby the parties attempted to safeguard their secular interests (for example, as far as property was concerned). The latter contracts might be oral or written.

MARRIAGE CONTRACTS

Following R. H. Helmholz in the previous chapter, I define a marriage contract as an agreement between a man and a woman (or between their legal representatives) expressing their obligation to be married or at least mentioning that obligation as one object of the agreement. What created a marriage that was valid and binding by canon law standards was a mutual oral agreement expressed in the present tense (*per verba de praesenti*). Gestures or written words were acceptable only in exceptional cases (for example, if one party was mute). A contract to marry expressed in the future tense (*per verba de futuro*) was sometimes called a marriage, but it was not

---

[4] X. 4.1.15. For comments on the development and dating of Alexander III's marriage decretals, see Charles Donahue, Jr., "The dating of Alexander the Third's marriage decretals: Dauvillier revisited after fifty years," *Zeitschrift der Savigny-Stiftung für Rechtsgeschichte, kanonistische Abteilung* 68 (1982): 70–124; and idem, "The policy of Alexander the Third's consent theory of marriage," in *Proceedings of the Fourth International Congress of Medieval Canon Law*, Stephan Kuttner, ed. Monumenta Iuris Canonici, Series C, Subsidia 5 (Città del Vaticano, 1976), 251–81, at 253–56.

binding in the same sense. It was what we might call an engagement or betrothal. But instead of promising to marry in the future or simply agreeing to marry with present effect, the partners might add conditions to their agreement (e.g., "if my father agrees"). The marriage would then meet canon law standards for a valid and binding marriage as soon as the condition was fulfilled (unless the condition was criminal or vitiated the ends of matrimony). Finally, a conditional marriage or a marriage expressed *per verba de futuro* (in modern terms, an engagement) was regarded by the church courts as a valid and binding marriage if the partners consummated their agreement by sexual intercourse. In theory, at least, their coitus expressed their present intent to marry. Hence the episcopal courts considered any stipulated conditions to have been waived if the parties subsequently had sexual intercourse.

Following Helmholz again, I distinguish between "spiritual" and "secular" marriage contracts. What I have described in the previous paragraph was the spiritual contract. But although a marriage contract and its associated negotiations might deal solely with "spiritual" matters, a contract might also deal with secular matters, such as the transfer of land or money. Secular contracts sometimes even regulated marital behavior. In contrast, the spiritual contract was exclusively concerned with those aspects of human life over which the church claimed jurisdiction because they concerned the salvation of souls, namely, the establishment of indissoluble marriage (which by this period the church regarded as a sacrament). Consistory courts, therefore, were interested only in spiritual contracts. The two kinds of contracts coexisted and were, in the main, complementary. They shared several points of similarity: for example, both made regular use of conditions, and both provided for arbitration. But whereas spiritual contracts were strictly oral (for reasons explained earlier), secular contracts were often (but not always) written down.

The cases outlined subsequently suggest that litigants in medieval English marriage disputes chose which jurisdiction to employ – secular or ecclesiastical – by deciding which was more likely to help them reach their desired goals. It mattered little to the litigants whether their case proceeded in the "lay" or the "spiritual sphere." What mattered was that a chosen instrument allowed them to achieve their goals, such as to enforce a marriage, to maintain control of land, to enforce a monetary payment, or to restrict or permit certain behaviors in marriage. Likewise, the laity recognized the existence of both written and spoken marriage contracts and gave equal weight and value to both types. Lay people were aware of, understood, and used both oral and written contracts in marrying and in litigation.

Spouses and their families frequently safeguarded marriage contracts by employing experts in law, who have left telling traces in the written evidence of the courts. People of all kinds could witness such contracts, but there was a clear preference in the consistory courts for what we should call "expert witnesses." Thus, notaries and priests often appeared before the consistory courts to give evidence. It is likely that the notaries would have consulted their notarial act books before giving oral testimony to the court, and that their oral evidence would often have been based on a copy of a written document, such as a secular contract. But although such act books survive from the Mediterranean regions, none has survived from Northern Europe.[5]

SELF-REGULATION IN PRACTICE: THE CAMEYS CASE (ROLLS OF PARLIAMENT, 1302)

I begin with a case that came before a secular court rather than an ecclesiastical one, namely, Parliament. If we accept the distinction between the two types of contract, respectively spiritual and secular, may we assume that secular courts dealt exclusively with secular contracts whereas ecclesiastical courts (i.e., the consistories) dealt exclusively with spiritual contracts? For the most part, the answer is yes, but the separation was not watertight. On the one hand, secular courts sometimes pronounced on the validity of a marriage bond (supposedly the exclusive domain of the spiritual contract and episcopal courts). On the other hand, litigants sometimes used the ecclesiastical courts to enforce the payment of dower (the property that a husband had named as belonging to his wife when marrying her) or of a dowry (the property that the wife brought with her to the marriage) – matters that a secular contract would have defined.

In the case that Margaret Cameys, the widow of John Cameys (a southern magnate), brought before parliament, not only did a secular court reject the decision of church courts regarding a marriage, but the lay parties in the case were sufficiently aware of the rules and instruments of law to try to use them for their own purposes. Parliament heard the Cameys case in 1302, and it was published in the 1782 *Rolls of Parliament*.[6] I have appended to this chapter a translation of the complete record, which, as always, was in Latin (see Appendix A).

The first scholar to refer to the case and to quote extracts from it was Frederic Maitland. Maitland took Parliament's summary as his point of departure for a robust declaration of how the Catholic church should not meddle in affairs of marriage.[7] Other extracts from the case have been printed in *English Historical Documents* and in Jennifer Ward's collection of sources for the history of women in

---

[5] Remarkably little is known about secular notaries in England. The most extensive study is C. R. Cheney, *Notaries Public in England in the Thirteenth and Fourteenth Centuries* (Oxford, 1972). An interesting but uneven study (which is not limited to Denmark) is Ole Fenger, *Notarius publicus: Notaren i latinsk middelalder* (Århus, 2000).

[6] Rotuli parliamentorum; ut et petitiones, et placita in parliamento in tempore Edwardi R. I, = vol. 1 of J. Topham et al. (eds.), Rotuli parliamentorum; ut et petitiones, et placita in parliamento (1275–1503) (London, 1783), 140–41.

[7] Frederick Pollock and Frederick W. Maitland, *The History of English Law before the Time of Edward I*, vol. 2 (Cambridge, 1909). Maitland's conclusion to the case reads (396): "After reading this judgment it is difficult to believe that ecclesiastical courts were preeminently fit to administer the law of marriage and divorce."

the Middle Ages.[8] None of these three translations reproduced the entire case, however, and therefore all three missed important legal points. A complete translation was not available until quite recently.[9]

The case concerned parts of the estate left by Sir John Cameys (1255–99) and the rights of his wife, Margaret, the daughter of John of Gatesden.[10] The documents reproduced in the *Rolls of Parliament* suggest that a marital breakdown between John and Margaret occurred when John was about thirty years of age. Their marital crisis coincided with the passing of the Second Statute of Westminster (1285), the thirty-fourth chapter of which stipulated that if a wife left her husband and was not reconciled with him (i.e., did not resume cohabitation and marital relations), then, regardless of intervention by the church, she was to forfeit her rights to her dower. The statute was a direct challenge to the jurisdiction of the church. It was also the basis of a legal challenge to Margaret's dower rights after John's death.

The exact dates of the events in the Cameys case are uncertain, and some of the circumstances are unclear. The written documents copied by Parliament include a letter of quitclaim that John Cameys had written some years before 1295 regarding her dower. In this letter, he allowed Margaret to retain all her goods and chattels (but not her lands), and he released her to the care of William Paynell, another Southern magnate. The letter shows that John regarded his marriage to Margaret as a matter that could be regulated privately, without recourse to the church. In a letter of 1289 John Cameys transferred all rights to the lands that he held in Sussex by right of his wife (i.e., her dower lands) to William Paynell for a period of one hundred years at a price of 100 marks. It is not clear whether the letter of quitclaim was a consequence of this transfer of the rights regarding Margaret's lands. (The quitclaim may, indeed, have predated the letter of 1289.)

These lands were probably the occasion for the unusual plea that Margaret and William Paynell presented before Parliament in 1302. John had died in 1299, and soon afterwards Margaret and William celebrated their nuptials. John Cameys had held lands from the crown, and one must presume that, as was standard practice at the time, the crown instituted a postmortem inquiry (*inquisitio post mortem*) into his holdings. This inquiry would have drawn attention to the unusual triangular relationship that had existed between John and Margaret Cameys and William Paynell. As a consequence, a royal claim threatened William's possession of Margaret's lands in Sussex.

---

[8] H. Rothwell (ed.), *English Historical Documents*, vol. 3: *1189–1327* (London, 1955), 448–49. Jennifer Ward (ed. and trans.), *Women of the English Nobility and Gentry, 1066–1500* (Manchester, 1995), 62–63.

[9] A new edition of the Parliamentary Rolls, with facing-page translations, has recently appeared on CD-ROM: C. Given-Wilson et al. (eds. and trans.), *The Parliament Rolls of Medieval England, 1275–1504* (Leicester, 2005). The translation of the Cameys case in the appendix, by Paul Brand, is taken from this edition.

[10] She died in 1313 and is buried in Trutton, Sussex. A monumental brass with her effigy can be seen at the following site: http://www.mbs-brasses.co.uk/pic_lib/Margaret_de_Camoys.htm.

In 1302, William and Margaret petitioned Parliament for the return of Margaret's dower lands, which consisted of "one third of the manor of Torpell with appurtenances." In support of their claim to enjoy rights over the estate as a married couple, and to demonstrate that Margaret had a claim to the lands in question, William and Margaret produced certificates from the bishop of Chichester and the archbishop of Canterbury showing that, while John was still alive, Margaret had been called before the consistory court in Chichester and William before the consistory court of Canterbury in 1288 to answer defamatory charges of adultery. They had defended themselves successfully. Margaret had been called to the court on the Saturday before the Purification of the Virgin 1296. Before the Dean and Treasurer of the cathedral and several other clerics and lay persons, she had denied and successfully compurgated herself of the crime of adultery with the help of the ladies Margaret Martel, Isabella Montfort (who was the prioress of the Augustinian priory of in Easebourne in Sussex), Hawisia Houtot, A. Corbet, and some other married women and ladies-in-waiting.[11]

In view of the value of the lands and rents that might be due to the crown as a consequence of John's death, it is not surprising that Parliament regarded the decision of the two church courts with suspicion and decided to uphold the secular laws entailed by the Second Statute of Westminster. Parliament found it impossible to believe that Margaret and William had lived together while John was alive without consummating their relationship.

Although this case concerns the dissolution of a contract rather than the formation of one, it sheds an interesting light not only on the marital ideology of John Cameys but also on the way in which the English Parliament regarded the institution of marriage and the respective jurisdictions of church and crown. The statute of Westminster had already subverted the distinction between secular and ecclesiastical jurisdictions. Its intention was to regulate marital behavior by punishing a wife who committed adultery or deserted her husband with a secular punishment: the loss of her dower.

In this case, the validity of the second marriage was not challenged. Parliament recognized that a legal marriage existed between William and Margaret. The case turned on whether they had committed adultery before John died. If they had done so, the argument went, her dower was forfeit. And in this respect Parliament explicitly rejected the verdict of the church that Margaret and William had *not* committed adultery.

Parliament could have gone further by asking the church to ascertain whether an "impediment of crime" had occurred, for the record stated that Margaret had

---

[11] William's letter from Canterbury simply stated that the church had investigated the claim of adultery and found him innocent: see *Rotuli Parliamentorum*, vol. 1, 141. The role of the named oath-helpers, married women, and ladies-in-waiting (*domicellae quamplures convicinae*) would have been like that of character witnesses today. Their function was to give general evidence as to the regularity of the union. Therefore they would not have given detailed evidence about the facts of the matter but, rather, would have testified that they did not believe Margaret and William were living in adultery.

intended to marry William when John died. If proven, that intention could have invalidated her second marriage. Yet despite its clear rejection of the church courts' acquittal of Margaret and William, Parliament chose not to challenge the validity of the marriage itself. Parliament's thinking here is quite understandable. On the one hand, the king's Parliament could not dictate to the church when to investigate a marriage case. Moreover, Parliament (or the royal exchequer of King Edward I) stood to gain little financially from pursuing this aspect of the case. On the other hand, Margaret and William seem to have kept within the bounds of canon law by not publicly declaring their intention to marry before John had died. Yet, in spite of the cautious language designed to avoid challenging the church's authority directly, Parliament flatly contradicted the findings of two church courts and applied its own understanding of the rules for marital conduct. Parliament judged that Margaret's and William's living arrangements had been implicitly adulterous, and that this was an unacceptable state of affairs that should have severe economic consequences.

The case confirms that, at least in the early fourteenth century, there were still clear differences between the lay and ecclesiastical understandings of marriage. John Cameys was entirely confident that marriage was a secular matter for him and his wife to regulate: he believed that it was up to him to decide whether to separate from his wife, and he drew up a legal document intended to clear the way for the separation. His wife and her partner seem to have agreed with him.

The three of them should have been successful: the church courts in Canterbury and Chichester had applied the high and ancient evidential rules of the church and demanded that the parties purge themselves from the accusations of adultery, not by swearing themselves (which might have made them perjurers) but through oath-helpers. Yet the lay tribunal required a different standard of proof. The compurgation of the parties, performed during the lifetime of Margaret's first husband, may have satisfied the church courts, but reasonably enough, Parliament was not willing to believe that Margaret and William lived a chaste life together while John was alive. Parliament was more inclined to admit "common sense" into consideration than the episcopal courts had been.

However one interprets the different outcomes in the two tribunals, the proceedings testify to lay people's confidence in their own right to regulate their marriage affairs without the interference of any court, whether secular or ecclesiastical. They also show how the three parties used negotiations and contracts, both oral and written, to settle marital matters that lay outside the focus of the spiritual contracts investigated by the consistory courts. John, Margaret, and William used written contracts to transfer Margaret's dower to her future second husband. This was not a matter of interest to the consistory courts of Chichester and Canterbury, but Parliament, which had a wider interpretation of the meaning of marriage, was certainly interested in such arrangements. Moreover, Parliament used other evidence collected by (but not of interest to) the consistory courts, as well as the quitclaim that John Cameys had written, to determine that William and Margaret's claim was false.

INDENTURED CONTRACTS: *PERCY C. COLVYLE* (CP E 12)

We have seen that in the Cameys case, a secular court rejected the written decisions of two church courts regarding an accusation of adultery. We turn now to another English case that subverted the barrier between secular and spiritual jurisdictions. Like the rest of the cases investigated in this essay, CP E 12 is preserved among the "cause papers" kept in the Borthwick Institute in York, which houses the provincial archives of the medieval archdiocese.[12] The series of cause papers (the preserved dossiers of cases heard before the York consistory courts), which begins in the year 1300, includes a case between Alexander Percy and Robert Colvyle heard in 1312.

The case was the consequence of the marriage of two noble children, John Percy and Elizabeth Colvyle. Their parents had agreed to the marriage in 1305, while the children were still underage. The children confirmed their marriage when they reached the age of discretion, but Elizabeth died approximately eighteen months later. Her father argued that Elizabeth's premature death released him from his obligation to pay her dowry.

The litigants in this case were not the spouses themselves but their fathers: Lord Alexander Percy and his tenant, Robert Colvyle. The cause papers mention oral marriage negotiations, a written secular contract, and an oral spiritual contract. For good measure, some witnesses added cohabitation as evidence for their belief in the existence of a legal marriage. The lay courts could have dealt with a case of nonpayment of dowry, yet Alexander Percy pleaded in an ecclesiastical court to enforce a secular contract and the payment of a sum of money. Another surprising aspect of the case is that the secular contract included specific noneconomic conditions that had to be met: The parties' children were to contract marriage (i.e., to conclude the spiritual contract), but they also had to cohabit for a period of at least two years. Hence a secular contract regulated the spiritual contract and the marital behavior that would follow it.

The Percy and Colvyle families had had a long-lasting association with each other – the Colvyle family had held Wheldrake manor from the Percys since 1086[13] – but it was in 1305 that the parents of John and Elizabeth agreed that the two children should marry, even though they were still underage at the time of the contract. It should be emphasized that the contract in question was between the parents. Because the agreement was complicated and economically significant, the parties

---

[12] The cases are calendared in D. M. Smith, *Ecclesiastical Cause Papers at York: The Court at York 1301–1399*, Borthwick Texts and Calendars 14 (York, 1988). The history of the archive is the subject of two articles by K. M. Longley: "Towards a history of archive-keeping in the Church of York: I The Archbishop's Muniments," *Borthwick Institute Bulletin* 1, no. 2 (1976): 59–75; and "Towards a history of archive-keeping in the Church of York: II The Capitular Muniments," *Borthwick Institute Bulletin* 1, no. 3 (1976): 103–19.

[13] See William Page (ed.), *Victoria County History of the County of Yorkshire* (= vol. 2 of *Victoria County History of England*) (London, 1913), 167, 262, and 293.

drew up a marriage contract in the form a written indenture[14] that was sealed in the manor of Sneton.[15] Although they are not mentioned by any of the witnesses, there must have been legal experts present at the drawing up of the contract between the Percy and Colvyle families: not only were the stipulations complex, but the means of preserving them included the legal form of an indenture. This could hardly have taken place without the presence of *jurisperiti*. The children's marriage contract became the subject of litigation in York in 1312, when Alexander Percy pursued a case of nonfulfillment of the dowry, for in the meantime Elizabeth had died. Between them, the parties produced eleven witnesses for the court, four of whom had been present at the marriage negotiations seven years earlier.

The libel of the case laid out Alexander Percy's position in detail:[16] that Robert Colvyle and Alexander Percy had agreed that John, Alexander's son and future heir, should contract marriage with Robert's heir, his daughter Elizabeth; that the children had contracted marriage later and had cohabited; that Robert promised to give Alexander 124 marks as Elizabeth's dowry and not for anything else; that Alexander should endow John and Elizabeth with the rents and incomes from a number of villages to the value of twenty-five marks annually; that Alexander had done so and had fulfilled everything else that the contract required; and that Alexander was to receive the 124 marks (the dowry) for the use and property of his son John, and not to pay off any existing debt. Alexander also alleged that Robert had acknowledged the debt "in the court of York" and had agreed that the money (the dowry) was to be paid to Alexander for his use.

Robert responded with a two-pronged defense. First, Elizabeth had not received the dower that had been agreed with Robert's express and voluntary consent. Second, the marriage was invalid for two reasons: Elizabeth had not been Robert's heir when the marriage contract was made, and John had been underage at the time of the contract.[17]

Alexander Percy's witnesses provided a more detailed description of the contents of the contract: it had stipulated that Sir Alexander would endow the couple with

---

[14] An indenture is a written contract, drawn up in two parts, one to be kept by each party. The text of the contract was written twice on a single piece of parchment, which was then divided by a jagged or indented cut. The two parts could be matched together as physical proof of authenticity.

[15] CPE12 (Walter de Yelmesley): "...conventum exitum et concordatum in tractatu." I have been unable to identify the modern-day name for Sneton, but I should suggest Stetton, which is near York. The CP (= "Cause Papers") references are those of the Borthwick archives.

[16] The libel is the plaintiff's initial written statement of his or her case.

[17] It is impossible to say whether this acknowledgment of the obligation to pay the money was heard before a lay or an ecclesiastical court. However, when the case was heard in 1312, Alexander produced three witnesses who confirmed that a written contract in the form of an indenture had been drawn up and sealed. The fourth witness, Walter Lange from Grimsby, does not mention the indentured written contract: he explained to the court that he saw the parties exchange vows seven or eight years earlier and that they contracted with "customary words, concerning which he does not recall at present [*verba consueta de quibus non recolit ad presens*]." But his deposition is in a poor state of preservation and its last part is missing. He may therefore have intended to indicate that he, too, saw a written marriage contract, as the other three witnesses had done.

the rents of the villages of Crathorn and Burton le Wald.[18] The couple received the income from the rents at once, whereas Robert Colvyle was to begin payment of the dowry after the marriage had been confirmed at the children's ages of discretion. The witnesses do not comment on the fact that this event was still five and a half years in the future at the time of the contract. Nevertheless, when John and Elizabeth did reach their ages of discretion, they lived together for eighteen months in several manors belonging to the Percy family in Crathorn, Ormesby, and Sneton. But Elizabeth died before two years had passed, and on her death Robert Colvyle had still not paid her dowry as he had promised.

The court in York, like most other church courts, was interested only in the oral narrative of witnesses, and not in written evidence. In the Cameys case Parliament saw, examined, copied, and filed both the written evidence of the spiritual courts and John Cameys's secular letter of quitclaim. But the consistory court in York did not wish to examine the written indenture. Even the evidence admitted for the existence of the indenture was purely oral: the witnesses testified to having *seen* the indenture, and in some cases they commented that they had its content explained to them. We are therefore hampered in our analysis of the contract.

Like the Cameys case, CP E 12 gives us a glimpse into the way wealthy Englishmen received, understood, and applied the law of marriage in the fourteenth century. Despite the probable involvement of legal experts, Robert Colvyle had the same attitude to the law as John Cameys: he attempted to interpret it to his own advantage. Robert Colvyle's nonpayment of the sum of money stipulated in the contract was a result of his own interpretation of the contract. Furthermore, despite the fact that the case revolved around the existence of a secular contract, the episcopal court in York was happy to hear this case.

THE SHADOWY PRESENCE OF EXPERTS: *WAGHEN* AND DEL *GARTH C. NEWTON* (CP E 245)

John Cameys and Robert Colvyle evidently regarded themselves as legal experts, but it is difficult to discern the presence of *professional* legal experts in the cause papers. Nevertheless, as the following case shows, their presence does become apparent if one looks carefully enough.

The decision to marry was an occasion fraught with great potential for things to go wrong. Therefore, the parties (or their parents or guardians) frequently tried to safeguard contracts by employing experts to negotiate the terms of the marriage and to witness the exchange of vows. (I discuss the role of experts subsequently.) The case of Agnes Waghen, a widow of York, and Thomas del Garth, a citizen of the same city, provides a glimpse of such marriage negotiations and contracts. They agreed to their marriage on the Saturday before the Purification of the Virgin

---

[18] Present-day Burton Leonard.

(January 28) 1391 in a house near Ouse Bridge in York that belonged to Agnes's father, Master William Cawod. The witness Master William Donnington typified the attitude that prevailed among the witnesses to marriage contracts. He dismissed "William Burton's clerk," one of the crucial witnesses to the contract, in an off-hand manner. William Burton himself was also interrogated about the event, but Donnington was the only witness to mention the clerk. Donnington (or the court scribe) distinguishes between the status of the clerk and that of the witnesses and parents: the latter are joined as a group by the conjunction *ac*, whereas the clerk is joined to this group with the stronger conjunction *et*: I have signaled this in the translation by adding parentheses and the word "also":

Concerning the first article he says that on the Saturday after the Purification of the Virgin just past, between the fifth and sixth stroke on the bell in the dwelling house of said William Cawod, the carnal father of said Agnes, in the presence of Master William Burton, Henry Sutton, the fellow witnesses of this witness; William Rufford, a butcher; and the father and mother of said Agnes (and also the clerk of said William Burton), said Thomas and Agnes contracted marriage with each other, with said Thomas taking her by the hand and saying, "here I accept thee, Agnes, as my wife and I give thee my pledge to this!" and her responding, "here I accept you as my man and I give you my pledge to this!"[19] And they stretched out their hands and kissed each other, and said Thomas placed a ring upon the finger of said Agnes, while she performed and received all these actions freely with a good face and great harmony and with a happy heart.[20]

The quality and learning of the small company of witnesses at this comparatively low-key occasion are beyond doubt. The exact number of witnesses to the exchange of vows is unclear, but in addition to William Cawod, the bride's father (who was a proctor of the court in York), five witnesses to the exchange were produced before the court: *magister* William Donnington, who was the master of the hospice of St. Mary's monastery by Bootham; William Burton, the vicar of St. Mary's, Bishopshill; two citizens of York; and the aforementioned "William Burton's clerk."

Unusually, it is possible to provide biographies both for the plaintiff herself and for most of the witnesses she produced. These biographies may explain why the consistory court regarded William Burton's clerk (who was presumably there to

---

[19] As is common in the York material, the contracting parties here used a mixture of formal and informal address: the man addressed the woman with the informal pronoun "thou," but the woman addressed him with the formal "you."

[20] Master William Donnington in CPE245: "Super primo articulo dicit quod die sabbati proximo post purificationem beate Marie virginis ultimo preteritum, inter [quintam] et sextam pulsationem campanili in domo habitationis dicti Willelmi Cawod, patris carnalis dicte Agnete, presentibus domino Willelmo de Burton, Henrico de Sutton, contestibus suis, Willelmo Rufford, carnifice ac patre et matre dicte Agnete et clerico dicti Willelmi de Burton, dicti Thomas et Agnes matrimonium adinvicem contraxerunt, dicto Thoma capiente eam per manum dexteram et dicente 'ego accipio te, Agnetam, in uxorem meam et ad hoc do tibi fidem meam,' et ipsa respondente, 'hic accipio vos in virum meum et ad hoc do vobis fidem meam' et strinxerunt manus et osculati [sunt] adinvicem et dictus Thomas imposuit anulum super digitum ipsius Agnetis, ipsa sponte et cum bona vultu et magna constantia et leto corde omnia predicta faciente et recepiente."

write down the terms of the contract) as relatively unimportant. Agnes Waghen was described in the libel as a widow. As such, she was probably a relatively wealthy woman. We do not know who her late husband was, but she was the daughter of William Cawod, who was a proctor of the consistory court and (at that time) the vicar general of the archdeaconry of Richmond.[21] William Cawood was an up-and-coming man in York: he held a licentiate in both laws, and a few years later he was appointed official of the episcopal court in York. From there he rose to become the archbishop's chancellor and one of the most influential members of his household.[22]

Because he was trained in law, William Cawod made certain that his daughter's second marriage was as unassailable as possible. In order to safeguard his daughter's choice of partner, he invited William Donnington and William Burton to the occasion. William's status as master of the hospice at St. Mary's made him a valuable witness to the contract. Although we can say little about their academic training, Donnington and Burton would certainly have had a good knowledge of the liturgical offices and would have been well acquainted with the church's teaching on marriage. They were probably personal friends of William Cawood, the bride's father (although the monastery of St. Mary's itself was the setting for many marriage contracts). As we have seen, William Burton, who was the vicar of the Church of St. Mary's (Bishopshill) and would therefore have been thoroughly familiar with the ritual of marriage, brought along his clerk. The clerk's function is not described, but he was probably there to notarize the marriage. He, too, was presumably familiar with marriage law.

The groom, Thomas del Garth, probably invited two other persons recorded as present at the marriage: Henry Sutton, a spicer, and William Rufford, a butcher. They may have been his personal friends. It is unlikely that either had any formal training in the law of the church. Of the two, it seems that only Henry Sutton gave evidence to the court, and he was the least informative of all the witnesses. Nevertheless, the parties contracted marriage according to the rules of canon law, and they clearly had excellent legal advice.

As it turned out, all of this legal knowledge was needed to protect the marriage. Thomas del Garth had a competitor – a squire by the name of John Newton – who challenged the legality of Thomas's and Agnes's marriage on grounds of prior contract. His case was strong enough for the dispute to be heard before the consistory court in York. William Cawod's care in safeguarding the marriage paid off.

---

[21] See A. Hamilton Thompson (ed.), *The Registers of the Archdeaconry of Richmond, 1361–1477*, reprinted from the *Yorkshire Archaeological Journal*, vol. 25 (Kendal, 1900), no. 158; and K. F. Burns, "The Medieval Courts," vol. 1 of *The Administrative System of the Ecclesiastical Courts in the Diocese and Province of York*, unpublished manuscript, Leverhulme Research Scheme (York, 1962), 142.

[22] The chancellor was formally the head of the archbishop's chancery or secretariat, but by the beginning of the fourteenth century at York (as at Canterbury and the other English dioceses), the archbishop's chancellor was mainly an attendant *jurisperitus*, serving the archbishop both as legal adviser and as judicial deputy in the audience and on visitations. See Thompson, *The Registers*, no. 150; and Burns, "The Medieval Courts."

Of all the surviving fourteenth-century cases in York, this was the one that saw the speediest conclusion. Agnes's case was initiated on April 3 and lasted for fewer than three weeks, reaching its conclusion on April 23, when the court decided in favor of Anges Waghen and Thomas del Garth.

The evidence suggests that William Donnington had been invited to the marriage ceremony specifically as a witness. The occasion was certainly not a social one, for Donnington informed the court that he did not like Thomas del Garth. But like the other witnesses, he accepted that the marriage was contracted with the free consent of both parties:

Asked if he was the promoter or the mediator of this marriage contract between Thomas and Agnes, he says no, but that this contract displeased him. Asked if they contracted once or several times he says only this once insofar as he was present. Asked whether said contract was initiated freely and willingly and whether with the consent of the parents and without either guile or evil intent of either party, he says yes, in so far as it manifestly appeared.[23] Further asked whether he heard said Alice swear to any matrimonial contract between her and John Newton, he says no, but he heard her – in the house of said William Burton, his fellow witness on the above-mentioned Saturday, before above-mentioned marriage contract was had between said Thomas and Agnes – expressly swear against it.[24]

[23] That William Donnington chose his words with great care is clear from his answers to a series of questions that required him to clarify his legal definitions: "Questioned 'what is *fama*?' 'what is *notorium*?' 'what is *manifestum*?' he says that *fama* is common talk, *notorium* is that which is believed to be true, but *manifestum* is that which is publicly known, as the witness says. He is neither suborned nor corrupted to say this, nor does he care who prevails in this case, as the witness says. [*Super tertio et ultimo requisitus, dicit quod continet veritatem in forma qua superius depositus. Interrogatus quid est fama, quid notorium, quid manifestum, dicit quod fama est communis locutio, notorium est illud quod creditur esse verum, sed manifestum est quod publice cognoscitur, ut dicit iste juratus, nec est subornatus vel corruptus ad sic deponendum in ista causa, nec curat quis optineat in eadem, ut dicit*]." Here I have translated the phrase *publice cognoscitur* literally as "publicly known," but the sense may be "publicly investigated." The suggestion that a public investigation is required before a contract is "manifest" is interesting and deserves more research. See Charlton T. Lewis, *A Latin Dictionary Founded on Andrews' Edition of Freund's Latin Dictionary Revised, Enlarged, and in Great Part Rewritten*, in collaboration with Charles Short (Oxford, 1987), s.v. *cognosco*.

[24] "Interrogatus an fuit promotor vel mediator huius contractus [sic] matrimonialis inter dictum Thomam et Agnetam, dicit quod non, sed quod contractus ille sibi displicuit. Interrogatus an semel vel plures contraxerunt, dicit quod sola illa vice, quatenus sibi constabat. Interrogatus an libere et sponte dictus contractus matrimonialis fuit initus et an consensus parentum et absque dolo et fraude alicuius partium predictarum, dicit quod sic, ut sibi evidenter apparuit. Interrogatus ulterius an audivit dictam Agnetem aliquem contractum matrimonialem inter ipsam et Johannem de Neuton, competitorem, fateri, dicit quod non, sed audivit eam in domo dicti domini Willelmi de Burton contestis sui, die sabbati antedicti post horam nonam ipsius diei, ante contractum matrimonialem predictum inter prefatum Thomam et Agnetem habitum, exprisse diffiteri." The text continues: "Interrogatus de causa scientie, dicit quod presens fuit ac vidit et audivit omnia et singula de quibus superius deposuit. Super secundo articulo diligenter examinatus, dicit quod continet veritatem quam ad contractum matrimonalem [habitum inter] dictos Thomas et Agnetem, et hoc dicit se scire quia interfuit et audivit ipsam Agnetem confiteri sponte et libere huius contractum in domo ipsius Agnetis quamplures et in aliis locis in presentia Johannis de Beverlay, Dominum Willelmum de Ottelay et aliorum diversis locis et temporibus."

Donnington's testimony suggests, as do other records among the York cause papers, that the process of contracting a marriage went through two stages. The process was concluded with a "spiritual" marriage contract (usually expressed *per verba de praesenti*), which created the indissoluble bond of marriage. Such was the contract that took place in William Cawod's house. But the evidence of the transcript suggests that the process of this marriage took place in two different locations: *negotiations* concerning the marriage contract had taken place in William Burton's house, whereas the *contracting* of the marriage itself took place later in William Cawod's house. It is highly likely that the negotiations in William Burton's house had dealt with the secular aspects of the marriage and concluded in a secular, prospective contract (expressed *per verba de futuro*). For the casual mention that a "clerk" was present on the second occasion suggests that the previous meeting in William Burton's house had marked the conclusion of a "secular" contract, which the clerk would have written down. The same clerk attended the conclusion of the proceedings, but on the second occasion, his presence was relatively unimportant.

This case demonstrates two important features that occur in most of the marriages documented in the fourteenth-century York cause papers. First, there were usually marriage negotiations that occurred before a final contract of marriage was concluded. Second, such negotiations were intended to safeguard the parties. In this case – as in many other preserved cases – witnesses were present on both occasions to help with the marriage negotiations and to bear detailed witness as to their conclusion. Master William Donnington was one such person: he had been invited to participate in the earlier negotiations, and he presented his detailed testimony of the subsequent spiritual contract despite his expressed dislike of the groom.

THE EXPERTISE OF WITNESSES

Because marriage affected a large majority of the population, it is not surprising that most people had at least a rough understanding of the consequences of entering into a marriage contract. To the modern observer, perhaps the most surprising aspect of medieval marriage cases as they appear in the court records is the frequent presence of negotiators and trained legal representatives for the parties. As in all other matters, the experts' level of expertise varied, from the sophisticated to the frankly ludicrous, as did their confidence in their own legal ability. But there seems to have been an easily accessible "pool of experts" whose services people frequently employed.

Marriage contracts could be complex, and in an effort to safeguard themselves, parties would ask such experts for help. Clerics or notaries witnessed many contracts: among approximately 560 witnesses whose accounts are preserved in the fourteenth-century York cause papers, 139 told the court what their occupation was. By far the largest group among these witnesses is made up of clerics: sixty-nine of them were active in the church in one capacity or other, of whom twenty-two were chaplains and sixteen were unspecified *clerici*. Among the remaining thirty-one clerics, six were parish priests, five were notaries public, and several were nuns, monks, and members of the courts.[25] The court's recording of the witnesses' occupations appears to have been a relatively late innovation: most of the information dates from the last three decades of the fourteenth century. If the first decades of the courts' existence conformed to the same trends, almost half of the witnesses heard by the courts were clerics of some sort, whether priests, notaries, nuns, or monks.

It is likely that the reason for this preponderance of clerics is that the court and the litigants themselves felt that their evidence carried a certain professional value. Litigants and courts alike assumed that because of their status, clerics would know which words created a legally binding marriage. Furthermore, as we saw in the case of the witness William Donnington mentioned earlier, their training made them sensitive to the subtle meanings of words, to the legal consequences of the vows that they heard, and to the significance of the words that their testimony passed on to the court. The partners getting married (or their parents) often called on such experts to recite the vows that made a marriage legally binding, so that by repeating them the parties could contract their marriage with exactly the legal consequences they sought. It was much to the advantage of litigants that courts took the existence of a marriage for granted if a cleric testified to it. Among the surviving recorded decisions of the court in York, there is no case in which the court ruled against the proper formation of a marriage when a priest or notary public testified that he had been present at an exchange of marriage vows in words of the present tense (*verba de praesenti*). If a cleric testified to his knowledge of the celebration of a marriage, the York court dissolved the marriage only if there were some proven impediment such as force and fear, consanguinity, or legal incapacity.

What Did Written Marriage Contracts Regulate?

It should come as no surprise that almost all the litigants who argued for the existence of a marriage claimed that the words of consent conformed almost verbatim to a standard pattern. Cause paper libels demonstrate the existence of a clear (if somewhat rough) understanding of the basics of the law, and the historian does well to notice when the words that were exchanged deviated from the standard

---

[25] The list of sixty-nine clerics may be divided thus: sixteen unspecified *clerici*, twenty-two chaplains, six vicars, five notaries public by apostolic authority (four of whom also described themselves as *clerici*, but I have not counted them among that group here), three clerks, three vicars choral, two guardians of hospitals (St. Mary's, Bootham, and St. Giles, Beverley), two nuns, two monks, one canon, one abbot (of St. Mary's Abbey, York), one clerk of the vestibule, one former official of the East Riding, one *janitor*, one *magister*, one *presbyter*, and one registrar of the court.

form. But as part of their collection of evidence, the courts were also interested in establishing *why* the witnesses had been present at the exchange of vows. Evidence from these parts of the depositions often provides further indications (albeit never a complete example) of what the parties had agreed to apart from their willingness to spend the rest of their lives together.

The following cases give some sense of what the parties tried to do by means of such negotiations and through related contracts, whether oral or written. This impressionistic evidence can provide some idea of what marriage meant to the parties and how they put safeguards around the marriage bond. These cases also confirm that there was not, as historians generally assume, a watertight separation between the secular and spiritual aspects of marriage.

Protecting a Young Girl's Virginity: Marrays c. Roucliff (CP E 89)

It was common for marriage contracts between the youngest litigants in the cause papers to be safeguarded by a contract between the intending groom and the bride's parents, or between the parents of the intending parties. We have already seen an example of this practice in the *Percy* c. *Colvyle* case. Many examples could be cited, but I have chosen the York case CP E 89, *Marrays* c. *Roucliff* (1364–65), in which the families negotiated a marriage contract when the bride was around nine or ten years of age. The documents of the case tell us how the contract was negotiated and witnessed by many people, and how the other members of the Marrays *familia* regarded the contract.[26] In several respects, however, the circumstances and the chain of events are obscure.

Because the parties to the agreement expected the girl to live in the household of the groom's sister, where the groom already lived, it is not surprising that the girl's mother was concerned to protect her physical well-being. It transpired during the case that the groom, John Marrays, had entered into an agreement with the bride's mother while the bride, Alice Roucliff, was still underage whereby he promised that he would not have sexual intercourse with Alice until she was ready. The parties safeguarded the promise by making John agree to pay a substantial fine if he did not wait until after the time to which he and Alice's mother had agreed. It is not clear when John and Alice's mother entered into this agreement, but it functioned as a condition added to the original contract. Because there was no basis in canon law for such a stipulation (with its penalty clause), we should regard it as a secular agreement, but the consummation of a marriage was a matter that was squarely within the purview of the canon law and ecclesiastical jurisdiction.

The case first came before the York consistory court at some time before September 27, 1365. On the latter date, the first business day after the court's summer recess, the court appointed Edward Cornwall, one of the court's proctors, as a guardian

---

[26] This case is extremely long and complex. Extensive excerpts are published in P. J. P. Goldberg (ed. and trans.), *Women in England c. 1275–1525: Documentary Sources*, Manchester Medieval Sources (Manchester, 1995), 58–80.

for Alice, the teenage daughter of Gervase Roucliff (or Roucliffe). Three weeks later, on October 14, the issue was joined in a written libel. The plaintiff in the case was the alleged husband, John Marrays, who wanted the court to uphold the marriage. He claimed in his libel that he had married Alice by words of present consent in the presence of the parents and family (*amici*) and with their express consent. He also maintained that she had "ratified" the contract on that occasion and by subsequent actions, and that Alice had later confirmed her intention, in front of several witnesses, to go through with the union "legally." John and his legal team were at pains to argue that Alice had reached the age of puberty when she confirmed the contract, but they do not state her age in years. The evidence of witnesses suggests that John was less certain of the legal status of the confirmed marriage than he made out in the libel. The basic legal issue might have been a fairly simple one of nonage, but there were also the rather unusual circumstances of the condition attached to the marriage agreement and provisions for a fine in the event of nonadherence to the contract. Moreover, the court seems to have been more concerned with whether Alice freely consented to the union than with her age.

The court interrogated twenty-three witnesses who appeared for John from November 16 to mid-December 1365.[27] They testified that John and Alice had celebrated marriage in front of witnesses at about Christmastime in 1364; that they had spent a night together in the nuptial bed; that they behaved like a married couple; and that Alice had been of sufficient age to contract marriage. One witness – John's sister, Annabile, the wife of Stephen Wastelyn – told the court how the ceremony had taken place in front of many witnesses in the room called "the Steward's chamber" in St. Mary's monastery in York.[28] Gervase, Alice's father, was not present. Among the witnesses produced before the court was a certain Master William Marrays, who was the abbot of the monastery, although he did not tell the court about the marriage contract itself and may not have been present at the conclusion of the contract. This ceremony seems to have been the occasion on which Alice confirmed the marriage, by which time she was supposedly of age.[29] But it becomes clear from the evidence that the import of the ceremony was unclear in the minds of both partners.

Most important among those present were Richard Bernard, in whose room the exchange took place; Master Adam Thornton, who was a notary public by apostolic authority; Alice's mother, Elena; and Robert Roucliff, who was presumably Alice's uncle. Richard Bernard had presided over the exchange of vows and prompted the

---

[27] The last recorded date for the interrogation of these witnesses is December 8, but a further four witnesses were heard before January 1366.

[28] Goldberg does not reproduce Annabile's evidence in *Women in England.*

[29] Unfortunately, we do not know when this time was supposed to arrive: even the plaintiff is not consistent in his application criteria for maturity: John's legal arguments sometimes mention that Alice had reached puberty, sometimes that she was twelve years of age.

parties with the correct words to be used. He could therefore confidently assert that the marriage had been contracted by *verba de presenti*. Richard Bernard's evidence suggests that the marriage was concluded at this early stage only because Alice's father, Gervase, was dying at the time.[30] The court paid special attention to the issue of whether Alice had been forced to contract against her will. Richard Bernard informed the court that Alice had contracted freely and with a happy face.[31] Alice's aunt, Katherine, the wife of Robert Roucliff, had been especially concerned about whether Alice understood the implications of marrying John. Alice had stayed with Katherine on the night before the marriage in St. Mary's, and Katherine had repeatedly inquired whether she was happy with the arrangements made. According to Katherine's testimony, "this witness then asked the same Alice if she was in good will to go away from her mother to Kennythorp, and she responded that 'yes' because she wanted, as she said, to go to any place where John wanted to send her."[32]

After the ceremony, the partners lay together in the same bed for at least one entire night on the night of the feast of the apostle Thomas (December 21, 1364) to ratify the marriage.[33] Master William Marrays, the abbot of St. Mary's, explained to the court that the parties had confirmed to him, and that he had had it confirmed as well by Alice's bedfellow (*socia in lecto*), that the two did attempt to go through with intercourse.[34]

After Christmas, Alice stayed in Annabile's household until the feast of St. James (July 25, 1365). During her stay at the Wastelyn estate she was widely regarded as John's wife because she continued to accept gifts from John "as if she were his wife." There can be little doubt that people both at the Wastelyn estate and elsewhere regarded her as such, but what behaving as his wife entailed is not entirely clear. Although the union created in the monastery of St. Mary was contracted, according

---

[30] His use of the phrase "Alicia, dudum filia Gervasii de Roucliff" probably indicates as much.

[31] CPE89 (Richard Bernard): "Fuerunt presentes in camera dicti jurati infra scepta monasterii beate Marie Eboracensis Johannes Marras, Alicia dudum filia Gervasii de Roucliff, dominus Adam de Thornton, Elena, mater carnalis dicte Alicie, Robertus de Roucliff et iste juratus, ubi et quum Johannes et Alicia matrimonium adinvicem per verba de presenti contraxerunt.... Et dicit in juramento suo quod dicta Alicia voluntarie et cum bona vultu ac nullius vi vel metu ducta contraxit ut supra deposuit."

[32] CPE89: "Et ipsa jurata interrogavit tunc eandem Aliciam an fuit in bona voluntate eundi apud Karthorp ab matre sua et illa respondit quod sic quia voluit ut dicit ire ad quemcumque locum ubi dictus Johannes voluit eam mitere." For a freer translation, see Goldberg, *Women in England*, 70.

[33] CPE89 (Annabile Wastelyn). William Marrays, the abbot of St. Mary's monastery in York, provided the court with the precise date: the night of the feast of the apostle Thomas (December 21, 1364). Annabile Wastelyn was less precise: cf. Goldberg, *Women in England*, 60–61, 63.

[34] Sleeping arrangements in the Middle Ages were very different from those of today. Beds were usually shared, and in some cases it is clear that the arrangements were longstanding. Both this case and CPE259 document a *socia in lecto* (literally, a [female] bedfellow). A *socia* naturally shared much knowledge about her fellow's emotional life. Such *sociae* may have been servants in the household, but they were roughly the same age as their partners.

to most witnesses, with legally binding words in the present tense, it is clear that to the inhabitants of the estate there was something not quite right about the contract. This may be why they looked for visible demonstrations of Agnes's consent to the union. Her acceptance of John's gifts (which were mundane) was clearly one such indicator.

The abbot of St. Mary's monastery in York, William Marrays, introduced evidence of another sort. He explained to the court that he had been told by Alice's bedfellow, Joanna de Rolleston (who was John's cousin),[35] and by John and Alice themselves, that the couple had intercourse at least two or three times in the countryside near the village of Grimston during the following Easter. Though the court in York interrogated Joanna, she had provided more details in conversation with William Marrays, to whom she reported that "she heard noises between them as if they were having intercourse and how Alice two or three times moaned quietly as if she had been hurt by the activity of the said John."[36]

Although the attempt clearly was painful to Alice, John's sister, Annabile Wastelyn, testified that Alice had been actively seeking the consummation of the marriage. Annabile explained that Alice had come to her, around the feast of the Epiphany,[37] and had explained to her that she and John had spent the night together, from bedtime to the next morning, in Annabile's house in Kennythorp. For this reason, Alice had requested that Annabile let the marriage be solemnized. "I am of sufficient age to be his wife, but not to be his lover," she exclaimed.[38] Instead of allowing Alice to continue speaking, Annabile asked her to wait and to repeat her statement to John when he returned home. Hence, later in the day, she repeated the request to John but added: "Master, I will not lie with you in bed any more until marriage is solemnized between us because I am sufficiently old that I might be your wife and not your 'friend' (in English: *lemman*)".[39]

---

[35] A certain *Alice* Rolleston, described in the deposition as a daughter of Annabile and more than fourteen years of age, gave evidence to the court on November 16. Although it is possible that the scribe who took down William Marray's deposition confused the name Johanna for Alice, William Marray's informant would appear not to have been the same as this Alice, given that Annabile Wastelyn also refers in her deposition to her daughter *Johanna*.

[36] CPE89 (William Marrays): "Audivit inter eosdem strepitum ad modum se adinvicem carnaliter cognoscentum et qualiter dicta Alicia bina vel trina vices reconquerabatur tacite propter opus dicti Johannis ac si fuisset tunc ex huius opere lesa." Compare with Goldberg, *Women in England*, 62, who translates "reconquerabatur tacite propter opus dicti Johannis" as "complained silently at the force on account of John's labor."

[37] The record specifies that date as a fortnight after the Saturday before Christmas.

[38] "Ego sum in sufficiente etate constituta et satis senex ad essendum uxor sed non amica sua, anglice *lemman*." CPE89 (Annabile Wastelyn). Compare Goldberg, *Women in England*, 70.

[39] CPE89 "Domine, ego nolo amplius jacere vobiscum in lecto antequam matrimonium sit inter nos solempnizatum quia satis sum senex ut sim uxor vestra et non amica, anglice *lemman*." Alice used the formal *vos* to address John. The word *amica* has a multitude of meanings, and the scribe was careful to put down the English word *lemman* to clarify its meaning: *lemman* has the clear connotation of a physical relationship. Goldberg, *Women in England*, 61 translates *amica* as "mistress," which is clearly the intended sense.

Annabile explained to the court that John had interrupted Alice and pointed out that he had entered into a contract with Alice's mother and kin according to which he would not consummate the marriage until a specific date. His statement implies that John regarded the marriage to be still *de futuro* even after the contract in St. Mary's and flatly contradicts not only Alice's mother[40] and the witnesses Adam Thornton and Richard Barnard (who were all at pains to point out that the marriage was contracted by *verba de praesenti*) but also the libel of the case. Annabile added that John also emphasized that he would have to pay a fine of "one hundred marks or pounds" to the family if he did not keep his side of the bargain.[41] The matter seems to have rested after this, although Alice clearly was dissatisfied and often repeated her wish that the question of the legality of the marriage be settled once and for all. Because the court was only interested in whether this incident proved that a binding marriage between John and Alice existed, it did not register Alice's reaction to John's statement. But according to John's witnesses, Alice did not protest and continued to accept gifts from John as if she was his wife.[42]

The witness accounts thus show considerable confusion about the legal status of the marriage. John Marrays (and possibly his sister as well) regarded the union as one that was yet to be confirmed, and Alice regarded it as incomplete and wanted to confirm it by having intercourse with John and by solemnization. As John saw it, the contract in the monastery of St. Mary's around Christmas 1364 was intended to protect Alice in her marriage, both from her husband and from herself. But how had this confusion come about? The circumstances of the marriage were unusual. Although many people appear to have attended the marriage at St. Mary's – one of them was even an apostolic notary – two, in particular, were conspicuous by their absence. One of these was William Marrays, the abbot of the monastery of St. Mary's and a member of the groom's family. In view of his status as abbot of the monastery of St. Mary's, it seems odd that he was not present at the contract. Notable, too, is the absence of Alice's father, Gervase Roucliff. Yet the latter's absence, and the seeming rush of the proceedings, may be explained if we take the descriptive phrase *dudum filia Gervasii de Roucliff* to mean that Alice's father was unexpectedly dying that Christmas. And the marriage then makes more sense as an emergency measure rushed into as a consequence of her father's unforeseen terminal illness: hence the ambiguity of Alice's age.

Alice was clearly confused by her new married state, and she shared that confusion with her alleged husband, John. We have already seen how John's sister,

---

[40] Goldberg, *Women in England*, 63, reproduces Alice's mother's deposition.

[41] CPE89/27 (Annabile Wastelyn): "Cui dictus Johannes respondit, dicens 'non dicas sic amplius. Tu scis conventionem inter matrem tuam et alios amicos tuos et me quod ego desponsabo te ad diem futuram ad quem ego servabo conventionem quia ego nolo perdere centum marcas vel centum libras'." Reproduced in Goldberg, *Women in England*, 61.

[42] For example, CPE89/27 (Annabile Wastelyn); William Marrays in Goldberg, *Women in England*, 61. Goldberg does not reproduce the part of William Marrays' deposition dealing with gifts.

Annabile, claimed that Alice actively sought her out and demanded that the marriage be consummated after the ceremony in the monastery of St. Mary in York. This demand was made despite the fact that John's uncle claimed to have been told by John and Alice and by Alice's bedfellow that John and Alice had, in fact, attempted to consummate the marriage. On the same occasion, John had spoken of an agreement that he would espouse her at some time in the future. Although we would probably not regard the attempted intercourse as consummation today, it could have been regarded as such by the fourteenth-century consistory court. Alice herself appears to have been unsure about the legal consequences of the attempt. We have already noted Alice's use of the English word *lemman*, which suggests that she was ashamed because she felt that she was John's mistress. But she went even further in her description of her status. William Potel, the carpenter on the Wastelyn estate who made the bed in which Alice and John were put after the ceremony in St. Mary's, related to the court how he became acquainted with her sharp tongue when he met Alice some time later. He asked her how she liked her new master. She replied that she was well satisfied, "and then this witness said to the said Alice: 'May you grow well so he can do to you what is fitting.' And she said, responding to him: 'I am fully sufficient to be his wife, but not to be his whore!'"[43] Alice's despair over her status is clearly evident in her use of the words *lemman* and (according to the Latin transcription) *meretrix* to describe what she did not want to be.

It is impossible to say what finally brought matters to a head, but at some point Lord Brian of Roucliff, an otherwise unknown local magnate, came to hear of the case.[44] Although he never appeared before the court, he clearly had an interest in Alice's fate. On July 25, 1365, during the summer recess of the York consistory court, his men rode to the Wastelyn estate and forcibly abducted Alice. The timing of the abduction seems to have been calculated to give Alice the longest possible breathing space away from John and his family, for it coincided almost perfectly with the York court's summer recess, and the case did not begin in earnest until after the court convened again in late September 1365.

It is clear that prior to the ceremony in St. Mary's, there had been negotiations about the terms of the marriage contract. Indeed, there had been an earlier contract (while Alice was still underage) to which a stipulation about consummation was appended, with a financial penalty clause. It is noticeable that the ceremony at St. Mary's was not the ostentatious, public occasion that one might have expected given the wealth of the parties. Perhaps this was because Alice's father was dying at the time. Among the many witnesses who gave evidence in the case was Adam

---

[43] CPE89 (William Pottel): "Et tunc dixit iste juratus eidem Alicia: 'crescas bene sic quod possit facere tecum sicut decet.' Ac illa sibi respondens dixit: 'Ego sum satis sufficiens ad essendam uxor sua, sed non meritrix sua'." Compare Goldberg, *Women in England*, 69–70.

[44] It is possible that Master Brian Roucliff was related to Alice. However, given that Rawcliff was one of the suburbs of York in the fourteenth century, it is probably that his surname was toponymic and that their sharing a name was merely coincidental.

Thornton, the apostolic notary. But, as we have come to expect from other cases, he only deposed on the subject of the spiritual contract that both lay and ecclesiastical guests had witnessed. Whatever was written down at any stage has now been lost, but, clearly, John respected the secular contract. It must have had "teeth" that would have helped to persuade him to observe it. He was certainly influenced by the prospect of having to pay what was undoubtedly a heavy fine for noncompliance with the stipulations of the contract.

The marriage contract between Alice Roucliff and John Marrays contained provisions that were intended to safeguard the interests of Alice. Indeed, the legal system did safeguard her, albeit with some difficulty, if, indeed, she wished to be his wife. Yet the outcome of the case as preserved in York is ambiguous. The court in York found for the validity of marriage, but the last document in the case, dated July 30, 1366, is a grant to Alice to take the case to the Apostolic See for an appeal.

Guaranteeing Fertility: Midelton and Frothyngham c. Welwyk (CP E 79)

Marriage contracts not only protected the interests of women. Robert Midelton persuaded Alice Welwyk (or Welewyke) to agree to a conditional contract whereby the marriage would be contingent on her conceiving by him within a year (see Appendix B). Robert Midelton's solution was creative and innovative, and the circumstances of the agreement regarding Alice differed in several respects from those considered previously. For one thing, the original contract had only one witness (for which reason alone, the court in York would have been predisposed to reject a claim for enforcement of the marriage), and that witness (Alice's servant) had little expert knowledge of canon law. Moreover, Robert made his pledge to her servant, and not to Alice Welwyk herself. The unusual agreement was well known in Beverley, and *Dominus* William Wetwang, a canon of Watre and chaplain of the hospital of St. Giles in Beverley, who was apparently a friend of Alice, was able to rehearse its terms to Robert when the latter and Alice sought William's advice.

There was another complication: Robert had married another (probably much wealthier) woman within a year of persuading Alice. Negotiations for the second contract were clearly complex and arduous, although the marriage itself was conventional and straightforward (see Appendix B.1). Many guests witnessed the subsequent marriage ceremony on April 17, 1351.[45]

The case progressed in York as follows: In late November 1358, Alice Welwyk appeared before the commissary general in York claiming that nine years earlier she had contracted marriage *per verba de futuro* with Robert Midelton, son of the late Henry Midelton of Bishop Burton, that they had subsequently had intercourse,

[45] CPE79 (Peter Frothyngham): "... [presentibus] tunc ibidem quampluribus bonis et gravis personis notis et amicis suis." *Dominus* Richard, the chaplain of Wynsted, explained that the wedding as well as the publication of the banns took place in Frysmersk, about a mile away from the Frothinghams' home, because the chapel there was large enough to hold all the guests: see Appendix B.2.

and that she had borne Robert Midelton a child. But Robert Midelton claimed to have contracted a valid marriage with Elizabeth Frothyngham, with the proper rites and with preceding marriage negotiations, eight years before the case was heard in York. Robert's unconventional contract with Alice had taken place before Easter in 1350: one year before his conventional marriage to Elizabeth, and nine years before the witnesses gave evidence to the court in York. If Alice's claims could be substantiated, Robert would be Alice's husband, and his marriage to Elizabeth would have to be annulled.

Robert had not wanted to marry Alice unless he could be sure that she would beget a child for him. Perhaps the recent outbreak of the plague had something to do his concerns. For a long time, between the feast of St. Michael (September 29, 1349) and the Saturday before Palm Sunday in the following year (i.e. March 20, 1350), he pleaded with Alice "in every manner that he could" to persuade her to have intercourse with him.[46] She resisted, insisting that they marry first. Because Robert did not want to marry her until he knew that she could become pregnant by him, he swore to marry her if she conceived their child. His precautions demonstrate that he had a precise knowledge of the canon law of marriage, and they show, too, his considerable cleverness in circumventing it. He explained that because he wanted to make sure that she could conceive by him, he could not promise to marry her, for if they exchanged a conditional vow and later had sex, they would be married as soon as they had intercourse regardless of any condition included in their vows. Instead, he suggested that he make the promise to someone else. Alice Welwyk agreed to this and summoned her servant, Alice Harpham, to receive Robert's oath that he would marry her (Alice Welwyk) if she conceived.

Their relationship lasted for just under a year. During that year Robert met Elizabeth Frothyngham and initiated marriage negotiations with her family. The family was unquestionably wealthy: the conclusion of the marriage negotiations and the contract *per verba de praesenti* took place in the private chapel of Amadus (or Hamadus) Frothyngham, and the solemnization of the marriage occurred three weeks later at Frysmersk, in the presence of more than one hundred guests. People knew about it in all the neighboring villages.[47] The witnesses do not say how long it took for the parties to agree on a marriage contract, but the record of Amadus Frothyngham's relief when he "finally" sent for a chaplain shows that the negotiations were involved and arduous.[48] The parties came to an agreement on

---

[46] CPE79 (Alice Harpham). See Appendix B.3.

[47] The witness Richard Wynsted (or de Wynestede) explained this when asked how he knew that they had married. See CPE79/13 (1358–60), or Appendix B.2. The village of Frysmersk is one of the lost villages of the Humber estuary: flooding began in the 1300s and in total 321 acres of arable, 100 acres of meadow, 152 acres of pasture (Chronica Monasterii de Melsa, III, pages 233–4) were lost. A map of the village's location can be found on http://www.fortunecity.com/greenfield/ecolodge/25/gord7.gif.

[48] CPE79: "Et habito consensu mutuo inter eos tandem istemet juratus misit pro quodam capellano vocato Ricardo de Wynstede ut eosdem Robertum et Elizabeth simul affidaret."

March 2, 1351. As in most other cases, the witnesses were silent on the contents of the secular contract. The courts wanted to know only about the circumstances of the vows and the words that were used to finalize the union.[49] Although this exchange of vows created a valid marriage, the marriage was solemnized three weeks later in the parish church of Frysmersk, after the publication of banns on three consecutive Sundays in the parishes of Frysmersk and Burton.

Alice seems to have been present on at least one of these occasions, when she did not object to the marriage, but Robert had secured her silence beforehand. *Dominus* William Wetwang, a canon and the master of the hospice of St. Giles in Beverley, deposed that Robert and Alice had come to see him there on an unspecified day before Robert was due to solemnize his marriage to Elizabeth Frothyngham. Robert was clearly in an apologetic mood when he turned to William Wetwang for counsel. Referring to William as Alice's best friend in the locality, he reminded him of the agreement between himself and Alice and of its circumstances. William was clearly familiar with the arrangement, and he opined that Robert was, indeed, deeply obligated to Alice, not least because she had, in fact, begotten a child by him.[50] The negotiations about compensation for Alice took place between Robert and William while Alice was silently present in the room. In the end, William and Robert agreed that Robert should pay Alice ten marks within a year. William commented that he was not sure why it was so important for Robert to make this covenant with Alice, but he added that it was probably to guarantee that Alice did not object to his marriage to Elizabeth Frothyngham.[51] It is frustrating for us, but entirely in keeping with the practice of the consistory courts, that the terms of the agreement have not been preserved. Hence we do not know how it was to have been enforced.

Robert Midelton presented a convincing case, and both judges who heard the case ruled against Alice Welwyk. Robert was able to produce three witnesses to his marriage negotiations with Elizabeth Frothyngham, one of whom was the cleric who guided their exchange of marriage vows in the family chapel, and who was apparently privy to the negotiations. But appearances were deceptive: although two judges passed sentence in favor of Robert and Elizabeth's marriage, and although Elizabeth and Robert had five children together, Alice persisted and appealed to the Apostolic See. Before the case could be transmitted to the Roman Curia, the court

---

[49] CPE79: "Et habito consensu mutuo inter eos tandem, istemet testis misit pro quodam capellano, vocato domino Ricardo de Wynestede, ut eosdem Robertum et Elizabetham simul affidaret. Qui quidem dominus Robertus statim postquam ibi venerat et intellexerat causam adventus sui, informavit dictas personas per que verba ipsi seinvicem mutue affidarunt, dicentes in hunc modum. Primo predictus Robertus, ad informationem dicti capellani, dixit sic: 'Ego accipio te Elizabetham in uxorem meam tenendam et habendam usque ad finem vite mee, et ad hoc do tibi fidem meam,' ac ipsa Elizabetha eodem modo respondebat sibi dicens, 'Hic accipio te Robertum in virum meum tenendum et habendum quousque mors nos seperaverit, et ad hoc do tibi fidem meam.'"

[50] CPE79 (William de Wetwang). See Appendix B.4.

[51] See Appendix B.4.

in York summoned Robert, where he acknowledged the validity of his marriage to Alice Welwyk. A memorandum of October 14, 1359, which was attached to the case, recorded that Robert had confessed that prior to his marriage with Elizabeth, there had been an exchange of vows regarding Alice Welwyk (albeit with the servant, Alice Harpham), that they had subsequently had intercourse, and that Alice Welwyk had had a child by him.[52] Despite this admission, the court passed sentence on December 11, 1359 in favor of his marriage to Elizabeth Frothyngham. The case did eventually pass to the Apostolic See.

Robert's behavior demonstrates that he had a good understanding of canon law, and it also tells us something about the oral nature of some contracts. Like the other litigants we have seen, he attempted to safeguard his interests by entering into a contract outside the essential "spiritual" one. In his case, there were two other contracts, both of which were apparently oral. The object of the first contract was to allow him to have intercourse with Alice Welwyk without creating a legally binding marriage. He cleverly made this contract in such a way that he did not contract with Alice directly. Instead, he made this oath to third party, who stood as guarantor for his intentions. The terms of the agreement were well known locally. The second oral agreement, pertaining to the dissolution of the union, was made between William Wetwang and Robert in Alice's presence. Its reported content fell squarely in the secular sphere. Its purpose was to provide for the child of Robert and Alice. But unlike most other agreements reported in the cause papers, this one had no witnesses present apart from Alice herself, who remained silent.

It is clear that Robert entered into prolonged and more traditional negotiations before his marriage to Elizabeth Frothyngham. Once again, we are unable to say what provisions were included in this secular agreement, but it is clear that the marriage was advantageous to Robert, for what necessitated the transference of the marriage ceremony from Elizabeth's home village (or manor) to Frysmersk was the large number of guests present. Although these guests did not depose to the consistory court in York, one must presume that some of them would have known about the contents of the secular marriage contract. Entirely in keeping with the procedure of the consistory courts, the shadowy presence of this contract is apparent only in the court's written record of the witnesses' oral recollections.

---

[52] CPE79: "Memorandum quod xiiiito die octobris anno domini millesimo cccmo lixmo Robertus de Midelton de Burton, juratus et ex officio per dominum officialem curie Eboracensis interrogatus, fuit solutus a quocumque contractu matrimoniali cum Elizabete, de quo in articulis memoratur, vel alia quacumque. Dixit in juramento suo quod promisit, Alicia de Harpham media, quod contraheret matrimonium cum Alicia de Welewyke in presentia eiusdem Alicia de Welewyke in eventu quod cognosceret carnaliter dictam Aliciam de Welewyke et de ea prolem suscitaret, prout in depositione eiusdem Alicia probatur. Et [dicit] in juramento suo quod ipsam Aliciam de Welewyke carnaliter cognovit et de ea prolem suscitavit, ut firmiter credit, antequam contraxit matrimonium cum qua nunc stat matrimonialiter copulatus, sed de forma contractus cum dicta Alicia de Harpham vel de verbis inter eosdem tunc prolatis non recolit, ut dicit."

Final Observations and Conclusions

It is clear that the cases heard by the church courts in England conformed to the model of marriage outlined in the canon law of the European church. We know most about the English church courts in York, Canterbury, and Ely (although we can find some supplementary material from fragmentary survivals in other dioceses).[53] At first reading, the documents may appear to show only how the courts focused their attention on the oral exchange that allegedly established the bond of marriage between the two litigating parties. Nevertheless, throughout the preserved cause papers there are indications that the exchange of vows could be the culmination of a lengthy process of negotiation and that the parties (or their legal guardians) tried to safeguard their interests by establishing a "secular" contract (oral or written) that supplemented the essential "spiritual" one. We also find that the spouses' families and friends were involved in establishing the terms of such contracts. A secular contract dealt with the worldly aspects of marriage – it might contain provisions for land and property transfer, and it might outline the husband's obligations toward the wife or make general provisions for the parties' life together – yet it might also include an agreement to marry. Such contracts were sometimes complicated, and they were often difficult for the parties to interpret. I have argued that the evidence of marriage contracts in late-medieval England shows that the contracting of marriage sometimes involved two phases, which concluded respectively first in a "secular" contract and later in a "spiritual" one.

Whereas spiritual contracts were oral, secular contracts might be oral or written. Although we know they existed, written marriage contracts have not survived in their original form among the surviving English ecclesiastical cause papers. In this essay I have used the records of witness accounts given before ecclesiastical courts to demonstrate not only that such contracts existed but also that they contained a wide range of provisions. Unfortunately for the modern historian, the procedure of the ecclesiastical courts, the cost of litigation, and social convention all worked

---

[53] Michael M. Sheehan's "The formation and stability of marriage in fourteenth-century England: Evidence of an Ely register," *Mediaeval Studies* 33 (1971): 228–63, has stood the test of time, as has R. H. Helmholz's concise analysis in his *Marriage Litigation in Medieval England* (London, 1974). Other useful studies of the practice of the court in York include Charles Donahue, Jr., "The policy of Alexander the Third's consent theory of marriage" (n. 4 earlier); idem, "Proof by witnesses in the medieval courts of England: An imperfect reception of the learned law," in Morris S. Arnold, et al. (eds.), *On the Laws and Customs of England: Essays in Honor of Samuel E. Thorne* (Chapel Hill, 1981), 127–58; Morris S. Arnold, "The canon law on the formation of marriage and social practice in the later Middle Ages," *Journal of Family History* 8 (1983): 144–58. The present chapter analyzes material from the York archives not found in Pedersen, *Marriage Disputes* (n. 3 earlier). On the methodological problems of interpreting such sources, see the Goldberg–Pedersen debate cited in n. 3 earlier, and see also Andrew J. Finch, "Parental authority and the problem of clandestine marriage in the later Middle Ages," *Law and History Review* 8 (1990): 189–204, and Charles Donahue, Jr., "'Clandestine' marriage in the later Middle Ages: A reply," *Law and History Review* 10 (1992): 315–22.

against the survival of written or notarized contracts: the courts were not interested in written contracts or in any written notarial evidence associated with them. Ecclesiastical judges wanted to know only whether the parties had used words or actions that had the requisite force to establish a marriage bond. For that they relied on the oral evidence of those who had witnessed or overheard the exchange of vows. Furthermore, the cost of producing documentation for the consistory courts was calculated on the basis of the number of lines in a document, a practice that encouraged the scribes and their clients to reproduce only what directly pertained to a marriage bond and to leave out any incidental information.[54] The inclusion of such information would only have added to the cost of litigation without strengthening the chances of success in the case. No cause papers included copies of written contracts, therefore, but it seems likely that a cleric or notary giving evidence about an exchange of marriage vows would have relied on his own written evidence when giving his oral deposition to a consistory court.

Since the publication of Georges Duby's *Medieval Marriage,* modern historians have conceived of medieval marriages as the subject of a struggle between two "models" of marriage, respectively secular (or "aristocratic") and ecclesiastical. Duby argued that the struggle between the two models was largely over by the end of the thirteenth century.[55] But the material investigated in this essay shows that there was a wider range of conceptions of marriage in thirteenth- and fourteenth-century England than Duby identified in his mainly French material. In England, it is doubtful whether there was really a "struggle" between the two systems, although there certainly was a distinction between them. Both Parliament and the consistory court in York examined cases that referred directly to the other "sphere." Moreover, Parliament examined the validity of the decision of the other jurisdiction, and the York consistory court examined and applied the provisions of "secular" marriage contracts. But it was not just the courts that tried to settle marriage disputes by reference to the contents of marriage contracts. Lay people, as well, understood and applied oral and written contracts. Examples of this include John Cameys's attempt

---

[54] According to Archbishop Greenfield's statutes of 1311, the two examiners of the York consistory court could conduct the interrogation of witnesses in court or out of court in the witnesses' home parish. Normally, the examiners were not to be paid more than 12 d. (pence) per witness examined, but if the litigants had handed in articles of excessive length, the examiners were allowed to charge 1 d. for every twelve lines of deposition taken down. The charge for copies of these or other documents was 1 d. for every 24 lines. Each line was to be written in a clear legible hand, ten inches long, and with adequate spacing between the lines. The examiners' fee was to be waived if the litigant for whom they performed the examination was a pauper or a "miserable person." See David Wilkins (ed.), *Concilia Magna Britanniae et Hiberniae a synodo Verolamiensi AD CCCCXLIV ad Londinensem AD MDC,* vol. 2 (London, 1737), 409.

[55] Georges Duby, *Medieval Marriage: Two Models from Twelfth-Century France* (Baltimore, 1978). Duby refined his argument in *Le chevalier, la femme et le prêtre: le mariage dans la France féodal* (Paris, 1981) (published in English as Barbara Bray [trans.], *The Knight, the Lady and the Priest: The Making of Modern Marriage in Medieval France* [New York, 1983]), but the basic argument remained the same.

to give legal validity to a private settlement of his marriage and to provide a written safeguard of his (illegal) divorce, Robert Midelton's attempts at contravening the rules of canon law, the Roucliff and Marrays families' attempt to protect an under-age girl from a too precocious entry into sexual activity, and the dispute between the Colvyle and Percy family about the obligation to pay a dowry. Frustratingly, these contracts do not survive, but the range of marital behavior that they regulated was wide.

Thus, the distinction or separation that we are so used to seeing between secular and ecclesiastical views of marriage was perhaps not as impermeable as we have grown accustomed to think. The cases examined in this essay demonstrate a will-ingness to put some sort of legal form to marital arrangements that ranged from what a contemporary *judicatio* would have called "illegal," through the complex indenture drawn up to protect the economic interests of the spouses' parents, to the ingenious circumvention of canon law proposed by Robert Midelton (perhaps in order to make sure that his marriage was fertile after the devastation of the plague). Common to all these cases is the litigants' willingness to engage opportunistically with the courts and the legal systems. The lay and ecclesiastical courts provided medieval litigants with a choice of venues and methods. The records of marriage litigation that we find in the spiritual jurisdiction may have been a part of a much larger and more complex system of arbitration in matters of marriage, wherein medieval people could pick and choose the venue for their conflict and the means to resolve it.

ᴄ∾

Appendix A: The Cameys Case (1302)[1]

From the Parliament at Westminster at the Octave of St. John the Baptist in the Thirteenth Year of the Reign of King Edward.

Proceedings on the petition of William Paynel and his wife Margaret, claiming her dower share of the manor of Torpel.

Concerning William Paynel and Margaret his wife. William Paynel and Margaret his wife previously, namely at the lord king's parliament at Westminster in the twenty-eighth year of his reign, requested the lord king through a certain petition that the same lord king be pleased to deliver to them a third part of the manor of Torpel with its appurtenances, as the dower of the same Margaret which belongs to her of the free tenement which belonged to John de Cameys, her first husband etc.

---

[1] Quoted from Paul Brand (ed. and trans.), "Edward I: Roll 11, Text and Translation," in *The Parliament Rolls of Medieval England*, C. Given-Wilson et al. (eds.), item 14, CD-ROM (Leicester, U.K.: Scholarly Digital Editions, 2005). The translation (which is Crown Copyright) is reproduced here by kind permission both of Dr. Brand and The National Archives (which holds the original document).

And Nicholas of Warwick, who sued on behalf of the lord king, said at that time that the aforesaid Margaret was not entitled to have her dower from this, nor ought she to be heard or admitted to claim any dower from it, since for a long time before the death of the said John, her former husband etc., she had freely and of her own accord left her same husband, and lived in adultery with the aforesaid William who is now her husband, during the lifetime of the aforesaid John, nor had she been reconciled by the same John before the same John's death.[2] As a result of which, in accordance with the terms of the statute of the lord king recently promulgated concerning women leaving their husbands and living with their adulterers and not reconciled freely and without ecclesiastical coercion before the deaths of their husbands, the aforesaid Margaret ought to be completely rejected from her aforesaid petition. And he asked for judgment on behalf of the king etc.

Whereupon the aforesaid William and Margaret produced a certain deed issued in the name of the aforesaid John de Cameys, her first husband etc., in these words:

To all Christ's faithful to whom the present deed will come, John de Cameys, the son and heir of lord Ralph de Cameys, greetings in the Lord. Know that I have given and demised of my own free will to lord William Paynel, knight, Margaret de Cameys, the daughter and heir of lord John of Gaddesden, my wife, and I have also given and granted to the same lord William, released and quitclaimed, all goods and chattels which the same Margaret has, or henceforth may have, and also whatever is mine of the aforesaid Margaret, her goods or her chattels with their appurtenances, so that neither I, nor anyone else in my name, can or may henceforth demand or claim anything in the aforesaid Margaret, or the goods or chattels of the same Margaret with their appurtenances. I will and grant, and by the present deed confirm, that the aforesaid Margaret is to live and remain with aforesaid lord William at the will of the same William. In testimony of which thing I have put my seal to this present deed. With these witnesses, Thomas of Repeston, John of Ferring, William of Iccomb, Henry le Brunz, Stephen Chamberlain, Walter le Blund, Gilbert of Batecombe, Robert de Bosco, and others.

And they said that the same Margaret lived with the same William under the terms contained in the said deed, and with the consent and by the will of the said John, then the husband of the same Margaret, during the lifetime of the same John, and through the surrender and grant of the same John, as can clearly be seen by the lord king and his court through the words contained in the same deed, and not with the same William as her adulterer. Whereupon they asked for judgment. And then the same William and Margaret were told to appear at the next parliament to hear their judgment there etc.

---

[2] Paul Brand gives his translation as "nor had she been reconciled to the same John before the same John's death." Though slightly awkward to a modern speaker of English, the present translation maintains the Second Statute of Westminster's insistence that the reconciliation be initiated by the *husband*.

Afterwards at the next parliament, namely at the parliament of the same lord king at Lincoln at the octave of Hilary in the twenty-ninth year of his reign, the aforesaid William appeared, and Margaret appeared through her attorney, and they pressingly requested the aforesaid dower of the same Margaret.

And they were adjourned to the next parliament etc.

Afterwards, at the next parliament of the same lord king, namely at Westminster at the octave of St. John the Baptist in the thirtieth year of his reign, the aforesaid William appeared, and likewise the aforesaid Margaret, through a certain Walter le Blund, the attorney of the same Margaret appointed before John Abel by virtue of a writ of the lord king. And they requested the aforesaid dower of the same Margaret, in the aforesaid form etc.

Whereupon, when the answer previously given on behalf of the same lord king had been read out before the same lord king and his council in full parliament, and when the tenor of the aforesaid deed previously produced by the same William and Margaret had also been heard and understood, and the aforesaid statute ordained by the same lord king and his council and put forward on behalf of the same king had likewise been read, heard and understood, in which it is expressly contained that, if a wife freely leaves her husband and goes to live with her adulterer, she is to lose in perpetuity her action for claiming her dower which might belong to her from her husband's tenements, if she is convicted of this, unless her husband is reconciled to her, freely and without ecclesiastical coercion, and allows her to live with him, the same William and Margaret then said that they were prepared to prove by a jury that the same Margaret did not live with the same William as her adulterer, during the lifetime of the aforesaid John her first husband etc. and they did not say anything else.

And because the same William and Margaret could not deny that the same Margaret, during the lifetime of the aforesaid John, her first husband, went and lived with the same William, completely abandoning her husband, namely the aforesaid John, and of her own accord, as is quite clear, since the same Margaret during the lifetime of the same John never objected to this, personally or through anyone else, in any detail or in any way, nor does she object to it now, but rather making clear her first spontaneous will, and continuing the affection which she had conceived for the same William during the lifetime of the aforesaid John, she allowed herself to be married to the same William after the death of the same John, and the same William and Margaret do not say or show anything through which the court can be shown that the aforesaid John, her first husband, reconciled her in any way during his lifetime,[3] and it appears clearly from the aforesaid deed produced by the same William and Margaret that the same Margaret during the lifetime of the said John was allowed through his grant and delivery to remain

---

[3] Paul Brand translates this as "through which the court can be shown that the aforesaid John, her first husband, was reconciled to her in any way during his lifetime." As in the previous change I have altered the translation to maintain the male agency in the reconciliation.

with the said William in perpetuity, and it is not necessary in the king's court to hold an enquiry by the country on things which the party cannot deny and which appear clear to the court, or on things which are stated and granted by the party in pleading, and it is more probable and more to be presumed, and more to be believed in the king's court and any other, that inasmuch as a man's wife, during her husband's lifetime, goes to live with some other man of her own accord, not objecting to or contradicting this in any way, she is living in adultery rather than in any other proper or lawful manner, and especially where such a clarification of the spontaneous will of the same wife follows afterwards as a marriage taking place between them after the husband's death, and nor does it pertain to the king's court to hold an enquiry by the country into adultery, it seems to the court that it is not necessary to proceed to hold any enquiry by the country, in the form which the said William and Margaret offer, in the face of such great and such manifest evidence, presumptions, proof and the admission of the aforesaid William and Margaret but rather that the aforesaid Margaret under the terms of the aforesaid statute ought not to be admitted or heard in her claim for her aforesaid dower, for the aforesaid reasons.

Amercement

And it is therefore adjudged that the aforesaid William and Margaret are to receive nothing from their aforesaid petition, but are to be amerced for their false claim etc.

Certain other letters were produced in court by the same William and Margaret: namely three, of which two concerned the canonical purgation of the same William and Margaret of the crime of adultery of which they were accused, and the third was about a certain annual rent of 80 marks, and the transcript of these remains in the wardrobe, and there is no mention of these letters in this judgment because they have no great relevance to this judgment, nor are judgments to be given in the king's court on the basis of the testimony of bishops, even though the bishops' letters have been produced in the king's court, unless the same bishops are writing back to the same king at the royal command. The tenor of the same letters, however, is given below:

To all Christ's faithful who will see or hear the present deed, John de Cameys, knight, eternal greetings in the Lord. Whereas previously I handed over and demised at farm to William Paynel and Henry of Didling my manors of Broadwater, Woolavington, Ditchling and Patching, and all the lands and tenements which I have in Grofham and Alversham, with their appurtenances in the county of Sussex, with the advowsons of the churches, chapels, and chantries of the aforesaid villages, for the entire lives of the aforesaid William and Henry, for £86 sterling to be paid to me annually, as is more fully contained in certain chirographed deeds made between us, know that I have received in the city of London, on the day of the writing of the present letters, from the aforesaid William and Henry £430 of good and legal sterling for a period of five years by way of the aforesaid farm, of which £430 I acknowledge that I have been fully paid, and I declare the aforesaid William and Henry quit of it, for myself and my heirs, and especially, after the aforesaid term of the aforesaid five years, I, the aforesaid John, depute and assign the aforesaid William and Henry to Margaret my wife and my children, for them to pay and render the aforesaid farm of £86, which they are to pay me annually after the aforesaid term of five years, to the aforesaid Margaret and to my aforesaid children for their support, annually at the terms contained in the aforesaid deeds, as fully as I am entitled to receive it after the passing of the aforementioned five years. In testimony of which thing I have put my seal to the present deed. Given at London on the day of St. Barnabas the Apostle in the thirteenth year of the reign of the lord king. With these witnesses, lords Adam de Bavent, Hamo Bonet, Henry de Liuns, knights, William of Lychepole, Thomas of Kepeston, Andrew of Lychepole, Valentine des Granges, John de la Grave, and others.

To all who will see the present letters, brother J. by divine permission archbishop of Canterbury, primate of all England, greetings in Christ. Know all of you that lord William Paynel, knight, has legally purged himself before us of the crime of adultery of which he was accused, which was allegedly committed with lady Margaret, the wife of lord John de Cameys, knight, through trustworthy men, knights and others: and therefore we, pronouncing him free from this crime, restore him to his former good name, by decree, and we have had these our letters patent strengthened with the protection of our seal, made for him in testimony of the aforesaid. Given at Slindon on 3 March in the year of the Lord 1287 (1288).

To all Christ's faithful who will see or hear the present letters, Gilbert by divine mercy bishop of Chichester eternal greetings in the Lord. We make it known to all of you by the present letters that, whereas lady Margaret de Cameys had been accused of the crime of adultery, committed, as was said, with lord William Paynel, knight, and for that reason had been called before our official at our command on a certain day at a certain place, the aforesaid lady Margaret appearing in person before the aforesaid official in the cathedral church of Chichester, on the Saturday before the feast of the Purification of the Blessed Virgin in the year of the Lord 1295 (1296) in the presence of lord William, the dean of the church of Chichester, master Robert, the treasurer of the said church, and other canons of the same place, and very many other clerks and lay persons, expressly denying the aforesaid crime of adultery of which she was accused, solemnly and canonically purged herself of it: namely through ladies Margaret Martel, Isabel de Montfort, the prioress of Easebourne, Hawise de Houtot, A. Corbet, and through many other married women and young maidens of the neighbourhood. We, having heard and learned of the aforesaid canonical purgation, approving it and considering the aforesaid lady Margaret de Cameys to be free from the aforesaid crime, as was just, restore her to her good name. In testimony of which thing we have had these letters patent, strengthened by our seal, made for the said lady. Given at Aldingbourne on the aforesaid day of the aforesaid year.

APPENDIX B: ROBERT MIDELTON AND ELIZABETH FROTHYNGHAM
c. ALICE WELWYK, FROM THE YORK CAUSE PAPERS (CP E 79)

To illustrate the proceedings of ecclesiastical courts, I have chosen to present four depositions from the York Cause Papers regarding the proceedings of *Robert Midelton and Elizabeth Frothyngham* c. *Alice Welwyk*. (The case had originally appeared in Beverley as *Alice Welwyk* c. *Robert Midelton*.)

The order in which the depositions are presented here is not chronological: Amadus Frothingham and Richard Wynsted, whose testimony appears first, were, in fact, interrogated after Alice Harpham and William Wetwang had made their depositions. (This explains the otherwise confusing references to the "first article" and "the above things" in the introduction to Amadus Frothyngham's deposition. The first introduction to a deposition in the case – namely, the one to Alice Harpham's interrogation – explains that she was "sworn in, examined, and diligently questioned concerning the articles appended to this roll.") The legal complexity of the case makes it desirable to present the fairly straightforward narratives of Amadus Frothingham and Richard Wynsted first. Their evidence provides a succinct narrative of the stages through which marriage negotiations went in this as in most other cases, and it also provides a good example of what the Cause Papers say about marriage contracts.

I decided not to include the account of Robert Richal, the priest who officiated over the solemnization of the marriage of Robert and Elizabeth, because the part of the roll that contains his deposition is in a poor state of conservation, with large parts having been eaten by mice. What remains from his deposition makes it clear that he confirmed the details of the marriage given by another cleric, Richard Wynsted.

In view of the relative simplicity of the exchange between Robert and Elizabeth, the understanding of canon law that Robert evinced in his earlier negotiations with Alice Welwyk (as displayed in the depositions of Alice Harpham and William Wetwang) may come as a surprise. It is impossible to say where he gained his legal know-how, but it was both sound and precise. Robert wanted to make his marriage to Alice conditional on her fertility but to avoid binding himself to her in indissoluble matrimony (by consummating a conditional marriage). He also wanted to persuade her that his intentions were (relatively) honest. An explanation for Robert's concern with Alice's fertility may be found in the date of the alleged vows: because of the onslaught of the Plague in 1348, 1350 must have been a year of devastation in the English countryside, and it is very likely that Robert believed that the recent mortality would have affected the availability or fertility of women. His solution (whereby he made his pledge to Alice Welwyk's servant) was ingenious and possibly unique.

I have retained the distinction between "thee/thou" and "you" throughout the translation. I have done so because Robert Midelton uses the formal second person plural ("you") to William Wetwang alone, and not to any of the other witnesses or in any of the other reported speeches and because Elizabeth Frothyngham addresses him using the informal "thou." I suggest that this distinction tells us two things about his character: he feels at ease addressing all lay people informally as "thou" (but he is clearly aware of the proper use of the honorific form, which he uses when he pleads with *Dominus* William Wetwang), and he is in a more equal role to Elizabeth Frothyngham than to (the virtually silent) Alice Welewyk.

Words or phrases that I have supplied to fill in lacunae in the original text are set in square brackets in the Latin transcriptions.

1. The Interrogation of Amadus Frothyngham on 30 April 1359 Concerning his Daughter's Licit Marriage to Robert Midelton[4]

Amadus Frothyngham, sworn in and examined about the above things, having been questioned about the first article says that he was present in his own chapel in the village of Frysmersk on the Wednesday in the first week of Lent eight years ago.[5] And there he and [Robert] Midelton and Elizabeth (concerning whom mention has been made), who is his daughter, as he says, agreed together about one thing, namely, that Robert ought to take said Elizabeth as his wife. And when at last there was mutual agreement between them, this witness sent for a certain chaplain, named Richard Wynsted, so that he could pledge the same Robert and Elizabeth together. That same *Dominus* Richard[6] Wynsted came at once thereafter, and when he had learned the reason for his coming, he instructed the said persons by which words they might pledge each other mutually, by speaking as follows: At first the said Robert, following the instruction of the said chaplain, said: "I take thee Elizabeth as my wife, to hold and to have until the end of my life, and on this I give thee my pledge." And said Elizabeth responded in the same manner, saying to him: "Here I take thee Robert as my husband to hold and to have until death has separated us, and on this I give thee my pledge." And it was around the third hour of the said Wednesday, as he recollects, but he does not remember the month. But he knows well that the parties were standing when they contracted in the manner mentioned. And at that time Peter (his son) and others were present in that place, as he says having been asked. Again, he says that banns between the aforesaid Robert and Elizabeth were afterwards published in the church of Frysmersk and in the church of Burton for three Sundays during

---

[4] As noted earlier, the witness accounts are not presented here in the original order. The first two witnesses heard in the case were Alice Harpham and William Wetwang, who gave evidence for Alice. Amadus Frothyngham and Richard Wynsted were interrogated some weeks later to prove the existence of the marriage between Elizabeth and Robert. But their accounts outline the canonically correct steps for establishing a licit marriage, whereas the events related by Amadus Frothyngham and Richard Wynsted demonstrate an unusual application of the law. The latter narrative might have been confusing to an unprepared reader if they came first.

[5] 2 March 1351.

[6] The scribe has written "Robert," but this is clearly an error.

solemn mass. Against these proclamations, Alice (concerning whom mention
has been made) did not object in any way. For this reason, this witness believes
that said Alice had no right to have said Robert as her husband. Furthermore,
the aforesaid marriage between the aforesaid Robert and Elizabeth was later
solemnized and plainly and publicly made in the church of Frysmersk, to
which solemnization the aforesaid Alice objected in no way. For which reason
he believes that she consented to the same solemnization which was made, as
he says, eight years ago, either near or around that time. And it was on the
Monday three weeks after Easter in the year concerning which he endeavored
to testify above, that is, after last Easter eight years had passed since the time
of the solemnization. Until the present day, the said Robert and Elizabeth are
living together and have lived together since then in bed and board, having
between them several children born during that time. And he says that the
aforementioned things are publicly known in the deaconry of Holderness and
Herthill and neighboring places, and now public voice and fame is laboring
concerning these things.

He does not know of any marriage contract or carnal coupling between
Robert and Alice Welwyk. He aims to win over said Alice in the present case,
as he says. And he says that she does not have right in her prosecution as he
believes

Latin Transcription:

Amadus de Frothyngham, juratus et examinatus super premissis. Super
primo articulo requisitus, dicit quod fuit presens in capella sua propria in
villa de Frysmersk die mercurii in prima septimana quadragesime ultima
preterita fuerunt octo anni elapsi. Et ibidem ipse et [Robertus] de Midelton
ac Elizabeth, de qua memoratur, que est filia sua, ut dicit, simul consen-
sierunt in unum, videlicet quod Robertus deberet ducere dictam Elizabethem
in uxorem. Et habito consensu mutuo inter eos tandem istemet testis misit
pro quodam capellano, vocato Ricardo de Wynestede, ut eosdem Robertum et
Elizabethem simul affidaret. Qui quidem dominus Robertus statim postquam
venerat. Et intellexerat causam adventus sui informavit dictas personas per
que verba ipsi seinvicem mutue affidarunt dicentes in hunc modum: primo
predictus Robertus, ad informationem dicti capellani, dixit, "Ego accipio te,
Elizabethem, in uxorem meam, tenendam et habendam usque ad finem vite
mee. Et ad hoc do tibi fidem meam," ac ipsa Elizabeth eodem modo respondebat, sibi dicens, "Hic accipio te, Robertum, in virum meum, tenendum et
habendum quousque mors nos seperaverit. Et ad hoc do tibi fidem meam."
Et fuit circa horam tertiam dicti diei mercurii, ut recolit, sed non recolit de
mensem. Sed bene scit quod dicte partes fuerunt stantes cum contraxerunt
modo quo prefertur. Et fuerunt tunc ibidem presentes, ut dicit interrogatus,
Petrus, filius suus et alii. Item dicit quod banna inter predictos Robertum et

Elizabethem postea fuerunt publice edita in ecclesia de Frysmersk et in ecclesia de Burton per tres dies dominicas infra missarum solempnia. In quibusquidem editionibus Alicia, de qua memoratur, nullatenus reclamavit. Per quod credit iste testis ipsam Aliciam nullum habuisse jus habendi dictum Robertum in maritum. Ac etiam predictum matrimonium postea fuit solempnizatum et palam ac publice factum in ecclesia de Frysmersk inter predictos Robertum et Elizabethem, cui quidem solempnizationi predicta Alicia nullatenus contradixit. Per quod credit ipsam consensisse eidem solempnationi que fuit facta, ut dicit, huic ab octo anni elapsi vel prope et circiter illud tempus. Et fuit in die lune ad tres septimanas post pascham in anno de quo supra nititur deponere – videlicet post pascham ultima preterita fuerunt octo anni elapsi a tempore huius solempnizationis – usque ad presentem diem predicti Robertus et Elizabeth ut vir et uxor in thoro et mensa simul cohabitarunt et adhuc cohabitavit plures proles inter se habentes medio tempore procreatos. Et dicit quod premissa sunt publica notoria in decanatu de Holdernes et Herthill et locis vicinis, et super hiis iam publica vox et fama laborat.

Nescit de aliquo contractu matrimoniali vel carnalis copula inter predictos Robertum et Alicia de Wellewyk. Affectat ipsam Aliciam succumbere in presenti causa, ut dicit, [et dicit ipsa] non habet jus in prosecutione sua, ut credit.

2. *The Interrogation of* Dominus *Richard Wynsted, a Chaplain, on 30 April 1359 Concerning the Licit Marriage Between Robert Midelton and Elizabeth Frothyngham*

Dominus Richard Wynsted, a chaplain, sworn in, examined, and diligently questioned about the articles attached to this roll, having been questioned about the first article says that it contains the truth. And he knows this because he was present, as he says, in the chapel of Amadus Frothyngham (the father of the Elizabeth about whom mention has been made) on a Wednesday around the third hour in the first week of Lent eight years ago, where and when he heard Robert and Elizabeth (concerning whom recollection has been made) contract marriage by words of mutual agreement expressed in the present tense, with said Robert at the prompting of this witness first saying as follows: "Elizabeth, here I take thee as my wife, to hold and to have until death has parted us, and on this I give thee my pledge." And said Elizabeth immediately responding to him spoke as follows, being prompted by this witness, as he says: "I take thee Robert as my husband until death separates us, and on this I give thee my pledge." And having stretched out their hands they kissed each other, as he says. And afterwards said Robert and Elizabeth had the banns between them published in the church [...] of Frysmersk for the three following Sundays, as this witness says he heard that they had been made. And afterwards they caused said marriage to be solemnized between them in the said church of Frysmersk on a certain Monday after the next Easter then following. And as he well remembers, that Monday was three weeks after the said feast of Easter, namely, eight years ago. And he does not know this because he was there, as he says, but rather because the said solemnization was so publicly and solemnly made in the presence of more than a hundred people that it could not escape the notice of anyone living in said village or in other villages close by. And this witness, as he says, was then present in a certain village called Wynsted, which is about one mile distant from said village of Frysmersk. And having been asked he says that the aforesaid Robert and Elizabeth were standing in said chapel at the time when they first contracted in the form that was mentioned and they were then present there with Amadus Frothyngham, Peter his son, and others. Also he says, having been asked, that the aforementioned solemnization concerning which he endeavored to depose was made by a certain *Dominus* Robert Richall, a chaplain, in the presence of many excellent and noble persons from those parts, as this witness says he knows from the report of those who were then present there. And finally, having been asked, this witness says that he knows this well because he saw that said Robert and Elizabeth lived together as man and wife in bed and board from the time of said solemnization, and in that time they had and still have offspring together, namely, five begotten children. Concerning any matrimonial contract entered into at any time between said Robert and Alice Welwyk, he does not know what to depose, nor concerning any carnal coupling between them.

He is not a blood-relative, not an affine, servant [or] familiar, of any of the persons between whom there is an action, nor does he care which party may win the present case, nor did he or will he receive anything for bearing his testimony. Having been asked, he says that the things that he deposed above concerning the matrimonial contract and its solemnization between the aforesaid Robert and Elizabeth are publicly known and manifest in the deaconry of Holderness and Herthill and in the neighboring places and public voice and rumor is laboring and has labored for a long time.

Latin Transcription:

Dominus Ricardus de Wynstedo, capellanus, juratus, examinatus et diligenter requisitus super articulis huic rotulo appensis. Super primo articulo requisitus, dicit quod continet veritatem. Et hoc scit per hoc quod presens fuit, ut dicit, in villa de Fryssemersk in capella Hamadi de Frothyngham, patris Elizabethe, de qua memoratur, in die mercurii circa horam tertiam in prima septimana quadragesime ultima preterita fuerunt octo anni elapsi. Ubi et quando audivit Robertum et Elizabethem, de quibus memoratur, contrahere matrimonium per verba mutuum consensum de presenti exprimentia, predicto Roberto ad informationem istemet testis primo dicente in hunc modum, "Elizabeth, hic accipio te in uxorem meam, tenendam et habendam quousque mors nos seperaverit. Et ad hoc do tibi fidem meam." Ac ipsa Elizabeth, incontinenter sibi respondens, dixit in hunc modum informata quod istemmet testem, ut dicit "Ego accipio te Robertum in virum meum quousque mors nos seper-abit. Et ad hoc do tibi fidem meam." Et distractis manibus eorum se mutuo osculabantur, ut dicit. Et postea iidem Robertus et Elizabeth fecerunt banna publice edi inter eos in ecclesia [...] de Frysmersk per tres dies dominicas subsequentes, prout iste testis dicit se audivisse factum fuisse, ac postea ipsi fecerunt dictum matrimonium solempnizari inter eos in dicta ecclesia de Frysmersk in quodam die lune post pascham tunc proxima sequente. Et, ut bene recolit, ille dies lune fuit tres septimanas post dictum festum pasche, videlicet ultimo iam fuerunt octo anni elapsi. Et scit non quia interfuit, ut dicit, sed quia dicta solempnizatio fuit ita solempniter et notorie facta in pre-sentia quamplurum centum homini quod non potuit alicui existenti in dicta villa vel in aliis villis propinque vicinis latere. Et istemet testis, ut dicit, fuit tunc presens in quadam villa vocatur *Wynestede* que vix distat a dicta villa de Frysmersk ad spatium unius miliar'. Et dicit interrogatus quod predicti Robertus et Elizabeth fuerunt stantes in dicta capella, tempore quo primo contraxerunt in forma qua prefertur, et fuerunt ibidem tunc presentes cum dictis Hamandus de Frothingham, Petrus, filius suus et alii. Item dicit inter-rogatus quod solemnizatio supradicta, de qua supra nititur deponere, fuit factum per quemdem dominum Robertum de Richall, capellanum, presen-tibus ibidem quampluribus probis et nobilis personis de illis partibus, prout iste testis dicit se scire per relatum eorundem ibidem tunc presentium. Et dicit iste testis ulterius requisitus quod ipse bene novit, quia vidit quod dicti Robertus et Elizabeth ut vir et uxor a tempore dicti solempnizationis in thoro et mensa simul cohabitarunt ac medio tempore proles inter se habuerunt et adhuc habent, videlicet quinque liberos procreatos. De aliquo contractu mat-rimoniali aliquo tempore inito inter dictum Robertum et Alicia de Welwyk nescit deponere, nec de aliqua carnali copula inter eos.

Non est consanguineus, affinis, domesticus, familiarius alicuius person-arum inter quas agitur. Nec curat que pars victoriam habeat in presenti causa. [Nec] aliquid recepit vel recepiet pro testimonio suo ferendo. Dicit requisitus quod ea que supra deponit de contractu matrimoniali et solempnizatione eiusdem inter predictos Robertum et Elizabethem sunt publica notoria et manifesta in decanatu de Holdernes et Herthill et locis vicinis et super hiis ibidem publica vox et fama laborat et a diu est laboravit [*sic*].

3. *The Interrogation of Alice Harpham, a Former Servant of Alice Welwyk, on 18 December 1358 Concerning the Illicit Marriage Between Alice Welwyk and Robert Midelton*

Alice Harpham, sworn in, examined and diligently questioned concerning the articles appended to this roll, having been questioned concerning the first article, says that nine years ago this witness was a servant of Alice Welwyk (about whom mention has been made) in the village of Beverley, and that she lived constantly with said Alice, serving her from the feast of St. Michael nine years ago until the feast of the translation of St. Thomas following. And she often saw Robert Midelton commonly come to the house of said Alice, her mistress, during that time, and she often saw at that time and term that Robert implored said Alice with all the inducements and ways that he could bring to bear that she allow him to know her carnally. And said Alice [Welwyk] always spoke with him about this matter. Whenever this witness heard, she [Alice Welwyk] always answered him that she would not let him know her carnally unless he first make her a guarantee that he would take her as his wife. And she well remembers as she says that on a certain day during this period, namely, the Monday after Palm Sunday nine years ago, the aforesaid Robert, in the manner noted, made a representation and spoke to said Alice in her aforementioned house situated in the neighborhood called Eastgate in Beverley. And said Alice replied to him in the same way [as she had done before], saying that she would not permit said Robert to know her carnally unless he made her a guarantee that he would take her as his wife. And said Robert immediately replied to her speaking in the following way: "I will not take thee as my wife unless I shall know that thou canst conceive and have offspring, and therefore if thou wilst permit me to go with thee and it happens that thou conceivest a child by me, for certain I will take thee as a wife, and I will make a guarantee that obliges me by my public oath to whomever thou may wish (and not to thyself) that I obligate myself in those things. But also, I will not do this now because if I do this and I bind myself to thee in the form that was mentioned, at once after the first night I shall have known thee thou wilst be my wife although thou wilst never have conceived. And therefore I want to make a guarantee to any another person thou wantest, but not to thee." To which said Alice responded saying that she was contented. And she made Robert call this witness to them speaking in this way: "Behold, Alice Harpham, such is the agreement between me and Alice Welwyk." And he recited in the form that is mentioned: "But this Alice Welwyk, thy mistress, wishes that I make a guarantee to thee about these things in her name, and I wish the same. And thou, Alice Harpham, accept my pledge here that I shall take said Alice Welwyk as my wife if it happens that she conceives and has offspring by me."

And she says that said Robert knew said Alice carnally on the following night and many other nights, because this witness saw them lie together in one and the same bed, single man with single woman, naked man with naked woman, in the house of said Alice with the intention, as she believes, that they come together carnally. And afterwards they did have a begetting. This she knows both by the confession of Robert and by public voice and fame, which labors thus in the village of Beverley and in the neighboring places. And the aforesaid things are publicly known and manifest as she says.

Asked about the persons present at the said matrimonial contract concerning which she endeavors to depose, she says that said contracting parties were present in the place that was mentioned. And it was around the hour of Vespers of said day. She does not know whose [...] is situated, nor is she able to depose about the matrimonial contract initiated with Elizabeth Frothyngham.

She is not hired, instructed, corrupted by payment or prayers, a servant or familiar of the aforementioned parties, nor does she care which party wins as long as justice is done, as she says in her oath.

Latin Transcription:

Alicia de Harpham, jurata examinata et diligenter requisita super articulis huic rotolo appensis. Super primo articulo requisita dicit quod a novem annis elapsis ipsemet testis fuit serviens Alicie de Welwyk, de qua memoratur, in villa Beverlaco. Et continue morabatur cum eadem Alicia, sibi deserviens, a festo Sancti Michaelis ultimo preterito nonem anni clapsi usque ad festum translationis Sancti Thome tunc sequens. Et vidit sepius tempore intermedio Robertum de Midelton communiter venire de domum dicte Alicie, tunc magistra sue. Et sepius vidit dicto tempore et termino ipsum Robertum precari dictam Aliciam et eam viis et modis quibus potuit inducere ut eum permisset ipsam carnaliter cognovisse. Ac eadem Alicia semper quum ipse simul loquebatur de ea materia, quotienscumque ista testis audivit, semper respondebat sibi dicens quod ipsa noluit permittere eum ipsam carnaliter cognoscere nisi primo faceret sibi securitatem quod eam duceret in uxorem. Et bene recolit, ut dicit, quod quodam die dicti temporis intermedii, videlicet die lune proxima post diem dominicam in ramis palmarum proxima futurum erunt nonem anni elapsi, predictus Robertus in modo que prefertur fecit et loquebatur predicte Alicie in domo sua supradicta, situata in vico vocatur *Estgate* Beverlacensis. Et ipsa Alicia eodem modo respondebat sibi in modo quo [...] dicens se nolle permittere ipsum Robertum eam carnaliter cognoscere nisi faceret sibi securitatem quod eam duceret in uxorem. Ac idem Robertus incontinenter respondebat sibi dicens in hunc modum, "Ego nollem ducere te in uxorem nisi sciram quod tu poteris de me concipere prolem[7] et habere. Et ideo si tu vis permittere me tecum coire [et con]tingat me prolem de te suscitare pro certo volo te tunc ducere in uxorem. Et super hoc volo facere

---

[7] The scribe has dotted out the word *filium* ("son") – i.e., cancelled it by putting dots under it – and replaced it with the gender-neutral term *proles* ("offspring"). The marriage theology of the Church emphasized *proles* as one of the three goods of marriage. This suggestive scribal correction makes it possible to argue that Robert wanted Alice to produce a *son* and that it was her failure to do so that caused the eventual break-up of their relationship outlined by the next witness.

securitatem [et] obligare me per fidem meam mediam cuicumque volueris quod me obligerem, preterquam tibimet. Sed etiam hec [nolem] facere ad presens quia, si sic facerem et me tibi obligarem in forma qua prefertur, statim prima nocte postquam, cognovero deceteres esses uxor mea licet prolem nuncquam conceperis. Et ideo volo facere securitatem [cum] alii cui volueris sed non tibi." Ad quod dicta Alicia respondebat dicens se fuisse contentam. Et fecit Robertus vocare istamet testes ad eos, dicens in hunc modum, "Ecce Alicia de Harpham, talis est [intentionem] inter me et ista Alicia de Welwyk." Et recitavit in forma qua prefertur, "At ipsa Alicia de Welwyk, magistra tua, vult quod ego faciam securitatem super premissis tibi nomine suo et sic volo ego. Et tu Alicia de Harpham accipe hic fidem meam quod ego ducam istam Aliciam de Welwyk in uxorem meam si contingat eam concipere et habere prolem de me." Et dicit quod idem Robertus dictam Aliciam in nocte proxima tunc sequente carnaliter cognovit, ac pluribus aliis noctibus postea sequentibus quia ista testis vidit eos simul jacere in uno et eodem lecto solus cum sola, nudus cum nuda in domo ipsius Alicia secundum eam intentionem, ut credit, ut seinvicem carnaliter commiscerunt [et] inter se habuerunt postea procreationem. Hec scit tam per confessione dicti Roberti quam [per vocem] et famam quam [*sic*] sic laboravit in villa de Beverlaco et locis vicinis. Et sunt premissa ibidem [publica notorie et manifeste,] ut dicit. Interrogata de presentibus in dicto contractu matrimoniali de quo nititur deponere dicit quod dicte partes [contrahentes] fuerunt presentes loco quo prefertur et sunt circa horam vesperum dicti diei. Nescit infra cuius [....] domus situata nec scit deponere de contractu matrimoniali inito cum Elizabeth de Frothyngham.

Non est conducta, informata, prece vel precio corrupta, domestica vel familiaris partis predictis [nec curat que pars] vincat dummodo justitia fiat, ut dicit in virtute juramenti sui.

4. The Interrogation of Dominus William Wetwang, Canon of Wartre, on 8 January 1359 Concerning the Illicit Marriage Between Alice Welwyk and Robert Midelton

Dominus William Wetwang, a canon of Watre, sworn in and examined about the aforesaid things, says when asked about the first article that concerning its contents he is unable to depose except from what others have said and from public voice and fame, which he heard labor over the truth of the contents in the manner and form that was recited to him in the village of Beverley and in neighboring places nine years ago, as he remembers. Asked concerning the second article, he says that on a certain day, which he does not remember for certain – but he knows well that it was before Robert and Elizabeth (concerning whom mention has been made) caused there to be solemnization between them – Robert Midelton and Alice Welwyk[8] came together to a certain dwelling called the hospital of St. Giles in Beverley where this witness was and still is the warden, as he says. And said Robert began to explain to this witness the reason for their coming and to speak[9] in this way, saying: "*Dominus* William, we come to you as the best friend[10] whom said Alice has in these parts, except for the prior of Wartre, the blood-relative of this Alice. And you ought to know that I am much obligated to her for diverse reasons and therefore I want to endow her with my goods as was covenanted between us,[11] which covenant I will recite before you and see if both you and she will still agree to it."[12] To which the witness responded in this way: "Robert, for certain, if it is as I have heard said, thou art in many ways obligated to her. Because it was said to me that thou promised that thou wouldst take this Alice as thy wife if it happened that she conceived offspring by thee (as indeed she did) – and that thou knewest her carnally after this promise and that thou hadst given thy pledge to Alice Harpham, then her servant, in her presence that thou shouldst do the aforementioned things under the condition that has now been met, as it is said." To which said Robert immediately answered, while said Alice Welwyk was present and hearing, speaking in this way: "For certain, I will not contradict that this happened, nor can I. But these things notwithstanding, I shall do and provide for her in such a way that she will consider herself well content." And afterwards they discussed among themselves what this Robert was to give to her, and they settled on ten marks, which he promised to pay to her within the next year. But as to the reason for which he made her that promise, this witness does not know what to testify for certain, since [he did not give] nor express any reason then except that he said that he was obligated to pay that amount. [....][13] that he made the aforesaid promise to her for this reason: lest said Alice should in any way object to the solemnization that he caused to be between him and said Elizabeth Frothyngham after that Saturday, concerning which he endeavored to depose above because public voice and fame labors (namely, from nine years ago and more) and it labored more in the village of Beverley that Robert had promised said Alice Welwyk that he would take her as his wife if he begat any offspring by her. And it was also known in the village of Beverley that he

---

[8] The MS has *Wetewang*, but this is clearly a scribal error.

[9] *recitare.*

[10] The scribe used the word *amicus*, which may also be translated as "family member" or "kinsman."

[11] The phrase is *conventum est*, which strongly implies "legally agreed."

[12] The Latin reads "velitis et velit" (second person plural, second person singular). Robert Midelton is addressing William Wetwang using the formal pronoun (second person plural), hence the duplication of the verb: the plural form refers to William, the singular form to Alice. The Latin verb *velle* means much the same here as the auxiliary verb "will" in English.

[13] There is a lacuna in the MS at this point.

did beget offspring by her long before the time when he contracted with said
Elizabeth.

Latin transcription:

Dominus Willelmus de Wetewang, canonicus de Wartre, juratus et examinatus
super premissis.

Super primo articulo requisitus dicit quod super contentis [nescit]
deponere nisi ex relatu aliorum et ex publica voce et fama quam audivit
laborare super veritatem contentorum in modo et forma sibi recitatum in
villa Beverlaco et locis vicinis huic a nonem annis elapsis, ut recolit.

Super secundo [articulo requisitus dicit quod] quodam die, de quo pro
certo non recolit (sed bene scit quod fuit antequam Robertus et Elizabeth, de
quibus memoratur, inter se solempnizari fecerunt) Robertus de Midelton et
Alicia de Wetewang [*sic*] venerunt simul ad quadam domum vocatur *Hospitale
Sancti Egidii* in Beverlaco, ubi ipsemet testis est custos et tunc fuit, ut dicit. Et
predictus Robertus incipit dicere isti testi causam adventus eorum[14] et recitare
in hunc modum, dicens, "domine Willelme, nos venimus ad vos tamquam ad
meliorem amicum quem ista Alicia habet in istis preter priorem de Wartre,
consanguineum ipsius Alicie, et debitis scire quod ego sum multum obligatus
sibi ex diversis causis. Et ideo volo innare ea cum bonis meis prout est conventum inter me et ipsam, quam quidem conventionem volo recitare coram
vobis et videre si vos et ipsa adhuc velitis et velit consentire." Cui iste juratus
respondit in hunc modum, "Roberte, pro certe, si ita sit prout audivi dici,
tu multis es obligatus sibi, quia dictum fuit michi quod tu ante hoc tempore
promisit quod tu deberes ipsam Aliciam ducere in uxorem, si contingeret eam
de te prole concipere – prout revera fecit – et quod tu, post huius promissionem, ipsam carnaliter cognosces, et quod tu dedisti fidem tuam Alicia de
Harpham, tunc servienti sua, in presentia sua, quod deberes premissa fecisse
sub predicta conditione, que iam est impleta, ut dicitur." Cui dictus Robertus
incontinenter respondit – ipsa Alicia de Welwike ibidem tunc presente et hoc
audiente–in hunc modum dicens, "pro certo, ego nolo contradicere quin ita
fuit, nec possum, sed hiis non obstantibus, ego ita faciam sibi et providebo
quod ipsa reputabit se bene contentam." Et tunc ulterius loquebatur inter
se quid idem Robertus esset dare sibi. Et convenerunt de decem marcas quas
promisit sibi solvere infra illum annum tunc sequentem. Sed ob quam causam
istam fecit sibi promissionem pro certo nescit deponere iste testis, ut dicit.
Quum […] ibidem aliquam causam et ibidem exprimere nisi quia dixit se
multum teneri ipsi […] sua, quod ipse predictam promissionem fecit illa
de causa ne ipsa Alicia aliquomodum [contradicit so]lempnisationi quam
fecit fieri inter ipsum et Elizabeth de Frothyngham post die sabbati, de quo

---

[14] Ms. *ad.* The scribe erroneously began to insert the word *ad[ventus]* in this place.

supra nititur deponere, quia publica vox et fama [laborat,] videlicet a novem annis elapsis et amplius laboravit in villa de [Beverlaco quod ipse] promiserat predicte Alicie de Welwyk quod ea duceret in uxorem si e[um prolem] ex ea suscitaret. Et fuit etiam notorium et manifestum in dicta villa de Beverlaco [quod prolem] suscitavit de ea diu ante illud tempus quo contraxit cum predicta Elizabeth.

CHAPTER NINE

Marrying and Marriage Litigation in Medieval Ireland

Art Cosgrove

Medieval Ireland, according to contemporaries, was a country divided into two "nations." On the one hand there were the descendants of the Anglo-Norman settlers of the late twelfth and early thirteenth century; on the other, the successors to the older Gaelic Irish population. The church could not avoid being affected by this division and itself became split into two sections, one *inter Anglicos* (among the Anglo-Irish), the other *inter Hibernicos* (among the Gaelic Irish).[1] We must therefore investigate marital behavior in the two parts of Ireland: the section of the country under English control and using English law, Anglo-Ireland; and the Gaelic Irish area where a different legal system, the old brehon law, still held sway. But first, a word about the context in canon law.

Church law on marriage was defined and clarified during the twelfth and early thirteenth centuries. Basic Christian teaching was straightforward: What God has united, man must not divide (Mark 10:10). But how do you know when God has united a man and a woman in matrimony? In other words, what constitutes a marriage? The attempts by theologians and canonists to formulate an answer to this question resulted in a definition of marriage that changed little between the thirteenth and sixteenth centuries.

The matrimonial bond was created by the consent of the two parties, freely given. The primacy of consent is made clear by the fact that words of consent expressed in the present tense (*verba de praesenti*) constituted a marriage tie even without consummation of the union. Conversely, if it could be shown that one or other partner had not consented to the union, then the marriage could be annulled. The

---

[1] J. A. Watt, *The Church and the Two Nations in Medieval Ireland* (Cambridge, 1974); and idem, "*Ecclesia inter Anglicos et inter Hibernicos*: Confrontation and coexistence in the medieval diocese and province of Armagh," in James Lydon (ed.), *The English in Medieval Ireland* (Dublin, 1984), 46–64.

This article was first published in Art Cosgrove (ed.), *Marriage in Ireland* (Dublin, 1985), 25–50. We reproduce it here (with minor revisions) by kind permission of the publisher – College Press, Dublin – and of that press's founder. We have added a new appendix of documents, which Prof. Cosgrove translated from Latin into English.

[332]

renowned twelfth-century canonist, Gratian, had enunciated the principle that "no woman should be coupled to anyone except by her free will."[2]

Preferably, the consent of the couple should be expressed in a public ceremony, and one of the consistent aims of the church was to have marriages publicly celebrated. The ideal procedure, in the church's view, would be initiated by a public betrothal of the couple. Following this, there would be a reading of the banns in the parish church: on three successive Sundays the local priest would inform the congregation of the proposed marriage so that any objections to it could be raised. If there were no objections or if these had been satisfactorily rebutted, then the marriage ceremony would take place at the door of the church. The partners expressed their willingness to marry, normally the groom gave a ring or other token to the bride, and the bridal party then entered the church for the nuptial mass.

Yet many marriages did not conform to this ideal. It must be stressed that no public ceremony was required to make a marriage valid and indissoluble. Because the consent of the partners rather than the church ceremony was the essential element, the church recognized unions that took place without its knowledge or blessing. Church authorities frequently condemned these "clandestine" marriages throughout the medieval period, but their validity was admitted until the decree *Tametsi* of the Council of Trent in 1563. The "private" celebration of marriage had obvious disadvantages, particularly if the partners subsequently disagreed. A public ceremony safeguarded the contract. Yet because many people believed that they could regulate their marriages for themselves, clandestine unions remained common and inevitably produced more disputes than those which observed all the formalities laid down by the church.[3]

The church also defined the impediments that prevented individuals from validly contracting marriage. Obviously, if one partner had married before and the spouse was still living, it was impossible to enter upon a second marriage. Those who had taken solemn religious vows or major holy orders were also prohibited from matrimony, and the parties to a marriage had to have reached the age of puberty (fourteen for boys, twelve for girls) before they could make a binding contract.

The church also forbade marriage between those who were considered to be too closely related. This prohibition had nothing to do with any fear of genetic disorders. Among the reasons advanced by Thomas Aquinas for the ban on such marriages was the danger to family life that could arise if the possibility of subsequent marriage fostered concupiscence among those of opposite sexes dwelling in the same household. More positively, he argued that the prohibition of marriage

---

[2] Words of consent expressed in the future tense (*verba de futuro*) effected a binding tie only if they were followed by consummation.

[3] Richard H. Helmholz, *Marriage Litigation in Medieval England* (Cambridge, 1974), 26–31; Michael M. Sheehan, "The formation and stability of marriage in fourteenth-century England: Evidence of an Ely register," *Mediaeval Studies* 33 (1971): 228–63; idem, "Marriage theory and practice in the conciliar legislation and diocesan statutes of medieval England," *Mediaeval Studies* 40 (1978): 408–60.

between relations tended to promote the multiplication of friendship and the propagation of love.[4]

Yet it is questionable if either of these arguments justified the wide-ranging nature of the prohibition. Even after the Fourth Lateran Council (1215) had reduced the prohibited degrees of blood relationship or consanguinity from seven to four, one was still prevented from marrying anyone descended from the same great-great-grandfather. In addition, there were the restrictions springing from the tie of affinity, which bound any man or woman and the blood relations of the partner with whom he or she had sexual intercourse. Lying behind the concept was the view that by copulation parties became "one flesh," and consequently the blood relations of one party became the relations by affinity of the other party. Because copulation rather than marriage was the key issue, affinity was considered to arise not only from lawful marriage but also from illicit intercourse. And because the impediment of affinity was co-extensive with that of consanguinity, that is, to the fourth degree, the result was that if a man had sexual relations with a woman, he could not subsequently marry her sister, or her first, second, or third cousin.[5] The bond of spiritual affinity must also be mentioned. This was forged between relations of the person who acted as sponsor for a child at baptism or confirmation and the family of the child. This impediment, for example, could prevent a widower from marrying the woman who had stood as godmother to a child by his first wife.[6]

The regulations on marriage were designed for universal application throughout the western church. Because it was the church that determined what constituted or did not constitute a valid marriage, both civil and ecclesiastical authorities accepted that marriage disputes should be heard only in church courts. How did people observe the regulations in Ireland between the thirteenth and sixteenth centuries?

The evidence on which the investigation is based is much less satisfactory than one would wish. Canon law required every ecclesiastical court to employ a notary or two other suitable men to record all the acts of the court. These act books, as they were termed, often provide a detailed record of marriage litigation in particular dioceses.[7] No such act book survives for any Irish diocese, however, and for the activity of an ecclesiastical court in marriage disputes, we are forced to rely on the incomplete and haphazard records of marriage litigation that appear among the registers of the medieval archbishops of Armagh.[8] Thus, from the late fourteenth

---

[4] *Summa theologiae* II\u1d43II\u1d43\u1d49, q. 154, a. 9.

[5] Francis X. Wahl, *The Matrimonial Impediments of Consanguinity and Affinity: An Historical Synopsis and Commentary*, Catholic University of America Canon Law Studies, 90 (Washington, D.C., 1934), especially 4–7, 19, 57, and 72–74.

[6] Helmholz, *Marriage Litigation*, 78.

[7] Ibid., 7–11.

[8] For a survey of the registers see W. G. H. Quigley and E. F. D. Roberts (eds.), *Registrum Iohannis Mey: The Register of John Mey, Archbishop of Armagh 1443–1456*, (Belfast, 1972) (hereafter, *Reg. Mey*), ix–xv.

to the early sixteenth century, we are provided with glimpses of an Irish ecclesiastical court dealing with marriage disputes. This, in itself, means that the evidence is biased, for it is unfortunately true that marital harmony tends to leave little trace in the records.

GAELIC IRELAND

Within Gaelic Ireland, marriage behavior had long been the target of criticism, especially from the clergy. Throughout the eleventh and twelfth centuries, church reformers within and without the country attacked a pattern of marital behavior that in their view was based not on the canon law of the church but on older, indigenous traditions. Thus, the Irish law on marriage – a law of fornication rather than a law of marriage, according to Archbishop Lanfranc of Canterbury – permitted a man to keep a number of concubines, allowed divorce at will followed by the remarriage of either partner, and took no account of canonical prohibitions regarding consanguinity or affinity.[9] It is not surprising to find, therefore, that one of the benefits that Pope Alexander III hoped might accrue from Henry II's visit to Ireland in 1171–72 was a reformation in Irish marriage customs.[10]

Yet traditional marriage behavior seems to have survived the coming of the Anglo-Normans, at least among the higher ranks of Gaelic Irish society; at any rate, that is what remarks by contemporaries suggest. One annalist went so far as to attribute the decline of a formerly great Gaelic Irish family to the sexual excesses of its leading member, who had laid claim to the high-kingship of Ireland in the period immediately preceding the Anglo-Norman incursions. The Annals of Connacht contain the following entry on the death of Áed Ó Conchobair in 1233:

Here ends the rule of the children of Ruaidhrí Ó Conchobair, king of Ireland. For the Pope offered him the title to [the kingship of] Ireland for himself and his seed for ever, and likewise six wives, if he would renounce the sin of adultery henceforth, and since he would not accept these terms God took the rule and sovereignty from his seed for ever, in punishment for his sin.[11]

The registers are preserved in Armagh Public Library. Transcripts are contained in TCD (Trinity College, Dublin) MS 557, 1–13.

[9] Katharine Simms, "The legal position of Irishwomen in the later middle ages," *Irish Jurist* n.s. 10 (1975): 96–111, at 97.

[10] Maurice P. Sheehy (ed.), *Pontificia Hibernica: Medieval Papal Chancery Documents Concerning Ireland, 640–1261*, vol. 1 (Dublin, 1962), 21.

[11] Alexander M. Freeman (ed.), *Annála Connacht: The Annals of Connacht (1224–1554 A.D.)*, (Dublin, 1944), 47. See William M. Hennessy (ed.), *The Annals of Loch Cé: A Chronicle of Irish Affairs from A.D. 1014 to A.D. 1590*, vol. 1 (London, 1871), 314–15.

Obviously Pope Alexander III would never have made the offer here attributed to him, but it is clear that people still did not regard monogamy as mandatory in Gaelic Ireland.[12]

Acknowledgment in Gaelic Irish sources of a continuation of traditional modes of behavior is matched by denunciation of them in hostile Anglo-Irish records. Among a long list of charges made against the Gaelic Irish in a letter from the Dublin government to Pope John XXII ca. 1331 is the accusation that men lived with their wives and their female relatives and had sexual relations indiscriminately with them, excusing their incest and adultery on the frivolous grounds that it was the custom of the country.[13]

Such a prejudiced source must be treated with some skepticism, but other, less biased, accounts confirm the continuing prevalence of uncanonical practices. The existence of formal contracts of concubinage is made clear by a regulation issued in the ecclesiastical province of Armagh in the mid-fourteenth century:

That no subject of the province of Armagh, lay or clerical, may hold women or concubines under the name of Cayf otherwise Choghie for obtaining their concubinage . . . if anything is given or promised to said woman or another with that occasion in mind directly or indirectly, the person giving and holding and receiving her falls into . . . sentence of greater excommunication.[14]

Many men and women among the aristocracy continued to have a succession of spouses, and this was a key factor in the proliferation of some of the major families. For example, Pilib Mág Uidhir, Lord of Fermanagh (d.1395), had twenty sons by eight mothers, and Toirdhealbach Ó Domhnaill, Lord of Tír Conaill, had eighteen sons by ten different women. On the basis of this and other evidence, Kenneth Nicholls concluded that "throughout the medieval period, and down to the end of the older order in 1603, what could be called Celtic secular marriage remained the norm in Ireland and Christian matrimony was no more than the rare exception grafted on to this system."[15]

---

[12] For commentary on the passage, see B. W. O'Dwyer, "The annals of Connacht and Loch Cé and the monasteries of Boyle and Holy Trinity," *Proceedings of the Royal Irish Academy* 72 (1972), Sect. C, 83–101, at 92–93; and cf. Freeman, *Annals of Connacht*, 77–79.

[13] " . . . et consanguineas suas cum uxoribus propriis in eadem domo commorantes, modo unam modo aliam indifferenter carnaliter cognoscentes consuetudinem in hiis ad modum patrie in eorum frivolosam excusationem pretendunt, incestus crimen et adulterii detestabiliter committendo. . . . " Quoted from J. A. Watt, "Negotiations between Edward II and John XXII concerning Ireland," *Irish Historical Studies* 10 (1956–57): 1–20, at 19.

[14] D. A. Chart (ed.), *The Register of John Swayne, Archbishop of Armagh and Primate of Ireland, 1418–1439* (Belfast, 1935) [hereafter, *Reg. Swayne*, 11; Simms, "The legal position of Irishwomen," at 101–102. " . . . mulieres et concubinas sub nomine cayf alias choghie pro concubinatu earundem obtinendo" (TCD MS 557, iii, 395–96). The terms *cayf* and *choghie* seem to be dialectal variants of *coibche*: see Donnchadh Ó Corráin, "Marriage in early Ireland," in Art Cosgrove (ed.), *Marriage in Ireland* (Dublin, 1985), 5–24, at 24 n. 35.

[15] Kenneth W. Nicholls, *Gaelic and Gaelicised Ireland in the Middle Ages* (Dublin, 1972), 11 and 73.

This sweeping statement needs some qualifications. Although it is true that the canon law was challenged throughout the medieval period in Gaelic Ireland by concepts of marriage that pre-dated the advent of Christianity, the impact of church teaching and regulation was not negligible. The failure to solemnize marriages in church need occasion no surprise: clandestine unions were common throughout Western Europe.[16] The marriage pattern outlined previously may have been confined to the upper reaches of Gaelic Irish society; lack of evidence prevents any estimate of marital behavior lower down the social scale. For the Gaelic Irish aristocracy, real difficulties were caused by canonical regulations on consanguinity and affinity. In a letter to the Pope in July 1469 seeking a dispensation from impediments of consanguinity to permit Énri Ó Néill to marry Johanna MacMahon, Archbishop Bole of Armagh made the general point that several of the leading men in Ireland "are living in incestuous relationships, because they can rarely find their equals in nobility, with whom they can fittingly contract marriage, outside the degrees of consanguinity and affinity."[17] And this reflects a similar situation in the Scottish highlands a century earlier, when it was claimed that "there is such a dearth of nobles that it is hard for them to marry except within the prohibited degrees."[18]

The impact of the church regulations on affinity and consanguinity was naturally much greater in small-scale societies like those in Gaelic Ireland and highland Scotland, and the frequency with which dispensations were sought is an indication of their effect. But, equally, the desire to be dispensed, often at considerable trouble and expense, shows that there were many who were not prepared to flout the church law in this regard. Even the most cursory survey of the Calendar of Papal Letters, particularly for the fifteenth century, reveals a steady demand for papal dispensations from Gaelic Irish as well as Anglo-Irish petitioners. It is true that many of these requests came from couples who had been cohabiting for some time and had already produced offspring. In some few instances, ignorance that their relationship was within the forbidden degrees was put forward as the cause of the delay, as in a case in 1290 in the diocese of Lismore, when the dispensation was granted to a couple who had married thirty years previously.[19] But many of those seeking dispensations had chosen to marry first and then to regularize their union. Presumably the fact that they were already living together increased the

---

[16] See Helmholz, *Marriage Litigation*, 27–30; George H. Joyce, *Christian Marriage: An Historical and Doctrinal Study*, 2nd edition (London, 1948), 103–16; and Beatrice Gottlieb, "Getting Married in Pre-Reformation Europe: The Doctrine of Clandestine Marriage and Court Cases in Fifteenth-Century Champagne" (Ph.D. diss., Columbia University, 1974).

[17] "... nonnullos nobiles proceres et magnates in terra Hibernie incestuose degentes eo quod raro possunt eorum pares in nobilitate extra gradus consanguinitatis et affinitatis sibi matrimonialiter copulandas commode reperire" (Reg. Octavian f. 203a, TCD MS 557, xi, 778–80).

[18] *Calendar of Entries in the Papal Registers relating to Great Britain and Ireland* (London, 1893), *Papal Letters 1362–1404*, p. 56.

[19] Ibid., *1198–1304*, p. 518.

likelihood of obtaining the necessary dispensation. Certainly few couples seemed prepared to delay cohabitation until the reception of the dispensation, and this was true in Anglo-Irish as well as in Gaelic areas. A marriage agreement in Galway in 1468 is revealing in this regard. John Blake entered into a settlement on behalf of his daughter Evelyn with Peter Lynch. Among its terms was an undertaking by Peter that he would obtain the dispensation necessary to allow him to wed Evelyn. However, the agreement went on to state that:

any issue begotten between the said Peter and Evelyn before the obtaining of the said dispensation and solemnization of said marriage [were] to be treated . . . as being as much legitimate as the issue begotten after the publication of the banns and the solemnization of said marriage.[20]

What was it that prompted couples to seek these dispensations even in so tardy a fashion? In the Anglo-Irish area, the desire to safeguard inheritance rights could well have been a factor, but this was less important for the Gaelic Irish aristocracy, among whom acknowledgment of paternity rather than canonical concepts of legitimacy determined hereditary entitlements.[21] The reasons for such dispensations still await investigation, but a troubled conscience or a wish to conform to church regulations may explain some of them. Certainly, there can hardly be any other reason for the dispensation sought in 1448 by Aedh Ó Conchobair (Odo Ochoncoir), described as a nobleman of the diocese of Kildare. Prior to his marriage to Honora Nic Ghiolla Phadraig he had sexual relations with both her sister and another woman related to her in the third degree of affinity, thus invalidating the union. But these affairs were unknown to Honora's friends and to all others, and the bishop of Kildare was therefore authorized to absolve Aedh, dispense from the impediments created by his premarital behavior, and permit the couple to contract marriage again.[22]

Only a small proportion of the material on marriage litigation in the Armagh registers comes from those parts of the diocese and province that lay *inter Hibernicos*. Appeals to the court of the archbishop against decisions reached in dioceses such as Clogher and Clonmacnoise[23] imply the existence of courts dealing with marriage disputes within those dioceses, but no records of them now survive. A number of cases were initiated by Gaelic Irish women who sought to have their husbands restored to them, sometimes after years of separation. When archbishop Colton made his visitation to the diocese of Derry in 1397, Una O'Connor sought redress from him: she had been dismissed by her husband, Manus Ó Catháin, without any court judgment and replaced by a concubine. Katherine O'Doherty

---

[20] Martin J. Blake (ed.), *The Blake Family Records*, 1st series: *1300–1600* (London, 1902), 39.

[21] Nicholls, *Gaelic and Gaelicised Ireland*, 77–78.

[22] *Calendar . . . Papal Letters 1447–55*, pp. 426–27.

[23] Reg. Prene ff. 102v, 142–142v, TCD MS 557, V, 361–64, vi, 106; *Reg. Mey* (n. 8 above), pp. 123–29, 213–14. For the appointment of a commissary to hear marriage disputes in the section of the Armagh diocese *inter Hibernicos*, see Reg. Cromer f. 60, TCD MS 557, xii, 487–88.

complained that her husband, Manus McGilligan, ignored the decision of the Derry diocesan court that she was his legitimate wife and openly consorted with other women.[24]

The attitude of Gaelic Irish men of rank toward the canon law and the ecclesiastical courts is best illustrated, perhaps, by the case involving Muircheartach Ruadh Ó Néill, head of the O'Neills of Clandeboye (1444–68). Ó Néill had married Margaret, daughter of Maghnus Mac Mathghamhna, and had subsequently deserted her for a woman named Rose White. In justification of his action he claimed that his marriage to Margaret was invalid by a tie of affinity because he had previously had sexual relations with Margaret's first cousin Maeve (Mewe). In support of his contention, he brought forward the explicit evidence of one Aine "new Owhityll," a fifty-year-old woman from the Down diocese.

In her deposition to the court, Aine stated that Muircheartach had been captured and detained by Maeve's father, Ruaidhri Mac Mathghamhna; during the period of captivity, Muircheartach often had Maeve with him in bed. The witness claimed that she herself had shared the same bed, that she had often seen the couple naked together, and that she was certain that sexual intercourse had taken place between them. She admitted that Maeve had not become pregnant, that she was uncertain about the date of the alleged incidents, and that they had taken place within Ruaidhri's dwelling without his knowledge.

Yet the court refused to accept this evidence, clearly taking the view that the story had been fabricated to provide a pretext whereby Muircheartach could escape from an unwelcome marriage. And although the case dragged on for more than two years, the eventual decision of the archbishop of Armagh in December 1451 was that the marriage between Muircheartach and Margaret was valid. Ó Néill was ordered, under pain of excommunication, to separate from Rose White and to accept Margaret as his legitimate wife.[25]

We do not know whether or not Muircheartach obeyed this injunction. In repudiating one wife and taking another without any adjudication on validity, Muircheartach was acting in a manner sanctioned by Gaelic Irish tradition. Yet, clearly, he felt that the canonical regulations could not be ignored; otherwise he would hardly have gone to the trouble of mounting his ultimately unsuccessful defense. Church teaching on marriage was not sufficiently influential to prevent the continuation of traditional practices, but the impact of church regulations was strong enough to persuade Gaelic Irish leaders that it was worthwhile attempting to clothe such practices in canonical respectability.

Nevertheless, the clash between two quite different concepts of marriage and its function in society continued throughout the Middle Ages. The issue at stake was not the promiscuity of the Gaelic Irish aristocracy, which could be paralleled or

---

[24] William Reeves (ed.), *Acts of Archbishop Colton in his Metropolitan Visitation of the Diocese of Derry A.D. MCCCXCVII, with a Rental of the See Estates at that Time* (Dublin, 1850), 33–40 and 48–49.
[25] *Reg. Mey*, 135, 210–11, 222–24.

surpassed by aristocracies elsewhere. The real problems lay in the fact that practices in Gaelic Ireland that elsewhere would be classified simply as illegal or uncanonical found a sanction in traditional law. Women regarded as concubines by the church often enjoyed the same legal and social status as wives, and the children of such women were accorded the same rights as those of the canonically recognized wife. Where no distinction is made between legitimate and illegitimate children, the difference between legal and illegal wives loses much of its force.

The point was fully appreciated by Sir Thomas Cusack when he expounded to the English council in 1541 the benefits to be expected from the enforcement among the Gaelic Irish leaders of the scheme known as Surrender and Regrant. Cusack believed that one element in the scheme, the acceptance of English laws of inheritance, would lead to a reformation in marriage practices:

Item, annother grete commoditie shall ensue by taking of ther landes, for when non of ther basterdes shall inherite, which is the cause whie that they doe not marie, but live diabolicallie withoute mariage, and knowing that non shall inherite but mulierly [legitimately] borne, it will cause them to marie and to lyve according the lawes of God.[26]

The scheme never achieved the widespread acceptance and implementation for which Cusack had hoped, but, ultimately, the extension of English law into Gaelic Irish territories was to undermine traditional practices in this, as in other areas of life.

ANGLO-IRELAND

Within Anglo-Ireland, the secular legal system presented no such challenge to the canon law. As in England, the common law accepted that cases concerning marriage and legitimacy should be determined in the ecclesiastical courts.[27] Church influence was clearly greater here than in Gaelic Ireland. In 1305, an inquisition in Waterford revealed that Henry Fitz-John, having been prevented from marrying a woman because of a tie of affinity, "kept her as his concubine in the parts of Connacht because the prelates of the bishopric of Waterford did not permit them to cohabit in that diocese."[28]

In the late-fifteenth century, when it became known that Patrick Goldsmith was living adulterously with Belle Barry in Dublin, the mayor expelled Belle from the

---

[26] *State Papers of the Reign of Henry VIII*, 11 vols. (London, 1830–52), vol. 2, 326–27.
[27] There was a significant difference between the two laws on the issue of legitimacy. Canon law recognized the legitimacy of children born prior to the marriage of the parents, whereas English common law acknowledged as legitimate only those children born after their parents' marriage. See Richard H. Helmholz, "Bastardy litigation in medieval England," *American Journal of Legal History* 13 (1969): 360–83. For an inheritance case that turned on the same issue, see Reg. Cromer ff. 108v–109, TCD MS 557, xii, 281–85.
[28] James Mills (ed.), *Calendar of the Justiciary Rolls, or Proceedings in the Court of the Justiciar of Ireland* (Dublin and London, 1905–1914), vol. 2 (for 1305–1307), 112–13.

city for a year. The measure had only a limited effect given that Patrick would secretly bring Belle from Kilmainham to his room at night, but it is indicative of a desire on the part of the municipal authorities to support church rulings.[29]

The Dublin administration did attempt to regulate marriage practices in one way. Concern about the threats to the security and cultural identity of the colonial settlement posed by intermarriage with those hostile to it led to restrictions on the choice of marriage partner. The ordinance of 1351 forbade marriage between the colonists and any enemies of the king, whether Gaelic or Anglo-Irish. Fifteen years later, the Statute of Kilkenny imposed a ban based solely on ethnic grounds, prohibiting any "alliance by marriage … concubinage, or by caif [*coibche*]" between the Anglo-Irish and the Gaelic Irish.[30]

Yet it was not within the competence or the power of the administration to enforce such regulations. It was simply not possible to prevent people from getting married and only an ecclesiastical court could determine whether or not a marriage was valid. All that the secular authorities could do was impose penalties after the event, the most celebrated instance being the confiscation of the property of the Anglo-Irish woman, Elizabeth de Veale, after she had married Art Mac Murchadha.[31] The legislation did little to discourage those Anglo-Irish who so wished from choosing a partner from the Gaelic Irish community. Popular attitudes rather than governmental directives were more responsible for restricting the number of marriages that bridged the ethnic and cultural divides between the two "nations." In a case before the Armagh ecclesiastical court in 1448, a witness to the clandestine marriage of John Brogeam and Katherine "Odobuy" claimed that John's friends were much displeased that John, the son of a good father, should marry such a Gaelic Irish woman ("quod talem Hibernicam in suam haberet uxorem"). Another witness confirmed that John had lost his friends on account of his love for Katherine and that he subsequently attached himself to Katherine's father, in whose service he now remained. But John's friends were persistent in their efforts to break up what they clearly regarded as an unsuitable match. Having ultimately detached John from Katherine, they arranged a marriage, with a church ceremony, between John and Mabina Huns. Because Katherine was still alive at the time of this wedding, Mabina was able to seek annulment on the grounds that John was already married.[32]

Though lacking the competence to adjudicate on the validity of marriage, the secular courts did have to deal with offences that arose out of marital strife. John Malvern was sentenced to be hanged in June 1310 for having killed his wife with an axe. In a quarrel between David Le Whyte and his wife Agatha in Dublin in 1306, David threw a knife that missed his wife but glanced off the wall and injured his

[29] Reg. Octavian f. 338b, TCD MS 557, xi, 1340–41.
[30] Henry F. Berry (ed.), *Statutes and Ordinances, and Acts of the Parliament of Ireland: King John to Henry V* (Dublin, 1907), 386–87 and 432–33.
[31] See Art Cosgrove, *Late Medieval Ireland 1370–1541* (Dublin, 1981), 14.
[32] Reg. Prene ff. 54–54v, TCD MS 557, v. 213–15.

daughter Margery in the head. A fight over a woman in Clonmel in 1312 led to the death of one of the participants. The court was told that when William O'Kelly was lying, embracing a woman, Richard Laudefey, moved by jealousy, took William by the feet and dragged him away from the woman. The two men then dug up sods and threw them at one another; one of the sods thrown by William contained a small stone and, when this struck Richard, he drew his sword and injured William. Thereupon the latter also drew his sword and fatally wounded Richard.[33]

The most notable case of this type was heard at Cork in May 1307. It concerned John Don, a wine merchant from Youghal, who married a woman called Basilia and shortly afterwards went abroad on business. During his absence, Stephen O'Regan came to John's house "asking Basilia that he might be her friend. She lightly consenting, they lay together . . . for the whole time that John was abroad." On his return John was informed by his neighbors about what had been going on and, naturally irate, he forbade Stephen to visit his house in future. Yet subsequently, when John was absent on a business trip to Cork, Stephen again came to the house and slept with Basilia.

When John learned of this second offence, he devised a plan to trap Stephen. He had, attached to his house, a tavern, and the keeper of this promised him that he would let him know if Stephen came to visit Basilia again. On a day following John pretended that he was going to Cork on business but instead went to another house in Youghal. That evening, Stephen and Basilia dined together with one Stephen Le Jeofne, who, unknown to the couple, seems to have been an ally of John. After supper Stephen O'Regan went to the tavern and drank some wine with the tavern keeper. While they were drinking, Basilia passed through the tavern to her bedroom. Stephen and the tavern keeper followed her. Aware now of the need for discretion, Stephen and Basilia attempted to buy the silence of the tavern keeper and Basilia's maid by offering the former the sum of five shillings and the latter a cow. Then Stephen proceeded to take off his shoes, clearly intending to spend the night with Basilia.

The tavern keeper, faithful to his prior agreement with his employer, now went to the house of Stephen Le Jeofne where John Don was waiting with a group of armed men. Once informed of what had happened, they proceeded to John's house, hoping to catch the guilty couple together. The noise of the armed men's approach alarmed Stephen and Basilia and they extinguished their candles. Stephen then decided to attempt an escape, but in the hall of the house he ran into John Don's armed men. They threw him to the ground, bound his hands and feet, and then castrated him.

Stephen succeeded in his action for assault and was awarded substantial damages of £20 against John Don and his associates. The latter avoided imprisonment by the

---

[33] *Calendar of the Justiciary Rolls . . . Ireland 1308–1314*, p. 148; ibid., *1305–1307*, p. 503; ibid., *1308–14*, p. 252.

payment of a fine of five marks (£3. 6s. 8d.). A week later, John Don counterclaimed against Stephen for compensation for goods destroyed or stolen from his house and was awarded £2 by the court.[34]

Almost all of the other evidence for marital behavior in Anglo-Ireland comes from the Armagh registers and is mainly concerned with the southern half of the Armagh diocese, which was *inter Anglicos,* mostly contained in the modern county Louth. One fact emerges clearly from an examination of the depositions in these court cases: the continuing prevalence of clandestine marriages despite frequent condemnation of the practice by the church authorities. In the late fourteenth century, a council under Archbishop John Colton attempted to encourage couples to solemnize their marriages in church by extending the period in which a church ceremony was available. Church weddings were not normally permitted between the beginning of Advent and 13 January, a period of six–seven weeks; from Septuagesima Sunday to the first Sunday after Easter (ten weeks); and from the first Rogation Day (the Monday before Ascension Thursday) to the Sunday after Pentecost (three weeks);[35] making a total of nineteen–twenty weeks in which solemnization was not possible. Colton's council allowed couples to contract matrimony in church "on all days of the year except from Palm Sunday to the Sunday after Easter,"[36] reducing the prohibited period to a mere two weeks.

Colton's concession seems to have had a limited impact. Couples continued to exchange consent in a variety of settings outside the church: in Robert Preston's tavern at Drogheda, in the hall of John Byford's house in Dunshaughlin, in the kitchen of White of Richardstown, on top of the rabbit-warren of Kilclogher, in a barn or storehouse, and (less surprisingly) in a bed.[37] Such unions came to the notice of the ecclesiastical court only if one or other partner disputed the fact that a marriage had taken place. As in English dioceses, many suits were initiated by parties (often women) seeking judgment that a valid marriage had already taken place, with them.[38]

Why did so many couples settle for clandestine unions and avoid a church ceremony that would have formalized and publicized the marriage? In some instances, the motivation was a desire to marry without the knowledge of parents or friends. In 1454, for example, it was alleged that Peter Waryn of Drogheda wanted to keep his wedding to Jenet Monteyne of Dunshaughlin a secret because he believed his parents and friends would be angry with him if they knew about it.[39] Evidence in the case brought by Anisia Fy John (FitzJohn) in January 1522, seeking to have John McCann declared her legitimate husband, reveals a clash between father and

---

[34] Ibid., *1305–1307*, pp. 376–77 and 398.
[35] William Lyndwood, *Provinciale, seu Constitutiones Anglie* (Paris, 1501), fol. 149.
[36] *Reg. Swayne,* 13–14.
[37] *Reg. Mey,* 141–42, 190–91, 356, and 412–13; Reg. Cromer ff. 59, 62–63, TCD MS 557, xii, 124–26, 135–38.
[38] Helmholz, *Marriage Litigation,* 31–73.
[39] *Reg. Mey,* 413.

son over the latter's choice of wife and also, perhaps, second thoughts on the son's part. The first witness in the case, Niall (Nellanus) Omoregan, a laborer who came, like the two principals, from Termonfeckin, stated that one night in the previous September, he had accompanied John McCann on his journey to meet Anisia. The three of them ended up in the garden of John Fy John where, while everyone else was asleep, John McCann and Anisia exchanged consent and Niall joined their hands together. Other witnesses testified to the subsequent displeasure of John's father, William McCann. But John was defiant and reportedly stated that even if his father cut off his head he would not deny that Anisia was his wife! And when, in mid-December 1521, John's brother Thomas sought him out in Walter Fy John's barn to help their father with plowing, he refused to go unless his father acknowledged his married status.

John's ardor must subsequently have cooled if Anisia found it necessary to bring a court case to prove the marriage. On examination, John did admit that he had exchanged words of consent with her, but declared that they had been in the future tense (*verba de futuro*) and thus constituted a promise to marry rather than an actual marriage. But because he also admitted that he had afterward had sexual relations with Anisia, the court adjudged that they were legitimately married, given that canon law laid down that an exchange of consent by *verba de futuro* followed by sexual intercourse made a binding union (see Doc. 1).[40]

Although some children did defy their parents' wishes in regard to marriage – one man expressly stated that he would not seek his parents' advice, as he wished to make his own choice of partner[41] – this would explain only a small proportion of clandestine unions. It has been suggested for other parts of Europe that clandestine marriages were cheaper because some priests attempted to charge a fee for officiating at a wedding ceremony,[42] but there is no evidence of this practice in Ireland. Indeed, the resolution of a marriage dispute arising out of a clandestine match could be quite costly. The court's normal fee was 10s. 6d., and this at a time when a carpenter's daily wage was 5d. and that of a mason, 9d.[43] There are some indications that in Ireland, as elsewhere in Europe,[44] people considered laymen as competent to perform a marriage ceremony. When, in October 1455, an English seaman, Richard Pymroke, wished to marry Matilda Austin in Drogheda, the couple went to the house of a notary in Drogheda around suppertime and the latter witnessed and recorded their marriage.[45] William Kelly of Slane was sought out

---

[40] Reg. Cromer ff. 102–03, TCD MS 557, xii, 258–62.

[41] *Reg. Mey*, 413.

[42] Jean Dauvillier, *Le mariage dans le droit classique de l'église, depuis le décret de Gratien (1140) jusqu'à la mort de Clément V (1314)* (Paris, 1933), 116–20.

[43] *Reg. Swayne*, 46; *Reg. Mey*, 10–11, 54–55, 57–59, 71–72; Reg. Prene ff. 49–49v, 128, TCD MS 557, v, 199–203, 473–74; Reg. Octavian ff. 243a–b, TCD MS 557, xi, 927–28. See James Lydon, "A fifteenth-century building account from Dublin," *Irish Economic and Social History* 9 (1982): 73–75.

[44] Dauvillier, *Le mariage dans le droit classique*, 107–108; Joyce, *Christian Marriage*, 106 and 113.

[45] *Reg. Swayne*, 200, TCD MS 557, iv, 516.

at night by Margaret Keran when she wished to marry John Leche. She brought him back to her home where John and his brother Thomas were waiting. William first made the brothers swear that John was not already married, and Margaret likewise took an oath that she was free to marry. Then William joined their right hands together and "married" them, the couple expressing their consent in the usual fashion. Afterward, they all spent some time drinking, and then Margaret and John went off to bed together (see Doc. 2).[46]

The availability of alternatives to priestly officiation was a further discouragement to marriage in church, but it seems probable that the main reason for the continuation of clandestine marriages was the deep-rooted belief that matrimony was a private rather than a public affair, of concern only to the individuals involved and their families. Some couples intended to have a future solemnization of their union, but given that this was not essential, the good intention must often have withered. Arguably, canon law made it too easy to get married. In theory, a valid exchange of consent could take place between a couple on their own without any witnesses, although in any future disagreement it would be very difficult, if not impossible, to establish what really happened.

In one instance, the Armagh court was forced to rely on eavesdroppers rather than witnesses in its attempts to discover the truth. Katherine Floskye sought a judgment from the court that she was validly married to John O'Lyne. Her case relied mainly on the testimony of her sister and the latter's two girl friends. All three girls had been lying in bed in a closed or locked room when they overheard a conversation between John and Katherine. They claimed that John told Katherine that he wished to have her as his wife. He came, he said, not to demean her but to make her a good woman and his wife. On that understanding they went to Katherine's bed and slept together. The girls also claimed that as a sign of the contract John had given Katherine a brass ("latyn") ring, a fact confirmed by a subsequent witness, who added that John had given Katherine 5s. to have her clothes mended in Drogheda and that he had heard them discussing wedding expenses, an indication that a more formal ceremony was envisaged (see Doc. 3).[47] The court's decision has not survived, but it seems likely that Katherine won her case.

Testimony put forward on behalf of the plaintiff in such cases could be challenged by the defense, which, having heard the evidence of witnesses, could frame a series of questions to test their veracity. This usually meant a detailed interrogation about the circumstances in which the alleged exchange of consent took place. If it occurred in a house or a barn, was it beside the window or beside the bed? What were the date and time of day? Was the weather good or bad? What were the parties wearing at the time? Were they sitting or standing? What were the actual words used in the making of the contract?

---

[46] "fecit eos insimul affidari" (*Reg. Mey*, 348).
[47] "ad faciendam ipsam bonam mulierem et uxorem suam" (*Reg. Mey*, 140–41).

The record of the court proceedings is in Latin but there are occasional reports of what was said in English. In a case from Drogheda in October 1449 in which Katherine Boys sought to prove that Henry Palmer was her husband, one witness gave the words used in the exchange of consent: "I Henry Palmer take the Kateryn Boys to my ryghtfull wyff to have and to hold unto my lyfes end and thereto y plyght the my trouthe." In the same case, another witness under questioning stated that it was a clear day and that he had been summoned away from harvesting to act as a witness to the marriage in the barn. Queries to him and other witnesses about the clothes worn by the couple elicited the information that Henry was clad in a blue gown, a short doublet of "fustayne" (coarse cotton), red hose, and a "blew velten hatt." Surprisingly, perhaps, Katherine's dress was described in less detail: she was said to be wearing a red tunic with a blue tunic underneath. All witnesses agreed that the couple had slept together in the barn on the night following the exchange of consent. The court found in Katherine's favor, though Henry entered an appeal against this decision (see Doc. 4).[48]

Suits to enforce marriage contracts formed one part of the court's business; it also had to deal with pleas for annulment: a declaration that a marriage contract had been invalid from the outset. Annulments were sought on a variety of grounds. As already noted, a plea that the parties were related within the forbidden degrees of consanguinity or affinity might be made. More often, the case was based on an allegation of pre-contract, that one party to a marriage contract was already validly married and thus disqualified from making a second marriage.

In cases in which pre-contract was alleged, the court had to establish not only the validity of the contract but also its date, so as to ensure that it was made prior to the second marriage agreement. It then had to determine whether the spouse of the first union was still alive at the time of the second contract. On occasion, this might involve the court in consideration of events that happened many years before.

It emerged from proceedings in the Armagh court in July 1440 that Agnes Herford, daughter of a butcher from Thomas Street, Dublin, had originally married John Hert at Kilmainham some fourteen years previously. The witness to this stated that he had not been present at the actual ceremony, but that he had been invited to the wedding breakfast in the house of Agnes's father. Five or six years later, presumably after John had deserted her, Agnes was married to William Beg in St. Peter's church in Drogheda. But John was still alive at the time of this ceremony: a witness testified that he met him subsequently to the Drogheda ceremony, in France. He had run off with the wife of a man from Sandwich and was living adulterously with her in Calais. In the circumstances, the court had no option but to declare the marriage between Agnes and William null and void. Because William was regarded as having acted in good faith, he was given permission to

---

[48] *Reg. Mey*, 190–91, 247, 253–54.

marry another woman and the children born to himself and Agnes were declared legitimate.[49]

A case in 1481 turned on evidence of what had occurred thirty years previously. Thaddeus Carpenter sought the annulment of his union with Juliana Maynaghe on the grounds of a valid pre-contract between Juliana and Roger Sarsfield. A number of witnesses claimed they had been present either at the church marriage ceremony or at the wedding feast of Roger and Juliana in Ardee thirty years before. The couple had lived together for some time, but Roger then left and went to live in England. He was unable to persuade his wife to join him there and she then contracted marriage with Thaddeus Carpenter "before the earl of Worcester came to Ireland," that is, prior to 1467. Roger's sister, Jeneta Sarsfield, testified that she knew that her brother was alive five years before because she had received a letter from him asking her to come to England. For good measure, she added that only three years earlier she had received a message from him via Milo Fleming, a merchant from Slane, requesting her to send her son to him in England.[50]

It is worth noting that the court always upheld the earlier valid contract. This it did even if the first marriage was made clandestinely and the second in church. Christiana Brown had exchanged words of consent with James Lepyng in front of a number of witnesses in the house of Marion Newton when both she and James were about fifteen years of age. Afterward, she had married John Waryng of Balrothery in a church ceremony and had several children by him. But the court declared her to be validly married to James Lepyng and nullified her marriage to John.[51]

Although consent rather than consummation made a marriage valid, it was possible, nevertheless, to secure the dissolution of the bond on the grounds of impotence. Usually the woman pleaded her desire to be a mother and the inability of her husband to fulfill that desire, and the Armagh court did award annulments on those grounds.[52] But the court was clearly aware of the danger of fraud or collusion and would not accept a plea of impotence without some form of substantiation, a precaution clearly justified in a case brought by Anisia Gowin in February 1521.

In the previous December, Anisia had failed in her bid to have her marriage to Nicholas Conyll nullified on the basis of pre-contract. She now charged her husband with impotence, a charge he denied. The court ordered that she was "to spend the night with Nicholas in the same bed, without any disturbance" and appointed nine men to carry out an inspection of Nicholas and report their findings. Their evidence left no doubt as to Nicholas's ability to perform his marital duties.[53] Even

---

[49] *Reg. Mey*, 9–11, 54–55.

[50] Reg. Octavian f. 144a, TCD MS 557, x, 574–76.

[51] *Reg. Mey*, 70–71; Reg. Prene f. 128, TCD MS 557, v, 473–74.

[52] *Reg. Swayne* f. 38v, TCD MS 557, iii, 134–35. Reg. Cromer ff. 21v–22v, TCD MS 557, xii, 54–60.

[53] "quod membrum habet satis magnum et ut apparet satis aptum ad coendum et ad copulam carnalem reddendam alicui mulieri" (Reg. Cromer f. 68, TCD MS 557, xxi, 159–61).

when a man admitted impotence the court demanded corroboration from seven witnesses.[54]

Because consent to a marriage had to be freely given, it followed that a union made under duress would be invalid. To get an annulment on this count, a party had to show that the element of compulsion was considerable, in canonical terms, that he or she had been subjected to "force or fear that could move a constant person." It had also to be demonstrated that the couple had not willingly cohabited subsequently, because this could be interpreted as consent by the supposedly unwilling partner.[55] Such formulations clearly left a good deal to the court's discretion.

In two instances, the Armagh court specifically cited the canonical ruling on force and fear in awarding an annulment on the grounds of defective consent. In 1488, the marriage between John McEgallogly of Castle town and Anna "Ny Keghurry" of Drogheda was dissolved for this reason. There was little doubt about Anna's unwillingness because John had been able to detain her only by keeping her in chains; once released, she ran away.[56] Earlier, in 1477, in annulling the marriage between Edmund Butler and Eleanor Taafe, the court found that both sets of parents had exercised threats and intimidation that amounted to "force and fear sufficient to move a constant person."[57]

Almost all pleas for annulment on these grounds were based on allegations of undue parental pressure, and this raises the general issue of the role played by parents in marriage arrangements. As we have seen, children could and did defy their parents' wishes in their choice of marriage partners. But such cases were probably exceptional, and compliance with parental desires, when these were expressed, was more usual.

Some parents did "arrange" marriages for their children. In one instance, it was claimed that discussions about a future marriage took place between parents when the partners were still children at school together (an interesting indication that some form of elementary education was available to girls).[58] Such discussions naturally concerned themselves with the financial details of the marriage settlement. In 1456, William Cashell, on behalf of his son Nicholas, and John Avell, acting for his daughter, Matilda, drew up such an agreement in a notary's house in Drogheda. Under its terms, the future bride's father was to give 40s. and a brass pot, and the future groom's father, 40s. The money and the pot were to be kept by William Cashell until the couple came of age and set up house together. If either of the

---

[54] Ibid., ff. 41v–42, pp. 83–85.

[55] Joseph V. Sangmeister, *Force and Fear as Precluding Matrimonial Consent: An Historical Synopsis and Commentary*, Catholic University of America Canon Law Studies 80 (Washington D.C., 1932), 61–64.

[56] Reg. Octavian f. 10a, TCD MS 557, ix, 57–58.

[57] "...vim et metum qui possunt cadere in constantem" (Reg. Octavian f. 242a, TCD MS 557, xi, 920–25).

[58] "ipis tunc parvulis in scolis insimul addiscendo" (*Reg. Mey*, 70).

parties to the wedding arrangement died beforehand, the father of the deceased party would have his contribution restored to him.[59]

What happened if a daughter refused to accept the husband chosen for her by her parents? On behalf of Isabella Heyron, it was claimed that on the day of her wedding to William Drake, she attempted to run away from home. When she was brought back, her father beat her and compelled her to come to the church. A witness was unable to say whether or not she gave her consent to the wedding because of the chatter of those present at the door of the church but did state that she wept a great deal and was unwilling after the ceremony to accept William as her husband.[60] In the case of Katherine McKesky, both her parents were alleged to have struck her in order to get her to marry John Cusack. Her mother was said to have beaten her so hard with a "bedoke" that she broke it, and her father knocked her to the ground because she disobeyed him.[61] In neither case has the decision of the court survived, but if the evidence given was accepted as true, it seems probable that annulments would have been allowed.

Yet, in this, as in other pleas, the court could be deceived. The final decision in a case from 1459 was that the couple involved had put forward a fraudulent allegation of coercion in order that they could separate and marry other partners.[62] The suspicion must naturally arise that lack of consent was put forward on occasion simply in an attempt to escape from a marriage that had not worked out.

What should we make of the plea of duress advanced in the proceedings that sought to annul a marriage that had united two of the leading families in county Louth, the Dowdalls and the Verdons? Katherine, daughter of Sir John Dowdall of Termonfeckin, had been married to Christopher Verdon but subsequently sought a dissolution on the grounds that she had been forced into the marriage. The key witness on her behalf was her own father.

In the course of his testimony, Sir John stated that at the time both of the betrothal and of the marriage he had coerced his daughter with harsh words and threats; she had made it clear through her tears and in other ways that she had gone through these ceremonies unwillingly and out of fear. Afterward, she refused to consummate the marriage. Although her father spoke harshly to her, called her various vile names, and threatened to break her bones, Katherine refused to go to bed with Christopher unless she had her sister or another woman with her. Sir John explained that the couple lay in an interior room within his room sometimes with and sometimes without a light, and that he was often able to observe their behavior. Never, he claimed, did he see him touch her nor her consent to him and at no stage did they act as man and wife. Sir John concluded his evidence by

[59] *Reg. Swayne*, 202–203.
[60] "propter presentes in ostio et garrulantes" (*Reg Mey*, 199–200).
[61] *Reg. Swayne*, 202–203.
[62] Reg. Octavian ff. 243a–b, TCD MS 557, xi, 925–29.

expressing his regret that they had not been able to agree. The marriage settlement had included favorable financial terms and, if it were now annulled, he would find it very difficult to make alternative provisions for Katherine; he had many daughters not yet disposed of and not very much money.

Sir John's wife supported his testimony and confessed that she herself, at the time of the betrothal, had beaten Katherine around the head and called her "javeyll" (rascal) and other names. During the betrothal ceremony, Katherine had wept and had never afterwards displayed any sign of consent to the union. Katherine's sister, Jenet, stated that she had lain in bed with the couple on several occasions and that she had never seen Christopher place his hand on her sister or show her any sign of affection. She added that when Christopher returned after a period of absence, this would turn Katherine's mood from joy to sadness. Katherine's nurse, Johanna Cryspy, testified that she had often chided the parents for marrying such a young girl against her will, but that she had been told that she did not appreciate the advantages of the match (see Doc. 5).[63]

The sentence of the court in this case has not survived. But if the court accepted this evidence of initial unwillingness on Katherine's part, coercion by parents, and subsequent refusal by Katherine to acknowledge Christopher as her husband, then it would have had little option but to annul the marriage.

Annulments were also granted on occasion to those pleading a tie of spiritual affinity, usually caused by acting as sponsor or godparent at baptism. In 1441, Matilda Ardagh's marriage to William Corbally was dissolved because "Matilda's father had lifted William from the sacred fount," that is, acted as godfather at his baptism. And in 1449, William Pumrell secured an annulment of his marriage on the grounds that his mother had acted as his wife's godmother at baptism.[64]

An alternative to annulment was a judicial separation *a mensa et thoro* (from table and bed) permitting a couple to live apart but without the right to remarry. This was granted when there were no grounds for declaring the marriage invalid but one or the other partner was guilty of heresy, adultery, or cruelty. In October 1450, Janet Swayne of Drogheda was granted such a separation from her husband because of his adultery with Agnes Bowyghere of Bristol. Margery Kelly's decree in Ardee in 1518 was given because of cruelty and fear of death. The court was told that her husband frequently struck her with an iron rake, a long knife, and other weapons, and that her life would be endangered if she remained with him. Less usual was the separation order to William Osere in 1484 when the court accepted that his wife was attempting to murder him.[65]

Overall, the surviving records of matrimonial litigation among the Armagh registers support the view that marriage practices in Anglo-Ireland did not differ

---

[63] *Reg. Mey*, 277–78.
[64] *Reg. Mey*, 57–59, 71–72, 143–44.
[65] *Reg. Mey*, 255–56; Reg. Cromer ff. 2v, 3, 75, TCD MS 557, xxi, 5–8, 170–71; Reg. Octavian, f. 156b, TCD MS 557, x, 616–17.

markedly from those elsewhere in Latin Christendom. In comparison with the evidence from England, which is much fuller, there seems to have been a greater number of pleas based on duress or lack of consent as well as a higher percentage of cases concerned with consanguinity and affinity. Despite the best efforts of the church authorities, marriage was still widely regarded as a personal matter subject to a private contract between the parties. Clandestine unions remained common, and even after the Council of Trent's decree outlawing such unions, clandestine marriage was to have a long history in Ireland.[66]

∽

Appendix: Depositions from the Armagh Registers

Document 1: *Anisia FitzJohn vs. John McCann, January, 1521*[1]

In the name of God, Amen. On the last day of the month of January in the year of our Lord 1521. Examination of the witnesses produced on behalf of Anisia FitzJohn of the parish of Holy Trinity in the matrimonial case undertaken between the same Anisia the plaintiff on the one hand, and one John McCann of the same parish the defendant on the other, in the presence of the Archdeacon of Armagh, President of the Court to the undersigned, etc.

First, Niall O'Moregan a laborer of the same parish aged twenty-three years, having been sworn in and carefully examined, testified that on certain night about fifteen days before the last feast of Michaelmas, at the beginning of the night, the aforesaid John brought him [Niall] with the same John from Donilston to Tananton. After they arrived at Tananton, John left the same Niall and Thomas, John's brother, in the road called in English "Abaytr" just outside Tananton. John went on to Tananton and brought Anisia to the garden of John FitzJohn where Niall met them, and when those present were silent the aforesaid John married the said Anisia and she similarly him with words

---

[66] Since this article was first published in 1985, several relevant studies have appeared. They include the following: Art Cosgrove, "The writing of Irish medieval history," *Irish Historical studies* 27 (1990), 97–111; Terence B. Barry, Robin Frame, and Katherine Simms (eds.), *Colony and Frontier in Medieval Ireland: Essays Presented to J. F. Lydon* (London, 1995); James Muldoon, *Identity on the Medieval J. F. Lydon Irish frontier* (Gainesville, Fla., 2003); W. David H. Sellar, "Marriage, divorce and the forbidden degrees: Canon law and Scots law," in W. N. Osborough (ed.), *Explorations in Law and History: Irish Legal History Society Discourses, 1988–1994* (Dublin, 1995), 59–82; and Christine Meek and Katherine Simms, eds., *The Fragility of Her Sex?: Medieval Irish Women in their European Context* (Dublin, 1996).

[1] From the Register of Archbishop Cromer, in John McCafferty, *The Act Book of the Armagh Diocese 1518–1522: A Text and Introduction* (published M.A. dissertation, Dublin, 1991), no. 128, pp. 142–43. All the following depositions have been translated from Latin. Where the recorder or notary has included a verbatim record in English within the text (which is otherwise in Latin), that record appears verbatim here as well, in the English of the period.

in the present tense, saying, "I take you as my wife," and she similarly, "I take you as my husband until death do us part." Asked who was present, he says that there was no one except the three of them and says that he the witness joined their hands together, neither out of a request nor for a reward.

Next, Patrick O'Donelly of the parish of Saint Fechin of Termonfeckin seeming to be aged about thirty years, having been sworn in and carefully examined, testified that on a certain day at Donilston about fifteen days before the last Christmas in the house of William McCann father of the aforementioned John, while said William was complaining to his aforementioned son about the said Anisia, the said John in response to his father said that whether he had twenty marks or had nothing except his cloak, Anisia was his wife. When the said father threatened his son John, the latter said that even if his father were to cut off his head he would not deny that she was his wife, and even if he were to lose his inheritance he would be content.

Next, Isabella Lales of the aforementioned Tananton, a woman of more than twenty years, having been sworn in and carefully examined, testified that on a certain day before the last Michaelmas having met John near Tananton she asked him whether or not he had contracted marriage with the said Anisia. John replied that it was so, and when she pressed him further about the truth, John said that if he were deprived of a foot or a hand on account of Anisia he would still not deny that she was his wife.

Again, Hugh Ordlin of the aforesaid Tananton seemingly thirty years of age, having been sworn in, testified that three weeks before the previous Sunday, as he recalled, Thomas McCann brother of the aforesaid John came to John at the haggard[2] of Walter FitzJohn in Tananton where John was at that time. When Thomas asked John to go to his father's field,[3] John responded that he would not go unless his father agreed to the [married] status that he now had. Thomas replied that he presumed his father would not agree. He did not know enough to testify further, neither out of a request nor for a reward.

Again, the aforesaid John McCann, having been sworn in and carefully examined, testified that he had contracted with Anisia by words spoken in the future tense, and having been asked whether he had afterwards known her bodily, he said that he had.

In the name of God, Amen. Having heard, seen, and fully understood the merits and circumstances of the matrimonial case between Anisia FitzJohn of the parish of the Holy Trinity, Termonfeckin in the Armagh diocese the plaintiff on the one hand, and John McCann of the same parish defendant on the other, a case that having been moved was left pending undecided for some time, we have found through confessions of parties made judicially before us and by means of other probative documents to which there was no

---

[2] That is, barn, storehouse. The word is still in use in Ireland.
[3] *Caruca*: either a plow or a field (i.e., a carucate).

canonical obstacle, that the aforesaid Anisia and John have jointly concluded a marriage by the expression of words of consent in the future tense and have consummated this marriage by bodily union. Therefore we Cormac Routh bachelor of Canon Law, President of the Metropolitan Court, invoking first the name of Christ and having him alone before our eyes and having considered the advice of those skilled in the law, judge that the said John is the legitimate husband of Anisia and that the same Anisia is now John's lawful wife. We decree and declare that the marriage contracted between John and Anisia is legitimate through this our definitive judgment, which through the mediation of justice we have put in writing herein, penalizing the side of the said John with the expenses of the Court, the assessment of which we reserve for later. This judicial sentence was read and promulgated in the Church of Saint Fechin in Termonfeckin on the third day of January in the year of our Lord 1521. Present were Thomas Drew of Termonfeckin, John FitzJohn of Tananton, Isabella Lales of the same place, and Richard Corkeran apparitor of the deanery of Drogheda.

DOCUMENT 2: *Margaret Keran vs. John O'Kele*[4]

Examination of the witnesses of Margaret Keran of Slane in the marriage case before and after between her and John Leche alias O'Kele and of the divorce between the same John and Matilda McKarmyk of Drogheda in the publication of the banns put forward on behalf of the said Margaret etc.[5]

William Kelly of Slane, the first witness, having been brought forward, admitted, sworn in, and carefully examined, says that at the request of the said Margaret who came, he says, at night in order to bring him a pot of ale which he bought, and earnestly requested him and did not stop until he went with her to her house, and she told him that the said John O'Kele wished to contract marriage with her. He says that he went there with her and finding him [John] there with his brother he enquired about the intentions of the said John, who replied that he wished to contract with the said Margaret as her lawful husband and to marry her. He [William Kelly], as he avers, considering both their intentions, first took the Book and as a precaution made both the said John and his brother Thomas O'Kele then present swear that the said John was entirely free from any matrimonial contract, that he had no obligation to any other woman, and similarly that Margaret had no obligation to any other man. Then, when this had been done, the right hands of the said Margaret and John having been joined together, the witness who speaks married them. Asked about the form of words, he said that it was: "I John take you Margaret

---

[4] From W. G. H. Quigley and E. F. D. Roberts (eds.), *Registrum Iohannis Mey: The Register of John Mey, Archbishop of Armagh, 1443–1456* (Belfast, 1972), no. 332, pp. 348–49.

[5] The published text reads, "in edicione bannorum per predictam Margaretam prohibitorum etc." I read *prehibitorum* ("put forward") instead of *prohibitorum*.

as my lawful wife and thereto I give you my faith," and that she in response said: "I Margaret take you John as my lawful husband and thereto I give you my faith." Then they kissed one another. As to the place, he says it was in the house of the said Margaret. As to the time, he says that it was before the feast of the Apostles Philip and James two years ago. As to whether they were sitting or standing, he says that they were standing. Asked who was present, he says that he the witness who speaks and Thomas the brother of the said John were there. When this was done as related they drank together. The said William after some time drinking with them left them and they spent the night there. Asked whether after the marriage of this kind[6] he [John] had had sexual relations with her, he said that it was so, on many occasions on that night and others, as he supposes (and this is the public opinion and gossip in the village of Slane and the neighboring places). Asked why he had testified as above, he said that it was only for the truth etc.

Thomas O'Kele, the second witness, having been brought forward, admitted, sworn in, and carefully examined, says that he was present but denies completely the oath and the contract of marriage, and notwithstanding diligent examination and investigation of him by the lord official, under the oath he had taken, he refused to say more than [was said] above or to give testimony.

DOCUMENT 3: *The Clandestine Marriage of John O'Lyne and Katherine Floskye*[7]

Examination of the witnesses of Katherine Floskye in the matrimonial case between Katherine and John O'Lyne.

Katherine Blosky, the first witness, having been brought forward, admitted, sworn in, and carefully examined, says that she the witness who is speaking along with Rosina Ythe and Katherine Floskye's sister were lying in the same bed in a single closed room within the same Katherine's house, when they heard Katherine Floskye and John O'Lyne talking and discussing together to the point where John promised by his faith that he came because he wished to have her as his wife and did not come to do harm to her, as he expressly put it, but to make her a good woman and his wife. On that condition they went together to the bed of the said Katherine where he slept with her and had sexual relations with her. Asked when, she says that it was the Sunday night immediately prior to last Christmas. She says that the same John as a sign of the contract and agreement gave to the said Katherine "1 latyn ryng,"[8] and she also heard them discussing the costs of the wedding that would take place. Asked whether there was any public knowledge of the contract of this kind among neighbors and those known to them, she said it was known

---

[6] That is, as described earlier.
[7] *Reg. Mey*, no. 148, pp. 141–42.
[8] Quotation recorded in English; "latyn" = "brass."

immediately on the next day and to some on the same night. As to why she gives evidence, she says only for the truth.

Lord Thomas Ball, chaplain of the parish of Tullyallen, the second witness, having been brought forward, admitted, sworn in, and carefully questioned about the public knowledge of the said contract, says that it was known by the following morning. The same John had dined with the said chaplain on that same Sunday, and after supper when he believed that John was spending the night with him John secretly left and visited Katherine, and as was made public the next morning spent the night there, slept with her, and made the contract with her. He gives this testimony only for the truth.

John Gilchrist, the third witness, having been brought forward, admitted, sworn in, and carefully examined, agrees about the public knowledge and about the ring and [says] that John gave to the said Katherine five shillings to have her clothes mended in Drogheda and that he heard them discuss the costs needed for a wedding. And he gives his testimony only for the truth.

Richard Ethe, the fourth witness, having been brought forward, admitted, sworn in, and carefully examined, agrees about the public knowledge and about the contract, as he heard from his daughter Rosina the following morning, and it was and is commonly spoken of and known. And he testifies solely for the truth.

Rosina Geth [Ethe?],[9] the last witness, having been brought forward, admitted, sworn in, and carefully examined, says in agreeing with the said Katherine Blosky that the witness who speaks, the said Katherine, and Alicia the sister of the aforementioned Katherine Blosky were lying together in the one bed in a closed room, and they heard the said John and Katherine contracting with one another, and afterwards they knew that they were spending the whole night sleeping together. She testifies that as a sign of the contract the said John gave Katherine "1 latyn ring,"[10] and she agrees as to the day and the place and [says] also that in the morning she told her father and others about the contract of this kind. Asked why she testifies to the above she says that she does so only for truth and for no other reason etc.

DOCUMENT 4: *Katherine Boys vs. Henry Palmer, October, 1449*[11]

Examination of the witnesses of Katherine Boys asking that Henry Palmer of Drogheda be adjudged to be her lawful husband on the grounds that he contracted marriage with her through words in the present tense expressing mutual consent with bodily union following, conducted by the Lord Official of the Armagh Court at Drogheda on October 17th in the year of our Lord 1449.

[9] Presumably the daughter of the fourth witness (Richard Ethe), and the same person as the Rosina Ythe mentioned earlier.

[10] Quotation recorded in English.

[11] *Reg. Mey*, no. 192, pp. 190–91.

John Fleming Senior, the first witness, having been brought forward, admitted, sworn in, and asked his age, says that he is over forty years of age. When asked if he knows Henry Palmer of Drogheda and Katherine Boys, he says that he had seen them on many occasions. Asked if he knows of any matrimonial contract between them, he says that he heard that they had expressed similar words for the purposes of a matrimonial contract and that they had said, namely,[12] "I Harry Palmer take thee Kateryn Boys to my ryghtfull wyf to have and to hold unto my lyfe's end and thereto y plyght thee my trouthe," she answering thus, "I Kateryn Boys take thee Harry Palmer to my lawfull spouse to have and to hold unto my lyfe's end and thereto y plyght thee my trouthe." Asked what they did next, he said that they kissed each other. As to whether they did these things sitting or standing, he said that they were standing. Again, as to whether they did this willingly or under duress, he said they were already in agreement before they came there. Asked about their clothing, he says it was long time ago and therefore he does not remember well. Again, asked whether he had been called or requested to act as a witness, he said that he been called by both of them. Again, asked when this happened, he said that this was on the first Monday after the feast of St. Bartholomew the Apostle two years ago. As to the time of day, he says it was in the afternoon. Again, asked about the weather on that day, as to whether it was clear or cloudy, he says that he does not remember. Again, asked where this took place, he says that it was at Rathbran in the storehouse[13] of the witness who speaks. And asked in which part of the building, he says that it was beneath the building.[14] Again, asked for what reason said Henry and Katherine came there, he knows not unless as he presumes it was for the same reason, and he adds that the wife of the witness who speaks had said to Henry that he had kinsfolk[15] and that it would be good for him first to have their advice in such an undertaking. Yet Henry expressly said that even if his father and mother were alive, he would not take their advice in the matter because he wished to contract [marriage] with his wife of his own free will. As to who was present, the witness who speaks says his son and John Boys. And as to whether he [Henry] had her on the subsequent night, he supposes that it was so. As to whether he was related by blood or other affinity to the said Katherine, he says that he is not related to her, and he is not against Henry because it would be improper, as he had said, on the grounds that Henry's mother acted as sponsor to the daughter of the witness who speaks at confirmation by the Bishop, nor did he make trouble when questioned before the Lord Official, but after his citation he came for the conduct of his examination. As to why he testifies as above, he says solely

---

[12] The following two quotations are recorded in English. Before Henry's words, a recorder has written but cancelled the Latin equivalent in the MS.

[13] Or "barn" (*orrium*, = *horreum*).

[14] Perhaps in a cellar?

[15] Or "friends": *amici.*

and entirely for the truth and for no other reason and because he had been called as a witness as stated before.

John Fleming junior, the second witness, having been brought forward, admitted, sworn in, and asked his age, says that he is over twenty-four years of age. And asked whether he knew the said Henry and Katherine, he says that he does. Again, questioned about the matrimonial contract between them, he says and agrees that he heard them contracting together by similar words expressing mutual consent as above. As to the day, the place, and those who were present, he confirms what was said above. And he adds, when asked about the weather, that it was a clear day, and that they sent for him from the harvesters so that he could act as a witness to the contract. Again, asked about their clothing, he says that Henry had a blue gown and "1 blew velten hatt,"[16] and that the aforesaid Katherine was wearing a single red tunic. Again, asked if they slept together, he believes that it was so on the same night following . . . [17] in the storehouse. As to how he is related to Katherine, he says not in any way. And as to why he testifies as above, he says entirely for the truth, and because he was requested to act as a witness as above.

John Boys, the third witness, having been brought forward, admitted, sworn in, and asked his age, says that he is over twenty-four years of age. And as to whether he knows Katherine and Henry, he says that he does. As to how he is related to the woman, he says that he is her brother. And regarding the contract and the precise form of words, he agrees as above; also regarding the place, the time, and those present, as above. He adds that it was near a window beneath the aforesaid storehouse. And as to their clothing, he says that Henry wore a single tunic "de light blewe cum 1 blew velten hatt, 1 short doblet of fustyane, and 1 payre of rede hossen,"[18] and that the woman wore a single red outer tunic with a blue tunic underneath. And he says that he had been asked as a witness. When questioned, he says that it was a good clear day. He also says when asked about bodily union that they slept together during the subsequent night in the same storehouse and that he knows well that he had her. And he testifies solely for the truth and for no other reason, because he was asked to be a witness, as above.

DOCUMENT 5: *A Divorce Case on the Grounds of Force and Fear: Katherine Dowdall vs. Christopher Verdon*[19]

The case of divorce between Christopher Verdon and Katherine Dowdall.

Examination of the witnesses of Katherine Dowdall in the case of divorce brought by her and pending before our Lord the Primate against Christopher Verdon, her de facto husband of the Armagh Diocese etc.

---

[16] Quotation recorded in English.
[17] Lacuna: the MS was worn at this point.
[18] Quotation recorded in English.
[19] *Reg. Mey*, no. 274, pp. 277–78.

Lord John Dowdall, knight, the first witness, having been brought forward, admitted, sworn in, and carefully examined as to whether he knows that Katherine had contracted marriage freely or under compulsion, and whether she had consented to her said husband or not, says that he knows well that at the time both of the betrothal and of the wedding, were it not that she had been compelled by her father and others with harsh words and threats she would otherwise not have wished to be present, and through her tears and other signs he knew that she had done this not willingly but out of fear. He was unable to get her to agree to go freely to bed with the said Christopher at any time except through the compulsion of her said father who, as he declares, spoke to her in many ways with harsh words, calling her different vile names and threatening that he would break her bones. Nevertheless, she never wished to go to bed with him unless she had her sister or some other woman with her. Because they slept in an inner chamber within the room of the said witness who is speaking, he often approached and scrutinized them, sometimes with a lamp, sometimes with the lamp extinguished, to see if he [Christopher] through any signs or in any other way knew her or had relations with her. He never saw or knew that he touched her, or that she consented to him or that she loved him, or, contrariwise, that he had treated her as his wife. He is much saddened, he asserts, that they have not been able to agree with one another because his father had left to him [Christopher] in his will [an estate] that far exceeded his own inheritance, in that he was the heir of Richard Verdon. If it happened that they were divorced, it would be hard for him to make alternative arrangements for the said Katherine, because he had many daughters undisposed of and did not have the benefit of much money. For these and other reasons he is sad, as above. He gives testimony solely for the truth in the form as above.

Lady Anna Bocun, wife of the said knight, mother of the aforesaid Katherine, the second witness, having been brought forward, admitted, sworn in, and carefully examined, says the same about the compulsion as above. She also adds that at the time of the marriage she not only compelled her with harsh words but also struck her and beat her around the head, saying "javeyll,"[20] and calling her by other different names, saying that she would never have believed that her daughter was going to have such a man for her husband.[21] She brought her in tears to the marriage ceremony and she never knew that she had freely consented to him at any time, even to go to bed with him unless compelled by her father and herself as above through fear. She never recognized through her expression or otherwise that she ever loved him or

---

[20] = "rascal."

[21] "nunquam eam crederet natam fore ad habendum sibi talem in maritum": that is, her mother never expected her to make such an advantageous match, for Katherine was marrying upward, at least in regard to wealth.

that he ever touched her with his hand or treated her with any other sign of affection as his wife. And she testifies only for the truth.

Jeneta Dowdall, wife of Henry,[22] the third witness, having been brought forward, admitted, sworn in, and carefully examined, says that for the entire time she stayed with them in the house, she never saw that Katherine, by her expression or other signs, had consented to the aforesaid Christopher or that she loved him. And she testifies solely for the truth.

Jeneta Dowdall, sister of the aforesaid Katherine, the fourth witness, having been brought forward, admitted, sworn in, and carefully questioned, agrees about the compulsion of the father and mother as above, and adds that the said Katherine never consented to the said Christopher nor loved him, as she knows from the several occasions on which the witness who is speaking lay in bed, as she asserts, with them. She never knew the said Christopher to place his hand on Katherine or to show any other sign of affection. She adds also that whenever Christopher arrived after even a long absence, if the said Katherine was in a good mood, once she had seen him she changed immediately to great despondency, and she did not know that she loved him in any way or consented to him, as above. And she testifies solely for the truth.

Johanna, wife of John Cryspy, nurse of the said Katherine, the fifth witness, having been brought forward, admitted, sworn in, and carefully examined, agrees about the compulsion of the father and mother, and adds that on many occasions, as much as she dared, she chided them that they would wish to dispose of such a young girl except with her own consent. They replied that she did not know what he [the father?] had in mind as he would not have believed that their daughter was ever going to have such a man for her husband.[23] And she testifies solely for the truth.

Henry Dowdall, brother of Katherine, the sixth witness, having been brought forward, admitted, sworn in, and carefully examined, agrees about the compulsion as above, and that he never knew that she loved him or consented to him at any time. And he testifies solely for the truth.

Alice Dowdall, the last witness, having been brought forward, admitted, sworn in, and carefully examined, agrees about this compulsion as above and adds that at the time of the wedding her mother beat her [Katherine] as above.

---

[22] Presumably Katherine's sister-in-law, the wife of Katherine's brother, the sixth witness.

[23] "nesciebat quid in facto consideraret quia non credidit ipsam unquam fore natam ad habendum talem in virum suum." Compare n. 19 earlier. Judging from the context, one might have expected the verbs to be in the plural (referring to both parents). Note that *virum suum* ("her husband") is an editorial correction: the MS had *uxorem suam*.

CHAPTER TEN

MARRIAGE CONTRACTS IN MEDIEVAL ICELAND

Agnes S. Arnórsdóttir

The small population of medieval Iceland and its wealth of documents make it an ideal setting for a case study of marriage that sheds light on how family and gender relations changed over a long period.[1] However, one should keep in mind the special characteristics of medieval Iceland. Although it was highly literate, Icelandic society remained decentralized: there were no towns, and the royal administrations in Norway and (after 1380) in Denmark were far away. Moreover, throughout the medieval period, Icelandic society was dependent on animal husbandry, and landed property was one of the main sources of power.

Chiefly because Icelanders documented all transfers of land, many Icelandic documents relating to property transactions are extant from the late Middle Ages. Among them are written marriage contracts, all of which are in Icelandic.[2] Although these contracts are concerned primarily with the transfer of property (especially the husband's gift called the *mundr* or brideprice), one cannot understand them

---

[1] The population of Iceland in the Middle Ages has been calculated to be about 40,000 to 60,000. The following abbreviations are employed: DI = *Diplomatarium Islandicum: Íslenzkt fornbréfasafn, sem hefir inni að halda bréf og gjörninga, dóma og máldaga, og aðrar skrár, er snerta Ísland eða íslenzka menn*, Jón Sigurðsson, Jón Þorkelsson, et al. (eds.), 16 vols. (Copenhagen and Reykjavík, 1857–1952); KLNM = *Kulturhistorisk Leksikon for Nordisk Middelalder fra Vikingtid til Reformasjonstid*, ed. A. Bugge, et al., 22 vols. (Oslo, 1956–78); NGL = *Norges gamle love indtil 1387*, ed. Rudoph Keyser, et al., 5 vols. (Christiania, 1846–1895); AM = *Den Arnamagnæanske Håndskriftsamling*, Arnamagnæanske Institut, Copenhagen. (Many old Icelandic documents are preserved in the Arnamagnean Institute in Copenhagen.) All translations from Icelandic in the main text are my own unless otherwise stated. I am grateful to Frederik Pedersen for comments on an earlier version of this chapter, and to Philip Reynolds for correcting my English.

[2] According to the law book known as *Jónsbók* (1281), all property transfers by marriage, as well as any other form of selling or transferring land, should be written down in a property contract called *kaupmáli* for marriage contracts or *kaupbréf* for general property transfers. See Ólafur Halldórsson (ed.), *Jónsbók: Kong Magnus Hakonssons Lovbog for Island, vedtaget paa Altinget 1281 og Réttarbætr, de for Island givne retterbøder af 1294, 1305 og 1314 Jónsbók og réttarbætr* (Copenhagen, 1904), 222. (All subsequent references to *Jónsbók og réttarbætr* are to this edition.) In no other Nordic country have so many marriage contracts survived from medieval times.

fully without appreciating the influence of canon law on the institution of Icelandic marriage during the twelfth and thirteenth centuries.[3] The oldest information about the making of marriage contracts in Iceland dates from the twelfth century.[4] These early contracts, which were not written but oral,[5] involved both economic and political agreements.[6] The thirteenth and fourteenth centuries saw a change in the way in which a marriage was contracted. This change was related both to economic agreements and to marriage rituals, a focus that, as time passed, contributed to a change in the meaning of Icelandic marriage.

One may divide this evolution into three stages. The first stage dates from the time of the episcopacy of Bishop Þorlákur Þórhallson (1178–93).[7] Þorlákur placed great emphasis on persuading spouses to be properly joined in holy matrimony, and as Auður Magnúsdóttir's study has shown, the church increasingly influenced the marital arrangements of Icelandic chieftains during the twelfth and thirteenth centuries.[8] The second stage involved changes at the legal level during the thirteenth century, when Icelandic marriage legislation evolved under the influence of canon law. One finds documentary evidence of this phenomenon in *Grágás*, the oldest collection of Icelandic law (dating from the twelfth and early thirteenth centuries),[9]

---

[3] Apart from my own research, Hrefna Róbertsdóttir's article, "Helmingarfélög hjóna á miðöldum," *Sagnir* 7 (1986): 31–40, still represents the only serious effort to analyze some of these marriage contracts. See also my own studies of marriage contracts in the Middle Ages: Agnes S. Arnórsdóttir, "Um brúðarkaup, kvennagiftingar og kanónískan rétt," in Inga Huld Hákonardóttir (ed.), *Konur og kristmenn: þættir úr kristnisögu Íslands* (Reykjavík, 1996), 65–89; eadem, "Two models of Marriage? Canon law and Icelandic marriage practice in late Middle Ages," in Mia Korpiola (ed.), *Nordic Perspectives on Medieval Canon Law* (Helsinki, 1999), 79–92; eadem, "Property and virginity: Change in the contract of marriage in the Middle Ages," in Richard Holt, Hilde Lange, and Ulrike Spring (eds.), *Internationalisation in the History of Northern Europe: Report of the Nordsaga '99 Conference, University of Tromsö, November 17-21, 1999* (Tromsö, 2000), 79–89; eadem, "Marriage in the Middle Ages: Canon law and Nordic family relations," in Per Ingesman and Thomas Lindkvist (eds.), *Norden og Europa i middelalderen: Rapporter til det 24. Nordiske historikermøde, Århus 9–13 august 2001, bd. 1*, Skrifter udgivet af Jysk selskab for historie 47 (Århus, 2001), 174–202; eadem, "'Ægte' eller 'uægte' ægteskab i middelalderren: et spørgsmål om definition," *Den Jyske historiker* 98–99 (2002): 13–23; and eadem, "Icelandic marriage dispensations in the late Middle Ages," in Kirsi Salonen and Christian Krötzl (eds.), *The Roman Curia, the Apostolic Penitentiary and the Partes in the Later Middle Ages*, Acta Instituti Romani Finlandiae 28 (Rome, 2003), 159–69.

[4] This information is to be found in the marriage legislation of the oldest Icelandic law. See Vilhjálmur H. Finsen (ed. and trans.), *Grágás: Islændernes lovbog i fristatens tid*, 4 vols. (Copenhagen, 1852–70). This law code cannot be traced further back than the early twelfth century.

[5] See especially information about marriage in *Grágás*, vol. 1, Ib, 29–75, II, 152–209.

[6] See Agnes S. Arnórsdóttir, *Konur og vígamenn: Staða kynjanna á Íslandi á 12. og 13. öld*, Sagnfræðirannsóknir (= Studia Historica) 12 (Reykjavík, 1995), 105–123.

[7] See Sveinbjörn Rafnsson, "Þorláksskriftir og hjúskapur á 12. og 13. öld," *Saga* 20 (1982): 114–29, at 114.

[8] See Auður G. Magnúsdóttir, "Ástir og völd: Frillulíf á Íslandi á þjóðveldisöld," *Ný Saga*, (1988): 4–12, especially 11–12. See also Auður Magnúsdóttir, *Frillor och fruar. Politik och samlevnad på Island 1120–1400* (Göteborg, 2001).

[9] There are changes in the marriage law of *Grágás* that can be explained by the influence of canon law. See Agnes S. Arnórsdóttir and Thyra Nors, "Ægteskabet i Norden og det europæiske perspektiv.

and also in legislation of the late thirteenth century. The third stage of development might be characterized as the internalization of Christian norms. It is not until the late Middle Ages that there is enough evidence from surviving sources for us to understand this last change fully.

In the following discussion, I explore how the extant written marriage contracts from late-medieval Iceland reveal changes in the meaning of marriage and in particular the influence of canon law. I aim to take into account not only how the composition of marriage contracts changed, but also the *meaning* of that change, especially in relation to the forging of social and religious bonds.

The Law of Marriage

Knowledge of canon law in medieval Iceland was widespread. Medieval sources provide information about the libraries at the sees of Hólar and Skálholt, where the registers mention many books of canon law. It is not clear how these books came to Iceland, but Bishop Árni Þorláksson probably had the *Liber Extra* with him when the archbishop of Norway sent him to Iceland in 1269.[10]

The influence of canon law is apparent in the provincial law and penitential practices of the Icelandic bishops. I have argued elsewhere that the earliest recorded marriage legislation of the country, which appears in *Grágás*, already reflects a process of convergence with the Christian understanding of marriage evident in the letters of popes and European archbishops by the end of the twelfth century.[11] We know, too, that at the end of the twelfth century in Iceland, clerics began to get involved in such issues as divorce and the marriage of close relatives.[12]

Following Georges Duby,[13] some have interpreted the changes in Scandinavian marriage practices during the Middle Ages as aspects of a struggle between two models of marriage, respectively secular and ecclesiastical.[14] On the one hand, the secular model of marriage emphasized the consent of the parents and regarded

Overvejelser om især danske og islandske normer for ægteskab i 12. og 14. Århundrede," in Kari Melby, Anu Pylkkänen, and Bente Rosenbeck (eds.), *Ægteskab i Norden fra Saxo til i dag* (Copenhagen, 1999), 27–54, at 34. The Commonwealth period is from ca. 930–1262/64, but the oldest part of *Grágás* cannot have been written earlier than 1118.

[10] See Sigurður Líndal, "Um þekkingu Íslendinga á rómverskum og kanóniskum rétti frá 12. öld til miðrar 16. aldar," *Úlfljótur afmælisrit* 50 (1997): 241–73.

[11] See Arnórsdóttir "Two models of marriage?" and compare to the discussion of marriage legislation in Denmark and Iceland in Arnórsdóttir and Nors, "Ægteskabet i Norden" (n. 9 earlier).

[12] See Magnús Stefánsson, "Frá goðakirkju til biskupakirkju," *Saga Íslands*, vol. 3 (Reykjavík, 1978), 150–51, 252; Jón Jóhannesson, *Íslendingasaga*, vol. 1 (Reykjavík, 1956), 193–94; and Magnús Stefánsson "Kirkjuvald eflist," *Saga Íslands*, vol. 2 (Reykjavík, 1975), 57, 68.

[13] See Georges Duby, *Medieval Marriage: Two Models from Twelfth-Century France*, translated by E. Forster (Baltimore, 1991), 1–22. Duby's term is "aristocratic" rather than "secular."

[14] See, e.g., Birgit Sawyer, *Kvinnor och familj i det forn- och medeltidiga Skandinavien*, Skriftserie fra Historisk Institutt 24 (Trondheim, 1998), 17–64. See Jenny Jochens, "Consent in marriage: Old Norse law, life, and literature," *Scandinavian Studies* 58 (1986): 142–76.

endogamy, concubinage, remarriage, and divorce as acceptable. According to this model, marriage was above all an alliance between two families, and it was based on an economic agreement that could be cancelled. On the other hand, the ecclesiastical model was based on the consent of the spouses themselves. The clergy also endorsed exogamy and monogamy, forbade divorce, and criminalized adultery.

Whereas there is some truth in the view that there was such a struggle in medieval Iceland, as there was elsewhere, consideration of the two models calls for an analysis of the discrepancy between the literature of canon law and its actual influence on social behavior. When one takes that into account, it becomes clear that the change in how people contracted marriage in Iceland was not so much a movement from a secular model to a rival ecclesiastical one as it was a slow assimilation of Christian doctrines affecting both spheres, which were interrelated in Icelandic culture. Many aspects of the secular model survived in the new ecclesiastical model, and both secular and ecclesiastical authorities were involved in redefining the institution of marriage in Iceland under the influence of European canon law.

The European ecclesiastical model of marriage was introduced into Norway and Iceland during the late twelfth and early thirteenth centuries. At the end of the thirteenth century, the model resulted in new marriage legislation that was much influenced by canon law. The *New Christian Law* of Bishop Árni Þorláksson in 1275 provides the earliest example.[15] Icelanders formally acknowledged canon law when the assembly in Þingvöllur accepted the *New Christian Law*.[16] However, Icelandic clerics had known about the consensual theory of marriage since almost a century earlier.[17]

The *New Christian Law* is extant in more than two hundred manuscripts, about fifty of which pre-date the Reformation. According to Icelandic historian Magnús Lyngdal Magnússon, this work was based partly on the *Christian Law* of the Norwegian archbishop Jón Rauði, partly on the *Old Christian Law* of *Grágás*, and partly on the *New Christian Law* of the Gulating in Norway. (The regional assembly of Gulating was, at one time, the main court of law for Southern and Western Norway, and Gulating law was first written down during the eleventh century.) The content of the *New Christian Law* was derived mainly from European canon law – from the *Liber Extra* as well as the *Decretum Gratiani* – but canon law probably came into Icelandic legislation via Norwegian law.[18] Iceland became subject to the Norwegian

---

[15] See DI II, 591 ff. I refer to items in DI by page numbers, not by the item number.

[16] See Sigurður Líndal, "Ægteskab. Island," in KLNM 20:495–501, at 498. The situation was different in Norway, where the central authority seems to have been much stronger than in Iceland. In 1268, the *New Christian Law* of Archbishop Jón was written, in which the consent of the partners was one of the requirements for a valid marriage, but the royal authority in Norway did not accept this law until a century later. Recently, the Icelandic historian Magnús Lyngdal Magnússon had argued that the sees of Skálholt and Hólar both accepted the Icelandic *New Christian Law* in 1275.

[17] DI I, 284–89. This is evident in this letter from Archbishop Eiríkur Ívarsson to the Icelanders concerning the canon law of marriage.

[18] Magnús Lyngdal Magnússon, "Kristniréttur Árna frá 1275: Athugun á efni og varðveislu í miðalda-handritum" (MA diss., University of Reykjavík, 2002), 4, 134. (This unpublished dissertation is available at the University and National Library in Reykjavík and in some libraries in Denmark.)

crown in 1262/64, but the Icelandic church had been a part of the archdiocese of Nidaros in Norway ever since the latter was established in 1153.

In Norway, the Gulating law and the new legislation of Archbishop Jón Rauði (the *Christian Law*) were associated intimately with the reform of Norwegian Legislation that King Magnús lagabætir ("Law Reformer") Hákonarson (1263–80) had initiated. In addition, Archbishop Jón Rauði had a *New Christian Law* drawn up for Norway. Although the Norwegian royal authorities did not accept this law, it provided another model for the Icelandic *New Christian Law* of Bishop Árni Þorláksson of Skálholt (1275).

The Scandinavians, including the Icelanders, adopted the rules of canon law in a distinctive way, for in their view, social consensus was important. Here is another reason why a division into ecclesiastical and secular models or domains can be misleading. As mentioned earlier, canon law became accepted in Iceland when the law council at the Alþingi in 1275 determined that the *New Christian Law*, instead of the *Old Christian Law* of *Grágás*, should be the valid law.

Árni's text of the *New Christian Law* of 1275 reveals a process of redefining the meaning of marriage in Iceland. It begins with a declaration that marriage is sacred only if it is made according to the laws of God, but it gives equal prominence to the church's demand for the mutual consent of the contracting partners and to the requirement of parental consent from earlier Icelandic legislation.[19] Norwegian and Icelandic clerics now promoted the consensual theory of marriage that Parisian scholars had defined in the twelfth century, but the Icelandic version of this theory also stressed the importance of making marriage agreements with the full acceptance of *all* the parties involved, including the parents. This emphasis on parental consent was related to a salient feature of secular marriage legislation in Iceland: the centrality of property.

Shortly after Iceland became part of the Norwegian kingdom in 1262/64, King Magnus initiated work on a new compilation of law. This effort in turn influenced the new civil legislation in 1281, later called *Jónsbók*. The latter law code and the new laws (*réttarbætr*) enacted in 1294, 1305, 1306, and 1314 provide our main sources for Icelandic civil legislation over the next four hundred years.[20]

The marriage law in *Jónsbók* reveals a close connection between the law of inheritance and the notion of what constituted a legally valid marriage. Only those children who were born to a marriage made with the consent both of the spouses *and* of their parents were counted as legal heirs.[21] The marriage section of *Jónsbók* incorporated many elements taken from the old law in *Grágás*, as well as elements from the laws of King Magnus the Law Reformer that were compiled in Norway in 1274.[22]

---

[19] See NGL 5:36–37.
[20] *Jónsbók og réttarbætr*, 176–77. See also the *réttarbót* for Iceland given by King Eirikur Magnusson in NGL 3:281–89; and the first and second *réttarbætr* for Iceland given by King Hakon Magnusson in NGL 3:289–92 and 293–99. Compare a part of the Norwegian *Retterbød* 2. mai 1313 in NGL 3:99–102.
[21] *Jónsbók og réttarbætr*, 78.
[22] See Magnús Már Lárusson, "Festermål: Island" KLNM 4:236–40 at 238.

In contrast to the *New Christian Law* of 1275, the secular law of *Jónsbók* stated no rules for the formation of marriage.[23] Yet *Jónsbók* does contain a chapter covering the financial contract of marriage and rules for the exchange of matrimonial gifts and for inheritance.[24] The church had claimed jurisdiction over marriage throughout Europe, and faithful to that principle, Bishop Árni Þorláksson and his clerics wanted the marriage law[25] and the general jurisdiction over marriage to be part of the *New Christian Law*.[26] Yet the Icelandic aristocracy did not accept this claim entirely. They demanded instead that the rules for property transfer between spouses and for inheritance should continue to be part of the secular law of *Jónsbók*. The economic rules concerning marriage thus became a part of secular law, although the aristocracy nonetheless accepted the church's jurisdiction over marriage.[27]

Even if part of the marriage legislation remained in the secular law of *Jónsbók*, those rules, as compared with older legislation, reflect a new understanding of marriage. According to the rules in *Grágás*, a wife did not need to share the property of the household jointly with her husband if she did not wish to do so.[28] Precisely the opposite is the case in *Jónsbók*, which explicitly states, "No wife shall deny her husband joint ownership."[29]

These opposing rules regarding the rights (or, later, the lack thereof) of wives to deny joint ownership to their husbands tell us something about how twelfth- and thirteenth-century marriage differed. In both periods, the property was ultimately at the husband's disposal, but there was a major difference regarding the legal status of the woman. On the one hand, the twelfth-century rule established separate ownership as the norm: at any time, a wife could take her property and return to her own family or relatives. On the other hand, the thirteenth-century rule established joint ownership as the norm. This rule strengthened the husband's control over his wife, while the influence of the woman's kinsfolk was correspondingly reduced (although the norm of joint ownership was not exclusive, and the two practices coexisted). In consequence, the husband acquired a stronger right to dispose of his wife's property.[30] One aim of the thirteenth-century legislation was to strengthen the legal position of the conjugal family (a relatively recent construct) against the claims of the couple's parents or kin groups. Another reason for favoring a marriage agreement according to the rule of joint possessions, rather than maintaining separate properties, pertained to the "new" strategy of Icelandic aristocracy when

---

[23] Sigurður Líndal, "Ægteskab: Island," KLNM 20:495–501.

[24] *Jónsbók og réttarbætr*, 70–118.

[25] Called "the marrying of women" (*Kvennagiptingar*): see *Jónsbók og réttarbætr*, 70.

[26] DI II, 206–8.

[27] Compare to *Jónsbók og réttarbætr*, 71.

[28] *Grágás*, vol. 1, Ib, 45–46, II, 75.

[29] *Jónsbók og réttarbætr*, 73, "Engi kona á at synja bónda sínum félags."

[30] See Randi Andersen, "Kvinnas økonomiske rettsstode i norsk mellomalder," in Hedda Gunneng and Birgit Strand (eds.), *Kvinnans ekonomiska ställning under nordisk medeltid. Uppsatser framlagda vid ett kvinnohistoriskt symposium i Kungälv 8.–12. oktober 1979* (Lindome, 1981), 81–88.

it got hold of properties left over after the Black Death. There is an example of an early fifteenth-century marriage contract for joint possession in the appendix at the end of this chapter (Doc. 1). (During the sixteenth century, it became common, once again, to make a contract whereby the partners would retain separate properties.)

Basing his case on the evidence of Norwegian legislation, Randi Anderson has argued that the principle of joint ownership of marital property should be seen as a consequence of the stronger position of the church and also of the king, "who wanted to break down a family right, appropriate to an older social organization."[31] That explanation is debatable, but what is important to note here is that in Norway, Iceland, and Denmark, the institution known as *félag* became stronger under the influence of canon law.[32] One may characterize *félag* as a communal principle whereby the spouses shared their marital wealth instead of retaining their individual properties. This communal principle strengthened the new ecclesiastical institution of marriage, for according to canon law, marriage should be based entirely on the spouses' own consent.

The marriage legislation of *Jónsbók* was the result of a compromise. *Jónsbók* still accepted certain elements of the financial contract of *Grágás*. Even though the communal principle of marriage was stronger, it was still possible for the wife to hold separate property. Yet the guardian or guardians of the bride (usually her father or closest relative) now had less influence than hitherto over the marital life of the new couple. Thus, at the end of the thirteenth century, one finds a preponderance of rules concerning joint ownership in marriage, whereas the role of separate ownership became less important in legislation. One may interpret this development as a shift toward a more communally based model of how marriages should be organized, and it confirmed the role of the church as a key power in late-medieval Iceland, as well as the growing role of the Norwegian king and his representatives.

I would argue, then, that the change in the Icelandic understanding of marriage during the Middle Ages was not a dramatic shift from a "secular" to an "ecclesiastical" model of marriage. Rather, it was a gradual movement (in both secular and church law) toward conformity with the Christian doctrine of marriage as defined by the twelfth- and thirteenth-century European clerics. Yet, although the basic idea of marriage as an institution evolved, many aspects of the secular model were included in the Icelandic version of ecclesiastical model.[33] Thus one should not interpret the marriage regulations in the *New Christian Law* of 1275 simply as

---

[31] Andersen, ibid., 117.

[32] The rules of *félag* are complicated and control how matrimonial wealth is divided among the heirs. On the equivalent institution in Danish law, see Stig Iuul, *Fællig og hovedlod: studier over formueforholdet mellem ægtefæller i tiden før Christian V's danske lov* (Copenhagen, 1940); and Frederik Pedersen, "The *fællig* and the family: The understanding of the family in Danish medieval law," *Continuity and Change* 7 (1992): 1–12.

[33] See Arnórsdóttir, "Two Models of Marriage?"

canon law that Icelanders had adopted from abroad, but rather as a text that the legislators had "translated" into a new context, so that it would be understandable to those who were supposed to follow it.

The secular marriage law of *Jónsbók* was, likewise, partly a result of this process of Christianization. Considered at its most basic level, *Jónsbók*'s law of marriage, which the law council accepted at the assembly of the Alþingi in 1275 and 1281, was the result of an interaction between clerical and secular traditions. These changes in marriage legislation were not isolated from some formative changes in how people made marriage contracts.

Changes in the Making of Marriage: From Oral to Written Tradition

The transition from oral tradition to written law in Iceland did not happen overnight. It is clear even from written documents that people could also prove ownership rights orally. But the use of written documents increased from the fourteenth century onward, and when written contracts became common, people used them, too, as proof of property rights. Royal and ecclesiastical authorities in Norway and Iceland used written records in their administration, and written documents became important evidence in disputes of all sorts.[34]

Most of the Icelandic marriage contracts and related documents that survive from the period 1300–1600 have been published.[35] These documents indicate that people followed certain formalities. They concluded settlements in accordance with the rules governing legal marriage. Marriage was to be made only with the consent of the partners, who also entered into an agreement about their financial affairs, called a *fékaup*. This was an essentially oral agreement, but it was confirmed in a document called a *kaupmálabréf* (a term that one might translate as "letter of marriage contract").[36] The *kaupmálabréf* was a record of the dotal arrangements of the partners regarding the value of the various marriage gifts (see Doc. 3).[37]

---

[34] Sveinbjörn Rafnsson, *Studier i Landnámabók: Kritiska bidrag till den isländska fristatstidens historia*, Bibliotheca historica Lundensis 31 (Lund, 1974), 109 ff.

[35] See DI I–XVI for the contracts until 1570. I have also looked at the unpublished charters from the period 1570–1600 and at those documented in *Alþingisbækur Íslands* (= *Acta Comitiorum Generalium Islandiæ*, Reykjavík), vols. 1–3, for the period 1570–1600. (This series, begun in 1912, covers records and correspondence of the Alþingi from 1570.) I have analyzed all these sources systematically, but among the sixteen volumes of the DI, II–XV are most relevant.

[36] Lárusson, "Festermål: Island," KLNM 4:236–40. The three elements of the term are as follows: *Kaup* = "purchase" (cf. the Norwegian Viking market town *Kaupang*), *Máli* = "agreement," and *bref* = "letter" or "record." Among related contracts that have survived from medieval Iceland is a contract to rent out landed property (similar to the Norwegian *bygsle* contract), and the *kaupbréf* of DI, which was a contract of land exchange or sale.

[37] See the marriage contract of Sigurður Þorleifsson and Kristín Finnbogadóttir, from 24 June, 1489, DI VI, 660–61.

TABLE 10.1. *Extant marriage contracts and
related documents, 1300–1600*

1301–1350	0
1351–1400	5
1401–1450	18
1451–1500	39
1501–1550	66
1551–1600	65
TOTAL	193

Sources: DI: Diplomatarium Islandicum I–XV, and
Alþingisbækur Íslands I–III.

In total, 193 documents pertaining to such settlements have survived. This number includes contracts proper, letters of witnesses concerning contracts, and a few summaries of judgments or declarations about contracts. The table shows how many documents of this sort can be found from each fifty-year period.

All such contracts involved people who owned property (mainly the ruling elite). The contracts vary in form, and one should understand them primarily as nonstandardized documents that were drawn up by the families involved and kept in family archives. Such documents reflect different stages in the process of a shift from oral to written marriage contracts. Normally, a person connected with either the royal or the ecclesiastical administration informally authorized the contract, either by writing it down or by serving as one of the witnesses.

Because the church redefined what constituted a valid marriage during the twelfth century, marriage contracts became important documents for proving inheritance rights. Even during the late Middle Ages, great uncertainty persisted in Iceland about what constituted a legally valid marriage. Changes in the legal regulations show that it took a long time for the older traditions of marriage to give way to the new trends.

It is important to take careful note of how this evolution in the formation of marriage took place. Part of the change entailed a transition from traditional oral marriage contracts to written contracts. The contracts gradually acquired written form during the fifteenth century. By the end of that time, a priest was required as one of the witnesses. We find the same development elsewhere in Europe during the Middle Ages, although practices differed from place to place.[38] For example, priests witnessed marriages in fourteenth-century France, even before blessings or church weddings became the rule.[39] It is clear that Icelanders observed a similar

---

[38] See James A. Brundage, *Law, Sex, and Christian Society in Medieval Europe* (Chicago, 1990), 508.
[39] See Philippe Aries and Georges Duby (eds.), *A History of Private Life*, vol. 2, *Revelations of the Medieval World* (Cambridge, Mass., 1988), 126.

practice during the fifteenth century.[40] The role of the priest in marriage contracts, according to Icelandic sources, was to announce the marriage publicly and to act as a witness.

In order to show what role clerics might have played in Icelandic marriages, we may cite the marriage of Ólafur and Vigdís in 1492 as an example. First, the priest Gunnsteinn Ásgrímsson testified in a document that he had been in the small sitting room of the farm Skarð in Skarðsströnd during the visitation of Bishop Stefán. The document states that the priest asked what kind of advice the bishop would give about this particular marriage.[41] The problem was that Ólafur had not been completely obedient to the bishop. The priest wanted the partners to delay their marriage until Ólafur had made his peace with the church.[42] It is not clear whether or not the partners waited to get absolution before they married. Be that as it may, five days after the visitation, Ólafur and Vigdís contracted marriage in a small sitting room in Ögur in Ísafjörður. The priest Gunnsteinn was one of the witnesses, although the agreement was not recorded in writing until 1496.[43]

The basically oral character of these written marriage contracts is quite clear. *Festingarorð*, the words of betrothal (i.e., in this context, the words that the partners spoke to establish the bond of marriage), were the last words to be proffered in the old formula for making marriage contracts.[44] Equivalent terms, denoting the marriage contract in various ways, include *festarmál*, *máli*, *kaupmáli*, and *mundarmál*.[45] A similar formula from *Grágás* was included in the *New Christian Law* of 1275.[46] According to *Grágás*, the formula is as follows:

A woman is legally betrothed if the bridegroom shows the financial contract [*mundarmál*]. And then the guardian and the man to whom the woman is to be betrothed should name witnesses. The man who is to be betrothed to the woman shall say, "We name witnesses to this, that you N. betroth N. to me by a legal betrothal and you give me [*handsalar*] the dowry."[47]

One often finds the same words of betrothal repeated in the written marriage contracts of the late Middle Ages. For example, in 1521, a man gave his daughter

---

[40] In most of the marriage contracts referring to witnesses in DI after 1450, both a priest and some laymen witnessed the marriage.

[41] DI VII, 138–39.

[42] Ibid., 136–37.

[43] The reason for this is probably that it had taken time for Ólafur and the bishop of Hólar to reach peace. A declaration has survived from 1498 from Bishop Stefán concerning the matter: see DI VII, 386; see also ibid., 313–14. Other documents that have survived regarding this marriage include an oath from Vigdís (DI VIII, 544), another testimony that she had made this oath (DI VIII, 545), and a clerical judgment concerning the legal status of the marriage (DI VIII, 506–9).

[44] Johan Fritzner, *Ordbog over det gamle norske sprog*, vol. 1 (Kristiania, 1886), 409.

[45] Lárusson, "Festermål: Island," KLNM 4:237.

[46] Ibid., 236–40. *Grágás* has a special chapter concerning marriage legislation. See *Grágás*, vol. 1, Ib, 29–75, II, 152–209.

[47] *Grágás*, vol. 1, II, 162.

legally in marriage, using the correct words of the betrothal formula and according to the "law of God."[48] Thus the written contracts of late-medieval Iceland were shaped in part by the older oral tradition.

Yet at the same time, the character of the formulae altered. The old betrothal formula in *Grágás*, quoted earlier, suggests that the bridegroom spoke the words of betrothal to the guardian of the bride. But several of the later formulae present a more personal picture, such that the agreement of betrothal is between the man and his bride rather than her father or other guardian, and the bridegroom speaks directly to the bride to establish their marriage. A formula from around 1300, found in a handbook for priests in the archdiocese of Nidaros, illustrates this point well:

But now should the free consent be witnessed in the hearing of God and holy Church and for me. Do you N. want to take this woman to be your wife, to keep her whether sick or healthy? Do you take this man to be your husband, keep him, and take care of him when he is sick as well as in good health? And no matter what happens to you while you live together, you should both keep this holy law and shall not disturb this joining. By the aforementioned marriage contract [*kaupmala*], I give you this woman in the name of God. [Then the bridegroom says:] And with this golden ring I marry you, and I give you this silver, and with myself I will honor you, and as long as I live I will keep you, with God's help and mercy.[49]

We may assume that this Norwegian formula was used in Iceland as well (although the grammatical style of the text is more Norwegian than Icelandic).[50] The text clearly shows how the Christian formula was added to the traditional formula for making an economic contract. The priest gave the bride to the man, to whom she was bound (*fest*) by virtue of the exchange of gold and silver.

Icelandic historian Magnús Már Lárusson has pointed out that this text from the archdiocese of Nidaros does not refer to a priest's blessing of the couple during what we should regard as a wedding (as the editors of the *Diplomatarium Islandicum* indicate). A priest was supposed to pronounce the formula quoted earlier at the church door, but the contract itself would already have been concluded, a contract that often took the form of a written deed outlining the financial obligations of the two families toward the couple.[51] It was part of the priest's role to establish that the marriage settlement had been made. Lárusson's interpretation is congruent with the general role of the clergy in marriages during the Middle Ages. Even the medieval marriage liturgy did not always include a formal blessing and joining

---

[48] DI VIII, 784.

[49] DI II, 328–29, from ca. 1300. This document is preserved in a manual for priests in the archdiocese of Nidaros (*handbók fyrir presta í Niðaróserkibiskupsríki*).

[50] DI II, 328.

[51] See Lárusson, "Festermål: Island," KLNM 4:239. Lárusson comments: "This does not concern the marriage itself, as the editors of the *Diplomatarium Islandicum* II thought, but rather the marriage (*festermålet*) that took place in front of the church door when all formal requirements had been met." [Editor's translation.]

of the couple in the context of a church service. Instead, the spouses, once their consent and the customary requirements for marriage had been confirmed at the church door, simply stood before the congregation as they attended mass.

Nevertheless, the role of the priest gave the agreement a new meaning, for it was he who was said to give the woman to the bridegroom. My study of Icelandic marriage contracts has revealed that the use of the word *gifta*, which originally denoted the giving of the bride to her future husband by her parents, altered during the fifteenth and, especially, during the sixteenth century. The change pertained to the priest's increased role in the making of a marriage agreement, whereby the priest became a central figure in the ritual. In the name of God, the priest (as well as the parents of the bride) would now *give* a woman to her husband-to-be.

As noted earlier, the formulae from the late Middle Ages emphasize the commitment that the bridegroom made to the bride, whereas earlier formulae, from the late twelfth through early thirteenth centuries, stress the contract between the men of the two families. This change was a consequence of Árni's *New Christian Law* of 1275. According to the new procedure, following the publication of the financial settlement (*fékaup*), the man would take the woman's hand in the presence of previously nominated witnesses, state her name, and declare that he was betrothed to her according to the law of God. The witnesses were supposed to hear the woman pronounce an audible "yes."[52] Thus, chapter 16 of the law says:

The one who shall become married to the girl or the woman shall hold her hand, name two witnesses or more, and say these words: "I betroth you to me as my proper wife by the law of God and in accordance with the sayings of the holy Fathers, and you are my proper legal wife."[53]

The witnesses needed to hear the woman's consent clearly, and the partners had to use the correct formula for a betrothal.[54]

Several other versions of marriage formulae from the late Middle Ages are extant. One formula from 1490 refers to a blessing of the bride.[55] Another version, from 1432, which is preserved as part of a marriage contract of Árni Steingrímsson and Ingunn Ólafsdóttir, gives us the words that the bridegroom spoke to the witnesses at the marriage.[56] A version contained in a marriage contract of Jón Narfason

---

[52] See Jenny Jochens, "Consent in marriage: Old Norse law, life, and literature," *Scandinavian Studies* 58 (1986): 142–76, at 144. See NGL 2:299–300, NGL 3:368, and NGL 5:37.

[53] Lárusson, "Festermål: Island," KLNM 4:236–40. This text comes from Chapter 16 (NGL 5:37) and was valid for the diocese of Skálholt. The text was not used in the diocese of Hólar until 1354.

[54] Ibid., 239. Compare to DI VII, 239, and also DI VII, 413, 425.

[55] AM 241 b, fol. 7, "Brudestykker af formularer til bruk ved brudevielser." This manuscript from ca. 1490 contains fragments of marriage formulae.

[56] DI IV, 495, from AM 235 4°, 42 (Copybook of Bishop Jóns Vilhjálmssonar): "God be our witness and the good men that are here present, that I Árni Steingrímson bind Ingunn Ólafsdóttir as my own wife according to the laws of God and this country and according to the sayings ["sentences"] of the holy fathers. God be with us."

and Sesselíu Bassadóttir from 1537 bears similarities to the 1432 version but with an interesting difference: here, the husband spoke the words directly to the bride rather than to the witnesses.[57]

It is not possible fully to reconstruct the relationship between the surviving formulae, on the one hand, and the ways in which people actually used them, on the other. Sometimes people married using forms of words that were centuries old, and they might use elements from more than one formula. Hence it is difficult to demonstrate a development of the forms of words used in contracting marriage. Nevertheless, the use of an old formula demonstrates the longevity of a particular custom, whereas conversely, one may interpret the introduction of new formulae as evidence of changing customs, of a break in tradition. The formula from the Nidaros handbook (ca. 1300) was probably an example of a break in tradition, whereas the following formula contained in the *Íslandslýsing* from the sixteenth century exemplifies the endurance of a long-lasting tradition. This sixteenth-century formula indicates a continuation of the old custom of *festar* from *Grágás*. Nevertheless, here that custom is combined with elements of later, more Christianized formulae:

God shall be my witness, and these kind men present. I NN-son marry you NN-daughter according to the laws of God and this country and the holy Fathers' sayings, with your witnesses NN-son and you NN-son and all those who hear my words. And now you are my legal wife.[58]

After he had made this pronouncement, the bridegroom kissed the bride. The kiss was supposed to be a symbol of "the love and duty of their joined minds."[59] This formula, more than any evidence we have seen thus far, expresses to what extent the church had managed to imbue marriage with new meaning by using the old rituals of entry into marriage while giving them a new Christian significance.

Another late–sixteenth-century formula gives an even clearer picture of this development. It is found in the work of the humanist and rector at Glaumbær, Gottskálkur Jónsson (d.1593), and is called *formáli yfir hjónum nokkr* ("formula for a certain couple"):[60]

---

[57] DI X, 116, from AM fasc. 49, 4° ("frumrit á skinni"): "I, Jón Narfason, betroth you, Sesselía Bessadóttir, to be my wife according to the law of God and according to the sayings ["sentences"] of the holy fathers, and by this you are my legal wife, in front of these witnesses who are testifying to the written contract, and other witnesses."

[58] Oddur Einarsson [or Sigurðr Stefánsson], *Íslandslýsing, qualiscunque descriptio Islandiae*, translated by Sveinn Pálsson (Reykjavík, 1971), 84. It is not certain whether Oddur Einarsson, Bishop of Skálholt (1559–1630), or Sigurðr Stefánsson (1570–95) was the author of this work. I have been unable to consult the original Latin version, and I have therefore used the Icelandic version of 1971, in which the work is ascribed to Oddur.

[59] Ibid.: "skyldusamrar ástar eða nánari og innilegri sameiningu huganna."

[60] The formula is found in an Icelandic MS in the British Library (11242 4°), and it is described in Jón Þorkelsson, "Islandske haandskrifter i England og Skotland," *Arkiv for nordisk filologi* 8 (1892): 199–237, at 225.

God, you who with the power and strength of your blessed Son created all things without matter and so wonderfully made marriage as a holy agreement, by which the Holy Spirit joined a man and a woman and by so doing made the world to be rich in people. Do you bless this couple by your holy hand and grant them mercy, so that they will love you day and night . . . and may they live long enough to see the birth of their grandchildren and great-grandchildren.[61]

In some ways, the written contract of the late Middle Ages took over the role of the witnesses, the *festarváttar*. According to *Grágás*, a marriage contract was valid as long as the witnesses were alive and no other agreement was made.[62] This did not mean that the contract became invalid if the witnesses died, but rather that their death would pose a problem if the validity of the marriage was questioned in court and there was no one to testify that the marriage had taken place. From the legal point of view, oral marriage contracts could be substantiated only as long as witnesses survived and could remember them (as had been the case according to the rules contained in *Grágás*). In the later laws, on the contrary, a contract lasted effectively as long as the written documentation was extant.

The written marriage contracts were legal documents about property transactions, but people could use them to prove the legality of a marriage as well as to prove property rights. They were sometimes significant for persons not directly involved in the transfer of property, and they became a necessary means of proving property claims many years after the marriage. For this reason, all agreements had to be taken down in writing and testified with seals.[63] Such marriage contracts were called *festingarbréf* or *kaupmálabréf*. They were preserved privately, and people soon learned how to use the contracts in court cases.[64]

In contrast to what Georges Duby found in France – that documents signed by the contracting partners themselves increasingly superseded written agreements signed by large family groups – the persons who signed medieval Icelandic marriage contracts were not the partners themselves but the witnesses to the contract.[65] The names of the witnesses were recorded as part of the marriage contract.[66] The priest came first in the list of witnesses. His signature or seal gave the document more value because it proved that the marriage had been contracted in accordance with the rules of the church. Next, several laymen could witness the contract, and often some of these were members of the Icelandic royal administration. In third place came the couple's close relatives.

---

[61] Lilli Gjerløw (ed.), *Liturgica Islandica*, 2 vols., = Biblotheca Arnmagnæana 35–36 (Copenhagen, 1980), vol. 1, 68–69.

[62] Compare to Agnes S. Arnórsdóttir, "Viðhorf til kvenna í Grágás," *Sagnir* 7 (1986): 23–30, at 26.

[63] See *Jónsbók og réttarbætr*, Chapter 12.

[64] On how the contracts could be used at court, see DI VII, 315.

[65] See Georges Duby, *Love and Marriage in the Middle Ages*, translated by J. Dunnett (Chicago, 1994), 110.

[66] See DI IV, 495 (a contract from 1420 "voru þessir festingarvottar a brullavpsdegi").

It was common for contracts not to be written down and witnessed until some time after the wedding ceremony, and sometimes the delay was considerable. For example, Bjarni Ólason and Margrét Ólafsdóttir started their married life in 1461, but their marriage contract was not written down until 1471. Such delay may have been associated with the gradual process of change from oral to written documentation, but it was not an exclusive trend: for example, the contract of Andrés Guðmundsson and Þorbjörg Ólafsdóttir in 1462 was published and confirmed on the day of their betrothal.[67]

Two types of written marriage contracts have survived. One type started with a sentence stating that the contract was made publicly and was confirmed (*lýstist og staðfestis*). The second type started with the announcement, "We make it known..." (*við gerum kunnugt*). The significance of the difference between these two types of documents relates in part to the document's function: whether (as in the first type) the document witnessed the event of marriage itself, or whether (as in the second type) it confirmed that the contract had already been made. In the first type of agreement, the names of the witnesses appeared at the end of the document,[68] whereas in the second type, the names of the witnesses appeared at the beginning.

An example of the first type of marriage contract is one from 1535 between Ormur Sturluson and Þorbjörg Þorleifsdóttir. (Doc. 4). At the end of the document, appear the names of all the witnesses. A marriage contract from 1465 between Eyjólfur Böðvarssonar and Guðrún Þorkelsdóttir, the daughter of a priest, is an example of the second type (Doc. 2).[69] Here the names of the witnesses appear at the beginning of the document. Then it declare that "the priest Þorkell Guðbjartsson [the father of the bride] had heard and seen the handclasp of the couple, and Eyjólfur on behalf of the other family, with the condition that Þorkell gave [*gipti*] his daughter Guðrún to Eyjólfur, with the consent of her mother." Next come the details of the financial settlement, and then the following confirmation: "and hereafter did Eyjólfur betroth Guðrún Þorkelsdóttir to be his legal wife according to the law of God, with the words that belong to that agreement."

This type of contract, as noted previously, began with the words, *við gerum kunnugt* ("we make it known"). A contract from 1467 exemplifies this kind of announcement, made between the "honest men" (*ærligra manna*)[70] Magnús Magnússon and Sigríður Jónsdóttir. The contract does not include any commentary on the religious function of marriage, but the priest testified to the contract, and his testimony would have guaranteed that the marriage had been made according to the law of God.[71]

---

[67] DI V, 372–73.

[68] DI V, 415. See DI V, 87–88.

[69] DI IX, 739-40, DI V, 454–55.

[70] This corresponds with a standard Latin phrase used across Europe (*honestis viris* or *bonis et honestis viris*), but all the Icelandic contracts were written in the vernacular.

[71] DI V, 506–7.

A letter of betrothal (*festingarbréf*) between Sumarliði Eiríksson and Guðrún Árnadóttir from 1468 provides also an example of this second type of contract. The priest and secular witnesses at a farm in Kalmanstunga declared that Sumarliði had betrothed Guðrún "to be his legal wife" in the honorable manner. They added: "we cannot find any hindrance to this according to our best knowledge."[72] This statement indicates one way in which clerics expressed their own proper concerns when a legal marriage took place. It also shows that members of the laity were involved in the reading of banns.

Several points are worth highlighting in summary. First, although the marriage customs outlined in *Grágás* were based on contractual arrangements, people at that time confirmed marriages by oral agreements. Second, at least from 1281, when *Jónsbók* required a mandatory written record concerning the financial settlements for a marriage,[73] the process of evolution from oral to written marriage contracts was under way. Nevertheless, oral and written contracts were based on much the same formulae. Third, the chief change in how people contracted marriages pertained to which persons were involved in the contracts. For the first time, women and priests became active participants in the formal drawing up of (written) contracts. It is noteworthy, too, that although some elements, such as the requirement in *Grágás* that the parties should have a certain minimum level of wealth before they married, were *removed* from the standard contract,[74] new elements were *added* to it, most notably the emphasis on the mutual consent of the partners themselves, including the bride.

Finally, one should note that even after written contracts had become commonplace, oral customs persisted. A letter of witness from 1600 confirms that the written contract was read aloud after it was made.[75] Indeed, to this day, the spoken word continues to have legal significance in weddings. In the modern wedding ceremony, the bride and the bridegroom are requested to say clearly whether they want to be joined together as loving wife and husband. The anticipated response, needless to say, is "I do."

THE MAKING OF NEW SOCIAL AND RELIGIOUS BONDS: FROM *HANDABAND* TO *HJÓNABAND*

By the end of the thirteenth century, the concept of marriage as an institution that was both ecclesiastical and secular was fully developed in the legal codes of Iceland, and Icelanders had added a Christian liturgy to the old kin-based family

---

[72] DI V, 532–33.

[73] *Jónsbók og réttarbætr*, 222.

[74] Nevertheless, the ritual of *festar* continued to take place.

[75] AM *dipl. isl. fasc.* 69, 8°. The phrase "og að þeirra Kaupmálabréf þar upplesnu" shows that the contract was to be read aloud.

agreement. There were corresponding changes in vocabulary and on the level of social bonding. The conspicuous element in the formation of a marriage had been the handclasp or joining of hands (*handaband*) between the two families. But from around the late thirteenth century, the significance of the handclasp changed. Moreover, there were now references to a *hjónaband*, a term signifying the bond between husband and wife, and in due course, the notion of *hjónaband* tends to supplant that of *handaband*. These changes in terminology and ritual reflected developments in the contractual and socio-economic aspects of marriage noted previously. In contrast to the older marriage agreement, which was between families, the *hjónaband* pertained to the personal relation between husband and wife.

In the oldest laws, recorded in *Grágás*, the contract of betrothal (*festar*) was made between male members of the two families involved. The future husband made the contract with the closest male relative of the bride, who acted on her behalf.[76] Thus, on the formal level, men seem to have dominated the making of such contracts, although the laws give the impression that the suitor might propose to the woman herself as well as discuss the proposal of marriage with her parents. (The woman could not propose to the man.)[77]

An essential part of the traditional ritual of marriage was the *handaband* between the woman's (male) guardian and either the future husband himself or his father. The *handaband* (literally, "joining of hands") was the usual way of confirming agreements of all kinds. Taken from the oral tradition, the practice continued in late-medieval contracts.[78] Indeed, the old practice of *handaband* existed throughout the late Middle Ages, but the significance of the handclasp in marriage changed. What created the contract was no longer a handclasp between men; rather, a handclasp between the bride and the bridegroom now confirmed the contract. Thus, the *New Christian Law* states: "The one who will become betrothed to a virgin or a woman shall hold her by the hand, name two witnesses or more, and say these words [of betrothal]."[79]

One finds the same new function of the joining of hands beautifully symbolized in fourteenth-century ring-shaped buckles from both Norway and Denmark and also in a Danish betrothal ring from the year 1500. (Men and women used ring-shaped buckles to close a neck opening and to fasten a belt.) A popular motif

---

[76] *Grágás*, vol. 1, II, 162.

[77] DI VI, 746. In a witness record of April 24, 1491, the witness being questioned testifies about a man who went to make a proposal to a woman. See also Arnórsdóttir, *Konur og vígamenn* (n. 6 earlier), 130–39, concerning this tradition during the twelfth and thirteenth centuries.

[78] See DI IV, 530. Women performed the *handaband* when they gave or sold property. Thus Solveig Þorsteinsdóttir gave half of Vatnsfjörður to her daughter and her daughter's son with the consent of her mother, Kristín Björnsdóttir (who was Solveig's heir), and that consent was confirmed with a handclasp.

[79] NGL 5:37.

on such buckles was a pair of joined hands, symbolizing the *handaband* of betrothal and marriage. The words *Ave Maria* often accompanied the motif. The same motif is found on the Danish betrothal ring from 1500, on which the hands are joined around a heart. The ring symbolized the indissolubility of the contract and the recognition that husband and wife were bound together forever by their *handaband*.[80]

A wedding ring, in these cultures as elsewhere, was a common token of marriage and a symbol (*signum*) of the union of two individuals.[81] In the ninth century, Pope Nicholas I described how the groom would give a ring to his bride and how she would accept it as a pledge of their fidelity.[82] By appreciating the symbolic meaning of the ring and its association with the linking of hands, one may understand more fully the context of the sacred contract in Iceland. A ring depicting the *handaband* symbolized what the *New Christian Law* described. It was the handclasp of the bride and the bridegroom that mattered, a joining of hands symbolizing their entry into indissoluble matrimony. Likewise, the ring signified something that could not be dissolved or broken.

The marriage contracts themselves reflect this change in the relationship between the spouses. Moreover, contracts from the late fourteenth and early fifteenth centuries indicate that by this stage, use of the word *hjónaband* had become common.[83] This development in language was closely related to the idea of engagement (*trúlofun*): the promise of a bond uniting the couple (the *hjón*). Their union, now called *hjónaband*, was based on the partners' promise to remain faithful to each other and to God. This was something new, for the old marriage contract (usually called a *hjúskapr*) had been soluble.

One can observe parallel changes in attitudes toward the bride. In the written Icelandic marriage contracts of the late Middle Ages, the woman had achieved a more prominent position than in previous contracts. This new prominence was

---

[80] See Poul Grinder-Hansen (ed.), *Margrete 1. Nordens frue og husbond: Kalmarunionen 600 år: Essays og Udstillingskatalog* (Copenhagen, 1996), 339 (ring-shaped buckle, no. 151), and 397 (ring brooch, no. 295). The buckle is in the Museum of Bergen, and the ring can be found in the National Museum of Copenhagen.

[81] One late-medieval Irish *vita* speaks of a wedding ring worn by a wife: see Lisa M. Bitel, *Land of Women: Tales of Sex and Gender from Early Ireland* (Ithaca, N.Y., 1996), 44. Bitel cites Charles Plummer, *Vitae Sanctorum Hiberniae*, 2 vols. (Oxford, 1910), 2:78, and refers also to Máirín O Daly's translation of *Cath Maige Mucrama: The Battle of Mag Mucrama*, Irish Texts Society 50 (Dublin, 1975), 66–67 (regarding the exchange between Art Mac Cuinn and the daughter of Olc Aiche).

[82] See Michael M. Sheehan, "The bishop of Rome to a barbarian king on the rituals of marriage," in James K. Farge (ed.), *Marriage, Family, and Law in Medieval Europe: Collected Studies* (Toronto, 1996), 278–91, esp. n. 32 on p. 287. For the relevant passage in Pope Nicholas's letter to King Boris of Bulgaria, see the articles by Philip L. Reynolds in this volume, at 4–5, 124–25.

[83] E.g., DI XII, 319. See Fritzner, *Ordbog* (n. 44 earlier), vol. 1, 834, on *hjúskapr*, and see also the examples that Fritzner cites for *hjúskaparband* (833), which he took from the *New Christian Law* of Bishop Árni.

partly a consequence of the change regarding who made the agreement. What people documented in a marriage was now a contract between husband and wife (as well as between the couple and God), whereas previously (according to the oral contracts) the agreement had been between the prospective husband and his future father-in-law.

Apart from the Danish laws of the late twelfth and early thirteenth centuries, all Nordic law codes emphasized the importance of the rituals associated with entering marriage. The man's payment of a *mundr* (in effect, a brideprice) was one element of the handclasp custom as found in the Icelandic law of *Grágás*.[84] Even if the new marriage legislation of the late thirteenth century changed the rules for entering marriage, it was still common in the fourteenth century to marry according to the formula of *Grágás*, which included the *mundr* (although the payment of *mundr* was no longer a legal requirement for a valid marriage).

Such continuity illustrates well how people in the fourteenth century still connected marriage agreements to other kinds of agreements concerning property transfer, rather than interpreting marriage as a sacrament. That is why a contract from 1380 informs us that fathers made the marriage agreement (*kayptu loglighu hiuskaparkaupe*) between their children. We find further evidence of this understanding (whereby people construed marriage primarily as a settlement over property) in terminology, for at the beginning of the fourteenth century, the same terminology (e.g., *kaupmáli* or *kaupmálabréf*) was used for contracts concerning property transfer (properly called *kaupbréf*) as well as for marriage contracts.[85] Accordingly, one can see how closely the people of the fourteenth century related marriage agreements to agreements about the transmission of property in general.

In contrast, it seems that by the end of the sixteenth century, the word *kaupmáli* no longer signified the transfer of landed property. This change of usage suggests that property transfer through marriage had come to be viewed differently from other types of property transfer and that marriage agreements no longer focused exclusively on property. The contract of *hjónaband* between wife and husband, by which she put her hand in his and they were joined together in matrimony, was becoming stronger during this period. One example of this development dates from a contract of 1521, in which witnesses confirmed the marriage contract between the future wife and husband.[86] Thus, by the late sixteenth century, people had accepted the idea of marriage as a personal contract between the spouses. It does not follow, however, that the parents had lost all of their influence over their children's marriages.

---

[84] See Stig Iuul, "Formuefællesskab," KLNM 4:487–91.
[85] See DI III, 65–66, where a property agreement of 1352 is called *kaupmáli*. There are examples of the word being used in this sense also from 1332 (DI II, 673–74) and from 1360 (DI III, 142–44). See also examples from 1372 (DI III, 274–75), 1377 (DI III, 315–16), and 1378 (DI III, 331–32).
[86] DI III, 351; DI VIII, 813.

THE ROLE OF THE PARENTS AND THE POSITIONS OF THE SPOUSES

There were also changes in the role of the parents in relation to the legal position of the spouses themselves. The earliest contracts from the late fourteenth century emphasize the role of the parents in the formation of a marriage, but as time passed, the position of the partners themselves became more important. The consent of the woman or the mutual consent of the partners themselves was a new element: there had been no mention of it as a feature of marriage-making in *Grágás*. By the end of the sixteenth century, the partners had achieved a more prominent role in the creation of the marriage contract, although parental consent continued to be important.[87]

The contracts of the sixteenth century are very different from those of the late fourteenth through fifteenth centuries. The partners themselves more commonly drew up or agreed to these contracts (Doc. 4),[88] whereas the earlier contracts had given equal weight to the consent of the parents and of the partners.[89]

For an example of a contract that the partners themselves drew up, one may consider the letter of betrothal (*festingarbréf*) of the *lögmaður* lawman Eggert Hannesson and Sesselía Jónsdóttir, dating from 1559.[90] It seems that he was either marrying for the second time or that there was some question about the woman's name, for a dispensation has also survived whereby the king granted Eggert permission to marry one Steinunn Jónsdóttir even if some impediment had been found, for she had been living with a relative of Eggert.[91] Two men, a priest and another witness, testified that they could find no objection to the relationship. Then Eggert asked:

the said Sesselía whether she would like to marry him, and she said yes, and so they shook hands and Eggert betrothed Sesselía with the words, "I Eggert Hannesson betroth you Sesselía Jónsdóttir to be my legal wife according to the law of God, and of the country, and of the holy Fathers, and by this you are my legal wife, and to this will you be witness, priest Árni Steinólfsson, and you Arngrímur Björnsson."[92]

As mentioned previously, it also is clear that during the sixteenth century, the word *gifta* had come to denote the act of getting married, rather than the act

---

[87] From as late as 1552, we find a marriage contract stressing the importance of the consent of both parents: see DI XII, 439. Another *kaupmálabréf* from the early seventeenth century (a contract from 1620 between Sveinn Símonarson on behalf of Magnús Gissurarson and Þóra Bjarnadóttir on the behalf of her daughter Þórkatla Bjarnadóttir) illustrates how strong the need for parental consent remained: see AM *dipl. isl. fasc.* LXI, 9.

[88] As well as the contract of 1535 between Ormur Sturluson lögmaður and Þorbjargar Þorleifsdóttir (DI IX, 739–40 [Doc. 4]), see the contract of 1529 between Þorsteinn Einarsson and Guðrúnu Bessadóttur in DI IX, 499: he betrothed himself to her *festir sér til eiginkonu* after they had had three children.

[89] See for example the formula from a marriage contract of 1432 in DI IV, 494–95.

[90] DI XIII, 440–41.

[91] DI XIV, 76.

[92] DI XIII, 440–41.

whereby a woman's guardian gave her away.[93] This new meaning of the word was related not only to the changing understanding of marriage discussed earlier, but also to changes in the social bonding of the spouses, pertaining to their altered position in relation to each other after marriage.

PARENTAL CONSENT IN THE LATE MIDDLE AGES

Yet at the same time as these changes were taking place, as if to confuse the issue, there was *more* emphasis in the documents on the role of the parents, both in giving consent and in making contracts on behalf of their children.[94] This apparent anomaly is not hard to explain. Hitherto, before marriage contracts had become contracts between the spouses themselves (as during the thirteenth and fourteenth centuries), it was not necessary to confirm the existence of parental consent, for it was the parents themselves who had made these contracts. When marriage became a contract between a future husband and wife, however, the documented consent of the parents acquired a new importance as a guarantee of those elements of the agreement concerning property.[95] The emphasis on the consent of both spouses did not alter the fact that marriage (at least among the wealthy elite) still conspicuously involved property transfer, wherein the parents of the spouses had a special interest.

The need for parental consent was greater for the parents of the bride than for the parents of the groom, given that the husband's participation in the creation of the marriage contracts was generally more active than the wife's. A 1537 contract (made between the partners) stated that the man contributed property both for *kaups* and for *kuonarmundar* (i.e., as the financial settlement and as the brideprice), whereas the father of the bride gave her to the husband.[96] In 1549, Örnólfur Jónsson and Steinunn Ólafsdóttir made a marriage contract that stated that to get her, he would contribute a certain amount of wealth as her financial settlement and brideprice (*til kaups og kvonarmundar*).[97] Örnólfur's easy access to wealth suggests that the bride was more dependent on her relatives' consent than the bridegroom was.

The marriage of Helga Aradóttir and Páll Jónsson in 1558 shows that a woman could seek permission to marry from other relatives when her guardian did not

---

[93] See the 1666 copy of a short *ágrip af kaupmáli* from 1533 in DI XI, 113. Here Jón Ólafsson, the bridegroom, married (*giftist*) his bride, Þóra Björnsdóttir. It is possible that such phraseology reflects the usage of 1666 rather than that of 1533, but it at least indicates that a change in usage had occurred by the later date.

[94] DI XI, 305.

[95] For example, in DI X, 421–22, from 1539, a man goes to make a marriage agreement with his intended with their parents' consent.

[96] DI X, 331–32.

[97] DI XI, 739.

approve of the marriage.[98] Þorleifur Grímsson, Helga's grandfather on her mother's side and her legal guardian, had previously given his consent in a written document, yet "now he did not want to have anything to do with the case."[99] But men of honor and the priest said that the woman could nevertheless get married because she had the consent of other relatives:

This is why Helga Aradóttir had asked her grandmother, Helga Sigurðardóttir, and the sister of her father, Þórunn Jónsdóttir, as well as the brother of her father, the priest Sigurður Jónsson, to consent that Helga Aradóttir really wanted to be the wife of Páll Jónsson.[100]

It seems that her grandfather and guardian, Þorleifur, did not care about the marriage. In the absence of his active blessing, Helga turned to her female relatives and to her uncle, a priest. Another letter from 1558 documents the same marriage. But this was a letter of witness from four priests and five laymen declaring that the priest Sigurður Jónsson (Helga's uncle) was her guardian.

The latter document contains valuable information regarding the general nature of marriage. Here Sigurður, now her guardian, asked for advice from the witnesses:

He thought that this marriage was not as good as he wished and therefore it was necessary to be aware that the woman would not lose her honor by marrying a man of lower rank. He told us that the man who wanted to marry her was from a high-ranking family, and that he was wealthy and a gentleman.[101]

The document demonstrates that it was important to establish clearly that the woman consented to the match, that the marriage was contracted without legal hindrance, and that it would be between two equal partners.[102] The partners in this case were judged to have been legally married, but the case also shows that women could rely on different relatives when necessary, a feature that is characteristic of bilateral family structure.

In a marriage contract from 1562, the bride's guardian (*giftingarmaður*) was her mother.[103] In most cases, parental consent was a matter for fathers, although the involvement of mothers was not precluded. The issue of parental consent was closely related to the properties involved in the marriage contract. Both *sets* of parents could perform the handclasp to confirm the marriage agreements of their children. Although the demand for paternal consent remained stronger than that for maternal consent, the mother's right to perform the handclasp reflected a

---

[98] DI XIII, 127–28, 270–73, 278–81.

[99] DI XIII, 271.

[100] Ibid.

[101] DI XIII, 279: "ad honum þætti hennar rád med spiollum fara. og þui naudsyn vera ad hun væri ej fjrd sijnu jafnrædi og sæmd. sagdi hann oss ad hennar villdi fa til ektaskapar(og eigenordz) eirn velborenn. fiadur og forsöktur heidarlegur dandess sveirn."

[102] DI XIII, 280–81.

[103] DI XIV, 15.

general strengthening of the wife's legal position in regard to all kinds of property agreements in Icelandic society. When we do find both parents (father and mother) consenting to marriage, it is usually the case that both had donated property toward their children's marriage settlement. By the late Middle Ages, therefore, control over marriage was *parental* rather than *paternal*, and this was true both for sons and for daughters.

Instances of paternal and parental control are common in the documents. One example is from 1281, which gives a list of reasons that a father could use to disinherit his son.[104] But a document from 1479 describes a *mother's* agreement to permit her daughter to marry a man to whom she was related in the fourth degree, as long as there was dispensation from the clerical authorities.[105] Another example from 1483 involves parents who did not agree to their daughter's marrying because she had chosen a potential husband without their consent. In this case, the parents stated that they forgave their daughter and accepted her into their family again, a statement that probably implied that she was their heir once more.[106] A further example comes from 1487, when Bishop Magnús of Skálholt gave landed property to his sister and agreed that she would give it to her son as long as the latter married with the consent of his mother and the bishop, as well as of his father.[107] It is clear from these examples that parental authority – or the right of family members to control the transfer of property by means of marriage – was not perceived to be in conflict with the understanding of what constituted a Christian marriage.

Conclusions

We have observed the form and evolution of Icelandic marriage settlements, beginning from the twelfth century, when we have the first evidence of *oral* marriage contracts. We have considered the written contracts in relation to Icelandic and Norwegian law codes and to the influence of European canon law. These written contracts (examples of which are extant beginning from the mid-fourteenth century) varied considerably in form and might be drawn up at the time of the settlement itself or afterwards (as a subsequent written record of an agreement that the parties had already entered into orally). An important shift occurred during the late thirteenth and early fourteenth centuries. In the older form, the compact was between the kinsfolk on both sides as well as between the partners themselves, the partners retained separate ownership of their respective properties, and the bond was soluble. In the new form, there was more emphasis on the agreement

---

[104] DI II, 234–35.
[105] DI VI, 182 (*Ólöf Loptsdóttir to Solveig and Páll*).
[106] DI VI, 475.
[107] DI VI, 604–5. See also DI X, 68–69, where the case discussed in Chapter 5 concerns a person who received a gift from his grandfather, but his grandmother did not give her consent to it.

of the partners themselves, they held the property in common (i.e., the wife normally would not retain her own property), and the bond was indissoluble. This change, I have argued, was a result of influence from contemporaneous European canon law. Yet church weddings and the involvement of clerics in nuptials were not legally necessary, and marriage-making continued to take place in a purely "secular" manner.

The changes in how medieval Icelanders viewed marriage and marriage-making are evident both in written contracts and in laws. Yet one should not construe these changes, I have argued, as representing a transition from a "secular" to an "ecclesiastical" model of marriage. The words that created a marriage could always be spoken anywhere, be it at a farm (when the financial contract was made) or in front of the church door. Yet the form of words used, which originally concerned only the woman and the financial arrangements, did change gradually in a process of Christianization. New symbolic gifts and acts expressed the sacred meaning of marriage, while the role of priests in marriage contracts became greater (although prior to the Reformation, the absence of a priest did not affect the legal validity of the contract, nor did the absence of any transfer of gifts).

As in Europe, what mattered subsequently was some extant testimony that a marriage contract had indeed been made "according to the law of God." People could take a written record of the contract to court and use it as proof that the partners had married legitimately, but there was no standardized form: nothing to dictate precisely which words or actions created a valid marriage. The evidence presented to the bishops or to secular lawmen at court (for the Icelandic marriage cases were often judged in "mixed" courts that included secular members as well as clerics) could take many forms. For example, there might be a letter from witnesses stating that the marriage had been contracted "according to the law of God," or outlining how the financial contract was made; there might be a formal written contract giving details of the transfer of property; or there might merely be a declaration that a given marriage had been "legally" contracted.

The evidence of marriage contracts from the fourteenth century is too sparse for one to be able to say anything confidently about general patterns in the making of marriage contracts during this period. Nevertheless, the material that does survive indicates that it was not the partners themselves who forged such contracts but rather their respective fathers (although one should not interpret that situation as evidence that people did not recognize the Christian rules for valid marriages).

All the surviving marriage contracts from the fourteenth century merely document the property agreements. They are stubbornly silent about the personal commitment established between the partners according to the law of God. There is no surviving written testament to the spiritual or religious commitment of spouses from this century. As the contracts from 1380 and 1381 show, the partners' fathers (or, in their absence, their grandfathers, uncles, or brothers) were the persons who agreed to the contract. In other words, the relatives of the couple, and not the spouses themselves, made the contracts. These contracts, therefore, still represent an older understanding of marriage, according to which contracting marriage was essentially a property agreement between two families.

Whereas the surviving marriage contracts from the fourteenth century confirm the sense of an older tradition of marriage-making, the sources from the next century indicate significant changes in the making of marriage contracts. Court cases indicate that during the fifteenth and early sixteenth centuries, the mutual consent of the partners themselves was something that people looked for and accepted as a norm. Yet once the requirement of mutual consent had become established, aristocratic families found it necessary to reassert their control. One may therefore interpret the marked emphasis on parental control and approval in this period as a conservative response to the new institution of marriage (ecclesiastical in origin), whereby the mutual consent of the partners themselves (expressed orally) was the essential element. There was no way in which an element of parental control could have disappeared completely in a society such as Iceland, where power was based almost entirely on landed property.

A study of the Icelandic marriage contracts from the late Middle Ages shows how a fundamental change in the law of marriage that had occurred at the end of thirteenth century slowly gained practical significance during the period that followed. One sees the results of this development both in documents related to court proceedings and in written marriage contracts. The survival of these sources was connected intimately to the marriage and inheritance strategies of the most powerful Icelandic families.[108] The church's redefinition of what constituted a legal marriage made it more important to preserve matrimonial documents, for they would be valuable if disputes arose over property.

The Icelandic marriage contracts of the late fifteenth and sixteenth centuries show that the old financial considerations and the new Christian values existed side by side. Little from the old formula of marriage as found in *Grágás* had disappeared, but there were new elements as well. Some documents speak of the religious significance of marriage, but more often they recognize ecclesiastical rules simply by stating that the contract was made "according to the law of God."

The most significant difference emerges when one compares these written contracts with the earliest laws, for the contracts now record the union of the spouses themselves, and not agreements between the brides' fathers and their future sons-in-law. This development toward a more personal, individualistic concept of marriage also heralded a new way of construing gender identity. The spouses (who had become the main subject of marriage) should love each other as well as their God. The meaning of marriage became a personal and spiritual matter, and not just a contract involving the transfer of wealth and the forging of social and political

---

[108] See discussion of this point in Arnórsdóttir, "Icelandic Marriage Dispensations," 159–69, and cf. Hrefna Róbertsdóttir, "Helmingarfélag hjóna á miðöldum," *Sagnir* 7 (1986): 31–40.

alliances. Thus marriage became the foundation for a new understanding of the relationship between the sexes and of gender roles in late medieval Iceland.

༈

APPENDIX: FOUR ICELANDIC MARRIAGE CONTRACTS*

The original texts of these charters are in Icelandic except for a few phrases in Latin (including Roman numerals) expressing the date or an invocation. The Latin phrases are indicated in the translations by italics.

DOCUMENT 1: *The Marriage Contract of Guðmundur Arason and Helga Þorleifsdóttir, October 7, 1423 in Vatnsfjörður (DI IV, no. 370, p. 312)*[1]

In the name of the Lord, Amen.

The following agreement [*kaupmáli*] between farmer Guðmundur Arason and Helga Þorleifsdóttir was made publicly [*lýstur*][2] and confirmed on their wedding day, the first Tuesday after Michaelmas, in Vatnsfjörður when there had elapsed since the birth of our Lord Jesus Christ *one thousand four hundred twenty* and three years: that the said Guðmundur had twelve hundred hundreds[3] in his own property for the financial agreement [*kaup*] with Helga. In return, Þorleifur Árnason gave his daughter Helga, for the financial agreement with Guðmundur, the land at the farm on Rauðasandur for one hundred hundreds and, in addition, one hundred hundreds in other land and one hundred hundreds in movable goods. The aforementioned Guðmundur gave the aforementioned Helga a one-fourth gift [*fjórðungsgjöf*][4] of those twelve hundred hundreds which he had for the financial agreement with her.

---

* [The following translations are by Kendra Willson (University of California at Berkeley), with a few modifications by the author. Notes are the author's. An English translation of *Grágás* is available: *Laws of Early Iceland: Grágás, the Codex Regius of Grágás with Material from Other Manuscripts,* translated by Andrew Dennis, Peter Foote, and Richard Perkins, 2 vols. (Winnipeg, 1980, 2000). For the section on "betrothals," see vol. 2, 53–81. At the time of going to press, a bilingual edition of *Jónsbók* is in preparation, edited by Jana K. Schulman, as *Bibliotheca Germanica* vol. 4 (AQ-Verlag, Saarbrücken).]

[1] This typical contract of joint possession is also an example of a marriage settlement between two powerful Icelandic families. A witness's letter about this marriage from three decades later (1453) has survived (DI V, p. 109).

[2] The term *lýstur* ("announced," "proclaimed"), although applied here to the contract itself on the occasion of the wedding, was usually applied to the banns, i.e., the announcement in church of the forthcoming marriage three Sundays previously, a requirement for a valid marriage.

[3] The term *eitt hundrað* signifies one hundred = 120 *alen vaðmál* (cloth) = about six cows. *Höfuðból,* the manor, was worth sixty hundreds or more.

[4] That is, a gift that was worth one fourth of his property.

Kristín Bjarnadóttir chose, with the approval and handclasp of Guðmundur himself and of Hrafn Guðmundsson, his father's brother, who was the most closely related to him [of those] there, her daughter [to be] a wife in a shared property agreement [*helmingarkona*][5] in Guðmundur's estate with respect to all property acquired and not yet acquired. The aforementioned Helga should continue to own, in addition to a half-share of Guðmundur's property, forty hundreds in decent goods with commercial value, which the aforementioned Guðmundur gave the aforementioned Helga as her bench gift.[6]

The witnesses to the wedding were these: Loftur Guttormsson, Hrafn Guðmundsson, Auðun Salómonsson, Árni Einarsson, Gamli [i.e., Old] Marteinsson, Gunnar Andrésson, and Helgi Guttormsson.

And in proof of this we the aforementioned men place our seals before this document, written in the same place and one year, two nights later than previously stated.

DOCUMENT 2: *The Marriage Contract of Eyjólfur Böðvarsson and Guðrún, Daughter of Pastor Þorkell Guðbjartsson, October 6, 1465 and April 28, 1468 in Laufás (DI V, no. 401, pp. 454–55)*

This do we, Rögnvaldur Ásgrímsson, Bergfinnur Jússason, pastors; Hrafn Brandsson, Eyvindur Eyvindsson, Kolli Vigfússon, and Ögmundur Hákonarson, laymen, make known to good men with this our open deed, that *in the 1465th year of grace* on the first Sunday after Michaelmas in Laufás in Eyjafjörður we were present, saw, and heard the words and handclasp of Reverend Þorkell Guðbjartsson for the first party and Eyjólfur Böðvarsson for the second party with the following agreement [*skildagi*]: that the aforementioned Reverend Þorkell gave the aforesaid Eyjólfur Guðrún, his daughter, with the approval of Valgerður Magnúsdóttir, her mother, with this gain in property: that he gave her fifty hundreds in land and movable property, these lands which are located in Bárðardalur in Lundarbrekka parish – one is called Sigurðarstaðir and the other Sandvík – for six hundred and twenty. And the aforementioned Valgerður, her mother, gave her ten hundreds. These sixty hundreds are her dowry [*heimanfylgja*]. And the aforementioned Eyjólfur counted for himself in return one hundred hundreds in land and movable property. The following properties were specified: Ysti Mór for thirty hundreds and half of Sjöundastaðir for fifteen hundreds. These properties are located in Fljót in the Bárðar assembly district. Eyjólfur gave the aforementioned Guðrún, his wife, twenty hundreds as a bridal gift [*tilgjöf*] and ten hundreds as a morning gift and bench gift. Reverend Þorkell Guðbjartsson

[5] The term implies that she is to be married according to the principle of joint possession, whereby husband and wife each own half of the matrimonial estate.
[6] The bench gift (*bekkjargjöf*) was given by the husband to the wife at the wedding feast.

chose Guðrún, his daughter, [to be] a wife retaining property of her own [*málakona*] in the estate of the aforementioned Eyjólfur and contributed this property [*máli*] of hers to his estate and the best property that he might come to own. And after this Eyjólfur Böðvarsson espoused [*festi*][7] Guðrún Þorkelsdóttir to be his lawful wife according to God's law with the appropriate words.

And in proof of this, we the aforementioned men place our seals before this document, which was made in the same place on the Thursday before the mass of the two apostles Philip and Jacob, *in the 1468th year of our Lord.*

DOCUMENT 3: *The Marriage Contract of Sveinn Sumarliðason and Guðríður Finnbogadóttir, September 11, 1485, April 20, 1486 in Þverá (DI VI, no. 489, pp. 547–49)*

To all those men who see or hear this document, Eiríkur Einarsson and Jón Gíslason, pastors, [and] Páll Brandsson, Þorsteinn Þorleifsson, Jón Arngrímsson, Tómas Sveinbjarnarson, Ásgrímur Hallsson, and Þormóður Þormóðsson, laymen, send God's greeting and their own, making known that *in the 1485th year of grace* on the first Sunday after *the Nativity of the Blessed Virgin Mary* at Þverá in Laxárdalur we were present, saw, and heard the words and handclasp of these men, Sumarliði Eiríksson and his son Sveinn, for the first party, and Finnbogi Jónsson and his daughter Guðríður, for the second, when it was stipulated, first, that they, Finnbogi and Sumarliði, gave these their children together according to law with the assent and consent of both, with the following conditions and financial agreement: that the said Sveinn Sumarliðason provided for the financial agreement [*kaup*] and his marriage [*eiginorð*] to the aforementioned Guðríður Finnbogadóttir all his property, that which he had then, and that which had come to him in inheritance and possession from the late Eiríkur Loftsson, his paternal grandfather. In this was specified, first, the entire property Grund in Eyjafjörður, Dalur, and Mörk under Eyjafjöll, with all the property, landed and movable, which belonged to it and which Eiríkur Loftsson owned when he died and has not since legally left [as his estate]; and likewise Helluland in Skagafjörður, Skáldalækur in Svarfaðardalur, Þóroddsstaðir on Svalbarðsströnd, and along with it all other property, land and movable goods, livestock and other property, which Eiríkur had at the time of his death and which had come to the aforementioned Sveinn as inheritance, whoever then possessed or controlled it. The aforementioned Sumarliði announced and calculated that Mrs. Ólöf Loftsdóttir had taken for herself and not relinquished four hundred hundreds of the property inherited from the aforementioned Eiríkur Loftsson. Sumarliði also calculated that Mrs. Soffía Loftsdóttir had taken for

[7] Literally, "bound."

herself and not relinquished another four hundred hundreds of the aforementioned inheritance from Eiríkur Loftsson.

In return, Guðríður Finnbogadóttir provided for the financial agreement
with the aforementioned Sveinn Sumarliðason the property Fellsmúli, which
is located in Rangárvellir, for eighty hundreds and in addition ten [times]
ten hundreds in useful property. The aforementioned Sveinn Sumarliðason
gave to the aforementioned Guðríður Finnbogadóttir for her full possession the entire property of Arnbjargarbrekka, which is located in Möðruvellir
parish in Hörgárdalur with those conditions that sixty hundreds was the legal
bridal gift [*tilgjöf*] and in addition forty hundreds for the counter-payment
[*gagngjald*] and gift, which are called morning gift and bench gift. Guðríður
should include these gifts in the estate of Arnbjargarbrekka. Hereafter, according to the counsel, will, terms, and approval of all the aforesaid people (first
and foremost Sveinn and Guðríður), Finnbogi and Sumarliði decided that
there should be a shared property agreement [*helmingafélag*] between the
aforementioned Sveinn Sumarliðason and Guðríður Finnbogadóttir. To this
joint property between them should be contributed all that they then owned
or might later come to own in real estate or movable property, as specified
in the legislative amendment of King Hákon, with these cessions of right
of inheritance [*arftak*] and conditions [*skildagi*]: that each of them should
acquire, with respect to the other, fully half of their property between them,
landed and movable, livestock and other property, which then shall last until
their deaths should come about. Then Sveinn or his heirs, namely, his legitimate children, father or siblings, can claim back disposition of the property
Grund in Eyjafjörður, and Guðríður or her heirs should then take, from the
portion which belonged to Sveinn or his heirs, for half of Grund one hundred
hundreds of the best property which shall be available and she or they would
themselves have chosen.

This entire deed [*gjörningur*], contract [*kaupmáli*], and agreement [*skildagi*]
took place with a handclasp between the aforementioned people, Sveinn
and Guðríður, Finnbogi and Sumarliði. And as proof of this we, the aforementioned people, place our seals before this document, made at Þverá in
Laxárdalur on the Thursday before the festival of Johannes the Bishop and
Confessor, one year later than previously stated.

DOCUMENT 4: *The Marriage Contract of Ormur Sturluson
and Þorbjörg Þorleifsdóttir August 4, 1535 at Möðruvellir
(DI IX, no. 613, pp. 739–40)*

In the name of the Lord, Amen.

The following agreement [*kaupmáli*] between Ormur Sturluson and
Þorbjörg Þorleifsdóttir was made publicly and confirmed on their wedding
day, the first Sunday after the first Mass of St. Ólafur [in the Fall] at Möðruvellir
in Eyjafjörður, when there had elapsed since the birth of our Lord Jesus Christ

1535 years: that the aforementioned Ormur Sturluson had for the financial agreement with the aforementioned Þorbjörg Þorleifsdóttir three hundred hundreds in real estate. In this was included and specified [the property called] Staðarfell and eighty milch cattle and eighty hundreds in all useful property, both animate and inanimate.

In return, the aforementioned Þorbjörg Þorleifsdóttir had two hundred hundreds in land and forty milch cows, twenty hundreds in silver and twenty hundreds in other useful property. Her maternal inheritance is included in this.

The aforementioned Ormur Sturluson gave to the aforementioned Þorbjörg Þorleifsdóttir as a bridal gift [*tilgjöf*]: sixty hundreds was specified: the property Skorravík thirty hundreds, and Holt for twenty hundreds, which is located in Staðarfell parish, and in addition ten milch cows. Þorbjörg's separate property [*máli*] is thus calculated as two hundred hundreds and eighty hundreds.

Farmer Þorleifur Grímsson chose his daughter Þorbjörg [to be] a wife retaining property of her own [*málakona*] in relation to Ormur Sturluson.

Farmer Daði Guðmundsson consented to this agreement as the legal representative of farmer Þorsteinn Finnbogason who then should have control over the property of his kinsman Ormur Sturluson.

These were the witnesses to the espousal and wedding [*festingarvottar og brúðkaupsvitni*]: Oddur Halldórsson, Egill Hallsson, Andrés Ásgrímsson, pastors; Páll Grímsson, Jón Þorláksson, and Þorvaldur Árnason, laymen. Each set his seal before this marriage contract [*kaupmálabréf*], which was made at the same place three days later than previously stated.

CHAPTER ELEVEN

CONTRACTING MARRIAGE IN RENAISSANCE FLORENCE

Thomas Kuehn

In May 1453, a clandestine wedding occurred in Florence. Two years later, it gave birth to a notorious lawsuit. The groom, Giovanni di ser Lodovico della Casa, denied that the ceremony had ever happened and that his relationship with Lusanna di Benedetto, widow of Andrea Nucci, was nothing more than sexual. The entire legal proceeding was ecclesiastical. The only secular complication was a suit to see if the *podestà* had jurisdiction, and that was settled early and without input from the parties. (If dowry had been at issue, the case would have come before a secular court.)[1] The subsequent judgment in favor of Lusanna made by the court of Archbishop Antonino, the sainted moral and legal reformer, shows that he placed credence in the fact of the wedding ceremony as well as in certain other bits of evidence (although the judgment was reversed on appeal to Rome). That ceremony presents us, therefore, with an interesting and illuminating point of entry into Florentine marital customs and their relation to canon law. We can come to appreciate what made this wedding secret, in contrast to those that were public knowledge; or, pressing a bit further, what would have rendered their relationship a marriage rather than concubinage, which was the most that Giovanni della Casa would admit.

The ceremony took place in Lusanna's brother's house and involved a small contingent of witnesses, even including a friar and a young novice summoned from Santa Croce, but not including any kin of the groom. Following a meal, the friar was asked to say a few words as the party formed a circle around him and the couple. Witnesses reported that the friar then asked Giovanni if he wished to take Lusanna as his wife, and that he posed the corresponding question to Lusanna.

---

[1] Gene A. Brucker has captured the entire incident in memorable fashion in his *Giovanni and Lusanna: Love and Marriage in Renaissance Florence* (Berkeley, 1986). On the lawsuit, see ibid., 39–75. On the significance of the affair, see also Thomas Kuehn, "Reading microhistory: The example of Giovanni and Lusanna," *Journal of Modern History* 61 (1989): 512–34. I wish to thank our editors, Philip Reynolds and John Witte, for their careful reading of and incisive comments on my paper and their exemplary management of the entire project.

The groom next placed a ring on her finger while Lusanna's brother held her hand as she received it. Kisses were exchanged. Giovanni presented gifts to Lusanna's relatives present, shared wine with them, and then retired upstairs with his bride, presumably to consummate their union.[2]

If there were witnesses and clergy present at the ceremony, what made the marriage clandestine? This was a wedding that was *meant* to be secret, or at least covert: to be kept from general public notice and, above all, from Giovanni's father and the rest of the della Casa. That was plain from the court testimony of Lusanna's brother to the effect that Giovanni refused to have a notary present (a member, in this case, of his father's profession and guild) to make a written legal record. Secrecy demanded as well that the bride and groom could not set up household together (though there was testimony as to their behavior while in *villeggiatura* in the countryside during the following summer). There was no dowry from the bride (at least not in any written and notarized form, as was common in Florence at the time, although she had 250 florins as dowry from her marriage to Andrea Nucci), nor from her family to Giovanni; nor was there any token marital gift (*donatio propter nuptias*) from him to her (beyond the gifts to her kin, which were, in fact, of no legal relevance).[3] In the absence of documentation, of the active participation of the groom's family, and of transfers of property, it was at least possible to contest the validity of the marriage in an ecclesiastical court.

Yet this was not an attempt to keep the union entirely secret because of something inappropriate or criminal in it, as might happen when people married secretly to hide legal impediments: it was not a wedding of underage children, for example. The social key to this wedding was its calculated misalliance. Giovanni della Casa was a scion of a fairly well-to-do family, of a lineage of some pedigree and prominence in Florence. At age thirty-three in 1453, active in banking and the silk trade, Giovanni was at the point in life when he could expect to marry a young girl of good family and begin to sire the children needed to carry the family's name, honor, and fortune.[4]

---

[2] The details are in Brucker, *Giovanni and Lusanna*, 16–21.

[3] In Florence, this was the Mediterranean form of dowry as elaborated in Roman law, as distinct from other forms of *dos* discussed by others in this volume. In the course of the twelfth century, the Roman form of dowry from the bride's father had displaced the Lombard institution of an endowment of the bride by her husband. On the legal and social background of the dowry in Tuscany and more generally in central and northern Italy, see Manlio Bellomo, *Ricerche sui rapporti patrimoniali tra coniugi: Contributo alla storia della famiglia medievale* (Milan, 1961); and Diane Owen Hughes, "From brideprice to dowry in Mediterranean Europe," *Journal of Family History* 3 (1978): 262–96. On the related *donatio propter nuptias* (from husband to bride) and the assimilation of various customs under this civil law heading, see Roberta Braccia, "*Uxor gaudet de morte mariti*: La *donatio propter nuptias* tra diritto comune e diritti locali," *Annali della Facoltà di Giurisprudenza di Genova* 30 (2000–2001): 76–128.

[4] On marriage ages in Florence (i.e., the average ages for a first marriage in both genders), see David Herlihy and Christiane Klapisch-Zuber, *Les toscans et leurs familles: Une étude du catasto florentin de 1427* (Paris, 1978), 393–419. (Canon law determined the minimum marriageable ages.) On marriage as social alliance, see Anthony Molho, *Marriage Alliance in Late Medieval Florence* (Cambridge, Mass., 1994); and Lorenzo Fabbri, *Alleanza matrimoniale e patriziato nella Firenze del 400: Studio*

Lusanna was of much more modest circumstances, and she was a widow to boot, and much older than the usual first-time bride in Florence. At stake in the secrecy of this union was reputation, to be sure, but also deniability, as is apparent from what happened afterwards. Giovanni could try simply to walk away from this relationship and to enter into a full, formal, public marriage – as he ultimately did, with a young woman of the prominent Rucellai lineage. His marriage to Marietta Rucellai, in contrast, passed through a number of formal, public processes and thus contained a number of elements missing from the clandestine union with Lusanna, especially a written legal instrument, a dowry (including, as well as the instrument, payment in cash or other valuables), and the establishment of the bride in the groom's household, all with the open participation of his kin and hers.

In what follows, using the nine documents in the appendix as examples, I consider the cardinal elements of the normal marriage process, elements that were significantly absent from the clandestine marriage of Giovanni and Lusanna.

FLORENTINE MARRIAGE DOCUMENTS

The surviving late-medieval and Renaissance documentation regarding marriage in Italy defies systematization. People married in a wide variety of places (occasionally even in a church) and under almost as wide a variety of forms. Some sort of exchange of consent, often accompanied by a ring, was common, and a bridal dowry (however modest) was normally involved; but one can generalize little beyond that much for Italy as a whole, or even for communities such as Florence.[5]

Had a notary been present at Giovanni and Lusanna's nuptials, he could have recorded at least one of the three types of written contract typically involved in Florentine marriages. The first was the betrothal contract, generally termed the *sponsalitium*. The second was an exchange of vows in the present tense with the placing of a ring on the bride's finger. In the fifteenth century, both the ritual itself and its documentary record were usually called *matrimonium*. The ritual (especially if there was written record of it) met the canon law requirements for marriage. The third type of document that one is likely to find in Florentine notarial marriage records is the dowry (*dos*), more precisely entitled *instrumentum dotale* or *confessio dotis*. I carefully analyze examples of all three.[6]

sulla famiglia Strozzi (Florence, 1991). Regarding inheritance ideology, if not practice, see Thomas Kuehn, "*Memoria* and family in law," in Giovanni Ciappelli and Patricia Lee Rubin (eds.), *Art, Memory, and Family in Renaissance Florence* (Cambridge, 2000), 262–74.

[5] See Silvana Seidel Menchi, "Percorsi variegati, percorsi obbligati: Elogio del matrimonio pre-tridentino," in Silvana Seidel Menchi and Diego Quaglioni (eds.), *Matrimoni in dubbio: Unioni controverse e nozze clandestine in Italia dal xiv al xviii secolo* (Bologna, 2001), 17–60, at 18–22.

[6] Early formulary versions of *confessio dotis, sponsalitium,* and *matrimonium* can be found in Silio P. P. Scalfati (ed.), *Un formulario notarile fiorentino della metà del Dugento*, Archivio di Stato di Firenze, Scuola di Archivisitica Paleografia e Diplomatica, no. 5 (Florence, 1997), 51–52, 83–85, and 149–51.

Documentation was part of what distinguished an honorable, socially recognized marriage both from clandestine marriage and from concubinage. Tuscan cities such as Florence and Pistoia did not enact laws dealing with clandestine marriage, unlike cities elsewhere in Italy. Daniela Lombardi speculates that this was because Tuscan cities did not demand paternal consent for marriage; instead, she argues, "the Tuscan statutes insist repeatedly on the obligation to contract marriage before a notary."[7] It is possible, on the contrary, that paternal oversight in Florence was assumed to make statutes about clandestine marriage more or less moot. Yet although proof of marriage, as in the case of Giovanni and Lusanna, fell to church courts and not to secular ones, such proof was always tricky in the absence of notarial documents.[8] In 1477, in the midst of a flurry of statutory reforms, the Florentine *Consiglio del Cento*, concerned to avoid the expense and mountains of paper required in litigation ("tolere multas expensas et prolixitatem scripturarum in litigiis"), decreed that in matters where proof was required regarding death, filiation, or time of marriage, a party who failed to appear to answer an assertion was judged to have agreed to the other side's premise. If the party appeared but claimed to have no certain knowledge ("non bene informatum"), he had only three days to become so informed.[9] Notarial texts, as well as family and business records and the recollections of witnesses, would have been the means to "inform" oneself.

Betrothal

The betrothals of Florence differed little from those throughout northern and central Italy.[10] The *sponsalitium* was an agreement struck between men, notarized and thus publicized, with guarantors and arbiters. It was an arrangement between families that promised a movement of property as well as a daughter to another house, and it involved the entire issue of family honor and reputation. Promises in the future tense to consent later in the present tense were carefully set out, on one side by the groom for himself (if of age) or by his father or guardian (if not), and on the other side by the father for his daughter. Our documents show that the bride herself was not present. The groom promised the *arrha* against the possibility of the wounded honor that would result if one party saw the other renege on the pledge by failing to give consent in the present tense in due course.

---

[7] Daniela Lombardi, *Matrimoni di antico regime* (Bologna, 2001), 59.

[8] Needless to say, notarial texts were subject to doubt at points, for all that they were otherwise "proof proven." See Laurie Nussdorfer, "Lost faith: A Roman prosecutor reflects on notaries' crimes," in Paula Findlen, Michelle M. Fontaine, and Duane J. Osheim (eds.), *Beyond Florence: The Contours of Medieval and Early Modern Italy* (Stanford, 2003), 101–14.

[9] Florence, Archivio di Stato [hereafter ASF], Consiglio del Cento 2, fols. 16v–17r (23 July 1477).

[10] See Christiane Klapisch-Zuber, "Zacharias, or the ousted father: Nuptial rites in Tuscany between Giotto and the Council of Trent," in eadem, *Women, Family, and Ritual in Renaissance Italy*, translated by Lydia G. Cochrane (Chicago, 1985), 178–212, at 183–84. (The article was first published as "Zacharie ou le père évincé: Les rituels nuptiaux toscans entre Giotto et le Concile de Trent," *Annales E. S. C.* 34 [1979]: 1216–43.)

The *sponsalitium* bore some resemblance to arbitration agreements (usually termed *compromissum*), for an arbiter was designated to determine in due course the (supposedly) appropriate amount for the dowry. Florentines saw engagements as potentially conflict-ridden events and used the language of compromise and arbitration, as Matteo di Niccolò Corsini did when he recorded that his son Piero "compromised for his legitimate wife [*chonpromise per la sua ligitima sposa*]," namely, Ghita, daughter of Stefano di Vanni di ser Lotto Castellani.[11] Research demonstrates that among written, notarized documents, betrothal contracts were much rarer than marriage contracts and tended to be used almost exclusively by elite families.[12] These families, in turn, were relying on statutes that imposed penalties on parties who contracted and broke betrothals, especially in multiple instances. They were also relying on the sums set as *arrhae* in the contracts themselves. Although canonists had some difficulty reconciling *arrhae* with the doctrinal necessity of free consent in marriage, the realities in Florence were that few notarized betrothals failed to culminate in marriages.[13]

A further general observation, in line with Lombardi, regarding the marital process in Florence and in Tuscany as a whole is that religious ritual or any other involvement of the church (as a place of worship or as clergy) was extremely limited.[14] Our documents make that abundantly clear. The observation is as true of betrothals as it is of weddings. At first sight, the betrothal agreement (*sponsalitium*) of March 11, 1413 (Doc. 1) seems to be a counterexample, for it notably occurred in the parish church of Santa Maria sopr'Arno (according to the notary's description of time, place, and witnesses). In fact, a parish church was the customary starting point of the typical notarized record of a betrothal. The notarized document thus has it that the parties met face to face in a sacred place to proclaim their promises to each other. Yet the church served merely as a socially public and neutral site in which to bring two families together. Thus, in 1356, the city government had decreed that *sponsalitia* should take place in a church in order to assure that public peace would be maintained.[15] In a city whose most famous factional quarrel hitherto,

---

[11] Armando Petrucci (ed.), *Il libro di ricordanze dei Corsini (1362–1457)* (Rome, 1965), 72.

[12] Samuel K. Cohn, Jr., *The Laboring Classes in Renaissance Florence* (New York and London, 1980), 19–23; Osvaldo Cavallar and Julius Kirshner, "Making and breaking betrothal contracts (*sponsalia*) in late Trecento Florence," in Orazio Condorelli (ed.), *Panta rei: Studi dedicati a Manlio Bellomo*, 5 vols., vol. 1 (Rome, 2004), 395–452.

[13] Cavallar and Kirshner, "Making and breaking betrothal contracts," passim.

[14] See Lombardi, *Matrimoni*, 70; and eadem, "Fidanzamenti e matrimoni: Norme e consuetudini sociali dal concilio di Trento alle riforme settecentesche," in Michela De Giorgio and Christiane Klapisch-Zuber (eds.), *Storia del matrimonio* (Bari, 1996), 215–50. Still valuable is Francesco Brandileone, *Saggi sulla storia della celebrazione del matrimonio in Italia* (Milan, 1906); but more pertinent are Jean Gaudemet, *Le mariage en Occident: Les moeurs et le droit* (Paris, 1987); Ottavia Niccoli, "Baci rubati: Gesti e riti nuziali in Italia prima e dopo il Concilio di Trento," in Sergio Bertelli and Monica Centanni (eds.), *Il gesto: nel rito e nel cerimoniale dal mondo antico ad oggi* (Florence, 1995), 224–47; and Herlihy and Klapisch-Zuber, *Les toscans* (n. 4 earlier), 488–95.

[15] A point made by the foremost recent student of Florentine marriage practices, Christiane Klapisch-Zuber, in her "Zacharias," at 193.

legend had it, had arisen from a repudiated engagement (of Buondelmonte dei Buondelmonti to the daughter of Oderigo Giantruffetti in 1215, culminating in the Guelf-Ghibelline division), such a provision probably seemed highly sensible. Though the parties may have been present in *a* church, therefore, the presence of *the* church was not essential in the *sponsalitium*. The pledge did not involve an oath made on Scripture or on a relic. In general, as Christiane Klapisch-Zuber has noted, "Florentine rituals persistently kept ecclesiastical presence and the religious consecration of marriages to a marginal role."[16]

There were witnesses present at a *sponsalitium*, as at any notarized legal event. In Document 1, they were men of substance from the neighborhood. The text declares that Lorenzo Gualterotti promised Francesco d'Arnaldo Mannelli that he would see to it that his daughter Ginevra would consent to be Francesco's wife, and that he would give Francesco whatever dowry was decided by the mutually chosen arbiter, Filippo Machiavelli. For his part, Francesco promised to consent to take Ginevra as his wife, to give her a ring, and to acknowledge (*confitere*) the dowry and his legal obligations regarding it. Interesting, at the end of the text, is the positing of 800 florins as an *arrha* (*nomine arrarum*): an earnest money pledged against the breaking of the contract, seemingly by either party.[17]

The *sponsalitium* that Zanobi de' Bardi and Giovanni Spinelli entered into two years later before the same notary (Doc. 4) follows the same pattern. The two parties (the groom and bride's father) gathered with witnesses outside but at (*iuxta*) the church of Santa Caterina, probably in the small piazza in front. Here, Zanobi promised his daughter Diana to Spinelli, with a dowry to be set by the "wise men" (*sapientes viros*) Francesco de' Bardi and Arrigo Sassolini. Giovanni promised to take Diana as his wife and to acknowledge the dowry. Here, again, a sum of 800 florins was set as the *arrha* or earnest money, although there is no overt mention of a ring. In that regard, this document contrasts with the agreement in 1441, drawn up by a different notary, of two more humble Florentines, Lorenzo di Giovanni di Domenico and Domenico di Matteo, (Doc. 7). That text stated with some care that Masa, Lorenzo's daughter, would accept Domenico's ring and that the latter would "give her a ring in symbol of true marriage [*eidem tradere anulum in signo veri matrimonii*]." Their earnest money was only 100 florins, and their dotal arbiters were men of their own profession, namely, spinners (*filatoiai*). The parties met in a church before neutral witnesses.[18]

The primacy of family in the making of marriage is evident in these examples of *sponsalitia*, but what is missing is all the preliminary and very much behind-the-scenes maneuvering that brought the parties to the point of a public contract of betrothal. Careful and quiet appraisals of likely prospects, especially for daughters,

---

[16] Ibid.

[17] Klapisch-Zuber, "Zacharias," 186, takes the term *subarratio per anulum* as meaning that the *bride* was pledged, yet it seems the groom, too, was bound.

[18] Another example: In an engagement of 1393 between a *farsettaio* and a *ricamatore*, the pledged amount was 250 florins (ASF, Notarile antecosimiano 9395, fols. 240v–41r, July 3, 1393).

must surely have been occurring constantly in the homes, shops, and streets of Florence, although they emerge to our notice only sporadically, as in the letters of the matriarch Alessandra Strozzi.[19] A professional go-between, known in Florence as a *sensale*, frequently acted as a marriage broker. Only after a certain basic agreement had been struck through the *sensale's* services would the men from the two families meet privately.[20] Then the engagement was established, and a notary would draw up the document at that moment or soon afterward. What stuck in Florentines' minds from such family encounters was the pacific and contractual gesture of the handclasp: what they called *impalmamento* or *toccamano*. Fathers recorded in their family accounts that they had *impalmato* their daughter. A related expression – *fermare il parentado* – stressed that the betrothal constituted an alliance between families who had now become kin to each other (*parenti*). Thereafter, the future groom might hasten to the natal home of his bride-to-be and present gifts, customarily receiving a special dinner (elements that also crop up in the case of Giovanni della Casa). This trip to her house was necessitated by the bride's absence from the betrothal. The groom may have had little or no contact with her prior to the engagement.

Matrimony

To return to the documentary trail: The next step in the typical Florentine marital process was the actual exchange of vows in the present tense and the groom's placing a ring on the bride's finger. This was the *matrimonium*. The corresponding notarial texts (examples are Docs. 2, 5, and 8) are consistently brief. These acts took place not in a church but just generally somewhere designated as being in a given church-denominated district, a *popolo* (e.g., in the *popolo* of San Jacopo sopr'Arno). That was how Florentines customarily located their residences. The usual place for matrimony was the bride's home. Masa's marriage to Domenico notably took place in her brother's house on the same day as the engagement. The entire party, including the notary, had proceeded from the neutral ground of the Church of Santo Stefano a Ponte to the house in the nearby parish of San Jacopo sopr'Arno. All three marriage documents simply reported that bride and groom had contracted marriage through the exchange of words of consent in the present tense (*per verba de presenti*), and through the giving and receiving of a ring (*per anuli dationem et receptionem*).

Within the context of a volume focusing on medieval marriage contracts (as problematic as the term "contract" may be in this context), what is interesting about these Florentine examples (broadly characteristic, as they can be claimed to be, of communities throughout northern and central Italy) is their essentially

---

[19] These are now available in a convenient bilingual form, *Selected Letters of Alessandra Strozzi: Bilingual Edition*, translated by Heather Gregory (Berkeley, 1997).

[20] In addition to Klapisch-Zuber, "Zacharias," 183, see Robert Davidsohn, *Storia di Firenze*, 7 vols., translated from the German by Eugenio Dupré-Theseider, vol. 4 (Florence, 1973), part 3, 675–79.

written quality. The typical *matrimonium* text, in which the very verb "to contract" appears conspicuously, was not at all about property, in contrast to the surviving written marriage contracts from England that R. H. Helmholz examines in this volume. Although oral exchange and the gesture of placing a ring on the bride's finger lay behind the text,[21] the moment was not generally left to oral tradition alone (where, in contrast, it had been deliberately left in the case of Giovanni and Lusanna). The influence behind such resolute textuality in Italy, which was singularly reliant on writing in proofs and procedures, was less that of the church (in any overtly religious or spiritualizing form) than that of learned law (the *ius commune*, composed from both civil and canon law, with some other ingredients). The notarized text also had the advantages of survival (in contrast to witnesses, who would disappear over time) and of portability (again in contrast to witnesses, who were possibly reluctant or unable to appear in court, or whose appearance was more costly than production of a document).

The concept of *verba de presenti* was, as is obvious in several essays in this volume, a canon law notion locating the essence of marriage in the actual mutual consent of the spouses.[22] Because church courts had jurisdiction over marriage disputes, such as that of Giovanni and Lusanna, it was more than pertinent for notaries to employ language easily recognizable to those courts. Notarial texts were not, in themselves, decisive in matrimonial cases in the absence of witness testimony or in the face of contradictory testimony, but they had high probative value nonetheless.[23]

The symbolism of the ring was polyvalent, encompassing in its shape and as a worn object the meaning of conjugal union (although because the husband alone gave one, it was a sign of marital affection and fidelity only in regard to the woman who received it).[24] The giving of a ring was, itself, a powerful gesture, with or without a written record. Niccolò Machiavelli's father, Bernardo, found his hand forced when Francesco di Giovanni d'Agnolo Vernacci gave his daughter a ring without any prior negotiation and certainly without Bernardo's leave to do so, and

---

[21] The ring is explicit in one notarial text: "in signum matrimonii predictus Francischus disponsavit predictam dominam Riccha<m> in digito anulleo manu dextra dicte domine cum uno anulo aureo" (ASF, Notarile antecosimiano 15218, September 29, 1377).

[22] On marriage as the effect of a mutual agreement between the spouses and as subject to ecclesiastical jurisdiction, see R. H. Helmholz, *Marriage Litigation in Medieval England* (London and New York, 1974); Martin Ingram, *Church Courts, Sex, and Marriage in England, 1570–1640* (Cambridge, 1987); Michael M. Sheehan, *Marriage, Family and Law in Medieval Europe: Collected Studies*, edited by James K. Farge (Toronto, 1996); John Witte, Jr., *From Sacrament to Contract: Marriage, Religion, and Law in the Western Tradition* (Louisville, 1997); Lombardi, *Matrimoni di antico regime*; Luigi Nuzzo, "Il matrimonio clandestino nella dottrina canonistica del basso medioevo," *Studia et Documenta Historiae et Iuris* 64 (1998): 351–96; and James A. Brundage, *Law, Sex, and Christian Society in Medieval Europe* (Chicago, 1987).

[23] See M. T. Clanchy, *From Memory to Written Record, England 1066–1307*, 2nd ed. (Oxford, 1993). Klapisch-Zuber, "Zacharias," 185, says that the notary officiated by posing the "questions prescribed by the Church."

[24] Klapisch-Zuber, "Zacharias," 197.

without Francesco's own father's leave, for that matter. The two fathers met and agreed that they had no choice but to resign themselves to now being relatives (although the girl's account in the Florentine dowry fund [*monte delle doti*] had not matured, so that her transfer to her husband's house was not imminent, or at least required certain levels of trust and commitment that the two fathers then attempted to negotiate). One assumes that this bestowal of a ring was sufficiently public to bring each man's honor into play and to make Bernardo Machiavelli feel himself "constrained by the truth" (*costretto dal vero*) to recognize that "thus it pleased God and it was not possible to turn back [*così piaciuto a Dio e che non potea tornare indrieto*]."[25]

A final observation about *matrimonium* involves its chronological relationship to the preceding engagement. The time frames vary in our three examples. Nuptials between Francesco Mannelli and Ginevra came six weeks later (March 11 versus April 23). Giovanni Spinelli married Diana more than four months after their engagement (August 15 versus January 23), whereas Domenico and Masa married on the same day. Robert Davidsohn argues that weddings in Florence typically followed engagement by between two days and two weeks, but his evidence hails largely from the late thirteenth and early fourteenth centuries, rather than from the fifteenth,[26] and Davidsohn also assumed that the dowry and marital gifts were all settled upon before or at the time of betrothal. The fifteenth-century documents that we have in hand do not indicate that such was necessarily the case. If we assume, as Davidsohn does, that a woman of marriageable age already had her trousseau and that a groom could easily and quickly acquire the clothing, jewelry, and other marital gifts he needed to bestow upon his bride (as we shall see, questionable presumptions in some degree), then we are left to face the fact that negotiation of the sum of the dowry or, perhaps more important, the actual gathering of that sum, might have been the more likely reason for the delays between *sponsalitium* and *matrimonium* that we see in the marriages of wealthier Florentines.[27] Dotal contracts usually come after the *matrimonium* in notarial records.

The Procession
The dowry was of enormous social and economic importance, but it was distinct from the most public moment of celebration of a marriage. That was instead the

---

[25] Bernardo Machiavelli, *Libro di ricordi*, edited by Cesare Olschki (Florence, 1954), 108–10. It was, in fact, three years before the dowry was paid out and the bride led off to her husband's house.

[26] Davidsohn, *Storia di Firenze*, vol. 4, part 3, 676–77.

[27] Here, by the way of a counterexample, one may cite another set of documents from the same notarial cartulary, ASF, Notarile antecosimiano 9038, fols. 27v–28r (July 9, 1412), where, on the same day, Cristoforo di Giovanni da Laterina engaged Madalena da Russia, a servant girl in the household of Giovanni di Teruccio de' Bardi, and acknowledged the 30 florin dowry paid by her employer. This was not so much a family alliance as an employer's following up on an agreement to provide a dowry and find a husband for a servant of modest background. See Christiane Klapisch-Zuber, "Female celibacy and service in Florence in the fifteenth century," in eadem, *Women, Family, and Ritual* (n. 10 earlier), 165–77.

visible movement of the bride and her goods, often in a procession accompanied by the groom and some of his kin and friends, through the streets of the city to his house (the *ductio* or *transductio: menare* in the vernacular). One may gauge the importance of this step for Florentines from Matteo Corsini's record of his son's marriage. Following his notation from December 31, 1386, about the engagement, he records in his next entry that on April 22, his son led (*menò*) his wife to their house and "there did the nuptials [*là fece le noze*]." Then he reported that a dowry of 1000 florins (880 in cash and 120 in *doni*) had changed hands.[28] Bernardo Machiavelli was exceptionally thorough in recording his daughter's marital procession (though there were irregularities in this situation, as we saw earlier). He listed by name seven women who accompanied the bride to Santa Reparata, and he indicated less fully the identity of four women (all kin of the groom) who accompanied her thence, after the service of vespers, to the groom's house.[29]

The bride was on display during the procession. The trousseau that she brought with her (variously known in different communities as *corredo, dona*, or *donora*) could be conspicuously displayed as she moved through the streets to her new home.[30] It included such items as personal garments, beddings and other linens, and ceremonial dress. Also on display in the course of the *ductio* was the husband's investment in "auspiciousness": the festivities, and the gifts, jewels, and clothing in which he adorned his bride and even the nuptial chamber for the sake of the talismanic, magical, and even sexual functions that such things possessed. Among elite Florentines, these gifts often amounted to between a third and two thirds of the value of the dowry.[31] A conspicuous example is that of Francesco di Matteo Castellani, who, in 1448, wed Elena di Francesco Alamanni, thanks to the mediation of Cosimo de' Medici (*mediante Cosmo di Giovanni de' Medici*), Florence's most conspicuous and powerful citizen. Castellani carefully recorded the subsequent five installments of his bride's dowry, paid over four months and totaling almost 600 florins. Yet, even before the first payment had reached him, as his next domestic record shows, he had contracted with a tailor to make her a dress with elaborate work in pearls and other ornamentation.[32]

Following the procession to the groom's house, there might be a celebratory meal with his family and finally (ideally on that night) consummation of the union. The *ductio* was commonly found in other Italian communities, with appropriate local variations. (In Venice, for example, the procession was usually by boat, for

---

[28] *Il libro di ricordanze dei Corsini*, 72.

[29] Machiavelli, *Libro di ricordi*, 185–86.

[30] See Julius Kirshner, "Materials for a gilded cage: Non-dotal assets in Florence (1300–1500)," in David I. Kertzer and Richard P. Saller (eds.), *Family Life in Italy from Antiquity to the Present* (New Haven, 1991), 184–207, at 185–86.

[31] Julius Kirshner, "*Li emergenti bisogni matrimoniali* in Renaissance Florence," in William J. Connell (ed.), *Society and Individual in Renaissance Florence* (Berkeley, 2002), 79–109, especially 87–96.

[32] Francesco di Matteo Castellani, *Ricordanze*, vol. 1: *Ricordanze A (1436–1459)*, edited by Giovanni Ciappelli (Florence, 1992), 116–18.

obvious reasons.)[33] This act of *menare a casa* was what made a marriage truly complete (*perfetto*), according to Klapisch-Zuber. Only then had it been suitably given public notice, even if by some measures, the festivities were really "something of an anticlimax."[34]

Anticlimactic or not, the *ductio* was not an essentially religious event, any more than any other phase of the marital process in Florence. No priest was asked to bless the procession. There was no requirement to stop at churches or shrines, although in a city such as Florence it was next to impossible to proceed through the streets for any distance without passing a church. The whole proceeding looked no more religious than the analogous departure after the wedding (which may have taken place in a church) and the subsequent reception that we commonly see today. Nevertheless, a priest might be called on to bless the marriage bed. That blessing may have imparted some spiritual quality or meaning to the consummation about to take place on the bed, but it also looked to fertility of the union.

One sign of the social or secular importance of the marital procession and festivities is the fact that these events were the objects of repeated sumptuary legislation regulating such things as the size of the meals, the number of guests, and total expenditures.[35] Here was where the groom's family especially tried to impress neighbors with their status and wealth and with the status of the newly established marital alliance. In his *Della vita civile,* the Florentine humanist Matteo Palmieri envisioned the city as a set of lineages interconnected by marriages that underwrote an idealized irenic moral universe.[36] In fact, longstanding conflicts between lineages were as apt to give them a sense of identity and social standing.[37] Still, the celebration of marriage left a powerful image of family for those involved and for those who observed it. "The transfer of the woman from her father's house to that of her husband was the culminating act, highly charged with material and symbolic meanings, of the marriage ritual; it was the *traductio* that rendered the event visible to the eyes of the community."[38] It was to make the *traductio* as visible as possible, and not for particularly religious reasons, that Florentines often chose to set these events on Sunday, when there were likely to be more observers.[39]

---

[33] See Elizabeth S. Cohen and Thomas V. Cohen, *Daily Life in Renaissance Italy* (Westport, Conn., 2001), 205.

[34] Klapisch-Zuber, "Zacharias," 186–87.

[35] Sumptuary laws typically regulated expenditures in family ceremonies such as weddings and funerals, as well as female dress, jewelry, and makeup. See Davidsohn, *Storia di Firenze*, vol. 4, part 3, 680–81; and Diane Owen Hughes, "Sumptuary law and social relations in Renaissance Italy," in John Bossy (ed.), *Disputes and Settlements: Law and Human Relations in the West* (Cambridge, 1983), 69–99.

[36] Matteo Palmieri, *Vita civile* edited by Gino Belloni (Florence, 1982), 161, on which see also Molho, *Marriage Alliance*, 344–45.

[37] See Thomas Kuehn, *Law, Family, & Women: Toward a Legal Anthropology of Renaissance Italy* (Chicago, 1991), 19–74, 143–56.

[38] Menchi, "Percorsi variegati, percorsi obbligati" (n. 5 earlier), 38.

[39] Klapisch-Zuber, "Zacharias," 188.

The transfer of the woman to her new home had enormous importance for Florentines, as Klapisch-Zuber has noted. This is apparent from the fact that by statute, only after a woman had been handed over (*tradita*) to her husband or led (*ducta*) by him was she deemed married for the purposes of the law absolving married women from paternal debts.[40] At that point she was no longer part of her father's household, and her dowry should have been paid over to her husband who, presumably, would otherwise not have taken her to his house.

There was a reverse process in the case of widows. Their kin (after the funeral of the husband) sometimes came to the house, especially if there were no children from the union (as Klapisch-Zuber has importantly shown), but sometimes even if there were children, to extract (*trarre*) the widow and to take her back to her natal home. This reverse *ductio* was an expression of the statutorily defined right of a widow to return (*tornata*) to her family. If she was still young enough to be attractive in the marriage market, it was also preparatory to her remarriage.[41]

Dowry

For all that, notarial texts do not record the procession through the streets. The notarial third act (after the betrothal and the exchange of marital vows), and easily the most legally involved, was the dowry. It is probable (although we have no way of knowing this from the notarial texts alone) that the husband did not bring his bride to their home until her kin had paid at least a portion of the agreed dowry to him.[42] Such payment required the elapse of some time following the marriage vows, and that elapse substantiated the union legally, even before property changed hands. Our two dotal instruments (Docs. 3 and 6) both occurred after some considerable delay. Francesco Mannelli and Ginevra married on April 23, but he did not "confess" the dowry of 880 florins until May 12. The delay was much greater in the other instance, in which the marriage occurred on January 23, 1415, but receipt of the dowry not until April 24, 1416. Generally (and there were exceptions), at least prior to a crucial revision of Florence's statutes in 1415 that shifted emphasis to

---

[40] *Statuta communis Florentiae anno salutis mcccxv*, 3 vols. (Freiburg [Florence], 1778–83), vol. 1, liber II, rubric CXIII, Quod filiae nuptae non teneantur pro debitis paternis, 1: 205.

[41] Christiane Klapisch-Zuber, "The 'cruel mother': Maternity, widowhood, and dowry in Florence in the fourteenth and fifteenth centuries," in eadem, *Women, Family, and Ritual* (n. 10 earlier), 117–31, at 123–24. On remarriage, see also Giulia Calvi, "Reconstructing the family: Widowhood and remarriage in Tuscany in the early modern period," in Trevor Dean and K. J. P. Lowe (eds.), *Marriage in Italy, 1300–1650* (Cambridge, 1998), 275–96; Isabelle Chabot, "Seconde nozze e identità materna nella Firenze del tardo medioevo," in Silvana Seidel Menchi, Anne Jacobson Schutte, and Thomas Kuehn (eds.), *Tempi e spazi di vita femminile tra medioevo ed età moderna* (Bologna, 1999), 493–523; eadem, "Lineage strategies and the control of widows in Renaissance Florence," in Sandra Cavallo and Lyndan Warner (eds.), *Widowhood in Medieval and Early Modern Europe* (Harlow, U.K., and New York, 1999), 127–44. Corsini, *Il libro di ricordanze*, 72, sadly reports the later death of his son, after only three years of marriage, and the return of the dowry to his departing widow.

[42] Kirshner, "*Emergenti bisogni*" (n. 31 earlier), 101, notes that Paolo Niccolini waited three years to *condurre a casa* because the dowry was not paid yet.

consummation to substantiate a husband's claim to the dowry of his predeceased wife, the interval between payment of the dowry and the husband's "leading" of his wife to his house was rather brief, with the dowry usually being paid just before the leading.[43]

In other respects, our two dotal instruments are very similar (and not just because the same notary happened to draw them up) and typical of the usual form. Before witnesses, the husband, often with his father or other kinsmen or friends as guarantors (Francesco di Jacopo Mannelli in Doc. 3, the husband's brother Jacopo and Lorenzo d'Antonio Spinelli in Doc. 6) acknowledged receipt of a stated sum from the bride's father or from someone representing him (Galeotto Mannelli represents Lorenzo Gualterotti in the first example) as her dowry. One cannot determine from the texts alone whether the husband actually received the stated sum in full at that time or, in reality, received less, or would receive the dowry only at a later date (for these were frequent occurrences in Florence).[44] The groom reciprocated with a *donatio propter nuptias* of 50 *lire* to the bride, a sum capped by Florentine statute (as alluded to in the notarial document). The groom and his guarantors then pledged under set penalties and various formulas to return the dowry to the wife or to her heirs (optimally their children, but such need not be and was far from always the case) in every instance in which it should be returned (i.e., usually when the death of one spouse dissolved the marriage). In this light the property of each spouse retained a legal separateness that is in marked contrast to the pooling of resources into a common fund, as in the *ravestissement* that Martha Howell examines in this volume.[45]

This is not the place to explore the intricacies of dowry law or the complex economic calculations that lay behind dowries,[46] but it is important for us to recognize how central dowry was in social concepts of marriage and in legal domains aside from canon law. "If a dowry was not a legal prerequisite of marriage [*matrimonium potest esse sine dote*], society nonetheless looked askance at dowerless marriages. A woman without a dowry was called 'unfortunate'."[47] The social importance of dowry in Florence – and it was little different elsewhere in Italy – was marked by several phenomena. One was the custom of charitable bequests of modest dowries

---

[43] Julius Kirshner, "*Maritus lucretur dotem uxoris sue premortue* in late medieval Florence," *Zeitschrift der Savigny-Stiftung für Rechtsgeschichte (Kanonistische Abteilung)* 77 (1991): 109–55, at 121.

[44] See Kirshner, "*Emergenti bisogni*," 102–09.

[45] On spousal property relations, see Kirshner, "Materials for a gilded cage" (n. 30 earlier); and idem, "Wives' claims against insolvent husbands in late medieval Italy," in Julius Kirshner and Suzanne F. Wemple (eds.), *Women of the Medieval World* (Oxford, 1985), 256–303; and Bellomo, *Ricerche* (n. 3 earlier), 131–62.

[46] See the magisterial work of Bellomo, *Ricerche* (n. 3 earlier), supplemented by several important studies of Julius Kirshner already cited, and Christiane Klapisch-Zuber, "The Griselda complex: Dowry and marriage gifts in the Quattrocento," in eadem, *Women, Family, and Ritual*, 213–46.

[47] Julius Kirshner, *Pursuing Honor While Avoiding Sin: The Monte delle Doti of Florence* (Milan, 1978), 9.

by wealthy Florentines for poor girls who had none.[48] The foundling homes of Florence, notably the Innocenti, similarly provided dowries to the unfortunates in their care who survived to marriageable age.[49] Most spectacularly in Florence the social necessity to capitalize dowries contributed in 1425 to the establishment of a public dowry fund, the *Monte delle doti*, which became implicated in the tortuous finances of city government over the life of the fund into the sixteenth century.[50]

MARRIAGE, HONOR, AND CONCUBINAGE

What lay behind the importance of dowry and the various practices clustering around it (perhaps most notably the practice of symbolic dowries, such as a flower, when all else failed) was the notion of honor. Contrariwise, concubinage was a relationship that brought no honor to a woman and yet was recognized in civil law.

Dowries were vitally linked to the preservation of family honor (*salvare lo onore*). To marry was to take a woman (whose sexuality, especially if she was adulterous, raised the fear of shame and dishonor) and to lead her to honor (*condurre ad honore*).[51] Conventionally, anthropologists see honor as conflicting in the main with Christian morality.[52] Honor certainly was not confined within the terms of theology or canon law. Procession of one's bride through the streets adorned in jewels and finery was a visible and practical, almost literal, expression of the sense of leading her to honor. The better her family and the more honorable her descent, the larger in all likelihood was her dowry.[53]

A woman's family looked to the honor and wealth of the groom's family, too. Alessandra Strozzi reported on the groom chosen for her daughter, Caterina, to the trusted relative, Marco Parenti, by describing his parentage, the marriage gift, and the sources from which it came, predicting (as she wrote in August 1447) that

---

[48] In addition to Kirshner, ibid., see Samuel K. Cohn, Jr., *Death and Property in Siena, 1200–1800: Strategies for the Afterlife* (Baltimore, 1988), 28–32, 55–56, and 212–14.

[49] See Anthony Molho, *Marriage Alliance*, 275–79; John Henderson, *Piety and Charity in Late Medieval Florence* (Oxford, 1994), 316; Philip Gavitt, *Charity and Children in Renaissance Florence: The Ospedale degli Innocenti, 1410–1536* (Ann Arbor, 1990), 78–79, 244–46.

[50] In addition to the works of Julius Kirshner and Anthony Molho cited earlier, see their preliminary collaborative essay, "The dowry fund and the marriage market in early Quattrocento Florence," *Journal of Modern History* 50 (1978): 403–38.

[51] Kirshner, *Pursuing Honor*, 8, 10–15.

[52] For a few examples, Julio Carlo Baroja, "Honour and shame: A historical account of several conflicts," in J. G. Peristiany (ed.), *Honour and Shame: The Values of Mediterranean Society* (Chicago, 1966), 79–137; Pierre Bourdieu, *Outline of a Theory of Practice*, translated by Richard Nice (Cambridge, 1977), especially 60–61, 181–82; J. K. Campbell, *Honour, Family and Patronage* (Oxford, 1964); J. Davis, *People of the Mediterranean: An Essay in Comparative Social Anthropology* (London, 1977); Julian Pitt-Rivers, *The Fate of Shechem: Essays in the Anthropology of the Mediterranean* (Cambridge, 1977).

[53] In this regard, for Venice, see Stanley Chojnacki, "Dowries and kinsmen in early Renaissance Venice," *Journal of Interdisciplinary History* 5 (1974–1975): 571–600, now reprinted in his *Women and Men in Renaissance Venice* (Baltimore, 2000), 132–52.

it would be three months yet before the bride would go to his house. When that happened, the bride would also be dressed and adorned such that "when she goes out she'll have more than four hundred florins on her back."[54] Money, honor, and social reputation are all promiscuously intermingled in this account.

As another example of the importance of dowry, leavened in this case by the hard-headed practicality of the merchant, we can look at the marriage entry in the *ricordi* of Paliano di Falco. This is not a notarial text, though its language reveals the influence of legal Latin, and merchants' books such as this had forensic probative value. Paliano's entry for August 3, 1390 (Doc. 9) was a *sponsalitium*. It would result in the ring ceremony exactly four months later. The two details that he carefully records about his bride in this record are her parentage (her mother's patronymic identity as well as her father's) and her dowry. He states the details of the *promised* dowry, of which the value was to be 1100 florins: there would be possessions worth 1000 florins, and 100 florins for the trousseau. We learn on the next folio that although he had received two farms, some farm animals, and a piece of vineyard, that property in total was worth only 900 florins. But Paliano's *ricordi* reveal the importance of dowry in another way, which is more pertinent here: its absence could be significant, too, and a feature that distinguished concubinage from marriage. For Paliano had also, years before marrying, been involved in a longstanding relationship of concubinage with a woman in Arezzo. He did not consider that relationship a marriage, and it is significant that he never gave her a ring or received a dowry. He had several children by her but carefully called them all illegitimate (*naturali*).[55]

Concubinage did not sit well with canon law and moral theology, but it was a relationship recognized in civil law. Although it could seem worse than casual fornication in moral terms because of its repeated and continual character,[56] it gave some limited rights and privileges to the concubine and to any children of the union (who were designated as *naturales*, in distinction to all other types of illegitimates, called *spurii*).[57] What made a relationship concubinage was that the man and woman had a steady sexual relationship while they were not married to others or otherwise prohibited from marrying each other (except by social recognition of a misalliance), and that they lived together "in marital affection" (*maritali affectu*).

[54] *Selected Letters of Alessandra Strozzi* (n. 19 earlier), 28–31.
[55] On this aspect of Paliano's life and the fate of his bastards, see Thomas Kuehn, "Inheritance and identity in early Renaissance Florence: The estate of Paliano di Falco," in Connell, *Society and Individual* (n. 31 earlier), 137–54.
[56] Regarding penalties for concubinage, see Lucia Ferrante, "Il valore del corpo, ovvero la gestione economica della sessualità femminile," in Angela Groppi (ed.), *Il lavoro delle donne* (Rome, 1996), 206–28.
[57] On what follows, see Thomas Kuehn, *Illegitimacy in Renaissance Florence* (Ann Arbor, 2002), 40–44. In general, on illegitimacy in law, see Anke Leineweber, *Die rechtliche Beziehung des nichtehelichen Kindes zu seinem Erzeuger in der Geschichte des Privatrechts* (Königstein, 1978); and Hermann Winterer, *Die rechtliche Stellung der Bastarde in Italien von 800 bis 1500* (Munich, 1978).

Their relationship was thus overt, insofar as it was known to others and in that sense public. What kept such a relationship from being matrimony was, on the one hand, the lack of any formal celebration or declaration of a marriage, and thus the lack of demonstrable mutual consent to be husband and wife, and on the other hand, the corresponding absence of a dowry, an absence that would point as well to the noninvolvement of kin on both sides. Those were precisely the elements that the sequences of events and notarial documents, in Florence and elsewhere, framed and highlighted: involvement of kin on both sides, in public places, with dowry and other property transfers; and exchange of consent with the giving and reception of a ring. Missing, too, was any notarial record.

Marriage had to be distinct from concubinage. Statutory insistence on notarial presence and records can thus be interpreted as a means to differentiate marriage from concubinage, rather than to ensure against clandestinity per se. An excellent example of Florentines' awareness of the difference between concubinage and marriage is the very same Francesco d'Arnaldo Mannelli whose marriage is set out in our documents. For some years prior to his wedding, he had a relationship with a lower-class woman whom he arranged to marry to another when he himself married.[58] Just as certainly, Lorenzo Alberti kept distinct his concubinage with a Genoese widow that resulted in the birth of his *naturalis* Battista, the famed humanist, from his later marriage to a Florentine woman, which was celebrated in lavish style.[59]

A woman might try to prove that their relationship met the requirements for marriage. For example, in the affair with which we began, Lusanna's case rested on an exchange of vows and the gift of a ring before witnesses, with further testimony that when together she and Giovanni treated each other as husband and wife, even referring to each other as such.[60] By a parallel process, a bastard child intent on wiping away the "stain" of illegitimate birth might argue through witnesses that the parents' relationship involved an exchange of vows or at least use of the words "husband" and "wife" toward each other. In an extreme case, one Florentine bastard of a well-to-do father tried to pass off a forged notarial marriage charter.[61] Canon law's emphasis on consent, as is well known, made it easier to marry informally and

---

[58] See Kuehn, *Illegitimacy*, 180, 182, 197–98.

[59] See Kuehn, *Law, Family, & Women* (n. 37 earlier), 157–75.

[60] Lombardi, *Matrimoni* (n. 7 earlier), 75, states that proof of marriage in the absence of ceremonial consent *per verba de presenti* or consummation following *verba de futuro* rested on the partners' open cohabitation and treatment of each other as husband and wife for ten years according to the *fama* of the neighbors. *Fama* operated with other indices of proof. Yet she also says that mere *fama* could establish the legitimacy of any children. A Florentine statute declares that four witnesses are necessary to prove fact or time of death, filiation, or paternity (*Statuta*, liber II, rubric II, De modo probandi mortem, filiationem, tabellionatum et iurisdictionem, 1: 115). These last two are not the same as legitimacy. See Kuehn, *Illegitimacy*, 37–39, and idem, "Fama as a legal status in Renaissance Florence," in Thelma S. Fenster and Daniel Lord Smail (eds.), *Fama: The Politics of Talk and Reputation in Medieval Europe* (Ithaca, 2003), 27–46.

[61] See Kuehn, *Illegitimacy*, 99–100.

privately (even if a priest were present),[62] and by the same token, the possibility that a church court might validate a clandestine marriage gave hope to women like Lusanna and to any children they may have had.[63]

Nevertheless, the absence of a dowry, the misalliance, and the woman's lack of honor in the typical relationship of concubinage might prevent the marriage from being recognized. Thus, although formal marriage of the parents after a child's conception or birth would result in the child's legitimization, the requirement in civil law for proof of such a marriage and of the parents' intent to legitimize their children was a dowry, and the dowry, as noted above, was bound up with honor.[64] Without a dowry, although the marriage might be valid in canon law, the civil law disabilities of illegitimacy would remain. And even if the rituals of consent and other formalities were observed, misalliance or dishonor, too, might work against the recognition of a marriage. As noted previously, Giovanni's "wedding" with Lusanna had to be secret because of the misalliance involved. And Giovanni's defense against Lusanna's claim that they were married did not rest on the absence of such formalities as a wedding procession, participation by his family, and written instruments, nor even the absence of a dowry. His witnesses gave evidence of her sexual dalliance with Giovanni while she was still married and of promises that she would marry Giovanni following her husband's death. That was an invalidating condition in canon law for a subsequent marriage with her lover,[65] but it is significant that he made his case by attacking her character.

MARRIAGE AND THE CLERGY

There remains one further element of the ceremony between Giovanni and Lusanna that is of special interest here: the presence of a friar officiating. In what ways were clergy usually involved in the formation of marriages? Klapisch-Zuber points out that the presence of a priest at the ring ceremony (as opposed to presence of a notary for the *sponsalitium* and the *dos*, neither of which occurred in the case of Giovanni and Lusanna) was more common among modest Florentines than among the elite.[66] In that regard, the ceremony staged by Lusanna and her brother in his house was not unusual, especially for people of their social status (except for the

[62] Roger Lee Brown, "The rise and fall of the Fleet marriages," in R. B. Outhwaite (ed.), *Marriage and Society: Studies in the Social History of Marriage* (New York, 1981), 117–36.
[63] See Giuliano Marchetto, "Matrimoni incerti tra dottrina e prassi: Un *consilium sapientis iudiciale* di Baldo degli Ubaldi (1327–1400)," in Menchi and Quaglioni, *Matrimoni in dubbio* (n. 5 above), 83–105.
[64] Kirshner, *Pursuing Honor* (47 earlier), 8–10.
[65] For Giovanni's tactics, see Brucker, *Giovanni and Lusanna*, 25–37. On adultery and remarriage, see Kuehn, *Illegitimacy*, 50; Laurent Mayali, "Note on the legitimization by subsequent marriage from Alexander III to Innocent III," in Laurent Mayali and Stephanie A. J. Tibbetts (eds.), *The Two Laws: Studies in Medieval Legal History Dedicated to Stephan Kuttner* (Washington, D.C., 1990), 55–75.
[66] Klapisch-Zuber, "Zacharias," 196.

total absence of Giovanni della Casa's kin). But here, too, much as with the custom of staging betrothal in or before a church, what mattered may have been the social neutrality of the priest and the fact that, like a notary, he was a public witness. There is no record of any particular prayers, blessings, or liturgical elements. And during legal proceedings, Giovanni's representative sought to blacken the reputation of the friar with an account of his public punishment and humiliation for unspecified crimes and misdeeds in Cortona before coming to Florence.[67] Such an assault on the friar's *fama* was designed to undermine his value as a witness.[68] It was not an attack on the propriety or necessity of his officiating.[69]

The church in Florence, particularly under Antonino's direction, sought to require that clergy should celebrate a conjugal mass to mark first marriages (although it is clear that Florentines did not generally follow that guideline). But the Florentine church was much more reticent about the clergy's blessing second marriages, and a local synod of 1346 forbade the practice.[70] Remarriages had moral and religious complications, notably so for widows, on whom preachers like San Bernardino urged acceptance of a "second virginity." It was also a socially difficult and even divisive process. There were the problems of caring for the children of the first marriage. There were complications of retrieving and reconstituting the dowry.[71] And there were the variously thwarted expectations of youth that gave vent to loud and embarrassing displays, most often at night, of "music" directed against second marriages (though usually when it was the husband's second and his young bride's first). This was the *mattinata*, or what came to be known in France as *charivari*. In Florence, where the church did not gain much control over marriage, *mattinata* and second marriages received little attention from synods, in contrast to France, where ecclesiastical control of marriage was more successful and synods were able to turn their attention to condemning such displays. In Italy, synods were still worried about the problems of banns and publicity of first marriages.[72]

---

[67] Brucker, *Giovanni and Lusanna*, 57.

[68] See Fenster and Smail (eds.), *Fama*; Francesco Migliorino, *Fama e infamia: Problemi della società medievale nel pensiero giuridico nei secoli xii e xiii* (Catania, 1985).

[69] David d'Avray, "Marriage ceremonies and the church in Italy after 1215," in Dean and Lowe (eds.), *Marriage in Italy* (n. 41 earlier), 107–15, disagrees with Klapisch-Zuber that marriage before a notary was perfectly legal in the eyes of the church, yet he also notes that there was no rule requiring the officiating of priests at marriages.

[70] Klapisch-Zuber, "The *mattinata* in medieval Italy," in eadem, *Women, Family, and Ritual* (note 10 earlier), 261–82, at 275–76. For synodal legislation in Florence, see Richard C. Trexler, *Synodal Law in Florence and Fiesole, 1306–1518* (Vatican City, 1971). George W. Dameron, *Florence and Its Church in the Age of Dante* (Philadelphia, 2005), 67–68, 72, and 222, notes that episcopal courts rarely handled marital cases, in contrast to usury.

[71] In Florence, there was the added complication after 1415 of a statute excluding the children of a woman's first marriage from inheriting her dowry if she had children and/or a surviving spouse from her second: cf. Chabot, "Seconde nozze" (n. 41 earlier), 502–3.

[72] Klapisch-Zuber, "Mattinata," 275–77.

The *mattinata* as noise and thus public display, which brought attention to second marriages, contrasts pointedly with the *ductio* festivities of first marriages. Remarriages of widows were kept discrete and quiet. Few gifts were exchanged. There was "none of the pomp and display" regularly found with first marriages.[73] Yet the notarized elements were the same. An engagement bargain was struck. There was an exchange of vows and a ring. There was a dowry. It was every bit as important to mark the second marriage legally as the first.

Still, though the evidence is spotty, anecdotal, and even pictorial, it is clear that people in Florence and other Italian cities sometimes called on priests at first weddings to bless the couple, the ring, or even the marriage bed. There was an effort, albeit not consistent, to lend some spiritual quality to marriage, which otherwise was resolutely terrestrial in its orientation. But these elements were rarely recorded because, as Luigi Nuzzo argues, they were of no legal value. Within society, when one thought of marriage, as he says,

one thought of the family's role in selection of the partner, of the redaction of the dotal instruments, and finally one reflected on the extraordinary importance of the wedding procession, symbol of the economic and social power of the families, which symbolized the woman's passage from her father's house to that of her husband, from one form of control to another, and rendered public – and thus proved – the bond that was created by means of the consent of the spouses.[74]

CONCLUDING OBSERVATIONS

Florentine nuptial rites and customs demonstrated the intention of the parties and their families behind a marriage. The church prescribed no particular forms, other than insisting that mutual consent be expressed freely, and therefore Florentines were able to devise their own marital customs.[75] The Florentine church had no particular role in influencing such customs, although it is very interesting to note that, in the wake of the Giovanni and Lusanna case, Archbishop Antonino tried to legislate that a nuptial mass be part of every first marriage in Florence.[76] Generally, historians think that the church extended its control over marriage following the Council of Trent, changing it from an entirely social process into one that was ecclesiastical as well.[77] Yet even then, it is arguable, according to Silvana Seidel Menchi,

[73] Ibid., 281. See also Isabelle Chabot, "La sposa in nero: La ritualizzazione del lutto delle vedove fiorentine (secoli xiv–xv)," *Quaderni storici* 86 (1994): 421–62; and apposite essays in Jacques Dupâquier (ed.) *Marriage and Remarriage in Populations in the Past* (London and New York, 1981).
[74] Nuzzo, "Matrimonio clandestino" (n. 22 earlier), 395.
[75] Klapisch-Zuber, "Zacharias," 179.
[76] D'Avray, "Marriage ceremonies," 110–11.
[77] See Kate Lowe, "Secular brides and convent brides: Wedding ceremonies in Italy during the Renaissance and Counter-Reformation," in Dean and Lowe, eds., *Marriage in Italy* (n. 41 earlier), 41–65,

that the conciliar decrees did not put priests into the sort of complete control that the Tridentine reformers intended.[78] Klapisch-Zuber has provocatively and perceptively opined that "as the fifteenth century progressed, the oblique solution to the problem of the dowry brought on by the *Monte delle Doti* did more to change nuptial ritual in upper-class Florentine society than did the policies of the church."[79] She finds evidence that, in the course of the fifteenth century, consummation of the marriage started to move up from the day of the *ductio* of the bride to her husband's house to the day of the ring ceremony and vows, the *matrimonium*, or to some point between the *matrimonium* and the *ductio*. Because the *Monte* made consummation a necessary condition for payment of the dowry to the husband, whereas the dowry had been the usual precondition for the *ductio* and subsequent consummation, the relationship among these events was reversed.

Florentine marital customs and documents emphasized the material aspects of the union: the pledging of resources and their exchange as dowry, as trousseau, and as wedding gifts and adornments. But they did so also in separate moments and directions. The property of each spouse remained distinct. Different rules applied to each side. In Florence, wives had no rights to inherit from their husbands. Husbands had rights to inherit from wives, but those rights had limits, were superseded by those of their children, if any, and were subject to the rules for returning the dowry. This separation of property made possible the claims of wives to retrieve dowries from the hands of bankrupt husbands, the separate inheritances or repudiations of inheritance by children to fathers and to mothers, and varying fiscal obligations.[80] Perhaps, then, the differences in marital customs between a Roman law city such as Florence and areas of northern Europe are also a reflection of matrimonial property regimes and the distinct personhoods of property owners. It is interesting, for example, to contrast the marriage process in Florence with that in London, as examined by Shannon McSheffrey. She finds that the English ensured that the intimate relationship of a couple was nonetheless public, for the exchange of consent was regularly ratified in a parish church.[81]

at 42; Menchi, "Percorsi variegati, percorsi obbligati (n. 5 earlier), passim; Diego Quaglioni, "*Sacramenti destestabili:* La forma del matrimonio prima e dopo Trento," in Menchi and Quaglioni, *Matrimoni in dubbio* (n. 5 earlier), 61–79; Gabriella Zarri, "Il matrimonio tridentino," in Paolo Prodi and Wolfgang Reinhard (eds.), *Il concilio di Trento e il moderno* (Bologna, 1996), 437–83.

[78] Menchi, "Percorsi," 53; Lombardi, *Matrimoni,* 16.

[79] Klapisch-Zuber, "Zacharias," 211. See also Kirshner, "*Emergenti bisogni,*" 96–109, and "*Maritus lucretur dotem,*" 132–36.

[80] See Kirshner, "Wives' Claims" (n. 45 earlier); Thomas Kuehn, "Law, death, and heirs in the Renaissance: Repudiation of inheritance in Florence," *Renaissance Quarterly* 45 (1992): 484–516; idem, "Daughters, mothers, wives, and widows: Women as legal persons," in Anne Jacobson Schutte, Thomas Kuehn, and Silvana Seidel Menchi (eds.), *Time, Space, and Women's Lives in Early Modern Europe* (Kirksville, Mo., 2001), 97–115.

[81] Shannon McSheffrey, "Place, space, and situation: Public and private in the making of marriage in late medieval London," *Speculum* 79 (2004): 960–90.

Although one can only agree that the Middle Ages did not share the modern liberal divorce between public and private spheres, and that, therefore, no sexual relationship was wholly private, still it seems that in Florence, in contrast to London, marriage lay a bit further toward the private end of a public–private continuum. At any rate, in comparison to the English evidence, Florentine marriages were more about family alliances than about household formation, at least among the elites.

Be that as it may, it also remains the case that Florentine marriages were social liaisons. Daniela Lombardi, in an exhaustive study of marital law and practices before and after Trent, examines a case from 1562 with close parallels to that of Giovanni and Lusanna over a century earlier. Lawyers in the 1562 case maintained that despite an exchange of consent and the gift of a ring before witnesses, the union was clandestine: "the solemnities were lacking and, above all, the brothers and relatives of the groom had not been informed." They surely would have protested against the social inequality of the spouses. The archepiscopal court agreed with them.[82] As the social stakes of marriage increased in Florence in proportion with an increasing aristocratization of its ruling class (overtly so with the coming of the Duchy of the Medici after 1530), and as fewer children of elite families married, fear of clandestine unions can only have increased as well.[83] In contrast to the church's marital ideology of the free consent of the spouses, the constraints on those marrying can only have grown and their "private feelings" have mattered less and less.[84]

Still, the distance between the ecclesiastical requirement of mutual consent and familial coercion was not as great as it may seem. We should not see this situation in terms of present day rights-based notions of consent. On the one hand, families looked to the willingness of children to marry and hoped for a growing sense of love and companionship. They did not want explosive suits giving vent to animosities between parents and children as to choice of marriage partner.[85] On the other hand, the clergy were not in favor of generalized free choice

---

[82] Lombardi, *Matrimoni*, 90–95.

[83] In general, on the Florentine elites under the Medici principate, see R. Burr Litchfield, *Emergence of a Bureaucracy: The Florentine Patricians, 1530–1790* (Princeton, 1986). For the situation in Venice, see Stanley Chojnacki, "Nobility, women and the state: Marriage regulation in Venice, 1420–1535," in Dean and Lowe (eds.), *Marriage in Italy*, 128–51. Note also Brian Richardson, "*Amore maritale*: Advice on love and marriage in the second half of the Cinquecento," in Letizia Panizza (ed.), *Women in Italian Renaissance Culture and Society* (Oxford, 2000), 194–208.

[84] The phrase is the Cohens', from *Daily Life in Renaissance Italy* (n. 33 earlier), 201.

[85] There has been some exceptional work on Venice in this regard: see Daniela Hacke, "*Non lo volevo per marito in modo alcuno*: Forced marriages, generational conflicts, and the limits of patriarchal power in early modern Venice, c. 1580–1680," in Menchi, Schutte, and Kuehn, eds., *Time, Space, and Women's Lives* (n. 80 earlier), 203–21; and Joanne M. Ferraro, *Marriage Wars in Late Renaissance Venice* (Oxford, 2001), 33–67.

independent of family concerns regarding parentage, property, and honor (especially after Trent, even if the church never satisfactorily resolved the relationship
between family need and individual consent). It is instructive that in Florence
the *matrimonium*, as an exchange of consent with bestowal of the ring, usually in
the bride's home, was kept distinct, documentarily and physically (if not always
chronologically), from the heavily familial moments of *sponsalitium* and *ductio*
(or of the *dos*, for that matter). By combining yet distinguishing between these
events, Florentine marriage customs operated, as Helmholz nicely has it, "in the
shadow" of the church's law.[86] Yet they also operated in the daylight of family
interests.

○○

APPENDIX: FLORENTINE MARRIAGE DOCUMENTS

DOCUMENT 1: *Betrothal by Lorenzo Gualterotti of Ginevra, his Daughter,
to Francesco Mannelli*[1]

Later the said year [1412/13] and indiction and the eleventh day of the month of
March. Done and recorded in Florence in the Church of Santa Maria sopr'Arno
of Florence, the witnesses called, involved, and asked to be present for these
matters, Barduccio Cherichini, money changer, and Parigi di Tommaso de'
Corbinelli and Francesco di messer Alessandro de' Bardi and Antonio di Vieri
degli Altoviti, Florentine citizens, and others.

The noble and prudent man Lorenzo, son of the late Totto, formerly of the
Bardi and now of the Gualterotti of Florence, promised etc. Francesco, son of
the late messer Arnaldo de' Mannelli of Florence, to do and take care etc. that
the lady Ginevra, daughter of the said Lorenzo, will consent to said Francesco
as her husband etc. and to give the dowry that Filippo, son of Lorenzo de'
Machiavelli of Florence, will declare etc. In return said Francesco promised to
consent to said lady etc. and to give a ring and to acknowledge the dowry etc.
in which Filippo etc. said parties agreed to settle their differences etc. as in
an arbiter and arbitrator etc. giving etc. full power etc. of rendering decision
etc. of law and of fact etc. With the clause that of the thing decided there is
understood to have been a suit etc. promising etc. to yield to what is decided
etc. and not to appeal etc. and they established and acknowledged that they
had for the sake of earnest money with each other 800 gold florins etc. which

---

[86] See in this volume, R. H. Helmholz, "Marriage contracts in medieval England," 267.
[1] Archivio di Stato, Notarile antecosimiano 9038 [1411–17], fol. 72v.

all etc. and restoration of damages etc. obligation of goods etc. renouncing etc. warranties[2] etc.

Item postea dictis anno [1412/13] et indictione et die undecima mensis Martii. Actum Florentie in ecclesia Sancte Marie supra Arnum de Florentia, presentibus testibus ad hec vocatis, habitis et rogatis Barduccio Cherichini, campsore, et Parigio Tommasi de Corbinellis et Francisco domini Alexandri de Bardis et Antonio Vieri de Altovitis, civibus florentinis et aliis.

Nobilis et discretus vir Laurentius olim Tocti olim de Bardis et hodie de Gualteroctis de Florentia promisit etc. Francisco olim domini Arnaldi de Mannellis de Florentia facere et curare etc. quod domina Ginevra filia dicti Laurentii consentiet in dictum Franciscum tanquam in eius virum etc. et dare dotem quam declarabit Filippus Laurentii de Machiavellis de Florentia etc. Et ex adverso dictus Franciscus promisit consentire in dictam dominam etc. et dare anulum et confiteri dotem etc. in quem Filippum etc. dicte partes compromiserunt etc. tanquam in arbitrum et arbitratorem etc. dantes etc. plenam baliam etc. laudandi etc. de iure et de facto etc. Cum pacto quod de laudatis intelligatur litem fuisse etc. promictentes etc. pareri laudatis etc. et non appellare etc. et constituerunt et confessi fuerunt se habuisse nomine arrarum invicem florenos octingentos auri etc. que omnia etc. et refectio dampnorum etc. obligatio bonorum etc. Renuntiantes etc. Guarantigia etc.

DOCUMENT 2: *Marriage of Ginevra to Francesco Mannelli*[3]

Later the said year and indiction and day. Done in Florence in the parish of Santa Maria sopr'Arno of Florence, present Francesco di Piero da Volognano and Benedetto di Lippaccio de' Bardi and Bartolomeo Neri, all of said parish, and Gerozzo di Francesco de' Bardi and Filippo di Lorenzo de' Machiavelli and other witnesses etc.

Lady Ginevra, daughter of Lorenzo di Totto de' Gualterotti of said parish of Santa Maria, for one part, and Francesco di messer Arnaldo de' Mannelli of Florence, for the other part, contracted [marriage] legitimately with each other by words of present tense and the giving and receiving of a ring. Asking me the undersigned notary to draw up a public instrument concerning the aforesaid.

---

[2] *Guarantigia:* This is a truly untranslatable term. Under Florentine statutory law, payment of sums such as the *arrha* was enforceable and thus an effective deterrent. A summary procedure known as *preceptum guarantigie* was used to compel the defaulting party to pay without undergoing time-consuming court procedures. Parties' willingness to submit to summary procedure was inserted into contracts, by which they waived their right to contest judgment ordering them to pay. In betrothal contracts, the breaching party was considered the debtor, who had to provide indemnity to the damaged party, the creditor.

[3] Ibid., fol. 81v.

Item postea dictis anno et indictione et die. Actum Florentie in populo Sancte Marie supra Arnum de Florentia, presentibus Francisco Pieri de Volognano et Benedicto Lippacci de Bardis et Bartolomeo Neri, omnibus dicti populi, et Gerozzio Francisci de Bardis et Filippo Laurentii de Machiavellis et aliis testibus etc.

Domina Ginevra filia Laurentii Tocti de Gualteroctis dicti populi Sancte Marie ex parte una et Franciscus domini Arnaldi de Mannellis de Florentia ex alia parte [per] verba de presenti et anuli dationem et receptionem ad invicem legitime contraxerunt. Rogantes me notarium infrascriptum ut de predictis publicum conficere instrumentum.

DOCUMENT 3: *Receipt of Ginevra's Dowry*[4]

Later the said year and indiction and the twelfth day of the month of May. Done in Florence in the parish of Santa Margherita, witnesses called, involved, and asked to be present for this, ser Marco di ser Niccolò Mazzetti, Florentine notary and citizen, and ser Filippo di Niccolò Nacci of Gambasso, Florentine notary, and Tommaso di Bernardo di Francesco, a dyer of the parish of San Frediano of Florence, and others.

The nobleman Francesco, son of the late noble knight messer Arnaldo de' Mannelli of Florence, and Francesco di Jacopo de' Mannelli of Florence, and each of them in entirety acknowledged and were content to have had and received from Galeotto di Niccolò de' Mannelli, giving and paying as a dowry and for sake of a dowry of the lady Ginevra, daughter of Lorenzo di Totto formerly de' Bardi and today de' Gualterotti of Florence, 880 gold florins of Florentine weight and coin, renouncing the exception of a dowry not specified in cash etc., and therefore said Francesco made a gift on account of marriage of 50 *lire di spiccioli*. Which dowry and gift the aforesaid Francesco di messer Arnaldo and Francesco di Jacopo and each of them in entirety promised said Galeotto, receiving, as above, on behalf of said lady Ginevra and her heirs to restore etc. in every case etc. and to hold the aforesaid firm etc. and not to act against etc. under penalty of double the said dowry etc. and restoration of damages etc. and obligation of property etc. Which they established to possess on request etc. giving leave to enter on her own authority etc. and with a dotal agreement etc. Renouncing etc. warranties etc.

Item postea dictis anno et indictione et die duodecima mensis Maii. Actum Florentie in populo Sancte Margherite, presentibus testibus ad hec vocatis, habitis et rogatis ser Macteo ser Nicholai Mazzetti, notario et cive florentino, et [82v] ser Filippo Nicholai Nacci de Gambasso, notario florentino, et

---

[4] Ibid., fol. 82r–v.

Tommaso Bernardi Francisci, tintore populi Sancti Fridiani de Florentia et aliis.

Nobilis vir Franciscus quondam nobilis militis domini Arnaldi de Mannellis de Florentia et Franciscus Jacopi de Mannellis de Florentia predictis et quilibet eorum in solidum fuerunt confessi et contenti se habuisse et recepisse a Galeocto Nicholai de Mannellis predictis, dante et solvente in dotem et nomine dotis domine Ginevre filie Laurentii Totti olim de Bardis et hodie de Gualteroctis de Florentia, florenos octingentos octuaginta auri ponderis et conii florentini, renuntiantes exceptionem non numerate dotis etc. et ideo dictus Franciscus fecit donationem propter nuptias de libris L sp. etc. Quas dotem et donationem prefati Franciscus domini Arnaldi et Franciscus Jacopi et quilibet eorum in solidum promiserunt dicto Galeocto recipienti, ut supra, pro dicta domina Ginevra et eius heredibus restituere etc. in omni casu etc. et predicta firma habere etc. et non contrafacere etc. sub pena duppli dicte dotis etc. et refectionem dampnorum etc. et obligationem bonorum etc. Que constituerunt precario possidere etc. dantes licentiam ingrediendi propria auctoritate etc. et cum pacto dotali etc. Renuntiantes etc. Guarantigia etc.

Document 4: *Betrothal by Zanobi Bardi of Diana, his daughter, to Giovanni Spinelli*[5]

Later said year, indiction, and the fifteenth day of August. Done in Florence in the parish of San Remigio of Florence above the Ponte Rubiconte, before the church of Santa Caterina, witnesses asked to be present etc. messer Giovanni di ser Ristoro, Florentine judge and attorney, and Niccolò di Benozzo of the parish of Santa Lucia de' Magnoli, and Francesco di Giovanni Cavallari of the parish of Santa Maria sopr'Arno and several others.

Zanobi, son of the late messer Andrea de' Bardi, of the parish of Santa Lucia de' Magnoli of Florence, promised Giovanni di Lorenzo degli Spinelli of Florence that Diana, daughter of said Zanobi, would consent to said Giovanni as her husband etc. and to give the dowry to be declared by the wise men Francesco, son of messer Alessandro de' Bardi, and Arrigo di Giovanni de' Sassolini, Florentine citizens etc. And in return said Giovanni promised said Zanobi to consent to said Diana as his wife etc. and to acknowledge the amount and terms of the dowry to be established by said Francesco and Arrigo, the aforesaid arbiters etc. in which Francesco and Arrigo said parties compromised as in arbiters and arbitrators etc. giving etc. said arbiters and arbitrators, both in agreement, full power and authority etc. to render decision etc. of law and of fact etc. with agreement etc. promising etc. and they acknowledged as earnest money for the betrothal from hence 800 gold florins etc. promising etc. to hold

---

[5] Ibid., fol. 194v.

firm etc. under penalty of double said earnest money etc. and restoration of damages etc. and obligation of property etc. renouncing etc. warranties etc.

Item postea dictis anno [1414] indictione et die quintadecima Augusti. Actum Florentie in populo Sancti Romigii de Florentia super pontem rubicontis, iuxta ecclesiam Sancte Katerine, presentibus testibus rogatis etc. domino Johanne ser Ristori, iudice et advocato florentino, et Nicholao Benozzi populi Sancte Lucie de Magnolis et Francisco Johannis Cavallari populi Sancte Marie supra Arnum et aliis pluribus.

Zenobius olim domini Andree de Bardis populi Sancte Lucie de Magnolis de Florentia promisit Johanni Laurentii de Spinellis de Florentia quod Diana, filia dicti Zenobii, consentiret in dictum Johannem ut in eius virum etc. et dare dotem declarandam per sapientes viros Franciscum domini Alexandri de Bardis et Arrigum Johannis de Sassolinis, cives florentinos, etc. Et ex adverso dictus Johannes promisit dicto Zenobio consentire in dictam Dianam tanquam in uxorem etc. et confiteri dotem declarandam per dictos Franciscum et Arrigum, arbitros predictos, etc. in quos Franciscum et Arrigum dicte partes compromiserunt tanquam in arbitros et arbitratores etc. dantes etc. dictis arbitris et arbitratoribus, ambobus in concordia, plenam licentiam et auctoritatem etc. laudandi etc. de iure et de facto etc. cum pacto etc. promictentes etc. et confessi fuerunt pro arris sponsalitiis hinc inde florenos octingentos auri etc. promictentes etc. firma habere etc. sub pena duppli dictarum arrarum etc. et refectionem dampnorum etc. et obligationem bonorum etc. renuntiantes etc. guarantigia etc.

DOCUMENT 5: *Marriage of Diana to Giovanni Spinelli*[6]

Later said year and indiction and day 23 of January. Done in Florence in the parish of Santa Lucia de' Magnoli of Florence, witnesses asked to be present etc. Giovanni di Tommaso di Salvestro and Niccolò di Benozzo, both of said parish, and several others.

Giovanni di Lorenzo degli Spinelli of the parish of San Jacopo tra le fosse of Florence, for one part, and the lady Diana, daughter of Zanobi di messer Andrea de' Bardi of Florence of the said parish of Santa Lucia, for the other, legitimately contracted marriage with each other by words of the present tense and the giving and receiving of a ring.

Item postea dictis anno [1414/15] et indictione et die xxiii Januarii. Actum Florentie in populo Sancte Lucie de Magnolis de Florentia, presentibus testibus rogatis etc. Johanne Tommasi Silvestri et Niccholao Benozzi, anbobus dicti populi, et aliis pluribus. [222r]

---

[6] Ibid., fols. 221v–22r.

Johannes Laurentii de Spinellis populi Sancti Jacopi inter foveas de Florentia ex parte una et domina Diana, filia Zenobii domini Andree de Bardis de Florentia dicti populi Sancte Lucie, ex alia per verba de presenti et anuli dationem et receptionem matrimonium ad invicem inter se legitime contraxerunt.

DOCUMENT 6: *Receipt of Diana's Dowry*[7]

Later said year and indiction the twenty-fourth day of April. Done in Florence in the parish of San Jacopo tra le fosse of Florence, witnesses asked to be present etc. Berto d'Angelo, butcher, and Bonaiuto di Nofri Morazzi, both of said parish etc.

Jacopo and Giovanni, brothers, and sons of Lorenzo degli Spinelli of Florence, and Lorenzo, son of the late Antonio, son of the said late Lorenzo degli Spinelli of Florence, and each in entirety acknowledged and were content to have had and received from Zanobi di messer Andrea de' Bardi, giving and paying in dowry and for the sake of dowry of the lady Diana, daughter of said Zanobi and wife of said Giovanni, 700 gold florins of Florentine weight and coin etc. renouncing the defense of nonpayment of the dowry etc. And so said Giovanni from his property made a gift on account of marriage to said Zanobi, receiving on behalf of said lady Diana, of 50 *lire di spiccioli*. Which dowry and gift etc. said Jacopo, Giovanni and Lorenzo, and each of them in entirety obligating promised etc. said Zanobi, receiving on behalf of said lady Diana and her heirs, in every case of restoring said dowry and paying the gift etc. and to hold firm all the aforesaid etc. under penalty of double said dowry etc. and restoration of damages etc. and obligation of the same men and each of them in entirety and of theirs and each of theirs property, present and future, which they established to possess on request etc. for said lady etc. giving leave to enter by her own authority etc. and to hold and take possession of fruits without calculating a share etc. renouncing etc. and with benefit of several defendants etc. warranties etc.

Item postea dictis anno [1416] et inditione et die vigesima quarta Aprilis. Actum Florentie in populo Sancti Jacopi inter foveas de Florentia, presentibus testibus rogatis etc. Berto Angeli, beccario, et Bonaiuto Nofrii Morazzi, ambobus dicti populi etc.

Jacopus et Johannes, fratres et filii Laurentii de Spinellis de Florentia, et Laurentius, filius olim Antonii olim dicti Laurentii de Spinellis de Florentia, et quilibet in solidum fuerunt confessi et contenti habuisse et recepisse a Zenobio domini Andree de Bardis, dante et solvente in dotem et nomine dotis domine Diane filie dicti Zenobii et uxoris dicti Johannis, florenos septingentos auri ponderis et conii florentini etc. renuntiantes exceptionem non numerate dotis etc. Et ideo dictus Johannes de suis bonis fecit donationem

---

[7] Ibid., fol. 334v.

propter nuptias dicto Zenobio recipienti pro dicta domina Diana de libris quinquaginta sp. Quas dotem et donationem etc. dicti Jacopus, Johannes et Laurentius et quilibet eorum in solidum etc. et se principaliter et in solidum obligando promiserunt etc. dicto Zenobio recipienti pro dicta domina Diana et eius heredibus reddere et solvere etc. dicte domine Diane et eius heredibus in omni casu restituende dicte dotis et solvende donationis etc. et predicta omnia firma habere etc. sub pena duppli dicte dotis etc. et refectione dampnorum etc. et obligatione ipsorum et cuiuslibet eorum in solidum et eorum et cuius-libet eorum bonorum presentium et futurorum que constituerunt precario possidere etc. pro dicta domina etc. dantes licentiam intrandi propria auc-toritate etc. et tenendi et fructus percipiendi minime in sortem computandi etc. renuntiantes etc. et benefitio de pluribus reis etc. guarantigia etc.

DOCUMENT 7: *Betrothal by Lorenzo di Giovanni of Masa, his Sister, to Domenico di Matteo*[8]

In the name of the Lord, amen. In the year 1441 from his salvation-bearing incarnation, fourth indiction, sixth day of the month of August. Done in Florence in the Church of Santo Stefano a ponte and witnesses present etc. Jacopo d'Andrea, a spinner of the parish of Santa Trinita, and Bernardo d'Andrea Lottini, saddle maker of the parish of San Jacopo sopr'Arno.

Lorenzo, son of the late Giovanni di Domenico, spinner of the parish of San Jacopo sopr'Arno, for himself and his heirs, promised Domenico, son of the late Matteo, spinner of the parish of San Lorenzo, present and receiving and contracting for himself and his heirs, that he will do and take care so and such that etc. the lady Masa, his sister and daughter of the late Giovanni di Domenico, at the requisite time will consent to said Domenico as her spouse and legitimate husband and for that by words of the present tense and receipt of a ring. And in return said Domenico di Matteo, spinner, for himself and his heirs, promised both by solemn covenant and by word to said Lorenzo, present, receiving and contracting for himself and for said lady Masa, his sister, at the requisite time to consent to said lady Masa as his wife and to hand her a ring in token of true matrimony and to contract marriage with her etc. and they do all and each of these and have said party done in these matters by agreement, at the time, place and with that dowry and amount of a dowry that just as and according as will be established by Giovanni d'Antonio and Jacopo di Matteo, spinners, both in agreement, in whom said parties compromised etc. present, accepting, giving etc. power etc. to declare and render decision etc. promising to stand etc. when they declare and render decision and from now said parties acknowledged together and to each other etc. in monetary penalty to have one brought forth to authority and conversely in the name

[8] Notarile antecosimiano 19069, fol. 217v.

of earnest money and penalty of the present betrothal 100 gold florins, which quantity of 100 gold florins, in the name of the aforesaid dowry, the party failing promised to restore etc. to the party observing etc. doubled etc. which all etc. promised etc. to each other under penalty of double etc. for which etc. obligation etc. renouncing to each other etc. to which etc. for warranties etc. asking etc.

In nomine domini amen. Anno ab eiusdem salutifera incarnatione mccccxli, inditione iiii, die sexto dicti mensis Augusti. Actum Florentie in ecclesia Santi Stefani ad pontem et presentibus testibus etc. Jachobo Andree, filatorario populi Sancte Trinitatis, et Bernardo Andree Lottini, bastario populi Santi Jachobi supra Arnum.

Laurentius olim Johannis Dominici, filatorarius populi Santi Jachobi supra Arnum, per se et suos heredes, promisit Dominico olim Mattei, filatorario populi Santi Laurentii, presenti et pro se et suis heredibus recipienti et stipulanti, se facturum et curaturum ita et taliter etc. quod domina Masa eius soror et filia olim Johannis Dominici debito tempore consentiet in dictum Dominicum tanquam in suum sponsum et virum legiptimum et ab eo per verba de presenti et anuli receptionem. Et ex adverso dictus Dominicus Mattei, filatorarius, per se et suos heredes, promisit et solepni stipulatione et verbo dicto Laurentio, presenti, recipienti et stipulanti pro se et dicta domina Masa, eius sorore, debito tempore consentire in dictam dominam Masam tanquam in suam uxorem et eidem tradere anulum in signo veri matrimonii et cum ea matrimonium contrahere etc. et hec omnia et singula faciunt et dictam partem fieri facere in illis pacto, tempore, loco et cum illa dote et quantitate dotis que et prout et sicut declarata fuerit per Johannem Antonii et Jachobum Mattei, filatorarios, ambos in concordia, in quos dicte partes compromiserunt etc. presentes acceptantes dantes etc. balia etc. declarandi et laudandi etc. promictentes stare etc. cum declarant et laudant et ex nunc dicte partes fuerunt sibi invicem et vicissim confessate etc. in pena numerata habuisse una pari a balia et converso nomine arrarum et pene presentis sponsalitii florenos centum auri qua quantitas florenorum centum auri, nomine dotis predicte, pars fallens restituere promisit etc. parti servanti etc. duplicata etc. que omnia etc. promisit etc. sibi invicem sub pena dupli etc. pro quibus etc. obligatio etc. sibi invicem renumptiantes etc. quibus etc. per guarantigia etc. rogantes. etc.

DOCUMENT 8: *Marriage of Masa to Domenico*[9]

Later said year, indiction and present the above written witnesses. Done in the parish of San Jacopo sopr'Arno, namely in the house of the above written Lorenzo.

---

[9] Ibid.

Said lady Masa, daughter of the late Giovanni di Domenico of said parish of San Jacopo sopr'Arno, for one part, and said Domenico di Matteo, spinner, for the other part, contracted marriage legitimately by words of present tense and the giving and receiving of a ring, mutual consent intervening. Asking etc.

Item postea dicti anno, inditione et presentibus suprascriptis testibus. Actum in populo Santi Jachobi supra Arnum, videlicet in domo suprascripti Laurentii.

Dicta domina Masa filia olim Johannis Dominici dicti populi Santi Jachobi supra Arnum ex parte una et dictus Dominicus Mattei, filatorarius, ex parte alia per verba de presenti et anuli dationem et receptionem, mutuo consensu interveniente, legitime matrimonium contraxerunt. rogantes etc.

DOCUMENT 9: *Paliano Falchi's Record of his Marriage to Margharita di Francesco Scodellai and of her Dowry* 1390[10]

In the name of God and of the virgin madonna, Holy Mary, and of all the saints, male and female, of the court of paradise, I record how this third day of August the aforesaid year, I swore and compromised and took for my legitimate wife Margharita, daughter of the late Francesco di Buto Scodellai and daughter of mona Laca de' Ristori, of which oath appears a charter from ser Francesco di ser Piero Mangiatrocie, notary of the quarter of San Giovanni; and on the third of December and the aforesaid manner I gave her the ring, charter by the hand of the aforesaid ser Francesco, and I slept with her in the house of mona Laca, her mother.

For dowry Domenico di Bartolino Scodellai and Giovanni di Filippo Rondinelli and Ristoro di Michele Ristori, and each in entirety, promised me for my dowry 1100 gold florins, that is 1000 florins in possessions that are worth that in cash, and 100 florins in cash; and these 1100 florins from henceforth remain to be given.

And the abovesaid Domenico and Giovanni and Ristoro and more, mona Lisabetta, wife of the late Niccolò Falconieri, promised me they would not for any reason demand from me nor cause me trouble over the possessions that were given me as dowry for the aforesaid Margharita, my wife.

mccclxxxx
Al nome di Dio e della vergine madonna Santa Maria e di tutti santi e sante della corte del paradiso, ricordo come questo dì iii d'Aghosto, anno sopradetto, giurai e compromisi e presi per mia legittima donna la Margharita, figluola che fu di Francesco di Buto Scodellai e figluola di monna Lacha de' Ristori, dello

---

[10] ASF, Carte strozziane, 2nd ser., 7, fol. 9v.

quale giuramento n'apare carta per ser Francesco di ser Piero Miangiatrocie, notaio del quartiere di San Giovanni; e a dì iii de dicembre e modo sopradetto le diè l'anello, carta per mano del sopradetto ser Francesco, e dormi con lei in casa monna Lacha sua madre.

Per dota mi promisono Domenicho Bartolini Scodellai e Giovanni di Filippo Rondinelli e Ristoro di Michele Ristori, e ciasquno in tutto, per mia dota fiorini mille ciento d'oro, cioè fiorini mille in posesioni, per quello che vagliono a di contanti, e fiorini ciento in danora; e questi fiorini mille ciento di insino a questo dì rest<an>o a dare m c.

E promisono mi e sopra detti Domenicho e Giovanni e Ristoro e più mona Isabetta, donna che fu di Niccholò Falconieri, per niuna cagione non a domandarmi ne darmi inpacio sopra le possesioni mi fossono date in dota per la sopradetta Margharita mia donna.

CHAPTER TWELVE

Marital Property Law as Socio-Cultural Text: The Case of Late-Medieval Douai

Martha C. Howell

The texts of marital property law are, by nature, reluctant witnesses to marriage's social and cultural meanings. The statutes, legal commentaries, litigation records, court judgments, and individualized documents such as marriage contracts and wills that make up this body of law are typically formulaic summaries of the rules governing property's transmission via marriage. Alone, any such record does not tell us much about whether the rules were followed or how they affected the way husbands and wives or parents and children related to one another. The scarcity of such records from premodern Europe compounds these problems of interpretation. Until the last centuries of the epoch, the surviving documents are widely scattered across geographic and chronological space, and, in any case, they treat only a tiny, elite sector of society, which almost surely cannot stand for the whole.

One of the rare exceptions to this rule in northern Europe is late-medieval Douai: an important French-speaking city in the medieval county of Flanders (and now part of France), and the home of a kind of marital property law especially favored in the North. Thanks to an extraordinary collection of documents left by the citizenry, we are able to look closely at how such property laws worked to express and construct marriage's meaning, not just in Douai but, by extension, in other areas where the record is much spottier: in French-speaking Flanders and northern France where the Douaisien story has immediate relevance, but also in nearby German- and Dutch-speaking areas and in parts of England.[1]

---

[1] For a discussion of this archive and its relationship to marital property law in the region, see in particular Robert Jacob, *Les époux, le seigneur et la cité: coutume et pratiques matrimoniales des bourgeois et paysans de France du Nord au moyen âge* (Brussels, 1990); Philippe Godding, *Le droit privé dans les Pays-Bas méridionaux du 12ᵉ au 18ᵉ siècle*, Mémoires de la Classe des Lettres, collection in 4°, 2nd series, pt. 1 (Brussels, 1987); Monique Mestayer, "Les contrats de mariage à Douai du XIIIᵉᵐᵉ au XVIᵉᵐᵉ siècle, reflets du droit et de la vie d'une société urbaine," *Revue du Nord* 61 (1979): 353–80; idem, "Testaments douaisiens antérieurs à 1270," *Nos Patois du Nord* 7 (1962): 64–77; and Martha C. Howell, *The Marriage Exchange: Property, Social Place and Gender in Cities of the Low Countries, 1300–1550* (Chicago, 1998).

Between about 1250 and 1550, we shall see, Douaisiens moved from a marital property regime radically privileging the conjugal pair to one privileging the lineal and collateral kin of each spouse. In the former, property from both the groom's and bride's sides was merged into the new household, as were all goods otherwise acquired, and the entire pool became the full property of both spouses. The surviving spouse had absolute rights to all of it if children had been born of the marriage and to half of it if there had been no live birth of the marriage, the rest going to parents and siblings of the deceased spouse. Only if there were no children alive after the death of both spouses (and no survivors of those children) would the families of origin have rights to the property. In the latter system, in contrast, property from each spouse's family was managed by the male head of the new household, but he did not own the property and his management of the property was supervised by the respective families of the spouses. Ultimate ownership resided with these families, not with the spouses themselves. Although it was typically provided that the property in the new household flowed to the next generation, the families of origin could set the terms of that descent, and, in any case, the property tended to stay in the male line.

In legal terms, the shift was from unwritten custom to written contract, a move that suppressed a form of community property law (entailing joint ownership and privileging the conjugal pair over kin) and introduced something akin to what legal historians call dotal marriage (in which the spouses, and their families of origin, retained separate ownership of the marriage gifts and other property in the new household). Although this complex legal history is the foreground of the story, a more fundamental history of social and cultural change lies beneath its surface. By situating the legal records carefully in time and place and by reading them against one another and against other kinds of sources from Douai, we can begin to uncover that deeper history. We can expose the social tensions inscribed in legal formulas, witness the ways that law sought to resolve the tensions, and in the process learn more about how the people of late-medieval Douai imagined and experienced marriage.

Marital Property Law and Marriage in Premodern Europe

No scholar working with the records of marital property law left by premodern Europeans can fail to recognize the hazards involved in reading marital property law for its social and cultural meaning. Although it is possible to use such sources to reconstruct the rules about how property entered marriage, was managed during it, and was passed on at the marriage's end, it is very difficult to assess the larger importance of that information, especially when we are studying a culture as distant from our own as premodern Europe's. Law is never an unmediated expression of cultural or social practices. It is a product of institutions with their own histories and powers. Only rarely is it the direct creation of people who live – or are supposed to live – under it. Hence, if we are to learn more from these records than something about abstract legal systems, we must know the law's institutional history. We must, for example, have some way of assessing the extent to which a legal text reflects the norms of the culture at large or only those of its rulers: local elites, central governments, or newly arrived conquerors. In the likely case that the law's authors are the society's most powerful members, we must determine the extent to which the legal norms were adopted by society as a whole, and with what effect. Thus, the question of "whose law?" is basic, and it is often very hard to answer.

It is risky also to assume that a marital property regime directly reflected the way wives and husbands, parents and children, or nuclear family and kin actually related to one another. Although it may be tempting to assume, for example, that a regime denying wives control of marital property implied a male-dominant gender system, we dare not leap to that conclusion unless we know much about women's property rights at different life stages and about social practices more generally. Did widows succeed their husbands as property owners? Could they take the property they acquired as widows into subsequent marriages? Did daughters inherit property from their own families that was somehow sequestered from the marital property fund? Did women marry as girls or as mature women? Did they marry men close to them in age? Did they have a major say in the marriage decision? What roles did they play in the marital household? What kind of kin or friendship networks did they sustain during marriage?

Although fully aware that marital property records cannot be treated as mirrors of sociocultural meaning, historians of marriage and family in premodern Europe have had little choice but to turn to them, for no other sources from the age take us so close to the actual practices of marriage. Unlike the memorable romances, lyric poems, or comic tales that tell us much about cultural imaginaries of the period, marital property records do not appear to deal with the imagined, but with the real. They also differ from the sources left by ecclesiastical authorities, which focus on marriage as a sacrament or seek to determine the criteria for legitimacy under canon law. In contrast, marital property records portray marriage as a profoundly secular and social event, thus exposing, as ecclesiastical records do not, property's importance in marriage. Wisely, historians have not dared to ignore the reality that these sources describe. To limit their studies to what canonists, theologians, or church courts thought marriage should be or what poets dreamed it might be, they have judged, would be to miss a great deal of what marriage actually was in that age: a property relationship.

Yet it is no easy task to get information about these property relations. Until the late Middle Ages – after 1200 in the South and not until almost 1500 in the North – we have distressingly few sources.[2] There are, to be sure, a few marriage

---

[2] The scholarly literature on the subject of medieval and early modern marital property law is vast. Some of the best overviews are Jean Brissaud, *A History of French Private Law* [translation of 2nd French edition] (Boston, 1912); Amy Louise Erickson, *Women and Property in Early Modern England*

contracts setting forth the terms of property exchange, some wills and other records of inheritance and bequest, a scattering of court cases in which such matters were adjudicated, the rare summary of practice, and a few narrative sources that describe the rituals of property exchange in marriage. Even in their totality, these sources do not provide the density necessary for confident generalizations; worse still, all but a very few of them are concerned with royalty or high nobility. For ordinary people everywhere – and, in fact, for most of the elite as well – we have almost nothing from these early centuries.

This situation is considerably worse for northern Europe than it is for the areas bordering the Mediterranean. As the chapters by Johnson and Kuehn in this volume make clear, the South was direct heir to legal institutions of the Roman Empire, and after the tenth century, southern Europeans revived many of those practices.[3] Among them were secular notaries (lawyers of a kind), who drafted and preserved agreements of many types, property agreements first among them. Thus, people in the South who had property to exchange in marriage or to pass on at death (even in small amounts) customarily hired a notary to record their wishes, and beginning about 1200 we have good evidence of how people across much of the social spectrum in that region organized property relations in marriage and how they passed on property at death. In contrast, northerners typically left few such records during the Middle Ages, and the scattered documents that we do have from this region usually involved people at the very top of the social order. Thus, what we know about northern people's conceptions of marriage itself in this age has, until recently, come more from church courts (where people argued about their marital status, arranged legal separations, or brought suits for violation of

---

(London, 1993); Lloyd Bonfield (ed.), *Marriage, Property, and Succession* (Berlin, 1992); Hans Planitz, *Deutsche Rechtsgeschichte*, 3rd edition (Graz, 1971); Jean Yver, *Égalité entre héritiers et exclusion des enfants dotés: Essai de géographie coutumière* (Paris, 1966); idem, "Les deux groupes de coutumes," *Revue du Nord* 35 (1953): 197–220; Paul Ourliac and Jehan de Malafosse, *Histoire du droit privé*, vol. 3, *Le droit familial* (Paris, 1968); Godding, *Le droit privé* (n. 1 earlier); John Gilissen, "Le statut de la femme dans l'ancien droit belge," *Recueils de la Société de Jean Bodin pour l'histoire comparative des institutions*, vol. 12, *La Femme* (Brussels, 1962), 255–321; Gabriel Lepointe, *La famille dans l'ancien droit*, 2nd edition (Paris, 1947); François Olivier-Martin, *Histoire de la coutume de la prévôté et vicomté de Paris*, 2 vols. (Paris, 1922–30; repr. Paris, 1972); Georges Chevrier, "Sur quelques caractères de l'histoire du régime matrimonial dans la Bourgogne ducale aux diverses phases de son développement," in *Mémoires de la Société pour l'histoire du droit et des institutions des anciens pays bourguignons, comtois et romands*, vol. 27, *Les droits des gens mariés* (1966), 257–84; and Diane Owen Hughes, "From brideprice to dowry in Mediterranean Europe," *Journal of Family History* 3 (1978): 262–96.

[3] On the late-medieval South, see Jean Hilaire, *Le régime des biens entre époux dans la région de Montpellier du début du XIIIe siècle à la fin du XVIe siècle* (Montpellier, 1957); Laurent Mayali, *Droit savant et coutumes: L'exclusion des fille dotées, XIième–XVIième siècles* (Frankfurt am Main, 1987); Jacques Lafon, *Les époux bordelais, 1450–1550: Régimes matrimoniaux et mutations sociale* (Paris, 1972); Dominique Favarger, *Le régime matrimonial dans le comté de Neuchâtel du XVe au XIXe siècle* (Neuchâtel, 1970); and Jean François Poudret, "La situation du conjoint survivant en pays de Vaud XIIIe–XVIe siècle," in *Mémoires de la Société pour l'histoire du droit et des institutions des anciens pays bourguignons, comtois et romands*, vol. 27, *Les droits des gens mariés* (1966), 3–38.

marital vows) than from any information we might tease out of marital property records.

The paucity of documents from the North, like the relative abundance of documentation from the South, reflects the region's legal history. Following older Germanic traditions, northerners allowed relations between private individuals (what legal scholars refer to as "private law") to be governed by custom or, to put it another way, by common practice. In this region, it was even casually said that "people make law," a phrase invoking the conviction that private law arose from the practices of the people, not from a lawyer's office, not from the sovereign's chancery, and not from the courtroom. Because everyone knew the local practice, there was, in principle, no need for written law or written records. As a result, custom remained local: it varied considerably from region to region and, unsurprisingly, it changed easily as circumstances changed.

It was not until the late Middle Ages, and especially after about 1500, that these customs were gradually written down, in the process being rendered considerably more stable and uniform. Judicial practice accomplished the first steps, as individuals brought their disputes about application or interpretation of local custom to court, leaving records that tell us something about the norms and how they evolved over time. We also have a limited number of statutes issued by territorial sovereignties that sought to regularize, change, or clarify custom. Yet it is not until almost the end of the Middle Ages that these became frequent, and not until later still that issuers acquired the authority necessary for reliable enforcement. There are also some written customals (summaries of local practice). Rare before about 1400, by the mid-sixteenth century, almost all regions and many localities had published such compilations, in response in part to pressures from territorial sovereigns who wished to regularize and publicize law in order to simplify governance.

In addition, as we shall see, people in this region occasionally turned to the marriage contract to make adjustments to customary rules or used the will for more than charitable gifts. Most often, these were the rich or the well connected, who were in a position to overwrite local custom or, in some cases, were able to invoke customs special to their class. Nevertheless, there were some occasions in the later Middle Ages when ordinary people in the North also used written documents to modify custom, and in a few exceptional cases they did so in great enough numbers to create an archive able to reveal the pattern of choices.

DOUAI AND NORTHERN EUROPEAN MARITAL PROPERTY LAW

Douai was one such exception. To my knowledge, it was the only place in northern Europe to have produced a significant number of such documents before 1500. To understand these sources, however, we must first understand the custom that they modified. The customary marital property regime in Douai was a version of what legal historians have labeled "community property law." In the classic communal regime, the property of both husband and wife was merged into one undifferentiated marital property fund over which the husband had full managerial control. In addition, these regimes recognized children as exclusive and inalterable heirs of their parents' communal property, granting them what in law are called devolutionary rights and allowing parents no latitude in the choice of heirs. "God chooses heirs," went the adage of the day. Such regimes also granted the widow succession rights to communal property (either some or all of it), in recognition of her position as replacement for her deceased husband. The common fund was thus an unspecified mass of property in which family members shared collective rights. Custom guaranteed each participant in the fund a proportional claim to it when the marriage ended (although it did not guarantee the amount or the kind of the property received). Thus, marriage agreements did not have to be written in order to regulate property relations between husband and wife, and wills did not have to be written in order to define the rights of heirs.

As we shall see, Douai adopted a radical version of this regime, but it was only one of thousands of places in the North, especially in the southern Low Countries, that adopted community property law. The precise origins of these customs cannot be traced, although versions existed throughout the Middle Ages, and many scholars have located them in certain aspects of early Germanic custom that tended to merge the property interests of husband and wife by means of gifts from the groom to the bride and the bride's family.[4]

In its original form, this northern-European, "Germanic" arrangement stood in stark contrast to the Roman system typical of southern Europe. There, marital property was divided into two separate accounts, one reflecting the wife's contribution to the marriage, and the other reflecting the husband's. Legal historians have labeled these "Roman" systems "dotal," because the wife's property was called her dowry (*dos* in Latin; *dot* in French). In the typical marriage contract written to set the terms of this arrangement, the bride's dowry was specifically listed (and often its monetary value was also expressed). It was separately managed during the marriage, and she was promised return of that amount upon her widowhood, typically along with an increase to be calculated as a percentage of the dowry itself. In structure, then, dotal regimes were "separatist," for they sought to distinguish a husband's property interests from his wife's and to protect hers by separating her property from his.

The "Germanic" system, in contrast, did not entail a separation of property but rather a merger created by the presentation of gifts from the groom to the bride or to the bride's family. The wife was thus incorporated into her husband's household and assigned to his care. By the twelfth century at the latest, certain of

---

[4] The groom's gifts included the morning gift (*Morgengabe* in German, or *morgangyha* in Frankish texts) and the so-called *donatio ex marito* or *donatio ante nuptias*. For a summary of the literature on such gifts, see Brissaud, *History of French Private Law*, and especially Régine le Jan, *Femmes, pouvoir et société dans le haut moyen âge*, Les médiévistes français 1 (Paris, 2001).

the gifts from the groom to the bride had evolved into what would by the fourteenth century be called, in French, the *douaire*. This was the widow's right to property from her husband's estate. The *douaire* was another way of expressing the husband's obligation to care for his wife. In the form that it had acquired by the thirteenth century, it referred, not to ownership rights, but to lifetime rights to the income from property the husband had brought to the marriage or specifically pledged by formal agreement.[5] A centerpiece of French customary law until the Revolution, the *douaire* also made an appearance elsewhere, including in English common law (as the "dower") and in those manorial customs that provided a widow with "freebench" (her right to occupy the marital home for the rest of her life).

Even after the *douaire* had become customary in northern France and elsewhere, it typically existed alongside community property law and was combined with it, sometimes in baroque ways. In such arrangements, a certain amount of property was reserved for each spouse respectively and thus was not contributed to the community account. In the Parisian region, for example, the community account was restricted to movable wealth brought to the marriage and all property acquired after the marriage. In contrast, immovable wealth brought to the marriage by either spouse (sometimes along with specially named movables, also contributed to the marriage) was held apart from the common fund, serving as the lineal property of each spouse respectively. The properties that the husband reserved were the source of his widow's *douaire*, but she also had a claim to part of the community fund as well as rights to her own lineal properties.

In some other areas (such as most of Dutch-speaking Flanders), even though no *douaire* was provided to widows, immovable property brought into the marriage was nevertheless not deposited in the communal account; instead, each spouse held that property separately during marriage, and it returned to his or her respective lineal families at death. Thus, here, too, custom constructed a dual system, in which part of the property of each spouse (typically inherited immovables) was held "separate" for the familial line, and the remainder (typically movables and immovables that had been acquired during marriage) was held jointly.

In a few areas, however, all property was considered communal. In what became the classic or so-called "universal" community property regime, no lineal properties were held apart and a widow received no dower; instead, all property was communal, under the husband's control during marriage. Yet the wife was firmly positioned as successor to her husband with respect to her share of communal property (typically fifty percent), she was able to block his ability to borrow against it or alienate it during his life, and she was automatically positioned as first "creditor" of his estate at his death.

Whatever the size of a community property fund, the couple was fully incorporated into it as an economic entity, a "community," with respect to the goods so

---

[5] See Le Jan, "Aux origines de douaire médiévale (VIe–Xe siècle)", in eadem, *Femmes, pouvoir et société*, 53–67.

shared. Wives, as subordinates in the unit, had no direct control over the property, for they were contained by their husbands, under what was known as *couverture* with respect to that fund. Douaisien texts of the late-medieval period articulate this conception directly, not only in the provisions for property, as we shall see, but also in the titles accorded to the head of household: as many of the Douaisien texts put it, he was his wife's "baron," or *maître et seigneur*.[6]

Nowhere was community property law more fully adopted than in the southern Low Countries, and nowhere in that region was it more radically interpreted than in Douai.[7] In fact, Douaisiens were so attached to the central principle of community property law, which gave the head of household full authority over community property, that they allowed him (or sometimes her) to make choices about use of those assets that deviated from other precepts of community property law. Thus, unlike almost all of their neighbors in the North, who were bound to obey the collectivity of practices making up local custom, Douaisien heads of household were free to write wills that distributed conjugal property in ways other than custom would have dictated, and they were free to write marriage documents that modified custom. Their aldermen (*échevins*) were the final arbiters of custom, but all the evidence that we have – litigation records, judicial rulings, statutes, and contracts or similar documents – indicates that citizens and their governors shared the same general understanding of custom's principles, agreeing that the head of household could manage the conjugal fund for the most part as he or she saw fit. The disputes that came to court were not about these matters, but about particular applications of the law. The archive that Douaisiens produced by writing their documents, arguing in court, or issuing ordinances and statutes to clarify custom, provides a rare view of community property law as it normally operated, and, as we shall see later, as it could be adapted in response to changed circumstances.[8]

This extraordinary collection is part of a larger archive in Douai of what the French call *actes de la pratique*, that is, legal instruments created to manage private affairs. For the period between about 1230 (the approximate date of the earliest documents) and 1500, some fifty thousand such records survive.[9] Chief among

---

[6] Similarly, the custom of Tournai placed her "under the power, responsibility and guardianship of her husband [*in de macht, plicht ende momboorije van heuren man*]": see Godding, *Le droit privé*, 80.

[7] The classic history of medieval Douai is Georges Espinas, *La vie urbaine de Douai au moyen âge*, 4 vols. (Paris, 1913). Espinas's major works on Douai also include *Les finances de la commune de Douai des origines au XVe siècle*, 2 vols. (Paris, 1902), and *Les origines du capitalisme*, 4 vols. (Lille, 1933–49), as well as numerous articles and edited source collections.

[8] For discussion and analysis of this collection, see the sources cited earlier in n. 1.

[9] For an overview of the documentary record in urbanized Europe, see Walter Prevenier, "La production et la conservation des actes urbains dans l'Europe médiévale," in Walter Prevenier and Thérèse de Hemptinne (eds.), *La diplomatique urbaine en Europe au moyen âge, Actes du congrès de la Commission internationale de diplomatique* (Leuven and Apeldoorn, 2000), 559–70. There are comparable collections for Cologne (the *Schreinsbücher*) and Ghent: see Hans Planitz and Thea Buyken (eds.), *Die Kölner Schreinsbücher des 13. und 14. Jahrhunderts*, Publikationen der Gesellschaft für Rheinische Geschichtskunde 44 (Weimar, 1937); and Marc Boone, Machteld Dumon, and Birgit Reusens,

them are contracts for purchase and sale of real property, pre-eminently houses and holdings. Alongside these contracts, there are records of movable property transactions (principally raw materials, livestock, and foodstuffs) and a huge collection of quitclaims. Finally, there are the testaments and the agreements about property relations in marriage: the documents of principal interest in this study. The marriage documents alone, numbering about five thousand documents (or about ten percent of this pre-1500 archive), are labeled *contrats de mariage*. As we shall see, many of the documents archived as *contrats de mariage* are not, in fact, *contracts* of marital property as historians of marital property law generally understand that term. Instead, many were mutual donations made by husbands and wives, what Douaisiens called *ravestissements par lettre*; others were hybrids, neither *ravestissements* nor marital property contracts strictly so called. Accompanying these agreements is a rich collection of litigation records covering disputes about marital property and inheritance arrangements, which provide invaluable evidence of the way Douaisiens interpreted and used these documents.

CUSTOM'S INSCRIPTION AND ITS LOGIC

A *ravestissement par lettre* was, in effect, a mutual donation in which each spouse granted his or her property to the survivor of the marriage. The etymology of the term *ravestissement* is unclear, although it may have been related to the verbs *vestir*, *investir*, and *revestir*. Written *ravestissements* were postnuptial agreements. A few of them contain information suggesting that they were written after the partners had been married for some considerable time, but there is no way of dating any of them in relationship to the wedding. Indeed, most are too general in language to tell us anything about that relationship.

The *ravestissement par lettre* was a Douaisien's written expression of custom's commitment to the marital community. In Douai, as in some of the areas nearby, a couple whose marriage had produced a live birth was considered to have formed a perfectly universal community property fund, one that included all property in the partnership; and in Douai the surviving spouse of the marriage, man or woman, succeeded to all of these assets. In the terminology of the region, such couples had created a *ravestissement par sang* (a mutual donation "by blood") as a result of

---

Immobiliënmarkt, fiscaliteit en sociale ongelijkheid te Gent, 1483–1503 (Courtrai, 1981). Cologne also has a collection of medieval wills: see Walther Stein (ed.), *Akten zur Geschichte der Verfassung und Verwaltung der Stadt Köln im 14. und 15. Jahrhundert*, Publikationen der Gesellschaft für Rheinische Geschichtskunde 10 (1893–95; repr. Dusseldorf, 1993). For other repositories in England and on the continent, see *Acts of Last Will*, = *Recueils de la Société Jean Bodin pour l'histoire comparative des institutions* 59–62 (Brussels, 1992–94). Leiden has preserved a few marriage contracts from the late fifteenth century and a richer collection from the sixteenth: see Gemeente Archief, Leiden, Rechterlijke Archief vóór 1811, 76A and 76B. The sheer size of Douai's archive accounts for much of its value.

having produced a child.[10] The *ravestissement par lettre*, therefore, was a written statement of custom's rules about marital property relations. It added to custom only inasmuch as it gave to infertile couples the customary privileges of fertile couples.

Radical in its devotion to conjugal property rights, the *ravestissement par lettre* appeared also to express a surprising commitment to gender parity, by positioning the husband and wife as exactly identical partners in the marriage, even using precisely parallel language to describe their respective donations:

Let it be known to all that Jacquemart De Lommel, who resides in Douai, has made and makes a *ravestissement* to Jehanne De Sanchy, his wife and spouse, of all that he has, will have, and might acquire, whether or not there is an heir, according to the law and custom of Douai. And in a like manner, the said Jeanne De Sanchy makes and has made a *ravestissement* to Jacquemart her husband, of all that she has and will have or might acquire, whether or not there is an heir, according to the law and custom of the city of Douai. . . . [11]

The first *ravestissement* that we have dates from 1228, but there are only four such documents surviving for the entire period from 1228 to 1259, and only sixty for the next fifty years.[12] The rate of issuance (or survival) did not grow appreciably for the next three quarters of a century, but the *ravestissement* retained its dominance throughout the period, constituting about eighty-six percent of the 166 marriage documents surviving from the 145 years between 1228 and 1373. Thereafter, as we shall see, its relative importance slowly declined as the marriage contract took hold in Douai, but in absolute terms the number of *ravestissements* in the archive grew steadily until about 1400, and the document never disappeared from the medieval archive.

So powerful did the *ravestissement* render the survivor of a marriage that he or she could even disinherit children, thus denying them the usual right to an equal share of marital property, one of the central principles of the usual community regime (and a principle of Douaisien custom in intestate deaths). Indeed, as Douai's first printed Customal of 1627 decisively put it:

when two spouses have made a *ravestissement* or a *ravestissement par lettre*, to the survivor of the two belongs each and every good, movable, chattel, and *heritage* [a term referring to heritable properties, generally understood as real property] which belonged to them and each to which the deceased spouse was heir at the date of his/her death; the survivor has the right to enjoy, use, and possess as heritable property, as his/her own

---

[10] The *ravestissement* was not unique to Douai. For a discussion of its appearance elsewhere in the region, see Godding, *Le droit privé*, 310–11, and the sources cited there.

[11] Archives municipales de Douai (hereafter AMD), FF 616/2374 (27 Dec. 1442). For the full text, see Appendix, Doc. 1 in this Chapter.

[12] See Jacob, *Les époux*, 192. This calculation includes modified *ravestissements* (i.e., those containing extra clauses).

[all these properties], and the children of the marriage or, in their absence, the kin of the deceased will have no rights whatever in these properties.[13]

The *ravestissement* was radical in its insistence on conjugal unity and independence, and the image that it conveyed was not merely an effect of the text. In seeming replication of the text's verbal message, the rituals of actually making a *ravestissement par lettre* enacted the themes of conjugal independence, unity, and power. Husband and wife alone produced the document, and together they had it drafted in the presence of two aldermen. No parents, siblings, or children accompanied the couple to the town hall where the document was drawn up, no neighbors or friends bore witness. Although a public act in the sense that it required public authority, the execution of a *ravestissement par lettre* was neither a communal ritual nor a familial ceremony. It was a private agreement, made solely between husband and wife, between the couple and the law.

Although Douai was unusual in its devotion to community property law, it was only one of the thousands of places in the North that adopted some version of this regime. Peasants throughout the medieval North, along with city dwellers of all classes and even some members of the nobility, similarly created community accounts out of marital goods, similarly privileged the male head of household, and similarly gave widows significant succession rights. Very few, as far as we know, so radically interpreted the principle granting authority to the head of household that he or she could deny children equal inheritance rights, but even in Douai the normal practice was to let custom rule, in which case all sons and daughters inherited equally.

Although some core ideas of a community property regime are visible in earlier Germanic customs, the region's adherence to and careful elaboration of these principles cannot be explained by legal tradition. Rather, commoners in northern Europe adopted and adapted these regimes because they accommodated the socio-economic realities of their lives. In the countryside, where these customs first took root, community property regimes provided peasants with a mechanism for preserving and protecting the *manse* or manorial holding on which they depended. The regime's emphasis on the conjugal family's control of the holding not only gave the members of the residential kin group full enjoyment of the asset; it also assigned responsibility for its management directly to them. It thus effectively bound all family members to the holding, providing a guaranteed work force but also giving all a stake in the asset and making all dependent on it and on each other. Community property law's traditional adherence to rules of succession and descent also gave the asset patrimonial status, for the rights of devolution assured that the asset would be available for the next generation, in perpetuity. At the same

---

[13] *Coutumes de la ville et eschevinage de Douay . . . en l'an mil six cents vingt-sept, le 16. septembre* (Ghent, 1777).

time, it assured continuity of leadership by delineating clear lines of succession from husband to his widow and then, automatically, to his children.[14]

Once carried into cities, these systems served equally well. The principal asset of city dwellers was not a *manse* or land rights; in fact, few of them owned any land or land rents at all. Instead, they lived from what was called movable wealth or chattels. Throughout the Middle Ages, chattels had been an important form of wealth for all people, whether as the equipment, furnishings, foodstuffs, and clothing vital in both the peasant and noble household, or as the jewels, plate, horses, armor, and other luxuries that also graced the noble dwelling. But for the merchants and artisans who made up the propertied classes of cities in the high and late Middle Ages, the category of movables was much larger, for it included the raw materials, inventories, equipment, and supplies that constituted the workshop, as well as the commercial goods, financial paper, and stashes of coin that filled the warehouses and offices of merchants. Very little real estate accompanied it. Until the early modern period, only the very richest urbanites held land or land rights outside the city. Although city people often owned urban real estate as well as chattels, that property consisted of warehouses and dwellings that were often treated in law as though they were movable, as, in a sense, they often were in fact: easily bought and sold, destroyed, and rebuilt in the course of a lifetime.

Urban people needed the freedom to manage such assets, for movable wealth required constant attention and had to be turned over regularly. As many scholars have pointed out, community property law provided exactly the flexibility necessary, for it allowed the head of the conjugal household, who was, in reality, the head of the workshop or the business on which the family was dependent, to merge most or all conjugal property into a common fund. He (or sometimes she) thus wrested control of it from the kin who had originally donated it to the new marital household and was able to buy and sell, deploy and re-deploy it as he (or she) saw fit. Authorized by community property law to manage the assets alone, the head of household was not obligated to explain to relatives why money had been moved from spices to wine, for example, or why a workshop had shifted from manufacture of wool cloth to silk, or why a son was being trained in banking rather than metalworking. Children anticipating their inheritance were equally powerless. They could not, for example, insist that the family shop or even the family home be held intact for them; they could only wait, knowing that they would receive their portion of whatever was left, but having no say in how that wealth was managed until then.

Community property law also neatly accorded with the sexual division of labor characteristic of both countryside and city, for women's labor was vital to the functioning of household economies in both locations. In late-medieval Douai,

---

[14] This argument is best articulated by Robert Jacob, "Les structures patrimoniales de la conjugalité au moyen âge dans la France du Nord: Essai d'histoire comparée des époux nobles et roturiers dans les pays du groupe de coutumes 'picard-wallon'," (PhD diss., Université de Paris 2, 1984).

marriage was synonymous with household formation (as it was in most northern cities of the period). Bride and groom, both of whom typically first married in their early to mid-twenties, almost never lived with their parents, and newly married couples ran their own shops and managed their own businesses. They were initially financed by their parents and often followed the same occupations, but married sons and daughters were not normally their parents' lodgers, employees, or junior partners.

Wives had chief responsibility for subsistence production in the household, for it was they who organized meals, saw to clothing and bedding, and kept house. Women also helped run family businesses and sometimes managed shops on their own. The extensive regulations issued by Douai's aldermen to control production quality in the supremely important wool cloth industry were often quite explicit on the latter point. Some ordinances were directed to the wives of craftsmen, as well as to the craftsmen themselves: "and if the wool were not dyed the color the draper had commanded the dyer, his wife or his journeyman . . . " reads one of them.[15] Many implied that women practiced the trade independently: "no dyer, whether male or female," may work with "*alun de glace*," intoned a thirteenth-century regulation.[16] Less hypothetical references to such businesswomen are equally plentiful. A 1324 list of fees paid by merchants who rented stalls in the Douaisien cloth halls named, for example, sixteen women among the sixty-three lessors, and in a list almost its duplicate, thirteen of fifty-two were women.[17] Seen as a reflection, even an encoding, of these social practices, the *ravestissement* and the custom that it inscribed thus acquire a deeper logic, and the text's positioning of husband and wife as mutually interchangeable partners seems in rough accordance with daily life.

To be sure, women were not imagined as creators of wealth *de novo*, but in that way they were just like men. Brides in Douai obtained much of their wealth from property given to them by their parents, just as grooms did, and daughters seem to have been treated about as well as sons in those distributions. Under custom, daughters received an exactly equal portion of the family property in intestate successions. Even when Douaisiens wrote wills, they tended to leave equal amounts to boys and girls. Richard Hucquedieu, a tanner, for example, left his son Jehan 200 francs, the same amount as he left to his son-in-law, heir of his deceased daughter and father of his only grandchildren, both girls.[18] Jacque Balloon, another tanner whose will comes from the same early fifteenth-century period, left his son Thomas a "little house" (*petite maison*); to a married daughter he gave a house with five

---

[15] Georges Espinas and Henri Pirenne (eds.), *Recueil de documents relatifs à l'histoire de l'industrie drapière en Flandre*, Part 1, *Des origines à l'époque Bourguignonne*, 4 vols. (Brussels, 1906), doc. no. 229 (32), dated c.1250. See also ibid., doc. no. 385 (11), in which a fuller's wife is similarly described as her husband's partner.

[16] Ibid., doc. no. 229/96 and 97, dated c. 1250.

[17] Ibid., doc. no. 338, dated c. 1324. These lists are from the *basse halle*, where cloth was sold in small lots: see Espinas, *La vie urbaine* (n. 7 earlier), vol. 2, 853–54, for a discussion of this institution.

[18] AMD, FF 869 (14 May 1401).

rasières and two *couppres* of land (about 5 1/2 acres), and to another married daughter he left a third house.[19] Like the distributions given to them at their parents' deaths, the marriage gifts given to daughters were approximately the same as those given to sons. From a collection of marriage contracts written in the mid-sixteenth century, for example, we know that rich women brought land to marriages as often as rich men did, and that people lower on the social ladder provisioned their marriageable daughters as well as they did their sons.[20]

The *ravestissements par lettre* issued in Douai sometimes explicitly expressed the importance of women's work and women's property. One from the 1550s, for example, put it this way:

Jean Vallain the elder, bourgeois of Douai, and Marie De Paradis his wife, who live in Douai . . . *because most of their goods, debts, rents and heritages consist of properties acquired in the course of their marriage through their common labor, industry and assets, for this reason* . . . these partners . . . wanted and want that, at the death of the first, the survivor has the entire and total enjoyment and use of all the goods, both patrimonial and after-acquired, which belong to them and of which they are the possessors on the day of the said death. . . .[21]

THE ILLOGIC OF CUSTOM

Yet although community property law accorded comfortably with the realities of daily life for peasant and city dweller alike, the law was laden with contradictions. The system of partible inheritance on which community property law insisted was perhaps the greatest source of tension. In the countryside, where the peasant's holding was almost the sole source of subsistence, it could become uneconomic to divide the holding equally among all the children. Over time, as social historians well know, these practices led to centuries of poverty and suffering in the early modern countryside, as holdings were divided so many times they became too small to support a family or to allow efficient agricultural methods.

The rules of partible inheritance could also inconvenience, indeed fatally injure, city people. Although it was relatively easy to divide movable property into heritable shares and parcel them out as premortem inheritances when the children married, it was very hard – almost impossible – to measure out the assets being transferred so as to preserve the rule of equality, simply because the value of an estate composed principally of movables was unstable. A daughter marrying in, let us say, 1300, might take 100 pounds as her share of the estimated estate and count herself well provided for. But what if the parent's business thereafter doubled in value, leaving the remaining children over twice as much to divide among themselves? To be

[19] AMD, FF 869 (19 Sept. 1403).
[20] Based on a sample of contracts from the 1550s: AMD, FF 655.
[21] AMD, FF 655/5564 (8 Nov. 1558), emphasis mine.

sure, some customs provided a solution: the child who had already received an inheritance as premortem marriage gift might return it to the fund and then take a proportionate share of the newly augmented account. But what if the fund had fallen in value? Was the daughter obliged to return to the common account and wind up with less than the amount with which she had started? Yes, according to such a custom, but what kind of burden would that place on the daughter's own marriage, and on the children whom she now helped to support?

Second and third marriages posed additional problems, both in the countryside and the city. By the logic of the law itself, a peasant's holding should have passed with the surviving spouse into the new marriage, and the children of the first marriage should have stood as equal heirs to the combined properties, along with any children born of the new marriage. And that, indeed, is what some customs provided. More commonly, though, customs required that the property be divided between the surviving spouse and the children when the new marriage took place, thus granting the children of the first marriage a claim to only half of the common property in the new marriage, which they would then split, head for head, with any children born of the new marriage. Other customs devised other schemes, such as a split according to the marriage (by "bed" in the vernaculars, rather than "by head"). Again, the variations were endless, the confusion and tensions obvious. For city people, the problems multiplied, because the value of the estate now being moved into a new household was certain to change, perhaps to rise, thus benefiting those who stood to inherit. Or perhaps it would fall, making it seem imperative that the children of the first marriage get their share before the new marriage. But who could predict which would be preferable or fairer? There were no easy answers, and no available remedies within the usual terms of community property law.

Another contradiction concerned gender, for the system contained two radically opposed notions regarding male–female relations. On the one hand, community property law implied a kind of gender parity, suggesting that marriages were based on mutual trust and respect, and that widows enjoyed independent rights granting them male-like autonomy. On the other hand, women enjoyed no parity during marriage at all, for such customs gave husbands absolute authority over conjugal property during their lives, effectively denying wives any property rights during marriage. The contradictions inherent in this notion of partnership were not lost on Douaisiens, and, in fact, they came to be expressed in most of the *ravestissements par lettre* written after about 1400, the very text which seemed otherwise to articulate a notion of gender parity. As though admitting the absurdity of a law that represented wives as free and equal agents, a strange and revealing clause came to be regularly inserted into the standard text, as in the following:

Let it be known to all that before the aldermen of the city of Douai have personally come Pierre Hardi and Jacque Huquedieu, his wife and spouse, to whom Pierre has made a *ravestissement* and by virtue of this document makes a *ravestissement* to Jacque his wife of all he has or will acquire during their marriage whether in goods, movables, chattels, or in heritable immovables, to enjoy after his death by his wife and her representatives. And likewise, this woman, *being sufficiently empowered by Pierre her husband, which empowerment she accepts as agreeable*, has made and makes a *ravestissement* to Pierre her husband of all she has or will acquire during their marriage whether in goods, movables, chattels, or immovables for him and his representatives to enjoy after her death, all according to the custom of Douai. . . . [22]

The clause that is italicized in the aforementioned quotation was nonsensical on the face of things, for why would a woman who was able to give her own property away need her husband's permission to do so, especially if she was giving it to him? Yet the clause nicely captures the contradiction between economic "sameness" and socio-legal distinction: wives were powerful creators and managers of property, and simultaneously, people with no independent claims to wealth.

The key word here is "wives," for it was only as wife that custom denied a Douaisien woman full property rights. Once widowed, a woman was fully empowered until she remarried. She could then act for her husband and for the household estate that she now represented. Custom was entirely unambiguous about this radical transformation: it openly acknowledged women's capacities to create wealth and to manage property, and it seemed fully to intend that widows exercise these powers. Still, an insidious inconsistency lurked beneath custom's serene exterior. The law granted widows this authority not as individuals but as representatives of the household, a household defined as male-headed. Hence, to do her job as custom envisaged it, a widow would have had to act for, and indeed to act *as*, her late husband. No widow could do so, even if she wanted to; and not all of them wanted to.

If she did not want to or was not able perfectly to represent her late husband, a widow was a dangerous person, for in succeeding to the communal account in a city like Douai she acquired unusual autonomy. If she remained single, she could use the money in almost any way she chose: to invest in new businesses, to purchase annuities and live off the proceeds, perhaps in a new town, in a new house. Unlike her neighbor in the countryside, she was not tied to the land that she had inherited: she was free to use her property as she wished, for movable wealth was, in fact, movable. It could be bought and sold with relative ease. She could give it away in pieces, in the form of gifts to charities, religious institutions, family, and friends. She could use it to buy luxuries or necessities according to whim. The possibilities, in theory, were endless, and the resultant anxieties were high. It is no wonder that many of the stories and songs and plays produced in those centuries featured widows who did or threatened to do just that: to take their deceased husbands' money and spend it foolishly, or to use it to exert unjust power over others, powers that no woman should have.

---

[22] AMD, FF 616/2346 (26 November 1441), emphasis mine.

When these women remarried, as most of those with property did, other problems arose. Whether the property that she took with her was the entire communal account, as was the custom in a few places like Douai, or only part of it, as was the more typical arrangement, it became, in effect, the property of her new husband, available to the children of her prior marriage only in part, for they would have to share it with any children born of the new match. This was the case in the countryside as well, but when the assets being transferred were movable, commercial wealth, the dangers were greater. The property being transferred would, in effect, disappear from view, sinking into a common fund made up of similar and similarly fungible goods the form and value of which would surely change over the course of the new marriage. How much the widow brought, what had become of it, where it went: none of this could be easily tracked or remembered. What might have been worth 100 pounds when the marriage occurred might have become 200 or fifty when the final accounting was done. There was no telling.

The issue in all these cases was not just property rights, although property was at its heart. Attending it was the problem of status itself, for with property went social and political status. To control the household's property was to control the household: to make decisions about production, distribution, and consumption, to direct the labor of others, to determine marriages and residential patterns, even to represent the household in civic affairs. To put a woman in this role was to violate all norms about gender, yet to deny her this role was to threaten the household unit, to abandon the notion that it existed through time free of the claims of collateral kin or lord, as the sole property of the conjugal unit and its successors.

Community property systems were, then, Janus-faced constructions. An almost perfect expression of peasant and urban social life, they were also the source of struggle for economic viability and for maintenance of gender hierarchy. People in this region (especially those in cities, where the tensions seem to have been greatest and the mechanisms for change closer at hand) gradually put in place a series of measures in response to the disorders latent in the logic of community property law. These measures were intended both to minimize the risks involved in a life lived from movable, commercial wealth and, simultaneously, to adjust the way in which community property law functioned.

Douaisien Custom in Motion: The Marriage Contract

Douaisiens have left an astonishingly rich record of their efforts to do exactly that. Their tool was custom itself or, more precisely, custom's willingness to allow the head of household to use and bequeath property as he (or she) wished. Deploying this authority with remarkable energy, Douaisiens began, as early as the midthirteenth century, to issue individual documents that modified the terms of custom itself. The *ravestissement par lettre* was one such document, for it changed custom by granting infertile couples the same inheritance rights that unwritten custom allowed fertile couples in the form of the *ravestissement par sang*. But the *ravestissement par lettre* was unique because it preferred the conjugal pair. All other documents written to intervene in custom worked to contrary ends.

First to pursue objectives in opposition to the norms of custom was the will, which Douaisiens began issuing in the late thirteenth century. They did so not just to care for their souls as their priests instructed, but also, and principally, to intervene in custom's inheritance practices. Even the earliest wills had these goals. All of the nine wills that were written by married or widowed men in the city's earliest collection (consisting of pre-1274 wills) were principally directed at changing custom's most basic rules about succession.[23] Simon Le Cras, for example, left everything to his wife, Marien, as custom would have decreed, but he required that she support their daughter Oede until the latter came of age and then pay her 13 *livres parisis*, a restriction that custom would not have imposed.[24] Aleaume Le Cambier left his chief residence to his wife Oedain but only until she remarried; in that event, the house would go to their children.[25] Nine of the sixteen married or widowed men who wrote wills dated between 1350 and 1367 similarly used the will to rearrange succession. All of the five married men in the group denied their wives some of the property that custom would have granted them; all the men who had children made unequal bequests to the children, thus appearing to overrule custom's preference for equal inheritances. Of twelve Douaisien men in a sample taken about a half century later, in the very early fifteenth century, all but one used the occasion not just to make gifts to the church but also, like their predecessors, to intervene in customary norms about succession.

Thus, to judge from these records, the shift from custom began with the will, yet by the late fourteenth century, what I shall call the marriage contract (as distinct from the *ravestissement*) had assumed that role by adopting a property regime closer in spirit to the dotal regimes of southern Europe. Sixty-two percent of a sample of marriage documents from Douai in that epoch were contracts (the rest being *ravestissements*). By the mid-fifteenth century, that proportion had risen to eighty-three percent, and it would rise again, to ninety-five percent, by the mid-sixteenth century. Unlike the *ravestissement*, the marriage contract was a prenuptial agreement, drawn up at least forty days before the wedding. It is hard to say how long before was typical. The duration probably varied, but it seems unlikely that the parties agreed to a contract long before the wedding because the documents are usually quite precise as to which rent, which piece of clothing, which house, which loom, and so on.

---

[23] These early wills contained no clauses granting alms or gifts for charity. Later ones generally did include charitable bequests and gifts to the church, but even those documents were primarily concerned with (re-)arranging inheritance and succession.

[24] FF 861, April 1263, in Monique Mestayer, "Testaments douaisiens antérieurs à 1270," *Nos Patois du Nord* 7 (1962), 73.

[25] FF 861, April 1248, in Mestayer, "Testaments douaisiens," 64.

By specifying that each spouse would bring a *portement* to the marriage (the name given to the collection of property contributed to the marriage by either the bride or the groom), the Douaisien marriage contract seemed resolved to abandon the idea of community that custom had clearly articulated. Although it resembled the *dos* in that it marked the women's contribution to the marriage, the woman's *portement* was, in legal terms, simply her contribution to the whole. Unlike the Roman *dos*, it was technically merged into the marital property fund during marriage, as was the husband's *portement*, unless explicit provision was made otherwise.[26] Nevertheless, as we shall see, her *portement* became the basis for an implicit separation of conjugal goods into his and hers, and for a marked distinction between male and female succession rights. Similar marriage contracts (separating a wife's properties from her husband's) were occasionally written elsewhere in the late-medieval North where community property laws also prevailed.[27]

Almost all marriage contracts from Douai specified the contents of the bride's *portement*. The contract for the marriage of Ysabel le Dent and Jean De Temple, written in 1441, was typical. The document began (after the usual formulas) with the statement of Le Dent's *portement*:

The said Ysabel Le Dent brings to the marriage, as a gift of her father, for one part, 200 *salus d'or* or the equivalent in cash, which her father is obligated to pay, that is to say: 100 *salus* in ready cash and the other 100 *salus* within the year before Easter 1442. And, for the other part of her *portement*, the said Ysabel brings, as a gift from her father, 28 *mencaudées* of tillable land or thereabouts, in the boundaries of Vaulz in Artois. And with this a manor and holding in the said city of Vaulz, abutting the holding of Ondart De Uumleville, this 28 *mencaudées* of land and the said manor, which itself contains about 2 *mencaudées* of land, will be in the possession of the said married couple and their heirs or representatives forever, but only after the death of Jean Le Dent; with it comes the obligation to pay perpetual rents due on the holding to the extent they exist. . . .[28]

---

[26] Because it provided the basis for calculation of the widow's *reprise* (and, indirectly, her *douaire, assene, et amendement*), it resembled the classic Roman *dos*, and worked, as I argue subsequently, to construct a similarly "separatist" regime.

[27] In Ghent, for example, we have records of one or two such marriage contracts per year in the *Jaarregisters van de Keure*. These registers contained financial agreements voluntarily brought to the aldermen for registration. They begin in 1339 and continue to 1679 with some interruptions. There are sixty-six folio volumes for the fourteenth and fifteenth centuries combined. The municipal archive of Ghent has published some indices of these folio volumes. Of the 1,427 entries in the *Jaarregisters* indexed for the six years 1339–40, 1343–44, 1345–46, 1349–50, 1353–54, and 1357–58, only eight marriage contracts are mentioned, two of which the aldermen later crossed out as inoperative. Among the 1,580 entries for the single year 1400–01, only one marriage contract is mentioned. See *Regesten op de Jaarregisters van de Keure* (Inventarissen en Indices gepubliceerd door het Archief, Stad. Gent.). The index of 1969 (edited by J. Boon), covers 1353–54 and 1357–58; that of 1968 (edited by J. Boon) covers 1339–40, 1343–44, 1345–46, and 1349–50; and the three indices from 1967, 1970, and 1972 (no named editor) cover 1400–01.

[28] AMD, FF 616/2321 (23 April 1441). There are several variants of the proper names in the sources (Ysabel/Isabel; Du Temple/De Temple; Jean/Jehan, etc.). Here and elsewhere, I have standardized in the main text spellings of the same names occurring in the same document, but I have transcribed names literally in the Appendix that follows.

These assets, along with any additional properties that Ysabel Le Dent would inherit from her *lez et coste* (her "side") during the marriage, were to be returned to her (as an amount called her *reprise*) when she became a widow. In addition, she would receive an increase that was called the *douaire* or the *douaire, assene, et amendement*. As a widow, Le Dent had absolute rights only to this *reprise* and *douaire*, although she was thereby free of the claims of her deceased husband's creditors and could take her *reprise* and *douaire* from the estate even before the creditors:

if it happens that after the marriage Jean De Temple dies before Ysabel without a living heir in existence or expected on the day of his death, the said Ysabel will have and can freely take, without obligation of any kind, all the *heritages* she brought to the marriage and all which came to her in its course, whether by gift, succession, inheritance or any other way if it was from her natal kin, with the rents and revenues well and sufficiently attached. And she takes without obligation as her *portement* in money and as *douaire, assene, et amendement* of the marriage the sum of 500 *francs*, at 33 Flemish *gros* for the franc. . . .

As a widow, therefore, Ysabel Le Dent received all the land and rents that she had contributed to the marriage (her *heritages*) plus a cash payment of 500 *francs*: almost double the cash amount she had brought to the marriage as her *portement* (i.e., 200 *salus d'or*, equivalent to about 290 *francs*). To assure Le Dent her *portement* (as her *reprise*) and her *douaire*, her groom pledged to secure their value in real property: "which 500 *francs* the said Jean De Temple has promised and is obligated to convert into land or rents situated in the city or territory of Douai within a year, for the security of the said Ysabel."

It was not Ysabel Le Dent alone who would have looked over Jean De Temple's shoulder to see that he kept her property safe. She was assisted by her *avoués*, the male relatives appointed by her father to oversee her affairs:

And all this with the counsel and advice of Ysabel's *advouez* named below, with the requirement that the "heritages" or rents bought by Jean De Temple may not be sold, given away, transferred, or alienated without the permission of Isabel and her *advouez*. If they are sold or [the rents] repurchased, the revenues therefrom must be reinvested in similar "heritages" or rent, as already required, for the profit of Isabel [sic].

One of the most surprising features of Douaisien custom is that it also allowed widows like Le Dent to "stay" (*demeurer* or *rester* in the French texts) rather than take their *reprise* and *douaire* as provided in a marriage contract. The marriage contract written for Jehenne Le Fevre and Jaquemart Dounoin in 1435, for example, carefully spelled out Jehenne's *portement, reprise,* and *douaire, assene et amendement*, but it also provided that if he died first, "she was counseled to give up her *portement* and marriage agreement mentioned above and stay, take, and seize the goods and *heritages* at their then present value in such portion as custom grants ... notwithstanding the conditions and terms above described."[29]

Although Lé Dent's contract does not specifically grant her such a right, we have court cases from the period in which widows were permitted to refuse their contractual rights and revert to custom's *ravestissement par sang*, even if their marriage contract had provided no such privilege. Franchoise Rohard, for example, renounced her *reprise* and *douaire* to position herself as full heir of her deceased husband, even though her marriage contract had given her no right to do so.[30] In texts written still later, this right "to stay" was typically called the *douaire coutumier*, inviting a comparison with the French *douaire*, which also provided the widow usufruct rights to a portion of the deceased husband's property.[31] Many contracts also provided that widows, whether they "stayed" or not, could claim their most personal property before any creditors did so: the clothing and jewels "of her body." This provision explicitly secured what custom apparently did not, for custom made every piece of property in the household – every object, every rent, every tool, every coin, every dress, every soup pot – part of the assessable estate.[32]

MARITAL PROPERTY LAW AND MARRIAGE'S MEANINGS

Ysabel Le Dent and Jean De Temple were prosperous members of Douaisien society. Ysabel's father owned a manor house and many acres of land in the region, and Jean was able to secure Ysabel's *douaire* with real property inherited from his family. Many of the couples who wrote such contracts were similarly well-off, and in this way the Douaisen story seems to resemble patterns more familiar from

---

[29] AMD, FF 613/2034 (3 May 1435). Compare the marriage contract of Magdelanne Pollet of 1522, which permitted her to "take on the debts and goods of her husband, according to custom" instead of demanding return of her *portement* and a *douaire assene et amendement* of 300 *livres parisis monnaie de flandre*: AMD, FF 649/5140 (14 Jan. 1522 ns).

[30] AMD, FF 289, fols. 19–19v, 31 v, and 134–37 (July 1434 to February 1435). Her marriage contract (AMD FF 600/1258 [29 May 1402]) provided only a *reprise* and *douaire*, although Franchoise Rohard claimed that "all the goods, movables, chattels, and *heritages* that was his [her late husband's] belong to me as his heir." Douai's aldermen and judges upheld her claim (AMD, FF 289, fol. 137): "it is our judgment that the defendant is heir and representative of her husband and has [the disputed property] to use as her own property."

[31] See, for example, FF 654/5539–41. The *douaire coutumier* in Douai applied to the entire marital estate, whereas the French *douaire coutumier* was collected only from the husband's reserved properties. In Douai, the *douaire coutumier* was the alternative to the *reprise* and its increase, which was called (confusingly) the *douaire* or the *douaire, assene et amendement*. On the origins of the Douaisien *douaire coutumier* (which acquired its name quite late) and its relation to the normal *douaire coutumier* of France and the dower of England, see Howell, *Marriage Exchange*, Appendix I.

[32] For example, Jehene De Hordain's contract of 1436 (AMD, FF 613/2069 [15 January 1436]) provided that "if after the wedding the said Hue [the groom] were to die before the said demoiselle Jehan [sic], with or without an heir of their marriage, she can take and carry out [of the estate] freely and without care or debt, her furnished bed chamber, her cloths, clothing, jewels, and ornaments for her body in whatever value they have on the day of Hue's death."

elsewhere in early modern Europe, where well-propertied urbanites similarly arranged marriages. However, the Douaisien story is more complex. Although the rich were disproportionately represented among late-medieval contract writers, ordinary people made up the majority. For example, some eighty percent of all writers of contracts identified by occupation in a late–fourteenth-century sample of marriage documents were artisans and retailers; thirty-three percent of all contracts in the sample were written by people of extremely modest economic status; and another forty-four percent were issued by men and women who had no significant real property beyond their home and shop.[33] Only about twenty-seven percent of contract writers from that sample belonged to Douai's economic and social elite. Although, as we shall see, ordinary citizens later seem to have slowly abandoned the marriage contract, they would dominate the archive for at least another 150 years. Seventy-five percent of all contracts from a mid-fifteenth century sample, for example, were written by people far below Le Dent on Douai's social ladder.

We cannot know exactly what compelled Douasiens to intervene in custom so aggressively. At one level, we can argue, they did so because they could: almost alone of other urbanites in the region, Douaisens had enormous freedom to amend custom, and they had a municipal government willing to assist them in that effort. That explanation is surely not enough, however. More fundamentally, the shift reflects a change in the nature of the Douaisien economy and the meaning of commercial wealth, although that story cannot be told through legal records, and to tell of its complicated history would require a book.[34] Instead, the legal records tell the story that accompanied, and surely helped fuel, the larger history of socio-economic change: the story of the stakes in play between men and women when they married.

Custom, as we have seen, constructed marriage as an inseparable union of husband and wife, imagining the couple as a single economic unit. But husband and wife were not considered equal; rather, husbands subsumed their wives, putting them under effective *couverture*. The women gained independent property rights only in their widowhoods, when they assumed their husbands' places. Yet it was at this point that the contradictions of the system became exposed. Wives, once so contained by their husbands that they needed their permission even to make a *ravestissement*, assumed male authority as widows. Whereas this role obviously benefited some women, giving them control over property and household, it burdened others with responsibilities that they could not manage and often could not afford, for many such widows were left with unpaid debts, insolvent businesses, and inefficient shops.

---

[33] For this data, see Howell, *Marriage Exchange* (n. 1 earlier), 78–79.
[34] For this story and its implications, see Howell, *Marriage Exchange* (n. 1 earlier).

The regime constructed by contract seems in many ways a direct response to these difficulties. It eliminated both the threat posed by the independent (and too merry) widow and the tragedy of the widow left destitute by bad luck or a husband's bad management. Now, widows could claim specified assets – those which they had brought to the marriage (or their equivalent), and those pledged as *douaire, assene, et amendement* – to shield them from creditors and assure subsistence. Alternatively, if the estate was solvent, they could "stay" in their husbands' estate, acquiring lifetime rights to the income that it generated. Thus, widows were safe. But in exchange they lost financial control and independence. They no longer shared in the gains of the marriage; no longer could they assume full managerial control over the conjugal fund when their husbands died, for the property was now explicitly marked for heirs and thus unavailable for sale or mortgage without the approval of those heirs.

Under the new regime, men did not suffer as costly a decrease in survivors' rights as women did, for if they outlived their wives, they acquired full ownership of all property in the marital estate except that which had been specifically marked for others by the terms of the marriage contract. Typically, those reserves included only a small provision for testamentary bequests and (in the absence of living descendent heirs) return of immovable property (the *heritages* she had brought to the marriage) to the woman's natal line. As husbands, though, men did less well, for a husband was constrained by special clauses that labeled specific items as the property of his bride, forbade their sale without her consent or the consent of men assigned by the marriage contract to look after her financial interests (the *avoués*), and required their return to her *lez et coste* (her kin) at her death if there were no children born of the marriage.

The marriage contract not only realigned property rights. It appeared to rewrite femininity itself. Unlike custom, which positioned women as creators of property and widows as powerful, independent managers of it, the marriage contract lodged managerial authority with men throughout every stage of a woman's life, and it seemed to position women as mere carriers of property. As a daughter, a woman was supervised by her father and, in his absence, by a group of male relatives from both her mother's and her father's sides. As a wife, she was jointly supervised by her male relatives or their representatives and by her husband; as a widow, a woman was subject to her children and to male supervisors from her family. Thus, under this new regime, women were treated as though they constantly needed protection. Perhaps people assumed that they were ignorant of financial affairs and dangerous if put in charge of male property. Even if they were technically free of *couverture* during marriage insofar as they had formally independent claims to property, they were never free of male supervision.

The new marital property regime had an even more profound effect on the meaning of marriage. In some ways, the marriage contract seemed to weaken the conjugal bond itself, for by abandoning the *ravestissement*, Douaisiens also appeared to have abandoned the idea that husband and wife could be made one through mutual property interests. What replaced it was an utterly different notion of marital economic interests, one based on a partial and limited partnership, on restrictions and withholdings, on boundaries. The result was a considerably less robust vision of the marital bond as constructed by shared wealth. As we shall see, this hardly implied a repudiation of marriage, but it did imply a re-imagining of the institution.

We can trace this conceptual shift in the language of the marital documents themselves. The original *ravestissement par lettre*, as we have seen, represented the husband and wife as one, even to the point of creating the absurdity of a wife's needing her husband's permission to make gifts to him. The marriage contract saw husband and wife differently, not as one but as two distinct entities; and it saw marriage between them as a complicated matter, hard to configure in the net of kinship. The text of the marriage contract itself perfectly expressed this complexity, in both language and form. Unlike the *ravestissement*, which imposed an austere simplicity on marriage, the marriage contract reveled in recounting the multiplicity of nuptial ties. In contrast to the short and tidy *ravestissement par lettre*, the contract was long, typically between 700 and 2,000 words; and although it was formulaic, like the *ravestissement*, its formulas were tortured, its special clauses and unusual provisions abundant.

Moreover, the ceremony it described was completely unlike the straightforward affair of the *ravestissement*. Whereas ostensibly, husband and wife alone composed the *ravestissement* in the presence of only two aldermen and their clerk, a crowd wrote the marriage contract. Men and women about to be married under contract were taken to the town hall by a huge group: always fathers, usually mothers, and very often grandparents, brothers, stepparents, children of first marriages, uncles, sisters, cousins, aunts, and "friends." Antoinette De Cantin, for example, was accompanied at the registration of her marriage contract with Ipoitie Berthe in 1570 by her father and mother, her grandfather, her maternal uncle, her grand uncle, her aunt, still another uncle, and another aunt. The groom was accompanied by his father, mother, uncle, and two aunts by marriage.[35] Once assembled, the large company oversaw the listing of the bride's *portement*, followed by the many clauses specifying the distribution of the estate. Then there was the matter of testamentary bequests made by either spouse and of how they were to be honored. And then came questions about the disposition of *heritages*.

In this way, the new marital property regime made marriage a messy arrangement. Its chief text, the marriage contract, looked less like a pact between partners in life than an exhaustive list of bargaining points among hostile participants. Yet it is perhaps the greatest paradox of a history filled with paradoxes that the legal texts that rewrote marriage as so precarious a financial union simultaneously rebuilt marriage on new and even more enduring foundations. They did so indirectly,

---

[35] AMD, FF 655/5586 (20 Oct. 1570).

subtly, and in ways recognizable only if placed within the cultural discourse of which they were a part.

Reflecting the notion that marriages were sacramental as well as secular unions, all the Douaisien contracts acknowledged the church's right to authorize these unions, using a formula to introduce the contract that seldom varied over the three centuries closing the Middle Ages, as in this example:

> To all present, now and in the future, let it be known that these are the agreements of marriage made and agreed to between Jaque Le Marie and Jehan Le Marie his nephew, on the one hand, and Jacque Le Werme and Robe Le Werme his daughter, whom the said Jehan intends to take as his wife and spouse within forty days, *if the holy church gives assent. . . .*[36]

Alongside this rather formal statement of marriage's religious significance came indirect notice that marriage was as much about personal ties as it was about property. Children, for example, came to figure prominently in the typical contract. Those written by widows or widowers commonly included clauses setting aside property from the new conjugal fund for these children when they reached majority or married, or the contracts simply labeled certain immovables as becoming the children's after the death of their natural parent. The 1437 contract between the widower Collart Tallon, a painter, and Marie Du Bosquiel, widow of Collart Bellot, included elaborate provisions for the children of their previous marriages. His daughter was to receive specified sums from Bosquiel when Tallon died, and the provisions were to be adjusted according to her age and marital state. The three children of Bosquiel received similar protections, and all four were guaranteed nurturance, housing, and education:

> It is provided and agreed among the said parties that each, Collart and Marie, is required at his or her expense to care for and raise their children, to send them to school, to have them learn a trade, to dress them, to give them what they need as drink, food, clothing, and lodging until they marry, are emancipated, or reach the age of 18 years. . . .[37]

Most contracts assigned the tasks of parenting to both husband and wife, but some added special instructions for the mother, admonishing her that, if she should survive her husband, she alone was obligated to care for the children "as a good mother should [*comme le doit une bonne mere*]." In this clause lies a telling commentary on the ideology of marriage then developing, for it suggests not only that marriage was being equated with parenthood, but that feminine virtue was coming to be associated with certain maternal tasks. Although this was hardly the first (or the last) European text that would link a woman's moral capacities to the quality of the care she gave her children (*comme le doit une bonne mere*), it does help signal the shift in the conception of marriage that was then underway in Douai.

---

[36] AMD, FF 585/162 (16 Nov. 1373), emphasis mine.

[37] AMD, FF 613/2082 (27 Apr. 1437).

In addition to marital reciprocity and parenthood, some of the texts spoke of love. Such language did not appear in the marriage contract, where we might expect to find it, but in those *ravestissements* written in the last years of our period. Presumably in an effort to justify what by that time was no longer the norm among propertied Douaisiens, partners who decided to give all their property to the surviving spouse without restriction spoke of the "conjugal love and affection they hold for one another."[38] Some other documents from the same period speak of their *bon amour mutuel* or *la bonne amour et affection naturelle et conjugalle.* Another document attempted more straightforwardly, if somewhat confusedly, to justify the *ravestissement*, explaining that the couple has chosen this agreement "for the good love which they have for one another and because they do not have child of their marriage ... and for many other reasons too [*pour la bonne amour eulx porturent de avouer reciproquement lun vers lautre aussi quilz navoient nulz enffans de leur corp ... et pour plussieurs aultres causes*]."[39]

As dramatic as the differences between the actual texts of the *ravestissement* and the marriage contract may be, it is hard to argue that Douaisiens who wrote the former had one conception (and experience of) marriage and those who first wrote the latter thought of marriage and its gender system in entirely different terms. The empirical record alone will not support this interpretation, for we know that until around 1450 some Douaisiens wrote *both* documents for the same marriage, drafting a marriage contract before the wedding and a *ravestissement* afterwards, presumably to assure that the property not explicitly covered in the marriage contract would be subject to the old rules of custom. We also know that the earliest marriage contracts often resembled *ravestissments* in form and to a certain extent in content, for they combined provisions from each kind of marital property regime in ways that seem entirely confused.[40] Therefore, we cannot conclude that the "medieval" marriage was entirely "conjugal," and the "early modern" marriage "separatist." Nor can we assume that Douaisiens saw these as incompatible regimes. Clearly, they often wanted the best of both: to facilitate management of the household and protect the property it acquired from the demands of outside kin, but at the same time, to protect widows from want and to assure husbands that their property went to their offspring. Hence they wrote *ravestissments* but inserted clauses excluding some property from the conjugal fund; or they wrote contracts covering only property brought to the marriage, not that acquired thereafter; or they fashioned still more baroque arrangements, leaving what appears to legal historians a confused record of "archaic" practice.

All propertied Douaisiens, even simple weavers and fullers or shoemakers and carpenters, took advantage of custom's willingness to be bent in these ways. If not quite at the same rate as their social betters, these people wrote contracts in

---

[38] AMD, FF 655/5564 (8 Nov. 1558).

[39] AMD, F 655/5551, 5 Mar. 1555; 5582 (1 Feb. 1567); and 5584 (25 Aug. 1570).

[40] Early *ravestissements* often appeared to bracket some property, treating it as privately owned by each spouse: see, e.g., Appendix, Doc. 4 (AMD FF 585/148 [8 Oct. 1443]).

considerably greater numbers than did the elites, and they continued to do so into the sixteenth century. By mid-century, however, the new "separatist" regime seems to have acquired especially firm place among Douai's securely propertied citizenry: the city's small class of newly ennobled bourgeoisie, its expanding class of educated bureaucrats, the rich financiers and merchants from the city's old families, and its most prosperous artisans and shopkeepers. For them, property linked families rather than spouses; and now it served lineages rather than households. At the same time, in contrast, ordinary Douaisiens were steadily abandoning the marriage contract. Whereas seventy-nine percent of the marriage contracts from a mid-fifteenth century sample were written by artisans and retailers, only forty-five percent of those in a sample from the 1550s were drawn up by such people.[41] The new regime's emphasis on lineal property, its assumptions that women were carriers rather than creators of property, and its tendency to lodge masculine authority in the line rather than the household: all this seems to have offered little to people who still thought of the household as a production unit and still needed wives to work with and on behalf of the household. For them, they must have decided, old custom best expressed the kind of economic and social relations they sought in marriage.

Douaisiens were not alone in this story of legal instability, although there is no doubt that their story is better documented and more dramatic than others in the region. One legal scholar has recently argued, for example, that the story in Douai was replicated throughout the *Nord* (the area of France to which Douai now belongs). In his words, "the constant principle of family law in the *Nord* in the late Middle Age [was] the retreat of the couple in the face of strengthened ties of lineage" and "accentuation of the masculine [i.e., patrilineal] bias of family law."[42] In other parts of northern Europe, the story is more complicated, but its fundamental theme is the same. In Flanders proper (what is now approximately Belgian Flanders), in the Isle de France, in Burgundy – everywhere, in fact, that scholars have been able to look – we find community property systems under pressure. Everywhere there is evidence that people with property, especially the rising class that historians would come to call bourgeois, were abandoning the rules of a strictly communal system, either surrounding it with provisions that undercut the size of the community, or alternatively, overwriting community property arrangements by means of contracts and wills, just as people in Douai were doing. In the end, if we take 1550 or thereabouts as the end, community property law had been significantly eroded, and in some individual cases had been entirely overwritten by arrangements that were more "dotal" and separatist in spirit, much more like those traditionally associated with the South, the so-called *pays d'écrit*.

Even in the South, there was instability of the same kind. Jean Hilaire's studies of late-medieval Montpellier and its region, where the principles and institutions of Roman law supposedly reigned supreme, describe a telling example of such

---

[41] See Howell, *Marriage Exchange* (n. 1 earlier), 85.
[42] Jacob, *Les époux* (n. 1 earlier), 319 and, similarly, passim.

instability. There, people writing marriage contracts to set the terms of the traditional dotal marriage regularly inserted clauses that created community accounts much like those that were customary in the North.[43] Yet, as in the North, these practices were not adopted across the social spectrum. Rather, community property arrangements in the South were always associated with simple people, those who shared both work and residence ("the same house, the same bread, the same wine"), and not with merchants and aristocrats.[44]

The Douaisien evidence helps us understand why marital property law was in motion elsewhere, even in the South, where written law and judicial systems were better established than they were in Douai. Marital property law, we have learned, does not inscribe social and personal relations; rather, it undergirds these relations by linking people to each other through claims to property. Yet it cannot rid those relationships of tension; in fact, property relations are themselves the source of many of the tensions imbedded in marriage. In Douai, as we have seen, community property law could not stabilize gender hierarchy; it could not render kin, conjugal, and generational interests identical; and it could not assure class continuity across generations, especially in a world where property itself was acquiring new meanings. The system that replaced custom, although resolving some of these tensions, created others. Most obviously, it separated husband from wife and she from him, not just by means of property rights but also in the way it defined their respective capacities to manage property.

As if in acknowledgment that the marriage thus founded was a feeble thing, not fit to its task of securing social and gender order, the very texts that so assiduously organized property relations came to supplement the rules of property. They called upon the church to bless unions, they gave marriage moral purpose by featuring parents' responsibilities to children, and they even introduced romance into what was formally only a material arrangement. In doing so, they seemed to confess, marriage, no matter how emphatically about property, was about more than that.

Appendix

Document 1: *Ravestissement from Mid–Fifteenth-Century Douai*[1]

Let it be known to all present and future that Jaquemart De Lommel who resides in Douai makes and has made a *ravestissement* to Jehanne De Sanchy, his wife and spouse, of all that he has, will have, or might acquire whether or not there is an heir, according to the law and custom of the city of Douai.

---

[43] Hilaire, *Le régime des biens*; idem, "Vie en commun, famille et esprit communautaire," *Nouvelle Revue historique de droit français et étranger*, 4th series, 51 (1973): 8–53.

[44] Hilaire, *Le régime des biens*, 312.

[1] AMD, FF 616/2374.

And in a like manner the said Jehanne De Sanchy makes and has made a *ravestissement* to Jaquemart her husband of all she has and will have or might acquire, whether or not there is an heir, according to the law and custom of the city of Douai.

This is recognized and passed before, as aldermen of the said city of Douai, Thomas Dauby and Thomas Du Clerc. It was passed the 27th day of December, year one thousand four hundred and forty-two.

DOCUMENT 2: *Marriage Contract from Late–Fourteenth-Century Douai*[2]

Let it be known to all present, now and in the future, that just as it is here and hereafter set forth, these are the "covenants" of marriage which are to be made between Jehan Aymon, for one part, and Gillotte Descaillon whom the said Jehan intends to take as wife and spouse within 40 days if the holy church assents, for the other part.

And the said Gillotte brings to the marriage with the said Jehan in goods, movables, and chattels and in coin the value of 75 *livres*, money of Flanders, in *francs royaulx*, [valued at] 37 shillings the piece; the said Jehan acknowledges himself to be "content" and well paid.

Further, it is to be known that it is agreed between the parties and by the "covenant" of marriage that if the said Jehan dies before the said Gillotte without an heir [born of the marriage] alive or expected at the day of death, the said Gillotte may have and take out [of the estate] freely and completely the said sum of 75 *livres* which she brought and is bringing to the marriage as stated above; and with that she will have, as *douaire, assenne et amendement* the amount of 25 *livres* of the said money, and she shall have this amount from the best goods, movables, chattels and *heritages* then remaining of the said Jehan['s property].

And if there are heirs of their bodies living or expected on the day of the said Jehan's death, they shall have, as theirs alone, the 25 *livres* of *douaire et amendement* described, and the said Gillotte may not ask for or have the 75 *livres* that she brought to the marriage.

And if the said Gillotte dies before the said Jehan and there is an heir or heirs of their bodies living or expected on the day of her death, this heir or heirs will have the 25 *livres* that is described above. And the entire remains and surplus of the property of Jehan and Gillotte will belong to Jehan as his own property.

If there is no heir of their bodies living or apparent on the day of Gillotte's death, the said 25 *livres* go to Sir Jehan Descaillon, priest, her father if he is then living. And if he is not living the said Jehan returns [the sum] to Willem Descaillon, the son whom he [Sir Jehan Descaillon] had of Jehanne Dillies, and to Saudrine Descaillon, his daughter whom he had of Mlle. Phellipe Crecque,

---

[2] AMD, FF 586/214.

in equal shares. And if one of the two, Willem or Saudrine, is not alive, the sum of 25 *livres* goes to the survivor of the two. And if both are dead, the sum goes to the closest living heir or heirs of the said Sir Jehan Descaillon.

All these things and each of them in their entirety this Jehan Anmon and his heirs freely commit to the said Jehan, Willem Fruchelet, and Jehan De Saille, son of Amkiel, *advouez* of the said Gillotte, or to the bearer of this letter, citizens of Douai. . . .

1 May 1375

Document 3: *Marriage Contract of Early Fifteenth-Century Douai*[3]

Let it be known to all present and future that as is set forth below these are the "covenants" of marriage which are to be made between Jehan Au Laudeluye for one part and Marie Le Libert, daughter of Jean Le Libert, whom the said Jehan intends to take as wife and spouse within 40 days if the holy church assents, for the other part.

First, the said Marie brings to the marriage with the said Jehan the sum of seventy *couronnes d'or* from the forge of our king on the condition that the said Jehan Au Laudeluye and Marie above named together obligingly declare themselves "content" and quit the said Jehn Le Libert, his heirs and representatives of the gift which was earlier given by the said Jehan Le Libert to the said Marie. That is to say, the sum of 20 *francs* and the fifth part of two houses and *heritages* which the said Jehan possesses in Douai in the street of Draques connecting on one side to the tenement of Martin Despres and on the other to the tenement of Pierot Du Cauquies, with which *portement* the said Jehan declares himself content.

Thus it is agreed and contracted between the parties and by the "covenants" of marriage that if it happens that during the espousals the said Jehan or Marie dies and that they have any children of their marriage living or expected on the day of the death of their father or mother, the children may justly have half of all the goods, movables, chattels and *heritages* remaining to the father or mother.

And in the case that the said Jehan and Marie do not have children living or expected on the day of the death of Jehan or Marie, the closest heirs or heir of the one who thus had died will have the third of all the goods, movables, chattels and *heritages* remaining of the one who had died.

Moreover it is agreed between the parties that and by the covenants of marriage that if it happens that the said Marie dies before Jehan with or without heirs she may give as alms, freely, wherever and to whom it pleases her before the sons and daughters of the holy church without the permission or consent of the said Jehan the sum of 10 *francs*, which the said

---

[3] AMD, FF 606/1628.

Jehan is obliged to pay in their entirety to the extent Marie has made these gifts. And the rest of the surplus and remainder that exists, the above said clauses and conditions having been met, belongs to the said Jehan as his own property.

All these "covenants" and each of them Jehan Au Laudeluye has sworn to honor in each point and to that end he obligates and has obligated all his goods with all the above mentioned goods, movables, non-movables, chattels and *heritages* present and future in order that the bearer of these letters may take possession and arrest and sell them and conduct the sale in any seigneurie and jurisdiction until the terms of this agreement are fulfilled. And with it to pay all costs, expenses and outlays whatever and all unsatisfied obligations. And, similarly, these agreements he will keep and complete by his oath and the guarantee of all his movables, chattels and *heritages* for this execution as above said.

This "covenant" of marriage is made and recognized before aldermen of the city of Douay, Jehan De Brebriere and Colle Le Wange. It is done the 20th day of January, in the year of our Lord one thousand four hundred and fifteen.

DOCUMENT 4: *Ravestissement with "Contract-Like" Clauses, from Mid–Fourteenth-Century Douai*[4]

Let it be known to all present now and future that Jehan Davennes, weaver of drapery, has made and makes a *ravestissement* to Maroie Loberille, his wife, of all he has, will have, and will acquire, whether or not there is an heir, according to the law of the city. And in exactly the same manner the said Maroie has made and makes a *ravestissement* to Jehan of all she has, will have, and will acquire, whether or not there is a heir, according to the law of the city.

And the said *ravestissment* which the said spouses have made is [subject to] the manner and condition that if the said Jean Davennes exits from this century before the said Maroie his wife, whether or not there is an heir, the said Maroie will have and take out 50 *florins d'or* from all the best goods which the spouses possessed on the day of the said Jehan's death. And the said Maroie [may] have and take her best furnished bed and all her draperies, linens, clothing, and jewels that she had for her body on the day of the death.

And in the case that the said Marioe dies before the said Jehan her husband she may give as alms to whomever she pleases all her draperies, linens, clothing, and jewels that she had for her body on the day of the death.

This *ravestissement* and all its elements set forth above were passed before the aldermen Jehan Li Kievre and Collars Painmoullies.

This was created the 28th day of the month of April, in the year one thousand three hundred and 62.

[4] AMD, FF 585/148.

Note on Document 4

This *ravestissement* provides the usual mutual donation ("Jehans Davennes tisser-ans de draps a ravesti et ravest maroie loberielle se feme de quanque il a et ara et avoir et acqueire poura a hoir et sans hoir permit le loy de la ville/et tout en tell maniere a laditte Maroie ravesa et raviest le dit Jehan Davennes sen mary de quanques elle a et ara et avoir et acquerre poura a hoir et sans hoir. . . . "). Yet it goes on to stipulate that if Jehan dies before Marioe, with or without an heir, she can take 50 gold florins from the estate along with her "best bed," her clothing and jewels; and in addition she is permitted to bequeath all her clothing and cloths, along with her jewelry, should she die before him. Presumably, the intent was to provide Marioe, should she survive Jehan, with property "off the top" of the estate (before creditors asserted their claims), but to require her to "stay" in the remaining estate. Should she predecease Jehan, she is permitted to extract (by means of her will) her personal goods from the estate for the benefit of friends and relatives, leaving Jehan with the remainder.

CHAPTER THIRTEEN

MARRIAGE CONTRACTS, LITURGIES, AND PROPERTIES IN REFORMATION GENEVA

John Witte, Jr.

Marriage was one of the hotly contested issues of the sixteenth-century Protestant Reformation and one of the first institutions to be reformed.[1] The leading Protestant theologians – Martin Luther and Philip Melanchthon, Thomas Cranmer and William Tyndale, Martin Bucer and John Calvin – all prepared lengthy tracts on the subject in their first years of reform. Scores of leading jurists took up legal questions of marriage in their *consilia* and commentaries, often working under the direct inspiration of Protestant theology and theologians. Virtually every city and territory that converted to the Protestant cause in the first half of the sixteenth century had new marriage laws on the books within a decade after accepting the Reformation.[2]

The Protestant reformers' early preoccupation with marriage was partly driven by their theology. Many of the core issues of the Reformation were implicated by the prevailing sacramental theology and canon law of marriage. The Catholic church's jurisdiction over marriage was, for the reformers, a particularly flagrant example of the church's usurpation of the magistrate's authority. The Catholic sacramental concept of marriage, on which the church predicated its jurisdiction, was for the reformers a self-serving theological fiction. The canonical prohibition on marriage of clergy and monastics stood sharply juxtaposed to Protestant doctrines of sexual sin and the Christian vocation. The canon law's long roll of impediments to

---

[1] This chapter represents work in progress on a multi-volume project with Robert M. Kingdon, *Sex, Marriage and Family in John Calvin's Geneva*. The first volume, subtitled *Courtship, Betrothal, and Marriage* was published in 2005; the second volume, *The Christian Household and School* is forthcoming in 2007. I wish to thank Professor Kingdon and Thomas Lambert for their expert commentary and criticisms, and M. Wallace McDonald for his diligent research and excellent translations of the consistory cases in the Genevan archives sampled in the last section of this chapter. I also wish to thank Professors R. H. Helmholz, Martha Howell, Thomas Kuehn, and Philip L. Reynolds for their helpful criticisms and comments on an earlier draft of this chapter.

[2] See sources and discussion in John Witte, Jr., *Law and Protestantism: The Legal Teachings of the Lutheran Reformation* (Cambridge, 2002), 177–256; idem, *From Sacrament to Contract: Marriage, Religion, and Law in the Western Tradition* (Louisville, 1997), 42–193.

betrothal and marriage, its prohibitions against complete divorce and remarriage, and its close regulations of sexuality, parenting, and education all stood in considerable tension with the reformers' understanding of the Bible. That a child could enter marriage without parental permission or church consecration betrayed, in the reformers' views, basic responsibilities of family, church, and state to children. Issues of marriage doctrine and law thus implicated and epitomized many of the cardinal theological issues of the Protestant Reformation.

The reformers' early preoccupation with marriage was also partly driven by their politics. A number of early leaders of the Reformation faced aggressive prosecution by the Catholic church and its political allies for violation of the canon law of marriage and celibacy. Among the earliest Protestant leaders were ex-priests and ex-monastics who had forsaken their orders and vows, many of whom had married shortly thereafter. Indeed, one of the acts of solidarity with the new Protestant cause was to marry or divorce in open violation of the canon law and in defiance of a bishop's instructions. As Catholic church courts began to prosecute these canon law offences, Protestant theologians and jurists rose to the defense of their co-religionists, producing a welter of briefs, letters, sermons, and pamphlets that denounced traditional norms and pronounced a new theology of marriage.

Protestant theologians treated marriage not as a sacramental institution of the heavenly kingdom but as a social estate of the earthly kingdom. Marriage, they taught, served the goods and goals of mutual love and support of husband and wife, mutual procreation and nurture of children, and mutual protection of both spouses from sexual sin. All adult persons, preachers and others alike, should pursue the calling of marriage, for all were in need of the comforts of marital love and of protection from sexual sin. When properly structured and governed, the marital household served as a model of authority, charity, and pedagogy in the earthly kingdom and as a vital instrument for the reform of church, state, and society. Parents served as "bishops" to their children. Siblings served as priests to each other. The household altogether – particularly the Christian household of the married minister – was a source of "evangelical impulses" in society.[3]

Though divinely created and spiritually edifying, marriage and the family remained a social estate of the earthly kingdom, of the present life. All parties could partake of this institution, regardless of their faith. Though it was subject to divine law and clerical counseling, marriage came within the jurisdiction of the magistrate, not the cleric; of the civil law, not the canon law. The magistrate, as God's vice-regent of the earthly kingdom, was to set the laws for marriage formation, maintenance, and dissolution.

---

[3] The quotation is from Gerald Strauss, *Luther's House of Learning: Indoctrination of the Young in the German Reformation* (Baltimore, Md., 1978), 112.

Political leaders rapidly translated this new Protestant gospel into civil law. Just as the civil act of marriage often came to signal a person's conversion to Protestantism, so the Civil Marriage Act came to symbolize a political community's acceptance of the new Protestant theology of marriage. These new civil laws included a number of important innovations triggered by the new Protestant theology of marriage. But they also ultimately retained a good deal of the medieval canon law and civil law.

Geneva followed this general pattern of Protestant reform. On May 21, 1536, the Genevan authorities renounced the canon law in favor of "the holy Evangelical Law and Word of God."[4] The local prince-bishop was forced to leave, along with the canon lawyers who had staffed the bishop's court and had applied the canon law of marriage in the diocese. Two months later, John Calvin arrived in Geneva, armed with a copy of his new *Institutes of the Christian Religion* in which he, too, renounced the traditional theology and canon law of marriage and called for the reformation of marriage "root, trunk, and branch."[5] The Genevan city councils began to issue new statutes on discrete marriage questions almost immediately thereafter. These early laws culminated in a detailed Marriage Ordinance, drafted by Calvin and others in 1545 and revised in 1546. The authorities also mandated the use of a new Marriage Liturgy that Calvin had drafted in 1542 and issued in expanded form in 1545. These and other laws were enforced both by the Council of Geneva and by the Consistory, a new institution composed of both ministers and magistrates.

These new Genevan ordinances introduced a number of important changes to the prevailing law of marriage. Betrothal and marriage contracts became harder to make and harder to annul. Both public banns and church weddings were made essential to the validity of a marriage. The wedding liturgy itself was reworked heavily to emphasize biblical instruction and congregational participation. The law of marital property – betrothal gifts, dower, and dowry – changed rather little, but the Genevan authorities would not annul engagement or marriage contracts that were conditioned on delivery of marital property, even if the betrothed parties and their families fell into bitter dispute.

---

[4] Emile Rivoire and Victor van Berchem (eds.), *Les sources du droit du canton de Genève*, 4 vols. (Aarau, 1927–35), vol. 2, item no. 701 [hereafter SD]. Only a decade before, the city council had confirmed unequivocally its support for the church's jurisdiction over marriage. Statute of December 20, 1528, in SD, vol. 2, item no. 621; see also ibid., item no. 571. See Walter Köhler, *Zürcher Ehegericht und Genfer Konsistorium*, 2 vols. (Leipzig, 1932–42), 2:514–15, 541–55.

[5] John Calvin, *Ioannis Calvini Institutio Religionis Christianae* (Basel, 1536), in Guillelmus Baum et al. (eds.), *Ioannis Calvini opera quae supersunt omnia*, 59 vols. (Brunswick, 1863–1900) (Corpus Reformatorum Series, vols. 29–87), 1:192–95 [hereafter CO], translated as John Calvin, *Institution of the Christian Religion*, by Ford L. Battles (Atlanta, 1975), 236–40.

Betrothal and Marriage Contracts

Calvin introduced most of the reforms of betrothal and marriage contracts in his 1546 Marriage Ordinance.[6] Like the medieval canonists, Calvin started with the principle of freedom of marital contract. Marriage, he insisted, depended in its essence on the mutual consent of both the man and the woman. Absent proof of free consent by both parties, there was no marriage. Calvin defended this principle repeatedly in his later commentaries and sermons. "While all contracts ought to be voluntary, freedom ought to prevail especially in marriage, so that no one may pledge his faith against his will."[7] "God considers that compulsory and forced marriages never come to a good end.... [I]f the husband and the wife are not in mutual agreement and do not love each other, this is a profanation of marriage, and not a marriage at all, properly speaking. For the will is the principal bond."[8] When a woman wishes to marry, therefore, she must not "be thrust into it reluctantly or compelled to marry against her will, but left to her own free choice."[9] "When a man is going to marry and he takes a wife, let him take her of his own free will, knowing that where there is not a true and pure love, there is nothing but disorder, and one can expect no grace from God."[10]

Also following medieval canonists, Calvin distinguished between contracts of betrothal and contracts of marriage: betrothals and espousals as he called them, following the tradition. Betrothals were future promises to be married. Espousals were present promises to be married. But, unlike the medieval canonists, Calvin removed the need for the parties to use specific formulaic words: any clear indication of consent would do. He softened the distinction and shortened the duration between betrothals and espousals. He insisted that these contracts be both public and private in nature. He would not declare a marriage valid merely on proof that a betrothed couple had consummated their union; a church wedding was still required.

Because the consent of the couple was the essence of the betrothal contract, Calvin took pains to secure it in the 1546 Marriage Ordinance. Betrothal promises had to be made "simply" and "honorably in the fear of God." Such betrothals were to be initiated by "a sober proposal" from the man, accepted by the woman, and witnessed by at least two persons of "good reputation." Betrothals made in secret, qualified with onerous conditions, or procured by coercion, fraud, or deceit were automatically annulled, and the couple themselves, and any accomplices in their

---

[6] The 1545 draft is in CO 10/1:33–44, the 1546 draft in Jean-Francois Bergier and Robert M. Kingdon (eds.), *Registres de la compagnie des pasteurs de Genève au temps de Calvin*, 2 vols. (Geneva, 1964), 1:30–38. The 1546 version was used by the authorities from the start, but it was not formally promulgated until 1561 as a section of *Les Ordonnances ecclesiastiques* (1561) in CO 10/1:91–124.

[7] Comm. Josh. 15:14.

[8] Serm. Deut. 25:5–12.

[9] Comm. Gen. 24:57.

[10] Serm. Deut. 25:5–12.

wrongdoing, could face punishment. Either party could petition to annul betrothals procured through trickery or "surprise," or made "frivolously, as when merely touching glasses when drinking together." Betrothal promises extracted by or from children below the age of consent were presumptively invalid, though children could confirm them upon reaching majority. Betrothals involving a newcomer to the city were not valid until the parties produced proof of the newcomer's integrity of character and eligibility for marriage. Absent such proof, the couple had to wait a year before they could marry.

The consent of the couple's parents, or their guardians, was also vital to the validity of the betrothal. The consent of fathers was the more critical; the consent of mothers was required only when fathers were absent and would be respected only if (male) relatives would concur with her views. In the absence of both parents, guardians would give their consent, again with priority for the male voice. Minor children – men under twenty, women under eighteen – who became betrothed without such parental consent could have their betrothals unilaterally annulled by either set of parents or guardians. Adult or emancipated children could proceed without their parents' consent, though "it is more fitting that they should always let themselves be governed by the advice of their fathers."

The Ordinance made clear that parental consent was a supplement to, not a substitute for, the consent of the two partners themselves. Parents were prohibited, on pain of imprisonment, from coercing their children into unwanted betrothals or marriages and from withholding their consent or payment of dowry until the child chose a favored partner. They were further prevented from forcing youngsters into marriage before they were mature enough to consent to and participate safely in the institution. Minor children "observing a modest and reverend spirit" could refuse to follow their parents' insistence on an unwanted partner or a premature betrothal. Other children, confronting a "negligent or excessively strict" father, could "have him compelled to give a dowry" in support of their marriage.

The consent of the broader state and church community also played a part in betrothals. Betrothed couples were to register with a local civil magistrate, who would post notices of their pending nuptials and furnish the couple with a signed marriage certificate. Couples were to file this registration thereafter with a local church, whose pastor was to announce their banns from the pulpit on three successive Sundays. Such widespread notice was an open invitation for fellow parishioners and citizens alike to approve of the match or to voice their objections. Any objections to the betrothal could be raised at this point. But all such objections had to be voiced privately to the Consistory, and only by citizens or by persons of good reputation. Such precautions helped to avoid the prospect of "defamation or injustice," particularly "to an honorable girl." The partners or their parents could sue for defamation those who objected in an untimely or improper manner. A final call for objections to the marriage came during the wedding liturgy.

While the Consistory was given wide discretion to review these objections, the strong presumption was that betrothal contracts, once properly made, could not be broken. Objections that raised formal impediments required closer scrutiny and sometimes could result in orders of annulment, or at least delay of the wedding. Of the numerous impediments to betrothal recognized at medieval canon law, the 1546 Marriage Ordinance listed only five: (1) infancy; (2) precontract; (3) incest; (4) contagious disease or physical deformity; and (5) physical desertion by either party. The Ordinance listed as an impediment to either betrothal or marriage: (6) discovery of the lack of presumed virginity. Though the Ordinance was silent on the question, in practice, Calvin and the Consistory also raised to the level of an impediment to betrothal: (7) lack of consent by either the man or woman; (8) lack of parental consent to a minor's marriage; (9) bodily fornication with another by either betrothed party; and (10) failure of conditions that went to the essence of marriage. The Ordinance did not list, and the Consistory did not recognize, various other impediments to betrothal recognized in canon law: expiration of time, cruelty or dissent towards a fiancé(e), special affinity, spiritual fornication, a man's entry into the clergy, either party's vow of chastity, or dissolution by mutual consent of the betrothed couple.

The removal of this last canon law impediment to betrothal, dissolution of the betrothal by mutual consent of the couple, was particularly surprising. The medieval canonists had introduced this impediment not to encourage transient troth but to give parties a final chance to walk away from the budding union if their relationship did not work out or if they and their families fell into dispute, say, over money or marital property, which were often points of real contention. Calvin and his colleagues provided no such escape. When the parties gave their mutual consent to engagement but then later changed their minds, the Consistory held them to their promises. Even if the parties were now fundamentally at odds and both wanted out of their engagement, Calvin and the Consistory often ordered them to marry in accordance with their betrothal promises. A betrothal contract, once made, could not be broken unless the parties could prove another impediment. If it had been formed properly, the engagement contract could not be dissolved even by mutual consent.

This rule underscored Calvin's teaching that both betrothals and marriages were "sacred contracts" that could not be put asunder easily. It also underscored Calvin's repeated counsel that parties must meet, become well acquainted, and deliberate carefully with each other and their parents and peers before they became engaged to be married.[11] To be sure, it was easier to get out of a betrothal than a marriage in Reformation Geneva, for the roll of impediments to betrothal was considerably longer than the roll of marital impediments. But it was even easier to get out of a courtship. Either courting party could simply leave, or the parties could mutually agree to sever their relationship. All this was a notable departure from the medieval tradition, which had allowed parties to dissolve engagement contracts by mutual

---

[11] This courtship ethic is detailed in Witte and Kingdon, *Sex, Marriage and Family*, vol. 1, ch. 3.

consent. What was a two-stage process in the medieval tradition now became a three-stage process in Reformation Geneva: courtship, betrothal, and marriage.

A Genevan couple, once properly betrothed, had little time to waste and little room to celebrate. Neither their publicly announced betrothal nor the civil registration of their marriage was sufficient to constitute a marriage. A formal church wedding had to follow within six weeks of betrothal. If the couple procrastinated in their wedding plans, they would be reprimanded by the Consistory; if they persisted in procrastinating, they would be "sent before the Council so that they may be compelled to celebrate it." If the prospective groom disappeared without cause, the woman was bound to her betrothal for a year. If the prospective bride disappeared, the man could break off the betrothal immediately – unless there was evidence that she had been kidnapped or involuntarily detained. Cohabitation and consummation, in the brief period prior to the wedding, were strictly forbidden to the parties, on pain of imprisonment. Pregnant brides-to-be, though spared prison, were required with their fiancés to do public confession for their fornication prior to the wedding, and to wear a veil but no flowers on their wedding day to signal their sin. Weddings were to be "modest affairs" "maintaining the decorum and gravity befitting Christians." Wedding parties were to be celebratory but sober, without drunkenness, dancing, or debauchery.

Marriage Liturgies

Calvin's 1545 Marriage Liturgy elaborated the rules and rites of weddings.[12] Marriages without weddings were invalid in Reformation Geneva. "The public and solemn" wedding ceremony was "essential" for a marriage to be "true and lawful," Calvin put it in the 1542 draft of his Marriage Liturgy.[13] "No marriages are lawful, except those that are rightly consecrated," he repeated in 1554.[14]

For Calvin and his colleagues, weddings were essential confirmations not only that the couple privately consented but also that the church and the state publicly consented to the marriage. As noted, all weddings had to be announced in advance by the publication of banns, and the banns were to be signed by a local magistrate and declared by a local minister for three successive Sundays before the wedding. Weddings took place either on Sunday or on a weekday when a public Bible lecture was scheduled, and in the church where the banns had been pronounced. Weddings could not be held on the same Sunday for which the Eucharist was scheduled lest "the honor of the sacrament" be impugned. The local minister presided over the

---

[12] CO 6:203–8. The 1545 edition largely repeats the 1542 edition but adds a lengthy preface and further instructions. Later editions of 1547, 1558, 1559, 1562, 1563, and 1566 are largely the same, except for small variations of wording.

[13] CO 6:203–04.

[14] Comm. Gen. 24:59.

wedding following a detailed liturgy that Calvin drafted. Marriages that had been secretly contracted or celebrated improperly elsewhere had to be announced and celebrated anew in a church wedding.

The banns were written announcements of the parties' pending wedding plans. The minister usually read them from the pulpit during the Sunday worship service. The publication of banns was an ancient practice of the church. What was new in Geneva, as compared to late-medieval Catholic practice, was that the publication of banns was mandatory for every wedding. Marriages were not valid without weddings, and weddings could not proceed without banns. What was also new in Geneva, compared with some other Protestant communities, was that banns were to be announced in the church, not in the public square or the city hall. A city official, called a syndic, had to sign the banns after the parties registered their betrothal in the local town hall. But the minister had to pronounce these signed banns in the church where the parties intended to be married. This underscored a central point of Calvin's marriage theology: that marriages were at once public and private, spiritual and temporal, ecclesiastical and political in nature.

The permission to celebrate weddings on any day, save on a Sunday when the Eucharist was celebrated, was a marked departure from the late-medieval Catholic tradition. Prior to the Reformation, the prince-bishop of Geneva prohibited weddings on any of the sixty-odd holy days of the medieval religious calendar, as well as throughout the period of Lent. Several local synods also prohibited weddings on Sundays and discouraged them on Fridays.[15] But when church weddings were celebrated, the Eucharist had to be included in the wedding liturgy. Calvin and his colleagues eliminated most holy days and softened considerably the Lenten restrictions, freeing up days for weddings.[16] But, more to the point, they allowed weddings on any days that the congregation gathered to hear biblical exposition, whether the Sunday sermon or the weekday lecture on biblical texts. This underscored an accent that Calvin's liturgy spelled out in more detail: weddings were congregational events that featured exposition of the Bible, not celebration of a sacrament.

Calvin's wedding liturgy moved in three phases: (1) biblical exhortation on marriage and its duties; (2) the consent of the couple and congregation and exchange of vows; and (3) blessing, prayer, and further exhortation. In the first phase, the minister offered the couple a rich mosaic of biblical teachings on marriage, citing and paraphrasing a dozen Old and New Testament passages. Man and woman were created for each other. The two shall become one flesh. Their voluntary union shall be permanent. The wife shall subject herself to her husband. Both husband and

---

[15] See examples in Jean-Baptise Molin and Protais Mutembe, *Le rituel du mariage en France du XIIᵉ au XVIᵉ siècle* (Paris, 1974); Kenneth W. Stevenson, *Worship: Wonderful and Sacred Mystery* (Washington, DC, 1992).
[16] Philip Benedict, *Christ's Churches Purely Reformed: A Social History of Calvinism* (New Haven and London, 2002), 495 ff.

wife shall surrender their bodies to each other. Marriage protects both parties from lust. Their bodies are temples of the Lord to be maintained in purity.

After this lengthy opening exhortation, the minister moved to the second phase, asking the man and the woman separately whether each consented to the marriage as so described. Part of the concern was to ensure that both the man and the woman fully and freely consented to the marriage and were not pursuing this marriage frivolously, fraudulently, or under any false illusions. Part of the concern was to ensure that each party had a detailed understanding of the nature and responsibility of the marriage institution that they were about to enter. The minister also asked the congregation whether they consented to the union or knew of any impediment. With all confirming their consent to go forward, the minister then administered the vows. Some of the phraseology of the vows will be familiar to Protestants today. But note that these vows were taken before God and the congregation, and that the parties were bound by God's word. Note, too, the disparities in the duties the husband and wife owe each other:

Do you, N., confess here before God and his holy congregation that you have taken and take for your wife and spouse N. here present, whom you promise to protect, loving and maintaining her faithfully, as is the duty of a true and faithful husband to his wife, living piously with her, keeping faith and loyalty to her in all things, according to the holy Word of God and his holy Gospel?

Do you, N., confess here before God and his holy assembly that you have taken and take N. for your lawful husband, whom you promise to obey, serving and being subject to him, living piously, keeping faith and loyalty to him in all things, as a faithful and loyal wife should to her husband, according to the Word of God and the holy Gospel?

The third phase of the liturgy combined blessing, prayer, and further biblical exhortation. The minister called on God to bless the new couple in the "holy estate" and "noble estate" to which "God the Father had called" them "for the love of Jesus Christ his Son." The minister quoted the familiar passage of Matthew 19:3–9, with its solemn warning, "what God has joined together, let no man put asunder." He enjoined the couple to live together in "loving kindness, peace, and union, preserving true charity, faith, and loyalty to each other according to the Word of God." The minister then led the couple and the congregation in a lengthy prayer. The prayer repeated much of the language of the opening biblical exhortation. It also called upon God to help the couple live together in holiness, purity, and uprightness, and to set good examples of Christian piety for each other and the broader community. The parties and congregation were then blessed with the final peace.

Compared with other Catholic and Protestant liturgies of the day, Calvin's wedding liturgy was long on instruction and short on ceremony. The liturgy was amply peppered throughout with choice biblical references, quotations, and paraphrases. The liturgy began and ended with lengthy biblical teachings on the respective duties of husband and wife. More biblical instruction was offered in the regular sermon for the day that followed immediately after the marriage liturgy. The lengthy vows again confirmed each party's godly duties in marriage, as did the concluding prayer. There was no Eucharist, no kneeling at the altar, no ritualistic clasping of hands, no lifting of the veil, no kissing of the bride, no exchange of rings, no delivery of coins, no music or singing – all of which were featured in other wedding liturgies of the day.[17] The Genevan wedding liturgy was to proceed, the preamble insisted, "respectably, religiously, and properly in good and decent order," so that the partners can "hear and listen to the holy Word of God that will be administered to them."

Calvin's wedding liturgy was a "beautiful collection of biblical texts," writes a leading historian of liturgy.[18] It was also a surprising collection, and not just because of its length and the number of biblical passages adduced. First, only two of the three traditional goods of marriage were referenced in the liturgy: mutual love and companionship and mutual protection from sexual sin. Nothing was said anywhere in the liturgy about the blessing and procreation of children. Though the liturgy referred to Genesis 1, it did not, like many other wedding liturgies, quote the familiar biblical instruction: "Be fruitful and multiply" (Gen. 1:28). Second, the natural qualities and duties of marriage were emphasized more than the spiritual. The opening exhortation did speak of "honorable holy matrimony instituted by God" and of the "sacred" obedience that a wife owed her husband. The final blessing did speak of the "holy estate" and "noble estate" of marriage. But much of the biblical exhortation, oaths, and final prayer were focused on the natural qualities of marriage: its origins in creation, the mandate of fleshly union, the need for mutual bodily sacrifice, the command of continence, the analogy of the body as the temple of God, the need for bodily purity. Not even the familiar analogies between marriage and the covenant between Yahweh and His elect or Christ and His Church were referenced. These emphases – together with the express prohibition on any Eucharistic celebration during the wedding, or even on the day of the wedding – underscored Calvin's fervent belief that marriage was both a natural and spiritual estate, but it was not a sacrament.

Calvin's marriage liturgy made it clear that the formation of marriage was a fundamental concern of the church community.[19] For three Sundays before the wedding, the church proclaimed the banns, which served as a general invitation not only for anyone to raise impediments but also for everyone to attend the wedding service. The wedding liturgy took place during a worship service. The wedding took place *in* the church, not at the church door, as was customary in some late-medieval liturgies, and certainly not in a private home, as was also

---

[17] See samples in Mark Searle and Kenneth W. Stevenson, *Documents of the Marriage Liturgy* (Collegeville, Minn., 1992); Molin and Mutembe, *Le rituel du mariage.*

[18] Kenneth Stevenson, *Nuptial Blessing: A Study of Christian Marriage Rites* (London, 1982), 131.

[19] Bryan D. Spinks, "The liturgical origins and theology of Calvin's Genevan marriage rite," *Ecclesia Orans* 3 (1986): 195–210, at 195, 208–10.

customary in some Protestant and Catholic communities.[20] The minister's duty, reads the preamble to the Marriage Liturgy, was "to approve and confirm this marriage before the whole assembly." The congregation was asked to consent to the marriage. Both husband and wife were asked to confirm their consent and to swear their vows again "before God and his holy assembly." The congregation was asked to join in congregational prayer for the blessing of the couple. While the minister presided at the wedding, he stood with the couple on the same level, not on the pulpit. His head was uncovered. He faced the couple and congregation throughout the ceremony. He made no turn to the altar as had been customary in medieval liturgies. And the entire liturgy was in the vernacular language, so that all could understand that in which they were participating. All this underscores that in Calvin's Geneva a wedding liturgy was very much a church affair, a public congregational event. Even the couple's parents and relatives had no special place in the wedding liturgy.

Calvin did not create his wedding liturgy from whole cloth. A good bit of this liturgy came from the "radical revision" introduced in Geneva by Guillaume Farel in 1533.[21] And Farel's wedding liturgy built, in part, on liturgical reforms introduced in the 1520s in Bern, Strasbourg, Zurich, and other Protestant cities.[22] Calvin downplayed the novelty of his wedding liturgy. When the Council of Bern later charged him with liturgical iconoclasm, Calvin insisted: "The form of marriage has always remained in its original state, and I follow the order which I found established like one who takes no pleasure in making innovations."[23] Calvin was being forgetful or perhaps too modest, for he had revised Farel's 1533 liturgy.[24] But Calvin also did not much care about the exact form of the liturgy. Wedding liturgies, he wrote, concerned "things indifferent [*adiaphora*], wherein the churches have a certain latitude of diversity." "[W]hen one has weighed the matter carefully, it may be sometimes considered useful not to have too rigid a uniformity respecting them, in order to show that faith and Christianity do not consist in that."[25] The event of a church wedding liturgy was essential to the validity of marriage. The exact form of the liturgy, however, was open to local variation.

---

[20] See examples in Steven Ozment, *When Fathers Ruled: Family Life in Reformation Europe* (Cambridge, Mass., 1983); idem, *The Bürgermeister's Daughter: Scandal in a Sixteenth-Century German Town* (New York, 1996); idem, *Ancestors: The Loving Family in Old Europe* (Cambridge, Mass., 2001).

[21] Searle and Stevenson, *Documents*, 227; Henri Vuilleumier, *Histoire de L'Église Réformée du pays de Vaud sous le régime Bernois*, 4 vols. (Lausanne, 1927–33), 1:310–314, 345–48.

[22] See also the influence of Bucer's reforms of marriage law, lore, and liturgy discussed in Elfriede Jacobs, *Die Sakramentslehre Wilhelm Farels* (Zurich, 1978); Herman J. Selderhuis, "Das Eherecht Martin Bucers," in Christoph Strohm (ed.), *Martin Bucer und das Recht* (Geneva, 2002), 185–99.

[23] April, 1555, CO 15:537–42. See also Letter to Ministers of Bern (February, 1537), CO 10/2:82–84.

[24] Spinks, "The liturgical origins."

[25] CO 15:537–42. On the meaning of *adiaphora* in Calvin's thought, see John L. Thompson, *John Calvin and the Daughters of Sarah: Women in Regular and Exceptional Roles in the Exegesis of Calvin, his Predecessors, and his Contemporaries* (Geneva, 1992), 227ff.

Marital Property

In sixteenth-century Geneva, as much as today, marriage was not only a union of persons. It was also a merger of properties: land, money, jewelry, clothing, household commodities, social titles, property rents, business interests, and sundry other "immovable" (real) property and "movable" (personal) property. When the parties were members of the aristocracy or the ruling class, a marriage could be the occasion for a massive exchange of power, property, and prerogatives that was distilled into lengthy written contracts. But even paupers who intended marriage generally made at least token exchanges of property and oral agreements about future transactions.

Although the marital property contract was often combined with a betrothal or marriage contract, these were actually independent agreements with different legal implications. For the marriage to be valid, a marriage contract, an oral or written agreement by the couple to marry, was essential. A marital property contract, an agreement to exchange property in anticipation or in consideration of marriage, was not essential. Indeed, a marital property contract could be negotiated and executed by other parties besides the couple, such as their relatives or guardians, with or without confirmation or even mention of the betrothal or marriage. To conjoin the marriage contract and marital property contract in one instrument was both prudent and efficient, but it was not legally necessary.[26]

Calvin and his fellow Genevan reformers made few changes in the prevailing *ius commune* on marital property.[27] The *ius commune* distinguished three types of marital property exchanges. First, a man accompanied his betrothal proposal with a gift to the woman of some sort and sometimes with a gift to her family as well. At minimum, the man offered the woman a token gift to signify his affection and to seal his betrothal promise: a ring, hat, flower, feather, kerchief, pin, bottle of wine, or some form of earnest money. A man of ample means could be more elaborate, offering expensive jewelry or clothing to his fiancée, or a horse and carriage to her or to her family. These gifts of betrothal to the prospective bride (or her family) may have been a carryover of a Germanic custom whereby a man paid a "purchase

---

[26] See chapter by R. H. Helmholz in this volume and idem, *Marriage Litigation in Medieval England* (London, 1974), 25–73.

[27] The sources at my disposal contain no special Genevan statutes on marital property, leading me to assume that the subject was governed by the canon law and civil law that prevailed in Geneva and in the Savoy, much of it comparable to prevailing French law in the neighboring regions. For detailed sources on this *ius commune* of marital property in this period, see Helmut Coing, *Handbuch der Quellen und Literatur der neueren europäischen Privatrechtsgeschichte*, 3 vols. (Munich, 1973–77), II/1:345–48. For particular local studies, see Antoine Flammer, *Le droit civil de Genève: ses principes et son histoire* (Geneva, 1875), 6–8, 13–16. For studies of early modern marital property law, see the chapter by Martha C. Howell in this volume and eadem, *The Marriage Exchange: Property, Social Place, and Gender in Cities of the Low Countries, 1300–1550* (Chicago, 1998); Alfred Havenkamp, *Haus und Familie in der spätmittelalterlichen Stadt* (Cologne, 1984).

price" to the woman's family for the right to marry her, often a rather hefty price. By the sixteenth century, this once lucrative windfall to the bride's family had become largely ceremonial.[28] To be sure, a few women (and their families) could still insist on a more elaborate betrothal gift, particularly if the woman was highly coveted or if a marital tie to her family was highly prized. But an elaborate betrothal gift was neither required nor customary in the sixteenth century.

If the betrothal ripened into marriage, the betrothal gift vested. It was now the woman's property (or her family's property, if they had received the gift), to be used or disposed of without interference from the donor man, even after the marriage. If the betrothal fell apart, it was customary for the woman (or her family) to return these gifts. Failure to return the gifts could lead to litigation in the secular courts for their recovery, particularly if the betrothal gift was an expensive piece of jewelry or clothing.

In the second type of marital property exchange, the woman and her family brought property into the marriage. This was called her dowry (*dos, dot*). The dowry consisted, at minimum, of the woman's clothing and personal effects, but the dowry usually involved a good deal more. Frequently, it included other movable property such as household furnishings and decorations, cooking utensils and linens, poultry and cattle, standing orders for newly harvested fruit and grain, and more. Sometimes, especially with an aristocratic marriage, the dowry was land, a house, a rental property, or a place of business. The type and value of the dowry were open to negotiation between the couple and their families (or representatives), but the dowry was often a very expensive proposition for the woman and her family. It was also an ample source of tension for the partners and their families during the marital property negotiations. It was not uncommon for the bride's family to give the woman (a portion of) her inheritance in advance to meet the high costs of a dowry.

Once delivered, the woman's dowry did not pass entirely beyond her control or that of her family. A portion of the dowry, called the "marriage portion," remained reserved to the woman and her family after the wedding; the remainder became the community property of the marriage. The type and the amount of dowry property included in the marriage portion were open to negotiation between the

---

[28] See Diane Owen Hughes, "From brideprice to dowry in Mediterranean Europe," in Marion A. Kaplan (ed.), *The Marriage Bargain: Women and Dowries in European History* (New York, 1985), 13–58. The betrothal or marriage gift, traditionally called the *pretium*, was sometimes called the dowry (*dos*), not to be confused with the kind of dowry discussed later in this chapter. According to Hughes, this gift was originally large and usually held by the family in Germanic law, but in due course, the gift grew smaller and was often held by the woman. See samples in *De Dot, tractatus ex variis iuris civilis interpretivis decerpti* (Louvain, 1569) and differentiation of terminology in Jack Goody, *The Development of the Family and Marriage in Europe* (Cambridge, 1983), 240–61. But note that even the Merovingian dotal charters in Zeumer's collection of Frankish formulae (discussed by Philip Reynolds in this volume) define a marriage gift (often called a *dos*), and sometimes a very large one, that went directly to the wife to confirm the betrothal.

couple and their families, but the marital property contract generally stipulated clearly that some portion (including the betrothal gift) was reserved. The wife could retain custody of this marriage portion (particularly her betrothal gift), but usually the husband controlled all the marital property, including the marriage portion. The property in the marriage portion, however, could not be sold, mortgaged, given away, or destroyed. The wife or her family had the right to retrieve the marriage portion when the marriage ended by annulment or death. They could also request the authorities to assign a *tuteur* over wastrel husbands who were suspected of squandering or damaging the wife's marriage portion. If the marriage portion had been invested, they could seek a portion of the profits as well, which was called the accrual (*addendum*). If the marriage portion had been damaged or destroyed, they could seek restitution of its value from the husband's own property. Once retrieved, the marriage portion and its accrual were redistributed within the wife's family, with priority given to the wife herself (if she survived) and to her children.

Third, not only did the wife reserve rights over a portion of her own property through the law of the marriage portion, but upon marriage, she also gained rights over a portion of her husband's property through the law of dower (*douaire*). Dower was a form of built-in insurance designed to provide for the wife upon her husband's death. If the wife became a widow, she would be entitled to one third to one half of all the movable property (not the land or immovable property) owned by her husband during the marriage. This was not just the movable property that the husband brought into the marriage or left at his death. Dower rights attached as well to any movable property that the husband acquired during the marriage, including, importantly, the movable property in his inheritance from his own family. The cumulative value of all that movable property was calculated on the husband's death, and the widow assigned her dower property. Typically the widow received a life estate or usufruct in this property: the right to use and possess the dower property for her lifetime, but with no right to sell or dispose of the property. This dower property would revert to the couple's children upon her death, or, in the absence of children, to her late husband's family. If the widow sold or gave away her dower property to third parties or damaged or destroyed it during her life estate, her children or her late husband's family could bring suits for its restitution when their reversionary interests vested.

Dower rights imposed an ample restriction on the husband's rights to dispose of his own movable property during the course of his married life. He could not simply sell, encumber, or give away his movable property without consideration of his wife's dower interests. Nor could he craft his last will and testament without taking these dower interests into account. After his death, his wife and the children could claim their dower rights against third parties who had acquired interests in the late husband's property without the wife's consent or without advance payment to her. Moreover, in cases in which a husband had squandered or misused all his movable property, or when he sought to give his entire estate to others, the wife could make priority claims on the balance of her husband's estate to have her dower interests made whole.

Although betrothed parties could negotiate about the types and amounts of property subject to dower, they could not renounce dower altogether. "To allow a woman to contract herself out of her [dower] rights would put her rights at the mercy of the unscrupulous."[29] The canon law, in particular, made dower mandatory and severely punished unscrupulous husbands who sought to avoid its effects through fancy property schemes. Only if the wife was convicted of adultery or malicious desertion of her husband – or, according to some canonists, if she was found guilty of mortal sin and excommunicated – would she forfeit her dower.[30]

A good illustration of this law of marital property can be seen in a 1536 marriage and marital property contract between a woman named Claude Bigot and the distinguished Genevan jurist Germain Colladon, who would later join Calvin in the leadership of the Genevan Reformation (Doc. 1). Germain Colladon was a well-heeled soul, son of an attorney and nephew of a judge in the nearby French city of Bourges. Bigot had lost her parents while still a youth, but she had inherited a good deal of money and property that was being held in trust by her grandmother. The grandmother was also Claude's guardian. The quite generous marital property agreement that she struck for Claude shows that she was a rather skilled negotiator.

The marital property contract was executed after the parties had executed their formal betrothal to marry. The agreement confirms that Germain and Claude promise to be married in the future (art. 2). Both their families give their consent to the pending union (art. 3) and become parties to the marital property agreement. The economics of the marriage, however, are the principal concern of the instrument. Claude, the future wife, promises to bring to the marriage an ample dowry of 1500 *livres*, composed of land, movables, and a yearly income drawn from Claude's inheritance. As a way of protecting themselves, Claude and her guardian grandmother agree to make the dowry payments in installments over two years, future payments presumably to be withheld if the marriage goes amiss or is annulled after the wedding. They also promise to furnish Claude's own clothing and ornaments (arts. 4, 5). They even promise substitute dowry payments if the projected yearly income from one of the dowry properties falls short (art. 11). One-third of this dowry (500 *livres*) is stipulated to become community property of the marriage, for the common use of husband and wife, which either party takes upon the death

---

[29] W. S. Holdsworth, *A History of English Law*, 17 vols. (London, 1922–66), 3:194–95. Contrary to the *ius commune* on the Continent, English common law dower attached to land and other immovable property, not to movable property, and it attached to one-third rather than to one-half of the husband's property.

[30] See an interesting case study of England, with comparative asides, in Paul Brand, "'Deserving' and 'undeserving' wives: Earning and forfeiting dower in medieval England," *Journal of Legal History* 22 (2001): 1–20.

of the other. Two-thirds of this dowry (1000 *livres*) is reserved as Claude's marriage portion (arts. 5, 6).

If Claude predeceases him, Germain, her future husband, promises to turn over to Claude's heirs this 1000 *livres* marriage portion, along with Claude's rings, clothing, and personal effects (art. 8). If Germain predeceases her and the couple has no children, Claude receives not only her 1000 *livres* marriage portion, but also her 500 *livres* contribution to the community property. Presumably, if there are children, the 500 *livres* goes to them. Moreover, Germain promises Claude a dower of one-half of his movable property of her choice, plus a stipulated monetary inheritance beyond this standard dower (arts. 7, 9). Germain's father also makes a gift of land to his son, in consideration of the marriage (art. 10). The *ius commune* would give Claude no rights over her husband's immovable property, and nothing in what survives of the contract changes that presumption.

Much of this traditional law and custom of marital property was unchanged by the Reformation in Geneva. Calvin may have written, or at least intended to write, more on the subject of marital property than has survived. The outline of his proposed Code of Civil Law and Civil Procedure for Geneva includes titles for separate entries on dower, dowry, and usufruct, as well as detailed titles on testamentary succession, which also would have dealt with the dower rights of widows.[31] It is unclear whether Calvin wrote these provisions in his proposed code; if he did, they have not survived. What has survived is a fragment of Calvin's proposed statute on the division of marital property in the event of a couple's formal separation (Doc. 2). But this fragment does not address the thorny question of dowry and marriage portion rights that a separation case would raise.

No other new statute on marital property was forged in Calvin's day. In 1568, however, which was four years after Calvin's death, the same Germain Colladon whom we encountered earlier prepared a lengthy new title on point for the new Civil Code of Geneva (Doc. 3). This was a sophisticated and comprehensive new legal code that remained in effect until the republican government of Geneva collapsed in 1792, as a result of the French Revolution.

The marital property provisions in the 1568 Civil Code largely repeated the traditional law of dowry that we have seen, yet it made one change that was potentially advantageous to women. The full amount of the dowry that the woman brought to the marriage was now presumptively her marriage portion, unless the parties stipulated otherwise. Her husband could use that property during their married life, but she was entitled to full recovery of all of it (arts. 3, 4, 6, 13) upon his death, as well as any accrued increase in its value (art. 5). Traditionally, a wife's marriage portion was on the order of one-third or one-half of the dowry.

The new marital property law also largely repeated the traditional law of dower. But it made two changes, both potentially harmful to widows. First, unless she could

[31] CO 10/1:130–31.

prove that her husband had deliberately sought to defraud her, a widow received no priority over other creditors in securing her dower interests from her late husband's estate (art. 17). This could well leave a widow with nothing, if her husband had been incompetent in managing his property or died heavily in debt. Second, a husband could order his heirs to support his widow upon his death. If she accepted their support, the widow would forfeit her dower interest and its accrued value. This provision could well expose widows to the designs of unscrupulous heirs. It was a notable departure from the canon law rule that a woman's dower rights could not be renounced under any condition, save her conviction for adultery or malicious desertion.

Not every marriage contract required the kind of detail that was set out in the 1568 Civil Code of Geneva. But the statute did seem to encourage Genevan parties to get their marital affairs in written order. Perhaps this reality dawned on the Genevan couple Michel Guichon and Pernette Cuvat, for in 1569, the year after the statute came into effect, the parties executed a simple marital contract to formalize a marriage they had already celebrated and consummated (Doc. 4). This was, evidently, a couple of modest means, and the partners agreed simply to merge their respective properties with full mutual rights of survivorship. In the event of children, Pernette would receive her stipulated marriage portion and then serve as trustee of the balance of the marital property, using it to support the children. All this was in perfect accord with the 1568 law.

Conditional Betrothal and Marriage Contracts

Although Calvin and his colleagues did not alter much of the law of marital property, the reformers did significantly change the laws governing contracts of betrothal or marriage that were made conditional on marital property transactions.

Conditional marriage contracts had become a rather complex topic by the early sixteenth century.[32] Late-medieval canonists and church courts regularly faced the question of what to do when a party contracted thus: I shall marry you "if my parents agree"; "after you have secured a job"; "provided you quit your military service"; "so long as the wedding takes place within six months"; "if we can live in my hometown"; "provided you pay me certain property"; "after my father dies"; "if God preserves me"; "so long as we have no children"; "if you can touch the sky"; "whenever a woman becomes pope"; "if you can drink the sea empty"; "provided you kill my rival" or any number of other such conditions. Did those promises automatically lapse if the condition was not met, or would the parties have to

---

[32] Rudolf Weigand, *Die bedingte Eheschliessung im kanonischen Recht*, 2 vols. (Munich, 1963–80), vol. 1; Bartholomew T. Timlin, *Conditional Matrimonial Consent: An Historical Synopsis and Commentary* (Washington, DC, 1934).

litigate? What if the conditions in question were impossible, silly, or downright illegal?

By the eve of the Reformation, the canonists had gathered a complex jurisprudence around these questions.[33] They herded conditional promises into a whole complex of categories. Three categories of conditions were the most important and common. "Honest possible" conditions ("if my parents consent," "so long as you move to Geneva by September 1," "provided you buy me a horse and carriage before the wedding") were valid, and betrothal or marriage promises could be voided on their breach. "Dishonest possible" conditions that vitiated an essential dimension of marriage ("so long as we have no children," "provided I may maintain a concubine," "so long as you remain unbaptized") were invalid and automatically voided the promises. All other conditions were generally disregarded, and the promises were enforced as if the condition had not been made. These included "dishonest possible" conditions that did not go to the essence of the marriage ("so long as you kill my rival") as well as conditions that were naturally or legally impossible ("if you empty the sea," "when a woman becomes pope").[34]

Calvin and his colleagues continued a good bit of the traditional law of conditions, though they simplified it considerably and explicitly outlawed the use of property conditions. The 1546 Marriage Ordinance had three provisions on conditional promises. Item 6 recognized that betrothal promises could be made "conditionally or otherwise." Item 14 made quite clear that property conditions would not be enforced: "Failure to pay a dowry or money or provide an outfit shall not prevent the marriage from coming into full effect, since these are only accessory." Item 15 was more ambiguous:

Although in discussing or arranging a marriage it is lawful to add conditions or reserve someone's consent, nevertheless when it comes to making the promise let it be pure and simple, and let a statement made conditionally not be regarded as a promise of marriage.

Read together with items 6 and 14, item 15 seems to say that betrothal contracts (those made "in discussing or arranging a marriage") could have non-property conditions attached to them, but marriage contracts had to be unconditional.

That was, in fact, how the Genevan authorities read and applied the 1546 Marriage Ordinance. Parties could seek annulment only of betrothal contracts, not of marriage contracts, on grounds of breach of condition. Those conditions not only had to be "honest and possible" but also had to go the essence of the budding marriage contract. Property or dowry payments were not considered essential conditions,

---

[33] Good early modern summaries are provided in Tómas Sánchez, *De sancto matrimonii sacramento disputationum* [1610] (Venice, 1712), bk. 5, disp. 1–19; Henry Swinburne, *A Treatise of Spousals, or Matrimonial Contracts* (London, 1686), 109ff.

[34] Helmholz, *Marriage Litigation*, 50ff.

and the Consistory disregarded them and enforced these betrothal contracts even if the parties had failed to deliver their promised property.

A good example of a valid conditional betrothal contract was the 1547 contract signed by a former Genevan named Helias who was now living in a nearby town of Neuchâtel (Doc. 5). No doubt instructed by counsel, Helias's fiancée had conditioned her marriage to him on proof that he was "not bound by any other marriage bond." The Neuchâtel authorities wanted to know from their Genevan counterparts whether Helias was already party to any betrothal or marriage contract. This condition did go to the essence of marriage, namely, whether Helias was, in fact, free to contract a new marriage. Calvin and his colleagues respected this condition. They certified to their Neuchâtel colleagues that Helias was not married or betrothed and thus was free to marry.

Another valid condition was for parties to accept betrothal proposals conditioned on the approval of their parents or guardians. The Genevan authorities usually respected these conditional betrothals, and annulled them when parental consent was not forthcoming. For parental consent, like individual consent, did go to the essence of the marriage, particularly if the party stipulating the condition was a minor. Indeed, in contracts involving minors (males under 20, females under 18), parental consent was as essential to the validity of the marriage as the consent of the couple.

In a 1552 case, for example, Pierre Sautier proposed to Rolanda in the presence of witnesses and gave her a golden ring (Doc. 6). She accepted his proposal, conditioned upon her parents' consent to the marriage. When her parents did not consent, Rolanda returned the ring to Pierre, who promptly became betrothed to another woman. When he was accused of bigamy, Pierre defended himself by saying that the first betrothal contract was voided automatically by the breach of the condition of parental consent. The authorities agreed. Similarly, in a 1556 case, a young woman named Guigonne conditioned her consent to Hugo Cant's proposal on the consent of her parents (Doc. 7). The parents dissented, and Guigonne petitioned the Consistory to annul her betrothal. Although her parents were Catholics (whose views were not much respected in Geneva), and Guigonne gave only hearsay testimony of their dissent, the Consistory respected this breach of condition and declared the betrothal contract "void and fraudulent."[35]

Contrast the conditions in these cases with the condition that new émigrés to Geneva frequently asked the Consistory to enforce: "I shall marry you, provided you move to Geneva with me." This was the issue in a 1554 case of Jean Philippe and Anne Renaud (Doc. 8). The Consistory did not respect this condition and upheld the betrothal contract of Jean and Anne. Their principal rationale was that the stipulated condition was a matter ancillary to the essence of marriage. Where

---

[35] It is not entirely clear from the record whether it was the lack of parental consent or the danger of interreligious marriage that motivated the Consistory. There is nothing to indicate why the contract was called "fraudulent."

a married couple would live after their wedding was hardly relevant to the core question whether they were fit, competent, and eligible to give their mutual consent to marriage. Jean and Anne had given their free and full consent, and they would have to proceed with their marriage, even if they ultimately lived elsewhere.

The Consistory dealt similarly with betrothal contracts that included property conditions. Already in a 1545 case, for example, the Consistory summoned Louis Piaget and his fiancée to inquire why they had not married (Doc. 9). It turned out that Louis was awaiting payment of a rather handsome dowry by his fiancée's master, and his fiancée had meanwhile returned to live with her father. The Consistory inquired closely whether the only issue was over property. When that proved to be the only obstacle, the Consistory ordered the couple to get married and sent the fiancée's master to the Council, who ordered him to pay the promised dowry.

The Consistory ruled similarly in two cases the following year. Jean de Landécy and Mia had become properly betrothed before witnesses (Doc. 10). Mia had promised Jean a dowry of money to be paid in installments. Because she had not been able to collect money owed to her, however, Mia had substituted various household items and tools for her first dowry installment. Jean had accepted the goods but evidently wanted his dowry money as well and threatened to break off the betrothal. Mia promised to try to fulfill her dowry demands. That was good enough for the Consistory to remand the case to the Council, with a recommendation that marriage be required. The Council ordered the couple to marry.

Similarly, Nicolard Adduard and Jehanne had been properly betrothed before witnesses (Doc. 11). Jehanne's uncle had made an unconditional promise of supplying a dowry of money, cattle, and all their household goods. When the uncle failed to deliver, Jehanne argued that she had been swindled and that she wished neither to marry nor to furnish substitute dowry. Nicolard wanted to marry only if he could get his hands on the promised dowry. The parties fell into bitter dispute and pled to be released from their betrothal. The Consistory would hear nothing of breaking the betrothal over a dowry dispute. They sent the parties to the Council. The Council ordered them to marry, notwithstanding Jehanne's continued protests.

The 1552–53 case of Thomas Bonna and Claudine de Loelmoz illustrates that a man could not condition his consent to marriage upon full and exact satisfaction of the dowry promise (Doc. 12). Thomas betrothed Claudine and gave her a golden ring, but he conditioned his promise on her delivery of a cash dowry – not land, goods, or other property. Claudine brought several casks of wine and other property. Thomas accepted them, but continued to insist on the promised cash dowry. When that was not forthcoming, he sought to annul the betrothal. The Consistory would hear none of it. The betrothal promise and the dowry promise were separate agreements, the Consistory insisted. Breach of the dowry promise could not be used as a ground for dissolving the betrothal, particularly if a man tendered a betrothal gift as Thomas had done. The case, which bounced back and forth between the Consistory and Council for more than a year, was an important precedent. Had Bonna prevailed, it would have been easy enough for a man or his father to demand perfect tender of a dowry before giving his consent to the marriage. This would defeat the principle on which Calvin had insisted – that questions of marital property were to remain ancillary to questions of the validity of the betrothal and marriage contract itself.

Summary and Conclusions

In Calvin's Geneva, as much as today, marriage was a contract between a fit man and a fit woman of the age of consent. Marriage was much more than a contract. It was also a spiritual, social, natural, and economic unit that could involve many other parties besides the couple. But marriage was never less than a contract. It could not be created unless both the man and the woman consented voluntarily to this union.

Calvin and his colleagues took pains to ensure the free and full consent of both parties. The 1546 Marriage Ordinance of Geneva required that engagement and marriage promises be made "simply" and "honorably," without "trick" or "surprise." The Consistory annulled engagement and marriage contracts procured by physical force or threat of force, or through fraud, deception, or seduction. They also annulled frivolous and drunken promises. The Consistory respected conditions to engagement contracts that went to the essence of marriage – such as conditioning one's own consent on the consent of one's parents. But they had no patience with other conditions about ancillary matters – such as conditioning one's consent on the other's delivery of marital property. These conditional engagement contracts were enforced regardless of whether the ancillary condition had been breached, and regardless, too, of whether this breach now put the couple at such odds that they both wanted out. The mutual consent of the parties was essential to form the engagement contract; but once properly formed, the engagement contract could not be dissolved even by mutual consent.

The wedding liturgy was the final essential step in the validation of marriage in Calvin's Geneva. It represented the community's consent to the marriage, as expressed by their magistrates and ministers. Magistrates voiced their consent through the signing and validation of the banns and the registration of the new couple's marriage contract and marital property. Ministers voiced their consent through the announcement of the banns and the celebration of the wedding liturgy.

Calvin took banns and weddings as seriously as he had taken the earlier stages of marriage formation. For him, wedding preparations and celebrations were solemn steps in the final divine confirmation and validation of a marriage. These final steps of marriage could not be rushed. Parties would have to start over if they failed to announce their banns or celebrate their weddings properly. These final steps of marriage also could not be ruined by subsequent drunkenness, dancing, or debauchery at the wedding party. This insulted the marital vows that the couple had just taken to be moral exemplars to each other and the community.

Calvin also took seriously the need for a delay between betrothals and weddings. The point of a public betrothal and waiting period was to invite others to weigh in on the maturity and compatibility of the couple, to offer them counsel and commodities, and to prepare for the celebration of their union and their life together thereafter. And it was to prepare their families and congregations to give their solemn consent to this budding union. Too long a betrothal would encourage the couple to fornication, but too short a betrothal would discourage them from introspection. Too secret a wedding would deprive couples of the essential counsel and commodities of their families and friends, but too open a wedding would deprive couples of the consent and confirmation of the community that counted. Too solemn a wedding ceremony would smother the joy that a new marital love should bring, but too raucous a wedding party would trespass the duties that the new marriages had just brought. Calvin thus strove to strike a judicious balance between betrothal and wedding, publicity and privacy, waiting and consummating, celebration and moderation.

These reforms of marriage contracts, ceremonies, and settlements were part and product of a much larger transformation of the theology and law of marriage in sixteenth-century Geneva and well beyond. Building on a generation of Protestant reforms, Calvin constructed a comprehensive new theology and jurisprudence that made marital formation and dissolution, children's nurture and welfare, family cohesion and support, and sexual sin and crime essential concerns for both church and state. Working with other jurists and theologians, Calvin drew the Consistory and Council of Geneva into a creative new alliance to govern domestic and sexual subjects. Together, these authorities outlawed monasticism and mandatory clerical celibacy and encouraged marriage for all fit adults. They set clear guidelines for courtship and engagement. They mandated parental consent, peer witness, church consecration, and state registration for valid marriage. They radically reconfigured weddings and wedding feasts. They reformed marital consent and impediments. They created new rights and duties for wives within the bedroom and for children within the household. They streamlined the grounds and procedures for annulment. They introduced fault-based divorce for both husbands and wives on grounds of adultery or desertion. They encouraged the remarriage of divorcées and widow(er)s. They punished rape, fornication, prostitution, sodomy, and other sexual felonies with startling new severity. They put firm new restrictions on dancing, sumptuousness, ribaldry, and obscenity. They put new stock in catechesis and education and created new schools, curricula, and teaching aids. They provided new sanctuary to illegitimate, abandoned, and abused children. They created new protections for abused wives and impoverished widows. Many of these reforms of sixteenth-century Geneva were echoed and elaborated in numerous Calvinist communities, on both sides of the Atlantic, and a good number of these reforms found their way into our modern civil law and common law of domestic relations.

What made this Calvinist reformation of sex, marriage, and family life so resolute and resilient was that it was a top-to-bottom reformulation of ideas and institutions, theology and law, learning and living. Calvin set out his legal reforms in scores of new statutes and consilia that were applied and adapted in hundreds of cases that came before the Genevan authorities. He set out his theological reforms in hundreds of sermons, commentaries, and systematic writings that were echoed and elaborated by a whole army of Reformed preachers and theologians in succeeding decades, ultimately on both sides of the Atlantic. He set out his pastoral advice in literally thousands of letters and pamphlets that ultimately catalyzed a whole industry of Protestant household manuals – the spiritual Dr. Spocks of their day – that would continue to be produced in the Anglo-American tradition until well into the nineteenth century.

Appendix

Document 1:
Marriage Contract of Germain Colladon and Claude Bigot (1536)[1]

1. Master Germain Colladon[2] the younger, attorney at law, of the one part, and the respectable Claude Bigot, daughter of the late honorable, respectable, and august Master Nicolas Bigot, during his lifetime counselor of our lord the king and lieutenant-general of the baliff of Berry, and of the respectable Cathérine Charrier his wife . . . by the respectable Guymon Thévernin, widow of the late Ythier Charrier, her maternal grandmother, for her of the other part.

2. Which parties have stated that a marriage by words *de futuro* has been agreed to between the said Master Germain Colladon and the said Claude Bigot according to the agreements, articles, and decisions which follow, by which the said Colladon, by the advice, counsel, and judgment of the honorable, respectable, and august Masters Germain Colladon, judge and warden of La Chastre, his father, Léon Colladon, attorney, counselor, and barrister of Bourges, his brother, [and] Urbain Chauveton, his brother-in-law . . . has promised to take the said Claude Bigot as wife and spouse.

---

[1] Original in Bourges, Arch. dép. E4453 (minutes of the notary Jean Ragueau), ancien: 4453, reprinted in Erich-Hans Kaden, *Le jurisconsulte Germain Colladon, ami de Jean Calvin et de Théodore de Bèze* (Geneva, 1974), 141–43. The ellipses and fragments are per the reprinted text.

[2] "Colladon" is rendered variously in the contract as "Collaidon" and "Coilhaidon."

3. Likewise the said Claude Bigot by the will... counsel of the said Guymon Thévenin, her said grandmother, and by the advice of the prudent and respectable Robert Bigot, paternal uncle of the said Claude, and of the honorable, respectable, and august Master Léon Colladon, Jean Artuys, [and] Jean Deschamps, brothers-in-law of the said Claude, has promised to take the said Master Germain Colladon as husband and spouse, if God, etc.

4. And in favor and expectation of the said marriage the said Guymon Thévenin, the aforesaid grandmother, having the administration of the bodies and goods of Masters Nicolas and Pierre Bigot..., of Etienne and Madeleine Bigot, and of the said Claude, all minor children of the said late Master Nicolas Bigot and the late Cathérine Charrier, has promised and promises to pay and give to the said future spouses from the goods fallen in by succession from the said deceased and which are common to the said minor children the sum of 1500 *livres tournois*, and this to cover all rights falling and payable to the said Claude by the said succession from the said deceased, that is:

(a) For the sum of 300 *livres tournois*, a house as it stands, situated in this city of Bourges on the rue d'Oron next to....

(b) Also for the sum of 200 *livres*, the sum of 13 *livres tournois* of rents....

(c) Also for the sum of 260 *livres tournois*, a body of land in several parcels situated near this city of Bourges, acquired by the said late Master Nicolas Bigot from the widow of the late Bélin.

(d) Also the sum of 140 *livres tournois* in movables.

(e) Also the sum of 600 *livres tournois* in cash, the sum of 400 *livres* on the day of the nuptial blessing by the said Guymon Thévenin, the aforesaid grandmother, and the sum of 200 *livres tournois* within two years, counting from the day and date of the present act.

(f) And the said widow shall clothe... the said Claude with wedding clothes and garments well and properly according to her estate, by the judgment and decision of herself and of the other relatives and friends of the said Claude.

5. And it was stated and agreed that of the said sum of 1500 *livres tournois*, the sum of 1000 shall be accounted a personal inheritance for the said future wife... and the sum of 500 *livres tournois* shall be accounted movables. And this... the goods, movables, and acquisitions... that they gain and acquire during the said marriage are and shall remain common to the said future spouses.

6. Also it was agreed between the said parties that if the said future wife should happen to pass from life to death before the said future husband without legitimate descendants of the said marriage, the said future husband shall be required to render to the heirs of the said future wife the said sum of 1000 *livres tournois* accounted as an inheritance, or the inheritance which shall have been acquired with the said sum, and the common goods of... and

the said sum of 500 *livres* accounted as movables or that which . . . shall have been . . . without the said heirs of the said Claude being able to claim any common right in the goods and joint estate of the said future husband.

7. Also if it happens that the said future husband passes from life to death before the said future wife without or with legitimate descendants of the said marriage, she shall have a right of choice and election of her common property from the goods, movables, and acquisitions of the said future husband along with the heirs of the said future husband, and in so choosing the said common goods, she shall take and have the sum of 500 *livres* only for her said inheritance and half of the movables and acquisitions, and in case she makes a choice and promise of marriage and does not wish to take her said community property, she shall have for an inheritance the said sum of 1000 *livres tournois*, and if . . . and the said 500 *livres* accounted as movables and the said. . . .

8. And whatever goods she chooses, she shall have in addition her jewelry and her . . . in whatever amount they may be and the dower . . . as a stipulated addition, and shall have time and space for making the said choice of three months, counted from . . . of the said husband, during which time she shall live off the community goods without . . . of her said choice.

9. And whichever choice she makes, the said future husband . . . one or the other,[3] in case there are children of the said marriage, of the sum of 30 *livres tournois* of rents only for the life of the said Claude, or the sum of 300 *livres* paid all at once, and in case there are no children of the said marriage, one or other of the said sum of 30 *livres tournois* of rents during her life or the sum of . . . 400 *livres tournois* paid all at once, at the choice and election of the said Claude Bigot.

10. And also the said Master Germain Colladon . . . in favor of the said marriage both gives and gives by act . . . by pure and simple and irrevocable gift . . . solemnly *inter vivos* to the said Master Germain Colladon, his said son, . . . and he accepts a meadow . . . located and situated in . . . [the] outskirts of La Chastre next to the road . . . going from . . . from the said town to Nevers . . . next to the meadow of Germain B . . . next to the vineyard of Simon and . . . and this as a marriage gift,[4] and also . . . to the said Master Germain Colladon and to his future . . . of the said Master Germain . . . of the said meadow. . . .

11. Also it was further stated and agreed that in case it is found that the rent of the said Orron house and for the said . . . and the said body of land in La Chastre do not come to the sums aforesaid at which they have been rated, in the said case the said widow . . . pay to the said future husband the sums and . . . at which they have been estimated and rated within three years, or the

---

[3] The French phrase is *douche et douche.*

[4] The French word is *préciput,* meaning in this case a sum given at marriage, without prejudicing his right to an equal inheritance with his siblings on his father's death.

lowest value . . . the said Claude shall promise to return in dividing with her said brothers and sisters . . . the aforesaid goods or that which . . . shall be.

12. . . . pledged . . . of the august Senate and given at Bourges the twenty-fifth day of the month of June of the year 1536 before the respectable Jean Ragueau . . . merchant residing in Bourges and the prudent and respectable François Deschamps, residing . . . to the witnesses summoned.

    Ragueau

DOCUMENT 2:
Fragment of Calvin's Draft Ordinance on Matrimonial Property (undated)[5]

Moreover, because otherwise we could not bring them to an agreement, we have ordered and order that beforehand and ahead of everything they must make an inventory both of their merchandise and of the business they do, debts, bonds, and everything else depending on it, and of their movables, utensils, common possessions, and purchased property. Let them settle and close their accounts and so arrange between them that there is a definite resolution, to put an end to all previous quarrels, and so that from this time on each may know what is his, so that there may be no retraction.

And we desire this to be done as soon as possible, at the latest within a year, without formal proceedings, but peaceably and with goodwill. If it happens that one of the parties does not want to consent to this – that is, to making such an inventory and settling their accounts without a suit or going to court – the other shall have the option and liberty of renouncing the present agreement and returning to his first course [of legal action?].

This being done, it shall be our desire that the two parties live together, keeping a common household as they have done until now, both for their own contentment and repose and to avoid the gossip of the world and the scandal that might result from their separation.

Nevertheless, since we cannot get them to agree to this, we order[6] that the separation be carried out when the accounts are finished, that is within a year. So that they must separate and each withdraw himself peaceably,[7] under penalty of returning to their previous condition, that is that each respectively should continue in the rights and actions he had taken as though this present agreement had never been made.

Nevertheless, if it happens afterwards that for the ease and convenience of the two parties or of one of them it seems proper to them to arrange and carry out a separation, we leave them at liberty to do this.

---

[5] CO 10/1:143–44.

[6] Calvin first wrote: "Nevertheless, if it cannot be done otherwise and both the parties prefer to live separately, or one of the two desires this, we order. . . . "

[7] Original text: "they are mutually obligated to separate, each at the other's request. . . . "

DOCUMENT 3:

Civil Edicts (January 29, 1568)[8]

Title XIV/Marriages, Dowries, Dowers, and Accrual[9]

1. The age, authority, and consent required for marriage are stated in the Ecclesiastical Ordinances [of 1561].

2. Guardians or trustees may not establish contracts or promises to marry between themselves or their relatives and those under their authority during the period of their authority and until they have surrendered their accounts and the residue of their trust; after having done so, they may not contract or make promises [of marriage] without the relatives' consent.

3. If there is no express provision of a dowry, conveyed and granted at the marriage, all of the wife's property will be deemed assigned and constituted as the dowry, and the husband will have its use and usufruct during the marriage to defray costs. And the husband must make an inventory of the property and give his wife proper acknowledgment of it, to serve her and hers in case of restitution.

4. The dowry provided, of whatever it consists and from whomever it derives, is assigned to the wife as her property to dispose of and devise to her heirs, unless there is a contrary agreement and exception in the contract establishing it.

5. The law of increase [addendum] and accrual is that, unless it is otherwise agreed, half of the value of the dower[10] will be given to the wife from her husband's assets as a life estate, she giving warranty that after her death the capital will be returned to be preserved for the children of the marriage, if there are any; otherwise it will belong entirely to her.

6. And if the dowry does not consist of money but of real property or other goods rather than money, the value of the goods will be appraised by knowledgeable people to establish and assess the said accrual at the rate of one third of the value of the goods which the husband will have had the use of because of his wife.

7. If a daughter married by her father has some property from her mother's side, and when providing the dowry her father does not state from whose

---

[8] SD, vol. 3, item no. 1081.

[9] The French word for dowry is *dot*, denoting the property that a woman brings into a marriage or sometimes receives at the time of marriage from her family. The French word for dower is *douaire*, denoting in this case a wife's (and widow's) life interest in a portion of her (late) husband's property – at least in theory, for although the statute's title makes this linguistic distinction, the text throughout uses only the term *dot/dottes*. Where it is obvious that the text is referring to "dower" rather than "dowry," we have translated *dot* as "dower."

[10] Here is an instance where *dot* seems to mean "dower," not "dowry." Item 4 had just indicated that the dowry (*dot*) is the wife's property to be disposed of at her will. Item 5 says that the dower (*dot*), however, is only a life estate interest, with remainder interest in the children.

property it is derived, the dowry will be presumed to come from the father's property, and her maternal property will be preserved to her.

8. And if a mother or grandmother, having authority over her daughter, provides a dowry on her marriage without declaring from whose property it derives, the said provision will be imputed to her paternal property; and if this does not suffice, the remainder of the dowry will be taken from the property of the mother or grandmother.

9. Those joined in marriage may not convey to each other during their lifetimes, at death, or by will more than half of their property derived from their parents to the prejudice of their parents in direct line or their brothers and sisters in collateral line. But they may dispose at will of the property they have acquired [during the marriage].

10. And if they have children they may not convey or devise to each other's benefit more than the usufruct of a third of their property. But the husband may leave to his wife the entire usufruct of all his property for the purpose of supporting his children, and this usufruct will last until the children reach the age of majority or marry.

11. Someone who marries a second time, having children by a previous marriage, may not convey property to his or her spouse for the said marriage or during it in excess of the portion of that one of his or her said other children to whom the least has been given.

12. What has been conveyed from one of those joined in marriage to the other whether by contract, will, or other disposition will revert to the children of the said marriage after the donee's death, even if the donation included the power to dispose of it at the donee's wish.

13. If a wife survives her husband she will have and retain the dresses, rings, and jewelry that she brought to her husband [at the marriage], to dispose of at her pleasure. As for dresses, rings, and jewelry that she received from her husband before or during the marriage, these, like her accrual, will be subject to restitution to the children, unless it has been stated otherwise in the marriage contract or the will.

14. But if the wife dies before her husband her heirs may demand of her husband only the dresses, rings, and jewelry found to be those that she brought to him on contracting or during the marriage, unless she has disposed of them differently.

15. A wife convicted of adultery will lose her dowry,[11] and the said dowry will be given to her husband unless she has children by a previous

---

[11] It is a closer question whether *dot* here means "dower" or "dowry." It was a commonplace of the *ius commune* that a wife sacrifices her dower interest if convicted of adultery or malicious desertion, but normally only the children of the present marriage, not those of her prior marriage, would inherit her dower interests. Thus it could well be that the statute is referring to her dowry (which all her legitimate children, by whatever marriage, would inherit).

marriage, in which case these children will receive only their own reserved portions.[12]

16. A widow, if she fornicates, will lose and render the accrued value of her dower to her husband's heirs. And if she was one of his heirs she will lose her inheritance to the designated substitute, or in default of such, to her husband's closest relatives.

17. Women owed dowers will not be preferred to creditors who hold previous bonds or mortgages, except for property that was expressly acquired using the dower money and without fraud.

18. If a wife, after the death of her husband, carries away or hides any goods belonging to her said husband, on being duly convicted of this she will be required to make restitution of three times the value of the goods taken, with deprivation of her accrual and of other goods given to her by her husband.

19. If a husband, by will or otherwise, has ordered that his wife be supported by his heirs during her widowhood, if she wishes to accept this provision, then during that time she may not recover either her dower [?][13] or its accrued value.

20. If a husband sells some of his wife's real property, even with her consent, she will be recompensed with the price set on it from her husband's property, unless the said amount has been used for her or for other purchases for her benefit.

21. If a husband has purchased property in his wife's name during their marriage she may not retain the said property unless she pays over its price or proves that it was purchased with her money.

DOCUMENT 4:
Marriage Contract of Michel Guichon and Pernette Cuvat (1569)[14]

Let it be known and manifest to all that a marriage was recently contracted and duly solemnized and carried out in the Christian church of this city between the Honorable Michel, son of the late François Guichon, of Mésigny, boatman, resident of Geneva on one part, and Pernette, daughter of the late Egrege Claude Cuvat of Geneva on the other part, without anything concerning the said marriage having been reduced to writing, as the parties state.

Now today, the fourth of the month of April, 1569, before me, the undersigned notary public, and the witnesses named below, there appeared personally the aforesaid Michel Guichon and Pernette Cuvat, his wife. The parties,

---

[12] The reserved portion (*légitime* in French) was the amount of an estate required to be left to a child or other natural heir, regardless of the amount willed elsewhere.

[13] Here it is not clear whether *dot* denotes dowry or dower. It was not uncommon in the day to calculate not only the original value of the dowry but also its accrued or increased value, which was called the *addendum*. See J. F. Poudret, "La situation du conjoint survivant en pays de Vaud XIIIᵉ–XVIᵉ siècle," *Mémoires de la societé pour l'histoire du droit des anciens pays bourguignons, comtois et romands* 27 (1966), 1.

[14] Archives d'État de Genève, Notaires, Aimé Santeur, v. 2, folios 128v–129v. Paragraph breaks have been added to the original.

in consideration of this marriage and following the agreement made when it was contracted, of their own free will, for themselves and all their heirs, have taken and take each other, for whatever goods they have at present or may have afterwards, whether movable, immovable, gold, silver, deeds, titles, or claims of any sort, so that the survivor will be and remain the sole and exclusive heir of the first decedent.

If, however, it pleases God to give them children by the present marriage, the wife after the death of her husband will take and receive from all the property of Guichon her husband the sum of fifty florins in all, together with the furnished bed she has brought to Guichon and all clothing, rings, and jewels and all movables she has brought to him, which are here taken to be specified. Guichon consents and is content that Pernette his wife will then act with a good and healthy conscience to manage and dispose of the whole [marital property] at her good pleasure and will.

So the said parties have promised and sworn by an oath taken before me, the undersigned notary, having agreed to keep good, firm, and valid the present act and to preserve, observe, and inviolably accomplish all its contents without ever contradicting or contravening it in any way or manner whatever. For this purpose, they have pledged and expressly hypothecated all their goods whatever, movable and immovable, present and future, which, for the complete observation of the present contract, they have submitted and submit to all the course and rigor of the law where they are found, renouncing all rules, laws, statutes, edicts, and privileges by which they might aid and serve themselves to contradict what is written above, notably the rule that says that a general renunciation is not valid if a specific one does not precede it. For which purpose the said parties have indeed asked that each of them be provided a contract made publicly according to the advice and correction of knowledgeable people, without changing its substance.

Concluded and enacted in Geneva in the house of the couple Claude Tosspot and Jean Bonnex, boatmen, citizens of Geneva, Jean Samoen, cobbler, and Jacques Marquis, also a cobbler, both residents of Geneva, being present as the required witnesses, and I, Aymé Santeur, the undersigned notary.

Santeur

DOCUMENT 5:
Letter of Attestation to Neuchâtel (1547)[15]

To the faithful servants and pastors of Christ in the church at Neuchâtel, both in the city and in the country, our beloved brethren and colleagues: Because our brother Helias who dwells among you wrote that a woman had betrothed herself to him on condition that, before the marriage was solemnized, he should certify to you by proper testimonies that he was not bound by any

---

[15] Philip E. Hughes (ed. and trans.), *The Register of the Company of Pastors of Geneva in the Time of Calvin* (Grand Rapids, 1966), 64.

other marriage bond, at his request we appointed two from our college to inquire into this matter. After investigation, they reported to us as follows: that six men and one woman of acknowledged repute declared with one voice that Helias was known to them in La Rochelle when he was a priest in the church first of St. Nicholas and afterwards of St. Bartholomew, that he lived honorably among men without any whisper of fornication, that he never publicly had a wife there, and that there was never any rumor of a private or secret marriage known to them. Accordingly, they hold him to be a man free from any marriage tie. We wished this to be testified to you lest we should fail in our duty to our brother.

DOCUMENT 6:
Case of Pierre Sautier (1552)[16]

(June 9, 1552) Pierre Sautier, a laborer from Chézery but now living in this city, was remanded by Master Raymond [Chauvet] because it is proved that he has promised [marriage to] two girls. He denied having broken off anything [with the first woman from Chézery] because she had conditioned [that is, she could not accept his proposal] if her parents did not consent. Afterwards he left this woman from Chézery, and she returned a sou he had given her for earnest money. As for the other [woman], who was from Présilly, he also left her because the lord of the town to which she is subject wanted to compel him to go live in the place and pay him homage, which he did not want to do. For the promise to the first woman, Mollex, Jaquet, and Grandjean were present at his house; for the promise to the second, there was a maid of Peytrequin's who was in the presence of the Peytrequin and his wife, and he told them he had sworn faith to the other woman and they had separated.

Decided: considering his confession, that we summon for Thursday the witnesses who were at the promise. He said there was also a carpenter named Pierre Bibet, a carpenter near the house of Master Amied Le Barbier, and Mollex, who has always been at all his promises, and Jaquet.

(June 16, 1552) Jaques Danton of Tagnigo, Jean Mollies of Beaumont, and Jean Bocquet of Peillonnex, laborer, witnesses against Pierre Sautier, were asked whether they know he is married. They said they were present when Sautier promised [marriage to] a girl named Rolanda, then a maid in Bon, who is from Chézery. It was at his house and about Christmas. They drank together and he gave her a sou; nevertheless she made a reservation that she wanted to inform her parents. Mollies further said that about three weeks ago he was at Peytrequin's, and he [Sautier] also promised [marriage to] a maid named Georges, drank, and gave her a sou also. But afterwards he and

---

[16] Robert M. Kingdon (gen. ed.), *Registres du Consistoire de Genève au temps de Calvin*, 21 vols. (Geneva, 1996–). Vols. 1–3 are in print. Vols. 4–21 are unpublished, but a transcription is available in the Meeter Center, Calvin College and Seminary, Grand Rapids, Michigan (hereafter R. Consist.). This case is in R. Consist. VII, 46, 48.

she did not keep their promise, and he made her return the earnest money. Afterwards he promised [marriage to yet] another woman named Pernette who was a maid of Plonjon's, for which banns are to be proclaimed. A laborer named Claudon, called Le Neyret, was present.

Decided: that he be remanded before the Council, asking them to get to the bottom of the case, since he has promised [marriage] to three wives [i.e., fiancées], and to have them called to learn the character of such separations, which are not to be tolerated. Also to learn who were present. Also Mollies was remanded, who was present at two promises. Also return them their banns. Note to compare [the records].

DOCUMENT 7:
Case of Guigonne Copponay and Hugo Cant (1556)[17]

(August 6, 1556.) Guigonne, daughter of Claude Copponay, and Hugo Cant who presented a petition concerning a promise of marriage [between the two of them]. The petition stated that she made a condition [of her promise to marriage] of having the advice of her parents and that they do not wish to consent to it. The aforesaid [Cant] said it is true, and denied the bulk of the petition.

Decided: that they return here for Thursday and bring her parents and that he bring Jean Bellet, their host, and the witnesses in her petition to settle it finally. She will bring them; apply to the basket-maker in the Mollard.

(Aug. 13, 1556.) Jean Bellot, Claude de Noyer, Tivent Tornier, and Guigonne Copponay were admonished that it has come to notice that they came to a tavern [at Bellot's] against the ordinances and commit insolences there. They said he has leave for it from the Lieutenant, for the day-laborers. They were also admonished that it has come to notice that in Bellot's cellar a certain promise of marriage was made. Bellot said that it is true that he saw both them and others who drank in his cellar. They called the girl who passed by and made her drink with a carter from the house of the host of the Bear. [The facts are] as [they are stated] in the contents of the petition on her behalf, except that she consented and was quite content, and she was admonished to ask her parents.

Decided: that De Noyer who ... proposed making such a marriage should also be remanded before the Council to be punished. And as for the marriage, it is void and fraudulent. Since the fiancé is from the papacy and she from St. Julien, let everyone proceed as they wish concerning them and their carter. Also Bellot is to be admonished for selling [wine] as in a tavern.

[*On August 17 the Council decided to examine the parties more fully, particularly whether Guigonne had stipulated that she must get the approval of her relatives. The record says nothing further about this examination.*]

---

[17] R. Consist. XI, 48, 49, 50.

DOCUMENT 8:

Case of Jean Philippe and Anne Renaud (1554)[18]

(Dec. 6, 1554.) Jean Philippe, Jaques Renaud, his wife, and their daughter Anne, all masons, were admonished that Philippe presented a petition, whose contents are that in the city of Paris they promised him the girl on condition of marrying her where they were going, and he gave her a silver ring in marriage. They confessed it, but now they do not want to consent to it, and as for the ring, she returned it to him, and he did not want to marry her there. The girl [Anne] said that she consented to it against the will of her mother, which the mother also said. She was asked separately whether she is promised to another; she said no, and as for another ring, said she bought it, asking that she be freed from such a promise, because he has boasted of leaving her.

Decided: that they be exhorted to accomplish the marriage; otherwise, if they do not wish to do it, let them be remanded before the Council, and no reason is known why such a marriage should be dissolved. The father said that he asks that he be given strict remonstrances, and that there would be no impediment according to God. Philippe was admonished separately that it has come to notice that he has maligned the [true] religion and the city. He denied it, and promised to be obedient to them.

DOCUMENT 9:

Case of Louis Piaget and Fiancée (1545)[19]

(Oct. 15, 1545.) Louis Piaget and the Bordons' maid were called to learn about their quarrel, because they are engaged, and how it happens that they have broken their promise and why they do not want to have the wedding. Levet's widow spoke certain verbose words about the girl, also about the Bordons. Also that Donne Claudine provided for him fully 200 florins p.p. [*petit poids*], and it was pledged by Monsieur Julian Bordon, or otherwise he did not make the promise, urging the need he has to provide in his business for what he owes and endures.

The girl was asked whether she agrees to marriage and whether the difference is only over money. [She testified that it was] because he says that her father obligated himself to Jullian for sum of 200 florins which Bordon had promised to [her prospective] husband Piaget.

Decided: [the prospective] husband was made to withdraw, and the fiancée was admonished for having gone back to her father and for having followed their papalist practice.

Decided: Monsieur Claude du Pan took on the duty of making Monsieur Julian Bordon, the father, to come here by Thursday, and then a good agreement can be reached.

[18] R. Consist. IX, 179.
[19] R. Consist. II, 2.

[*A week later Bordon was remanded before the Council for October 26. On that date the Council ordered that the marriage should go into effect and that Bordon should pay the "marriage" (that is, the dowry) within three weeks afterwards.*]

DOCUMENT 10:
Case of Jean de Landécy and Mia (1546)[20]

(March 4, 1546.) [The parties] were admonished to give the reason why they have come. Jean said that the woman promised him in marriage about two to three hundred florins, and there were present at the house of Bernard Cloye, tailor, . . . Bernard and Claude Roch, baker, and Pierre Pricqua. Mia said she had given him various household goods and carpenter's tools, as is stated in a list she has presented to us that has been read.

Decided: he confessed having almost all the contents [on the list]. Nevertheless, he said he will not marry her if she does not give him what she promised. They were remanded here to Thursday to bring the witnesses.

(March 11, 1546.). Claude Roch, baker, was admonished and asked to tell the truth about what he knows and that he was present at the promise of marriage of Jean de Landécy. He answered that it is true that his fiancée promised to provide him about two hundred florins in one way or another – 80 florins cash on the announcement, the rest afterwards or at the wedding. Asked whether a promise of marriage was made, he said yes, and that they both swore on the bread.

Pierre Priccatz was also asked about the above. He said it is true that Master Claude [Roch] asked the fiancée, that is Mia, whether she wanted Jean. Then she said yes, and the promise was made on the bread, and they drank together. Asked whether it was stated that if he did not have the [dowry] money he would not marry her, he said he did not hear anything said about that.

Decided: that they be remanded before the Council and that the promise appears to be valid, and that the Council should order the woman to give what she promised to her husband.

The fiancée was called, and was admonished that she was to keep the promise that she promised. She said she wanted to do it. Asked whether she did not say that she would give 24 florins immediately to her husband, she said she will certainly do it, and that it [the promise] is secured by a piece of land at Cruscilles. She said further that Guillaume Coustel owes her a certain sum that he denies, and that Coustel asks her for proof [of his debt], and that it is on his conscience.

Jean, the fiancé, was summoned, and was admonished that the marriage and promise were made and that he should carry them out and that the woman will give him all she can; if not, they are remanded to Monday before the Council.

[20] R. Consist. II, 38, 40.

[*On March 23 the Council summoned them for the following Monday, but the resulting decision is not reported. In January, 1547, Jean de Landécy, grave-digger, had still not married Mia. He was then suspected of theft, and was released on condition that he marry Mia, which he did.*]

DOCUMENT 11:
Case of Nicolas Adduard and Jehanne Pyto (1546)[21]

(April 8, 1546.) Nicolard Adduard of Esserts and Jehanne, widow of the late Jean Pyto of Neydens, were admonished and asked the reason why they are here. He responded that he swore faith to and drank in the name of marriage with her. She denied it, and said she was swindled. Asked whether there were any people present at the promise, the husband said there were eight people, among which company was an uncle of hers who promised him six score florins and all of their household goods and cattle. She excused herself, producing an excusatory petition.

Decided: that the marriage should not go into effect and that the woman should have the two she would most like to have speak about it come, that is her uncle, and with him also two of those who were at the promise. She answered that she cannot bring him because he does not dare to cross the bridge because of certain debts. Here on Thursday.

(April 15, 1546.) Two witnesses produced by Nicolas Adduard of Esserts: Michel Gillard of Germagnet and Nicolas Marchant of Esserts [appeared]. Claude, widow of Petet of Neydens, was called, and was asked whether she knows anything against these witnesses and whether they are relatives of Nicolas Adduard. She said they are respectable people; she does not know about [whether they are] relatives. Gillard answered that he was present in the company when the parties drank together in marriage together, and it was stated that she would give him six score florins and more and a cow. Asked whether there was any reservation made, he said no, except that she begged that no one yet disturb her brother about it, because he would be angry.

Asked the reason why he does not complete the marriage begun, he [Nicolas Adduard] answered that it is not his fault. Asked whether he would take her, he said does not want her because he would get no money. He said it depends on the decision of the Council. She does not want to accept marriage. They were admonished because Nicolas told her that he had only three children, and he has four. Also she promised him six score florins p.p. and can give him nothing. They are both found to have lied and cheated.

Decided: that they be remanded before the Council, declaring to them that there is a marriage and about the lies on one side and the other, and praying our lords to give consideration to having edicts [published] concerning marriages.

---

[21] R. Consist. II, 48v, 50v.

[*The following Monday, when called before the Council, Jehanne still opposed the marriage, but Nicolas wanted the marriage. On April 19, the Council finally decided that the marriage should be recognized and celebrated.*]

DOCUMENT 12:

Case of Thomas Bonna and Claudine de Loelmoz (1552–53)[22]

(Aug. 30, 1552.) Thomas Bonna was admonished why he does not proceed to marry his fiancée. He answered that when he made such a promise she had not reached her [age of] majority, and he told them [her family] that he did not want goods but money, and did not want land or lawsuits. He would otherwise not marry her until they gave him what they promised, and meanwhile he would serve his uncle Bienvenu until they gave him the money.

Decided: that for Thursday he be remanded before the Council, and despite all his excuses it is found that he should proceed with the banns. And let him bring his witnesses before the Council and everything he may use to assist him....

(Sept. 21, 1553.) Thomas Bonna and Claudine de Loelmoz [appeared]. Claudine produced the [Council's] orders given previously, asking that action be taken on it so the matter may be properly concluded. Thomas still alleges that he did what he did under the condition that he get cash. Afterwards he was read a schedule stating how this same Bonna gave [Claudine] golden rings, and that he made her sell stored wine and chests, when she was brought to his house. Bonna said indeed he gave her rings, and as for the chests, he did not receive them, but it was done without his command.

Considering all the procedures and examinations and orders given in Council, including the last, [the marriage promise is valid]. Thomas confesses the promise of marriage, but maintains that the condition [to marriage has not been met]. But considering the gift of rings, [and] that he made her mistress and governor of his goods and house, he broke his claimed condition, not holding to it. And it is evident that he promised [marriage], as he confesses.

It was decided unanimously by the Consistory that it does not appear to them at all that this [engagement] may be dissolved. There is a marriage here that cannot be broken off according to God for the reasons given by Thomas. Also considering that he gave her a procuration as from a fiancé to a fiancée, as the procurator Gallatin, who received this procuration, has stated here. And therefore he is remanded to Monday before the Council with the decision aforesaid.

---

[22] R. Consist., VII, 71; VIII, 54v, 55, omitting intervening Consistory discussions of Council procedure on December 1 and 8, 1552 and January 12 and September 13, 1553, reported in R. Consist. VII, 103, 106, 127; VIII, 54v.

INDEX

abduction, 57–58, 73, 126, 308

act books, 334

acta
deeds: as documentation, 41
princely: as teaching, 175
publica: registration requirements, 49, 66, 71, 86
royal: and dating of sacred preambles, 134

Adams, Norma, 263, 288

Adduard, Nicolas, 487–488

adultery
as criminal offense, 48
definition, 50
and dower lands, 293–294
and separation, 350

affectio maritalis. See marital affection

affection
in dotal charters, 127
and gifts, 65, 464
in marriages, 359, 446

affinity and Gaelic Irish, 334, 337

age of bride
and devolution, 240
in Rome, 47
and virginity, 303

age of consent, 47, 457

age of discretion, 295

age of puberty, 333

agreement to marry. *See also* consent
as act of mutual consent, 3
and dotal charters, 39
as expressed in betrothal, 4
and force and fear impediment, 14–15
with future or present effect, 10
in present tense (*See* consent in present tense)

and sacramental marriage, 10

Alberigo, Giuseppe, 25

Alessandro, John A., 6, 288

Alexander III (pope), 12–13, 272, 335

allegory
of church as valiant women, 109
of marriage as Christ and Church, 110–111

alliances. *See also* misalliance
of Anglo-Irish and Gaelic Irish, 341
and betrothal, 396
and castellany sphere of influence, 191–192
and dowry strategy, 182, 195
and Occitanian women, 217
of Roman elites, 59
in secular model of marriage, 363

Amargier, Paul, 238

Ambrose, bishop of Milan, 56, 57, 62, 91, 96

Ambrosiaster, 19, 146

analogy in preambles, 147

Anastasius, 92

ancillary rites, 18–19, 22, 271

Andecavenses Formulae, 148–150

Anderson, David, 53

Anderson, Gary, 136

Anderson, Randi, 365, 366

Anderson, W. B., 77

Andorlini, Isabella, 83

angels and human beings, 140, 141

Anglo-Ireland
dispensation and inheritance, 338
marriage regulation and enforcement, 340–351

Anglo-Norman nuptial liturgy, 23–25

Anglo-Saxon marriage agreements, 274–275

Anné, Lucien, 65, 66

marriage settlement(s)
  between aristocratic families, 233–235
  and definition of marriage contract, 262
  and Frankish dowry, 118
  Iceland, evolution of, 382–385
  and property settlements, 268
marrying
  and dissolubility and indissolubility of
    compact, 10
  documentation and dotation, 37–40
  in Ireland, 332
  as process, 5–6
  process in Frankish tradition, 121–124
  ritual process in southern and northern
    France, 248
  in Roman North Africa, 95–113
  as three state process, 459
  women's role in, 245
Martène, Edmond, 181
Martínez, Tomás M., 72
Mary, 6, 8
Mason, Emma, 275
Maspero, J., 83
Matecki, Bernard, 9
Mateline, 202
Matfred, Pierre, 231–233
Matfred, Pontia, 231–233
Mathghamhna, Maghnus Mac, 339
Mathilde d'Epagny, 188–189
Mathisen, Ralph W., 47, 53
matrimonial contracts. *See* marriage contracts
matrimonial rituals. *See* ritual(s)
matrimonial settlement. *See* marriage
    settlement(s)
matrimonial strategies, 181–186
matrimonium
  as contract, 397
  as distinct event, 411
  and engagement, 398
  and legitimate children, 50
  as record of present tense vows, 392
matrimony. *See also* marriage
  documentation in Florence, 396–398
  as a private affair, 315–316
  symbols of, 377
  as union in dower charters, 174–181
Matringe, Guillaume, 54, 55, 58, 61
Matthews, John, 45, 59, 86
mattinata and second marriages, 407–408
Mayali, Laurent, 406, 424
Maynaghe, Juliana, 347
McCafferty, John, 351
McCann, John, 344, 351–353
McCarthy, Conor, 261

McFarlane, K. B., 265
McGinn, Thomas A. J., 50, 51, 52
McKendrick, Neil, 260
McSheffrey, Shannon, 14, 40, 266, 273, 409
Meek, Christine, 351
Meens, Rob, 21
Meigne, Maurice, 72
Melby, Kari, 361
men
  authority over women, 443–444
  English marriage contracts and conduct of,
    269
  Gaelic Irish and ecclesiastical courts, 339
  of high-rank and low ranking women, 93
  and marriage contracts in Douai, 443
Menchi, Silvana Seidel, 264, 392, 400, 401, 406,
    408, 409, 410
Merdinger, Jane E., 102
Merea, Paulo, 55
Messalina, 75
Mestayer, Monique, 263, 421, 438
Metz, René, 18
Metzger, Marcel, 99
Meyer, Elizabeth, 63, 66, 74, 76, 84, 86
Meyer, Paul, 45, 46
Michaud, Francine, 241
Midelton, Robert, 309–312, 323–331
Migliorino, Francesco, 407
Millar, Fergus, 90
Mills, James, 340
Mingroot, E. Van, 7
ministers in Calvin's wedding liturgy, 461
misalliance. *See also* unequal unions
  and clandestine marriages in Florence,
    391–392, 406
  and concubinage, 13
  and valid marriage in Rome, 3
Mithilde d'Épagny, 197
models of marriage
  as alliances in secular, 363
  as aristocratic and ecclesiastical, 15–16
  of clergy, 15
  of Duby, 314
  and family structure, 229
  in Iceland, 362–363
  as individual and social, 272–273
  individualistic, 272
  laity and church's, 272–273
Mohlberg, Leo C., 19, 22
Molho, Anthony, 391, 400, 403
Molin, Jean-Baptiste, 17, 18, 20, 21, 24, 25, 26, 125,
    131, 137, 172, 173, 226, 238, 460, 462
Mommsen, Theodor, 44, 45, 46, 63
monetization and marital practices, 224–225